# British Government Publications;
# an index to chairmen and authors, 1900—1940

Compiled by
Stephen Richard

LONDON
The Library Association
Reference, Special and Information Section

1974

ISBN    0 85365 427 1

Price    £4.40    (£5.50 to non-members)

Printed by Howard Jones Associates, Swansea

## CONTENTS

# INTRODUCTION

This index covers the period 1900-1940; thus, with A. M. Morgan's index[1], extending the coverage of indexes of chairmen and authors from 1900-1966. Another index is planned by A. M. Morgan for the period 1967-1971. An index of chairmen and selected authors for the nineteenth century is being compiled by me. Thus, this index of chairmen for the 1900-1940 period forms part of a group of existing or planned indexes of chairmen of British government publications for the nineteenth and twentieth centuries.

The background to the preparation of this index for the first 40 years of the twentieth century dates from the beginning of my involvement with government publications. The complexity of publication and similarity of titles of British government publications leads to a reliance on names of chairmen to identify publications. As it was not until the 1940's that the Stationery Office began including chairmen's names, it is sometimes difficult to locate papers known only by the chairman's name and a vague subject field. After the appearance of and experience with A. M. Morgan's index for the 1941-1966 period, I contacted the Reference, Special and Information Section of the Library Association and began work on compiling the index in the Summer of 1972, which I completed in May 1973

The purpose of this index is to serve as a reference work for students, researchers and everyone wanting to consult commission and committee reports known by the chairmen. The success of the index by A. M. Morgan has shown the felt need by libraries and others to provide an easily accessible reference source for locating government reports by the chairman's names. This index also has been a preliminary to the longer index of chairmen nineteenth century British government publications. An index of this kind also has some interest for those studying the chairmanship activity and possible influence of M.P.'s and others in the government of the country. It cannot. of course, be a decisive or major measure of influence and activity as are H. Berrington's studies[2]. In biographical researches the index can provide an indication of the person's range of interest and activity. It is for the reason of use in the study of individuals that the entry is under the surname rather than the title.

## METHOD

This index has been compiled from the publications themselves and checked against the Fords' breviates[3]. J. E. Pemberton's guide to British official publications[4] and the H.M.S.O. lists for the period. The collections used were those in Edinburgh University Library and the National Library of Scotland who both hold excellent collections of parliamentary papers. The National Library of Scotland's collection of non-parliamentary papers is almost complete for the period. The few missing publications were consulted in the British Museum State Paper Room.

The materials included in the index are most easily described by a note of the exclusions. All H.M.S.O. publications except serials of a non-monographic character were checked. F. Rodgers' work[5] was used to determine which items were serials. The following types of material were also excluded: parliamentary standing committees, committees on bills, catalogues and guides, reprints, technical reports and communications, museum publications, accident reports (ships, railway, mining, explosions), statements of ministers and government representatives, and works by more than two authors.

This index is arranged by surname followed by christian names and titles. Thus Lord Riverdale is filed under his surname: Balfour, Arthur, *1st Baron Riverdale,* with a reference from the title. The order of items following each name is alphabetical by committee or title of report, except where an alternative order, e.g. numerical, is the obvious choice. The arrangement of each entry is: title, date of signature or printing, and location details. Parliamentary papers are given the sessional year; command (Cd. or Cmd.) numbers, House of Commons numbers (in round brackets), House of Lords numbers (H.L. in round brackets); volume number, and responsible body of government. Non-parliamentary papers have the responsible body of government following the date of signature or printing. Series are given in round brackets after the date.

E.*g.* Ridley, Matthew White, *3rd Viscount Ridley.*
> Interdepartmental committee on the rent restriction acts.
>> Report. 6 Dec.1937. 1937/38 Cmd. 5621 xv. Ministry of Health.

Ritchie, Alfred
> The food and feeding habits of the haddock in Scottish waters. 1937. (Sci. Invest., 1937, no. 2) Fishery Board for Scotland.

The use of printing and signature dates in this index means that the items signed or printed in the latter part of one year may appear in the Consolidated List of Government Publications for the following year. This applies to both non-parliamentary and parliamentary papers. When a signature date for parliamentary papers has been unavailable, I have used the date of the order to print or the H.M.S.O. details relating to the time of printing. This means the session of a parliamentary paper is not affected, although the year of the Consolidated List in which it appears may be the following year to the one of signature or order to print.

I would like to acknowledge the assistance of several persons and organisations in the compilation of this index. My thanks are due to Diana Marshallsay for looking over the draft and making many valuable suggestions; Edinburgh University Library for leave of absence and other assistance; the National Library of Scotland and especially Mr. Rodgers for his assistance in the use of their collection of British government publications; the publications sub-committee of the R.S.I.S.; Mrs. K. MacKenzie for typing and my family for putting up with thousands of cards over the period of compilation. Any omissions or other faults are, of course, my responsibility.

Edinburgh
June 1974.

[1] A. M. Morgan, ed. *British government publications; an index to chairmen and authors, 1941-1966.* London, Library Association, Reference, Special and Information Section, 1969.

[2] H. Berrington. *Backbench Opinion in the House of Commons, 1955-59.* Oxford, Pergamon Press, 1973. H. Berrington uses early day motions in these two studies. There are other measures used, such as the division lists as used by J. P. Mackintosh, and others in this area of research. H. Berrington's studies are given as an example of the more rigorous, statistical approach.

[3] Ford, P. *and* Ford, G. *Abreviate of parliamentary papers, 1900-1916.* Oxford, Blackwell, 1957. Reprinted: Shannon, Irish University Press, 1969.

---*Abreviate of parliamentary papers, 1917-1939.* Oxford, Blackwell, 1951. Reprinted: Shannon, Irish University Press, 1969.

[4] John E. Pemberton. *British Official Publications,* 2nd ed. Oxford, Pergamon Press, 1973.

[5] F. Rodgers. *Serial Publications in British Parliamentary Papers, 1900-1968; a bibliography.* London, Library Association, 1971.

# ABBREVIATIONS

The following list indicates the abbreviations used throughout in addition to the standard abreviations for months of the year.

| | |
|---|---|
| ( ) | House of Commons paper number |
| *Bn.* | Baron |
| B.R.B. | Building Research Board |
| Bull. | Bulletin |
| C.B. | County Borough |
| Cd., Cmd. | Command papers |
| D.C. | District Council |
| Dip.cons. reports: misc. ser. | Diplomatic and Consular Reports: miscellaneous series |
| *E.* | Earl |
| F.I.B. | Food Investigation Board |
| F.P.R. | Forest Product Research |
| F.R.B. | Fuel Research Board |
| G.B. | Great Britain |
| Geophys. Mem. | Geophysical Memoirs |
| (H.L.) | House of Lords paper number |
| I.H.R.B. | Reports of the Industrial Fatigue Research Board. 1919-1929; Reports of the Industrial Health Research Board, 1929- |
| *M.* | Marquis |
| M.O. | Meteorological Office Publication |
| Mem. Geol. Surv. | Memoirs of the Geological Survey |
| Mem. Geol. Surv., Paleont. | Memoirs of the Geological Survey, Paleontology |
| Mem. Geol. Surv., Scotland | Memoirs of the Geological Survey, Scotland |
| Memo. | Memorandum |
| Misc. | Miscellaneous |
| Mono. Min. Resour. | Monographs on mineral resources with special reference to the British Empire |
| N.D. | Navy Department |
| no. | number |
| Occ. paper | Occasional paper |
| Prof. Notes | Professional notes |
| R.D. | Rural District |
| R. com. | Royal Commission |
| R.R.B. | Radio Research Board |
| Rep. | Report |
| Rep. Insp. Food | Reports of Inspectors of Foods |
| Rep. Med. Insp. | Reports of Medical Inspectors |
| Rep. Min. Ind. | Reports of the Mineral Industry of the British Empire and foreign countries. |
| Rep.Pub.Health & Med. Subj. | Reports on Public Health and Medical Subjects |
| Road res. | Road research |
| S.M.R.B. | Safety in Mines Research Board |
| S.R.S. | Special Report Series, Medical Research Council |
| Salmon Fish. | Salmon Fisheries. Fishery Board for Scotland |
| Sci. Invest. | Scientific investigations |
| Stat. Rep. | Statistical reports |
| U.D. | Urban District |
| U.K. | United Kingdom |
| *Vct.* | Viscount |

ABBOT, A.
Trade schools on the continent, Oct. 1932 (Educational pamphlets, no.91). Board of Education.

Aberconway, *Lord. SEE:* M'Laren, C.B.B., *1st Baron.*

ABSALOM, H. W. L.
Report on the observations of terrestrial magnetism made in the British Isles on the occasion of the total solar eclipse of June 29, 1927. Feb. 1930. (Prof. Notes, no.55). Meteorological Office.

ACKLAND, Thomas G.
Report on the estimated financial effect of amendments introduced in Part II of the National Insurance Bill in committee. 24 Nov.1911. 1911 Cd.5980 lxxiii. Board of Trade.

Report on the scheme for insurance against unemployment embodied in Part II of the National Insurance Bill. 4 May 1911. 1911 (162) lxxiii. Board of Trade.

ACLAND, Arthur Herbert Dyke
Consultative committee of the Board of Education.
Report on attendance, compulsory or otherwise, at continuation schools.
Vol.1: Report and appendices. 7 May 1909. 1909 Cd.4757 xvii.
Vol.2: Summaries of evidence. 1909. 1909 Cd.4758 xvi. Board of Education.

Report on devolution by county education authorities. 28 Feb. 1908. 1908 Cd.3952 lxxxii. Board of Education.

Report on examinations in secondary schools. 16 Dec. 1911. 1911 Cd.6004 xvi. Board of Education.

Report on practical work in secondary schools. 9 June 1913. 1913 Cd.6849 xx. Board of Education.

Report on school attendance of children below the age of five. 2 July 1908. 1908 Cd.4259 lxxxii. Board of Education.

Report on scholarships for higher education. Interim report. 14 June 1916. 1916 Cd.8219 viii (no other reports identified, *see* Ford). Board of Education.

Departmental committee on sight tests.
Report. 28 May 1912. 1912/3 Cd.6256 xlvi.
Minutes of evidence and Appendices. 1912/3 Cd.6319 xlvi. Board of Trade.

ACLAND, Francis Dyke
Committee on the Exchequer and Audit Departments Act, 1866.
Report. 23 June 1921. 1921 Cmd.1383 xi. Treasury.

Committee on the extent and gravity of the evils of dental practice by persons not qualified under the Dentists Act.
Report. 5 Feb.1919. 1919 Cmd.33 xiii, part 1, Privy Council.

Departmental committee on accidents in places under the factory and workshop acts.
Report. 1 Feb.1911. 1911 Cd.5535 xxiii.
Minutes of evidence and appendix. 1911 Cd.5540 xxiii. Home Office.

Indian wheat committee.
Report. 1915 and 1916. 10 Nov.1917. 1918 Cd.9090 viii. Board of Agriculture and Fisheries.

Reconstruction committee. Forestry subcommittee.
Report. May 1917. 1917/8 Cd.8881 xviii. Ministry of Reconstruction.

Select committee on luxury duty.
Report, proceedings and appendices. 1 Aug.1918. 1918 (101) iv. House of Commons.

Select committee on teachers in grant-aided schools (superannuation).
Report, proceedings and evidence. 30 May 1922. 1922 (106) vi. House of Commons.

ACTON, *Lord.* SEE: Dalberg-Acton, R.M., *2nd Baron Acton.*

ACWORTH, William Mitchell
Committee on the administration and working of Indian railways.
Report. 22 Aug.1921. 1921 Cmd.1512 x. India Office.

Safeguarding of industries committee.
Report on aluminium hollow-ware. 9 March 1922. Board of Trade.
Report on plain and enamelled baths. 31 March 1922. Board of Trade.
Report on wrought enamelled hollow-ware. 30 March 1922. Board of Trade.

ADAM, Frank Forbes
Report of the Board of Trade railway conference. May 1909. 1909 Cd.4677 lxxvii. Board of Trade.

ADAMI, John George
Special committee on the standardisation of pathological methods.
Interim report: The Wasserman Test. 13 Nov. 1917. (S.R.S. no.14).
Second interim report: Laboratory diagnosis of gonococcal infections. Aug. 1918. (S.R.S. no.19).
Third interim report: Methods for the detection of spirochaetes. Aug. 1918. (S.R.S. no.19).
Fourth report: The diagnostic value of the complement fixation test in syphilis, commonly known as the Wasserman test. Nov. 1918. (S.R.S. no.21). Medical Research Committee.

ADAMS, Dorothy Rose
Dark adaptation (of the eyes); a review of the literature. 20 April 1929. (S.R.S. no.127). Medical Research Council.

ADAMS, Edward William
Report on recent researches upon the nature and therapy of pernicious anaemia. July 1934. (R.Pub.Health & Med.Subj., no.75). Ministry of Health.

A review of certain aspects of a recently recognized disease of the blood (Agranulocytosis or Agranulocytic Angina). March 1935. (R.Pub.Health & Med.Subj., no.70). Ministry of Health.

ADAMS, S.
Effect of eyestrain on the output of linkers in the hosiery industry. Feb.1927. (I.H.R.B.Rep., no.40). Medical Research Council.

The effect of lighting on efficiency in rough work (tile pressing). June 1935. Medical Research Council.

On the relief of eyestrain among persons performing very fine work. April 1928. (I.H.R.B. Rep., no.49).

Further experiments on the use of special spectacles in very fine processes. Aug. 1929. (I.H.R.B. Rep., no.57). Medical Research Council.

ADAMS, S. (continued)
The performance of weavers under varying conditions of noise. 11 Jan. 1935. (I.H.R.B. Rep., no.70). Medical Research Council.

ADAMSON, Harvey
Indian trade enquiry.
Reports on lac, turpentine and rosin. Nov. 1919. Imperial Institute.

Addington, *Lord. SEE:* Hubbard, J. G., *3rd Baron.*

ADDISON, Christopher
British workshops and the war. 1917. Ministry of Information.

Fishing industry sub-committee of the committee on civil research.
First interim report. 19 Dec.1929. 1929/30 Cmd.3473 viii.
Report 27 Dec. 1931. 1931/2 Cmd.4012 ix. Treasury.

National park committee.
Report. 23 April 1931. 1930/1 Cmd.3851 xvi. Treasury.

Special investigation committee on the incidence of phthisis in relation to occupations.
First report: The boot and shoe industry. Nov.1915 (S.R.S. no.1) (No further reports identified.) Medical Research Council.

ADEANE, C. R. W.
Military manoeuvres commission, 1912.
Report. 1912. 1912/3 Cd.6504 li. War Office.

ADKINS, William Ryland Dent
Consultative council on local health administration.
Report on procedure for proposals for the extension of boroughs, *etc.* Jan. 1921. 1921 Cmd.1113 xiii. Ministry of Health.

Departmental committee on old age pensions.
Report. 7 Nov. 1919. 1919 Cmd.410 xxvii.
Evidence. 1919 Cmd.411 xxvii. Treasury.

Departmental committee on sexual offences against young persons.
Report. 2 Dec. 1925. 1924/5 Cmd.2561 xv. Home Office.

AHRONS, A. M.
Reports on the Shops Act, 1912 as it applies to refreshment premises. 30 Dec.1912. 1912/3. Cd.6579 xxvi. Home Office.

AITKEN, George Atherton
Departmental committee on superannuation of officers of reformatory and industrial schools.
Report. 22 Jan. 1916. Home Office.

AJAX *(pseud.)*
The German pirate and his methods. 1918. Ministry of Information.

AKENHEAD, D.
Viticultural research; a memorandum. Nov. 1928 (E.M.B.,11). Empire Marketing Board.

AKERS-DOUGLAS, Aretas
Committee on education and training of officers of the army.
Report and appendix. March 1902. 1902 Cd.982 x.
Minutes of evidence. 1902 Cd.983 x. War Office.

Departmental committee on the Board of Manufacturers (Scotland).
Vol.1: Report. 8 Aug. 1903. 1904 Cd.1812 xxx.
Vol.2: Minutes of evidence and appendices. 1904 Cd.1813 xxx. Scottish Office.

Select committee on House of Commons accommodation.
Report, proceedings, minutes of evidence and appendix. 26 June 1901. 1901 (234) vi. House of Commons.

Select committee on House of Commons (ventilation).
First report, proceedings, evidence and appendix. 25 June 1903. 1903 (227) v.

Report, proceedings, evidence, appendix and index for 1902/3. 28 July 1903. 1903 (283) v. House of Commons.

ALEXANDER, Henry
Scottish housing advisory committee.
Report on the rehousing of aged persons. 8 June 1938. 1937/8 Cmd.5798 xii. Scottish Office.

Report on rural housing in Scotland. 27 Feb. 1937. 1936/7. Cmd.5462 xi. Scottish Office.

ALLAN, J. K.
The economic geology of the Fife coalfields.
Area 1: Dunfermline and west Fife. 23 Oct. 1930 (Mem.Geol.Surv.Scotland). Geological Survey, Scotland, 1931.
Area 2: Cowdenbeath and central Fife. 1 March 1933. (Mem.Geol.Surv.Scotland) Geological Survey, Scotland.

ALLEN, Arthur Acland
Departmental committee on reformatory and industrial schools in Scotland.
Report. 27 March 1915. 1914/6. Cd.7886 xxxiv.
Evidence and appendices, 1914/6 Cd.7887 xxxiv. Scottish Office.

ALLEN, Charles P.
Select committee on parliamentary debates.
Report, proceedings, evidence, appendix and index. 4 July 1907. 1907 (239) vii. House of Commons.

ALLEN, E. J.
Advisory committee on fishery research.
First report. Sept.1914. 1914 Cd.7200 xxx. (no further reports identified). Board of Agriculture and Fisheries.

Inter-departmental committee on crabs and lobsters.
Interim report. March 1926.
Interim report with further data regarding lobsters. July 1930. (No further reports identified) Ministry of Agriculture and Fisheries *and* Scottish Office.

ALLEN, Robert
Bismuth ores. July 1925 (Mono.Min.Resour.). Imperial Institute.

Chrome ore and chromium. 1940 (Rep.Min.Ind.). Imperial Institute.

Copper ores. 1923 (Mono.Min. Res.). Imperial Institute.

ALLEN, William
Sound transmission in buildings; practical notes for architects and builders. Nov. 1939. Department of Scientific and Industrial Research.

Allerton, *Baron. SEE:* Jackson, W.L., *1st Baron Allerton.*

ALLISTON, Frederick Prat
Preliminary statement of the central executive committee of the London Unemployed Fund, prepared at the request of the President of the Local

ALLISTON, Frederick Pratt (continued)
Government Board. 14 April 1905. 1905 Cd.2561 lxxiii. Local Government Board.

ALLSOP, G.
The ignition of firedamp by broken electric lamp bulbs: the appearance of the filaments. Oct. 1934 (S.M.R.B., Paper no.89). Mines Department.

The ignition of firedamp by the filaments of broken electric lamp bulbs. Nov. 1933 (S.M.R.B. Paper, no.80). Mines Department.

A new method of measuring pressures. Sept. 1925 (S.M.R.B. Paper no. 16). Mines Department.

The pressures produced by electric arcs in closed vessels. Aug. 1927 (S.M.R.B. Paper no.39). Mines Department.

The pressures produced on blowing electric fuse links. July 1927 (S.M.R.B. Paper no.38). Mines Department.

The pressures produced on blowing electric fuse links: the effect of the surrounding atmosphere. Feb. 1930 (S.M.R.B. Paper no.67). Mines Department.

The pressure produced on blowing electric fuse links and striking electric arcs in closed vessels. Jan. 1929 (S.M.R.B. Paper no.52). Mines Department.

A recording manometer having a low inertia. Jan. 1935. (S.M.R.B. Paper no.91). Mines Department.

Alness, *Baron. SEE:* Munro, R., *1st Baron Alness.*

Alverstone, *Baron. SEE:* Webster, R.E., *1st Baron.*

ALVIELLA, Goblet d'
The true and the false pacifism. 1917. Ministry of Information.

AMAN, Dudley Leigh, *1st Baron Marley*
Departmental committee on garden cities and satellite towns.
Report. 22 Dec. 1934. Ministry of Health.

Interdepartmental committee on the rent restriction acts.
Report. 11 July 1931. 1930/1 Cmd.3911 xvii. Ministry of Health.

AMERY, Lempold Charles Maurice Stennett
Advisory tribunal on a financial settlement between India and Burma.
Report. 15 March 1935. 1934/5 Cmd.4902 viii. India Office.

West Indian shipping committee.
Report. 15 Aug. 1919 Cmd.372 xxx. Colonial Office.

AMERY, William Bankes.
Report on the group settlements in Western Australia. June 1926. 1926 Cmd.2673 ix. Colonial Office.

Amulree, *Lord. SEE:* MacKenzie, W.W., *1st Baron.*

Ancaster, *Lord. SEE:* Willoughby, G.H.D., *2nd Earl.*

ANDERSON, Adelaide M.
Memorandum on subsidiary health and kindred services for women; prepared for the Women's Employment Committee. 27 Dec. 1917. Ministry of Reconstruction.

Special report on dangerous or injurious processes in the tinning of metals with an experimental investigation by G. Elmhirst Duckering. 26 June 1908. 1908 Cd.3793 xii. Factory Department, Home Office.

ANDERSON, Alan Garrett
Committee on pay, *etc.* of state servants.
Report. 25 July 1923. Treasury.

Departmental committee on fixed trusts.
Report. 29 July 1936. 1935/6 Cmd.5259 x. Board of Trade.

Joint committee on gas prices.
Report, proceedings and evidence. 21 April 1937. 1936/7 (110) vii. House of Commons.

ANDERSON, Andrew Macbeth, *Lord*
Court of inquiry concerning the threatened stoppage of work at the coal exporting ports of Great Britain, 1924.
Report. 26 May 1924. 1924 Cmd.2149 xi. Ministry of Labour.

Glasgow tribunal of inquiry, 1933.
Report on allegations of bribery and corruption in the civic and municipal administration of the Corporation of the City of Glasgow. 9 June 1933. 1932/3 Cmd. 4361 xii. Scottish Office.

ANDERSON, David
Air raid shelter policy.
Report. 20 Dec.1938. 1938/9 Cmd.5932 ix. Home Office.

ANDERSON, David Murray
Commission of government on the economic situation of Newfoundland.
Report 18 Dec.1934. 1934/5 Cmd.4788 vii. Dominion Affairs Office.

Commission of government on the unemployment situation in Newfoundland.
Report. 9 May 1935. 1934/5 Cmd.4910 vii. Dominion Affairs Office.

ANDERSON, E. M.
The economic geology of the Ayrshire coalfields. Area 2: Kilmarnock basin. 6 May 1925 (Mem.Geol.Surv., Scotland). Geological Survey, Scotland.

Economic geology of the central coalfield of Scotland. Area 6: Bathgate, Wilsontown and Shotts. 7 May 1923. (Mem.Geol.Surv.,Scotland). Geological Survey, Scotland.

The geology of mid-Strathspey and Strathearn (Sheet 74). 1915 (Mem.Geol.Surv.,Scotland). Geological Survey, Scotland.

The geology of Staffa, Iona and Western Mull (Sheet 43). 4 May 1925 (Mem.Geol.Surv.,Scotland). Geological Survey, Scotland.

ANDERSON, Eleanor J. M.
Identification of *Bacillus salmonicida* by the complement-fixation test; a further contribution to the study of furunculosis of the salmonidae. 1930. (Salmon Fish.,1930,no.1). Fishery Board for Scotland.

ANDERSON, J. G. C.
The granites of Scotland. 24 July 1939. (Special reports on the mineral resources of G.B., vol.32) (Mem.Geol.Surv.). Geological Survey.

High-grade silica rocks of the Scottish highland and islands. Aug.1940 (Wartime pamphlets). Geological Survey.

ANDERSON, John
Commission on the use of opium in the Straits Settlements and the Federated Malay States.
Vol.1: Report and annexures. 15 June 1908. 1909 Cd.4521 lxi.

ANDERSON, John (continued)
Vol.2: (not printed)
Vol.3: Analysis of evidence, appendices and subject index. 1909 Cd.4522 lxi. Colonial Office.

Committee on evacuation.
Report. 26 July 1938. 1937/8 Cmd.5837 xi. Home Office.

ANDERSON, R. Wherry
The romance of air-fighting. 1917. Ministry of Information.

ANDLER, Charles
German theory and practice of war. 1915. Ministry of Information.

Pan-Germanism; its plans for German expansion in the world. 1915. Ministry of Information.

ANDREW, George
Report on the Gemeindeschulen of Berlin and Charlottenburg. June 1904. 1904 Cd.2120 xxii. Board of Education.

ANDREWES, Frederick William
Advisory committee on bacteriological studies of cerebro-spinal fever during the epidemic of 1915. 13 Jan. 1916 (S.R.S. no.2). Medical Research Committee.

Committee on pathological methods.
Report on the laboratory diagnosis of acute intestinal infections, including the principles and practice of the agglutination test. June 1920 (S.R.S., no.51). Medical Research Council.

The haemolytic streptococci; their grouping by agglutination. 21 June 1932. (S.R.S., no.169). Medical Research Council.

A study of the serological races of the Flexner group of dysentery bacilli. 28 Oct. 1919. (S.R.S., no.42). Medical Research Committee.

ARBERRY, A. J.
The library of the India Office: a historical sketch. 1938. India Office.

Specimens of Arabic and Persian palaeography. 1939. India Office. Library.

ARCHER, William
Colour-blind neutrality; an open letter to Dr. George Brandes. 1916. Ministry of Information.

Shirking the issue; a letter to Dr. George Brandes. 1917. Ministry of Information.

Six of one and half-a-dozen of the other; a letter to Mr. L. Simons of the Hague. 1917. Ministry of Information.

To neutral peacelovers; a plea for patience. 1916. Ministry of Information.

ARDERN, E.
Treatment of sulphur fumes of the proposed Battersea electric power station.
Interim report on tests of proposed treatment. 9 Aug.1929. 1929/30 Cmd.3442 xvii.
Second report. 2 June 1930. 1930/1 Cmd.3714 xvii. Ministry of Transport.

ARKWRIGHT, Joseph A.
Foot-and-mouth disease research committee.
First progress report. July 1925.
Second progress report. Jan. 1925.
Third progress report. June 1928
Fourth progress report. Aug. 1931.
Fifth progress report. Feb. 1937. Ministry of Agriculture and Fisheries.

ARMITAGE-SMITH, Sydney Armitage
Financial mission to the Leeward Islands and St.Lucia.
Report. 31 Oct. 1931. 1931/2 Cmd.3996 vi. Colonial Office.

Report on a financial mission to Tanganyika. 26 Sept. 1932. 1931/2 Cmd.4182 vii. Colonial Office.

ARMSTRONG, Charles Herbert
Indian trade enquiry.
Reports on oil-seeds. 7 Feb.1918. Imperial Institute.

ARNOLD, Matthew
Reports on elementary schools, 1852-1882, new ed. Aug. 1908. Board of Education.

ARNOLD-FORSTER, Hugh Oakley
Committee on arrears of shipbuilding.
Report. 13 Feb. 1902. 1902 Cd.1055 lxi. Admiralty.

Lands settlement commission, South Africa.
Report, 28 Nov.1900. 1901 Cd.626 xxiv.
Part II: documents, evidence etc. 1900 Cd.627 xxiv. Colonial Office.

Particulars regarding the proposed army re-organisation scheme.
1 Aug. 1904. 1904 Cd.1910 li. War Office.

ASBURY, W.
Advisory committee on the welfare of the blind.
Report of the sub-committee on marketing and other matters affecting the employment and vocational training of blind persons. 29 Dec.1933. Ministry of Health. 1934.

ASHBY, A. W.
Committee on stabilization of agricultural prices.
Report. 26 Jan. 1925. (Economic series, no.2). Ministry of Agriculture and Fisheries.

Ashby, St.Ledgers, *Lord. SEE:* Guest, I.C., *1st Baron.*

ASHLEY, Wilfred William, *1st Baron Mount Temple*
Military manoeuvres Commission 1935.
Report. Feb.1936. 1935/6 Cmd.5103 xvi. War Office.

ASHLEY, William James
Agricultural tribunal of investigation.
Interim report. 29 March 1923. 1923 Cmd.1842 ix.
Second interim report. 10 Nov. 1923. 1923 Cmd.2002 ix.
Final report. 7 May 1924. 1924 Cmd.2145 vii. Ministry of Agriculture and Fisheries.

Safeguarding of industries committee.
Report on domestic, illumination and mounting glassware. 18 Feb. 1922. Board of Trade.

ASHLEY-COOPER, Anthony
National advisory council for juvenile employment. *SEE:* Goschen, G. J.

Ashmore, *Lord. SEE:* Wilson, J., *Lord Ashmore*

ASHTON, Thomas Gair, *1st Baron Ashton-of-Hyde.*
Departmental committee on the night employment of male young persons in factories and workshops.
Report. 13 Nov. 1912. 1912/3 Cd.6503 xxvi.
Minutes of evidence and appendices. 1913 Cd.6711 xxiii. Home Office.

ASKWITH, George Ranken, *1st Baron*
Accounts of expenditure of wage-earning women and girls. 1911. 1911 Cd.5963 lxxxix. Board of Trade.

ASKWITH, George Rauken, *1st Baron,* (continued)
Industrial council.
Report on enquiry into industrial agreements.
24 July 1913. 1913 Cd. 6952 xxviii.
Minutes of evidence. 1913 Cd.6953 xxviii. Board
of Trade.

Malta Royal commission.
Report. 29 Jan. 1932. 1931/2 Cmd.3993 vi.
Minutes of evidence. (Colonial, no.68). 1932.
Colonial Office.

Report of an enquiry into the cost of living in
American towns. April 1911. 1911 Cd.5609 lxxxviii.
Board of Trade.

Report of an enquiry into the earnings and hours of
labour of work people of the United Kingdom.
1: Textile trades in 1906. March 1909. 1909
Cd.4545 lxxx.
2: Clothing trades in 1906. Aug. 1909. 1909
Cd.4844 lxxx.
3: Building and woodworking trades in 1906.
March 1910. 1910 Cd.5086 lxxxiv.
4: Public utility services in 1906. June 1910.
1910 Cd.5196 lxxxiv.
5: Agriculture in 1907. Nov. 1910. 1910
Cd.5460 lxxxiv.
6: Metal, engineering and shipbuilding trades.
July 1911. 1911 Cd.5814 lxxxviii.
7: Railway service. 1912. 1912/3 Cd.6053
cviii.
8: Paper, printing, *etc.* trades; pottery, brick,
glass and chemical trades; food, drink and
tobacco trades; and miscellaneous trades.
1913. 1912/3 Cd.6556 cviii. Board of
Trade.

Report of an enquiry into working class rents,
housing and retail prices together with the rates of
wages in Belgium. 24 Feb.1910. 1910 Cd.5065 xcv.
Board of Trade.

Report on matters connected with the establishment
and working of railway conciliation boards, set up in
accordance with the agreement of 6 November 1907.
Feb.1909. 1909 Cd.4534 lxxvii. Board of Trade.

Report on the Industrial Disputes Investigation Act
of Canada, 1907. 9 Dec. 1912. 1912/3 Cd.6603 xlvii.
Board of Trade.

ASPINALL-OGLANDER, Cecil Faber
History of the Great War. Military operations.
Gallipoli. text, maps and appendices. 1928. 7 vols.
1929 and 1932. War Office.

ASQUITH, Herbert Henry
Committee on salaries of the principal posts in the
civil service.
Report. 20 July 1920. 1921 Cmd.1188 ix.
Treasury.

A free future for the world. 1916. Ministry of
Information.

Royal commission on Oxford and Cambridge
Universities.
Report. 1 March 1922. 1922 Cmd.1588 x.
Appendices. 1922.

Select committee of privileges (intervention of peers
at parliamentary elections).
Report and proceedings. 21 Sept.1909. 1909
(281) viii. House of Commons.

Select committee on procedure (anticipatory
motions).
Report, proceedings, evidence and appendix. 23
July 1907. 1907 (264) vii. House of Commons.

Select committee on vacation of seat (member
holding contract).
Special reports. 27 Nov.1912, 19 Dec.1912, 22
Jan.1913. 1912/3 (379), (406), (452) ix. House
of Commons.

Sub-committee of the Committee of Imperial
Defence on certain questions of naval policy raised
by Lord Charles Beresford.
Report. 12 Aug.1909. 1909 (256) liv. War
Office.

What Britain is fighting for: a reply to the German
Chancellor. 1916. Ministry of Information.

ASTOR, Waldorf, *2nd Viscount Astor*
Committee on Empire migration.
Report. 11 July 1931. 1931/2 Cmd.4015 ix.
Economic Advisory Council.

Committee on the production and distribution of
milk.
Interim report. 8 June 1917. 1917/8 Cd.8608
xvi.
Second interim report. 30 Nov.1917. 1917/8
Cd.8886 xvi.
Report. 9 May 1918. 1918 Cd.9095 xxii.
Third interim report. 5 Nov.1918. 1919
Cmd.315 xxv.
Final report. Dec.1919. 1919 Cmd.483 xxv.
Board of Agriculture & Fisheries.

Departmental committee on tuberculosis.
Interim report. April 1912. 1912/3 Cd.6164
xlviii.
Final report, vol.1: report. March 1913. 1912/3
Cd.6641 xlviii.
vol.2: Appendix. 1912/3 Cd.6654 xlviii.
Treasury.

Inter-departmental committee on infectious diseases
in connection with demobilisation.
Note on prophylaxis against venereal disease.
August 1919. 1919 Cmd. 322 xxx. Ministry of
Health.

Athlone, *Earl. SEE:* Cambridge, A. A. F., *1st Earl of
Athlone*

Atholl, *Duchess of. SEE:* Stewart-Murray, K. M.

Atholl, *Duke. SEE:* Stewart-Murray, J. G. *8th Duke of
Atholl.*

ATKEY, Albert Reuben
Advisory committee on water.
Report on measures for the protection of
underground water. 9 Jan.1925. Ministry of
Health.

Report on rural water supplies. March 1929.
Ministry of Health.

Second report of the legislation sub-committee.
Sept.1929. Ministry of Health. (no other reports
identified)

Technical sub-committee.
Report on the assessment of compensation
water. April 1930. Ministry of Health.

Joint advisory committee on river pollution.
First report, July 1928.
Second report: the reception of trade effluents
into the sewers of the local sanitary authorities.
April 1930.
(Third report not published, *see:* Ford)
Fourth report: machinery of administration of
the law as to river pollution. 2 July 1937.
Ministry of Health.

ATKIN, James Richard, *Baron*
Committee on insanity and crime.
Report. 1 Nov.1923. 1923 Cmd.2005 xii, pt.1. Lord Chancellor's Office.

Committee on the legal interpretation of the term "period of the war".
Reports. 2 May 1918. 1918 Cd.9110 xiv. Ministry of Reconstruction.

Legal education committee.
Report. July 1934. 1933/4 Cmd.4663 xi. Lord Chancellor's Office.

War cabinet committee on women in industry.
Report. 30 April 1919. 1919 Cmd.135 xxxi. Summaries of evidence, *etc.* Sept.1918. 1919 Cmd.167 xxxi. Prime Minister's Office.

ATKINSON, Cyril
Committee on official shorthand writers in the supreme court.
Report. 28 July 1936. 1936/7 Cmd.5395 ix. Lord Chancellor's Office.

ATKINSON, Edward Tindal
Royal commission on existence of corrupt practices at the last election for the city of Worcester.
Report. Vol.1: 22 Nov. 1906. 1906 Cd.3268 xcv. Minutes of evidence. Vol.2: 1906. 1906 Cd.3269 xcv.

ATKINSON, William Nicholas
Departmental committee on first aid certificates for purposes under the Coal Mines Act, 1911.
Report. 25 July 1914. 1914/6 Cd.7647 xxvii. Home Office.

ATTLEE, Clement Richard
Committee of privileges.
Report, proceedings, evidence and appendices. 9 Oct.1940. 1939/40 (164) iii. House of Commons.

AUSTEN, Ernest Edward
Tsetse-flies; their characteristics, distribution and bionomics with some account of possible methods for their control. July 1922. Imperial Bureau of Entomology.

AUSTEN, R. M.
Report on the oil industry of Echigo, Japan. April 1911. (Dip.cons.reports: Misc.ser., no.679) 1911 Cd.5466 lxxxix. Foreign Office *and* Board of Trade.

Avebury, *Lord. SEE:* Lubbock, J., *1st Baron.*

AVES, Ernest
Report on the Acts for the regulation of the hours of employment in shops in Australia and New Zealand. 20 April 1908. 1908 Cd.4168 lxxi. Home Office.

Report on the wages boards and industrial arbitration Acts of Australia and New Zealand. 30 March 1908. 1908 Cd.4167 lxxi. Home Office.

AVORY, Horace Edmund
Committee on the responsibility of wife for crimes committed under the coercion of husband.
Report. June 1922. 1922 Cmd.1677 vii. Lord Chancellor's Office.

BAGENAL, Hope
The reduction of noise in buildings; recommendations to architects. March 1933. (B.R.B. Bull., no.14) Department of Scientific and Industrial Research.

BAGNALL-WILD, Ralph Kirkby
Notes on iron and steel. May 1924. Air Ministry.

BAILEY, Edward Battersby
The geology of Ben Nevis and Glen Coe. (Sheet 53) 16 April 1915. (Mem.Geol.Surv.,Scotl.) Geological Survey, Scotland.

The geology of Staffa, Iona and Western Mull. (Sheet 43) 4 May 1925. (Mem.Geol.Surv.,Scotl.) Geological Survey, Scotland.

The pre-tertiary geology of Mull, Loch Aline and Oban. (parts of Sheets 35, 43, 44, 45 and 52) 12 June 1924. (Mem.Geol.Surv.,Scotl.) Geological Survey, Scotland.

Tertiary and post-tertiary geology of Mull, Loch Aline and Oban. (parts of Sheets 43, 44, 51 and 52) 12 June 1924. (Mem.Geol.Surv.,Scotl.) Geological Survey, Scotland.

BAILEY, George William
Standing committee on prices. Sub-committee on the prices, costs and profits of drugs and medicinal tablets.
Findings and decisions. 5 March 1920. 1920 Cmd. 633 xxiii. Board of Trade.

Standing committee on prices.
Report of a sub-committee on the sale and hire of gas apparatus. 2 May 1921. 1921 Cmd.1381 xvi. Board of Trade.

BAILEY, R. A.
Report on the safety of certified mine signalling bells when connected in parallel. 23 Oct.1928. Mines Department.

BAILEY, Rowland
Departmental committee on the drug tariff under the National Insurance Acts.
Vol.1: Report. 14 Sept.1913. 1914/6 Cd.8062 xxix.
Vol.2: Evidence. 1914/6 Cd.8063 xxix. National Health Insurance Joint Committee.

BAILEY, T. Lewis
Report on an investigation regarding the emission of fumes from artificial silk works. Jan.1929. Ministry of Health.

BAILEY, William Frederick
The present condition of tenant purchasers under the Land Purchase Acts.
Report. 25 March 1903. 1903 (92) lvii.Irish Secretary's Office.

BAILHACHE, Clement Meacher
Committee on the administration and command of the Royal Flying Corps., *etc.*
Interim report. 3 Aug.1916. 1916 Cd.8192 iv. Final report. 17 Nov.1916. 1916 Cd.8194 iv. War Office.

BAILLIE, James Black
Committee on the regulation of wages and conditions of service in the road motor transport industry (goods).
Report, 24 April 1937. 1936/7 Cmd.5440 xv. Minutes of evidence, 1st-11th days. 10 parts. 1936-7.
Appendices and index. 1937. Ministry of Labour *and* Ministry of Transport.

Court of inquiry on the dispute in the Hull fishing industry.
Report. 28 May 1935. 1934/5 Cmd. 4917 ix. Ministry of Labour.

BAINES, Frank
Report on the condition of the roof timbers of Westminster Hall, with suggestions for maintaining the stability of the roof. June 1914. 1914 Cd.7436 xlix. Board of Works.

**BAIRD, John Lawrence, *1st Viscount Stonehaven***
Civil aerial transport committee.
>Reports with appendices. 7 Feb.1918. 1918 Cd.9218 v. Air Council.

Committee on the administration of the Cinematograph Act. 1909.
>Report on the position of slow-burning films under the Act. 26 April 1939. Home Office.

Committee on the employment of women on police duties.
>Report. 24 July 1920. 1920 Cmd.877 xxii.
>Evidence and index. 1921 Cmd.1133 xvi. Home Office.

Departmental committee on the training, appointment and payment of probation officers.
>Report. 30 Jan.1922. 1922 Cmd.1601 x. Home Office.

**BAKER, G. E.**
Departmental committee on navigational warnings and gale warnings.
>Report. 1 May 1925. Board of Trade.

Report by the delegates on the International Labour Conference.
>8th Session, Geneva, 26 May to 5 June 1926. Oct.1926. 1926 Cmd.2749 xxx.
>9th Session, Geneva, 7 to 24 June 1926. Oct.1926. 1926 Cmd.2750 xxx. Ministry of Labour.

**BAKER, G. S.**
The effect of bilge keels on the rolling of lightships. Aug.1924. National Physical Laboratory. Department of Scientific and Industrial Research.

**BAKER, H. A.**
Geological investigations in the Falkland Islands.
>Final report. 1922. (no other reports identified.) Colonial Office.

**BAKER, J. E.**
Standing committee on trusts.
>Report of a sub-committee on the electrical cable industry. 12 May 1921. 1921 Cmd.1332 xvi. Board of Trade.

**BAKEWELL, B.**
The estimation of free calcium oxide and hydroxide. Sept.1931 (B.R.B. Special rep., no.17). Department of Scientific and Industrial Research.

Jointless (magnesium oxychloride) floors. Aug.1925 (B.R.B. Bull., no.1). Department of Scientific and Industrial Research.

**BALDWIN, Stanley**
Committee of privileges.
>Report and proceedings. 11 April 1933. 1932/3 (95) ix. House of Commons.

Select committee of privileges.
>Special report. 29 March 1926. 1926 (55) vii. House of Commons.

Balfour of Burleigh. *SEE:* Bruce, A. H., *6th Baron and* Bruce, G. J. G., *7th Baron*

**BALFOUR, Arthur, *1st Baron Riverdale***
Committee on industry and trade.
Survey of industrial relations. Feb.1926. Board of Trade.
 Survey of industries.
>Part 1: Factors in commercial efficiency. Dec.1926.
>Part 2: Further factors in industrial efficiency. Jan.1928.
>Part 3: Survey of textile industries. Jan.1928.

>Part 4: Survey of metal industries (including coal). Jan.1928.
>Part 5: Survey of overseas markets. June 1925. Final report. 29 Jan.1929. 1928/9 Cmd.3282 vii. Minutes of evidence. 3 vols. 1930-31. Board of Trade.

Departmental committee on fire brigade services.
>Report. 25 May 1936. 1935/6. Cmd.5224 x. Home Office.

Safeguarding of industries committee.
>Report on toys. 13 March 1922. Board of Trade.

Transport development and cotton growing in East Africa. Memorandum submitted by the Committee on Industry and Trade. 2 July 1925. 1924/5 Cmd.2463 xxi. Board of Trade.

United Kingdom trade mission to Egypt.
>Report. 17 April 1931. Department of Overseas Trade.

**BALFOUR, Arthur James, *1st Earl***
The British blockade. 1915. Ministry of Information.

National and imperial defence committee.
>Recommendations on the relations of the Navy and the Air Force, and the co-ordination of the defence forces. 21 July 1923. 1923 Cmd.1938 xv. War Office.

Report of the British delegates on the third assembly of the League of Nations. 16 Oct.1922. (Misc.,no.2, 1923) 1923 Cmd.1807 xxiv. Foreign Office.

Select committee on the imprisonment of a member.
>Reports, proceedings, minutes of evidence, and appendices. 30 July 1902. 1902 (309) vi. House of Commons.

**BALFOUR, Gerald William**
Committee on ichthyological research.
>Report, minutes of evidence, appendix and index. 24 Sept.1902. 1902 Cd.1312 xv. Board of Agriculture and Fisheries.

Committee on the National Physical Laboratory.
>Report. 16 Dec.1908. 1908 Cd.3926 xxix.
>Minutes of evidence, appendices and index. 1908 Cd.3927 xxix. Treasury.

Royal commission on lighthouse administration.
>Vol.1: Report. 28 Jan.1908. 1908 Cd.3923 xlix.
>Vol.2: Minutes of evidence, appendices and index. 1908 Cd.3937 xlix.

Select committee on imprisonment of a member (P.A. M'Hugh).
>Report and special report, proceedings, minutes of evidence and appendix. 30 July 1902. 1902 (309)vi. House of Commons.

**BALFOUR, Isaac Bayley**
Report on tree pruning in the Royal parks and gardens. 28 April 1911. 1911 Cd.5823 lxiii.

**BALFOUR, Robert, *1st Bt.***
Committee on the mode of issuing the dollar in the East.
>Vol.1: Report. 21 July 1913. 1913 Cd.6973 lxvii.
>Vol.2: Minutes of evidence. 1913 Cd.6974 lxvii. Treasury.

**BALFOUR-BROWNE, J. H.**
Committee on road conveyance by railway companies.
>Report. 8 March 1921. 1921 Cmd.1228 xvii. Ministry of Transport.

**BALLANTYNE, Henry**
Royal commission on the housing of the industrial population of Scotland.
>Report. 11 Sept.1917. 1917/8 Cd.8731 xiv.
>Special report on various types of small dwelling-houses in Scotland by John Wilson. 1917/8 Cd.8760 xiv.
>Minutes of evidence. 3 vols. 1921.
>Appendices and index. 1921.

**BALLEINE, A. E.**
Report on the International Dairy Congress held at Paris in October 1905 with an appendix. 31 July 1907. 1907 Cd.3689 xvii. Board of Agriculture & Fisheries.

**BANBURY, Frederick George**
Select committee on national expenditure.
>Reports, proceedings, evidence and appendices. 22 Dec.1919. 1919 (245) v.
>Reports, proceedings, evidence and appendices. 24 Dec.1920. 1920 (248) vii. House of Commons.

Select committee on navy and army canteens.
Report, evidence and appendices. 25 July 1923. 1923 (117) vii. House of Commons.

**BANKS, John Eldon**
Committee on persons in government offices not of British or allied parentage.
>Report. 14 Feb.1919. 1919 Cmd.195 xi. Prime Minister's Office.

Departmental committee on the public system of education in Wales in relation to the needs of rural areas.
>Report. Education in Rural Wales. 23 July 1930. Board of Education. Welsh Department.

Inquiry on the interrogation by the police of Miss Savidge.
>Report of the tribunal. 11 July 1928. 1928 Cmd.3147 xii. Home Office.

Royal commission on the private manufacture of and trading in arms.
>Report. 24 Sept.1936. 1935/6 Cmd.5292 vii.
>Minutes of evidence. 1935-6.
>Index. 1936. Home Office.

**BARBER, Charles Alfred**
Tropical agricultural research in the Empire, with special reference to cacao, sugar cane, cotton and palms. Sept.1927. (E.M.B.2). Empire Marketing Board.

**BARBER, David Miller**
Report on the finances of the Transvaal and the Orange River Colony. 29 March 1901. 1901 Cd.628 xlviii. Colonial Office.

Royal commission on London traffic.
>Vol.1: Report. 26 June 1905. 1905 Cd.2597 xxx.
>Vol.2: Minutes of evidence, index and digest. 1906 Cd.2751 xi.
>Vol.3: Appendices to the evidence. 1906 Cd.2752 xli.
>Vol.4: Appendices to the report. 1906 Cd.2987 xlii.
>Vol.5: Maps and diagrams. 1906 Cd.2798 xliii.
>Vol.6: Maps and diagrams. 1906 Cd.2799 xliv.
>Vol.7: Report by the Advisory Board of Engineers. 1906 Cd.2743 xlv.
>Vol.8: Appendix to the report by the Advisory Board of Engineers. 1906 Cd.2744 xlvi.

Straits settlements currency committee.
>Report. 17 March 1903. 1903 Cd.1556 xliv.
>Minutes of evidence and appendices. 1903 Cd.1585 xliv. Colonial Office.

**BARCLAY, R. B.**
Report on the methods of administering poor relief in certain large town parishes of Scotland. 1905. 1905 Cd.2524 lxviii. Local Government Board for Scotland.

**BARCROFT, Joseph**
Haemoglobin committee.
>Report on the acid-base equilibrium of the blood. 20 Dec.1922 (S.R.S., no.72). Medical Research Council.

**BARDSWELL, Noel Dean**
Pulmonary tuberculosis: mortality after sanatorium treatments. 21 June 1919. (S.R.S., no.33). Medical Research Committee.

**BARFIELD, R. H.**
A discussion of the practical systems of direction-finding by reception. May 1923 (R.R.B. Special rep., no.1). Department of Scientific and Industrial Research.

**BARHAM, George**
Departmental committee on milk and cream regulations.
>Report. 20 Feb.1901. 1901 Cd.491 xxx.
>Minutes of evidence, appendices and index. 1901 Cd.484 xxx. Board of Agriculture.

**BARING, Evelyn, *1st Earl Cromer***
Committee on proposed school of oriental languages in London.
>Interim report and appendices. 14 June 1911. 1911 Cd.5967 xviii. India Office. (no further identified)

**BARING, Francis George, *2nd Earl Northbrook***
Select committee on the prices fixed by the Ministry of Food for milk production.
>Report, proceedings and evidence. 4 Aug.1919. 1919 (H.L.161) vii. House of Lords.

**BARING, John, *2nd Baron Revelstoke***
Royal commission on the port of London.
>Report. 16 June 1902. 1902 Cd.1151 xliii.
>Minutes of evidence. 1901 Cd.4152 xliii.
>Appendices. 1902 Cd.1153 xliv.

**BARING, Rowland Thomas, *2nd Earl Cromer***
Royal commission on the Dardanelles.
>First report 12 Feb.1917. 1917/8 Cd.8490 x.
>Supplement. 1917/8 Cd.8052 x.
>Final report: conduct of operations, *etc.,* with appendix of documents and maps. 4 Dec.1917. 1919 Cmd.371 xiii, pt.1.

**BARKER, A. H.**
Tests on ranges and cooking appliances. April 1922 (F.R.B. special rep., no.4). Department of Scientific and Industrial Research.

**BARKER, Ernest**
Linguistic oppression in the German Empire. 1918. Ministry of Information.

The relations of England and Holland. 1917. Ministry of Information.

**BARKER, J.**
Annotated bibliography on bitter-pit. Nov.1934. (Occ.Paper, no.3) Imperial Bureau of Fruit Production.

The prevention of wastage in New Zealand apples. May 1930 (F.I.B. special rep.,no.39). Department of Scientific and Industrial Research.

BARKER, J. (continued)
Wastage in imported fruit; its nature, extent and prevention. May 1930. (F.I.B. special rep., no.38) Department of Scientific and Industrial Research.

BARKER, James
Report on technical and commercial education in East Prussia, Poland, Galicia, Silesia and Bohemia. 1900. 1900 Cd.419 xxii,pt.2. Board of Education.

BARKER, Sydney George
Coir; report on the attributes and preparation of coconut fibre. Sept.1933 (E.M.B.71). Empire Marketing Board.

Sisal; a note on the attributes of the fibre and their industrial significance. May 1933 (E.M.B.64). Empire Marketing Board.

Wool; a study of the fibre. Sept.1929 (E.M.B.21). Empire Marketing Board.

Wool quality; a study of various contributory factors, their significance and the technique of their measurement. Dec.1931. Empire Marketing Board.

BARLOW, E. W.
The upper air circulation of the Atlantic Ocean. Jan.1925. (Prof.Notes,no.39). Meteorological Office.

BARLOW, Montague
Interdepartmental committee on tuberculosis sanatoria for soldiers.
Report. August 1919. 1919 Cmd.317 xxx. Ministry of Health *and* Ministry of Pensions.

Royal commission on the distribution of the industrial population.
Report. Dec.1939. 1939/40 Cmd.6153 iv.
Minutes of evidence. 1937-9.

Select committee on pensions.
First special report. 28 July 1919. 1919 (149) vi.
Second special report, proceedings, evidence, appendices, index and digest of evidence. 23 Dec.1919. 1919 (247) vi. House of Commons.

BARNARDISTON, W. N.
Handbook of the French Army, rev.ed. June 1901. War Office.

BARNES, George Nicoll
Commission of enquiry into industrial unrest.
Report of the commissioners for the north-eastern area, (no.1 division). 12 July 1917. 1917/8 Cd.8662 xv.
Report of the commissioners for the north-western area including a supplement on the Barrow-in-Furness district, (no.2 division). 16 July 1917. 1917/8 Cd.8663 xv.
Report of the commissioners for the Yorkshire and east Midlands area, (no.3 division). 17 July 1917. 1917/8 Cd.8664 xv.
Report of the commissioners for the west Midlands area, (no.4 division). 11 July 1917. 1917/8 Cd.8665 xv.
Report of the commissioners for the London and south-eastern area (no.5 division). 12 July 1917. 1917/8 Cd.8666 xv.
Report of the commissioners for the south-western area (no.6 division). 12 July 1917. 1917/8 Cd.8667 xv.
Report of the commissioners for Wales including Monmouthshire, (no.7 division). 12 July 1917. 1917/8 Cd.8668 xv.
Report of the commissioners for Scotland, (no.8 division). 10 July 1917. 1917/8 Cd.8669 xv.

Summary of the reports of the commission. 17 July 1917. 1917/8 Cd.8696 xv.
Committee on the claims of professional ex-ranker officers.
Report. 1 May 1924. 1924 Cmd.2124 vii.
Evidence. 1924 Cmd.2205 vii. War Office.

Committee of inquiry into the work of the employment exchanges.
Report. 10 Nov.1920. 1920 Cmd.1054 xix.
Minutes of evidence. 1921 Cmd.1140 xi. Ministry of Labour.

Standing committee on merchandise marks.
Report on grave monuments and enclosures of granite and parts thereof. 27 Nov.1928. 1928/9 Cmd.3246 viii. Board of Trade.

Report on spring balances. 27 Nov.1928. 1928/9 Cmd.3251 viii. Board of Trade.

BARNES, George Stapylton
Lace, embroidery and silk industries committee.
Interim report: machine-made lace and embroidery industries. 7 Nov.1923.
Final report: the silk industry. 13 Dec.1923. Board of Trade.

Profit sharing and labour co-partnership in the U.K.
Report, Nov.1912. 1912/3 Cd.6496 xliii. Board of Trade.

Safeguarding of industries.
Report of the lace and embroidery committee. 27 April 1925. 1924/5 Cmd.2403 xv. Board of Trade.

BARNES, H. F.
Insects and other pests injurious to the production of seed in herbage and forage crops. June 1937 (Bull., no.20). Imperial Bureau of Plant Genetics: Herbage Plants.

BARNES, Henry Gorell, *2nd Baron Gorell*
Royal commission on divorce and matrimonial causes.
Report. 2 Nov.1912. 1912/3 Cd.6478 xviii.
Minutes of evidence. 3 vols. 1912/3 Cd.6479, Cd.6480, Cd.6481 xviii, xix, xx.
Appendices, 1912/3 Cd.6482 xx.

BARNES, John Gorell, *1st Baron Gorell*
Committee on county court procedure.
Report. 19 Feb.1909. 1909 (71) lxxii. Home Office.

Committee on the law of copyright.
Report. Dec.1909. 1910 Cd.4976 xxi.
Minutes of evidence, appendix and table of contents. 1910 Cd.5051 xxi. Board of Trade.

BARNES, Ronald Gorell, *3rd Baron Gorell*
Civil Aviation Advisory Board.
First (and last) report on imperial air mail services. 25 July 1922. 1922 Cmd.1739 xi. Air Ministry. *See also:* Moore-Brabazon, J. T. C.

Committee on art and industry.
Report. 16 March 1932. Board of Trade.

Committee on the control of flying.
Report. 6 Feb.1939. 1938/9 Cmd.5961 ix. Air Ministry.

Committee on the production of civil aeroplanes.
Report. 6 Feb.1939. 1938/9 Cmd.6038 ix. Air Ministry.

Imperial education conference. Committee on the use of the cinematograph in education.
Report. March 1924. Board of Education.

BARNETT, P. W.
Jointless (magnesium oxychloride) floors. Aug.1925 (B.R.B.Bull.,no.1). Department of Scientific and Industrial Research.

Mechanical properties of bricks and brickwork masonry. April 1934 (B.R.B. special rep.,no.22). Department of Scientific and Industrial Research.

The reduction of noise in buildings; recommendations to architects. March 1933 (B.R.B.Bull., no.14). Department of Scientific and Industrial Research.

BARR, James
Committee on Scottish building costs.
Report. 18 March 1939. 1938/9 Cmd.5977 ix. Department of Health for Scotland.

Select committee on capital punishment.
Report, proceedings, evidence, appendices and index. 9 Dec.1930. 1930/1 (15) vi. House of Commons.

BARRAN, John N.
Departmental committee on telegraphists' cramp.
Report, appendices and index. 31 Oct.1911. 1911 Cd.5968 xli. Post Office.

BARRES, Maurice
The soul of France: visit to invaded districts. 15 May 1915. Ministry of Information.

BARROW, George
The geology of the Cheadle coalfield. 12 March 1903 (Mem.Geol.Surv.) Geological Survey.

The geology of the country around Blair Atholl, Pitlochry and Aberfeldy (sheet 55). 4 April 1905 (Mem.Geol.Surv.,Scotl.). Geological Survey, Scotland.

The geology of the country around Lichfield. (Sheet 154) 7 June 1918. (Mem.Geol.Surv.) Geological Survey.

The geology of the districts of Braemar, Ballater and Glen Clova. (Sheet 65) 16 Aug.1912. (Mem.Geol.Surv.,Scotl.) Geological Survey, Scotland.

The geology of the Isles of Scilly. (Sheets 357 and 360) 21 Feb.1906. (Mem.Geol.Surv.) Geological Survey.

The geology of upper Strathspey, Gaick and the Forest of Atholl. (Sheet 64) 12 Feb.1913. (Mem.Geol.Surv.,Scotl.) Geological Survey, Scotland.

Records of London wells. 8 Oct.1912. (Mem.Geol.Surv.) Geological Survey.

BARROW-DILLON, A.
The system of education in British Honduras. 31 Jan.1913 (Imperial education conference papers). Board of Education.

BARRY, John Wolfe
Report on experiments made to measure the vibrations at St. Paul's Cathedral. May 1913. Home Office. National Physical Laboratory.

BARTON, Bertram H.
Departmental committee on the decline of dairying in Ireland.
Report. 12 May 1920. 1920 Cmd.808 ix. Department of Agriculture and Technical Instruction for Ireland.

BASHFORD, E. F.
Report on the second international conference on cancer research held at Paris from 1st to 5th October, 1910. 14 Feb.1911. 1911 Cd.5590 lxiii. Privy Council.

BASSOMPIERRE, Albert de
The night of August 2-3, 1914 at the Belgian Foreign Office. 1916. Ministry of Information.

BATEMAN, Alfred Edmund
Advisory committee on commercial intelligence.
Report on proceedings. 24 March 1904. 1904 Cd.2044 xxiii. Board of Trade.

Committee on the participation of Great Britain in great international exhibitions.
Report and appendices. 17 Aug.1907. 1908 Cd.3772 xlix.
Minutes of evidence, appendices and index. 1908 Cd.3773 xlix. Board of Trade.

Memorandum on the position of British firms in foreign countries. Feb.1902. 1902 Cd.971 civ. Board of Trade.

Southampton harbour commission.
Report with appendices and map. 12 June 1912. 1912/3 Cd.6347 xlvii. Board of Trade.

BATESON, R. G.
Kiln-drying schedules. Oct.1938 (F.P.R. Records, no.26). Department of Scientific and Industrial Research.

Methods of kiln operation. July 1937 (F.P.R. Records, no.19). Department of Scientific and Industrial Research.

Timber seasoning. Oct.1935 (F.P.R. Records, no.4). Department of Scientific and Industrial Research.

Types of timber kilns. Nov.1936 (F.P.R. Records, no.13). Department of Scientific and Industrial Research.

BATHURST, Charles, 1st Viscount Bledisloe
Departmental committee on the re-assessment of annual grants to institutions providing higher agricultural education in England and Wales.
Report. 7 April 1927. Ministry of Agriculture and Fisheries.

Royal commission on land drainage in England and Wales.
Report. 5 Dec.1927. 1927 Cmd.2993 x.
Minutes of evidence, 1st to 11th days. 1927.

Royal commission on Rhodesia and Nyasaland.
Report. 1 March 1939. 1938/9 Cmd.5949 xv.

Select committee on House of Commons ventilation.
Report, proceedings and evidence. 12 Aug.1913. 1913 (290) vii.
Report and proceedings. 10 Aug.1914. 1914 (445) viii. House of Commons.

BATTLEY, Harry
Single finger prints; a new and practical method of classifying and filing single finger prints and fragmentary impressions. May 1930. Home Office.

BAXANDALL, Frank E.
Comparison of the spectra of rigelian, cracian and alnitamian stars. May 1914. Solar Physics Committee. Board of Education.

Researches on the chemical origin of various lines in solar and stellar spectra. Oct.1910. Solar physics committee. Board of Education.

BAYLIS, P. G. S.
Report on a course for the training of visiting teachers held at Toro and Gombe, Northern Provinces Nigeria, 1936-8. 24 June 1938 (Colonial, no.174). 1940. Colonial Office.

Beach, M. E. H. SEE: Hicks-Beach, M. E.

BEACHCROFT, Charles Porten
Report on detainees and internees in Bengal. 31 Aug.1918. 1918 Cd.9198 viii. India Office.

BEADLE, John Field
Wheat Act, 1932. Standard price committee.
Report. 6 June 1935. 1934/5 Cmd.4932 xi. Ministry of Agriculture and Fisheries.

BEADLE, Ormond Alec
The intervertebrae discs; observations on their normal and morbid anatomy in relation to certain spinal deformities. 23 Oct.1931 (S.R.S., no.161). Medical Research Council.

BEARD, E. H.
Strontium minerals. 1937 (Rep.Min.Ind.). Imperial Institute.

BEATTIE, James Martin
On the destruction of bacteria in milk by electricity. 20 Feb.1920 (S.R.S., no.49). Medical Research Committee.

BEAUCHAMP, J. W.
Advisory committee on domestic supplies of electricity and methods of charge.
Report. 17 July 1926. Ministry of Transport.

BEAUCHAMP, William Lygon, *7th Earl*
Joint select committee on lotteries and indecent advertisements.
Report, proceedings, evidence, appendices and index. 29 July 1908. 1908 (275) ix. House of Commons.

Select committee on life insurance companies.
Report, proceedings, evidence and appendix. 31 July 1906. 1906 (H.L. 194). House of Lords.

Beaufort, *Lord. SEE:* Somerset, H.A.W.F., *9th Duke*

BECK, Arthur Cecil Tyrrell
Select committee on land values.
Report, proceedings, evidence and appendices. 22 Dec.1919. 1920 Cmd.556 xix. House of Commons.

BECKER, Ludwig
The climatology of Glasgow. 20 Sept.1921 (Geophys.Mem., no.23). Meteorological Office.

BECKETT, H. E.
Ultra-violet window-glazing. Aug.1930 (B.R.B.Bull., no.8). Department of Scientific and Industrial Research.

BEDFORD, T.
Preliminary notes on atmospheric conditions in boot and shoe factories. March 1921 (I.H.R.B. Rep., no.11). Medical Research Council.

Two studies on rest pauses in industry. Feb.1924 (I.H.R.B. Rep., no.25). Medical Research Council.

The warmth factor in comfort at work; a psychological study of heating and ventilation. July 1936 (I.H.R.B. Rep., no.76). Medical Research Council.

BEDIER, Joseph
German atrocities from German evidence. 1915. Ministry of Information.

BEGBIE, Sydney D.
Standing committee on prices.
Report of a sub-committee on brushes and brooms. 8 April 1921. 1921 Cmd.1275 xvi. Board of Trade.

Standing committees on prices and trusts.
Report of a sub-committee on dyeing and cleaning. 3 May 1921. 1921 Cmd.1361 xvi. Board of Trade.

BEILBY, George Thomas
Report on gas standards, by the Fuel Research Board. 29 Jan.1919. 1919 Cmd.108 xxii. Board of Trade *and* Department of Scientific and Industrial Research.

BELASCO, J. E.
The effect of variation in relative wind force on the readings of wet and dry bulb thermometers. July 1930 (Prof.Notes, no.57). Meteorological Office.

BELL, Archibald Colquhon
History of the Great War. A history of the blockade of Germany, Austria-Hungary, Bulgaria and Turkey, 1914-1918. 1 March 1937. War Office. 1961.

BELL, E. Seymour
Report on the cement industry in the United States. 28 May 1900. (Dip.Cons.rep.: misc.ser., no.556). 1901 Cd.430-11 lxxx. Foreign Office.

Report on the coal and coke trade of the United States. 3 July 1901. (Dip.Cons.rep.: misc.ser.,no.562). 1901 Cd.430-17 lxxx. Foreign Office.

Report on the coal industry of the United States. 18 Dec.1902. (Dip.Cons.rep.: misc.ser., no.587). 1903 Cd.1387 lxxvi. Foreign Office.

Report on the coal industry of the United States, 1903. 21 Feb.1905. (Dip.Cons.rep.: misc.ser., no.631). 1905 Cd.2237-12 lxxxvi. Foreign Office.

Report on the coal industry of the United States, 1904. 9 Jan.1906. (Dip.Cons.rep.: misc.ser., no.643). 1906 Cd.2683-7 cxxii. Foreign Office.

Report on the iron and steel exhibits at the St.Louis Exhibition. Feb.1905. (Dip.Cons.rep.: misc.ser., no.626). 1905 Cd.2237-7 lxxxvi. Foreign Office.

Report on the rice industry in the United States. 5 Dec.1904. (Dip.Cons.rep.: misc.ser., no.625). 1905 Cd.2237-6 lxxxvi. Foreign Office.

Report on the turpentine industry in the United States. 12 Mar.1906. (Dip.Cons.rep.: misc.ser., no.647). 1906 Cd.2683-11 cxxii. Foreign Office.

BELL, Gertrude Margaret Lowthian
Review of the civil administration of Mesopotania. 3 Dec.1920. 1920 Cmd.1061 li. India Office.

BELL, Henry Hesketh
Report on a tour through the eastern province of Uganda. 11 Sept.1908. (Colonial reports, misc. no.,57) 1909 Cd.4524 lix. Colonial Office.

Report on the introduction and establishment of the cotton industry in the Uganda protectorate. 14 Sept.1909. (Colonial reports, misc., no.62). 1909 Cd.4910 lix. Colonial Office.

Report on the measures adopted for the suppression of sleeping sickness in Uganda. 17 Nov.1909 (Colonial reports, misc., no.65). 1910 Cd.4990 lxv. Colonial Office.

BELL, Hugh
Departmental committee on the Science Museum and the Geological Museum.
Report. 22 March 1911. 1911 Cd.5625 xviii. Board of Education.
Report, (part 2). 19 April 1912. 1912/3 Cd.6221 xxii. Board of Education.

BELL, J. D.
Report on certain valuations in connection with Sir Alexander Binnie's report on the Bann and Lough Neagh drainage. 6 April 1907. 1907 Cd.3534 lxvii. Irish Secretary's Office.

BELL, Robert Duncan
Commission on the financial position and further development of Nyasaland. 4 July 1938. (Colonial no.152). Colonial Office.

BELL, Thomas
Oil fuel committee.
Report on conditions to prevent the danger of fire on passenger ships burning oil fuel. 11 Aug.1920. 1920 Cmd.944 xxi. Board of Trade.

BELLHOUSE, Gerald
Civil war workers committee
First (interim) report. July 1918. 1918 Cd.9117 xiv.
Second to fifth interim reports. March to Sept.1918. 1918 Cd.9192. xiv.
Final report. 7 Nov.1918. 1918 Cd.9228 xiv. Ministry of Reconstruction.

Departmental committee on the hours and conditions of employment of van boys and warehouse boys.
Report. 2 May 1913. 1913 Cd.6886 xxxiii.
Minutes of evidence. 1913 Cd.6887 xxxiii. Home Office.

Departmental committee on the occurrence of epitheliomatous ulceration among mule spinners.
Report. Feb.1926. Home Office.

Report of the conference on the prevention of accidents at docks. Feb.1924. Home Office.

Report on conferences concerning fencing of machinery, prevention of accidents and temperature in cotton spinning mills. 22 July 1912. Home Office.

Report on the transmission of certain diseases in weaving sheds by means of "shuttle-kissing". April, 1912. 1912/3 Cd.6184 xxvi. Home Office and Local Government Board.

BELPER, Henry Strutt, 2nd Baron
Departmental committee on the jurisdiction of the Metropolitan Police magistrates and county justices in the Metropolitan Police Court district.
Report, minutes of evidence, appendices and indices. 18 Aug.1899. 1900 Cd.374 xl. Home Office.

Departmental committee on Metropolitan police court jurisdiction in Middlesex.
Vol.1: Report. 16 July 1904. 1904 Cd.2215 xxxiv.
Vol.2: Minutes of evidence. 1904 Cd.2216 xxxiv. Home Office.

BENN, Arthur Shirley
Select committee on transport. Irish Sub-committee. SEE: Wilson-Fox, H.

BENNETT, A. Percy
Report on the Austro-Hungarian currency. 27 Nov.1901. (Dip.cons.reports: misc.ser., no.571). 1902 Cd.787-7 ciii. Foreign Office.

Report on the industrial development of Italy. 2 May 1904. (Dip.cons.reports: misc.ser., no.610). 1904 Cd.1767-14 xcvi. Foreign Office.

Report on the mineral resources of Greece. 31 Mar.1902. (Dip.cons.reports: misc.ser., no.576) 1902 Cd.787-12 ciii. Foreign Office.

BENNETT, Norman Godfrey.
Committee on dental disease. Investigation into the influence of diet on caries in children's teeth.
Interim report. 1 Aug.1931 (S.R.S., no.159).
Final report. 24 June 1936. (S.R.S., no.211). Medical Research Council.

Committee on dental disease. Report on the incidence of dental disease in children. Nov.1925 (S.R.S., no.97). Medical Research Council.

BENSON, Edward Frederick
Deutschland über Allah. 1917. Ministry of Information.

Poland and Mittel-Europa. 1918. Ministry of Information.

BENTINCK, Henry Cavendish, Lord
Inter-departmental committee on the grading and marking of beef.
Report. Aug.1930. 1929/30 Cmd.3648 viii. Ministry of Agriculture and Fisheries and Scottish Office.

Bentinck, W.J.A.C.J.C. SEE: Cavendish-Bentinck. W.J.A.C.J.

BENTLEY, Francis Joseph
Artificial pneumothorax; experience of the London County Council. 27 July 1936. (S.R.S., no.215) Medical Research Council.

BERRY, John
Notes on the migration of salmon smolts from Loch Ness, summer 1932. 1933 (Salmon Fish., 1933, no.1). Fishery Board for Scotland.

Report of an investigation of the migration of smolts in the River Tay during Spring 1931. (Salmon Fish., 1931, no.6). Fishery Board for Scotland.

BESANT, Arthur Digby
Unemployment insurance statutory committee.
Report on draft regulations. 23 March 1936. Ministry of Labour.

BESSEY, G. E.
The estimation of free calcium oxide and hydroxide. Sept.1931. (B.R.B. Special rep., no.17) Department of Scientific and Industrial Research.

Sand-lime bricks. Feb.1934. (B.R.B. Special rep., no.21) Department of Scientific and Industrial Research.

BEST, A. C.
Abnormal visibility at Malta. July 1939. (Prof. Notes, no.89) Meteorological Office.

Transfer of heat and momentum in the lowest layers of the atmosphere. July 1935. (Geophys.Mem., no.65) Meteorological Office.

BETTERTON, Henry Bucknall
Committee on the staffing and methods of work of the Royal Commission on Sugar Supplies.
Report. 14 Aug.1920. 1920 Cmd.1069 xxv. Prime Minister's Office.

Departmental committee on the non-ferrous mining industry.
Report. 17 March 1920. 1920 Cmd.652 xxi. Board of Trade.

Interdepartmental committee on public assistance administration.
Report. 20 Dec.1923. 1924 Cmd.2011 xii. Ministry of Labour and Ministry of Health.

Report of the British delegates on the International Labour Conference, seventh session, May to June 1925. July 1925. 1924/5 Cmd.2465 xxxii. Ministry of Labour.

BEVAN, Edwin
German war aims. 1917. Ministry of Information.

BEVERIDGE, William Henry
    Letter on the unemployment fund general account. 4 Nov.1937. 1937/8 Cmd.5603 xxi. Ministry of Labour.

    Standing committee on prices.
        Report on prices, costs and profits of the biscuit trade. 8 July 1920. 1920 Cmd.856 xxiii. Board of Trade.

    Standing committee on trusts.
        Report on the soap industry. 23 Dec.1920. 1921 Cmd.1126 xvi. Board of Trade.

    Unemployment insurance statutory committee.
        Memorandum on excepting certain employments as inconsiderable. 7 May 1935. Ministry of Labour.

    Unemployment insurance advisory committee.
        Report on draft regulations. 12 Aug.1933. 1932/3 Cmd.4407 xv. Ministry of Labour.

    Unemployment insurance statutory committee.
        Report on draft regulations. 9 June 1936. Ministry of Labour.

        Report on draft regulations. 17 July 1936. Ministry of Labour.

        Report on draft regulations. 12 Oct.1936. Ministry of Labour.

        Report on draft regulations. 22 Oct.1936. Ministry of Labour.

        Report on insurance against unemployment of persons engaged in agriculture. 20 Dec.1934. 1934/5. Cmd.4786 xiv. Ministry of Labour.

        Report on the draft Unemployment Insurance (Anomolies) (Seasonal Workers) Order, 1935. 5 July 1935. 1934/5 (123) xiv. Ministry of Labour.

        Report on the draft Unemployment Insurance (Anomolies) (Seasonal Workers) (Amendment) Order, 1936. 5 June 1936. 1935/6 (125) xviii. Ministry of Labour.

        Report on the draft Unemployment Insurance (Benefit) (Amendment) Regulations, 1936. 27 Jan.1937. Ministry of Labour.

        Report on the draft Unemployment Insurance (Benefit) (Amendment) (No.2) Regulations, 1937. 30 April 1937. Ministry of Labour.

        Report on the draft Unemploment Insurance (Benefit) (Miscellaneous Provisions) Regulations, 1938. 28 April 1938. Ministry of Labour.

        Report on the draft Unemployment Insurance (Contributions) (Amendment) Regulations, 1939. 27 April 1939. Ministry of Labour.

        Report on the draft Unemployment Insurance (Crediting of Contributions) (Amendment) Regulations, 1937. 9 Dec.1937. Ministry of Labour.

        Report on the draft Unemployment Insurance (Inconsiderable Employments) Regulations, 1935. 10 July 1935. Ministry of Labour.

        Report on the draft Unemployment (Insurable Employments) Regulations, 1937. 14 Oct.1937. Ministry of Labour.

        Report on the draft Unemployment Insurance (Inconsiderable Employments) (Amendment) Regulations. 10 June 1937. Ministry of Labour.

        Report on the draft Unemployment Insurance (Inconsiderable Employments) (Persons Under Sixteen) Regulations. 5 March 1935. Ministry of Labour.

        Report on the draft Unemployment Insurance (Insurable Employments) Regulations, 1936. 10 Jan.1936. Ministry of Labour.

        Report on the draft Unemployment Insurance (Insurable Employments) (No.2) Regulations, 1937. 14 Jan.1938. Ministry of Labour.

        Report on the draft Unemployment Insurance (Insurable Employments) (Agriculture) Regulations, 1938. 5 March 1938. Ministry of Labour.

        Report on the draft Unemployment Insurance (Mixed Employment) Regulations. 5 Feb. 1937. Ministry of Labour.

        Report on the draft Unemployment Insurance (Special Arrangements) Regulations, 1937. 11 Nov.1937. Ministry of Labour.

        Report on the draft Unemployment Insurance (Special Schemes) (Transfer) Regulations, 1939. 25 May 1939. Ministry of Labour.

        Report on the extension of unemployment insurance to outdoor private domestic servants. 23 Oct.1937. Ministry of Labour.

        Report on the extension of unemployment insurance to private gardeners. 3 July 1936. 1935/6 (157) xvii. Ministry of Labour.

        Report on holidays and suspensions in relation to unemployment insurance. 7 Oct.1938. Ministry of Labour.

        Report on remuneration limit for insurance of non-manual workers. 7 Feb.1936. Ministry of Labour.

        Report on shore fishermen in relation to the unemployment scheme. 22 Oct.1936. Ministry of Labour.

BHOWNAGGREE, Mancherjee Merwanjee.
    The verdict of India. 1916. Ministry of Information.

BIDDULPH, Robert
    Proceedings of a court of enquiry on the administration of the army remount department. 22 Aug.1902. 1902 Cd.993 lviii.
        Evidence and appendices. 1902 Cd.994 lviii. War Office.

BIGG, W. H.
    Ice formation in clouds in Great Britain. Dec.1937. (Prof. Notes, no.81) Meteorological Office.

BIGGER, Edward Coey
    Irish public health council.
        Report on the public health and medical services in Ireland. 10 May 1920. 1920 Cmd.761 xvii. Irish Secretary's Office.

BIGHAM, Charles Clive, *2nd Viscount Mersey*
    Select committee on agriculture (damage by rabbits).
        Report, proceedings and evidence. 25 Feb.1937. 1936/7 (H.L.58) iv. House of Lords.

    Select committee on auctioneers', house agents' and valuers' licences.
        Report, proceedings, evidence and appendix. 18 July 1935. 1934/5 (H.L.134) vi. House of Lords.

BIGHAM, John Charles, *1st Baron Mersey*
    Commission of inquiry into the casualty to the British steamship "Empress of Ireland" in the River St. Lawrence on 29 May 1914.

BIGHAM, John Charles, *1st Baron Mersey.* (continued)
Report. 11 July 1914. 1914 Cd.7609 lxx. Board of Trade.

Departmental committee on law and practice with regard to juries.
Vol.1:   Report. May 1913. 1913 Cd.6817 xxx.
Vol.2:   Minutes of evidence and appendices. 1913 Cd.6318 xxx. Home Office.

Departmental committee on the Salford Hundred court of record.
Report, minutes of evidence, appendices and index. 22 Dec.1910. 1911 Cd.5530 xl. Privy Council.

Formal investigation into the foundering on 28 March 1915 of the British steamship "Falaba" of Liverpool.
Report. 8 July 1915. 1914/6 Cd.8021 xxvii. Board of Trade.

Formal investigation into the foundering on 7 May 1915 of the British steamship "Lusitania" of Liverpool after being torpedoed off the Old Head of Kinsale, Ireland.
Report. 17 July 1915. 1914/6 Cd.8022 xxvii.
Proceedings *in camera.* 1919 Cmd.381 xxv. Board of Trade.

Report on the loss of the "Titanic" (S.S.). 30 July 1912. 1912/3 Cd.6352 lxxxvi. Board of Trade.

BILES, John Harvard
Departmental committee on boats and davits.
Interim report. 9 Dec. 1912. 1912/3 Cd.6558 xxxviii.
Report. 15 May 1913. 1913 Cd.6846 xviii. Board of Trade.

BILHAM, E. G.
Changes of zero in spirit thermometers. Feb.1929. (Prof. Notes, no.51). Meteorological Office.

The effect of variation in relative wind force on the readings of wet and dry bulb thermometers. July 1930. (Prof. Notes, no.57) Meteorological Office.

The effects of obstacles on sunshine records. June 1937. (Prof. Notes, no.76) Meteorological Office.

The frequency of days with specified duration of sunshine. July 1935. (Prof. Notes, no.69) Meteorological Office.

A height-computer for use in aerological work. March 1938. (Prof. Notes, no.80) Meteorological Office.

Pressure type in relation to fog frequency at Scilly during summer months. Oct.1924. (Prof. Notes, no.37) Meteorological Office.

The structure of the atmosphere over Benson (Oxon) on 3 March 1920. June 1921. (Prof. Notes, no.21) Meteorological Office.

BILLETT, H.
The South Wales tornado of 27 October 1913. 22 Sept.1914. (Geophys.Mem., no.11) Meteorological Office.

BILSLAND, Alexander Steven
Council for art and industry, Scottish committee.
Report on design in the Scottish woollen industry. July 1936. Board of Trade.

Report on education for the consumer; art in general education in Scotland. Aug.1935. Board of Trade.

Report on exhibitions of school crafts in Scotland. April 1939. Board of Trade.

BILSLAND, William
Departmental committee on inebriates detention in reformatories and retreats, Scotland.
Report. 23 June 1909. 1909 Cd.4766 xxvi.
Minutes of evidence, *etc.* 1909 Cd.4767 xxvi. Scottish Office.
*See also :* Dickson-Poynder, J.P.

Bingley, *Lord. SEE:* Lane-Fox, G. R., *1st Baron.*

BINNIE, Alexander Richardson
Arterial drainage commission (Ireland).
Report. 23 Feb.1907. 1907 Cd.3374 xxxii.
Appendix. 1907 Cd.3467 xxxii. Irish Secretary's Office.

Report on Bann and Lough Neagh drainage. 16 Jan.1906. 1906 Cd.2855 xcvi. Irish Secretary's Office.

BIRCHENOUGH, Henry
Advisory council, section 2.
Final report on anti-dumping legislation. 17 Oct.1918. 1919 Cmd.455 xxix. (no others identified) Ministry of Reconstruction.

Committee of chairmen on electric power supply.
Report. 14 Oct.1918. 1919 Cmd.93 xxix. Ministry of Reconstruction.

Departmental committee on the textile trades after the war.
Report. 22 May 1917. 1918 Cd.9070 xiii. Board of Trade.

Empire cotton growing committee.
Report. 22 Oct.1919. 1920 Cmd.523 xvi. Board of Trade.

Report on the present position and future prospects of British trade in South Africa. 21 Aug.1903. 1904 Cd.1844 lxi. Board of Trade.

BIRKETT, William Norman
Interdepartmental committee on abortion.
Report. March 1939. Ministry of Health.

BIRRELL, A.
Committee on retrenchment in public expenditure.
*SEE:* McKenna, R.

BJERKNES, J.
Practical examples of polar-front analysis over the British Isles in 1925-6. July 1930. (Geophys.Mem., no.50) Meteorological Office.

BJORKLUND, Charles J.
Memorandum on Mexican imports from the United Kingdom and Germany. July 1907. (Dip.cons.reports: misc.ser.no.662) 1907 Cd.3284-6 lxxxvii. Foreign Office *and* Board of Trade.

Report on livestock in Mexico. 26 April 1904. (Dip.cons.reports: misc.ser. no.614) 1904 Cd.1767-18 xcvi. Foreign Office.

Report on the Federal District of Mexico. 23 Oct.1899. (Dip.cons.reports: Misc.ser.no.517) 1900 Cd.2 xci. Foreign Office.

BLACK, Archibald Campbell
Scottish departmental committee on the training of nurses.
Report. Feb.1936. 1935/6 Cmd.5093 xi. Department of Health for Scotland.

BLACKBURN, J. M.
The acquisition of skill; an analysis of learning curves. March 1936. (I.H.R.B. Rep., no.73) Medical Research Council.

BLACKBURN, Robert L.
Departmental committee on fees exigible in the courts of session and justiciary and in the sheriff courts.
Report. 8 May 1922. Scottish Office.

Departmental committee on procurators-fiscal, sheriff-clerks, the commissary clerk, the sheriff-clerk of Chancery, and their respective staffs.
Report. 20 Dec.1920. Scottish Office.

BLACKLOCK, John William Stewart
Tuberculosis disease in children; its pathology and bacteriology. 28 July 1932. (S.R.S., no.172) Medical Research Council.

BLACKSHAW, J. F.
Departmental committee on rationing of dairy cows.
Report. 13 Aug.1925. Ministry of Agriculture and Fisheries.

BLACKTIN, S. C.
Spontaneous electrification in coal-dust clouds. March 1931. (S.M.R.B. Paper no.71) Mines Department.

Spontaneous electrification in dust clouds. March 1928. (S.M.R.B. Paper no.43) Mines Department.

BLAIR, E. W.
The production of formaldehyde by oxidation of hydrocarbons. July 1927. (Chemistry research special rep., no.1) Department of Scientific and Industrial Research.

BLAKE, Herbert Acton
Report of the conference on the system of marking wrecks. 22 March 1923. Board of Trade.

Blake, Isobel. SEE: Williamson, I. J. F.

BLACK, John Hopwood
The geology of the country around Reading. (Sheet 268) 25 March1925. (Mem.Geol.Surv.) Geological Survey.

The water supply of Berkshire from underground sources. 29 July 1901. (Mem.Geol.Surv.) Geological Survey.

BLAKEMORE, Felix J.
Standing committee on trusts.
Report of a sub-committee on yeast. 3 March 1921. 1921 Cmd.1216 xvi. Board of Trade.

BLAKEY, J.
Report on the mortality of government life annuitants. 12 Oct.1910. 1912/3 (298) xlix. National Debt Office, Treasury.

Blanesburgh, Baron. SEE: Younger, Robert, Baron Blanesburgh.

Bledisloe, Baron. SEE: Bathurst, C. 1st Viscount Bledisloe.

BLENKINSOP, Layton John
History of the Great War. Veterinary Services. 21 April 1924. War Office.

BLOMFIELD, Reginald
Committee on the treatment of the gallery and staircase leading to the lecture theatre in the Victoria and Albert Museum.
Report. June 1912. 1912/3 Cd.6355 xxii. Board of Education.

Royal fine art commission.
Report on the proposed St. Paul's bridge. 8 July 1924. 1924 Cmd.2228 ix.

BLUNDELL, F. N.
Reorganisation commission forEngland and Wales.
Report on eggs and poultry. 24 Jan.1935

(Economic Series, no.42). Ministry of Agriculture.

Reorganisation commission for G.B.
Report on eggs and poultry. 5 Dec.1935. (Economic Series, no.43). Ministry of Agriculture.

BLYTH, James, 1st Baron
Report on agriculture and viticulture in South Africa. June 1909 (Colonial Reports misc., no.61). 1909 Cd.4909 lix. Colonial Office.

Blythswood, Lord. SEE: Campbell, A. C. 1st Baron.

BODKIN, Archibald Henry
Committee on alterations in criminal procedure (indictable offences).
Report. 6 Dec.1921. 1923 Cmd.1813 x. Lord Chancellor's Office.

Departmental committee on share-pushing.
Report. 27 July 1937. 1936/7 Cmd.5539 xv. Board of Trade.

Departmental committee on the statutory definition and classification of firearms and ammunition.
Report. 8 Nov.1934. 1934/5 Cmd.4758 viii. Home Office.

Quarter sessions committee.
Report. 17 July 1936. 1935/6 Cmd.5252 viii. Lord Chancellor's Office.

BOLAM, Robert
Departmental committee on the training and employment of midwives.
Report. 10 July 1929. Ministry of Health.

Bonar Law. A. SEE: Law, A. B.

BOND, Charles Hubert
Committee on nursing in county and borough mental hospitals.
Report. 25 July 1924. Board of Control.

BONFIELD, Margaret Grace
Report by the British delegates on the International Labour Conference, 11th session, 10-28 June 1930. Jan.1931. 1930/1 Cmd.3774 xxxv. Ministry of Labour.

Report from the delegation to obtain information regarding the system of child migration and settlement in Canada. 18 Nov.1924. 1924/5 Cmd.2285 xv. Colonial Office.

BONN, Max J.
London Advisory Council for juvenile employment.
A guide to employment for London boys and girls. March 1928. Ministry of Labour.

A guide to employment for boys and girls in greater London. July 1938. Ministry of Labour.

BONNELL, D. G. R.
The prevention of pattern staining of plasters. Feb.1931 (B.R.B.Bull., no.10). Department of Scientific and Industrial Research.

BONNER, George Albert
Report on draft regulations for spinning flax and tow. 25 Jan.1906. 1906 Cd.2851 xv. Home Office.

BOOTH, Alfred Allen
Departmental committee on shipping and shipbuilding industries after the war.
Reports. March 1918. 1918 Cd.9092 xiii. Board of Trade.

BORSA, Mario
England and her critics. 1917. Ministry of Information.

Boscawen, A. S. T. G. *SEE:* Griffith-Boscawen, A. S. T.

BOSCAWEN, Evelyn Hugh, *8th Viscount Falmouth*
Committee of Imperial Defence. Sub-committee on oil from coal.
    Report. 31 Jan.1938. 1937/8 Cmd.5665 xii.
    Ministry for the Co-ordination of Defence.

Departmental committee on the imposition of penalties by marketing boards and other similar bodies.
    Report. 20 March 1939. 1938/9 Cmd.5980 xiv. Treasury.

BOSWELL, Percy George Hamnall
The geology of the country around Ipswich. (Sheet 207) 29 Oct.1927. (Mem.Geol.Surv.) Geological Survey.

The geology of the country around Sudbury, Suffolk. (Sheet 206) 27 Oct. 1928. (Mem.Geol.Surv.) Geological Survey.

The geology of the country around Woodbridge, Felixstowe and Oxford. (Sheets 208 and 225) 3 March 1928. (Mem.Geol.Surv.) Geological Survey.

BOTTOMLEY, William Cecil.
Colonial survey committee.
    Special report on the triangulations of eastern and central Africa. June 1928. (Colonial, no.33). Colonial Office.

BOURNE, Robert Croft
Committee on common form clauses in private bills.
    Report. 31 July 1936. 1935/6 (162) v. House of Commons.

BOVINGDON, H. H. S.
Report on the infestation of cured tobacco in London by the cacao moth *ephestia elutella HB*. July 1933. (E.M.B.67) Empire Marketing Board.

BOWDEN, John
Commission of enquiry on the De Vecchis beet sugar process.
    Report. 4 Feb.1925. 1924/5 Cmd.2343 ix. Ministry of Agriculture and Fisheries.

BOWERMAN, Charles William
Committee to select the best faces of type and modes of display for government printing.
    Report. 4 July 1922. Treasury.

BOWLES, Henry F.
Select committee on workmen's trains.
    Report, proceedings, minutes of evidence and appendix. 3 Aug.1904. 1904 (305) vii. House of Commons.

    Report, proceedings, evidence and appendix. 27 July 1905. 1905 (270) viii. House of Commons.

BOWMAN, Alexander
Biological exchanges between the Atlantic and the North Sea.
    No.1. The relationships of the Genus arnoglossus. 1922. (Sci.invest., 1922, no.2) (No further reports identified) Fishery Board for Scotland.

Danish seine-net fishing in the Moray Firth. 1928. (Sci.invest., 1928 no. 2) Fishery Board for Scotland.

The distribution of plaice eggs in the northern North Sea. 1921 (Sci.invest., 1914, no.2). Part 2. March 1921 (Sci.Invest., 1921, no.1) Fishery Board for Scotland.

Distribution of the larvae of the eel in Scottish waters. 1912 (Sci.invest., 1912, no.2). Fishery Board for Scotland.

Lemon soles; marking experiments 1919-1931. 1935 (Sci.invest., 1935, no.1). Fishery Board for Scotland.

Line fishing in the Moray Firth during the period 1904-1916. 1927 (Sci.invest., 1927, no.2). Fishery Board for Scotland.

Review of the cod net fishing in the Moray Firth. 1928 (Sci.invest., 1928, no.1). Fishery Board for Scotland.

The spawning areas of sand-eels in the North Sea. 1913 (Sci.invest., 1913, no.3). Fishery Board for Scotland.

Spawny haddocks; their occurrence and the locus and extent of herring spawning grounds. 1922 (Sci.invest., 1922, no.4). Fishery Board for Scotland.

BOWYER, George
Select committee on the civil service (employment of conscientious objectors).
    Report. 10 April 1922. 1922 (69) iv. House of Commons.

BOYCOTT, A. E.
Report on the diagnosis of ankylostoma infection with special reference to the examination of the blood. May 1904. 1904 Cd.2066 xiii. Home Office.

BOYD, Elizabeth M.
A preliminary investigation of the food of the sea trout. 1930 (Salmon Fish., 1930, no.3). Fishery Board for Scotland.

A second investigation of the food of the sea trout. 1932. (Salmon Fish., 1932, no.2). Fishery Board for Scotland.

A third investigation of the food of the sea trout, with a note on the food of the perch. 1934 (Salmon Fish., 1934, no.2). Fishery Board for Scotland.

BOYD, John Alexander
Supply handbook for the Army Service Corps. Feb.1904. War Office.

BOYS, Charles Vernon
Committee on acetylene generators.
    Report. 30 Oct.1901. 1902 Cd.952 x. Home Office.

Brabazon, J. T. C. M. *SEE:* Moore-Brabazon, J. T. C.

BRABROOK, E. W.
Report on the Outdoor Relief (Friendly Societies) (no.2) Bill, 1900. 1903 (H.L.60) xi. Treasury.

BRADBURY, John Swanwick, *1st Baron Bradbury of Winsford*
Committee on currency and Bank of England note issues.
    Report. 5 Feb.1925. 1924/5 Cmd.2393 ix. Treasury.

Committee on municipal savings banks.
    Report. 28 Nov.1927. 1928 Cmd.3014 ix. Treasury.

Committee on the organisation and staffing of government offices. Committee on staffs.
    Interim report. 5 April 1918. 1918 Cd.9074 vii.
    Second interim report. Oct.1918. 1918 Cd.9219 vii.
    Third interim report. 5 Nov.1918. 1918 Cd.9220 vii.
    Fourth interim report. 21 Feb.1919. 1919 Cmd.61 xi.
    Final report. 21 Feb.1919. 1919 Cmd.62 xi. Treasury.

BRADBURY, John Swanwick, *1st Baron Bradbury of Winsford*. (continued)
Court of inquiry concerning steel houses.
Report. 23 April 1925. 1924/5 Cmd.2392 xiii. Ministry of Labour.

Food council.
Report on fish prices. 18 Nov.1927. Board of Trade.

Report on short weight and measure in the sale of foodstuffs. 5 Feb.1926. 1926 Cmd.2591 x. Minutes of evidence. 4 vols. 1925-1926. Board of Trade.

Report on wholesale tea prices. 15 Oct.1926. Board of Trade.

BRADFORD, Edward R. C.
Committee on Post Office wages.
Part I: Report. 9 May 1904. 1904 Cd.2170 xxxiii.
Part II: Minutes of evidence, summary, appendices and indexes. 1904 Cd.2171 xxxiii. Post Office.

BRADY, F. L.
The corrosion of steel by breeze and clinker concretes. April 1930 (B.R.B. Special rep., no.15). Department of Scientific and Industrial Research.

The durability of slates for roofing. Feb.1932 (B.R.B. Bull., no.12). Department of Scientific and Industrial Research.

External rendered finishes; a survey of continental practice. Aug.1938. (B.R.B. Bull., no.16). Department of Scientific and Industrial Research.

Fire resistant construction. Jan.1927. (B.R.B. Special rep., no.8). Department of Scientific and Industrial Research.

Pozzolanas. Oct.1927 (B.R.B. Bull., no.2). Department of Scientific and Industrial Research.

The prevention of corrosion of lead in buildings. Oct.1929 (B.R.B. Bull., no.6). Department of Scientific and Industrial Research.

Slag, coke, breeze and clinker as aggregates. July 1927 (B.R.B. special rep., no.10). Department of Scientific and Industrial Research.

BRAME, John Samuel Stratford
Report of the proposed revision of bye-laws for regulating the transport of petroleum spirit in the Port of London. 9 May 1928. Ministry of Transport.

BRAMSDON, Thomas Arthur
Select committee on business premises.
Report, proceedings, evidence and appendices. 14 Dec.1920. 1920 (237) vi. House of Commons.

BRANCKER, William Sefton
Committee on West Indian air transport.
Report on the opportunities for civil air transport in the West Indies. 25 Oct.1926. 1927 Cmd.2968 xii. Air Ministry.

BRAND, David
Social condition of the people of Lewis in 1901 compared with twenty years ago.
Report by the Crofters Commission. 31 March 1902. 1902 Cd.1327 lxxxiii. Crofters Commission.

BRAND, E.
Report on prospects for growing cotton in the East Africa protectoriate. 22 Jan.1904. (Dip.cons. reports: misc.ser., no.606) 1904 Cd.1767-10 xcvi. Foreign Office.

BRAND, James
Report on the veterinary survey of Northern Nigeria. 5 Aug.1909. 1910 Cd.4973 lxvi. Colonial Office.

BRAND, Robert Henry
The financial and economic future. 1919. (National economy series, no.2) National War Savings Committee.

BRANFOOT, M. H.
A critical and historical study of the pectic substances of plants. July 1929. (F.I.B. special rep., no.33) Department of Scientific and Industrial Research.

BRANSON, George Arthur Harwin
Public trustee (infants damages) committee.
Report. 28 April 1923. 1923 Cmd.1870 xii, pt.2. Lord Chancellor's Office.

BRANTHWAITE, Robert Welsh
Committee on the diet of patients in mental hospitals.
Report. 20 May 1924. Board of Control.

Report on an outbreak of enteric fever at Brentry certified inebriate reformatory. Feb.1908. 1908 Cd.3938 xii. Home Office.

BRAY, R. A.
The problem of juvenile employment after the war. April 1918. Ministry of Labour.

BRAZELL, J. H.
The relation between the blueness of the sky and (a) the polarity of the air and (b) the gradient wind. Dec.1938. (Prof.Notes, no.85) Meteorological Office.

Breadalbane, *Lord. SEE*: Campbell, G. *1st Marquis of Breadalbane.*

BREND, William Alfred
The mortalities of birth, infancy and childhood. 30 Aug.1917. (S.R.S.,no.10) Medical Research Committee.

BRETT, Reginald Baliol, *2nd Viscount Esher*
Committee on His Majesty's Osborne estate in the Isle of Wight.
Report. 6 Dec.1902. 1902 Cd.1384 lxxxiii. Privy Council.

Committee on the administration and organisation of the Army in India.
Report. 22 June 1920. 1920 Cmd.913 xiv. India Office.

Committee to discuss certain militia questions with representative officers of militia.
Report. July 1906. 1907 Cd.3513 xlix. War Office.

War Office (reconstitution) committee.
Report. Part 1, 11 Jan.1904; Part 2, 26 Feb.1904; Part 3, 9 March 1904. 1904 Cd.1932, Cd.1968, Cd.2002 viii. War Office.

BRIDGE, Cyprian Arthur George
Committee on the evidence relating to the tactics employed by Nelson at the battle of Trafalgar.
Report. 17 July 1913. 1914 Cd.7120 liv. Admiralty.

Inquiry into the circumstances connected with the North Sea incident, 21-22 October 1904.
Report. 7 March 1905. 1905 Cd.2451 lxiv. Board of Trade.

BRIDGE, John Crosthwaite
Departmental committee on medical arrangements for the diagnosis of silicosis.
Report. 27 June 1929. Home Office.

BRIDGEMAN, William Clive, *1st Viscount*
Committee on enquiry on the Post Office.
Report. 10 Aug.1932. 1931/2 Cmd.4149 xii.
Post Office.

Departmental committee on the employment of
policewomen.
Report. 25 July 1924. 1924 Cmd.2224 xii.
Minutes of evidence. 1924. Home Office.

Interdepartmental committee on meat supplies.
Report. 16 Sept.1919. 1919 Cmd.456 xxv.
Board of Trade.

Regulation of coal mines.
Report by the Board of Trade under section 17,
Mining Industry Act, 1920. 7 Feb.1922. 1922
Cmd.1583 viii. Mines Department.

BRIGHT, R.
Official report of the British section of the Uganda-
Congo Boundary Commission, 1907-8. Aug.1909.
Colonial Office.

Brise, E. J. R. *SEE:* Ruggles-Brise, E. J.

BRITTON, C. E.
A meteorological chronology to A.D.1450. June
1937 (Geo.Phys.Mem.,no.70). Meteorological
Office.

Brock, A. C. *SEE:* Clutton-Brock, A.

BROCK: G. L.
Departmental committee on sterilisation.
Report. 8 Jan.1934. 1933/4 Cmd.4485 xv.
Ministry of Health.

BRODRICK, William St. John Freemantle
Committee appointed to consider the reorganisation
of the army and Indian nursing service.
Report. 1902. 1902 Cd.792 x. War Office.

Committee appointed to consider the reorganisation
of the army medical services.
Report. 1902. 1902 Cd.791 x. War Office.

BROMEHEAD, C. E. N.
The geology of the country around Holmfirth and
Glossop. (Sheet 86) 6 Oct.1932 (Mem.Geol.Surv.).
Geological Survey.

The geology of the country around Huddersfield and
Halifax. (Sheet 77) 14 Nov.1929. (Mem.Geol.Surv.)
Geological Survey.

The geology of the country around Windsor and
Chertsey. (Sheet 269) 21 Sept.1914. (Mem.
Geol.Surv.) Geological Survey.

The geology of north London. (Sheet 256) 1
Jan.1925. (Mem.Geol.Surv.) Geological Survey.

The geology of south London. (Sheet 270) 27 May
1921. (Mem.Geol.Surv.) Geological Survey.

Tungsten and manganese ores. 16 Nov.1915.
(Special reports on the mineral resources of G.B.,
vol.1) (Mem.Geol.Surv.) Geological Survey.

BROMLEY-DAVENPORT, William
Committee on the business of Territorial Force
Associations.
Report. 21 Feb.1913. 1913 Cd.6694 xlii. War
Office.

BROOKS, C. E. P.
Classification of monthly charts of pressure anomaly
over the northern hemisphere. 1926.
(Geophys.Mem., no.31) Meteorological Office.

The climate and weather of the Falkland Islands and
South Georgia. Feb.1920. (Geophys.Mem., no.15)
Meteorological Office.

The distribution of mean annual maxima and
minima of temperature over the globe. Nov.1928.
(Geophys.Mem., no.44) Meteorological Office.

The distribution of thunderstorms over the globe.
March 1925. (Geophys.Mem., no.24) Meteorological Office.

The effects of fluctuations of the Gulf stream on the
distribution of pressure. Dec.1926. (Geophys.Mem.,
no.34) Meteorological Office.

The influence of the Arctic ice on the subsequent
distribution of pressure over the eastern North
Atlantic and Western Europe. July 1928.
(Geophys.Mem., no.41) Meteorological Office.

The relation between the duration of bright sunshine
and the estimated amount of cloud. Oct.1929.
(Prof.Notes, no.53) Meteorological Office.

Regression equations with many variations.
Dec.1927. (Prof.Notes, no.47) Meteorological
Office.

A study of the atmospheric circulation over tropical
Africa. Oct.1932. (Geophys.Mem., no.55)
Meteorological Office.

Sunspots and the distribution of pressure over
Western Europe. July 1928. (Prof.Notes, no.49)
Meteorological Office.

The variation of meteorological elements at
St.Helena and some other places in the Atlantic
region. Dec.1926. (Geophys.Mem., no.33)
Meteorological Office.

Variations in the levels of the central African lakes,
Victoria and Albert. Aug.1923. (Geophys.Mem.,
no.20) Meteorological Office.

Variations of pressure distribution in the northern
hemisphere during the period 1904-13. Dec.1929.
(Prof.Notes, no.54) Meteorological Office.

The winds in Berbera. April 1934. (Prof.Notes,
no.65) Meteorologivcal Office.

BROOKS, F. T.
The "black spot" of chilled and frozen meat. April
1921. (F.I.B. special rep., no.6) Department of
Scientific and Industrial Research.

Mould growths upon cold-store meat. 1 July 1923.
(F.I.B. special rep., no.17) Department of Scientific
and Industrial Research.

BROOKS, Herbert E.
Joint advisory committee on river pollution. Second
report. *SEE:* Atkey, A. R.

BROWN, Alfred Ernest
Select committee on procedure.
Report, proceedings, evidence and index. 10
Nov.1932. 1931/2 (129) v. House of Commons.

Select committee on procedure on public business.
Special report. 7 Oct.1931. 1930/1 (161) viii.
House of Commons.

BROWN, C. H.
Deep currents of the North Sea.
*SEE:* Thompson, D. W. North Sea fisheries
investigation committee. 4th report for first
report.
Second report. 1913. (Sci.invest., 1913, no.2)
Fishery Board for Scotland.
Additional notes. 1916. (Sci.invest., 1916, no.2)
Fishery Board for Scotland.

Brown, F. G. *SEE:* Gore-Browne, F.

BROWN, Harold George
Committee on the production of civil aeroplanes.
Report. 29 April 1939. 1938/9 Cmd.6038 ix. Air Ministry.

BROWN, Henry Coddington
Epidemic catarrhal jaundice. May 1927. (R.Pub.Health & Med.Subj., no.42) Ministry of Health.

BROWN, Thomas Graham
Committee on the physiology of hearing.
Reports.  1: Localisation of sounds in the median plane. 29 Feb.1934 (S.R.S., no.166).
2: Some factors in auditory location. 29 Feb.1934. (S.R.S., no.166).
3: The localisation of sound. 13 Dec.1935. (S.R.S., no.207).
4: The use of hearing aids. 14 Dec.1936. (S.R.S., no.219).
5: Hearing and speech in deaf children. 26 Jan.1937. (S.R.S., no.221). Medical Research Council.

BROWN, Vernon
Report on the loss of the aircraft G-ADUU "Cavalier" between New York and Bermuda on 21 Jan.1939. 28 Feb.1939. 1938/9 Cmd.5975 ix. Air Ministry.

Browne, F. G. SEE: Gore-Browne, F.

BROWNE, Thomas John
Report on shellfish layings on the Irish coast, as respects their liability to sewage contamination. Aug.1903. 1904 Cd.1900 xxvii. Local Government Board for Ireland.

BROWNING, Ethel
Toxicity of industrial organic solvents; summaries of published work. Sept.1937. (I.H.R.B.Rep., no.80). Medical Research Council.

BROWNLEE, John
An investigation into the epidemiology of phthisis in G.B. and Ireland.
Parts 1 and 2. Aug.1918 (S.R.S., no.18).
Part 3. 12 Jan.1920. (S.R.S., no.46). Medical Research Committee.

The use of death-rates as a measure of hygienic conditions. Jan.1922. (S.R.S., no.60) Medical Research Council.

BROWNLIE, J. T.
Report on the output of munitions in France. Dec.1915. 1916 Cd.8187 xiii. Ministry of Munitions.

BRUCE, Alexander Hugh, 6th Baron Balfour of Burleigh
Committee on commerical and industrial policy.
Interim report on essential industries. 16 March 1917. 1918 Cd.9032 xiii.
Interim report on importation of goods from the present enemy countries after the war. 9 Nov.1916. 1918 Cd.9033 xiii.
Interim report on exports from the U.K. and British overseas possessions and conservation of resources of the Empire during the transitional period after the war. 14 Dec.1916. 1918 Cd.9034 xiii.
Final report. 3 Dec.1917. 1918 Cd.9035 xiii. Board of Trade and Treasury.

Departmental committee on procedure of royal commissions.
Report. 25 June 1910. 1910 Cd.5235 lviii. Home Office.

Interdepartmental committee on cable communications.
First report. 8 August 1902. 1902 Cd.958 xi.
Report. 26 March 1902. 1902 Cd.1056 xi.
Minutes of evidence with appendix and index. 1902 Cd.1118 xi. Treasury.

Report on the Clyde munitions workers. Dec.1915. 1914/6 Cd.8136 xxix. Ministry of Munitions.

Royal Commission on Local Taxation.
First report: Local rates in England and Wales, valuation and collection. 1899 C.9141 xxxv.
Second report: Tithe rent charge valuation and rating. 1899 C.1942 xxxv.
Evidence, vol.1: 1898 C.9863 xli.
Appendices to vol.1, 2 parts: 1898 C.8764 and C.8765 xlii.
vol.2: 1899 C.9150 xxxvi.
vol.3: Scotland. 1899 c.9319 xxxvi.
vol.4: 1900 Cd.201 xxxvi.
vol.5: Ireland. 1900 Cd.383 xxxvi.
Classification and incidence of imperial and local taxes, etc. 1899 C.9528 xxxvi.
Final report: England & Wales. 28 May 1901. 1901 Cd.638 xxiv.
Report on valuation in Ireland. 14 Feb.1902. 1902 Cd.973 xxxix.
Final report on local taxation. Ireland. 11 April 1902. 1902 Cd.1068 xxxix.
Final report on local taxation. Scotland. 10 April 1902. 1902 Cd.1067 xxxix.
Appendix to final report on local taxation. England and Wales. 1902 Cd. 1221 xxxix.
Index. 1903 Cd.1480 xxiii.

Royal Commission on supply of food and raw material in time of war.
Vol.1: Report. Aug.1905. 1905 Cd.2643 xxxix.
Vol.2: Minutes of evidence. 1905. 1905 cd.2644 xxxix.
Vol.3: Appendices. 1905 Cd.2645 xl.

Royal Commission on trade relations between Canada and the West Indies.
Part 1: Report. 19 Aug.1910. 1910 Cd.5369 xi.
Part 2: Minutes of evidence taken in Canada. 1910 Cd.4991 xi.
Part 3: Minutes of evidence taken in the West Indies. 1910 Cd.5370 xi.
Part 4: Minutes of evidence taken in London. 1910 Cd.5371 xi.

BRUCE, David
Commission on the nature, pathology, causation, and prevention of dysentery and its relationship to enteric fever.
Report. Nov.1901. 1903 Cd.1498 x. War Office.

BRUCE, Edward James, 10th Earl of Elgin and Kincardine
National advisory councils for juvenile employment (England and Wales, and Scotland).
Joint report on the organisation and development of the vocational guidance service in G.B. 29 May 1934. Ministry of Labour.

BRUCE, George John Gordon, 7th Baron Balfour of Burleigh
Central housing advisory committee.
Report of the house management and housing associations sub-committee. 6 April 1938. Ministry of Health.

BRUCE, George John Gordon, *7th Baron Balfour of Burleigh.* (continued)

Report of the house management and housing associations sub-committee. The operations of housing associations. 2 Jan.1939. Ministry of Health.

Committee on Straits settlements ordinance, no.15 of 1927 (women and girls protection amendment ordinance) and Federated Malay States enactment, no.18 of 1927 (women and girls protection amendment enactment).
Report. 8 Feb.1929. 1928/9 Cmd.3294 v. Colonial Office.

BRUCE, Victor Alexander, *9th Earl of Elgin and Kincardine*

Committee on Scottish universities.
Report, with appendices. Aug.1909. 1910 Cd.5257 xxvi.
Minutes of evidence with index. 1910 Cd.5258 xxvi. Treasury.

Departmental committee on Scottish prisons.
Report. 26 May 1900. 1900 Cd.218 xlii.
Minutes of evidence. 1900. 1900 Cd.219 xlii. Scottish Office.

Military manoeuvres commission, Fife.
Report. 1910. 1911 Cd.5479 xlvii. War Office.

Royal commission appointed under the Churches (Scotland) Act, 1905 (allocation of property between the Free Church and the United Free Church in Scotland).
Vol.1: Report. 23 Dec.1909. 1910 Cd.5060 xiii.
Vol.2: Minutes of proceedings and appendix. 1910 Cd.5061 xiii.
*See also:* J. Cheyne.

Royal commission on churches (Scotland).
Vol.1: Report. 12 April 1905. 1905 Cd.2494 xxiii.
Vol.2: Minutes of evidence and appendices. 1905 Cd.2495 xxiii.

Royal commission on salmon fisheries.
Part I: Report. 10 July 1902. 1902 Cd.1188 xiii.
Part II: Minutes of evidence and indexes. 1902 Cd.1269 xiii.
Part III: Appendix; section 1: England and Wales. 1902 Cd.1280 xiv.
Appendix; section 2: Scotland. 1902 cd.1281 xiv.

Royal commission on the war in South Africa.
Report. 9 July 1903. 1904 Cd.1789 xl.
Minutes of evidence. Vol.1: 1904 Cd.1790 xl.
Vol.2: 1904 Cd.1791 xli.
Appendices. 1904 Cd.1792 xlii.

BRUCE, William Napier
Committee on the organisation of secondary education in Wales.
Report. 20 Sept.1920. 1920 Cmd.967 xv. Board of Education.

Welsh in education and life.
Report of the departmental committee on the position of the Welsh language and its promotion in the educational system of Wales. 4 July 1927. Board of Education, Welsh Department.

BRUEN, Edward Francis
Committee on pay, allowances and pensions of the Royal Navy and Royal Marines.

Report of the sub-committee on half pay. 9 May 1919. 1919 Cmd.270 xxxiii. Admiralty.

BRUNET, Émile
German calumnies: the Anglo-Belgian conventions. 1916, Ministry of Information.

BRUNYATE, James Bennett
Safeguarding of industries.
Report of the committee on packing and wrapping paper. 25 Nov.1925. 1924/5 Cmd.2539 xv. Board of Trade.

BRYAN, J.
Experiments on the preservation of mine timber. Aug.1935. (F.P.R.records, no.3) Department of Scientific and Industrial Research.

Methods of applying wood preservations. Part 1: non-pressure methods. April 1936. (F.P.R.records, no.9) Department of Scientific and Industrial Research.

BRYAN, J. M.
The corrosion of the tin-plate container by food products. Feb.1931. (F.I.B. special rep., no.40).
Second report. Nov.1936. (F.I.B. special rep., no.44) Department of Scientific and Industrial Research.

BRYCE, James, *1st Viscount Bryce*
Committee on alleged German outrages.
Report. Aug.1915. 1914/6 Cd.7894 xxiii.
Appendix. 1914/6 Cd.7895 xxiii.
Evidence and documents. 1915. Home Office.

Committee on local records.
Report. 29 Oct.1902. 1902 Cd.1335 xlix.
Appendices. 1902 Cd.1333 xlix. Treasury.

Conference on the reform of the second chamber.
Report. April 1918. 1918 Cd.9038 x. Prime Minister's Office.

Treatment of Armenians in the Ottoman Empire, 1915-16. 1 June 1916. (Misc., no.31, 1916) 1916 Cd.8325 xxxiii. Foreign Office.

The truth about German atrocities; founded on the report of the Committee on Alleged German Outrages. Aug.1915. Parliamentary Recruiting Committee.

BRYCE, Roland L'E.
Report on political conditions in Montenegro. 16 Dec.1920. (Misc., no.2, 1921) 1921 Cmd.1124 xliii. Foreign Office.

BRYSON, Samuel
Report on the incidence of silicosis in the pottery industry. 26 July 1926. Home Office.

Report on the occurrence of silicosis among sandstone workers. 7 Nov.1928. Home Office.

Report on an inquiry into the occurrence of disease of the lungs from dust inhalation in the slate industry in the Guryrfai District. June 1930. Mines Department.

Buccleuch, *Lord. SEE:* Scott, J. C. M. D., *7th Duke.*

BUCHAN, Norman Macleod, *18th Earl of Caithness*
Committee on farm workers in Scotland.
Report. 29 June 1936. 1935/6 Cmd.5217 vii. Scottish Office.

BUCHAN, Stevenson
The water supply of the County of London from underground sources. 27 Aug.1937. (Mem. Geol.Surv.) Geological Survey.

BUCHAN, William
Memorandum on steam boilers. March 1911. Home Office.

BUCHANAN, George Seaton
Report on administration in London with regard to meat of pigs affected by tuberculosis. 7 Dec.1905. (Rep.Med.Insp., no.225) Local Government Board.

Reports on the application of formaldehyde to meat. 28 July 1909. (Rep.Pub.H. & Med.Subj., no.12) Local Government Board.

Report on certain imported meat foods of questionable wholesomeness. 31 Dec.1907. (Rep. Insp.Food, no.3) Local Government Board.

Report on the changes in certain meat essences kept for several years in tins. 4 Dec.1906. (Rep. Insp.Foods, no.1) Local Government Board.

Report on epidemic enteric fever in the Borough of Falmouth. 30 Jan.1900. (Rep.Med.Insp., no.148) Local Government Board.

Report on epidemic smallpox in the Union of Orsett, 1901-2. 1 Dec.1902. (Rep.Med.Insp., no.182) Local Government Board.

Report on the presence of tin in certain canned foods. 18 Dec.1908. (Rep.Insp.Foods, no.7) Local Government Board.

Report on the prevalance of enteric fever in the Urban District of Sheerness. 26 April 1925. (Rep. Med.Insp., no.215). Local Government Board.

Report on the recent epidemic of arsenical poisoning attributed to beer. 25 Jan.1901. 1901 Cd.459 ix. Local Government Board.

Report on re-inspection of the Borough of Falmouth. 10 June 1902. (Rep.Med.Insp., no.176) Local Government Board.

Report on smallpox in Gateshead and Felling, 1903-4 in relation to Sheriff Hill Hospital. 21 Nov.1904. (Rep.Med.Insp., no.201) Local Government Board.

Spirochaetal jaundice. 15 March 1927. (S.R.S., no.113). Medical Research Council.

BUCHANAN, Thomas R.
Select committee on House of Commons (Admission of Strangers), 1908.
Report, proceedings and evidence. 16 Dec.1908. 1908 (371) ix. House of Commons.

BUCKINGHAM, Henry Cecil
Standing committee on trusts.
Report of a sub-committee on the explosives industry. 11 May 1921. 1921 Cmd.1347 xvi. Board of Trade.

BUCKLEY, Henry Burton, 1st Baron Wrenbury.
Company law amendment committee.
Report. 15 July 1918. 1918 Cd.9138 vii. Board of Trade.

Select committee of the House of Lords on the Women's Royal Air Force: inquiry on Miss Violet Douglas-Pennant.
Report, proceedings, evidence and appendices. 4 Dec.1919. 1919 (H.L.243) vii. House of Lords.

BUCKMASTER, Stanley Owen, 1st Baron Buckmaster of Cheddington.
Committee on the position of British manufacturers and merchants in respect of pre-war contracts.
Report. 12 Jan.1918. 1918 Cd.8975 vii. Board of Trade.

Court of inquiry concerning the dispute in the building industry, 1924.
Report. 15 July 1924. 1924 Cmd.2192 xi. Ministry of Labour.

Court of inquiry concerning the wages position in the coal mining industry.
Report. 8 May 1924. 1924 Cmd.2129 xi. Ministry of Labour.

Report on bye-laws made on 29 January 1910, by the London County Council under the Employment of Children Act, 1903. 18 Nov.1910. 1911 Cd.5497 lxiv. Home Office.

BUCKNILL, Alfred Townsend
Tribunal of enquiry into the loss of H.M.S. "Thetis".
Report. 31 Jan.1940. 1939/40 Cmd.6190 v. Prime Minister's Office.

BULL, G. A.
A note on the bumpiness at Cranwell, Lincolnshire, December 1925 to April 1926. March 1927. (Prof. Notes, no.46) Meteorological Office.

Weather conditions over the central and western Mediterranean, 10 to 14 February 1929. Dec.1930. (Prof. Notes, no.60) Meteorological Office.

BULLOCH, William
Committee on anaerobic bacteria and infections.
Report on the anaerobic infections of wounds and the serological problems arising therefrom. Sept.1919. (S.R.S., no.39) Medical Research Committee.

BULLRICH, E. J.
International Labour Conference. Committee on the reduction of hours of work.
Report to the 17th session. July 1933. 1932/3 Cmd.4389 xxviii. Ministry of Labour.

BULSTRODE, Herbert Timbrell
Report on alleged oyster-borne enteric fever and other illnesses following the Mayoral banquets at Winchester and Southampton and upon enteric fever occurring simultaneously elsewhere, also ascribed to oysters. 14 May 1903. (Rep.Med.Insp., no.185) Local Government Board.

Report on an outbreak of diptheria in Burnham on Crouch U.D. and Burnham D.C. 29 Oct.1902. (Rep.Med.Insp., no.180) Local Government Board.

Report on outbreak of enteric fever in the Borough of Whitehaven. 16 July 1902. (Rep.Med.Insp., no.177) Local Government Board.

Report on sanitary conditions of Dunmow R.D. 4 Aug.1908. (Rep.Med.Insp., no.307) Local Government Board.

Report on sanitary conditions of Durham R.D. Re-inspection 11 June 1907. (Rep.Med.Insp., no.237) Local Government Board.

Report on the sanitary conditions of East Elloe R.D. 13 Nov.1908. (Rep.Med.Insp., no.319) Local Government Board.

Report on the sanitary conditions of Halstead U.D., Essex. 20 Aug.1908. (Rep.Med.Insp., no.309) Local Government Board.

Report on the sanitary conditions of Holbeach U.D. 5 Nov.1908. (Rep.Med.Insp., no.316) Local Government Board.

Report on the sanitary conditions of the Isle of Wight R.D. 28 Aug.1905. (Rep.Med.Insp., no.219) Local Government Board.

BULSTRODE, Herbert Timbrell (continued)
Report on the sanitary conditions of Itchen U.D. and on the prevalence of enteric fever therein. 11 Oct.1904. (Rep.Med.Insp., no.199) Local Government Board.

Report on the sanitary conditions of Long Sutton U.D. 4 Nov.1908. (Rep.Med.Insp., no.314) Local Government Board.

Report on the sanitary conditions of St. Helens U.D., Isle of Wight. 7 June 1901. (Rep.Med.Insp., no.160) Local Government Board.

Report on sanitary conditions of the Borough of Windsor. 29 June 1900. (Rep.Med.Insp., no.152) Local Government Board.

BUNKER, H. J.
A review of the physiology and biochemistry of the sulphur bacteria. Dec.1935. (Chemistry research special rep., no.3) Department of Scientific and Industrial Research.

BURBIDGE, Richard Woodman
Committee on the Royal Aircraft Factory.
Report. 12 May 1916. 1916 Cd.8191 iv. War Office.

BURDEKIN, J. T.
Report on the safety of mining telephones of the magneto ringing type. July 1933. Mines Department.

BURDWOOD, John
Sun's true bearing, or azimuth tables. Jan.1900. Admiralty, Hydrographic Department.

BURGESS, M. J.
Firedamp explosions: the projection of flame. May 1926. (S.M.R.B. Paper no.27).
Firedamp explosions: the projection of flame. Part 2. March 1928. (S.M.R.B. Paper no.42).
Firedamp explosions. Part 3: the effect of branch galleries and of bends. Jan.1934. (S.M.R.B. Paper no.83) Mines Department.

The ignition of firedamp by the heat of impact of coal-cutter picks against rocks. Jan.1931. (S.M.R.B. Paper no.70) Mines Department.

The ignition of firedamp by the heat of impact of hand picks against rock. Sept.1930. (S.M.R.B. Paper no.62) Mines Department.

The ignition of firedamp by the heat impact of metal against rock. April 1929. (S.M.R.B. Paper no.54) Mines Department.

The ignition of firedamp by the heat impact of rocks. May 1928. (S.M.R.B. Paper no.46) Mines Department.

The limits of inflammability of firedamp and air. Sept.1925. (S.M.R.B. Paper no.15) Mines Department.

The prevention of ignition of firedamp by the heat of impact of coal-cutter picks against hard rocks. July 1933. (S.M.R.B. Paper no.81) Mines Department.

Burghclere, *Lord. SEE:* Gardner, H. C., *1st Baron.*

Burleigh of Balfour. *SEE:* Bruce, H. A., *6th Baron.*

BURN, Joshua Harold
Reports on biological standards: pituitary extracts. 20 Oct.1922. (S.R.S., No.69) Medical Research Council.

BURNETT, Frank Marsden
Use of the developing egg in virus research. 10

Dec.1936. (S.R.S., no.220) Medical Research Council.

BURNETT, Isabel
An experimental investigation into repetitive work. July 1925. (I.H.R.B. Rep., No.30) Medical Research Council.

Burnham, *Lord. SEE:* Lawson, H. L. W., *1st Viscount.*

BURNS, John
Conference on arterial road communication in greater London.
Report of conference. 25 Nov.1913.
Report of sectional conferences, 9-18 March 1914, 1 May 1914.
Report of sectional conferences, (second series) 29 June—8 July 1914, Sept.1914.
Report of sectional conferences, (third series) 10 May—24 Aug.1915. Local Government Board.

BURRELL, Lancelot Stephen Topham
Report on artificial pneumothorax. 21 June 1922. (S.R.S., no.67) Medical Research Council.

BURRIDGE, L. W.
The prevention of pattern staining of plasters. Feb.1931. (B.R.B. Bull., no.10) Department of Scientific and Industrial Research.

BURY, John B.
Germany and Slavonic civilisation. 1914. Ministry of Information.

BUSHE, Henry Gratton
Commission of inquiry into the administration of justice in Kenya, Uganda and Tanganyika Territory in criminal matters.
Report and correspondence. 27 May 1933. 1933/4 Cmd.4623 ix.
Minutes of evidence and memoranda. (Colonial, no.96) 1934. Colonial Office.

BUTCHER, John George
Departmental committee on bond investment companies.
Report. 30 Oct.1905. 1906 Cd.2769 xcvii.
Appendices. 1906 Cd.2770 xcvii. Board of Trade.

BUTLER, C. V.
Village survey-making; an Oxfordshire experiment. July 1928. (Educational pamphlets no.61) Board of Education.

BUTLER, George Gay
Studies on the cultivation of vaccinia on the chorio-allantoic membranes of chick embryos. Oct.1938. (R.Pub.Health & Med.Subj., no.87) Ministry of Health.

BUTLER, Spencer Harcourt
Indian states committee.
Report. March 1929. 1928/9 Cmd.3302 vi. India Office.

BUTLER, William Francis
Committee on sales and refunds to contractors in South Africa.
Report with appendices. 22 May 1905. 1905 Cd.2435 ix.
Minutes of evidence. 1905 Cd.2436 ix. Army Council, War Office.

BUTLIN, K. R.
The biochemical activities of the acetic acid bacteria. Dec.1935. (Chemistry Research special rep., no.2) Department of Scientific and Industrial Research.

BUTTER, Archibald Edward
Report on the survey of the proposed frontier between British East Africa and Abyssinia. 7 Nov.1904. 1905 Cd.2312 lvi. Foreign Office.

BUTTERFIELD, W. J. A.
Report on carbon monoxide in public gas supplies. 6 Feb.1924. Board of Trade.

BUTTERWORTH, W. T.
Departmental committee on disinfection of wool costs.
    Vol.1:  Report. 25 April 1928.
    Vol.2:  Appendices. Nov.1928.
    Vol.3:  Supplementary Report. 18 June 1931. 1932. Home Office.

BUXTON, Charles Roden
Select committee on shop assistants.
    Special report, proceedings, evidence and index. 30 July 1930. 1929/30 (176) vii.
    Vol.1:  Report and proceedings. 18 Sept.1931. 1930/1 (148) ix.
    Vol.2:  Appendices. 1930/1 (148) ix.
    Vol.3:  Minutes of evidence and index. 1930/1 (148) ix. House of Commons.

BUXTON, Sydney Charles, *1st Earl Buxton.*
Committee on colonial governors, with special reference to pensions.
    Report. 23 Jan.1928. 1928 Cmd.3059 vii. Colonial Office.

Committee on Rhodesia.
    First report. 12 April 1921. 1921 Cmd.1273 xxiv.
    Second report. 29 April 1921. 1921 Cmd.1471 xxiv.
    Minutes of proceedings. 1921. Colonial Office.

Joint select committee of the House of Lords and the House of Commons on the sittings of Parliament.
    Report, proceedings, evidence and appendix. 26 June 1924. 1924 (112) vi. House of Commons.

BUZZARD, Edward Farquhar
Committee on injuries of the nervous system.
    First report. The diagnosis and treatment of peripheral nerve injuries. July 1920. (S.R.S., no.54).
    Second report. Injuries of the spinal cord and cauda equna. Oct.1924. (S.R.S., no.88) Medical Research Committee.

CADMAN, John, *1st Baron*
Committee of inquiry into civil aviation.
    Report. 8 Feb.1938. 1937/8 Cmd.5685 viii. Air Ministry.

Enquiry into the protection of oil storage tanks against lightning.
    7 Jan.1919. (Petroleum Executive Bull., no.1) Petroleum Executive.

Enquiry into ventilation of coal mines and the methods of examining for fire damp. 10 Nov.1909. 1909 Cd.4551 xxxiv. Royal Commission on Mines.

CADOGAN, Edward Cecil George
Departmental committee on corporal punishment.
    Report. 19 Feb.1938. 1937/8 Cmd.5684 ix. Home Office.

CAHILL, J. R.
Report of an enquiry into agricultural credit and agricultural co-operation in Germany with some notes on German livestock insurance. March 1913. 1912/3 Cd.6626 xi. Board of Agriculture and Fisheries.

CAINE, William
Monsieur Segotin's story. 1917. Ministry of Information.

CAIRNS, David S.
Christianity and *Macht-Politik*. 1918. Ministry of Information.

CAIRNS, Hugh
A study of intracranial surgery. 7 Dec.1928. (S.R.S., no.125) Medical Research Council.

Caithness, *Earl. SEE:* Buchan, N. M. *18th Earl.*

CALDER, James Charles
Safeguarding of industries. Committee on hosiery.
    Report. 10 July 1926. 1926 Cmd.2726 xv.
    Second report. 18 Feb.1928. 1928 Cmd.3078 xii. Board of Trade.

CALDERWOOD, W. L.
The artificial and the natural breeding of salmon. 1924. (Salmon Fish., 1924, no.2) Fishery Board for Scotland.

The common eel and its capture. Jan.1918. Scottish Freshwater Fisheries Committee.

Infrequency of spawning in the salmon. 1910. (Salmon Fish., 1910, no.1) Fishery Board for Scotland.

Results of salmon and sea trout marking in sea and river. 1922. (Salmon Fish., 1922, no.1) Fishery Board for Scotland.

Results of salmon marking, seventh paper. 1910. (Salmon Fish., 1910, no.2)
    Eighth paper. 1912. (Salmon Fish., 1911, no.2)
    Ninth paper. 1914. (Salmon Fish., 1913, no.2). Fishery Board for Scotland. 1911.

Salmon passes: a second paper. 1926. (Salmon Fish., 1926, no.2) Fishery Board for Scotland.

Salmon research in 1913; sea netting results. 1913. (Salmon Fish., 1913, no.1) Fishery Board for Scotland. 1914.

Salmon research in 1914; sea netting results. 1914. (Salmon Fish., 1914, no.3) Fishery Board for Scotland. 1915.

Salmon research in 1915; sea netting results. 1915. (Salmon Fish., 1915, no.1) Fishery Board for Scotland. 1916.

The spawning mark on salmon scales; a review. 1913. (Salmon Fish., 1913, no.3) Fishery Board for Scotland. 1914.

CALLWELL, Charles Edward
Small wars; their principles and practice, 3rd ed. 1 Jan.1907. War Office.

CALVERT, H. T.
Committee on methods of chemical analysis as applied to sewage and sewage effluents.
    Report. June 1929. Ministry of Health.

CAMBRIDGE, Alexander Augustus Frederick William Alfred George, *1st Earl Athlone.*
Interdepartmental committee on nursing services.
    Interim report. 20 Dec.1938. (no further reports identified) Ministry of Health.

Post-graduate medical committee.
    Report. 31 May 1921. Ministry of Health.

CAMERON, Thomas Wright Moir
Helminthology in its application to live-stock. 1932. (Notes and memo., no.7) Imperial Bureau of Agricultural Parasitology.

CAMMAERTS, Emile
To the men behind the armies. 1917. Ministry of Information.

CAMPAGNAC, E. T.
Report on the school trainingand early employment of Lancashire children. Nov.1903. (Special reports on Educational Subjects, supplement to vol.8.) 1904 Cd.1867 xix. Board of Education.

CAMPBELL, Archibald, *1st Baron Blythswood.*
Committee on steel rails.
Report. March 1900. 1900 Cd.174 lxxvi. Board of Trade.

CAMPBELL, Charles William
Report on a journey in Mongolia. 15 May 1903. (China, no.1, 1904) 1904 Cd.1874 cx. Foreign Office.

CAMPBELL, Frederick Archibald Vaughan, *3rd Earl Cawdor.*
Joint select committee on the High Court of Justice (Kings Bench Division).
Report, proceedings, evidence, appendices and index. 2 Dec.1909. 1909 (333) viii. House of Commons.

CAMPBELL, Gavin, *1st Marquis of Breadalbane.*
Scottish freshwater fisheries committee.
Interim report. 25 July 1917.
Second interim report. 27 March 1918. (no further identified) Scottish Office.

CAMPBELL, Gerald
Report on the mining industry in the State of Minas Geraes, Brazil. April 1908. (Dip.cons.report: misc.ser., no.667) 1908 Cd.3728-3 cviii. Foreign Office and Board of Trade.

CAMPBELL, Henry Cooke
Native affairs commission, Natal, 1906-7.
Report. 25 July 1907. 1908 Cd.3889 lxxii. Colonial Office.

CAMPBELL, Janet Mary
High maternal mortality in certain areas. July 1932. (R.Pub.Health & Med.Subj., no.68) Ministry of Health.

Infant mortality. July 1929. (R.Pub.Health & Med.Subj., no.55) Ministry of Health.

Maternal mortality. March 1924. (Rept.Pub.Health & Med.Subj., no.25) Ministry of Health.

Notes on the arrangements for teaching obstetrics and gynaecology in the medical schools. March 1923. (Rept.Pub.Health & Md.Subj., no.15) Ministry of Health.

The protection of motherhood. Oct.1927. (R.Pub.Health & Med.Subj., no.48) Ministry of Halth.

The training of midwives. July 1923. (Rept.Pub. Health & Med.Subj., no.21) Ministry of Health.

CAMPBELL, John Ritch
Departmental committee on the Irish butter Industry.
Vol.1: Report. 11 March 1910. 1910 Cd.5092 vii.
Vol.2: Minutes of evidence, appendices and index. 1910 Cd.5093 viii. Department of Agriculture and Technical Instruction for Ireland.

Departmental committee on the Irish flax-growing industry.

Report. 20 Jan.1911. 1911 Cd.5502 xxvi.
Minutes of evidence, appendices and index. 1911 Cd.5503 xxvi. Department of Agriculture and Technical Instruction for Ireland.

Report on agricultural education in Scotland. 29 Nov.1927. Board of Agriculture for Scotland.

CAMPBELL, Reginald John
A letter to an American friend. 1918. Ministry of Information.

Campbell-Hepworth, M. W. *SEE:* Hepworth, M. W. C.

Camperdown, *Lord. SEE:* Haldane-Duncan, R. A. P., *3rd Earl.*

CANTRILL, T. C.
The geology of the south Wales coalfield.
Part 3: the country around Cardiff. 27 April 1902. (Mem.Geol.Surv.) Geological Survey.

Part 6: the country around Bridgend. 4 Nov.1904. (Mem.Geol.Surv.) Geological Survey.

Part 12: the country around Milford. 11 June 1914. (Mem.Geol.Surv.) Geological Survey.

Iron ores: sundry unbedded ores of Durham, east Cumberland, north Wales, Derbyshire, the Isle of Man, Bristol district and Somerset, Devon and Cornwall. 13 Dec.1918. (Special reports on the mineral resources of G.B., vol.9) (Mem.Geol.Surv.) Geological Survey.

CARDEW, Alexander Gordon
Indian jails committee.
Report. Nov.1920. 1921 Cmd.1303 x. India Office.

CARLYLE, Robert Warrand
Indian trade enquiry.
Reports on timbers and paper materials. 14 June 1918. Imperial Institute.

CARMICHAEL, James
Committee on the building industry after the war.
Report. 4 Nov.1918. 1918 Cd.9197 vii. Ministry of Reconstruction.

CARNEGIE, Lancelot Douglas
Report on the beer-brewing industry of Bavaria, Germany. 10 Oct.1903. (Dip.cons.reports: misc.ser., no.599) 1904 Cd.1767-3 xcvi. Foreign Office.

Carnock, *Lord. SEE:* Nicolson, F. A., *2nd Baron.*

CARNWATH, Thomas
The bacteriological examination of water supplies. March 1934. (R.Pub.Health & Med.Subj., no.71) Ministry of Health.

Report on an outbreak of enteric fever at Oakenshaw in Willington U.D. 9 Jan.1912. (Rep.Pub.H. & Med.Subj., no.59) Local Government Board.

Report on the sanitary conditions of Padiham U.D. 14 Aug.1914. (Rep.Pub.H. & Med.Subj., no.101) Local Government Board.

CARPENTER, H. C. Harold
Committee on the staffs of government scientific establishments.
Report. 25 Sept.1930. Treasury.

Committee on welded containers.
Report. June 1930. Department of Scientific and Industrial Research.

Gas cylinders research committee.
First report: cylinders for transport of

"permanent" gases. Nov.1921.
Second report: periodical heat treatment. June 1926.
Third report: alloy steel light cylinders. Jan.1929.
Fourth report: cylinders for liquefiable gases. Jan.1929. Department of Scientific and Industrial Research.

Welding of steel structures.
Report of the welding panel of the steel structures research committee. Dec.1937. Department of Scientific and Industrial Research.

CARPMAEL, E.
Report on the census of Weihaiwei, 1911. 17 July 1911. (Colonial reports, misc., no.78) 1911 Cd.5897 lii. Colonial Office.

CARR, R. H.
Military service committee.
Report on the headquarters staff of the Ministry of Munitions. 12 Oct.1916. 1916 Cd.8411 xiii. Ministry of Munitions.

Carrington, *Lord. SEE:* Wynn-Carrington, C. R. *1st Earl*

CARRINGTON, Robert C.
Table for converting meters into British feet and fathoms (from 1-2,000). April 1932. (Hydrographic Publication H.D.311) Admiralty.

CARRUTHERS, R. G.
Barytes and Witherite. 16 Nov.1915. (Special reports on the mineral resources of G.B., Vol.2.) (Mem.Geol.Surv.) Geological Survey.

The economic geology of the central coalfield of Scotland, Area 8, East Kilbride and Quarter. 27 July 1916. (Mem.Geol.Surv.,Scotl.) Geological Survey, Scotland.

Fluorspar. 20 Dec.1915. (Special reports on the mineral resources of G.B. Vol.4.) (Mem.Geol.Surv.) Geological Survey.

The geology of Alnwick district. (Sheet 6) 15 Feb.1930. (Mem.Geol.Surv.) Geological Survey.

The geology of Caithness. (Sheets 110 and 116 with parts of 109, 115 and 117.) 6 Jan.1914. (Mem.Geol.Surv.,Scotl.) Geological Survey, Scotland.

Geology of the Cheviot hills. (Sheets 3 and 5.) 4 Jan.1932. (Mem.Geol.Surv.) Geological Survey.

Lead and zinc ores of Durham, Yorkshire and Derbyshire, with notes on the Isle of Man. 17 May 1922. (Special reports on the mineral resources of G.B., vol.26.) (Mem.Geol.Surv.) Geological Survey.

CARTER, William Morris
Kenya land commission.
Report. 7 July 1933. 1933/4 Cmd.4556 x.
Evidence and memoranda. May 1934. (Colonial no.91) 3 vols. Colonial Office.

CARTWRIGHT, K.St.G.
The causes of stain and decay in imported timber. June 1937. (F.P.R.Records, no.18) Department of Scientific and Industrial Research.

A decay of sitka spruce timber caused by *trametes serialis, Fr.;* a cultural study of the fungus. June 1930. (F.P.R.Bull., no.4) Department of Scientific and Industrial Research.

Principal decays of softwoods used in Great Britain.

Sept.1938. Department of Scientific and Industrial Research.

The principal rots of English oak. April 1936. Department of Scientific and Industrial Research.

CASSEL, Felix
Committee on compulsory insurance.
Report. 19 July 1937. 1936/7 Cmd.5528 xii.
Minutes of evidence and index, 1936-7. Board of Trade.

CASSON, T. C.
The system of education in Nyasaland Protectorate. 17 Dec.1912. (Imperial Education Conference papers) Board of Education.

CATHCART, Edward Provan
Committee on quantitative problems in human nutrition.
Report on the nutrition of miners and their families. 2 June 1924. (S.R.S., no.87) Medical Research Council.

Committee on Scottish health services.
Interim report: water supplies. 28 March 1934.
Report. June 1936. 1935/6 Cmd.5204 xi. Department of Health for Scotland.

A dietary survey in terms of the actual foodstuffs consumed. 15 Dec.1936. (S.R.S., no.218) Medical Research Council.

The energy expenditure of the infantry recruit in training. Dec.1919. War Office.

A study in nutrition; an inquiry into the diet of 154 families of St.Andrews. 1 Dec.1930. (S.R.S., no.151) Medical Research Council.

CAUSTON, Richard Knight, *1st Baron Southwark*
Committee on superannuation and similar funds of railway companies.
Report. 22 Aug.1910. 1910 Cd.5349 xlvii.
Minutes of evidence. 1911 Cd.5484 xxix. Board of Trade.

CAUTLEY, Henry Strother
Select committee on betting duty.
Report, proceedings, evidence, appendices and index. 15 Nov.1923. 1923 (139) v. House of Commons.

CAVE, Charles John Phillip
Soundings with pilot balloons in the Isles of Scilly, November and December 1911. Feb.1920. (Geophys.Mem., no.14.) Meteorological Office.

CAVE, George, *1st Viscount*
Committee of enquiry into the working and effects of the Trade Boards Acts.
Report. 11 April 1922. 1922 Cmd.1645 x.
Minutes of evidence. 1922. Ministry of Labour.

Committee on government machinery for dealing with trade and commerce.
Report. 10 July 1919. 1919 Cmd.319 xxx. Board of Trade.

Report of inquiry into the evidence given by the police at the trial of Stinie Morrison. 11 April 1911. 1911 Cd.5627 xxxviii. Home Office.

Report of the tribunal on the alleged instructions by an officer of the Ministry of Munitions as to the destruction or concealment of documents. 30 May 1921. 1921 Cmd.1340 xv. Home Office.

Voluntary hospitals committee.
Interim report. 9 March 1921. 1921 Cmd.1206 xiii.
Final report. 31 May 1921. 1921 Cmd.1335 xiii. Ministry of Health.

CAVENDISH, Richard Frederick
　　Royal commission on electoral systems.
　　　　Report with appendices. May 1910. 1910
　　　　Cd.5163 xxvi.
　　　　Minutes of evidence. 1910 Cd.5352 xxvi.

CAVENDISH, Spencer Compton, *8th Duke Devonshire*
　　Royal commission on the Paris international
　　exhibition, 1900.
　　　　Report. 1901. 2 vols. 1901 Cd.629, Cd.630
　　　　xxxi.

CAVENDISH, Victor Christian William, *9th Duke
Devonshire*
　　Joint select committee on the Local Government
　　Acts 1888 and 1894 and the Local Government
　　(Scotland) Acts 1889 and 1894 (financial
　　adjustments).
　　　　Report, proceedings, minutes of evidence and
　　　　appendices. 8 Aug.1911. 1911 (246) vii. House
　　　　of Commons.

Cawdor, *Earl. SEE:* Campbell, F.A.V., *3rd Earl.*

CAWSTON, John Westerman
　　Committee on the Customs waterguard service and
　　the Customs watchers.
　　　　Report. 22 May 1912. 1912/3 Cd.6290 xvii.
　　　　Minutes of evidence. 1912/3 Cd.6299 xvii.
　　　　Customs and Excise Board.

CECIL, Edgar Algernon Robert, *1st Viscount Cecil.*
　　Committee on the improvement of mountain and
　　moorland breeds of ponies.
　　　　Report. 12 Aug.1912. Board of Agriculture and
　　　　Fisheries.

　　Departmental committee on combinations in the
　　meat trade.
　　　　Report and appendices. 28 April 1909. 1909
　　　　Cd.4643 xv.
　　　　Minutes of evidence, appendices and index.
　　　　1909 Cd.4661 xv. Board of Trade.

　　Report of the British delegates to the League of
　　Nations.
　　　　Fourth assembly. 1 Dec.1923. (Misc., no.1,
　　　　1924) 1924 Cmd.2015 xxvii.
　　　　Sixth assembly. 26 Nov.1925. (Misc., no.1,
　　　　1926) 1926 Cmd.2576 xxx.
　　　　Seventh assembly. 19 Nov.1926. (Misc., no.12,
　　　　1926) 1926 Cmd.2780 xxx.
　　　　Tenth assembly. 15 Nov.1929. (Misc., no.13,
　　　　1929) 1929/30 Cmd.3458 xxxii.
　　　　Eleventh assembly. 31 Dec.1930. (Misc., no.4,
　　　　1931) 1930/1 Cmd.3771 xxxv.
　　　　Twelfth assembly. 30 Oct.1931. (Misc., no.21,
　　　　1931) 1931/2 Cmd.3986 xxvii. Foreign Office.

　　Report on the council of the League of Nations.
　　　　Twenty-fifth session. 12 July 1923. (Misc.,
　　　　no.4, 1923) 1923 Cmd.1921 xxiv.
　　　　Twenty-sixth session. 16 Oct.1923. (Misc.,
　　　　no.2, 1924) 1924 Cmd.2017 xxvii.
　　　　Twenty-seventh session. 29 Dec.1923. (Misc.,
　　　　no.3, 1924) 1924 Cmd.2018 xxvii. Foreign
　　　　Office.

　　Report on the League of Nations' Committee of the
　　Council on article 11 of the Covenant. 16 March
　　1927. (Misc., no.5, 1927) 1927 Cmd.2889 xxvi.
　　Foreign Office.

　　Report on the League of Nations' Preparatory
　　Committee for the Disarmament Conference, third
　　session, March 21 to April 26, 1927. 17 May 1927.
　　(Misc., no.4, 1927) 1927 Cmd.2888 xxvi. Foreign
　　Office.

CECIL, Evelyn, *1st Baron Rockley*
　　Departmental committee on deaths from gas
　　poisoning.
　　　　Report. 22 Jan.1930. Board of Trade.

　　Departmental committee on the treatment of young
　　offenders.
　　　　Report. 17 March 1927. 1927 Cmd.2831 xii.
　　　　Home Office.

　　Eastern mail service committee.
　　　　Report. 22 Jan.1904. 1904 Cd.2082 xxiii. Post
　　　　Office.

　　Royal commission on safety in coal mines.
　　　　Report. 2 Dec.1938. 1938/9 Cmd.5890 xiii.
　　　　Minutes of evidence. 3 vols. 1936-8.
　　　　Appendices. 1938.

　　Select committee on steamship subsidies.
　　　　Report, proceedings, minutes of evidence,
　　　　appendix and index. 1 Aug.1901. 1901 (300)
　　　　viii. House of Commons.

　　　　Report, proceedings, minutes of evidence,
　　　　appendix and index. 3 Dec.1902. 1902 (385) ix.
　　　　House of Commons.

　　Select committee on the telephone service.
　　　　Report, proceedings, evidence and index. 27
　　　　July 1921. 1921 (191) vii. House of Commons.

　　　　Report, and proceedings. 20 March 1922. 1922
　　　　(54) vi. House of Commons.

CECIL, Hugh Richard Heathcote, *Lord Hugh Cecil.*
　　Select committee on procedure (members'
　　unofficial business).
　　　　Report, evidence and appendix. 25 July 1927.
　　　　1927 (102) vi. House of Commons.

　　Select committee on procedure (members'
　　unofficial business).
　　　　Report, proceedings and evidence. 18 July
　　　　1929. 1929/30 (12) vii. House of Commons.

CECIL, James Edward Hubert Gascoyne, *4th Marquess
of Salisbury*
　　Committee of imperial defence. Sub-committee on
　　national and imperial defence.
　　　　Report. 15 Nov.1923. 1924 Cmd.2029 x. War
　　　　Office.

　　Committee on the operation of the rent restriction
　　acts.
　　　　Rqort. 31 March 1920. 1920 Cmd.658 xviii.
　　　　Minutes of evidence. 1920. Ministry of Health.

　　Housing advisory panel for England and Wales.
　　　　Memorandum on the emergency problem.
　　　　Oct.1917. 1918 Cd.9087 xxvi. Ministry of
　　　　Recmstruction.

Cecil, *Lord* Robert. *SEE:* Cecil, E. A. R., *1st Viscount
Cecil.*

CHADWICK, Robert Burton
　　Committee on the Safeguarding of Industries Act,
　　1921, part 1.
　　　　Report. 29 March 1926. 1926 Cmd.2631 xv.
　　　　Board of Trade.

CHALK, L.
　　British hardwoods; their structure and
　　identification. Aug.1929. (F.P.R.Bull., no.3.)
　　Department of Scientific and Industrial Research.

CHALMERS, Mackenzie Dalzell
　　Committee of inquiry into the liquor trade in
　　Southern Nigeria.
　　　　Part 1: Report. 17 Sept.1909. 1909 Cd.4906
　　　　lx.

CHALMERS, Mackenzie Dalzell (continued)
Part 2: Minutes of evidence, *etc.* 1909 Cd.4907 lx. Colonial Office.

Departmental committee on control of certain therapeutic substances.
Report. 24 Dec.1920. 1921 Cmd.1156 xiii. Ministry of Health.

Departmental committee on the law relating to coroners and coroners' inquests, and into the practice in coroners' courts.
First report. 16 June 1909. 1909 Cd.4781 xv.
Evidence and appendices. 1909 Cd.4782 xv.
Second report. 31 Dec.1909. 1910 Cd.5004 xxi.
Evidence. 1910 Cd.5139 xxi.
Evidence and appendices. 1911 Cd.5492 xiii.
Report on deaths resulting from the administration of anaesthetics. 18 March 1910. 1910 Cd.5111 xxi.
Report on the dangj arising from the use of flannelette for articles of clothing. 23 Aug.1910. 1910 Cd.5376 xxi. Home Office.

CHALMERS, Robert, *1st Baron of Northian*
Committee on research in the colonies.
Report. 6 April 1921. 1921 Cmd.1472 xxiv. Colonial Office.

CHAMBERLAIN, Arthur Neville
Committee of privileges.
Report and proceedings. 30 June 1938. 1937/8 (146) vii. House of Commons.

Committee on inland waterways.
(First interim report not published)
Second interim report. 10 June 1921. 1921 Cmd.1150 xiv. (no further reports identified) Ministry of Transport.

Committee on living-in on canal boats.
Report. 5 May 1921.
Minutes of evidence. 1921. Ministry of Health.

Select committee on the civil list.
Report, proceedings and an appendix. 7 April 1936. 1935/6 (74) v. House of Commons.

Report, proceedings and an appendix. 28 April 1937. 1936/7 (114) vi. House of Commons.

Unhealthy areas committee.
Interim report. 29 March 1921.
Second and final report. 20 April 1921. Ministry of Health.

Chamberlain, Austen. *SEE:* Chamberlain, Joseph Austen.

CHAMBERLAIN, Joseph Austen
Committee on a national guarantee for the war risks of shipping.
Report. 24 March 1908. 1908 Cd.4161 lviii.
Minutes of evidence and appendices. 1908 Cd.4162 lviii. Treasury.

Report of the British delegates on the League of Nations, special assembly, Geneva, March 8 to 17, 1926. (Misc. no.5, 1926) 19 April 1926. 1926 Cmd.2648 xxx. Foreign Office.

Report on the council of the League of Nations.
Thirty-second session. 1 Jan.1925. (Misc., no.3, 1925) 1924/5 Cmd.2336 xxxii.

Thirty-third session. 23 March 1925. (Misc., no.6, 1925) 1924/5 Cmd.2402 xxxii.

Thirty-fourth session. 6 July 1925. (Misc., no.10, 1925) 1924/5 Cmd.2471 xxxii.

Thirty-fifth session. 1 Nov.1925. (Misc., no.13, 1925) 1924/5 Cmd.2528 xxxii.

Thirty-sixth session. 12 Nov.1925. (Misc., no.14, 1925) 1924/5 Cmd.2543 xxxii.

Thirty-seventh session. 1 Feb.1926. (Misc., no.2, 1926). 1926 Cmd.2594 xxx.

Thirty-ninth session. 14 April 1926. (Misc., no.4, 1926) 1926 Cmd.2646 xxx.

Fortieth session. 5 July 1926. (Misc., no.8, 1926) 1926 Cmd.2694 xxx.

Forty-first and forty-second sessions. 18 Oct.1926. (Misc., no.9, 1926). 1926 Cmd.2761 xxx.

Forty-third session. 26 Jan.1927. (Misc., no.1, 1927) 1927 Cmd.2799 xxvi.

Forty-fourth session. 1 June 1927. (Misc., no.6, 1927). 1927 Cmd.2894 xxv.

Forty-fifth session. 25 July 1927. (Misc., no.7, 1927) 1927 Cmd.2925 xxvi.

Forty-sixth and forty-seventh sessions. 25 Nov.1927. (Misc., no.2, 1928) 1928 Cmd.3009 xxvi.

Forty-eighth session. 17 Jan.1928. (Misc., no.3, 1928) 1928 Cmd.3021 xxvi.

Forty-ninth session. 23 April 1928. (Misc., no.4, 1928) 1928 Cmd.3098 xxvi.

Fiftieth session. 21 July 1928. (Misc., no.5, 1928) 1928 Cmd.3171 xxvi.

Fifty-third session. 25 Jan.1928. (Misc., no.2, 1929) 1928/9 Cmd.3270 xxiii.

Fifty-fourth session. 10 April 1929. (Misc., no.3, 1929) 1928/9 Cmd.3314 xxiii. Foreign Office.

Royal commission on Indian finance and currency.
Interim report. 6 Aug.1913. 1914 Cd.7068 xix.
Final report. 24 Feb.1914. 1914 Cd.7236 xx.
Minutes of evidence. 1914 Cd.7069, 7237 xix, xx.
Appendices. 1914 Cd.7070, Cd.7071, Cd.7238 xx.
Index to minutes of evidence and appendices 1914 Cd.7072 xx.

Index to the two volumes of evidence and the three volumes of appendices. 1914 Cd.7239 xx.

Chamberlain, Neville. *SEE:* Chamberlain, Arthur Neville.

CHAMBERS, E. G.
The prognostic value of some psychological tests. May 1936. (I.H.R.B. Rep., no.74) Medical Research Council.

A psychological study of individual differences in accident rates. Nov.1926. (I.H.R.B. Rep., no.38) Medical Research Council.

A study of accident proneness among motor drivers. Dec.1939. (I.H.R.B. Rep., no.84) Medical Research Council.

A study of personal qualities in accident proneness and proficiency. Aug.1929. (I.H.R.B. Rep., no.55) Medical Research Council.

CHAMBERS, Edmund Kerchever
Departmental committee on the Royal College of Art.
Report with appendices. 3 July 1911. 1911 Cd.5810 xviii. Board of Education.

CHAMBERS, Theodore Gervase
Committee on agricultural credit.
Report. 20 Jan.1923. 1923 Cmd.1810 ix.
Ministry of Agriculture and Fisheries.

Champneys, W. D. SEE: Dalrymple-Champneys, W.

CHANCELLOR, John Robert
Provisional committee on hops.
Report. 21 June 1934. 1933/4 Cmd.4628 xii.
Ministry of Agriculture and Fisheries.

CHANDAVARKAR, Narayen Ganesh
Report on detainees and internees in Bengal. 31
Aug.1918. 1918 Cd.9198 viii. India Office.

CHANNELL, Arthur M.
Royal Commission on Sir John Jackson, Ltd.
Report. 30 March 1917. 1917/8 Cd.8518 xv.

CHAPLIN, C. J.
Empire timbers for structural design. British
Columbia Douglas fir. Oct.1932. Department of
Scientific and Industrial Research.

Mechanical and physical properties of timbers:
tests of small clear specimens. Jan.1928.
Department of Scientific and Industrial Research.

Strength tests of structural timbers.
Part 1: general principles with data on redwood
from Gefle and Archangel. Aug.1935. (F.P.R.
records, no.2).
Part 2: general procedure of selecting and
testing joists. Jan.1936. (F.P.R. records, no.8).
Part 3: development of safe loads and stresses.
Jan.1937. (F.P.R. records, no.15)
Part 4: development of a minimum structural
grade for redwood. May 1939. (F.P.R. records,
no.28). Department of Scientific and Industrial
Research.

Tests of some home-grown timbers in their green
and seasoned conditions. Sept.1929. Department of
Scientific and Industrial Research.

Tests of some home-grown timbers in their green
condition. Feb.1928. Department of Scientific and
Industrial Research.

CHAPMAN, A. W.
Rural education conference.
Report on consolidation of rural elementary
schools. 20 Nov.1911. 1912/3 Cd.6055 xi.
Board of Agricultural and Fisheries and Board
of Education.

CHAPMAN, Austin
Royal commission on old-age pensions (Australia).
Report. 16 Feb.1906. 1907 Cd.3341 lvi.
Colonial Office.

CHAPMAN, S. R.
An investigation of a rotating radio beacon.
Dec.1927. (R.R.B.special rep., no.6) Department
of Scientific and Industrial Research.

CHAPMAN, Sydney John
Mid-Scotland ship canal committee.
Report. 11 July 1930. 1930/1 Cmd.3657 xv.
Ministry of Transport.

CHAPMAN, W. Percy
Report on the agriculture of Tuscany, Italy. 30
March 1906. (Dip.Cons.reports: misc. ser. no.
648) 1906 Cd.2683-12 cxxii. Foreign Office.

Report on the changes which have taken place in
the distribution of works of art in the Royal
Galleries of Florence. 5 March 1904.
(Dip.cons.report; misc.ser., no.605) 1904 Cd.1767-9
xcvi. Foreign Office.

Report on the condition of the Italian silk trade and
on the yield of cocoons in Italy in 1904. 3 March
1905. (Dip.cons.reports: misc.ser., no.632) 1905
Cd.2237-13 lxxxvi. Foreign Office.

Report on the industries of the province of
Florence, Italy. 15 Oct.1901. (Dip.cons.reports:
misc.ser., no.570) 1902 Cd.787-6 ciii. Foreign
Office.

Report on the mineral wealth of the provinces of
Siena and Grosseto, Italy. 6 April 1905.
(Dip.cons.reports: misc.ser., no.633) 1905
Cd.2237-14 lxxxvi. Foreign Office.

CHATWIN, C. P.
British regional geology: East Anglia and adjoining
areas. 1937. Geological Survey.

British regional geology: the Hampshire basin and
adjoining areas. 1936. Geological Survey.

CHEESMAN, E. E.
Banana breeding at the Imperial College of
Tropical Agriculture; a progress report. Dec.1931.
(E.M.B.47) Empire Marketing Board.

Chelmsford, Baron. SEE: Thesiger, F. J. N., 1st
Viscount.

CHESHIRE, R. W.
Constructional data of small telescope objectives.
1915. National Physical Laboratory.

CHESTERTON, Gilbert Keith
How to help annexation. 1918. Ministry of
Information.

CHETWODE, Philip Walhouse
Indian military college committee.
Report. 15 July 1931. India Office.

CHEYNE, John
Departmental commission on the Free and United
Free Churches, Scotland.
Interim report. 17 Dec.1904. 1905 Cd.2510 ci.
Scottish Office. See also: Bruce, V. A. 9th Earl
Elgin.

CHILCOTT, R. E.
Report on the navigability of tributaries of the
upper Yangtse from Chung King to Ho Chau on
the Kialing Kiang and from Ho Chau to Ngan Dhu
Shien on the Fu Kaing. 24 July 1902.
(Hydrographic Publication H.D.188) Admiralty.

CHREE, Charles
Absolute daily range of magnetic declination at
Kew Observatory, 1858 to 1900. Sept.1923.
(Geophys.Mem., no.22) Meteorological Office.

Commission for terrestrial magnetism and
atmospheric electricity.
Report of meeting, September 1926. June 1927.
(M.O.296) Meteorological Office.

Comparison of magnetic standards at British
observatories. Feb.1926. (Geophys.Mem., no.30)
Meteorological Office.

A comparison of the records from British magnetic
stations, underground and surface. May 1927.
(Geophys.Mem., no.35) Meteorological Office.

Log in marine barometers on land and sea. May
1914. (Geophys.Mem.; no.8) Meteorological Office.

The regular diurnal variation of magnetic
declination at Kew Observatory, 1859-1894.
Dec.1928. (Geophys.Mem., no.43) Meteorological
Office.

Simultaneous values of magnetic declination at
different British stations. May 1921.

CHREE, Charles (continued)
(Geophys.Mem., no.17) Meteorological Office.

CHRISTIE, Ethel M.
The haemolytic streptococci; their grouping by agglutination. 21 June 1932. (S.R.S., no.169) Medical Research Council.

CHRYSTAL, R. Neil
The Douglas fir chermes (chermes cooleyi). July 1922. (Bull., no.4) Forestry Commission.

The silver fir chermes. Jan.1926. (Bull. no.7) Forestry Commission.

CHURCHILL, Winston Leonard Spencer
Committee on promotion of officers (not in regular army).
    Report. 9 May 1917. 1917/8 Cd.8642 iv. War Office. *For* Second report *see:* Lawson, H.L.W.

Chuter-Ede, J. *SEE:* Ede, J. C.

CLAPHAM, John Harold
Safeguarding of industries committee.
    Report on gold and aluminium bronze powders. 29 May 1922. Board of Trade.

Safeguarding of industries committee.
    Report on gold leaf. 21 Feb.1922. Board of Trade.

Clapon, J. E. Lane. *SEE:* Lane-Clapon, J.E.

Clarendon, *Earl. SEE:* Villiers, G. H. H., *6th Earl.*

CLARK, John Brown
Advisory council of the Scottish Education Department.
    Report on the position of technical education in the day school system of Scotland. 22 Jan.1937. Scottish Education Department.

    Report on the training of the woman primary school teacher. 9 July 1934. Scottish Education Department.

CLARK, Robert S.
Rays and skates; a revision of the European species. 1926. (Sci.invest., 1926, no.1) Fishery Board for Scotland.

CLARK-KENNEDY, Alexander K.
Reports on the Shops Act, 1912 as it applies to refreshment premises. 30 Dec.1912. 1912/3 Cd.6579 xxvi. Home Office.

CLARKE, Edward
Report upon the disputes affecting transport workers in the Port of London and on the Medway with minutes of evidence of the inquiry. 27 May 1912. 1912/3 Cd.6229 xlvii. Board of Trade.

CLARKE, Frederick Seymour
Report on state encouragement to industry in Hungary. July 1907. (Dip.cons.reports: Misc., ser., no.663) 1907 Cd.3284-7 lxxxvii. Foreign Office.

CLARKE, George Herbert
Why the United States of America entered the war. 1917. Ministry of Information.

CLARKE, George Sydenham, *1st Baron Sydenham of Combe*
Royal Commission on venereal diseases.
    First report. 8 June 1914. 1914 Cd.7474 xlix.
    Appendix; evidence. 7 Nov.1913 to 6 April 1914. 1914 Cd.7475 xlix.
    Final report. 11 Feb.1916. 1916 Cd.8189 xvi.
    Appendix: evidence, 27 April 1914 to 21 June 1915, index to evidence and digest of evidence. 1916 Cd.8190 xvi.

CLARKE, J. C.
Observations on experimental infection of trout by *B.salmonicida.* 1931. (Salmon Fish., 1931, no.7) Fishery Board for Scotland.

CLARKE, S. H.
Gurjun, apitong, keruing, kapur and allied timbers. April 1937. (F.P.R. records, no.16) Department of Scientific and Industrial Research.

Home grown timbers; their anatomical structure and its relation to physical properties. Elm. Aug.1930. (F.P.R. Bull., no.7) Department of Scientific and Industrial Research.

Seraya, meranti and lavan. Sept.1936. (F.P.R. records, no.12) Department of Scientific and Industrial Research.

Claughton-Scott, H. *SEE:* Scott, H. C.

CLAUSON, Albert Charles
Departmental committee on the Assurance Companies Act, 1909.
    Interim report. 30 June 1925. 1924/5 Cmd.2474 ix.
    Report. 21 Feb.1927. 1927 Cmd.2820 vii. Board of Trade.

CLAY, H. A.
Compulsory continuation schools in Germany. May 1910. (Educational pamphlets, no.18) Board of Education.

CLEARY, Henry william, *Bishop of Auckland 1910-1914*
Prussian militarism at work; a letter. 1917. Ministry of Information.

CLEGG, W. H.
Commission on Hong Kong currency.
    Report. 10 May 1931. 1930/1 Cmd.3932 x. Colonial Office.

CLENNELL, Walter J.
Report on a journey in the interior of Kiangsi (China). 5 Aug.1905. 1906 Cd.2762 cxxxvi. Foreign Office.

CLERK, Dugald
Committee on education for the engineering industry.
    Report. 17 July 1930. Board of Education.

Committee on facilities for education in coal-mining at the universities and technical schools in Britain.
    Report. 17 Nov.1922. Mines Department.

CLIFFORD, Hugh
Committee on trade and taxation for British West Africa.
    Report. 15 Dec.1921. 1922 Cmd.1600 xvi. Colonial Office.

CLIFFORD, John
Our fight for Belgium and what it means. 1918. Ministry of Information.

Clinton, *Lord. SEE:* Trefusis, C.J.R.H-S.F., *21st Baron Clinton*

Clive, R. G. W. *SEE:* Windsor-Clive, R. G., *14th Baron*

CLOAKE, P. C.
Red discolouration on dried salted fish. Oct.1923. (F.I.B. special rep., no.18) Department of Scientific and Industrial Research.

Cloan, *Lord. SEE:* Haldane, R.B., *1st Viscount.*

CLODE, Walter Baker
Railway pool committee.
Report. 27 July 1932.
Proceedings. 1932. Ministry of Transport.

CLOSE, Charles Frederick
A sketch of the subject of map projections.
Dec.1901. War Office.

Text book of topographical and geographical
surveying, 2nd ed. Nov.1913. War Office.

CLOUGH, C. T.
The economic geology of the central coalfield of
Scotland. Area 5: Glasgow east, Coatbridge and
Airdrie. 5 April 1916. (Mem.Geol.Surv., Scotl.)
Geological Survey, Scotland.

The economic geology of the central coalfield of
Scotland. Area 7: Rutherglen, Hamilton and
Wishaw. 5 May 1919. (Mem.Geol.Surv., Scotl.)
Geological Survey, Scotland.

The geology of East Lothian (Sheet 33 and parts of
34 and 41). 20 Sept.1909. (Mem.Geol.Surv., Scotl.)
Geological Survey, Scotland.

The geology of the Glasgow district. (Glasgow
district map, including parts of sheets 30, 31, 22
and 23). 13 March 1911. (Mem.Geol.Surv., Scotl.)
Geological Survey, Scotland.

The geology of West-Central Skye with Soay (Sheet
70). 28 May 1904. (Mem.Geol.Surv., Scotl.)
Geological Survey, Scotland.

CLUTTON-BROCK, Arthur
Our common purpose; the economics of peace.
1919. National War Savings Committee.

CLYDE, James Avon
Royal commission on the Court of Session and the
office of Sheriff Principal.
Vol.1:    Report. 25 Jan.1927. 1927 Cmd.2801 viii.
Vol.2:    Summary of evidence. 1927.

CLYNES, John Robert
Committee of the Economic Advisory Council on
the cotton industry.
Report. 4 June 1930. 1929/30 Cmd.3615 xii.
Treasury.

Select committee on House of Commons gallery
accommodation.
Report, proceedings, evidence and appendix.
24 July 1923. 1923 (116) vi. House of
Commons.

COATES, Edward Clive
Select committee on telephone charges.
Report, proceedings and evidence. 20
Dec.1920. 1920 (247) viii. House of Commons.

COBB, Cyril Stephen
Committee on the administration of public mental
hospitals.
Report. July 1922. 1922 Cmd.1730 viii.
Ministry of Health.

Select committee on nursing homes registration.
Report, proceedings, evidence, appendices and
index. 6 July 1926. 1926 (103) vii. House of
Commons.

COCHRANE, Thomas H. A. E.
Interdepartmental committee on provision of funds
for reformatory and industrial schools.
Vol.1:    Report and appendices. 3 Aug.1906.
1906 Cd.3143 liv.
Vol.2:    Minutes of proceedings. 1906 Cd.3144
liv. Home Office.

COCKBURN, A. W.
Reorganisation commission for England.
Report on hops. 29 April 1938. (Economic
Series, no.46). Ministry of Agriculture.

COHEN, Benjamin Arthur
Departmental committee on the law and practice
relating to industrial insurance.
Report. 30 June 1933. 1932/3 Cmd.4376 xiii.
Minutes of evidence, 1st—24th days, and
index. 1931-33.
Appendix 1: Memorandum by the Association
of Industrial Assurance Companies and
Collecting Friendly Societies. 1931.
Appendix 2: Memorandum by the Prudential
Assurance Co. Ltd. Oct.1931.
Appendix 3: Memorandum by the National
Union of Life Assurance Workers. 26 Sept.
1931.
Appendix 4: Memorandum by the Insurance
Unions Congress. Dec.1931. 1932.
Appendix 5: Memorandum by the Association
of Industrial Assurance Companies and
Collecting Friendly Societies. 1932.
Appendix 6: Memorandum by the Wesleyan
and General Assurance Society. 1932.
Appendix 7: Memorandum by the Trades
Union Congress General Council. 1932.
Treasury.

Committee on safeguarding of industries.
Report on light leather goods and metal
fittings. 23 Dec.1926. 1927 Cmd. 2837 xii.
Board of Trade.

Royal Commission on shipping rings.
Vol.1:    Report. 18 May 1909. 1909 Cd.4668
xlvii.
Vol.2:    Appendices. 1909 Cd.4669 xlvii.
Vol.3:    Minutes of evidence, days 1—19. 1909
Cd.4670 xlvii.
Vol.4:    Minutes of evidence, days 20—36.
1909 Cd.4685 xlviii.
Vol.5:    Report of the sub-commission upon
evidence taken in South Africa with minutes of
evidence and appendices. 1909 Cd.4686 xlviii.

COHEN, Israel
Anti-semitism in Germany. 1918. Ministry of
Information.

The German attack on the Hebrew schools in
Palestine. 1918. Ministry of Information.

The Turkish persecution of the Jews. 1918.
Ministry of Information.

COHN, August
Some aspects of the war as viewed by naturalised
British subjects. 1916. Ministry of Information.

COLE, Alfred Clayton
Departmental committee on accounts and
statistical returns rendered by railway companies.
Report. 25 May 1909. 1909 Cd.4697 lxxvi.
Minutes of evidence. 1910 Cd.5052 xlvi. Board
of Trade.

COLE, Grenville Arthur James
Memoir and map of localities of minerals of
economic importance and metaliferous mines in
Ireland. Jan.1921. (Mem.Geol.Surv., Ireland.
Mineral Resources) Department of Agriculture and
Technical Instruction for Ireland.

COLEBROOK, Dora Challis
Irradiation and health; two experimental studies. 6
Aug.1929. (S.R.S., no.131) Medical Research
Council.

COLEBROOK, Dora Challis (continued)
The source of infection in puerperal fever due to haemolytic streptococci. 14 Nov.1935. (S.R.S., no.205) Medical Research Council.

COLEBROOK, F. M.
An investigation of the interference caused by transmissions from radio stations. 1928. (R.R.B. special rep., no.8) Department of Scientific and Industrial Research.

Magnetic materials at radio frequencies; a critical survey of present knowledge. Jan.1934. (R.R.B., special rep., no.14) Department of Scientific and Industrial Research.

A theoretical and experimental investigation of high selectivity tone-corrected receiving circuits. 1 Sept. 1932. (R.R.B. special rep., no.12) Department of Scientific and Industrial Research.

Valve oscillators of stable frequency; a critical survey of present knowledge. Dec.1933. (R.R.B., special rep., no.13) Department of Scientific and Industrial Research.

COLEBROOK, Leonard
A study of some organic arsenical compounds with a view to their use in certain streptococcal infections. 12 Jan.1928. (S.R.S., no.119) Medical Research Council.

COLEFAX, Arthur
Court of enquiry concerning the stoppage of the London tramway and omnibus services, 1924.
Interim report. 24 March 1924. 1924 Cmd.2087 xi.
Report. 3 April 1924. 1924 Cmd.2101 xi. Ministry of Labour.

COLES, F. E.
Dust-storms in Iraq. Nov.1938. (Prof. Notes, no.84) Meteorological Office.

COLES, P. B.
Recent educational developments in Sweden. June 1930. (Educational pamphlets, no.81) Board of Education.

COLLENS, J. H.
The system of education in Trinidad and Tobago. 15 Feb.1913. (Imperial Education Conference Papers) Board of Education.

COLLIER, Robert
Report on Prussian railways. 13 Jan.1902. (Dip. cons.reports: misc.ser., no.574) 1901 Cd.787-10 ciii. Foreign Office.

Report on United States railways. 24 Dec.1904. (Dip. cons. reports: misc., ser., no.627) 1905 Cd.2237-8 lxxxvi. Foreign Office.

COLLINGS, Jesse
Select committee on fire brigades.
Report. . . with the proceedings. 16 July 1900. 1900 (278) vi. House of Commons.

COLLINS, Godfrey P.
Committee of inquiry on metal artificial limbs. 29 July 1925. Ministry of Pensions.

Select committee on members' expenses.
Report, proceedings, evidence and appendices. 22 Dec.1920. 1920 (255) vii. House of Commons.

COLLINS, Richard Henn
Committee of inquiry into the case of Mr. Adolf Beck.
Report, minutes of evidence, appendix and facsimilies of various documents. 14 Nov.1904.

1905 Cd.2315 lxii. Home Office.

War relief funds committee.
Report. 28 May 1900. 1900 Cd.196 xlii.
Minutes of evidence, appendices and index. 1900 Cd.248 xlii. Treasury.

COLLINS, William Job
Select committee on the hop industry.
Report, proceedings, evidence, appendix and index. 6 July 1908. 1908 (213) viii. House of Commons.

COLLIS, Edgar Leigh
Report of an inquiry in Dupuytren's contraction as a disease of occupation with special reference to its occurrence among minders of lace machines. 4 June 1912. Home Office.

Report on conditions under which bronzing is carried on in factories and workshops. July 1910. 1910 Cd.5328 xxix. Home Office.

Report on conditions of employment in the manufacture of tinplates with special reference to the process of tinning. 27 Aug.1912. 1912/3 Cd.6394 xxvi. Home Office.

Report on manufacture of silica bricks and other refractory materials used in furnaces. 14 Aug.1917. Home Office.

Report on miners' 'beat knee', 'beat hand' and 'beat elbow'. 15 July 1924. (S.R.S., no.89) Medical Research Council.

Special report on dangerous or injurious processes in the smelting of materials containing lead. Jan.1910. 1910 Cd.5152 xxix. Home Office.

COLVIN, Richard Beale
Select committee on performing animals.
Report, proceedings, evidence and index. 11 Aug.1921. 1921 (214) vii. House of Commons.

Select committee on performing animals.
Report, proceedings and evidence. 18 May 1922. 1922 (89) v. House of Commons.

Colwyn, *Lord. SEE:* Smith, F. H., *1st Baron Colwyn*

COMPSTON: John Albert
Court of inquiry on hours of labour of coal tippers and trimmers.
Report. 4 June 1920. Ministry of Labour.

Court of inquiry on hours of labour of coal tippers and trimmers in South Wales.
Report. June 1923. 1923 Cmd.1948 xii pt.1. Ministry of Labour.

Court of inquiry on the dispute at Covent Garden and the threatened stoppage of work at the ports and elsewhere arising therefrom.
Report. 11 Sept.1924. 1924 Cmd.2244 xi. Ministry of Labour.

CONACHER, H. M.
Committee on farm accounting and economics.
Report. 14 May 1926. Board of Agriculture for Scotland.

Economics of small farms and small holdings in Scotland.
Interim report. Dec.1919.
Report on agricultural credit and organisation in France, with suggestions for a Scottish scheme of agricultural credit. June 1920. Board of Agriculture for Scotland.

CONDELL, C. F.
The system of education in St. Lucia. Dec.1912. (Imperial Education Conference Papers) Board of Education. 1915.

CONSTABLE, Andrew Henderson Briggs, *Lord*
Committee on the rent restriction acts.
Report. 20 May 1925. 1924/5 Cmd.2423 xv.
Scottish Office.

Departmental committee on the organisation and finance of agricultural education and research in Scotland.
Report. 12 Sept.1924. Scottish Office.

CONYBEARE, Ernest Thomas
A report on outbreak of food poisoning due to salmonella, type 'Dublin' and conveyed by raw milk. March 1938. (R.Pub.Health & Med.Subj., no.82) Ministry of Health.

COOK, Duncan
Medical report on Pitcairn Island. 1938. (Colonial, no.155) Colonial Office.

COOK, Edward Tyas
How Britain strove for peace; a record of Anglo-German negotiations, 1898 to 1914, told from authoritative documents. 1914. Ministry of Information.

COOK, Frederick Charles
Departmental committee on street lighting.
Interim report. Sept.1935.
Final report. Aug.1937. Ministry of Transport.

Technical advisory committee on experimental work.
Report on concrete in road construction. June 1933. Ministry of Transport.

Report on methods of providing traffic lines in Great Britain. June 1933. Ministry of Transport.

COOKE, Henry A.
Report on Russian railways. 14 Feb.1900. (Dip.cons.reports: misc.ser., no.522) 1900 Cd.2—5 xci. Foreign Office.

Report on the coal crisis in Russia and the main sources of native supply. 5 March 1900. (Dip.cons.reports: misc.ser., no.523) 1900 Cd.2—6 xci. Foreign Office.

Report on the condition and prospects of British trade in Siberia. April 1905. 1905 Cd.2518 lxxxv. Board of Trade.

Report on the mineral and metallurgical industries of Russia. 20 May 1901. (Dip. cons. reports: misc.ser., no.555) 1901 Cd.430—10 lxxx. Foreign Office.

Report on the trade of Siberia. 21 Oct.1902. (Dip.cons. reports: misc.ser., no.585) 1902 Cd.787-21 ciii. Foreign Office.

Report on the trans-Siberian railway. 18 June 1900. (Dip.cons.reports: misc.ser., no.533) 1900 Cd.2—16 xci. Foreign Office.

COOPER, H. I.
Report of special inquiry into the expenditure of the guardians of the Parish of Poplar borough. 10 May 1922. Ministry of Health.

COOPER-KEY, Aston McNeill Cooper
Committee on dry powder fire extinguishers.
Report. 27 April 1916. 1916 Cd.8250 lx. Home Office.

Departmental committee on cylinders for dissolved acetylene.
Report and appendices. 30 Nov.1917. Home Office.

Departmental committee on the heat test as applied to explosives.
First report with appendices. 2 Feb.1914.
Memorandum. 2 Feb.1914. Home Office.

Inter-departmental committee on gas in substitution for petrol and petroleum products.
Report. 30 June 1919. 1919 Cmd.263 xxii. Petroleum Executive.

COPE, Alexander C.
Departmental committee on Glanders.
Report. 16 Dec.1902. 1903 Cd.1396 xxiii. Board of Agriculture.

COPEMAN, Sydney Arthur Monckton
Diet and cancer. Oct.1926. (R.Pub.Health & Med.Subj., no.36) Ministry of Health.

Report on enteric fever in the Borough of Harwich and its neighbourhood, 1912/3. 7 Aug.1913. (Rep. Pub.H. & Med.Subj., no.83) Local Government Board.

Report on infestation of the human subject by the nematode worm, *ascaris lumbricoides*. June 1925. (Rept.Pub.Health & Med.Subj., no.31) Ministry of Health.

Report on an outbreak of enteric fever at Belmont Asylum for Imbeciles, Sutton, Surrey. 18 Oct.1906. (Rep.Med.Insp., no.248) Local Government Board.

Report on an outbreak of enteric fever at Fulbourne Asylum near Cambridge, with special reference to risk of pollution of underground water supplies by the sewage of the asylum. 21 Feb.1906. (Rep.Med. Insp., no.229) Local Government Board.

Report on an outbreak of enteric fever in the Borough of Eccles, Lancashire, due to the consumption of ice-cream. 10 May 1911. (Rep.Pub.Health & Med.Subj., no.51) Local Government Board.

Report on an outbreak of enteric fever in the Borough of Workington. 30 Oct.1908. (Rep.Med. Insp., no.315) Local Government Board.

Report on an outbreak of epidemic skin disease at the Central London Sick Asylum, Hendon. 18 April 1904. (Rep.Med.Insp., no.194) Local Government Board.

Report on the sanitary conditions of Alcester R.D. 9 July 1901. (Rep.Med.Insp., no.162) Local Government Board.

Report on the sanitary conditions of the Borough of Boston. 29 Jan.1901. (Rep.Med.Insp., no.157) Local Government Board.

Report on the sanitary conditions of Brixworth R.D., Northamptonshire. 23 May 1908. (Rep.Med.Insp., no.303) Local Government Board.

Report on the sanitary conditions of Ely R.D. 6 Aug.1910. (Rep.Pub.Health & Med.Subj., no.39) Local Government Board.

Report on the sanitary conditions of Hanley C.B., and the prevalence of infectious diseases. 1 May 1905. (Rep.Med.Insp., no.217) Local Government Board.

Report on the sanitary conditions of Ely U.D. 6 Aug.1910. (Rep.Pub.Health & Med.Subj., no.38) Local Government Board.

Report on the sanitary conditions of Langport R.D., with special reference to outbreaks of diptheria and smallpox. 9 March 1906. (Rep.Med.Insp., no.230) Local Government Board.

COPEMAN, Sydney Arthur Monckton (continued)
Report on the sanitary conditions of Shirebrook, in Blackwell R.D., with reference to the continued prevalence of enteric fever. 2 Aug.1900. (Rep.Med.Insp., No.151) Local Government Board.

Report on the sanitary conditions of Sutton Bridge U.D., 22 Jan.1908. (Rep.Med.Insp., no.299) Local Government Board.

Report on the sanitary conditions of Whittlesey U.D. and R.D. 22 April 1904. (Rep.Med.Insp., no.196) Local Government Board.

Report on the sanitary conditions of Wigan C.B., with special reference to infantile mortality and to endemic prevalence of enteric fever and diarrhoea. 1 Jan.1907. (Rep.Med.Insp., no.246) Local Government Board.

CORBETT, Julian Stafford.
History of the Great War. Naval operations. 1920. vols. 1—3 and maps, 5 vols. 1920-23. War Office. *For further vols. see:* Newbolt, H.

The League of Peace and a free sea. 1917. Ministry of Information.

CORLESS, R.
On the radiation records obtained in 1911 at South Kensington and comparison with those at Kew Observatory. July 1912. (Geophys.Mem., No.4) Meteorological Office.

CORNWALLIS, Fiennes Stanley Wykeham, *1st Baron Cornwallis.*
Committee on the metropolitan police courts and juvenile courts.
Report. 9 May 1929. Home Office.

COSGROVE, J. R.
Empire timbers from home and overseas for building and structural purposes. April 1932. (F.P.R. Leaflet, no.5) Department of Scientific and Industrial Research.

COTTON, Charles P.
Committee to inquire into the public health of the city of Dublin.
Report. 14 May 1900. 1900 Cd.243 xxxix.
Minutes of evidence with appendices. 1900 Cd.244 xxxix. Local Government Board for Ireland.

COULSON, William
Committee on the standardisation and simplification of the requirements of local authorities. *SEE:* Shelley, A. N. C.

COURTHOPE, George Lloyd
Departmental committee on swine fever.
Part 1: Interim report. 8 May 1911. 1911 Cd.5671 ix.
Part 2: Minutes of evidence, index and appendix. 1911 Cd.5680 ix.
Part 3: Second interim report, minutes of evidence and appendix. 26 Jan. 1914. 1914 Cd.7247 xii.
Part 4: Final report, evidence and appendix. 12 Aug.1915. 1914/6 Cd.8045 xxxv. Board of Agriculture and Fisheries.

COURTNEY, Leonard Henry
Royal commission on superannuation in the civil service.
Report. 10 Aug.1903. 1903 Cd.1744 xxxiii.
Minutes of evidence, appendices and index. 1903 Cd.1745 xxxiii.

COUTTS, Francis James Henderson
Report on an inquiry into cases of anthrax suspected to be due to the use of infected shaving brushes. April 1917. (Rep.Pub.Health & Med.Subj., no.112) Local Government Board.

Report on an inquiry on condensed milks; with reference to their use as infants' foods. Aug.1911. (Rep.Pub.Health & Med.Subj., no.56) Local Government Board.

COWARD, H. F.
The ignition of fire damp. July 1925. (S.M.R.B. Paper no.8) Revised, May 1929. (S.M.R.B. Paper no.53) Mines Department.

The limits of inflammibility of firedamp in atmospheres which contain black-damp. Nov.1925. (S.M.R.B. Pqper no.19) Mines Department.

The movement of flame in firedamp explosions. June 1933. (S.M.R.B. Paper no.82) Mines Department.

COWPER, A. D.
Lime and lime mortars. Jan.1927. (B.R.B. Special rep., no.9) Department of Scientific and Industrial Research.

Pozzolanas. Oct.1927. (B.R.B. Bull., no.2) Department of Scientific and Industrial Research.

COX, H. A.
A handbook of Empire timbers. July 1939. Department of Scientific and Industrial Research.

CRAIB, William Hofmeyr
The electrocardigram. Nov.1930. (S.R.S., no.147) Medical Research Council.

CRAIG, Charles Curtis
Departmental committee on the fire at Highbury Hospital, Birmingham and on fire precautions generally.
Report. 27 July 1923. Ministry of Pensions.

CRAIG, E. H. Cunningham
The geology of Colonsay and Oronsay with part of the Ross of Mull. (Sheet 35 and part of 27) 3 Jan.1911. (Mem.Geol.Surv., Scotl.) Geological Survey, Scotland.

The geology of the districts of Braemar, Ballater and Glen Clova. (Sheet 65) 16 Aug.1912. (Mem.Geol.Surv., Scotl.) Geological Survey, Scotland.

CRAIG, John Herbert McCutcheon
Committee on subsistence allowances, *etc.*
Report on *per noctem* rates of subsistence allowance. 11 June 1929. Civil Service National Whitley Council, Treasury.

Report on removal expenses. 24 Oct.1925. Civil Service National Whitley Council, Treasury.

Joint general purposes committee. Sub-committee on promotions procedure.
Report. 27 June 1938. Civil Service National Whitley Council, Treasury.

CRAIGIE, James
Further investigations on the variola-vaccinia flocculation reaction. 30 April 1931. (S.R.S., no.156) Medical Research Council.

CRAIK, Henry
Departmental committee on the remuneration of teachers in Scotland.
Report. 14 Nov.1917. Scotch Education Department.

CRAMB, Alexander C.
Committee on uniformity of electricity charges and tariffs.
Report. 3 July 1930. Electricity Commission. Ministry of Transport.

CRAMP, William Dawkins
Departmental committee on dangers attendant on building operations. (Building accidents committee)
Report, draft for regulations, evidence and appendices. 15 Oct.1907. 1908 Cd.3848 xi Home Office.

CRAMPTON, C. B.
The geology of Caithness (Sheets 110 and 116 with parts of 109, 115 and 117) 6 Jan.1914. (Mem.Geol. Surv., Scotl.) Geological Survey, Scotland.

Crawford, *Lord. SEE:* Lindsay, D. A. E., *27th Earl.*

CRAWFORD, Donald
Departmental committee on fiars prices in Scotland.
Report. 32 May 1911. 1911 Cd.5763 xxiv.
Minutes of evidence, appendices and index. 1911 Cd.5764 xxiv. Scottish Office *and* Board of Agriculture and Fisheries.

Departmental committee on whaling and whale-curing in the north of Scotland.
Vol.1: Report. July 1904. 1904 Cd.2138 xlii.
Vol.2: Evidence. 1904 Cd.2153 xlii. Scottish Office.

Report on complaints of Ruchill Fever Hospital, Glasgow and on its administration and management. 19 Feb.1908. Local Government Board for Scotland.

CRAWFORD, R. F.
Report on the cultivation and drying of chicory in Great Britain and Belgium. 2 March 1904. 1904 Cd.2169 xvi. Board of Agriculture and Fisheries.

Report on the Dutch brined vegetable industry. 20 Oct.1902. 1902 Cd.1368 civ. Board of Agriculture.

Crewe, *Earl. SE—E:* Crewe-Milnes, R. O. A., *Earl.*

CREWE-MILNES, Margaret, *Marchioness of Crewe*

Central committee on women's training and employment.
Interim report. March 1915. 1914/6 Cd.7848 xxxvii.
Second interim report. Aug.1923. (no further identified) Board of Trade *and* Ministry of Labour.

CREWE-MILNES, Robert Offley Ashburton, *1st Earl Crewe*
Committee on home administration of Indian affairs.
Report. 29 June 1919. 1919 Cmd.207 xx. India Office.

Committee on the production of fuel oil from home sources.
Report. 1918. 1918 Cd.9128 x. Ministry of Munitions.

Committee on the position of classics in the educational system of the United Kingdom.
Report. 7 June 1921. Board of Education.

Joint select committee on municipal trading.
Report, proceedings, minutes of evidence and appendix. 27 July 1900. 1900 (305) vii. House of Commons.

Report, proceedings, minutes of evidence, appendix and index. 23 July 1903. 1903 (270) vii. House of Commons.

Select committee of the House of Lords on the Chantrey Trust.
Report, proceedings, evidence and appendix. 12 Aug.1904. 1904 (357) v. House of Commons.

CRICHTON, Ian M.
Scale-absorption in salmon and sea trout. 1935. (Salmon Fish., 1935 no.4) Fishery Board for Scotland.

CRIDER, F. J.
Collection of native grass seed in the great plains, U.S.A. Sept.1937. (Bull. no.24) Imperial Bureau of Plant Genetics: Herbage Plants.

CRIPPS, Charles Alfred, *1st Baron Parmoor*
Committee on industrial assurance companies and collecting societies.
Report. 19 Feb.1920. 1920 Cmd.614 xviii.
Evidence. 1920 Cmd.618 xviii. Board of Trade.

Committee on the history and constitution of the French Protestant Church of London.
Report, evidence and appendices. 27 Oct.1913. 1914 Cd.7138 xxix. Home Office.

Report of the British delegates on the League of Nations, Fifth assembly. 1 Nov.1924. (Misc., no.1, 1925) 1924/5 Cmd.2330 xxxii. Foreign Office.

Report of the British delegates on the League of Nations, Fifth assembly, relating to the protocol for the peaceful settlement of international disputes. 1 Nov.1924. (Misc., no.21, 1924) 1924/5 Cmd.2289 xxxii. Foreign Office.

Report on the council of the League of Nations.
Twenty-eighth session. 26 March 1924. (Misc., no.4, 1924) 1924 Cmd.2094 xxvii.

Twenty-ninth session. 27 June 1924. (Misc., no.11, 1924) 1924 Cmd.2187 xxvii.

Thirtieth session. 1 Nov.1924. (Misc., no.20, 1924) 1924/5 Cmd.2287 xxxii.

Thirty-first session. 1 Dec.1924. (Misc., no.2, 1925) 1924/5 Cmd.2333 xxxii. Foreign Office.

CRIPPS, Lucy Davis
The application of the Air Force physical efficiency tests to men and women. 25 March 1924. (S.R.S., no.84) Medical Research Committee.

CROMBIE, John William
Select committee on official publications.
Report, proceedings, minutes, appendix and index. 23 July 1906. 1906 (279) xi. House of Commons.

Select committee on publications.
Report, proceedings, evidence and index. 26 July 1907. 1907 (272) vii. House of Commons.

Cromer, *Lord. SEE:* Baring, E., *1st Earl; and* Baring, R. T., *2nd Earl.*

CRONIN, Archibald Joseph
Investigations in first-aid organisation at collieries in Great Britain. Oct.1925. Mines Department.

CRONSHAW, H. B.
Oil shales. Nov.1921. (Mono.Min.Resour.) Imperial Institute.

Petroleum. July 1921. (Mono.Min.Resour.) Imperial Institute.

Silver ores. July1921. (Mono.Min.Resour.) Imperial Institute.

CROOKHALL, R.
British regional geology. Bristol and Gloucester disgict. 1935. Geological Survey.

The Kidston collection of fossil plants; with an account of the life and work of Robert Kidston. 1938. (Mem.Geol.Surv.) Geological Survey.

CROOKS, William
The British workman defends his home. 1917. Ministry of Information.

CROSS, S.
Merchant Shipping Advisory Committee.
Report of the sub-committee on line-throwing appliances for use on ships in cases of shipwreck or distress at sea, with appendices. 4 Dec.1908. 1909 Cd.4552 lxxviii. Board of Trade.

CROSSLEY, Arthur William
Fabric co-ordinating research committee. *SEE:* Pickard, R. H.

CROSTHWAITE, Charles Hawkes Todd
Committee of inquiry on the expediency of maintaining the Royal Indian Engineering College
Reports and correspondence. 17 Aug.1903. 1904 Cd.2055 lxiv.
Minutes of evidence, analysis and index. 1904 Cd.2056 lxiv. India Office.

CROSTHWAITE, P. M.
Report on prevention of contamination of the supply of water furnished by the Cambridge University and Town Waterworks Co. 12 Oct.1908. Local Government Board.

Report on rivers Lee and Stort flooding. 30 June 1919. Local Government Board.

CROWDEN, Guy Pascoe
The physiological cost of the muscular movements in barrow work. March 1928. (I.H.R.B. Rep., no.50) Medical Research Council.

CROWE, E. T. F.
Report on habutae (Japanese manufactured silk). Jan.1909. (Dip.cons.reports: misc., ser., no.672) 1909 Cd.4447 xcii. Foreign Office *and* Board of Trade.

Report on the gold mines of Formosa. May 1906. (Dip.cons.reports: misc.ser., no.649) 1906 Cd.2683-13 cxxii. Foreign Office.

CROWE, J. H. V.
Handbook of the armies of Sweden and Norway. June 1901. War Office.

CROWELL, Benedict
American aviation mission.
Report. 19 July1919. 1919 Cmd.384 x. Air Ministry.

CROWLEY, Ralph Henry
Committee on partially sighted children.
Report. June 1934. Board of Education.

CROZIER, Thomas Henry
Departmental committee on the carriage of dangerous goods and explosives in ships
Report. 2 March 1933. Board of Trade.

Report of the loss of life at the Glen Cinema, Paisley, 31 December 1929. 5 May 1930. Scottish Office.

Report on the proposed revision of bye-laws for regulating the transport of petroleum spirit in the Port of London. 9 May 1928. Ministry of Transport.

CRUICKSHANK, A. E.
Report for the half-year ending December 31, 1903 on the country produce traffic on the Uganda railway. 28 Jan.1904. (Dip.cons.reports: misc.ser., no.607) 1904 Cd.1767-11 xcvi. Foreign Office.

CRUICKSHANK, John Norman
The causes of neo-natal death. 25 March 1930. (S.R.S., no.145) Medical Research Council.

Maternal syphilis as a cause of death of the foetus and of the new born child. Feb.1924. (S.R.S., no.82) Medical Research Council.

CRUICKSHANK, Lewis D.
Interim report on artificial light and X-ray therapy. Nov.1925. (no further reports identified). Scottish Board of Health.

CUFFE, Hamilton John Agmondesham, *5th Earl of Desart*
Inter-departmental committee on sleeping sickness.
Report. 13 March 1914. 1914 Cd.7349 xlviii.
Evidence. 1914 Cd.7350 xlviii. Colonial Office.

CULLEN, William James
Committee on the bankruptcy law of Scotland and its administration.
Vol.1: Report. 6 June 1910. 1910 Cd.5210 ix.
Vol.2: Minutes of evidence, appendix and index. 1910 Cd.5202 ix. Scottish Office.

Departmental committee on the effect of the recent rise in fiars prices.
Report. 26 July 1917. Scottish Office.

CULLINAN, Frederick Fitzjames
Inter-departmental committee on the employment of children in street trading in Ireland.
Report, evidence and appendices. 10 June 1902. 1902 Cd.1144 xlix. Irish Secretary's Office.

CULMAN, F.
German tendencies with regard to the preparation and development of an action. July 1908. War Office

CULPIN, Millais
The nervous temperament. Dec.1930. (I.H.R.B. Rep., no.61) Medical Research Council.

CUNLIFFE, Joseph Herbert
Committee on the supervision of charities.
Report. 9 March 1927. 1927 Cmd.2823 vii.
Minutes of evidence. 1927. Home Office.

CUNLIFFE, Walter, *1st Baron Cunliffe of Headley*
Committee on currency and foreign exchanges after the war.
First interim report. 15 Aug.1918. 1918 Cd.9182 vii.
Final report. 3 Dec.1919. 1919 Cmd.464 xiii, part 1. Treasury.

CUNNINGHAM, J. T.
Report on the fisheries of St. Helena. 1 Aug.1909. (Colonial reports: misc., no.69) 1910 Cd.4998 lxv. Colonial Office.

CUNNINGHAM, W. B.
Report on the coal mines of Kyushu, Japan. Oct.1907. (Dip.cons.reports: misc.ser., no.666) 1908 Cd.3728-2 cviii. Foreign Office *and* Board of Trade.

Cunningham-Craig, E. H. *SEE:* Craig, E. H. C.

Cunninghame, H. H. S. *SEE:* Cunynghame, H. H. S.

CYNYNGHAME, Henry Hardinge S.
Committee on explosions in mines.

35

CYNYNGHAME, Henry Hardinge S. (continued)
First report. 21 June 1912. 1912/3 Cd.6307 xxv.
Second report. Oct.1912. 1912/3 Cd.6431 xxv.
Third report on influence of incombustible dusts on the inflamation of gaseous mixtures. 11 March 1913. 1913 Cd.6704 xxxv.
Fourth report on coal dust explosions. 9 April 1913. 1913 Cd.6791 xxxv.
Fifth report. 22 Oct.1913. 1914 Cd.7132 xxix.
Sixth report. 23 Dec.1914. 1914/6 Cd.7638 xxi.
Sevenh report: effects of inhaling dusts applicable for stone-dusting in coal mines, by J. S. Haldane. 23 July 1915. 1914/6 Cd.8122 xxi. Home Office.

Departmental committee on bobbinite.
Report. 5 March 1907. 1907 Cd.3423 xxxii.
Minutes of evidence. 1907 Cd.3465 xxxii. Home Office.

Departmental committee on notification of industrial accidents.
Report. 4 Dec.1902. 1902 Cd.998 x. Home Office.

Departmental committee on petroleum spirit.
First report and appendices. 3 May 1910. 1910 Cd.5175 xliv.
Minutes of evidence, vol.1. 1910 Cd.5176 xliv.
Final report. 11 Feb.1913. 1912/3 Cd.6565 xlii.
Minutes of evidence and appendices, vol.2. 1912/3 Cd.6644 xlii. Home Office.

Departmental committee on the use of electricity in mines.
Report. 19 Jan.1904. 1904 Cd.1916 xxiv.
Minutes of evidence, wppendices and index. 1904 Cd.1917 xxiv. Home Office.

Interdepartmental committee on the employment of school children.
Report. 25 Nov.1901. 1902 Cd.849 xxv.
Evidence, appendices and index. 1902 Cd.895 xxv. Home Office.

Report of a conference on justices' clerks' fees and salaries. 22 Dec.1908. 1914 Cd.7495 xxxvi. Home Office.

Royal commission on metalliferous mines and quarries.
First report. 31 July 1912. 1912/3 Cd.6389 xli.
Minutes of evidence, index and appendices, vol.1. 1912/3 Cd.6390 xli.
Second report. 12 June 1914. 1914 Cd.7476 xlii.
Evidence, index and appendices, vols. 2 and 3. 1914 Cd.7477, Cd.7478 xlii.

Royal commission on mines. SEE: Monkswell, R. C.

CURPHEY, W. S.
Report on rivers pollution, Scotland. 17 March 1908. 1908 Cd.4407 xciii. Scottish Board of Health.

Report on the pollution of the River Leven, Dumbartonshire. 22 Oct.1907. 1908 Cd.3942 xciii. Scottish Board of Health and Local Government Board for Scotland.

CURRIE, George Welsh
Committee of inquiry into the high cost of building working class dwellings in Scotland.
Report. June 1921. 1921 Cmd.1411 xiii. Scottish Board of Health.

CURRIE, John Ronald
Report on housing accommodation available for workers at Rosyth Naval Base. 14 Aug.1912. 1914 (147) lxix. Scottish Office and House of Commons.

CURTIS, A. H.
Manganese ores. June 1919. (Mono.Min.Resour.) Imperial Institute.

CURTIS, Lionel
Letters to the people of India on responsible government. 1918. Ministry of Information.

CURZON, George Nathaniel, 1st Earl Curzon
Committee of the National Gallery trustees.
Report. 13 Dec.1913. 1914/6 Cd.7878 xxix.
Minutes of evidence. 1914/6 Cd.7879 xxix.

Cushendun, Lord. SEE: McNeill, R. J., 1st Baron

CUSTANCE, Reginald Neville
Committee on the education and training of cadets, midshipmen and junior officers of His Majesty's fleet.
Reports and enclosures. March 1913. 1913 Cd.6703 xliii. Admiralty.

CUTFORTH, A. E.
Reorganisation commission.
Report on milk. 6 Nov.1936 (Economic Series, no.44) Ministry of Agriculture.

CUTLER, G. A.
Report on the safety of miners' electric cap lamps when the battery is short-circuited. 9 April 1929. Mines Department.

D'Abernon, Lord. SEE: Vincent, E., 1st Baron

DALBERG-ACTON, Richard Maximillian, 2nd Baron Acton
Report on the German colonial estimates for the year 1901. 18 March 1901. (Dip.Cons. reports: misc. no.549) 1901 Cd.430-4 lxxx. Foreign Office.

Report on Netherlands nationality laws and liability to military service. Nov.1910. (Misc., no.1, 1911) 1911 Cd.5475 lxiii. Foreign Office.

DALE, F. H.
Report on intermediate education in Ireland. 15 Feb.1905. 1905 Cd.2546 xxviii. Board of Education.

Report on primary education in Ireland. Nov.1903. 1904 Cd.1981 xx. Board of Education.

DALE, Henry Hallett
Committee on cinchona derivatives and malaria.
Report on clincial comparisons of quinine and quinidine. Aug.1925. (S.R.S., no.96) Medical Research Council.

Reports on biological standards: pituitary extracts. 20 Oct.1922. (S.R.S., no.69) Medical Research Council.

DALGETY, W. R.
Report on the navigation of the Han Kiang (Yangtse); with sailing directions and a map. Dec.1902. (Hydrographic publication H.D.187) Admiralty.

DALRYMPLE-CHAMPNEYS, Weldon
Memorandum on the accommodation for the sick provided at certain public schools for boys in England. Sept.1928. Ministry of Health.

Report on the supervision of milk pasteurising plants. May 1935. (R.Pub.Health & Med.Subj., no.77) Ministry of Health.

Undulant fever. Aug.1929. (R.Pub.Health & Med.Subj., no.56) Ministry of Health.

DALTON, R. W.
Report on the trade of the Fiji Islands. Sept.1918. 1919 Cmd.201 xxxvi. Department of Overseas Trade.

Report on the trade of Western Samoa and the Tongan Islands. 19 Aug.1918. 1919 Cmd.200 xxxvi. Department of Overseas Trade.

D'Alviella, Goblet *SEE:* Alviella, Goblet d'

DAMPIER, William Cecil
Committee of inquiry into land settlement. 26 July 1939. Ministry of Labour.

Dairy research; a report to the Board. Nov.1931. (E.M.B.44) Empire Marketing Board.

DARBYSHIRE, Frederick James
Report on cancer of the rectum; an analysis of the literature with special reference to the rsults of operation. Dec.1927. (R.Pub.Health &Xed.Subj., no.46) Ministry of Halth.

DARLING, Charles
Committee on the law and procedure regulating military courts-martial.
Report. 29 July 1919. 1919 Cmd.428 x. War Office.

DARLING, Frank Fraser
A bibliography of the works of James Cossar Ewart. 1934. Imperial Bureau of Animal Genetics.

DARLINGTON, Thomas
Education in Russia. Aug.1909. 1909 Cd.4812 xviii. (Special reports on educational subjects, vol.23) Board of Education.

Darra Mair, L. W. *SEE:* Mair, L. W. D.

DAVENPORT, F. R.
Safeguarding of industries.
Report of the committee on aluminium hollow-ware. 12 Nov.1925. 1924/5 Cmd.2530 xv. Board of Trade.
Committee on enamelled hollow-ware.
Report. 31 March 1926. 1926 Cmd.2634 xv.
Second report. 19 May 1928. 1928 Cmd. 3115 xii. Board of Trade.

DAVEY, Horace, *Baron Davey of Fernhurst*
Report to accompany statutes and regulations made by the commissioners . . . [for] the University of London, with an appendix of correspondence. 27 Feb.1900. 1900 Cd.83 lxvi. Board of Education.

DAVEY, Norman
Bonding new concrete to old. Aug.1930. (B.R.B. Bull., no.9) Department of Scientific and Industrial Research.

Construction joints in concrete; bonding new concrete to old. Oct.1930. (B.R.B. special rep., no.16) Department of Scientific and Industrial Research.

Effect of temperature on the setting times of cements, and on the strength of cements, mortars and concretes. Jan.1929. (B.R.B. Special rep. no.13) Department of Scientific and Industrial Research.

Hot cement. Jan.1930. (B.R.B. Bull., no.7) Department of Scientific and Industrial Research.

DAVIDSON, D. DuB.
Committee on the problems of adjusting between authorities, the expenditure incurred by them in respect of evacuated school children.
Report. 31 Jan.1940. Board of Education.

DAVIDSON, John Colin Campbell, *1st Viscount*
Departmental committee on the Ordnance Survey.
Interim report.21 Dec.1935.
Final report. 3 Feb.1938. Ministry of Agriculture.

Indian states enquiry committee.
Report. 1 July 1932. 1931/2 Cmd.4103 viii. India Office.

Report of investigation into the industrial conditions in certain depressed areas. 1: West Cumberland and Haltwhistle. 2 Aug.1934. 1933/4 Cmd.4728 xiii. Ministry of Labour.

DAVIDSON, John Humphrey
Select committee on training and employment of disabled ex-service men.
Report. 2 Aug.1922. 1922 (170) vi. House of Commons.

DAVIES, E. F.
British and German finance. 1915. Ministry of Information.

The finances of Great Britain and Germany. 1916. Ministry of Information.

DAVIES, Edward Clement
Committee of inquiry into the anti-tuberculosis service in Wales and Monmouthshire.
Report. 13 Oct.1938. Ministry of Health.

DAVIES, G. M.
Tin ores. July 1919. (Mono.Min.Resour.) Imperial Institute.

DAVIES, Rhys John
Departmental committee on medical examination of young persons for factory employment.
Report. 30 April 1924. 1924 Cmd.2135 ix. Home Office.

Report of the British delegates on the International Labour Conference, Sixth session, June-July 1924. Feb.1925. 1924/5 Cmd.2325 xxxii. Ministry of Labour.

Select committee on the hours of meeting and rising of the House. 21 May 1930. 1929/30 (126) v. House of Commons.

DAVIES, W. Tudor
Committee on control of employment.
Report on a draft Control of Employment (Advertisements) Order, 1940. 21 March 1940. 1939/40 (107) iv. Ministry of Labour.

DAVIES, William
The grasslands of the Argentine and Patagonia. Nov.1940. (Bull., no.30) Imperial Bureau of Pastures and Forage Crops.

DAVIS, A. H.
The reduction of noise in buildings. June 1939. (B.R.B. special rep., no.26) Department of Scientific and Industrial Research.

DAVISON, Edward
West Indian Conference held in London, May to June 1926.
Report of proceedings. 4 June 1926. Colonial Office.

DAVY, James Stewart
Departmental committee on workhouse accounts.
Report with appendix. 17 June 1902. 1903 Cd.1440 xxvi. Local Government Board.

Memorandum on pauperism in Poplar. May 1906. Local Government Board.

DAVY, James Stewart (continued)
Memorandum on public health and social conditions. May 1909. 1909 Cd.4671 ciii.

Report on the Popular Union. 30 Oct.1906. 1906 Cd.3240 civ. Local Government Board.

Transcript of notes of the public inquiry on the general conditions of the Popular Union, its pauperism, and the administration of the guardians and their officers. Aug.1906. 1906 Cd.3279 cvi. Local Government Board.

DAWE, M. T.
Report on the economic resources of Uganda. 5 March 1906. 1906 Cd.2904 lxxx. Colonial Office.

DAWES, Charles G.
Reports of the expert committees appointed by the reparation commission.
Report from the first committee of experts (on balancing the budget and currency stabilisation). 9 April 1924. 1924 Cmd.2105 xxvii. Foreign Office.

DAWES, J. C.
The collection and disposal of refuse and street cleansing by local authorities in England and Wales.
Report of a conference on methods of keeping costing accounts. March 1925. Ministry of Health.

DAWKINS, Clinton E.
Committee on war office organisation.
Report. 9 May 1901. 1901 Cd.580 xl.
Minutes of evidence . . . appendices, digest and index. 1901 Cd.581 xl. War Office.

DAWSON, Bertrand, *1st Baron Dawson of Penn*
Consultative council on medical and allied services.
Interim report on the future provision of medical and allied services. May 1920. 1920 Cmd.693 xvii. (no further reports identified). Ministry of Health.

DAWSON, Shepherd
Intelligence and disease. 26 Nov.1931. (S.R.S., no.162) Medical Research Council.

DAWSON, William Harbutt
School doctors in Germany. Feb.1906. (Educational pamphlets, no.4) Board of Education.

DAY, Charles
Lathe tools research committee.
Report. Oct.1922. Department of Scientific and Industrial Research.

DAY, W. R.
Spring frosts; with special reference to the frosts of May 1935. May 1937. (Bull., no.18) Forestry Commission.

DEANE, H. E.
Handbook of elementary physiology for Army school teachers. Nov.1901. War Office.

DE COURCY-PERRY, Gerald R.
Report on the flax industry of Courtrai, Belgium. 11 Dec.1899. (Dip. and cons. reports: misc.series no.519) 1900 Cd.2-2 xci. Foreign Office.

Report on the present state of the Belgian coal, metal and glass industries. 22 June 1900. (Dip. and cons. reports: misc.ser., no.534) 1900 Cd.2-17 xci. Foreign Office.

De La Warr, *Earl. SEE:* Sackville, H.E.D.B., *9th Earl de la Warr*

DELÉPINE, Sheridan
Report on the effects of certain condensing and drying processes used in the preservation of milk on its bacterial contents. Dec.1914. (Rep.Pub. Health & Med.Subj., no.97) Local Government Board.

DELEVINGNE, Malcolm
Departmental committee on the employment of women and young persons on the two-shift system.
Report. 16 May 1935. 1934/5 Cmd.4914 x. Home Office.

Inter-departmental committee on the rehabilitation of persons injured by accidents.
Interim report. 6 May 1937.
Final report. Aug.1939. Home Office, Ministry of Health *and* Scottish Office.

Report by the British delegates on the International Labour Conference, eleventh session, Geneva, 30 May to 16 June 1928. Nov.1928. 1928/9 Cmd.3226 xxiii. Ministry of Labour.

Report by the British delegates on the International Labour Conference, twelfth session, Geneva, 30 May to 21 June 1929. April 1930. 1929/30 Cmd.3558 xxxii. Ministry of Labour.

Report on the International Conference on Opium and Dangerous Drugs held at Geneva, November 1924 to February 1925. May 1925. (Misc., no.8, 1925) 1924/5 Cmd.2461 xxxii. Foreign Office.

DE MONTMORENCY, J. E. G.
School excursions and vacation schools. Dec.1907. 1908 Cd.3866 xxvii. (Special reports on educational subjects, vol.21) Board of Education.

DENARO, L. F.
External rendered finishes; a survey of continental practice. Aug.1938. (B.R.B. Bull., no.16) Department of Scientific and Industrial Research.

Denbigh, *Earl. SEE:* Fielding, R.R.B.A.A., *9h Earl.*

DENIS, E.
Who wanted war? The origin of the war according to diplomatic documents. 1915. Ministry of Information.

DENMAN, Gertrude Mary, *Lady Denman*
Practical education of women for rural life.
Report of the sub-committee. April 1927. Ministry of Agriculture and Fisheries *and* Board of Education.

DENNY, Archibald
Committee on the sub-division of merchant ships.
First report: Foreign-going passenger steamers. 3 Nov.1914. 1914/6 Cd.7743 xxvii.
Diagrams. 1914/6 Cd.7809 xxvii.
Second report: Home-trade passenger steamers and cargo steamers. 6 Aug.1915. 1914/6 Cd.8080 xxvii. Board of Trade.

Informal committee on bulkheads and waterpght sub-division of passenger steamships.
Reports. 15 Nov.1922, 4 April 1923 and 7 Jan.1924. Board of Trade.

DENT, J. J.
Report on industrial and agricultural co-operative societies in the U.K. Feb.1912. 1912/3 Cd.6045 lxxv. Board of Trade.

Report on workmen's co-operative societies in the U.K. 1901. 1901 Cd.698 lxxiv. Board of Trade.

Derby, *Lord. SEE:* Stanley, E. G. V. *17th Earl*

Desart, *Lord. SEE:* Hamilton, J. A. *5th Earl.*

Desborough, *Lord. SEE:* Grenfell, W. H. *1st Baron.*

DESBOROUGH, A. P. H.
Report on visits to certain explosives factories and testing stations in Belgium, Germany and Holland. 29 May 1905. 1905 Cd.2650 x. Home Office.

DESTRÉE, Jules
The deportations of Belgian women. 1917. Ministry of Information.

To the Italian armies. 1917. Ministry of Information.

DE VILLIERS, John Henry
Report to the respective parliaments of the delegates to the South African convention, 1908-9, with a copy of the draft South Africa Constitution Bill. 3 Feb.1909. 1909 Cd.4525 lx.
Second report . . . with copy of the draft South Africa Constitution Bill as finally passed by the convention. 11 May 1909. 1909 Cd.4721 lx. Colonial Office.

Devonshire, *Lord. SEE:* Cavendish, S.C., *8th Duke and SEE:* Cavendish, V.C.W., *9th Duke*

DEVONSHIRE, James Lyne
Safeguarding of industries.
Report of the committee on cutlery. 23 Nov.1925. 1924/5 Cmd.2540 xv. Board of Trade.

DEWAR, John Alexander
Highlands and islands medical service committee.
Report. 24 Dec.1912. 1912/3 Cd.6559 xlii.
Minutes of evidence. 1913 Cd.6920 xxxvii. Treasury.

DEWAR, Thomas Finlayson
Report on house accommodation available for workers employed at Rosyth and for their families and on the provision for sickness and accident. 11 July 1911. Local Government Board for Scotland.

Report on the incidence of opthalmia neonatorum in Scotland. 3 June 1912. Local Government Board for Scotland.

DEWEY, Henry
Arsenic and antimony ores. 12 May 1919. (Special reports on the mineral resources of Great Britain, vol.15) (Mem.Geol.Surv.) Geological Survey.

British regional geology: South-west England. Geological Survey.

Copper ores of Cornwall and Devon. 4 Jan.1923. (Special reports on the mineral resources of Great Britain, vol.27) (Mem.Geol.Surv.) Geological Survey.

Copper ores of the Midlands, Wales, the Lake district and the Isle of Man. 30 Dec.1924. (Special reports on the mineral resources of Great Britain, vol.30) (Mem.Geol.Surv.) Geological Survey.

The geology of the country around Dartford. (Sheet 271) 4 July 1924. (Mem.Geol.Surv.) Geological Survey.

The geology of the country around Windsor and Chertsey. (Sheet 269) 21 Sept.1914. (Mem.Geol.Surv.) Geological Survey.

The geology of south London. (Sheet 270) 27 May 1921. (Mem.Geol.Surv.) Geological Survey.

Lead and zinc ores in the pre-carboniferous rocks of Shropshire and north Wales. 1 July 1921. (Special reports on the mineral resources of Great Britain, vol.23) (Mem.Geol.Surv.) Geological Survey.

Lead, silver-lead and zinc ores of Cornwall, Devon and Somerset. 12 March 1921. (Special reports on the mineral resources of Great Britain, vol.21) (Mem.Geol.Surv.) Geological Survey.

Tungsten and manganese ores. 16 Nov.1915. (Special reports on the mineral resources of Great Britain, vol.1.) (Mem.Geol. Surv.) Geological Survey.

DICK, Frederick J.
Report on the drainage of Lough Neagh and the lower Bann. 31 May 1904. 1904 Cd.2205 lxxix. Public Works Commissioners in Ireland.

DICKEY, Edward Montgomery O'Rorke
Industry and art education on the Continent. Dec.1934. (Industry series, no.14, Educational Pamphlet no.102) Board of Education.

DICKINSON, John
Departmental committee on rules and forms under the Criminal Justice Administration Act, 1911.
Report and supplemental report. 28 Jan.1914, and 5 March 1915. 1914/6 Cd.7853 xiii. Home Office.

DICKSON, Charles Scott
Committee on the management of Bellahouston Hospital.
Report. 6 Oct.1929. Ministry of Pensions.
Departmental committee on Sheriff Court procedure.
Report, minutes of evidence, appendix and index. Nov.1904. 1905 Cd.2287 lxiv. Scottish Office.

DICKSON, H. N.
A gazeteer of meteorological stations of the first, second and third order. Feb.1922. (Prof. Notes, no.27) Meteorological Office.

DICKSON, Spencer S.
Report on the coffee trade of Colombia. 11 Sept.1903. (Dip.cons.reports: misc.ser., no.598) 1904 Cd.1767-2 xcvi. Foreign Office.

DICKSON-POYNDER, John Poynder, *1st Baron Islington*
Departmental committee on inebriates detention in reformatories and retreats. (England and Wales)
Report. 18 Dec.1908. 1908 Cd.4438 xii.
Minutes of evidence, appendices and index. 1908 Cd.4439 xii.
Home Department. *SEE ALSO:* Bilsland, W.
Royal commission on the public services in India.
Vol.1: report. 14 Aug.1915. 1916 Cd.8382 vii.
Vols.2-11: evidence and appendices. 1914 Cd.7293, Cd.7578, Cd.7294, Cd.7579, Cd.7580, Cd.7296, Cd.7581, Cd.7582, Cd.7583 xxi, xxii, xxiii, xxiv.
Vols.12-20: evidence and appendices. 1914/6 Cd.7900-7908 xv, xvi, xvii.
Select committee on radiotelegraphic convention.
Report, proceedings, evidence, appendix and index. 8 July 1907. 1907 (246) viii. House of Commons.
Standing joint committee on Indian affairs.
First report. 21 April 1921. 1921 (86) vi.
Second report. 31 May 1921. 1921 (125) vi.
Third report. 20 July 1921. 1921 (177) vi.
Proceedings, 17th March to 13 July 1921. 1921 (180) vi. House of Commons.
Standing joint committee on Indian affairs.
First report. 29 May 1922. 1922 (102) v.
Second report. 13 July 1922. 1922 (136) v. House of Commons.

**DIGBY, Kenelm Edward**
Committee of inquiry into the provisions of the Agriculture and Technical Instruction Act, 1899.
Report. 30 May 1907. 1907 Cd.3572 xvii.
Minority report. 17 June 1907. 1907 Cd.3575 xvii.
Minutes of evidence. 1907 Cd.3574 xviii.
Appendix. 1907 Cd.3573 xviii. Irish Secretary's Office.

Departmental committee on ambulance service in the metropolis.
Vol.1: Report and appendices. 1 March 1909. 1909 Cd.4563 xxxi.
Vol.2: Minutes of evidence with index. 1909 Cd.4564 xxxi. Home Office.

Departmental committee on pilotage.
Report. 14 March 1911. 1911 Cd.5571 xxxviii.
Minutes of evidence and appendices. 1911 Cd.5572 xxxviii. Board of Trade.

Departmental committee on workmen's compensation.
Vol.1: Report and appendices. 1 Aug.1904. 1904 Cd.2208 lxxxviii.
Vol.2: Minutes of evidence and index. 1905 Cd.2334 lxxv.
Vol.3: Supplementary appendix: memorandum on foreign and colonial laws relating to compensation for injuries to workmen. 1905 Cd.2458 lxxv. Home Office.

Humber Conservancy Commission report. 14 July 1906. 1906 Cd.3076 xcviii. Board of Trade.

Interdepartmental committee on acts relating to naturalization.
Report with an appendix. 16 July 1901. 1901 Cd.723 lix. Home Office.

Northern Nigeria lands committee.
Report and despatches. 29 July 1908. 1910 Cd.5102 xliv.
Minutes of evidence and appendices. 1910 Cd.5103 xliv. Colonial Office.

**DIGBY, Lettice**
Bacteriological and clinical observations on pneumonia and empyemata, with special reference to pneumococcus and to serum treatment. Aug.1923. (S.R.S., no.79) Medical Research Council.

**DILKE, Charles Wentworth**
Select committee on income tax.
Report, proceedings, evidence, appendix and index. 29 Nov.1906. 1906 (365) ix. House of Commons.

**DILL, Samuel**
Vice-regal committee of inquiry into primary education, Ireland.
First report. 16 May 1913. 1913 Cd.6828 xxii.
Appendix: minutes of evidence, 13 Feb. to 12 March 1913. 1913 Cd.6829 xxii.
Second report. 31 Dec.1913. 1914 Cd.7228 xxviii.
Appendix: evidence, 13 March to 25 June 1913. 1914 Cd.7229 xxviii.
Third report. 24 Jan.1914. 1914 Cd.7479 xxviii.
Appendix: evidence, 26 June to 17 Sept.1913. 1914 Cd.7480 xxviii.
Final report. 27 Jan.1914. 1914 Cd.7235 xxviii. Irish Secretary's Office.

Dillon, A. B. *SEE:* Barrow-Dillon, A.

**DINES, H. G.**
The geology of the country around Aldershot and Guildford. (Sheet 285) 17 Dec.1928. (Mem.Geol.Surv.) Geological Survey.

The geology of the country around Reigate and Dorking. (Sheet 286) 29 Sept.1933. (Mem.Geol. Surv.) Geological Survey.

The geology of the country around Romford. (Sheet 257) 24 Aug.1925. Geological Survey.

**DINES, J. S.**
Meteorological conditions associated with high tides in the Thames. June 1929. (Geophys.Mem., no.47) Meteorological Office.

Soundings with pilot balloons in the Isles of Scilly, November and December 1911. Feb.1920. (Geophys.Mem., no.14) Meteorological Office.

**DINES, L. H. G.**
A comparison between the dry bulb temperature in the climatological screen at Valencia observatory. Sept.1921. (Prof.Notes, no.23) Meteorological Office.

A comparison between the geostrophic wind, the surface wind, and upper winds derived from pilot balloons, at Valentia observatory, Co.Kerry. Nov.1938. (Prof.Notes, no.83) Meteorological Office.

The Dines balloon meteorograph and the method of using it. Dec.1929. (M.D.321) Meteorological Office.

The rates of ascent and descent of free balloons, and the effects of radiation on records of temperature in the upper air. July 1935. (Prof. Notes, no.67) Meteorological Office.

**DINES, William Henry**
The characteristics of the free atmosphere. July 1919. (Geophys.Mem., vol.13) Meteorological Office.

The free atmosphere in the region of the British Isles.
First report. Dec.1909. (M.O.202)
Second report. 1911 (Geophys.Mem., no.2)
Third report. Jan.1914. (Geophys.Mem., no.6)

Observations on radiation from the sky. May 1921. (Geophys.Mem., no.18) Meteorological Office.

**DINHAM, C. H.**
The economic geology of the central coalfield of Scotland. Area 8: East Kilbride and Quarter. 27 July 1916. (Mem.Geol.Surv., Scotl.) Geological Survey, Scotland.

The economic geology of the Stirling and Clackmannan coalfield. 25 Nov.1931. (Mem.Geol.Surv. Scotl.) Geological Survey, Scotland.

**DITTMAR, Frederick**
Report on the conditions in Scotland in respect of provision of public slaughterhouses and methods of meat inspection. Aug.1907. Local Government Board for Scotland.

Report on the incidence of enteric fever in the larger towns of Scotland. 1 March 1911. Local Government Board for Scotland.

Report on the pollution of the River Leven, Dumbartonshire. 22 Oct.1907. 1908 Cd.3942 xciii. Scottish Board of Health *and* Local Government Board for Scotland.

DITTMAR, Frederick
Report on the sanitary condition of the Lews. 10 April 1905. 1905 Cd.2616 xxxiv. Local Government Board for Scotland.

DIXON, Arthur Lewis
Committee on the grant of a non-pensionable addition to the pay of the police in England and Wales in consideration of the increase in the cost of living.
Report. 24 Sept.1920. Home Office.

Committee on the pay of new entrants to the police.
Report. 16 Dec.1924. Home Office.

Committee on police conditions of service.
Report. 15 Jan.1925. Home Office.

Committee on police uniform clothing.
Report. 16 Jan.1934.
Illustrations of garments, headdress and other articles of uniform. July. Home Office.

Committee on rent allowances for the police. 1 Nov.1923. Home Office.

Committee on the scheme for the establishment of a police college.
Report. 30 Aug.1930. Home Office.

Departmental committee on detective work and procedure.
Report. Sept.1938. 5 vols. Home Office.

DIXON, E. E. L.
The geology of the Carlisle, Longtown and Silloth districts. (Sheets 11, 16 and 17) 2 Nov.1925. (Mem.Geol.Surv.) Geological Survey.

The geology of the south Wales coalfield. Part 13; the country around Pembroke and Tenby. 14 March 1921. (Mem.Geol.Surv.) Geological Survey.

DIXON, F. E.
The aurora of January 25 to 26, 1938 and associated magnetic storm. 1939. (Geophys.Mem., no.81) Meteorological Office.

Fog on the mainland and coasts of Scotland. March 1939. (Prof.Notes, no.88) Meteorological Office.

DIXON, Harold Bailey
The ignition of firedamp by compression. July 1935. (S.M.R.B. Paper no.93) Mines Departments.

DIXON, Stephen Mitchell
The deterioration of haulage ropes in service. Dec.1934. (S.M.R.B. Paper, no.92) Mines Department.

Measurements of the kinetic loads on colliery winding ropes. Oct.1932. (S.M.R.B. Paper no.78) Mines Department.

Tests on pit props. Sept.1931. (S.M.R.B. Paper no.72) Mines Department.

Wire ropes research committee.
Report on wire ropes for mines; some notes regarding their manufacture and use. 20 Dec.1927. (S.M.R.B. Paper no.41) Mines Department.

DOBELL, Clifford
Amoebic dysentery and the proto-zoological investigation of cases from the eastern Mediterranean. Jan.1917. (S.R.S., no.4) Medical Research Committee.

DOBSON, Gordon
A comparison of the electrical conditions of the atmosphere at Kew and Eskdalemuir. Jan.1914. (Geophys.Mem., no.7) Meteorological Office.

DODD, William Huston
Report on the Belfast prison inquiry. 25 Feb.1919. 1919 Cmd.83 xxvii. Irish Secretary's Office.

DODDS, Elliott
For all prisoners and captives. The work of the Prisoners of War Information Bureau. 1917. Ministry of Information.

DOMVILE, Compton
Committee on naval boilers.
Interim report. 2 Aug.1901. 1901 Cd.503 xlii.
Report. 28 May 1902. 1902 Cd.1158 lx.
Vol.1: Report. 12 June 1904. 1904 Cd.2207 liii.
Vol.2: Report on trials of H.M.S. "Medusa" and H.M.S. "Medea". 1904 Cd.2207-I liii.
Vol.3: Diagrams. 1904 Cd.2207-II liii.
Vol.4: Report on trials of H.M.S. "Hermes". 1904 Cd.2207-III liii. Admiralty.

DONALD, G. H.
The manufacture of charcoal in portable kilns. May 1939. (F.P.R.Records, no.29) Department of Scientific and Industrial Research.

DONALD, Robert
Imperial Wireless Telegraphy committee.
Report. 22 Feb.1924. 1924 Cmd.2060 xii. Post Office.

DONALDSON, H. F.
Committee on standard leading screws for screw-cutting lathes.
Report. 27 April 1905. War Office.

DONALDSON, James
Council for Agriculture for England.
Report on agricultural policy. 6 Aug.1925. Ministry of Agriculture and Fisheries.

DONKIN, S. B.
Lubricants and lubrication inquiry committee.
Report. Oct.1920. Department of Scientific and Industrial Research.

Donoughmore, *Lord. SEE:* Hely-Hutchinson, R. W. J., *6th Earl.*

DOODSON, Arthur Thomas
Instructions for analysing tidal observations. Feb.1928. Admiralty.

Report on Thames floods. June 1929. (Geophys.Mem., no.47) Meteorological Office.

DORINGTON, John Edward
Departmental committee on allowances to prosecutors and witnesses in criminal prosecutions.
Report. 28 April 1903. 1903 Cd.1650 lvi.
Evidence and appendices. 1903 Cd.1651 lvi. Home Office.

Douglas, A. A. *SEE:* Akers-Douglas, A.

DOUGLAS, Anne
Committee on women in agriculture in Scotland.
Report. Feb.1920. Board of Agriculture for Scotland.

DOUGLAS, Charles E.
Report on the cultivation, treatment and prospects of rice in British Guiana. Aug.1930. (E.M.B., 32) Empire Marketing Board.

DOUGLAS, Charlotte Ann
Report on maternal morbidity and mortality in Scotland. June 1935. Department of Health for Scotland.

DOUGLAS, Henry Percy
Report on the tides, currents and tidal streams in the southern part of the Torres Strait. Dec.1930. (Hydrographic publication, H.D.302) Admiralty.

DOUGLAS: Stewart Ranken
Tuberculin committee.
Report on tuberculin tests in cattle with special reference to the intradermal test. March 1925. (S.R.S., no.94) Medical Research Council.

Second report on tuberculin tests in cattle with special reference to the intradermal test. 11 June 1928. (S.R.S., no.122) Medical Research Council.

DOUGLAS-HAMILTON, George Nigel, *Lord*
Commissioner for special areas in Scotland.
Report. Dec.1938. 1938/9 Cmd.5905 xii.

DOUGLAS-JONES, Crawford Douglas
British Guiana constitutional commission.
Report. 12 Sept.1927. 1927 Cmd.2985 vii. Colonial Office.

DOVE-WILSON, John Carnegie
Departmental committee on persistent offenders.
Report. 30 April 1932. 1931/2 Cmd.4090 xii. Home Office.

DRAGE, Geoffrey
Wages and conditions of employment in agriculture.
Vol.1: General report. 18 Oct.1918. 1919 Cmd.24 ix.
Vol.2: Reports of investigators. 1918. 1919 Cmd.25 ix. Board of Agriculture and Fisheries.

DRUMMOND, J. C.
The relative values of cod liver oils from various sources. Dec.1930. (E.M.B.35) Empire Marketing Board.

DUCKHAM, A. N.
Grass and fodder crop conservation in transportable form; a memorandum. March 1928. (E.M.B.8) Empire Marketing Board.

DUCKHAM, Arthur McDougal
Standing committee on mineral transport.
First report. 21 Oct.1929. 1929/30 Cmd.3420 xvi. (no further reports identified) Ministry of Transport *and* Mines Department.

Dudley, *Lord. SEE:* Ward, W. H., *2nd Earl.*

DUDLEY, Sheldon Francis
The Schick test, diptheria and scarlet fever: a study in epidemiology. 20 Feb.1923. (S.R.S., no.75) Medical Research Council.

The spread of droplet infection in semi-isolated communities; a study in the ecology of parasites. 18 Oct.1926. (S.R.S., no.111) Medical Research Council.

DUFFON, A. F.
Heat transmission. Dec.1928. (B.R.B. special rep., no.11) Department of Scientific and Industrial Research.

DUNCAN, Andrew Rae
Advisory committee for coal and the coal industry.
Report on economies in the costs that make up the price of coal to the consumer. 14 Dec.1922. Mines Department.

Sea Fish Commission.
First report. The herring industry. Aug.1934. 1933/4 Cmd.4677 xii.
Second report. The white fish industry. 1935/6 Cmd.5130 x. Ministry of Agriculture and Fisheries.

Duncan, R. A. P. H. *SEE:* Haldane-Duncan, R.A.P., *3rd Earl Camperdown*

DUNDAS, Henry Charles Clement
Report on German East Africa, 1 July 1892 to 31 July 1899. Aug.1900. (Dip.Cons.reports: misc.ser., no.535) 1900 Cd.353 xci. Foreign Office.

DUNDAS, Lawrence John Lumley, *Earl of Ronaldshay*
Committee on private enterprise in British tropical Africa.
Report. Nov.1923. 1924 Cmd.2016 viii. Colonial Office.

Dunedin, *Lord: SEE:* Murray, A. G., *1st Baron*

Dunfermline, *Baron. SEE:* Shaw, Thomas, *Baron Shaw of Dunfermline*

Dunluce, *Lord. SEE:* M'Donnell, R. M. K., *Viscount Dunluce.*

DUNNICO, Herbert
Select committee on private bills.
Report, minutes of evidence, appendices and index. 14 July 1930. 1929/30 (158) vii.

DUNNING, Leonard
Report of inquiry on the St. Helen's County Borough police force held in November 1927. 15 Nov.1927. 1928 Cmd.3103 xii. Home Office.

DUNSTAN, Wyndham Rowland
Agricultural resources of Cyprus, with special reference to cotton cultivation.
Report. Sept.1905. 1906 Cd.2717 lxxvii. Colonial Office.

Cotton cultivation in the British Empire and in Egypt.
Report. April 1904. 1904 Cd.2020 lxxxvii. Colonial Office.

Cotton, gum and other economic products of Northern Nigeria.
Report. Nov.1905. (Colonial reports: misc., no.31) 1906 Cd.2778 lxxvi. Colonial Office.

Indian trade enquiry. Drugs and tanning materials committee.
Reports on cinchoria bark and myrobalans. Oct.1919 and Dec.1920. Imperial Institute.

Indian trade enquiry.
Reports on hides and skins. 30 March 1917. Imperial Institute.

Mineral survey of Ceylon, 1904-1905
Report on the results. Nov.1906. (Colonial reports: misc., no.37) 1906 Cd.3190 lxxvi. Colonial Office.

Mineral survey of Ceylon, 1905-6.
Report on the results. 24 June 1907. (Colonial reports: misc., no.42) 1908 Cd.3762 lxx. Colonial Office.

Mineral survey of Ceylon, 1906-7 and 1907-8.
Report on the results. Oct.1910. (Colonial reports: misc., no.74) 1910 Cd.5390 lxv. Colonial Office.

Mineral survey of Ceylon, 1912-3.
Report on the results. Jan.1914. (Colonial reports: misc., no.87) 1914 Cd.7175 lix. Colonial Office.

Mineral survey of Northern Nigeria, 1904-5.
First report on results. April 1906. (Colonial reports: misc., no.32) 1906 Cd.2875 lxxvi.
Second report on results. 10 Dec.1907. (Colonial reports: misc., no.46) 1908 Cd.3914 lxx. Colonial Office.

Mineral survey of Northern Nigeria, 1905-6.
Report on the results. 10 Dec.1907. (Colonial

DUNSTAN, Wyndham Rowland (continued)
    reports: misc., no.47) 1908 Cd.3915 lxx.
    Colonial Office.

    Mineral survey of Northern Nigeria, 1906-7.
        Report on the results. 5 May 1909. (Colonial
        reports: misc., no.59) 1909 Cd.4719 lix.
        Colonial Office.

    Mineral survey of Northern Nigeria, 1907-8 and
    1908-9.
        Reports on the results. Sept.1911. (Colonial
        reports: misc., no.79) 1911 Cd.5899 lii.
        Colonial Office.

    Mineral survey of the Nyasaland Protectorate,
    1906-7.
        Report on the results. 7 Jan.1908. (Colonial
        reports: misc., no.48) 1908 Cd.3916 lxx.
        Colonial Office.

    Mineral survey of Nyasaland Protectorate, 1907-8.
        Report on the results. 29 July 1909. (Colonial
        reports: misc., no.60) 1909 Cd.4908 lix.
        Colonial Office.

    Mineral survey of Nyasaland, 1908-9.
        Report of the results. July 1911. (Colonial
        reports: misc., no.80) 1911 Cd.5900 lii.
        Colonial Office.

    Mineral survey of Southern Nigeria for 1903-4 and
    1904-5.
        Reports. April 1906. (Colonial report: misc.,
        no.33) 1906 Cd.2876 lxxvi. Colonial Office.

    Mineral survey of Southern Nigeria, 1905-6.
        Report on the results. Jan.1910. (Colonial
        reports: misc., no.67) 1910 Cd.4994 lxv.
        Colonial Office.

    Mineral survey of Southern Nigeria, 1906-7.
        Report on the results. Jan.1910. (Colonial
        reports: misc., no.68) 1910 Cd.4995 lxv.
        Colonial Office.

    Mineral survey of Southern Nigeria, 1907-8
        Report on the results. 27 Jan.1911. (Colonial
        reports: misc., no.76) 1911 Cd.5517 lii.
        Colonial Office.

    Mineral survey of Southern Nigeria, 1908-9.
        Report on the results. Nov.1911. (Colonial
        reports: misc., no.81) 1911 Cd.5901 lii.
        Colonial Office.

    Mineral survey of Southern Nigeria, 1910.
        Report on the results. Aug.1912. (Colonial
        reports: misc., no.83) 1912/3 Cd.6425 lix.
        Colonial Office.

    Mineral survey of Southern Nigeria, 1911.
        Report on the results. Sept.1913. (Colonial
        reports: misc., no.85) 1914 Cd.7067 lix.
        Colonial Office.

    Mineral survey of Southern Nigeria, 1912.
        Report on the results. Nov.1913. (Colonial
        reports: misc., no.86) 1914 Cd.7110 lix.
        Colonial Office.

    Mineral survey of Southern Nigeria, 1913.
        Report on the results. Aug.1914. (Colonial
        reports: misc., no.89) 1914 Cd.7567 lix.
        Colonial Office.

Report on agriculture in Asia Minor, with special
reference to cotton cultivation. Oct.1908. 1908
Cd.4324 cvii. Colonial Office.

Reports on the quality of cotton grown in British
possessions May 1908. (Colonial reports: Misc.,
no.50) 1908 Cd.3997 lxx. Colonial Office.

DU PARCQ, Herbert
    Report on the recent disorder at Dartmoor convict
    prison. 3 Feb.1932. 1931/2 Cmd.4010 vii. Home
    Office.

DUPIERREUX, Richard
    To the Italian armies. 1917. Ministry of
    Information.

Durham, *Lord. SEE:* Lambton, J. G., *3rd Earl.*

DURHAM, F. M.
    Alcohol and inheritance: an experimental study. 15
    June 1932. (S.R.S., no.168) Medical Research
    Council.

DURKHEIM, E.
    Who wanted war? The origin of the war according
    to diplomatic documents. 1915. Ministry of
    Information.

DURST, C. S.
    The winds in Berbera. April 1934. (Prof.Notes,
    no.65) Meteorological Office.

DURWARD, J.
    Bumpiness on the Cairo-Basra air route. Oct.1929.
    (Prof.Notes, no.52) Meteorological Office.

    A comparison of temperatures inside and outside
    the meteorological enclosure, Ismailia, Egypt.
    March 1931. (Prof.Notes, no.61) Meteorological
    Office.

    Diurnal variation in wind velocity and direction at
    different heights. March 1921. (Prof.Notes, no.15)
    Meteorological Office.

    Diurnal variation of temperature as affected by
    wind velocity and cloudiness. Aug.1922.
    (Prof.Notes, no.30) Meteorological Office.

    The investigation of the winds in the upper air from
    information regarding the place of fall of pilot
    balloons and the distribution of pressure. Oct.1925.
    (Prof.Notes, no.42) Meteorological Office.

    Upper winds at Nicosia, Crete. March 1939. (Prof.
    Notes, no.87) Meteorological Office.

    Upper winds at Wadi Halfa, Sudan. Aug.1936.
    (Prof.Notes, no.72) Meteorological Office.

    Upper winds measured at M/Y Imperia, Mirabella
    Bay, Crete. Nov.1937. (Prof.Notes, no.79)
    Meteorological Office.

    The variation of wind with place. July 1921.
    (Prof.Notes, no.24) Meteorological Office.

DYER, Reginald Edward Harry
    Statement on disturbances in the Punjab. 3 July
    1920. 1920 Cmd.771 xxxiv. War Office.

DYKE, William Hart.
    Consultative committee of the Board of Education.
        Report on higher elementary schools. 24 May
        1906. Board of Education.

EARLE, Lionel
    Petroleum filling stations committee.
        Report. 8 May 1929. 1928/9 Cmd.3330 ix.
        Supplementary report. 22 July 1929. 1929/30
        Cmd.3370 xvi. Home Office.

EAST, William Norwood
    Report on the psychological treatment of crime.
    Dec.1938. Home Office.

EASTWOOD, Arthur
    Comparative histological and bacteriological
    investigations. Dec.1909.
        (Vol.5: Appendix to the final report of the
        Royal Commission on human and animal
        tuberculosis). Dec.1909. 1911 Cd.5975 xliv.

EASTWOOD, Arthur (continued)
Report on American methods for the control and improvement of milk supply. 25 March 1909. (Rep.Pub.Health & Med.Subj., no.1) Local Government Board.

Report on localised tuberculosis in swine. 9 Feb.1914. (Rep.Pub.Health & Med.Subj., no.91) Local Government Board.

EASTWOOD, T.
British regional geology: northern England. 1935. Geological Survey.

Copper ores of the Midlands, Wales, the Lake District and the Isle of Man. 30 Dec.1924. (Special reports on the mineral resources of Great Britain, vol.30) (Mem.Geol.Surv.) Geological Survey.

The geology of the country around Birmingham. (Sheet 168) 9 Feb.1925. (Mem.Geol.Surv.) Geological Survey.

The geology of the country around Coventry. (Sheet 169) 7 Oct.1922. (Mem.Geol.Surv.) Geological Survey.

The geology of the Maryport district. (Sheet 22) 25 June 1930. (Mem.Geol.Surv.) Geological Survey.

The geology of the southern part of the south Staffordshire coalfield. 28 Aug.1926. (Mem.Geol.Surv.) Geological Survey.

The geology of the Whitehaven and Workington District. 30 Jan.1931. (Mem.Geol.Surv.) Geological Survey.

The lead and zinc ores of the Lake District. 31 May 1921. (Special reports on the mineral resources of Great Britain, vol.22) (Mem.Geol.Surv.) Geological Survey.

EATOCK, Eric Richard
Report of an inquiry on Dupytren's contraction as a disease of occupation with special reference to its occurrence among minders of lace machines. 4 June 1912. Home Office.

ECCLES, William Henry
Wireless telegraphy commission. *SEE:* Mitchell-Thomson, W.

EDE, James Chuter
Departmental committee on private schools and others not in receipt of grants from public funds.
    Report. 10 March 1932. Board of Education.

EDEN, Robert Anthony
Report on the Council of the League of Nations, sixty-seventh session. 29 June 1932. (Misc., no.10, 1932) 1931/2 Cmd.4134 xxvii. Foreign Office.

Report of the United Kingdom delegates on the League of Nations, fifteenth assembly. 30 Nov.1934. (Misc., no.8, 1934) 1934/5 Cmd.4772 xxiv. Foreign Office.

Report of the United Kingdom delegates on the League of Nations, sixteenth assembly. 9 Dec.1935. (Misc., no.5, 1935) 1935/6 Cmd.5053 xxvii. Foreign Office.

EDLMANN, Edith
Education and peasant industry: some State-aided trade schools in Germany. Dec.1912. (Educational pamphlets, no.26) Board of Education.

EDMONDS, C. H. W.
Committee on light signals (on railways).
    Report. 28 Oct.1921. Ministry of Transport.

EDMONDS, James Edward
Handbook of the German Army, 2nd ed. Nov.1900. War Office.

History of the Great War; military operations. France and Belgium, 1914. 2 vols. and 2 vols. maps. April 1922—10 Oct.1924. War Office.

History of the Great War; military operations. France and Belgium, 1915. 2 vols. and 2 vols. maps. 1927-8. War Office.

History of the Great War; military operations. France and Belgium, 1916. Text, appendices and maps. 4 vols. 1932 and 1938. War Office.

History of the Great War; military operations. France and Belgium, 1918. 5 vols. 1935-1947. War Office.

EDMUNDS, F. H.
British regional geology: the central England district. 1936. Geological Survey.

British regional geology: the Wealden district. 1935. Geological Survey.

The geology of the country around Aldershot and Guildford. (Sheet 285) 17 Dec.1928. (Mem.Geol.Surv.) Geological Survey.

The geology of the country around Reigate and Dorking. (Sheet 286) 29 Sept.1933. (Mem.Geol.Surv.) Geological Survey.

The geology of the country around Romford. (Sheet 257) 24 Aug.1925. (Mem.Geol.Surv.) Geological Survey.

Water supply of Wiltshire from underground sources. 19 Oct.1925. (Mem.Geol.Surv.) Geological Survey.

Wells and springs of Sussex. 27 March 1928. (Mem.Geol.Surv.) Geological Survey.

EDWARDS, Wilfred
Geology of the country around Wakefield. (Sheet 70) 15 Aug.1940. (Mem.Geol.Surv.) Geological Survey.

Wells and springs of Dorset. 8 April 1926. (Mem.Geol.Surv.) Geological Survey.

EGERTON, Walter
Departmental committee on the colonial medical services.
    Report. 1 July 1920. 1920 Cmd.939 xiii. Colonial Office.

EICHHOLTZ, A.
A study of the deaf in England and Wales, 1930 to 1932. Nov.1932. Board of Education *and* Ministry of Health.

ELDER, James
Report of the Scottish conference on agricultural policy. June 1925. Board of Agriculture for Scotland.

EL-GHUSEIN, Fâiz
Martyred Armenia. 1917. Ministry of Information.

Elgin and Kincardine, *Lord. SEE:* Bruce, V. A., *9th Earl and SEE:* Bruce, E. J., *10th Earl*

ELLIOT, Walter
Agricultural economics in the Empire.
    Report of a committee. Oct.1927. (E.M.B.I.) Empire Marketing Board.

Committee on the mineral content of natural pastures.
    Sixth report. 24 Nov.1930.
    Seventh report. 1 Oct.1931. (no others identified) Economic Advisory Council. Treasury.

ELLIOTT, Frank Lloyd Dumbell
Committee on the licensing of partially disabled men as drivers of public motor vehicles.
Report. 1 July 1916. 1916 Cd.8314 xxii. Home Office.

Committee to review the decisions of the committee on the licensing of partially disabled men as drivers of public vehicles which reported in July 1916.
Report. 1919. 1919 Cmd.312 xxv.
Evidence. 1919 Cmd.333 xxv. Home Office.

ELLIOTT, Ivo D'Oyly
Commission on the financial situation of Mauritius.
Report. 23 Dec.1931. 1931/2 Cmd.4034 vii. Colonial Office.

ELLIOTT, Thomas Henry
Committee on the conditions of service and superannuation of the warder classes in prisons and criminal lunatic asylums.
Report. April 1919. 1919 Cmd.313 xxvii. Treasury.

Inter-departmental committee on proposals for facilitating the payment through the post of benefits under the National Insurance Act.
Report. 11 Dec.1913. 1914 Cd.7245 lxxii. Treasury.

ELLIS, John Edward
Select committee on infant life protection.
Report, proceedings, evidence, appendix and index. 24 March 1908. 1908 (99) ix. House of Commons.

Select committee on police forces (weekly rest-day).
Report, proceedings, evidence, appendices and index. 8 Dec.1908. 1908 (353) ix. House of Commons.
Report and proceedings. 4 May 1909. 1909 (132) viii. House of Commons.

ELLIS, O. C. deC.
The study of flame movement. Nov.1926. (S.M.R.B. Paper no.32) Mines Department.

ELLIS, Robert Geoffrey
Committee on the Safeguarding of Industries Act, 1921 (part 1) and the Finance Act, 1926 (section 10).
Report. 18 Dec.1935. 1935/6 Cmd.5157 xiv. Board of Trade.

ELLIS, Walter D.
Committee on improved and increased production of palm oil and palm kernals.
Report. 31 Aug.1924. (Colonial no.10) 1925. Colonial Office.

Eltisley, *Lord. SEE:* Newton, G. D. C., *1st Baron.*

ELTON, P. M.
An analysis of the individual differences in the output of silk-weavers. Jan.1922. (I.H.R.B. Rep., no.17) Medical Research Council.

Study of output in silk-weaving during the winter months. Aug.1920. (I.H.R.B. Rep., no.9) Medical Research Council.

EMMENS, C. W.
Variables affecting the estimation of androgenic and oestrogenic activity. 27 April 1939. (S.R.S., no.234) Medical Research Council.

EMMOTT, Alfred, *1st Baron Emmott of Oldham*
Committee to collect information on Russia.
Interim report. 4 Nov.1920. (Misc., no.13, 1920) 1920 Cmd.1041 xxv.
Report. 22 Feb.1921. (Russia, no.1, 1921) 1921 Cmd.1240 xliii. Foreign Office.

Departmental committee on the currency of the British West African colonies and protectorates.
Report. 5 June 1912. 1912/3 Cd.6426 xlviii.
Minutes of evidence. 1912/3 Cd.6427 xlviii. Colonial Office.

Departmental committee on the superannuation of school teachers.
Report. 30 July 1923. 1923 Cmd.1962 x. Treasury.

Royal commission on decimal coinage.
Report. 23 Feb.1920. 1920 Cmd.628 xiii.
Evidence and appendices. 1920 Cmd.719 xiii.

EMMOTT, Gertrude, *Lady Emmott*
Housing advisory council.
Report of the sub-committee on co-operative and communal arrangements. 6 May 1921. Ministry of Health.

Women's advisory committee on the domestic service problem.
Report. 1 March 1919. 1919 Cmd.67 xxix. Ministry of Reconstruction.

Women's housing sub-committee of the Housing Advisory Council.
First interim report. May 1918. 1918 Cd.9166 x.
Final report. 17 Jan.1919. 1918 Cd.9232 x. Ministry of Reconstruction.

EMTAGE, William Thomas Allder
The system of education in Mauritius. Dec.1914. (Imperial education conference papers) Board of Education.

ENFIELD, R. R.
Report on agricultural credit. 1927. (Economic series, no.8) Ministry of Agriculture.

ENGLEDOW, F. L.
West India Royal Commission.
Report on agriculture, fisheries, forestry and veterinary matters. 21 Dec.1939. 1944/5 Cmd.6608 vi.

ENNOS, F. R.
Refractory materials: fireclays.
Analyses and physical tests. 8 May 1924. (Special reports on the mineral resources of Great Britain, vol.28) (Mem.Geol.Surv.) Geological Survey.

ENTWISTLE, F.
The diurnal and seasonal variations of fog at certain stations in England. Aug.1923. (Prof.Notes, no.33) Meteorological Office.

EPPS, George Selby Washington
Report on the assets and liabilities of approved societies.
Fourth valuation. 23 April 1937. 1936/7 Cmd.5496 xiv. Ministry of Health. *For previous reports see:* Watson, A. W.

Report on the financial provisions of the Old Age and Widows' Pensions Bill, relating to contributory pensions and health insurance. 7 Feb.1940. 1939/40 Cmd.6169 v. Ministry of Health.

Report on the financial provisions of the Widows', Orphans' and Old Age Contributory Pensions (Voluntary Contributors) Bill, 1937. 19 March 1937. 1936/7 Cmd.5415 xxi. Ministry of Health.

ERICSON, Carl
Some Swedish reflections in these momentous times. Nov.1915. Ministry of Information.

ERIKSON, Dagny
Pathegenic aerobic organisms of the actinomyces group. 25 Sept.1935. (S.R.S., no.203) Medical Research Council.

Pathogenic anaerobic organisms of the actinomyces group. 19 Feb.1940. (S.R.S., no.240) Medical Research Council.

ERNST, Edward G.
British Guiana refugee commission.
Report to the Advisory Committee on political refugees appointed by the President of the United States of America. 19 April 1938. 1938/9 Cmd.6014 ix.
Appendices. 1938/9 Cmd.6029 ix. Colonial Office.

ERSKINE, T. E.
Report on education in Chicago. 5 Nov.1900. (Dip.cons.reports: misc. ser., no.544) 1900 Cd.353-9 xci. Foreign Office.

Report on St. Joseph Missouri. 22 Nov.1902. (Dip.cons.reports: misc. ser., no.586) 1902 Cd.787-22 ciii. Foreign Office.

Report on shipping and shipbuilding on the American lakes. 30 April 1900. (Dip.cons.reports: misc.ser., no.526) 1900 Cd.2-9 xci. Foreign Office.

Report on the cattle and meat trade of the United States. 16 Sept.1902. (Dip.cons.reports: misc.ser., no.581) 1902 Cd.787-17 ciii. Foreign Office.

Report on the Chicago summer vacation schools. 17 Aug.1904. (Dip.cons.reports: misc.ser., no.620) 1905 Cd.2237-1 lxxxvi. Foreign Office.

Report on the coal industry of the consular district of Chicago. 4 Sept.1902. (Dip.cons.reports: misc.ser.,fo.580) 1902 Cd.787-16 ciii.Foreign Office.

Report on the hose industry in the United States. 4 July 1901. (Dip.cons.reports: misc.scr., no.563) 1901 Cd.430-18 lxxx. Foreign Office.

Report on the iron ore industry of the United States. 25 Sept.1902. (Dip.cons.reports: misc.ser.,no.583) 1902 Cd.787-19 ciii. Foreign Office.

Esher, *Lord. SEE:* Brett, R. B., *2nd Viscount.*

ESSEN, Leon van der
A short account of the German invasion and occupation of Belgium. 1918. Ministry of Information.

EVANS, Gwilym
Technique of grassseed production at the Welsh plant breeding station. Aug.1937. (Bull., no.22) Imperial Bureau of Plant Genetics: Herbage Plants.

EVANS, John William
Directions for the collection of Geological Specimens. July 1914. Colonial Office.

EVANS, P. M.
Advisory committee on the welfare of the blind.
Report of the sub-committee on the unemployable blind. 10 July 1935. Ministry of Health.

EVANS, William
The course of the oesophagus in health, and in disease of the heart and great vessels. 5 March 1936. (S.R.S., no.208) Medical Research Council.

EWING, James Alfred
Bridge stress committee.
Report. 4 Oct.1928. Department of Scientific and IndustrialResearch.

Committee on the mechanical testing of timber.
Report. 20 May 1934. Department of Scientific and Industrial Research.

Engineering committee
Measurement of humidity in closed spaces.Sept.1925. (F.I.B. special report, no.8)Department of Scientific and Industrial Research.

EYLES, V. A.
The economic geology of the Ayrshire coalfields. Area 3:Ayr, Prestwick, Mauchline, Cumnock, and Muirkirk. 23 Dec.1929. (Mem.Geol.Surv., Scotl.) Geological Survey, Scotland.

EYRE, John William Henry
Special committee upon pathological methods.
Report of the sub-committee on the reaction of media. Aug.1919. (S.R.S., no.35) Medical Research Committee.

FAIRGRIEVE, J.
On the relation between the velocity of the gradient wind and that of the observed wind. Aug.1914. (Geophys.Mem., no.9) Meteorological Office.

Falls, Cyril Bentham
History of the Great War: military operations. Egypt and Palestine. Text and maps. 1930. 4 vols. War Office.

History of the Great War: military operations.France and Belgium, 1917. 1940. War Office.

History of the Great War: military operations. Macedonia. Text and maps, 4 vols. 1933 and 1935. War Office.

Falmouth, *Lord. SEE:* Boscawen, E. H., *8th Viscount Falmouth.*

Faringdon, *Lord. SEE:* Henderson, A., *1st Baron.*

FARMER, Eric
A comparison of different shift systems in the glass trade. Jan.1924. (I.H.R.B.Rep., no.24) Medical Research Council.

Motion study in metal polishing. Oct.1921. (I.H.R.B.Rep., no.15) Medical Research Council.

The prognostic value of some psychological tests. May 1936. (I.H.R.B. Rep., no.74) Medical Research Council.

A psychological study of individual differences in accident rates. Nov.1926. (I.H.R.B.Rep., no.38) Medical Research Council.

A study of accident proneness among motor drivers. Dec.1939. (I.H.R.B.Rep., no.84) Medical Research Council.

A study of personal qualities in accident proneness and proficiency. Aug.1929. (I.H.R.B.Rep., no.55) Medical Research Council.

Time and motion study. Oct.1921. (I.H.R.B.Rep., no.14) Medical Research Board.

FARMER, Florence A.
Council on art and industry.
Report on design in the pottery industry. March 1937. Board of Trade.

FARNDALE, Josh
Committee on traffic problems.
Report. 3 March 1925. Home Office.

FARQUHARSON, J. S.
Observations of the blueness of the sky. March 1936. (Prof.Notes, No.70) Meteorological Office.

FARRAR, Reginald Anstruther

Report on accommodation for strawberry pickers in the Dartford R.D. 6 Nov.1907. (Rep.Med.Insp., no.293) Local Government Board.

Report on an outbreak of enteric fever associated in some cases with cerebro-spinal symptoms, at Fincham, in the Downham R.D., Norfolk. 18 July 1905. (Rep.Med.Insp., no.238) Local Government Board.

Report on an outbreak of enteric fever in the Borough of Basingstoke. 16 Nov.1905. (Rep.Med.Insp., no.221) Local Government Board.

Report on inquiries in China and Siberia on pork and bacon exported to England. 25 Oct.1911. (Rep.Pub.Health & Med.Subj., no.577) Local Government Board.

Report on re-inspection of the Borough of Whitehaven. 8 Aug.1905. (Rep.Med.Insp., no.197) Local Government Board.

Report on the accommodation of navvies engaged in the construction of the Brooklands motor-racing track, with some suggestions relating to constructional works in general. 11 July 1907. 1907 Cd.3694 lxviii. Local Government Board.

Report on the cases of cerebro-spinal meningitis occurring in Irthlingborough Northamptonshire. 8 Aug.1905. (Rep.Med.Insp., no.218) Local Government Board.

Report on the conditions under which persons are employed in pea-picking. 24 June 1909. (Rep.Pub.Health & Med.Subj., no.11) Local Government Board.

Report on the lodging and accommodation of hop-pickers and pickers of fruit and vegetables. 21 Feb.1907. (Rep.Med.Insp., no.252) Local Government Board.

Further report on the lodging and accommodation of hop-pickers. 22 July 1914. (Rep.Pub.Health & Med.Subj., no.99) Local Government Board.

Report on the lodging of workmen employed in construction of public works. 14 Aug.1909. (Rep.Pub.Health & Med.Subj., no.14) Local Government Board.

Report on the outbreak of enteric fever at Denaby Main, Doncaster Rural District. 1 May 1905. (Rep.Med.Insp., no.216) Local Government Board.

Report on the sanitary conditions of Axbridge R.D. 17 Jan.1910. (Rep.Pub.Health & Med.Subj., no.21) Local Government Board.

Report on the sanitary conditions of Bakewell R.D·. 6 Aug.1910. (Rep.Pub.Health & Med.Subj., no.37) Local Government Board.

Report on the sanitary conditions of Beverley Borough with special reference to the prevalance of enteric fever and diarrhoea in the Borough. 9 Dec.1904. (Rep.Med.Insp., no.205) Local Government Board.

Report on the sanitary circumstances of Cwn R.D., Salop. 8 Dec.1905. (Rep.Med.Insp., no.222) Local Government Board.

Report on the sanitary circumstances of Darlaston U.D., Staffordshire. 10 Sept.1906. (Rep.Med.Insp., no.243) Local Government Board.

Report on the sanitary circumstances of Durham R.D. 8 April 1905. (Rep.Med.Insp., no.213) Local Government Board.

Report on the sanitary circumstances of Ebbw Vale U.D., with special reference to the prevalence of infectious diseases therein. 16 March 1907. (Rep. Med.Insp., no.255) Local Government Board.

Report on the sanitary circumstances of Emley, Farnley Tyas, Gunthwaite-and-Ingbirchworth, Hoylandswaine and Thurstonland U.D.'s., West Riding of Yorkshire, with suggestions for the formation of joint sanitary districts. 2 Jan.1908. (Rep.Med.Insp., no.297) Local Government Board.

Report on the sanitary circumstances of Howden R.D. 22 Dec.1904. (Rep.Med.Insp., no.206) Local Government Board.

Report on the sanitary circumstances of Oldham Borough. 28 May 1909. (Rep.Pub.Health & Med.Subj., no.7) Local Government Board.

Report on the sanitary circumstances of Pontefract Borough. 23 March 1910. (Rep.Pub.Health & Med.Subj., no.24) Local Government Board.

Report on the sanitary circumstances of Southwell R.D., Notts. 14 Oct.1908. (Rep.Med.Insp., no.312) Local Government Board.

Report on the sanitary circumstances of the Valley R.D., Anglesey. 10 May 1906. (Rep.Med.Insp., no.235) Local Government Board.

Report on the sanitary circumstances of Whitby R.D., especially those portions which are resorted to by summer visitors. 17 Nov.1908. (Rep.Med.Insp., no.320) Local Government Board.

Report on the sanitary circumstances of Whitby U.D. 18 Oct.1907. (Rep.Med.Insp., no.287) Local Government Board.

Report on the sanitary circumstances of Wigton R.D., U.D. and Holme Cultran U.D. 30 March 1914. (Rep.Pub.Health & Med.Subj., no.95) Local Government Board.

FARRER, Thomas Cecil, *2nd Baron*

Departmental committee on the encouragement of the life insurance system of the Post Office.
Report and minutes of evidence. 6 May 1908. 1908 (311) xxv. Post Office.

Departmental committee on Post Office facilities for insurance under the workmen's compensation acts.
Report. 5 June 1907. 1907 Cd.3568 lxviii.
Minutes of evidence. 1907 Cd.3569 lxviii. Post Office.

FARWELL, George

Royal commission on war stores in South Africa.
Report with appendices. 31 July 1906. 1906 Cd.3127 lvii.
Evidence. 2 vols. 1906 Cd.3128 lvii.
Report with appendices of Messrs. Annan, Kirby, Dexter & Co., Chartered Accountants, vol.3. 1906 Cd.3130 lviii.
Report on South African contractors. vol.4. 1906 Cd.3131 lviii.

FAULKNER, Alfred Edward

Committee on the increased use of coal for bunkering purposes.
Report. 1 July 1938. Mines Department.

FAWCETT, Edmund Alderson Sandford

Advisory committee on water.
Report of the technical sub-committee on the assessment of compensation water. April 1930. Ministry of Health.

Committee on water pipes and fittings.
Report. 11 Nov.1925.

FAWCETT, Edmund Alderson Sandford (continued)
Model specification. 1 Oct.1924. Ministry of Health.

The purification of the water of swimming baths. Aug.1929. Ministry of Health.

Report on the influence of the Brynmawr U.D. Council's sewage works on the health of the parish of Lanelly through pollution of the local water supplies. Nov.1901. Local Government Board.

Report on the water supply of Holderness in the East Riding of Yorkshire. 30 Jan.1905. Local Government Board.

FAWCETT, Millicent Garrett
Committee on concentration camps in South Africa.
Report. 12 Dec.1901. 1902 Cd.893 lxvii. War Office.

FAYLE, C. Ernest
History of the Great War: seaborne trade. Vols.1-3 and maps. 4 vols. 1920-24. War Office.

FEDELE, Pietro
Why Italy is at war. 1915. Ministry of Information.

FEETHAM, Richard
Committee on division of functions in the government of India.
Report. 26 Feb.1919. 1919 Cmd.103 xvi. India Office.
*For complete report SEE:* Hopwood, F. J. S.

Irish boundary commission.
Report. 9 Dec.1925. Cabinet Office. Published: Irish University Press, 1969.

FEILDING, Rudolph Robert Basil Aloysius Augustine, *9th Earl of Denbigh*
Why Germany made war. 1918. Ministry of Information.

FELLOWES, Ailwyn Edward
Departmental committee on foot and mouth disease.
Report. 22 May 1912. 1912/3 Cd.6222 xxix.
Minutes of evidence, appendices and index. 1912/3 Cd.6244 xxix. Board of Agriculture and Fisheries.

FENWICK, Edward N. F.
Departmental committee on musical copyright.
Report, evidence and appendix. 8 Feb.1904. 1904 Cd.1960 lxxix. Home Office.

Ferguson, M.R.C. *SEE:* Munro-Ferguson, R. C.

FERGUSSON, Charles
West Indies closer union commission.
Report on Leeward Islands, Windward Islands, Trinidad and Tobago. 7 April 1933. 1932/3 Cmd.4383 xv. Colonial Office.

FERGUSSON, James
Chairmen's panel.
Special report (on the proceedings of standing committees on bills) 24 July 1905. 1905 (261) vii. Home Office.

Select committee on national expenditure.
Report, proceedings, minutes of evidence, appendix and index. 4 Dec.1902. 1902 (387) vii.
Report, proceedings, evidence and appendix. 7 July 1903. 1903 (242) vii. House of Commons.

FERGUSSON, R. Menzies
Departmental committee on tinkers in Scotland.
Report. 25 Feb.1918. Scottish Office.

FETHERSTONE-GODLEY, Francis William Crewe
Special committee on the problem of prematurely aged ex-servicemen.

Report. 23 Nov.1937. 1937/8 Cmd.5738 xi. Prime Minister's Office.

FIELD, J. H.
A survey of the air currents in the Bay of Gibraltar, 1929-30. Nov.1933. (Geophys.Mem., no.59) Meteorological Office.

FIELD, William
Departmental committee on warble fly pest.
Report. 7 July 1926. Ministry of Agriculture and Fisheries.

FILDES, Paul Gordon
An analysis of the results of Wassermann reactions in 1,435 cases of syphilis or suspected syphilis. 30 Dec.1918. (S.R.S., no.23) Medical Research Committee.

Report on the prevalence of congenital syphilis among the newly-born of the East End of London. 20 May 1915. (Rep.Pub.Health & Med.Subj., no.105) Local Government Board.

Finch, J. C. W. *SEE:* Wynne-Finch, J. C.

FINDLAY, Leonard
Poverty, nutrition and growth. Studies of child life in cities and rural districts of Scotland. 4 May 1926. (S.R.S., no.101) Medical Research Council.

FINDLAY, W. P. K.
Decay of timber and its prevention. Nov.1938. (F.P.R. Records, no.27) Department of Scientific and Industrial Research.

Dry rot investigations in an experimental house. Jan.1937. (F.P.R. Records, no.14) Department of Scientific and Industrial Research.

Principal decays of softwoods used in Great Britain. Sept.1938. Department of Scientific and Industrial Research.

The principal rots of English oak. April 1936. Department of Scientific and Industrial Research.

FINLAY, Robert Bannatyne, *1st Viscount Finlay of Nairn*
Committee on the Finance Act, 1894.
Report. Feb.1900. 1900 Cd.89 xlvii. Treasury.

Royal commission on the importation of store cattle.
Report. 30 Aug.1921. 1921 Cmd.1139 xviii.
Appendices with indices of witnesses and subjects. 1921 Cmd.1541 xviii.

FINLAY, William, *2nd Viscount Finlay of Nairn*
Circuit towns committee.
Report. Aug.1936. 1935/6 Cmd.5262 viii. Lord Chancellor's Office.

Committee on legal aid for the poor.
First report. 29 March 1926. 1926 Cmd.2638 xiii.
Final report. 2 Jan.1928. 1928 Cmd.3016 xi. Lord chancellor's Office *and* Home Office.

FIRTH, A. R.
Report on agriculture and horse and cattle breeding in Kagoshima Prefecture, Japan. 19 Sept.1900. (Dip.cons.reports: misc.ser., no.539) 1900 Cd.353-4 xci. Foreign Office.

FIRTH, Algernon Freemen
Sub-committee of the Advisory Committee on commercial intelligence on British trade after the war.
Report. 11 Jan.1916. 1916 Cd.8181 xv.
Summaries of evidence. 1916 Cd.8275 xv. Board of Trade.

**FISHENDEN, Margaret White**
The calculation of heat transmission. July 1931. Department of Scientific and Industrial Research.

The coal fire. Aug.1920. (F.R.B. special rep., no.3) Department of Scientific and Industrial Research.

Heat transmission. Dec.1928. (B.R.B. special rep., no.11) Department of Scientific and Industrial Research.

**FISHER, C. B.**
Standing committee on trusts.
Report of a sub-committee on milk. 2 Nov.1920. 1920 Cmd.1102 xxiii. Board of Trade.

Travelling commission of enquiry into the cost of production of milk.
Interim report on the establishment of differential zones and the estimated cost of production of milk in the summer of 1919. April 1919. 1919 Cmd.205 xxv.
Report. 20 May 1919. 1919 Cmd.233 xxv. Ministry of Food.

**FISHER, Herbert Albert Laurens**
Select committee on the General Nursing Council.
Report, proceedings and evidence. 6 Aug.1925. 1924/5 (167) vii. House of Commons.

**FISHER, Norman Fenwick Warren**
Board of enquiry on certain statements affecting civil servants.
Report. 25 Feb.1928. 1928 Cmd.3037 vii. Prime Minister's Office.

Committee on the medical branches of the defence services.
Report. 19 July 1933. 1932/3 Cmd.4394 xi. Treasury.

Committee on the system of appointment in the Colonial Office and Colonial Services.
Report. 24 April 1930. 1929/30 Cmd.3554 viii. Colonial Office.

Departmental committee on pensions for members of the House of Commons.
Report. 30 Nov.1937. 1937/8 Cmd.5624 xii. Prime Minister's Office.

Industrial transference board.
Report. 26 June 1928. 1928 Cmd.3156 x. Ministry of Labour.

**FISHER, Ronald C.**
*Lyctus* powder-post beetles. June 1928. (F.P.R.Bull., no.2) Department of Scientific and Industrial Research.

Fisher, Warren. *SEE:* Fisher, N. F. W.

**FISHER, William Hayes**
Departmental committee on the welfare of the blind.
Report. 20 July 1917. 1917/8 Cd.8655 vii.
Evidence, appendices and index. 1917/8 Cd.8659 vii. Local Government Board.

**FITZALAN-HOWARD, Henry** *15th Duke of Norfolk*
Royal commission on the militia and volunteers.
Report. 20 May 1904. 1904 Cd.2061 xxx.
Minutes of evidence. 2 vols. 1904 Cd.2062, Cd.2063 xxx, xxxi.
Appendices. 1904 Cd.2064 xxxi.

**FITZGIBBON, Gerald**
Commission on Trinity College, Dublin, Estates.
Report. 29 April 1905. 1905 Cd.2526 xxvii.
Appendix: minutes of evidence, appendices, and maps. 1905 Cd.2527 xxvii. Irish Secretary's Office.

**FITZMAURICE, R.**
Principles of modern building.
Vol.1: Walls, partitions and chimneys. Aug.1938.
Vol.2: Floors and roofs. 1961. Department of Scientific and Industrial Research.
Sound transmission in buildings; practical notes for architects and builders. Nov.1939. Department of Scientific and Industrial Research.

**FITZROY, Almeric William**
Departmental committee on the working of the Midwives Act, 1902.
Vol.1: Report and appendices. 10 Aug.1909. 1909 Cd.4822 xxxiii.
Vol.2: Minutes of evidence and index. 1909 Cd.4823 xxxiii. Privy Council.

Interdepartmental committee on physical deterioration.
Vol.1: Report and appendix. 20 July 1904. 1904 Cd.2175 xxxii.
Vol.2: Witness and evidence. 1904 Cd.2210 xxxii.
Vol.3: Appendix and general index. 1904 Cd.2186 xxxii. War Office.

Flannery, J. F. *SEE:* Fortescue-Flannery, J.

**FLAVELLE, Joseph Wesley**
Canada and its relation to the British Empire. 27 April 1917. Ministry of Information.

**FLEMING, Arthur Percy Morris**
Industrial research in the United States of America. May 1917. Department of Scientific and Industrial Research.

**FLEMING, David Pinkerton,** *Lord*
Committee on existing law relating to contracts of hire-purchase in Scotland.
Report. 16 Sept.1931. Scottish Office.

Committee on registration of writs in the Sasines Office, Edinburgh.
Report. 23 June 1928. Scottish Office.

**FLEMING, James**
Inter-departmental committee on the rates of drawback on tobacco.
Report, appendices and evidence. 12 March 1904. 1904 Cd.2133 xxxix. Treasury.

**FLEMING, James Alexander**
Burden of the existing rates and the general financial position of the Outer Hebrides.
Report on the parishes of Barra, North Uist, South Uist, and Harris. 15 Jan.1906. 1906 Cd.3014 civ. Local Government Board for Scotland.
Departmental committee on sexual offences against children and young persons in Scotland.
Report. 2 Feb.1926. 1926 Cmd.2592 xv. Scottish Office.

**FLEMING, R. M.**
A study of growth and development; observations in successive years on the same children. 18 Oct.1933. (S.R.S., no.190) Medical Research Council.

**FLETCHER, Walter**
Memorandum on a visit to the United States, May 1921. Dec.1921. University Grants Committee. Treasury.

**FLETCHER, Walter Morley**
Medical Research Committee.
Interim report on work in connection with the war. 12 May 1915. 1914/6 Cd.7922 xxxi. (no other reports identified.) National Health Insurance Joint Committee.

FLETCHER, Wilfred William Ernest
A contribution to the study of chronicity in dysentery carriers. May 1919. (S.R.S., no.29) Medical Research Committee.

Report on an outbreak of enteric fever in Coleford U.D. and in the West Dean R.D. 18 May 1900. (Rep.Med.Insp., no.149) Local Government Board.

Report on the sanitary conditions of Aberayron R.D. comprising Aberayron R.D. and Aberayron and New Quay U.D.'s. 17 Sept.1907. (Rep.Med.Insp., no.283) Local Government Board.

Report on the sanitary circumstances of Ashton-under-Lyne Borough. 4 July 1907. (Rep.Med.Insp., no.271) Local Government Board.

Report on the sanitary circumstances of Audenshaw U.D. 19 June 1907. (Rep.Med.Insp., no.270) Local Government Board.

Report on the sanitary conditions of Brockley Borough and R.D. 18 March 1910. (Rep.Pub.Health & Med.Subj., no.26) Local Government Board.

Report on the sanitary conditions of the Brandon and Byshotts U.D., with special reference to the prevalence of enteric fever. 22 May 1907. (Rep.Med.Insp., no.260) Local Government Board.

Report on the sanitary conditions of the Bywell registration sub-district of Hexham Rural District and upon the continued prevalence of infectious disease. 18 Nov.1904. (Rep.Med.Insp., no.207) Local Government Board.

Report on the sanitary conditions of Chester-le-Street R.D. 29 Nov.1906. (Rep.Med.Insp., no.250) Local Government Board.

Report on the sanitary conditions of Farnworth registration sub-district of the Bolton (Lancs) R.D., and on the Farnworth and Kearsley U.D.'s. 1 Dec.1900. (Rep.Med.Insp., no.154) Local Government Board.

Report on the sanitary conditions of Gildersome U.D. and on the recent prevalence of enteric fever therein. 12 Nov.1901. (Rep.Med.Insp., no.168) Local Government Board.

Report on the sanitary circumstances of Halstead R.D. 22 March 1905. (Rep.Med.Insp., no.211) Local Government Board.

Report on the sanitary conditions of Heacham and certain other coast villages on the northern and western littoral of the Docking R.D. 2 Nov.1907. (Rep.Med.Insp., no.294) Local Government Board.

Report on the sanitary conditions of Leyburn R.D. 9 Sept.1907. (Rep.Med.Insp., no.279) Local Government Board.

Report on the sanitary conditions of Middlesborough C.B., with reference to the persistently high general death rate and infantile mortality and their causes. 22 Sept.1910. (Rep. Pub.Health Med.Subj., no.42) Local Government Board.

Report on the sanitary circumstances of Mossley Borough. 19 June 1907. (Rep.Med.Insp., no.265) Local Government Board.

Report on the sanitary conditions of Nantyglo and Blaina U.D. and on the prevalence of infectious disease in the district. 6 April 1905. (Rep.Med.Insp., no.212) Local Government Board.

Report on the sanitary conditions of Newport

Pagnell R.D. 26 Sept.1912. (Rep.Pub.Health & Med.Subj., no.72) Local Government Board.

Report on the sanitary conditions of Pewsey R.D. 18 April 1905. (Rep.Med.Insp., no.214) Local Government Board.

Report on the sanitary conditions of Romney Marsh R.D. and on the Borough of New Romney and Lydd. 22 Nov.1901. (Rep.Med.Insp., no.169) Local Government Board.

Report on the sanitary conditions of St.Asaph R.D., Flintshire and St.Asaph R.D., Denbighshire. 15 June 1908. (Rep.Med.Insp., no.305) Local Government Board.

Report on the sanitary conditions of Southwick-on-Wear U.D., and on recent prevalence of zymotic disease in the district. 28 Sept.1906. (Rep.Med. Insp., no.245) Local Government Board.

Report on the sanitary conditions of the village of Coggeshall, Braintree R.D., and alleged prevalence of infectious disease. 22 Sept.1906. (Rep.Med.Insp., no.244) Local Government Board.

Report on the sanitary conditions of Wimborne and Cranborne R.D. 3 Feb.1908. (Rep.Med.Insp., no.300) Local Government Board.

FLETT, John Smith
The first hundred years of the Geological Survey of Great Britain. July 1936. Geological Survey.

The geology of the Land's End district. (Sheets 351 and 358) 11 May 1907. (Mem.Geol.Surv.) Geological Survey.

The geology of the Lizard and Meneage. (Sheet 359) 26 Mar.1912. (Mem.Geol.Surv.) Geological Survey.

FLOWER, William D.
An investigation into the variation of the lapse rate of temperature in the atmosphere near the ground at Ismailia, Egypt. April 1937. (Geophys.Mem., no.71) Meteorological Office.

Sand devils. Aug.1936. (Prof.Notes, no.71) Meteorological Office.

Temperature and relative humidity in the atmosphere over lower Egypt. May 1937. (Prof.Notes, no.75) Meteorological Office.

FOOT, Isaac
Committee on firedamp detector regulations. Report. 25 Feb.1938. Mines Department.

FORBES, A. W.
Report on the sugar industry of Bohemia. 7 May 1901. (Dip. and cons. reports: misc.ser., no.554) 1901 Cd.430-9 lxxx. Foreign Office.

FORBES, James Graham
The prevention of diptheria. 21 March 1927. (S.R.S., no.115) Medical Research Council.

FORD, E.
Preparation of dog-fish for market. 1923. Fishery Board for Scotland.

FOREMAN, F. W.
The changes produced in meat extracts by the bacterium *staphylococcus aureus*. March 1928. (F.I.B. special rep., no.31) Department of Scientific and Industrial Research.

The control of reaction in cultures and enzymic digests. March 1928. (F.I.B. special rep., no.32) Department of Scientific and Industrial Research.

FORRESTER, R. B.
The fluid milk market in England and Wales.

FORRESTER, R. B. (continued)
Report. Aug.1927. (Economic Series, no.16) Ministry of Agriculture.

Milk price margins. June 1932. (E.M.B. 51) Empire Marketing Board.

Forster, H. O. A. *SEE:* Arnold-Forster, H. O.

FORSTER, John
Commission on the Trinidad and Tobago disturbances, 1937.
Report. 30 Dec.1937. 1937/8 Cmd.5641 xv. Colonial Office.

Court of inquiry concerning the stoppage of the London Central Omnibus services.
Interim report. 6 May 1937. 1936/7 Cmd.5454 xii.
Report. 21 May 1937. 1936/7 Cmd.5464 xii. Ministry of Labour.

The effects of working conditions upon the health of London Central busmen.
Report of conferences. 31 Aug.1939. Ministry of Labour.

FORSYTH, James Noel
Departmental committee on livestock and agriculture in the congested districts in Scotland.
Report. 24 Nov.1910. 1910 Cd.5457 xxi. Scottish Office.

Departmental committee on the work of the Congested Districts (Scotland) Commissioners for the Improvement of Agricultural Livestock.
Report. 24 Nov.1910. 1910 Cd.5457 xxi.
Minutes of evidence and index. 1911 Cd.5509 xiii. Scottish Office.

FORSYTH, Peter Taylor
The roots of a world-commonwealth. 1918. Ministry of Information.

FORTESCUE-FLANNERY, James
Departmental committee on Mr. A. W. Gattie's proposals for handling goods and traffic. (Gattie Committee)
Report. 16 Dec.1919. 1919 Cmd.492 xxx.
Minutes of proceedings and index. 1920 Cmd.580 xxiii. Ministry of Transport.

FOSTER, Michael
Committee on the ventilation of the House of Commons.
Report and recommendations. July 1906. 1906 Cd.3035 xciv.
Appendix: report by M. H. Gordon on an investigation of the ventilation of the debating chamber of the House of Commons. 1906 Cd.3068 xciv. Commissioners of Works and Public Buildings.

Departmental committee on botanical work and collections at the British Museum and at Kew.
Report and minutes of evidence. 11 March 1901. 1901 (205) lix. Treasury.

Royal Commission on human and animal tuberculosis. *SEE:* Power, W. H.

FOSTER, Walter, *1st Baron Ilkeston*
Departmental committee on the pay and classification of the Ordnance Survey staff.
Report. 20 July 1911. 1911 Cd.5825 xxxvii.
Minutes of evidence, appendices, index and analysis of evidence. 1911 Cd.5825 xxxvii. Board of Agriculture and Fisheries.

FOUNTAIN, Henry
Report of the imperial customs conference, 28 February to 17 March 1921. April 1921. 1921 Cmd.1231 x. Board of Trade.

FOWLER, A.
The geology of Berwick-on-Tweed, Norham and Scremerston. (Sheets 1 and 2) 21 Aug.1925. (Mem. Geol.Surv.) Geological Survey.

The geology of the country around Rothbury, Amble and Ashington. (Sheets 9 and 10) (Mem.Geol.Surv.) Geological Survey.

FOX, Arthur Wilson
Report of an enquiry into working class rents, housing and retail prices, together with the rates of wages in the principal industrial towns of America. April 1911. 1911 Cd.5609 lxxxviii. Board of Trade.

Report of an enquiry into working class rents, housing and retail prices, together with the rates of wages in the principal industrial towns of Belgium. March 1910. 1910 Cd.5065 xcv. Board of Trade.

Report of an enquiry into working class rents, housing and retail prices, together with the rates of wages in certain occupations in the principal industrial towns of France. 24 Dec.1908. 1909 Cd.4512 xci. Board of Trade.

Report of an enquiry into working class rents, housing and retail prices, together with rates of wages in the principal industrial towns of the German Empire. 10 April 1908. 1908 Cd.4032 cviii. Board of Trade.

Report of an enquiry on the cost of living of the working classes, United Kingdom, with an introductory memorandum. Dec.1907. 1908 Cd.3864 cviii. Board of Trade.

Report on rules of voluntary conciliation and arbitration boards and joint committees. Sept.1907. 1908 Cd.3788 xcviii. Board of Trade.

Wages and earnings of agricultural labourers in the United Kingdom.
Report. Aug.1900. 1900 Cd.346 lxxxii.
Second report. Feb.1905. 1905 Cd.2376 xcvii. Board of Trade.

Fox, G. R. L. *SEE:* Lane-Fox, G. R., *1st Baron Bingley*

FOX, H. H.
Memorandum on Chinese mines. June 1911. (Dip. cons.reports: misc.ser., no.680) 1911 Cd.5466-I lxxxix. Foreign Office *and* Board of Trade.

FOX, John Jacob
Treatment of chimney gases at the Battersea power station. *SEE:* Robertson, R.

FOX-STRANGWAYS, C.
The geology of the country between Atherstone and Charnwood Forest. (Sheet 155) 9 July 1900. (Mem. Geol.Surv.) Geological Survey.

The geology of the country between Derby, Burton-on-Trent, Ashby-de-la-Zouch and Loughborough. (Sheet 141) 24 Jan.1905. (Mem.Geol.Surv.) Geological Survey.

The geology of the country between Whitby and Scarborough. (Sheets 35 and 44 N.S.) 1881 and 1915. (Mem.Geol.Surv.) Geological Survey.

The geology of the country near Leicester. (Sheet 156) 11 Feb.1903. (Mem.Geol.Surv.) Geological Survey.

The geology of the country north of Harrogate. (Sheet 62) 2 Sept.1908. (Mem.Geol.Surv.) Geological Survey.

**FOX-STRANGWAYS, C.** (continued)

The geology of the Leicestershire and South Derbyshire coalfield. 16 July 1907. (Mem.Geol.Surv.) Geological Survey.

Water supply from underground sources of the East Riding of Yorkshire together with the neighbouring vales of York and Pickering. 23 Feb.1906. (Mem. Geol.Surv.) Geological Survey.

**FRANCIS, W.**

The spontaneous combustion of coal: the most readily oxidizable constituents of coal. July 1926. (S.M.R.B. Paper no.28) Mines Department.

**FRANCQUI, Emile**

Committee of experts on reparations.
Report. 7 June 1929. 1929/30 Cmd.3343 xvii. Treasury.

**FRANK, Howard**

Committee on crown lands and government lands.
Interim and final reports. 11 Jan. and 11 May 1922. 1922 Cmd.1689 vii. Treasury.

**FRASER, Andrew Henderson Leith**

Indian police commission.
Report and resolution of the government of India. 30 May 1903 and 21 March 1905. 1905 Cd.2478 lvii. India Office.

**FRASER, G. K.**

Studies of Scottish moorlands in relation to tree growth. May 1933. (Bull. no.15) Forestry Commission.

**FRASER, Simon Joseph,** *16th Baron Lovat*

Committee on agricultural research and administration in the non-selfgoverning dependencies.
Report. Feb.1927. 1927 Cmd.2825 vii. Colonial Office.
Committee on the Colonial agricultural service.
Report. 8 Feb.1928. 1928 Cmd.3049 vii. Colonial Office.
Committee on the colonial veterinary service.
Report. Nov.1928. 1928/9 Cmd.3261 v. Colonial Office.
Committee on local expenditure in Scotland.
Report. 2 Nov.1932. 1932/3 Cmd.4201 xiv. Scottish Office.
Departmental committee on the nature and cause of grouse disease.
Report. Aug.1911. 1911 Cd.5871 xxvi. Board of Agriculture and Fisheries.

**FRASER, Thomas R.**

Indian Plague Commission 1898-99.
Minutes of evidence, vols.1-3, 1900 Cd.139, Cd.140, Cd.141, xxx, xxxi, xxxii.
Vol.4: Indices to the evidence. 1902 Cd.809 lxxii.
Vol.5: Report with appendices and summary. 26 July 1901. 1902 Cd.810 lxxii. India Office.

**FREDERICK, G. C.**

Memorandum on constructing a harbour of refuge on the north coast of Cornwall. 28 April 1904. 1904 Cd.2086 lxxxvi. Board of Trade.

**FREEMAN, William Marshall**

Standing committee on prices.
Report of a sub-committee on pottery. 3 May 1921. 1921 Cmd.1360 xvi. Board of Trade.
Standing committee on prices.
Report of a sub-committee on repairing of boots, shoes and footwear. 6 May 1921. 1921 Cmd.1345 xvi. Board of Trade.

**FREEMAN-THOMAS,** Freeman, *1st Viscount Willingdon*

Advisory committee on China indemnity.
Report. 18 June 1926. (China, no.2, 1926) 1926 Cmd.2766 viii. Foreign Office.

**FREEMANTLE, T. F.**

Report on Swiss rifle ranges. 1901. 1901 Cd.523 xl. War Office.

**FREER-SMITH, Hamilton Pym**

Departmental committee on humidity and ventilation in cotton weaving sheds.
Report. 7 Jan.1909. 1909 Cd.4484 xv.
Minutes of evidence and appendices. 1909 Cd.4485 xv.
Second report, minutes of evidence and appendices. Jan.1911. 1911 Cd.5566 xxiii. Home Office.

Departmental committee on humidity and ventilation in flax mills and linen factories.
Report and appendices. May 1914. 1914 Cd.7433 xxxvi.
Evidence. 1914 Cd.7446 xxxvi. Home Office.

Illustrations of methods of dust extraction in factories and workshops. June 1906. 1906 Cd.3223 cx. Home Office.

Textile factories labour committee on factory labour in India.
Report and appendices. 5 April 1907. 1907 Cd.3617 lix. India. Department of Commerce and Industry. India Office.

**FRY, Edward**

Committee on the working of the Patent Acts on certain specified questions.
Report. 10 Jan.1901. 1901 Cd.506 xxiii.
Appendices and minutes of evidence. 1901 Cd.530 xxiii. Board of Trade.

Royal commission on Trinity College, Dublin, and the University of Dublin.
First report. 31 Aug.1906. 1906 Cd.3174 lvi.
Appendix: statements and returns. 1906 Cd.3176 lvi.
Final report. 12 Jan.1907. 1907 Cd.3311 xli.
Appendix, minutes of evidence and documents. 1907 Cd.3312 xli.

**FULTON, Thomas Alexander Wemyss**

Report on herring trawling investigations. June 1922. (Sci.invest., no.2, 1921). Fishery Board for Scotland.

Report on the marking experiments on plaice, made by the S.S. "Goldseeker" in the years 1910-13. 1919. (Sci.Invest., no.1, 1919) Fishery Board for Scotland.

**FUNCH, C. H.**

Report on the Danish system of taxation. April 1907. (Dip.cons.reports: misc.ser., no.659) 1907 Cd.3284-8 lxxxvii. Foreign Office.

**FUSSELL, G. E.**

Chronological list of early agricultural works in the Library of the Ministry. Jan.1930. Ministry of Agriculture and Fisheries.

**FYFE, Thomas Alexander**

Commission of enquiry into industrial unrest.
Report of commissioners for Scotland. *SEE:* Barnes, G. N.

**GADDUM, John Henry**

Methods of biological assay depending on a quantal response. 12 May 1933. (S.R.S., no.183) Medical Research Council.

GAGE, F. H.
Localisation of sounds in the median plane. 1931. (S.R.S., no.166) Medical Research Council.

GALLOWAY, I. A.
Borna disease and enzootic encephalo-myelitis of sheep and cattle. 28 July 1928. (S.R.S., no.121) Medical Research Council.

GALLOWAY, James
Advisory board for Army medical services. The treatment of venereal disease and scabies in the Army.
First report. June 1904.
Second report. March 1905.
Third report. Aug.1905.
Final report. Feb.1906. War Office.

Report on the physical examination of men of military age by National Service Medical Boards from November 1, 1917 to October 31, 1918.
Vol.1. Dec.1919. 1919 Cmd.504 xxvi. Ministry of National Insurance.

GAMBLE, Edward Harpur
Committee on signalling between His Majesty's ships and British merchant vessels.
Report. Feb.1906. Admiralty.

GANZONI, Francis John Childs
Select committee on medicine stamp duties.
Special report. 21 July 1936. 1935/6 (151) vi.
Report, proceedings, evidence and index; and proceedings of the 1935/6 committee. 18 Feb.1937. 1936/7 (54) viii. House of Commons.

GARBETT, Cyril Forster, *Bishop of Winchester, 1932-1942*
Central housing advisory committee.
Report of the demolition procedure sub-committee. Demolition of individual unfit houses in rural areas. 2 June 1938. Ministry of Health.

Central housing advisory council.
Report of the rural housing sub-committee. 22 July 1936.
Second report. 16 Dec.1936. Ministry of Health.

Gardner, H. T. *SEE:* Horridge, T. G.

GARDNER, Herbert Coulston, *1st Baron Burghclere*
Departmental committee on the Fertilisers and Feeding Stuffs Act, 1893.
Report. Feb.1905. 1905 Cd.2373 xx.
Minutes of evidence, appendices and index. 1905 Cd.2386 xx. Board of Agriculture and Fisheries.

GARNER, R. J.
The frameworking of fruit trees. April 1938. (Occ.Paper, no.5) Imperial Bureau of Fruit Production.

GARNETT, W. J.
Report of a journey through the provinces of Shantung and Kiangsu, (China). 23 Nov.1906. 1907 Cd.3500 xcix. Foreign Office.

GARRAN, Robert Randolph
Tribunal on defence expenditure in dispute between the government of India, the War Office and the Air Ministry.
Report. 17 Jan.1933. 1933/4 Cmd.4473 xi. India Office.

GARRETT, A. W.
Committee on the fencing of heavy power presses.
Report. 28 April 1939. Home Office.

GARSTIN, William
Report on the basin of the Upper Nile. July 1904. 1904 Cd.2165 cxi. Foreign Office.

GASKELL, William
Commission on the financial situation of British Guiana.
Report. 1 June 1931. 1930/1 Cmd.3938 x. Colonial Office.

GASTRELL, William Shaw Harriss
Extension of German subsidised mail steamers to South Africa. Aug.1900. (Dip.cons.reports: misc.ser., no.536) 1900 Cd.353-1 xci. Foreign Office.

Memorandum on and translation of the new German sickness and old age insurance law. 22 Dec.1899. (Dip.cons.reports: misc.ser., no.518) 1900 Cd.2-1 xci. Foreign Office.

Memorandum on commerce in the Netherlands. 27 Nov.1900. (Dip.cons.reports: misc.ser., no.543) 1900 Cd.353-8 xci. Foreign Office.

Memorandum on German imports and exports of "Iron and ironware" and "implements, machines, *etc.*" from 1897 to 1899. 14 May 1900. (Dip.cons. reports: misc.ser., no.525) 1900 Cd.2-8 xci. Foreign Office.

Memorandum on the German iron trade in 1899 and 1900. 7 May 1901. (Dip.cons.reports: misc.ser., no.553) 1901 Cd.430-8 lxxx. Foreign Office.

Memorandum on the German iron trade in 1900 and 1901. 17 March 1902. (Dip.cons.reports: misc.ser., no.575) 1902 Cd.787-11 ciii. Foreign Office.

Gattie's Committee. *SEE:* Fortescue-Flannery, J.

GAW, Francis
Performance tests of intelligence. May 1925. (I.H.R.B. Rep., no.31) Medical Research Council.

GEDDES, Auckland Campbell
Memorandum on the subject of the effects of prohibition in the United States. 14 June 1923. (United States, no.1, 1923) 1923 Cmd.1915 xxv. Foreign Office.

Report on conditions at Ellis Island immigration station. 18 Jan.1923. (United States, no.2, 1923) 1923 Cmd.1940 xxv. Foreign Office.

Royal commission on food prices.
First report with evidence and appendices. 23 April 1925. 1924/5 Cmd.2390 xiii.
Vol.2: Minutes of evidence 1925.
Vol.3: Appendices. 1925. (no further reports identified) Board of Trade.

Geddes, E. C.
Committee on national expenditure. *SEE:* May, G. E.

GEIKIE, Archibald
The geology of central and western Fife. (Sheet 40 and parts of 32 and 48) 1 June 1900. (Mem.Geol. Surv., Scotl.) Geological Survey, Scotland.

The geology of eastern Fife. (Sheet 41 and parts of 40, 48 and 49) 1902. (Mem.Geol.Surv., Scotl.) Geological Survey, Scotland.

Royal commission on the University of Dublin, Trinity College.
Report. 12 Nov.1920. 1920 Cmd.1078 xiii.
Appendix: extracts from evidence and documents. 1921 Cmd.1167 xi.

George, D. Lloyd. *SEE:* Lloyd George, D.

GEORGE, T. Neville
British regional geology: North Wales. 1935. Geological Survey.

British regional geology: South Wales. 1937. Geological Survey.

GETTINGS, Harold Salter
An investigation of the Flexner-Y group of dysentery bacilli. 18 Oct.1918. (S.R.S., no.30) Medical Research Committee.

GETTY, Arthur
Report on cold storage and refrigeration in Chicago. 3 Dec.1900. (Dip.cons.reports: misc.ser., no.545) 1901 Cd.430 lxxx. Foreign Office.

GIBB, Alexander
Light railways investigation committee.
Report. 26 July 1921.
Appendices. 1921. Ministry of Transport.

GIBB, George Stegmann
Committee on the report of the select committee of the House of Commons on Post Office servants, 1912/3.
First report. 25 June 1915. 1914/6 Cd.7995 xxxii.
Second report. 29 March 1916. 1916 Cd.8244 xiv. Post Office.

GIBB, Maurice Sylvester
Departmental committee on examinations of engineers in the mercantile marine.
Report. Dec.1937. Board of Trade.

GIBB, Roger
Report on railway rates and finance in Kenya, Uganda and Tanganyika Territory. 24 Sept.1932. 1932/3 Cmd.4235 x. Colonial Office.

**GIBBON, Ioan Gwilym**
Committee on floods from the River Thames in the county of London.
Report. 22 Feb.1928. 1928 Cmd.3045 xii. Ministry of Health.

The housing problem in Germany. May 1919. Local Government Board.

Infant welfare in Germany during the war. March 1918. Local Government Board.

Mothers' pensions in the United States of America. Nov.1918. Local Government Board.

The welfare of the children of women employed in factories in France and Germany. Nov.1918. Local Government Board.

GIBBONS, Sydney G.
*Calanus finmarchicus* and other copepods in Scottish waters in 1933. 1936. (Sci.invest., 1936, no.2) Fishery Board for Scotland.

A study of the biology of *calanus finmarchicus* in the north-western North Sea. 1933. (Sci.invest., 1933, no.1) Fishery Board for Scotland.

GIBBS, Philip
The Germans on the Somme. 1917. Ministry of Information.

GIBLETT, M. A.
A comparison of minimum temperatures for the period 17h to 9h and 17h to 17h. July 1921. (Prof.Notes, no.22) Meteorological Office.

The structure of wind over level country. April 1932. (Geophys.Mem., No.54) Meteorological Office.

GIBSON, Arnold Hartley
Construction and operation of a tidal model of the Severn Estuary.

Two reports. May 1929 and Oct.1932.
Diagrams, *etc.* 1933. Economic Advisory Council. Treasury.

GIBSON, Henry James
Interdepartmental committee on the appointment of audit staff under Part 1 of the National Insurance Act.
First report. 22 May 1912. 1912/3 Cd.6232 xlii.
Second report. 23 May 1912. 1912/3 Cd.6243 xlii. Treasury.

GIBSON, Walcot
Cannel coals, lignite and mineral oil in Scotland. 28 Mar.1922. (Special reports on the mineral resources of Great Britain, vol.24) (Mem.Geol.Surv.) Geological Survey.

The concealed coalfield of Yorkshire and Nottinghamshire. 25 Feb.1913. (Mem.Geol.Surv.) Geological Survey.

Geology of the country around Nottingham. 16 March 1910. (Mem.Geol.Surv.) Geological Survey.

The geology of the country around Stoke-upon-Trent. (Sheet 123) 19 July 1902. (Mem.Geol.Surv.) Geological Survey.

The geology of the north Staffordshire coalfields. 6 Jan.1905. (Mem.Geol.Surv.) Geological Survey.

The geology of the northern part of the Derbyshire coalfield. (Sheet 112 and the southern part of Sheet 100) 14 June 1913. (Mem.Geol.Surv.) Geological Survey.

The geology of the south Wales coalfield. Part 2: the country around Abergavenny. 16 June 1900. (Mem. Geol.Surv.) Geological Survey.

The geology of the southern part of the Derbyshire and Nottinghamshire coalfield. (Sheet 125) 15 Oct.1907. (Mem.Geol.Surv.) Geological Survey.

GIFFARD, Hardinge Stanley, *1st Earl of Halsbury*
Select committee of the House of Lords on the charges against Lord Murray of Elibank.
Report, proceedings, evidence and appendices. 29 April 1914. 1914 (H.L. 66) House of Lords.

GIFFEN, Robert
Committee on trade records.
Report. July 1908. 1908 Cd.4345 xxv.
Minutes of evidence, appendices and index. 1908 Cd.4346 xxv. Board of Trade.

GILKS, John Langton
The physique and health of two African tribes. 9 March 1931. (S.R.S., no.155) Medical Research Council.

GILL, David
A history and description of the Royal Observatory, Cape of Good Hope. 24 April 1913. Admiralty.

GILL, Thomas Patrick
Departmental committee on Irish forestry.
Report. 6 April 1908. 1908 Cd.4027 xxiii.
Minutes of evidence, appendices and index. 1908 Cd.4028 xxiii. Department of Agriculture and Technical Instruction for Ireland.

Report on foot-and-mouth disease in Ireland in the year 1912. 10 Sept.1913. 1914 Cd.7103 xii. Department of Agriculture and Technical Instruction for Ireland.

GILLETT, George Masterman
Commission on special areas, England and Wales.
First report. July 1935. 1934/5 Cmd.4957 x.
Second report. Feb.1936. 1935/6 Cmd.5090 xiii.

GILLETT, George Masterman (continued)
> Third report. Nov.1936. 1936/7 Cmd.5303 xii.
> Fourth report. Nov.1937. 1937/8 Cmd.5595 xii.
> Report. Dec.1938. 1938/9 Cmd.5896 xii.
> Ministry of Labour.

GILLIES, John
> Anaesthesia in casualty service. Aug.1940.
> Department of Health for Scotland.

GILMOUR, John
> Committee on Scottish administration.
>> Report. 4 Sept.1937. 1936/7 Cmd.5563 xv.
>> Scottish Office.
>
> Imperial wireless and cable conference, 1928.
>> Report. 6 July 1928. 1928 Cmd.3163 x.
>> Treasury.
>
> Select committee on Official Secrets Acts.
>> First report. 28 Sept.1938. 1937/8 (173) vii.
>> Report, proceedings, evidence, appendix and
>> index. 5 April 1939. 1938/9 (101) viii. House of
>> Commons.

GIRDLER, F. M.
> Report of delegates to enquire as to openings in
> Canada for women from the United Kingdom.
> Nov.1919. 1919 Cmd.403 xxxi. Colonial Office.
>
> Report of delegates to enquire as to openings in New
> Zealand for women from the United Kingdom.
> Aug.1920. 1920 Cmd.933 xxii. Colonial Office.

GLADSTONE, Herbert John, *1st Viscount Gladstone*
> Committee on recruitment for the civil service after
> the war.
>> Interim report. 28 Feb.1918. 1919 Cmd.34 xi.
>> Second interim report. 17 May 1918. 1919
>> Cmd.35 xi.
>> Third interim report. 30 Oct.1918. 1919
>> Cmd.36 xi.
>> Final report. 22 April 1919. 1919 Cmd.164 xi.
>> Treasury.

GLANVILLE, W. H.
> Mechanical properties of bricks and brickwork
> masonry. April 1934. (B.R.B. special report, no.22)
> Department of Scientific and Industrial Research.

GLAZEBROOK, Richard Tetley
> Committee on education and research in
> aeronautics.
>> Report. 12 Dec.1919. 1920 Cmd.554 ix. Air
>> Ministry.
>
> Departmental committee on accidents to
> monoplanes.
>> Report. 3 Dec.1912. 1912/3 Cd.6506 li. War
>> Office.
>
> Departmental committee on lighting in factories and
> workshops. *SEE:* Wilson, D. R.
>
> Engineering committee. Sub-committee on
> insulation.
>> Report on heat insulators. Dec.1921. (F.I.B.
>> special rep., no.5)
>> Report on the transmission of heat by radiation
>> and convection. Oct.1922. (F.I.B. special rep.,
>> no.9) Department of Scientific and Industrial
>> Research.
>
> Report on experiments made to measure the
> vibrations at St. Paul's Cathedral. May 1913. Home
> Office. National Physical Laboratory.

GLENNY, W. J.
> Report and resolutions of the British Empire
> statistical conference, 1920. 26 Feb.1920. 1920
> Cmd.648 xxv. Board of Trade.

GLOVER, James Allison
> Committee of inquiry into problems relating to
> children with defective hearing.
>> Report. July 1938. Board of Education.
>
> A report on chronic arthritis; with special reference
> to the provision of treatment. April 1928. (R.Pub.
> Health & Med.Subj., no.52) Ministry of Health.

GLYNN, Ernest Edward
> Bacteriological and clinical observations on
> pneumonia and empemata, with special reference to
> pneumococcus and to serum treatment. Aug.1923.
> (S.R.S., no.79) Medical Research Council.

GODBERT, A. L.
> The analysis of mine dusts. Nov.1938. (S.M.R.B.
> Paper no.101) Mines Department.
>
> The combustion of coal dust. April 1931. (S.M.R.B.
> Paper no.73) Mines Department.
>
> Laboratory methods of determining the
> inflammability of coal dusts. Sept.1926. (S.M.R.B.
> Paper no.31) Mines Department.
>
> The relative inflammability of coal dusts: a
> laboratory study. May 1929. (S.M.R.B. Paper
> no.56) Mines Department.
>
> The routine method for determining the
> inflammability of mine dusts: a modified form of the
> test. April 1934. (S.M.R.B. Paper no.87) Mines
> department.
>
> A routine test of the inflammability of mine dusts.
> June 1931. (S.M.R.B. Paper no.68) Mines
> Department.

GOLD, Ernest
> Aids to forecasting: types of pressure distribution.
> Feb.1920. (Geophys.Mem., no.16) Meteorological
> Office.
>
> The falling time of marine barometers. Feb.1928.
> (Prof.Notes, no.48) Meteorological Office.
>
> The international kite and balloon ascents.
> Aug.1913. (Geophys.Mem., no.5) Meteorological
> Office.
>
> Maximum day temperatures and the tephigram.
> May 1933. (Prof.Notes, no.63) Meteorological
> Office.
>
> Report on the calculation of wind velocity from
> pressure distribution. April 1908. (M.O.190)
> Meteorological Office.

GOLDIE, Archibald Hayman Robertson
> Characteristics of rainfall distribution in
> homogeneous currents and at surfaces of
> discontinuity. June 1931. (Geophys.Mem., no.53)
> Meteorological Office.
>
> Depressions as vortices. April 1939.
> (Geophys.Mem., no.79) Meteorological Office.
>
> Kematical features of depressions. May 1937.
> (Geophys.Mem., no.72) Meteorological Office.
>
> Rainfall at fronts of depressions. June 1936.
> (Geophys.Mem., no.69) Meteorological Office.
>
> Wind records from the Bell Rock lighthouse.
> Jan.1935. (Geophys.Mem., no.63) Meteorological
> Office.

GOMPERS, Samuel
> Commission on international labour legislation.
>> Report. 24 March 1919. (*In* Labour and the
>> peace treaty) Ministry of Labour.

GOODENOUGH, Francis William
Committee on education for salesmanship.
Interim report: British marketing overseas. 12 Nov.1929.
Second interim report: modern languages. 21 May 1930.
Final report. 3 July 1931. Board of Education.

GOODEY, T.
The genus *Anguillulina* Gerv. & v.Ben., 1859 vil *Tylenchus* Bastian, 1865. June 1932. Imperial Bureau of Agricultural Parasitology.

The nematode parasites of plants catalogued under their hosts. 1940. Imperial Bureau of Agricultural Parasitology.

GOOLD-ADAMS, Henry Edward Fane
The nitrogen problem and the work of the nitrogen products committee. 1 Nov.1917. Ministry of Munitions.

Nitrogen products committee.
Final report. 10 May 1919. 1919 Cmd.482 xxvi.
Statistical supplement. June 1921. Ministry of Munitions.

GORDON, Arthur Hamilton, *1st Baron Stanmore.*
Select committee of the House of Lords on the Palace of Westminster.
Report, proceedings and evidence. 20 Dec.1906. 1906 (H.L.256) ix. House of Lords.

Select committee of the House of Lords on the Palace of Westminster.
Report and proceedings. 10 July 1907. 1907 (H.L.104) vii. House of Lords.

GORDON, Edward Lillingston Stewart
Report on the Hokkaido, Japan. June 1908. (Dip. cons.reports: misc.ser., no.668) 1908 Cd.3728-4 cviii. Foreign Office *and* Board of Trade.

GORDON, Hugh
Mental and scholastic tests among retarded children. June 1923. (Educational pamphlets, no.44) Board of Education.

GORDON, James Scott
Departmental committee on the Irish pig-breeding industry.
Report. 27 April 1915. 1914/6 Cd.7890 vi.
Evidence, appendices and index. 1914/6 Cd.8004 vi. Department of Agriculture and Technical Instruction for Ireland.

GORDON, John
Departmental committee on state purchase and control of liquor trade in Ireland.
Report. 16 Jan.1918. 1918 Cd.9042 xi. Irish Secretary's Office.

GORDON, Mervyn Henry
Bacteriological studies in the pathology and preventive control of cerebro-spinal fever among the forces during 1915 and 1916. Jan.1917. (S.R.S., no.3) Medical Research Committee.

Report of an investigation of the ventilation of the House of Commons and recommendations. Dec.1904. 1905 Cd.2404 lxii. Works and Buildings Commissioners.

Report on an experimental investigation in relation to mumps or epidemic parotitis. 21 April 1914. (Rep.Pub.Health & Med.Subj., no.96) Local Government Board.

Report on the micrococcus of epidemic cerebro-spinal meningitis and its identification. 18 Feb.1907. Local Government Board.

Studies of the viruses of vaccinia and variola. 28 Aug.1925. (S.R.S., no.98) Medical Research Council.

GORE, Charles, *Bishop of Oxford 1911-1919*
The League of Nations: the opportunity of the Church. 1918. Ministry of Information.

GORE-BROWNE, Frank
Rates advisory committee.
Report on coastwise shipping and exceptional rates. 31 May 1921. 1921 Cmd.1372 xv. Ministry of Transport.

Report on the general revision of railway rates and charges. 22 Dec.1920. 1920 Cmd.1098 xxiv. Proceedings, etc. 1920. Ministry of Transport.

Report on the interim revision of railway rates, and charges. 23 July 1920. 1920 Cmd.857 xxiv.
Part 2: goods. 30 July 1920. 1920 Cmd.886 xxiv.
Part 3: fares lower than ordinary and services free or at nominal charges. 18 Nov.1920. 1921 Cmd.1148 xvii. Ministry of Transport.

Rates advisory committee.
Report on the navigation of the River Thames. 11 March 1920. 1920 Cmd.677 xxv. Ministry of Transport.

Report on the rates for conveyance of goods, minerals and merchandise. 16 Dec.1919. 1920 Cmd.525 xxiv. Ministry of Transport.

Report on recommendations on demurrage. 26 Nov.1919. 1920 Cmd.526 xxiv. Ministry of Transport.

Report on regulations for the new general railway classification of goods by merchandise trains. 17 Nov.1921. Ministry of Transport.

Gorell, *Lord. SEE:* Barnes, H. G. *2nd Baron*
Barnes, J. G., *1st Baron*
Barnes, R. G., *3rd Baron*

GORING, Charles
The English convict, a statistical study. Aug.1912.
Schedule of measurements and general anthropological data. July 1913. Home Office.

GORST, Eldon
Report on the system of British commercial attachés and commercial agents. 6 July 1907. (Commercial, no.8, 1907) 1907 Cd.3610 lxxxvii. Foreign Office.

GOSCHEN, George Joachin, *2nd Viscount*
Departmental committee on the registration of accountants.
Report. 31 July 1930. 1929/30 Cmd.3645 viii.
Minutes of evidence. 1930. Board of Trade.

Departmental committee on trade marks.
Report. 20 April 1934. 1933/4 Cmd.4568 xv.
Minutes of evidence. 1934. Board of Trade. Ministry of Labour.

Joint committee on the petition of the state of Western Australia.
Report, proceedings and speeches by counsel. 22 May 1935. 1934/5 (88) vi. House of Commons.

National advisory council for juvenile employment (England and Wales).
First report. Sept.1929.
Second report: age of entry into unemployment insurance. 1 Nov.1929. 1929/30 Cmd.3427 xv.
Third report: provision of courses of instruction for unemployed boys and girls. 19 July 1930. 1929/30 Cmd.3638 xv.
Fourth report: hours of employment of boys and

GOSCHEN, George Joachin, *2nd Viscount* (continued)
girls in "unregulated occupations". 13 Jan.1932.
Fifth report: provision of courses of instruction for unemployed boys and girls. 20 Jan.1934.
Sixth report: operation of the scheme of authorised courses of instruction for unemployed boys and girls. 26 April 1937. Ministry of Labour.

National advisory councils for juvenile employment (England, Wales and Scotland).
Joint report on the organisation and development of the vocational guidance service in Great Britain. 29 May 1934. Ministry of Labour.

GOSCHEN, William Henry Neville
Committee on housing finance.
Interim report. 27 Nov.1919. 1919 Cmd.444 xxii. (no further reports identified) Treasury.

Committee on schemes of assistance to necessitous areas.
Report. 19 March 1926. 1926 Cmd.2645 xiv. Treasury.

GOSLING, Harry
Peace: how to get and keep it. 1917. Ministry of Information.

GOUGH, C. M.
The use of asphalt mastic for roofing. Oct.1936. (B.R.B. special rep., no.25) Department of Scientific and Industrial Research.

Gower, G. G. S. L. *SEE:* Leveson-Gower, G. G. S.

GOWERS, Ernest Arthur
Coal mines reorganisation commission.
Report. 28 Nov.1933. 1933/4 Cmd.4468 xiv.
Report. 13 Jan.1936. 1935/6 Cmd.5069 xiv.
Mines Department.

Report on an enquiry into the reasons why certain insured persons became deposit contributors. 23 June 1913. 1913 Cd.7034 xxxvi. National Health Insurance Joint Committee.

GRAHAM, Maxtone
Report by accountants on the costs of production and financial results in the shale industry carried on by Scottish Oils, Ltd. 29 Oct.1925. 1924/5 Cmd.2538 xv. Board of Trade.

GRAHAM-CAMPBELL, Rollo Frederick
Committee on the regulation of street trading in the Metropolitan police district.
Report. 18 Feb.1922. 1922 Cmd.1624 x. Home Office.

GRAHAM-SMITH, George Stuart
The changes produced in meat extracts by the bacterium *staphylococcus aureus*. March 1928. (F.I.B. special rep., no.31) Department of Scientific and Industrial Research.

The control of reaction in cultures and enzymic digests. March 1928. (F.I.B. special rep., no.32) Department of Scientific and Industrial Research.

GRAHAME, George Dixon
Report on the 55th session of the Council of the League of Nations. 1 July 1929. (Misc., no.4, 1929) 1929/30 Cmd.3377 xxxii. Foreign Office.

Granard, *Lord. SEE:* Forbes, B.A.W.P.H., *8th Earl*

GRANT, E. C. H.
Report on Swiss rifle ranges. 1901. 1901 Cd.523 xl. War Office.

GRANT, Henry Clark
Barley survey. March 1933. (E.M.B.62) Empire Marketing Board.

Grant-Wilson, J. S. *SEE:* Wilson, J. S. G.

GRAY, Alexander
Court of inquiry concerning disputes between plasterers and joiners in Scotland.
Report. 25 Aug.1937. 1936/7 Cmd.5554 xii. Ministry of Labour.

GRAY, James Hunter
Departmental committee on gas incombustibles.
Report. 12 Aug.1921. 1921 Cmd.1492 xii. Board of Trade.

GRAY, John
A study of nephritis and allied lesions. 14 Feb.1933. (S.R.S., no.178) Medical Research Council.

GRAY, Thomas
Investigation as to coking coal in Scotland; tables of analyses. Aug.1918. Ministry of Munitions.

GREAVES, Richard Henry
Chromium steels. Sept.1935. Department of Scientific and Industrial Research.

GREEN, H. L.
Physical methods for the estimation of the dust hazard in industry. 18 Jan.1935. (S.R.S., no.199) Medical Research Council.

GREENE, Wilfred Arthur
Committee on restraint of trade.
Report. 7 July 1931. Board of Trade.

Company law amendment committee.
Report. 8 May 1926. 1926 Cmd.2657 ix.
Minutes of evidence. 1925. Board of Trade.

United Kingdom sugar industry inquiry committee.
Report. 13 March 1935. 1934/5 Cmd.4871 xi. Ministry of Agriculture and Fisheries.

GREENHILL, Alfred George
Notes on dynamics. 2nd ed. Oct.1908. War Office.

GREENLY, Edward
The geology of Anglesey. 2 vols. April 1919. (Mem. Geol.Surv.) Geological Survey.

GREENWALD, H.P.
Coal dust explosions. The effect of release of pressure on their development. Sept.1925. (S.M.R.B. Paper no.14) Mines Department.

GREENWELL, Allan
The application of stone dust in coal mines. July 1923. (S.H.R.B. Paper, no.2) Mines Department.

GREENWOOD, A. C.
Advisory committee on nutrition.
Memorandum on the criticism and improvement of diets. 5 Dec.1931. Ministry of Health.

Report on diets in poor law children's homes. 30 Nov.1931. Ministry of Health.

Committee on miners' nystagmus.
Third report. 22 Sept.1932. (S.R.S., no.176) Medical Research Council. *For previous reports SEE:* Haldane, J. S.

Diet and cancer. Oct.1926. (R.Pub.Health & Med. Subj., no.36) Ministry of Health.

The incidence of industrial accidents upon individuals with special reference to multiple accidents. Aug.1919. (I.R.B.Rep., no.4) Medical Research Committee.

GREENWOOD, A. C. (continued)
An inquiry into the composition of dietaries, with special reference to munition workers. 31 Dec.1917. (S.R.S., no.13) Medical Research Committee.

An inquiry into the prevalence and aetiology of tuberculosis among industrial workers, with special reference to female munition workers. 18 Oct.1918. (S.R.S., no.22) Medical Research Committee.

Postgraduate medical education committee.
> Report. 23 Jan.1930. 1929/30 Cmd.3535 xiv. Ministry of Health.

A report on the natural duration of cancer. June 1926. (Rep.Pub.Health & Med.Subj., no.33) Ministry of Health.

Report on the causes of wastage of labour in munitions factories employing women. May 1918. (S.R.S. no.16) Medical Research Committee.

GREENWOOD, Arthur
Standing committee on trusts.
> Report by a sub-committee on iron and steel products. 22 March 1921. 1921 Cmd.1268 xvi. Board of Trade.

GREENWOOD, Hamar
Departmental committee on the medical service of the Metropolitan police.
> Report. 13 Aug.1919. 1919 Cmd.336 xxvii. Home Office.

GREER, Arthur
Foreign judgments (reciprocal enforcement) committee.
> Report. 12 Dec.1932. 1932/3 Cmd.4213 x. Lord Chancellor's Office.

GREER, Harry
Merchandise marks committee.
> Report. 7 June 1920. 1920 Cmd.760 xxi.
> Minutes of evidence. 1920. Board of Trade.

GREGORSON, John A.
Report of delegation of the Economic Advisory Council on the industrial conditions in the iron and steel industries in France, Belgium, Luxembourg, Germany and Czechoslovakia. 16 April 1930. 1929/30 Cmd.3601 xii. Treasury.

GREGORY, Holman
Committee on suspension of retired pay of naval officers when recalled for service in war.
> Report. 24 July 1924. Admiralty.

Court of inquiry concerning the dock labour dispute, 1924.
> Report. 21 Feb.1924. 1924 Cmd.2056 xi. Ministry of Labour.

Court of inquiry concerning railway shopmen of the Great Northern section of the London and North Eastern Railway.
> Report. 15 April 1924. 1924 Cmd.2113 xi.
> Report. 8 Feb.1926. 1926 Cmd.2583 xi. Ministry of Labour.

Departmental committee on workmen's compensation for injuries.
> Report. 7 July 1920. 1920 Cmd.816 xxvi.
> Evidence, vol.1. 30 July to 9 December 1919; vol.2. 10 December 1919 to 28 May 1920. 1920 Cmd.908, Cmd.909 xxvi. Home Office.

Royal commission on unemployment insurance.
> First report. 1 June 1931. 1930/1 Cmd.3872 xvii.
> Minutes of evidence. 40 parts. 1931-2.
> Appendices. 9 parts. 1931-2.

Guide and index to the evidence. 1933.
> Final report. 27 Oct.1932. 1931/2 Cmd.4185 xiii.

GREIG, E. F.
Some problems connected with the determination of the fineness of coal dust. Aug.1926. (S.M.R.B. Paper no.25) Mines Department.

GREIG, Robert Blyth
Report on farm and agricultural schools and colleges in France, Germany and Belgium. Nov.1912. (Educational pamphlets, no.25) Board of Education.

GRENFELL, William Henry, *1st Baron Desborough*
Committee on the police service of England, Wales and Scotland.
> Report, part 1. 1 July 1919. 1919 Cmd.253 xxvii.
> Part 2. 1 Jan.1920. 1920 Cmd.574 xxii.
> Evidence. 1920 Cmd.874 xxii. Home Office.

Committee on the standard conditions of service in the police forces of Great Britain.
> Report. 4 March 1924. 1924 Cmd.2086 xii. Home Office.

Freshwater fisheries committee.
> Interim report. 1 Aug.1917.
> Second report: eel fisheries. 21 Dec.1917.
> Final report. 23 March 1920. Board of Agriculture and Fisheries.

GRESLEY, Herbert Nigel
Steering gear committee.
> Report. 3 March 1936. 1935/6 Cmd.5120 xiii.
> Second report. 29 June 1936. 1935/6 Cmd.5225 xiii. Board of Trade.

GRETTON, John
Committee of inquiry into government printing establishments.
> Report. 2 March 1927. 1927 Cmd.2828 ix.
> Minutes of evidence. 1927. Treasury.

Select committee on the conduct of a member.
> Special report. 5 Nov.1939. 1939/40 (172) iii.
> Special report. 17 Nov.1939. 1939/40 (177) iii.
> Report, proceedings, evidence and appendices. 18 Dec.1940. 1940/1 (5) ii. House of Commons.

GREY, Albert Henry George, *4th Earl*
Committee on the existing conditions of canteens and regimental institutions.
> Report and appendices. 3 Oct.1902. 1903 Cd.1424 x.
> Minutes of evidence. 1903 Cd.1494 x. War Office.

GREY, Edward, *1st Viscount Grey of Fallodon*
Great Britain's measures against German trade; a speech. 26 Jan.1916. Ministry of Information.

Naval reserves committee.
> Report. 9 Jan.1903. 1903 Cd.1491 xl. War Office.

Why Britain is in the war and what she hopes from the future; a speech. 23 Oct.1916. Ministry of Information.

GRICE, C. S. W.
The estimation of firedamp; flame caps. May 1927. (S.M.R.B. Paper no.37) Mines Department.

Firedamp explosions within closed vessels: "pressure piling". March 1928. (S.M.R.B. Paper No.49) Mines Department.

Flameproof electrical apparatus for use in coal mines.

GRICE. C. S. W. (continued)
Second report: perforated plate protection. Feb.1926. (S.M.R.B. Paper no.21) Mines Department.

Mine rescue apparatus: the S.M.R.B. gas mask. July 1929. (S.M.R.B. Paper no.57) Mines Department.

GRICE, J. Watson
The resources of the Empire. 1917. Ministry of Information.

GRIFFITH, Arthur Stanley
Investigation of viruses obtained from cases of human tuberculosis (other than lupus). June 1910. (Vol.1, Appendix to final report of Royal Commission on human and animal tuberculosis) 1911 Cd.5790 xlii. Royal Commission on Tuberculosis.

Investigation of viruses obtained from cases of lupus. July 1910. (Vol.2, Appendix to the final report of the Royal Commission on human and animal tuberculosis). 1911 Cd.5791 xliii. Royal Commission on Tuberculosis.

Studies of protection against tuberculosis; results with B.C.G. vaccine in monkeys. 21 Jan.1931. (S.R.S., no.152) Medical Research Council.

GRIFFITH, Ellis Jones
Departmental committee on compensation for industrial diseases.
Report. 21 July 1913. 1913 Cd.6956 xviii.
Minutes of evidence. 1913 Cd.6957 xviii. Home Office.
Departmental committee on reformatory and industrial schools.
Report. 4 May 1913. 1913 Cd.6838 xxxix.
Evidence. 1913 Cd.6839 xxxix. Home Office.

Select committee on employment of military in cases of disturbances.
Report and proceedings. 25 Aug.1914. 1914 (454) vii. House of Commons.

GRIFFITH, Frederick
Investigations into the tuberculosis occurring naturally in certain animals other than man; and modification experiments. Dec.1908. (Vol.4, appendix to final report of the Royal Commission on human and animal tuberculosis). 1911 Cd.5894 xliv.

Preliminary report on the pathology of bovine actinomycosis. 2 June 1915. (Rep.Pub.Health & Med.Subj., no.107) Local Government Board.

Report on localised tuberculosis in swine. 9 Feb.1914. (Rep.Pub.Health & Med.Subj., no.91) Local Government Board.

GRIFFITH, John Purser
Irish peat inquiry committee.
Report on the winning, preparation and utilisation of peat for fuel and other purposes. 26 Feb.1918. Fuel Research Board, Department of Scientific and Industrial Research.

Water power resources committee. Ireland sub-committee.
Report. 6 Dec.1920. Board of Trade.

GRIFFITH-BOSCAWEN, Arthur Sackville Trevor
Departmental committee on the fruit industry of Great Britain.
Report. 9 June 1905. 1905 Cd.2589 xx.
Minutes of evidence, appendices and index. 1906 Cd.2719 xxiv. Department of Agriculture and Fisheries.

Inter-departmental committee on road safety among school children.
Report. 15 Jan.1936. Board of Education and Ministry of Transport.

Report on the inter-allied conference for the study of professional re-education, etc., for soldiers and sailors disabled in the war, Paris, 8-12 May 1917. 4 June 1917. Ministry of Pensions.

Royal commission on transport.
First report: The control of traffic on roads. 19 July 1929. 1929/30 Cmd.3365 xvii.
Second report: The licensing and regulation of public service vehicles. 18 Oct.1929. 1929/30 Cmd.3416 xvii.
Final report: The co-ordination and development of transport. 19 Dec.1930. 1930/1 Cmd.3751 xvii.
Minutes of evidence. 3 vols. 1929-30. Ministry of Transport.

Transport advisory council.
Report on accidents to cyclists. June 1938. Ministry of Transport.

Report on periods of validity of carriers' licences. 16 Dec.1937. Ministry of Transport.

Report on proposals of the main line railway companies on the conveyance of merchandise by rail. 24 March 1939. Ministry of Transport.

Report on service and rates. 22 July 1937. Ministry of Transport.

Report on service and rates (coastwise shipping). 7 July 1938. Ministry of Transport.

GRIFFITHS, Edgar
The handling and transport of fish. 1925. (F.I.B. special rep., no.25) Department of Scientific and Industrial Research.

GRIFFITHS, Ezer
Heat transmission through walls, concretes and plasters. July 1923. (B.R.B. special rep., no.7) Department of Scientific and Industrial Research.

GRIGG, Edward
Reorganisation commission.
Report on milk. 27 Jan.1933. (Economic series no.38) Ministry of Agriculture and Fisheries.

GRIGG, Richard
Report on the conditions and prospects of British trade in Canada. 1 Dec.1907. 1908 Cd.3868 lxxi. Board of Trade.

Report on conditions and prospects of British trade in Newfoundland. 24 Feb.1908. 1908 Cd.4153 lxxiii. Board of Trade.

GRIMSHAW, H. C.
The ignition of firedamp by coal-mining explosives.
1: gallery experiments. Jan.1931 (S.M.R.B. Paper no.69)
2: sheathed explosives. Oct.1934. (S.M.R.B. paper no.90) Mines Department.

GRINDLE, Gilbert Edmund Augustine
Inter-departmental committee on income tax in the colonies.
Report. Dec.1922. 1923 Cmd.1788 x. Colonial Office.

GRINDLEY, C. G.
Psychological factors in peripheral vision. 31 Oct.1931 (S.R.S., no.163) Medical Research Council.

GROVE, Coleridge
Committee on promotion to colonel and general.
Report. 29 Jan.1906. 1906 Cd.2995 lxvii. War Office.

GROVES, A. W.
Manganese. 1938. (Rep.Min.Ind.) Imperial Institute.

GUEDALLA, Herbert
Departmental committee on artificial limbs.
Report. 20 May 1919. Ministry of Pensions.

GUEST, Ivor Churchill, *Viscount Wimbourne*
Committee on the extension of medical benefit under the National Insurance Act to Ireland.
Report. 18 July 1913. 1913 Cd.6963 xxxvii.
Minutes of evidence, *etc.* 1913 Cd.7039 xxxvii. Treasury.

Report on recruiting in Ireland. 14 Jan.1916. 1914/6 Cd.8168 xxxix. War Office.

Royal commission on coast erosion and the reclamation of tidal lands in the United Kingdom.
Vol.1, part 1: First report. 1 Aug.1907. 1907 Cd.3683 xxxiv.
Vol.1, part 2: Minutes of evidence and appendices. 1907 Cd.3684 xxxiv.
Vol.2, part 1: Second report. 4 Jan.1909. 1909 Cd.4460 xiv.
Vol.2, part 2: Minutes of evidence and appendices. 1909 Cd.4461 xiv.
Vol.3, part 1: Third and final report. 31 May 1911. 1911 Cd.5708 xiv.
Vol.3, part 2: Minutes of evidence and appendices accompanying the third report. 1911 Cd.5709 xiv.

GUILLEBAUD, W. H.
Rate of growth of conifers in the British Isles. June 1920. (Bull., no.3) Forestry Commission.

GUINNESS, Walter Edward, *1st Baron Moyne*
Departmental committee on cinematograph films.
Report. 11 Nov.1936. 1936/7 Cmd.5320 ix.
Minutes of evidence, appendices and index. 2 vols. 1936. Board of Trade.

Departmental committee on housing.
Report. 19 July 1933. 1932/3 Cmd.4397 xiii. Ministry of Health.

Report on certain financial questions in Kenya. 17 May 1932. 1931/2 Cmd.4093 vi. Colonial Office.

Royal commission on the University of Durham.
Report. 22 Jan.1935. 1934/5 Cmd.4815 viii.

West India Royal commission.
Recommendations. 16 Feb.1940. 1939/40 Cmd.6174 v.
Report on agriculture, fisheries, forestry and veterinary matters. 21 Dec.1939. 1944/5 Cmd.6608 vi.
Report. 21 Dec.1939. 1944/5 Cmd.6607 vi. Colonial Office.

GULLY, William Court, *1st Viscount Selby*
Royal commission on motor cars.
Vol.1: Report. July 1906. 1906 Cd.3080 xlviii.
Vol.2: Minutes of evidence, appendices and index. 1906 Cd.3081 xlviii.

Royal commission on vivisection.
First report. 26 Jan.1907. 1907 Cd.3325 xli.
Appendix: minutes of evidence, October to December 1906. 1907 Cd.3326 xli.
Second report. 15 April 1907. 1907 Cd.3461 xli.
Appendix: minutes of evidence, February to March, 1907. 1907 Cd.3462 xli.

Third report. 29 July 1907. 1908 Cd.3756 lvii.
Appendix: minutes of evidence. 1908 Cd.3757 lvii.
Fourth report. Dec.1907. 1908 Cd.3954 lvii.
Appendix: minutes of evidence. 1908 Cd.3955 lvii.
Fifth report. 28 May 1908. 1908 Cd.4146 lvii.
Appendix: minutes of evidence, appendices and index. 1908 Cd.4147 lvii.
Sixth report. 29 Feb.1912. 1912/3 Cd.6112 xlviii.
Appendix: further papers, 1906-10. 1912/3 Cd.6113 xlviii.
Final report. 1 March 1912. 1912/3 Cd.6114 xlviii.

GUNN, W.
The geology of Belford, Holy Island and the Farne Islands. (Sheet 4) 25 Nov.1899. (Mem.Geol.Surv.) Geological Survey.

The geology of north Arran, south Bute and the Cumbraes with parts of Ayrshire and Kintyre. (Sheet 21) 28 March 1903. (Mem.Geol.Surv., Scotl.) Geological Survey, Scotland.

GUNN, William Cooper
The bed bug; prevention of house infestation. A study for public health purposes. Aug.1933. Department of Health for Scotland.

GUPPY, Eileen M.
Chemical analyses of igneous rocks, metamorphic rocks and minerals. 2 March 1931. (Mem.Geol. Surv.) Geological Survey.

GUTHRIE, Charles John, *Lord Guthrie,*
Departmental committee on house-letting in Scotland.
Vol.1: Report. 20 Aug.1907. 1907 Cd.3715 xxxvii.
Vol.2: Minutes of evidence and appendices with index. 1908 Cd.3792 xlvii. Scottish Office.

GWATKIN, H. M.
Britain's case against Germany; a letter to a neutral. 1917. Ministry of Information.


HACKING, Douglas Hewitt
Committee on the conditions of licensing, *etc.,* of taxicabs.
Report. 16 Dec.1927. Home Office.

HADOW, William Henry
Consultative committee of the Board of Education.
Report on books in public elementary schools. 26 July 1928. Board of Education.

Report on differentiation of the curriculum for boys and girls in secondary schools. 29 Sept.1922. Board of Education.

Report on education of the adolescent. 28 Oct.1926. Board of Education.

Report on infant and nursery schools. 27 July 1933. Board of Education.

Report on psychological tests of educable capacity and their possible use in the public system of education. 27 March 1924. Board of Education.

Report on the primary school. 28 Nov.1930. Board of Education.

Departmental committee on qualifications, recruitment and training of local government officers.
Report. 10 Jan.1934. Ministry of Health.

HAGGARD, Henry Rider
Report on the Salvation Army colonies in the United States and at Hadleigh, England. June 1905. 1905 Cd.2562 liii. Colonial Office.

HAGGARD, William Henry Doveton
Report on a journey, October 1912, in the South of Brazil. March 1913. 1913 Cd.6666 lxix. Foreign Office *and* Board of Trade.

HAIG, Douglas *1st Earl*
King's Roll national council on the employment of disabled ex-servicemen.
Interim report. 17 July 1923. 1923 Cmd.1919 xii, pt.1. (no further published.) Ministry of Labour.

HAILEY, Malcolm, *1st Baron*
Conference on air raid shelters.
Report. 6 April 1939. 1938/9 Cmd.6006 ix. Lord Privy Seal's Office.

Hailsham, *Lord. SEE:* Hogg, D. M., *1st Viscount*

HAINES, R. B.
Microbiology in the preservation of animal tissues. Oct.1937. (F.I.B. special rep., no.45) Department of Scientific and Industrial Research.

Microbiology in the preservation of the egg. March 1939. (F.I.B. special rep., no.47) Department of Scientific and Industrial Research.

The storage of meat in small refrigerators. Aug.1933. (F.I.B. special rep. no.43) Department of Scientific and Industrial Research.

HALDANE, D.
The economic geology of the central coalfield. Area 1: Kilsyth and Kirkintilloch. 27 July 1937. (Mem. Geol.Surv., Scotl.) Geological Survey, Scotland.

The economic geology of the central coalfield. Area 3: Bo'ness and Linlithgow. 2 Aug.1932. (Mem.Geol. Surv., Scotl.) Geological Survey, Scotland.

The economic geology of the Fife coalfields. Area 1: Dunfermline and west Fife. 23 Oct.1930. (Mem. Geol.Surv.Scotl.) Geological Survey, Scotland.

The economic geology of the Stirling and Clackmannan coalfield. 25 Nov.1931. (Mem.Geol. Surv., Scotl.) Geological Survey, Scotland.

HALDANE, John Scott
Departmental committee on ventilation of factories and workshops.
First report. 15 Aug.1902. 1902 Cd.1302 xii.
Second report. 17 May 1907. 1907 Cd.3552 x.
Appendix. 1907 Cd.3553 x. Home Office.

Effects of inhaling dusts applicable for stone-dusting in coal mines. 23 July 1915. (Seventh report of the Explosions in Mines Committee.) 1914/6 Cd.8122 xxi. Home Office.

Miners' nystagmus committee.
First report. 14 Dec.1921. (S.R.S., no.65)
Second report. July 1923. (S.R.S., no.80)
Medical Research Council. *(For third report see Greenwood, M.)*

Report on an outbreak of ankylostomiasis in a Cornish mine. 24 Nov.1902. 1902 Cd.1318 xvii. Home Office.

Report on ankylostomiasis in Westphalian collieries. Nov.1903. 1904 Cd.1843 xiii. Home Office.

Report on the destruction of rats and disinfection on shipboard. 10 Nov.1904. (Rep.Med.Insp., no.201) Local Government Board.

Report on the health of Cornish miners. April 1904. 1904 Cd.2091 xiii. Home Office.

HALDANE, Richard Burdon, *1st Viscount Haldane of Cloan*
Advisory committee on university colleges (Great Britain) (Grant in aid).
First, second and third reports. 19 Dec.1904, 23 Feb.1905. 1905 Cd.2422 lx. Treasury.

Coal conservation committee.
Interim report on electric power supply in Great Britain. 17 April 1918. 1917/8 Cd.8880 xviii.
Final report. 23 Jan.1918. 1918 Cd.9084 vii. Ministry of Reconstruction.

Committee on the education and training of officers.
Report. 28 June 1923. 1924 Cmd.2031 vii. War Office.

Departmental committee on the property and endowments of the Church of Scotland.
Report. 4 April 1923. Scottish Office.

Departmental committee on the Royal College of Science (including the Royal School of Mines).
Preliminary report. 20 Feb.1905. 1905 Cd.2610 lxi.
Final report. Vol.1. 8 Jan.1906. 1906 Cd.2872 xxxi.
Minutes of evidence. Vol.2. 1906 Cd.2956 xxxi. Board of Education.

Machinery of government committee.
Report. 14 Dec.1918. 1918 Cd.9230 xii. Ministry of Reconstruction.

Memorandum by the Army Council on the existing Army system and on the present state of the military forces in the United Kingdom. 31 May 1909. 1909 Cd.4611 li. War Office.

Memorandum on Army reorganisation. 30 July 1906. 1906 Cd.2993 lxvii. War Office.

Royal commission on university education in London.
First report. 21 April 1910. 1910 Cd.5165 xxiii.
Minutes of evidence, July 1909—April 1910 with appendices and index. 1910 Cd.5166 xxiii.
Second report. 2 Feb.1911. 1911 Cd.5527 xx.
Appendix: minutes of evidence, June—November 1910. 1911 Cd.5528 xx.
Third report. 4 Oct.1911. 1911 Cd.5910 xx.
Appendix: minutes of evidence November 1910—July 1911. 1911 Cd.5911 xx.
Fourth report. 15 Dec.1911. 1912/3 Cd.6015 xxii.
Fifth report. 26 June 1912. 1912/3 Cd.6311 xxii.
Appendix: minutes of evidence, October 1911 to January 1912, with appendices and index. 1912/3 Cd.6312 xxii.
Final report. 27 March 1913. 1913 Cd.6717 xl.
Minutes of evidence, February to December 1912, with appendices and index. 1913 Cd.6718 xl.

Royal commission on university education in Wales.
First report. 8 March 1917. 1917/8 Cd.8500 xii.
Appendix: evidence, October to November 1916, appendices and index. 1917/8 Cd.8507 xii.
Second report. 20 July 1917. 1917/8 Cd.8698 xii.
Appendix: evidence, December 1916 to March 1917, appendices and index. 1917/8 Cd.8699 xii.
Final report. 6 Feb.1918. 1918 Cd.8991 xiv.
Appendix: evidence, March to June 1917, appendices and index. 1918 Cd.8993 xiv.

HALDANE-DUNCAN, Robert Adam Philips, *3rd Earl Camperdown*
Committee on mercantile cruisers.
Report. 9 July 1902. 1902 Cd.1379 xcii. Admiralty.

Joint select committee of the House of Lords and House of Commons on housing of the working classes.
Report, proceedings, minutes of evidence, appendix and index. 4 Aug.1902. 1902 (325) v. House of Commons.

Halifax, *Lord. SEE:* Wood, E. F. L., *3rd Viscount*

HALL, Arthur John
Sub-committee on the Sheffield outbreak of epidemic encephalitis in 1924.
Report. 20 Sept.1926. (S.R.S., no.108) Medical Research Council.

HALL, G. A.
The system of education in the Federated Malay States. 14 Dec.1912. (Imperial education conference papers) Board of Education.

The system of education in the Straits Settlements. 12 Dec.1912. (Imperial education conference papers) Board of Education.

HALL, Mordaunt
Some naval yarns. 1917. Ministry of Information.

HALLIBURTON, William Dobson
Committee on the causes of dental disease.
Report: The structure of teeth in relation to dental disease. Nov.1922. (S.R.S., no.70) Medical Research Council.
*(For further reports see:* Bennett, N. G.

HALLIDAY, James Lorimer
An inquiry into the relationship between housing conditions and the incidence of fatality of measles. 25 Jan.1928. (S.R.S., no.120) Medical Research Council.

HALLIMOND, A. F.
Iron ores: bedded ores of England and Wales. Petrography and chemistry. 4 Dec.1924. (Special reports on the mineral resources of Great Britain, vol.29) (Mem.Geol.Surv.) Geological Survey.

Halsbury, *Lord. SEE:* Giffard, H. S., *1st Earl of Halsbury*

HALSE, Edward
Antimony ores. 1925. (Mono.Min.Resour.) Imperial Institute.

Cobalt ores. 1924. (Mono.Min.Resour.) Imperial Institute.

Mercury ores. 1923. (Mono.Min.Resour.) Imperial Institute.

HALSEY, Lionel
Committee on pay, allowances and pensions of the Royal Navy and Royal Marines.
Report of the sub-committee on the pay of officers. 9 May 1919. 1919 Cmd.270 xxxiii. Admiralty.

Hambleden, *Lord. SEE:* Smith, W. F. D., *2nd Viscount Hambledon*

HAMBLING, Herbert
Civil air transport subsidies committee.
Report on government financial assistance to civil air transport companies. 15 Feb.1923. 1923 Cmd.1811 ix. Air Ministry.

HAMBLY, W. D.
Preliminary notes on atmospheric conditions in boot and shoe factories. March 1921. (I.H.R.B., Rep., no.11) Medical Research Council.

HAMILL, John Molyneux
Commission on the conditions of production of milk in the Netherlands and Denmark.
Report. 18 Oct.1927. 1927 Cmd.3004 xi. Ministry of Health.

Diet in relation to normal nutrition. Sept.1921. (Rep.Pub.Health and Med.Subj., no.9) Ministry of Health.

Notes of the pasteurisation of milk. July 1923. (Rep. Pub.Health & Med.Subj., no.17) Ministry of Health.

Report on "facing" and other methods of preparing rice for sale. 21 May 1909. (Rep.Pub.Health Med. Subj., no.4) Local Government Board.

Report on the bleaching of flour and the addition of so-called "improvers" to flour. 3 April 1911. (Rep. Pub.Health & Med.Subj., no.49) (Food reports, no.12) 1911 Cd.5613 xxxii. Local Government Board.

Report on the nutritive value of bread made from different varieties of wheat flour. Aug.1911. (Rep. Pub.Health & Med.Subj., no.55) (Food reports, no.14) 1911 Cd.5831 xxxii. Local Government Board.

Report on the preparation and sale of vinegar, in relation to the administration of the Sale of Food and Drugs Acts. 6 Jan.1908. (Rep.Insp.Foods, no.5) Local Government Board.

Report on the presence of calcium sulphate in baking powder and self-raising flour. 3 April 1911. (Rep.Pub.Health & Med.Subj., no.46) (Food reports, no.13) 1911 Cd.5614 xxxii. Local Government Board.

Report on the use of preservatives in cream. 11 Aug. 1909. (Rep.Pub.Health & Med.Subj., no.13) Local Government Board.

HAMILTON, David James
Departmental committee on louping-ill and braxy (diseases of sheep).
Part 1: General report. 10 April 1906. 1906 Cd.2932 xxiv.
Part 2: Details of investigation. 1906 Cd.2933 xxiv.
Part 3: Summary of suggestions. 1906 Cd.2934 xxiv. Board of Agriculture.

HAMILTON, Edward W.
Departmental committee on the financial aspects of the proposals made by the select committee of the House of Commons of 1899 about the aged deserving poor.
Report. 9 Jan.1900. 1900 Cd.67 x. Local Government Board.

HAMILTON, Frederick Tower
Committee on the conditions of deep water diving.
Report with index, appendices and illustrations. Aug.1907. Admiralty.

HAMILTON, George Francis, *Lord.*
Royal commission on the operations of war in Mesopotamia.
Report and appendices. 17 May 1917. 1917/8 Cd.8610 xvi.

Royal commission on the poor laws and relief of distress.
Report. 4 Feb.1909. 1909 Cd.4499 xxxvii.
Report on Ireland. 14 April 1909. 1909 Cd.4630 xxxviii.

HAMILTON, George Francis, *Lord.* (continued)

Report on Scotland. 13 Oct.1909. 1909 Cd.4922 xxxviii.

Appendix, vol.1: Evidence mainly of the Officers of the Local Government Board for England and Wales. 1909 Cd.4625 xxxix.

Vol.1A: Appendices to the evidence in Vol.1. 1909 Cd.4626 xxxix.

Vol.1B: Index to Vols.1 and 1A. 1909 Cd.4627 xxxix.

Vol.2: Evidence (with appendices) mainly of London witnesses. 1909 Cd.4684 xl.

Vol.2A: Index to Vol.1. 1909 Cd.4704 xl.

Vol.3: Evidence (with appendices) mainly of critics of the poor law and of witnesses representing poor law and charitable associations. 1909 Cd.4755 xl.

Vol.3A: Index to Vol.3. 1909 Cd.4764 xl.

Vol.4: Evidence (with appendices), oral and written, of the British Medical Association and of witnesses from Liverpool and Manchester districts, West Yorkshire, Midland towns. 1909 Cd.4835 xli.

Vol.4A: Index to Vol.4. 1909 Cd.4836 xli.

Vol.5: Evidence (with appendices), oral and written, of witnesses from South Wales and North Eastern Counties. 1909 Cd.4888 xli.

Vol.5A: Index to Vol.5. 1909 Cd.4889 xli.

Vol.6: Evidence (with appendices) relating to Scotland. 1910 Cd.4978 xlvi.

Vol.6A: Index to Vol.6. 1910 Cd.4982 xlvii.

Vol.7: Evidence (with appendices) containing the evidence from various rural centres in the South Western, Western, and Eastern Counties, from the Parish of Poplar Borough and from the National Conference of Friendly Societies. 1910 Cd.5035 xlvii.

Vol.7A: Index to Appendix, vol.7. 1910 Cd.5036 xlvii.

Vol.8: Unemployment; evidence (with appendices) relating chiefly to the subject of "Unemployment". 1910 Cd.5066 xlviii.

Vol.8A: Index to appendix, Vol.8. 1910 Cd.5067 xlviii.

Vol.9: Unemployment; evidence (with appendices) relating to the subject of Unemployment, *etc.* 1910 Cd.5068 xlix.

Vol.9A: Index to appendix, vol.9. 1910 Cd.5069

Vol.10: Evidence (with appendices) relating to Ireland. 1910 Cd.5070 l.

Vol.10A: Index to appendix, vol.10. 1910 Cd.5071 l.

Vol.11: Miscellaneous papers; communications from Boards of Guardians and Others, *etc.* 1910 Cd.5072 li.

Vol.12: Reports, memoranda, and tables prepared by certain of the Commissioners. 1910 Cd.4983 li..

Vol.13: Diocesan reports on the methods of administering charitable assistance and the extent and intensity of poverty in England and Wales. 1909 Cd.4850 xlii.

Vol.14: Report on the methods and results of the present system of administering indoor and outdoor poor law medical relief in certain Unions in England and Wales, by Dr. McVail. 1909 Cd.4573 xlii.

Vol.15: Report on the administrative relation of charity and the poor law, and the extent and the actual and potential utility of endowed and voluntary charities in England and Scotland, by Mr. A. C. Kay and Mr. H. V. Toynbee. 1909 Cd.4593 xlii.

Vol.16: Reports on the relation of industrial and sanitary conditions to pauperism, by Mr. Steel Maitland and Miss R. E. Squire. 1909 Cd.4653 xliii.

Vol.17: Reports on the effect of outdoor relief on wages, and the conditions of employment, by Mr. Thomas Jones and Miss Williams. 1909 Cd.4690 xliii. (see also Vol.36 in 1910.)

Vol.18: Report on the condition of the children who are in receipt of the various forms of poor law relief in certain Unions in London and in the Provinces, by Dr. Ethel Williams and Miss Longman and Miss Phillips. 1910 Cd.5037 lii.

Vol.19: Report on the effects of employment or assistance given to the unemployed since 1886 as a means of relieving distress outside the poor law in London, and generally throughout England and Wales, by Mr. Cyril Jackson and Rev. J. C. Pringle. 1909 Cd.4795 xliv.

Vol.19A: Report on the effects of employment or assistance given to the unemployed since 1886 as a means of relieving distress outside the poor law in Scotland, by the Rev. J. C. Pringle. 1910 Cd.5073 lii.

Vol.19B: Report on the effects of employment or assistance given to the unemployed since 1886 as a means of relieving distress outside the poor law in Ireland, by Mr. Cyril Jackson. 1909 Cd.4890 xliv.

Vol.20: Report on boy labour in London and certain other towns, by Mr. Cyril Jackson, with a memorandum from the General Post Office on the conditions of employment of telegraph messengers. 1909 Cd.4632 xliv.

Vol.21: Reports on the effect of the refusal of out-relief on the applicants for such relief, by Miss G. Harlock. 1910 Cd.5074 lii.

Vol.22: Report on the overlapping of the work of the voluntary general hospitals with that of poor law medical relief in certain districts of London, by Miss N. B. Roberts. 1909 Cd.4631 xlv.

Vol.23: Report on the condition of the children who are in receipt of the various forms of poor law relief in certain parishes in Scotland, by Dr. C. T. Parsons and Miss Longman and Miss Phillips. 1910 Cd.5075 lii.

Vol.24: Report on a comparison of the physical condition of "ordinary" paupers in certain Scottish poorhouses with that of the able-bodied paupers in certain English workhouses and labour yards, by Dr. C. T. Parsons. 1910 Cd.5076 lii.

Vol.25: Statistical memoranda and tables relating to England and Wales, prepared by the Staff of the Commission and by Government Departments, and others, and actuarial reports. 1910 Cd.5077 liii.

Vol.26: Documents relating more especially to the administration of charities. 1910 Cd.5078 liv.

Vol.27: Replies by distress committees in England and Wales to questions circulated on the subject of the unemployed workmen act, 1905. 1909 Cd.4944 xlv.

Vol.28: Reports of visits to poor law and charitable institutions and to meetings of local authorities in the United Kingdom. 1910 Cd.4974 liv.

Vol.29: Report on the methods of administering charitable assistance and the extent and

HAMILTON, George Francis, *Lord.* (continued)
intensity of poverty in Scotland, prepared by the Committee on Church Interests appointed by the General Assembly of the Church of Scotland. 1910 Cd.5243 liv.
Vol.30: Documents relating specially to Scotland. 1910 Cd.5440 liv.
Vol.31: Statistical memoranda and tables relating to Ireland, *etc.* 1910 Cd.5244 liv.
Vol.32: Report on visits paid by the Foreign Labour Colonies Committee of the Commission to certain institutions in Holland, Belgium, Germany, and Switzerland. 1910 Cd.5199 liv.
Vol.33: Foreign and colonial systems of poor relief, with a memorandum on the relief of famines in India. 1910 Cd.5441 lv.
Vol.34: Alphabetical lists of oral and non-oral witnesses. 1910 Cd.5442 lv.
Vol.35: Index to the report on England and Wales. 1909 Cd.4945 xxxvii.
Vol.36: Some industries employing women paupers; a supplement to appendix, Vol.17, by Miss Constance Williams and Mr. Thomas Jones on the effect of outdoor relief on wages and the conditions of employment for women. 1910 Cd.5200 lv.
Vol.37: General index. 1910 Cd.5443 lv., Pt.II.

HAMILTON, John Andrew, *Baron Sumner*
British cellulose enquiry committee.
Report. 31 July 1919. 1919 Cmd.306 xi. Treasury.

Committee on British and foreign legal procedure and the enforcement of judgments and awards.
Report. May 1919. 1919 Cmd.251 xxiv. Lord Chancellor's Office.

Committee on working classes cost of living.
Report. 23 Oct.1918. 1918 Cd.8980 vii. Treasury.

Departmental committee on state purchase and control of the liquor trade in England and Wales.
Report. 31 Oct.1917. 1918 Cd.9042 xi. Home Office.

Report of a public inquiry held under the Education Acts at Swansea, 31 July and 1 August 1908. 30 Sept.1908. Board of Education.

Report of a public inquiry on Oxford Street (Church of England) School, Swansea. 30 Sept.1908. 1909 Cd.4542 xviii. Board of Education, Welsh Department.

Royal commission on compensation for suffering and damage by enemy action.
First report. 22 Jan.1923. 1923 Cmd.1798 x.
Final report. 26 Feb.1924. 1924 Cmd.2066 ix.

Select committee on peerages in abeyance.
Report, proceedings, evidence and documents. 1 Dec.1926. 1926 (H.L.190) vi. House of Lords.

HAMMOND, Frederick Dawson
Report on the Nyasaland railways and proposed Zambesi bridge. 31 May 1927. (Colonial, no.27) Colonial Office.

HAMMOND, John
Report on cattle-breeding in Jamaica and Trinidad. Aug.1932. (E.M.B. 58) Empire Marketing Board.

HAMMOND: Laurie
Committee on the delimitation of constituencies in India.
Vol.1: Report. 23 Jan.1936. 1935/6 Cmd.5699 ix.

Vol.2: Proposals for delimitation. 1935/6 Cmd.5100 ix.
Vol.3: Selections from evidence. 1932. India Office.

Report on the delimitation of constituencies in Burma. 23 Jan.1936. 1935/6 Cmd.5101 ix. India Office.

HAMMOND, S. A.
Education in the Windward and Leeward Islands. Report of the education commissioners. 1938. (Colonial, no.164) Colonial Office.

HANBURY, Robert William
Joint select committee of the House of Lords and the House of Commons on the Queen Anne's Bounty Board.
Report, proceedings, minutes of evidence, appendix and index. 22 July 1901. 1901 (276) vii. House of Commons.

HANCOCK, George Charles
Report on outbreak of dysentery in the urban district of Lynton, Devon. July 1923. (Rep.Pub.Health & Med.Subj., no.20) Ministry of Health.

Report on an outbreak of illness at Poplar suspected to be due to pollution of the water supply. March 1927. (Rep.Pub.Health & Med.Subj., no.41) Ministry of Health.

Report on the composition of commoner British wines and cordials (alcoholic and non-alcoholic). April 1924. (Rep.Pub.Health & Med.Subj., no.24) Ministry of Health.

Report on the occurrence of glass fragments in foods packed in glass containers. Jan.1927. (Rep.Pub.Health & Med.Subj., no.37) Ministry of Health.

Report on the sanitary conditions of the Borough of Haverfordwest, and on the recent prevalence of enteric fever therein. 21 July 1906. (Rep.Med.Insp., no.239) Local Government Board.

HANSELL, E. W.
Bankruptcy committee.
Report. 22 Jan.1925. 1924/5 Cmd.2326 ix. Board of Trade.

HANSFORD, C. G.
Mould growths upon cold-store meat. 1 July 1923. (F.I.B. special rep., no.17) Department of Scientific and Industrial Research.

Hanworth, *Baron. SEE:* Pollock, E. M., *1st Baron*

HARBIN, John
The system of education in Grenada. 17 May 1913. (Imperial education conference papers) Board of Education.

HARCOURT, Lewis, *1st Viscount*
Army agricultural committee.
Report. 8 July 1919. 1919 Cmd.308 x. War Office.

HARDEN, Arthur
Report on the results of a chemical investigation. 1913 (Royal commission on human and animal tuberculosis, final report, part 2, appendix, vol.6.) 1913 Cd.6904 xl.

HARDING, Thomas Walter
Commission on Belfast health.
Report and appendices. 10 April 1908. 1908 Cd.4128 xxxi. Local Government Board for Ireland.

**HARDING, W. E.**
Report on conferences between employers, operatives and inspectors concerning the fencing of machinery, other safety precautions, health and welfare in tinplate factories. 30 March 1938. Home Office.

**HARDINGE, Henry Charles,** *3rd Viscount*
Royal commission on the rebellion in Ireland.
> Report. 26 June 1916. 1916 Cd.8270 xi.
> Evidence. 1916 Cd.8311 xi.

**HARDY, George F.**
Actuarial report on the position of persons in the naval and military service of the Crown. (Clause 36 of the National Insurance Bill) 26 July 1911. 1911 Cd.5809 lxxiii. Treasury.

Actuarial report on proposed government amendments to clause 36 of the National Insurance Bill (special provision with regard to persons in the naval and military service of the Crown). 6 Nov.1911. 1911 Cd.5943 lxxiii. Treasury.

Report of the actuaries in relation to the National Insurance Bill as amended in committee. 28 àov.1911. 1911 Cd.5983 lxxiii. Treasury.

Report of the actuaries in relation to the scheme of insurance against sickness, disablement, *etc.*, embodied in the National Insurance Bill, 1911. 20 May 1911. 1911 Cd.5681 lxxiii. Treasury.

Report by the actuaries on the preparation of the superannuation scheme for teachers. 15 March 1911. 1911 Cd.5982 lix. Scotch Education Department.

Report of the actuaries on the rate of sickness prevailing in the agricultural districts of Scotland. 16 Nov.1911. 1911 Cd.5966 lxxiii. Treasury.

**HARDY, Laurence**
Departmental committee on the dipping and treatment of sheep.
> Report. Aug.1904. 1905 Cd.2258 xxi.
> Minutes of evidence and appendices. 1905 Cd.2259 xxi. Board of Agriculture and Fisheries.

Select committee on premium bonds.
> Report, proceedings, evidence and appendices. 16 Jan.1918. 1917/8 (168) iii. House of Commons.

**HARE, A. E. C.**
Radium treatment in cancer of certain sites.
> Preliminary report. Nov.1934. (no further reports identified) National Radium Commission. Treasury.

**HARKER, Alfred**
The geology of the small isles of Inverness-shire. (Sheet 60) 9 Nov.1907. (Mem.Geol.Surv., Scotl.) Geological Survey, Scotland.

The geology of west-central Skye with Soay. (Sheet 70) 28 May 1904. (Mem.Geol.Surv., Scotl.) Geological Survey, Scotland.

**HARKER, J. A.**
Statistical supplement to the final report of the nitrogen products committee. June 1921. Ministry of Munitions. *(For report see:* Goold-Adams, H. E. F.)

**HARMSWORTH, Cecil Bisshopp**
Committee on applications of the Devon and Cornwall Local Fisheries. Committees for grants to fishermen to install motor power in their boats.
> Report and appendices. April 1913. 1913 Cd.6752 xxiv. Board of Agriculture and Fisheries.

Committee on clerical and commercial employment.
> Report. 9 Nov.1915. 1914/6 Cd.8110 xiii. Home Office.

Committee on shops.
> Report and appendices. Oct.1915. 1914/6 Cd.8113 xxxv. Home Office.

Committee on the conditions of retail trade which can best secure that the further enlistment of men or their employment in other national services may not interfere with the operations of that trade ("shops committee").
> Report. Oct.1915. 1914/6 Cd.8113 xxxv. Home Office.

**HARPER, John Ernest Troyte**
Reproduction of the record of the battle of Jutland. 10 May 1927. 1927 Cmd.2870 xv. Admiralty.

**HARREL, David**
Committee of inquiry into the Royal Irish Constabulary and Dublin Metropolitan Police.
> Report. 22 May 1914. 1914 Cd.7421 xliv.
> Appendix containing evidence and appendices. 1914/6 Cd.7637 xxxii. Irish Secretary's Office.

Departmental committee on Irish inland fisheries.
> Report. 25 Sept.1912. 1912/3 Cd.6433 xxvii.
> Minutes of evidence, appendices and index. 1912/3 Cd.6545 xxvii. Department of Agriculture and Technical Instruction for Ireland.

Memorandum on the proceedings of the committee on production, May 1918—November 1918. 9 Nov.1918. 1919 Cmd.70 xxvii. Ministry of Munitions.

Report of a court of inquiry on the dispute in the tramway industry. 25 Feb.1921. 1921 (37) xiv. Ministry of Labour.

Report of a court of inquiry on the electrical trades dispute, Penistone. 17 Sept.1920. 1920 Cmd.990 xix. Ministry of Labour.

Royal commission on the railway conciliation and arbitration scheme of 1907.
> Report. 18 Oct.1911. 1911 Cd.5922 xxix.
> Minutes of evidence, appendices and index. 1912/3 Cd.6014 xlv.

**HARRIS, Charles**
Army finance; two lectures. March 1925. War Office.

**HARRIS, George Robert Canning,** *4th Baron of Seringapatam and Mysore and of Belmont, Kent.*
Committee on the organisation, arms, and equipment of the yeomanry force.
> Report. 2 Jan.1901. 1901 Cd.466 xl. War Office.

**HARRIS, Henry Percy**
Select committee on pensions.
> Report, proceedings, evidence and appendices. 9 Aug.1920. 1920 (185) viii. House of Commons.

**HARRIS, P.**
Circular saws. Dec.1937. (F.P.R. Records, no.22) Department of Scientific and Industrial Research.

**HARRIS, Sidney West**
Departmental committee on the social services in courts of summary jurisdiction.
> Report. March 1936. 1935/6 Cmd.5122 viii. Home Office.

**HARRISON, Charles A.**
Departmental committee on deep excavations.
> Report, minutes of evidence and appendix. July 1912. 1912/3 Cd.6261 xviii. Home Office.

**HARRISON, F. C.**
Committee on financial risks attaching to the holding to trading stocks.

HARRISON, F. C. (continued)
Report. 5 Dec.1918. 1918 Cd.9224 xiii. Ministry of Reconstruction.

HARRISON, H. W. B.
Report on the mining industry in Spain for the year 1901. 16 July 1902. (Dip.cons.reports., misc.ser., no.579) 1901 Cd.787-15 ciii. Foreign Office.

HARRISON, John Burchmore
The katamorphism of igneous rocks under humid tropical conditions. 28 Dec.1933. Imperial Bureau of Soil Science.

HARRISON, Lawrence Whitaker
Anti-venereal measures in certain Scandinavian countries and Holland. Jan.1938. (Rep.Pub.Health & Med.Subj., no.83) Ministry of Health.

The treatment of syphilis; a survey of records from St. Thomas's Hospital. 19 April 1929. (S.R.S., no.132) Medical Research Council.

HARRISON, William
Standing committee on prices.
Report of a sub-committee on agricultural implements and machinery. 20 April 1921. 1921 Cmd.1315 xvi. Board of Trade.

HART, Philip Montague D'Arcy
The value of tuberculin tests in man, with special reference to the intracutaneous test. 21 Dec.1921. (S.R.S., no.164) Medical Research Council.

HART, William Edward
Departmental committee on Thames flood prevention.
Report. July 1933. 1932/3 Cmd.4452 xv. Ministry of Health.

HARTLEY, G. W.
Salmon caught in the sea; the Island of Soay and Ardnamurchan, 1938. 1939. (Salmon Fish., 1939, no.1) Fishery Board for Scotland.
Salmon caught in the sea; north-west Sutherland, 1936. 1937. (Salmon Fish., 1937, no.3) Fishery Board for Scotland.
Salmon caught in the sea; west Sutherland, 1937. 1938. (Salmon Fish., 1938, no.2) Fishery Board for Scotland.

HARTLEY, Harold
Committee on emergency conversion of motor vehicles to producer gas.
Report. 13 Dec.1939. Mines Department.

HARTLEY, Harold Brewer
British mission to visit enemy chemical factories in the occupied zone in Feb.1919.
Introduction to the report. April 1921. 1921 Cmd.1137 xx. War Office.

HARTWELL, F. J.
The limits of inflammability of firedamp in atmospheres which contain blackdamp. Nov.1925. (S.M.R.B. Paper, no.19) Mines Department.

HARVEY, C. O.
The determination of iodine in biological substances. 21 May 1935. (S.R.S., no.201) Medical Research Council.

HARVEY, Leonard C.
Pulverised coal systems in America. May 1919. (F.R.B.special rep., no.1) Department of Scientific and Industrial Research.

HARWARD, J.
The system of education in Ceylon. 28 Dec.1912. (Imperial education conference papers) Board of Education.

HARWOOD, J.
The ignition of firedamp by compression. July 1935. (S.M.R.B. Paper, no.93) Mines Department.

HASLAM, J. F. C.
Schistosomiasis and malaria in relation to irrigation. May 1929. (E.M.B.17) Empire Marketing Board.

HATCH, Ernest Frederick George
Committee of inquiry into the conditions of employment in the linen and other making-up trades in the north of Ireland.
Report and evidence. Nov.1912. 1912/3 Cd.6509 xxxiv. Home Office.

Committee on the application of the National Insurance Act to outworkers.
Vol.1: Report. 7 May 1912. 1912/3 Cd.6178 xlii.
Vol.2: Evidence and appendices. 1912/3 Cd.6179 xlii. National Health Insurance Joint Committee.

Committee on the application of the National Insurance Act to outworkers in Ireland.
Vol.1: Report. 27 July 1914. 1914/6 Cd.7685 xxxi.
Vol.2: Evidence and appendices. 1914/6 Cd.7686 xxxi. National Health Insurance Joint Committee.

Departmental committee on Belgian refugees.
First report. Dec.1914. 1914/6 Cd.7750 vii.
Minutes of evidence. 1914/6 Cd.7779 viii. Local Government Board.

Departmental committees on checkweighing in chalk quarries and cement works and limestone quarries and limeworks.
Reports, evidence and appendix. 18 Feb.1908. 1908 Cd.4002 xi. Home Department.

Departmental committee on checkweighing in the iron and steel trades.
Report. 15 Nov.1907. 1908 Cd.3846 xi.
Minutes of evidence. 1908 Cd.3847 xi. Home Department.

Departmental committee on the checking of piece-work wages in dock labour.
Report. 7 Oct.1908. 1908 Cd.4380 xxxiv.
Minutes of evidence. 1908 Cd.4381 xxxiv. Home Department.

Departmental committee on the reception and employment of the Belgian refugees in this country.
First report. Dec.1914. 1914/6 Cd.7750 vii.
Evidence. 1914/6 Cd.7779 vii.
Report on the work undertaken by the British government in the reception and care of Belgian refugees. 18 Dec.1919. Local Government Board and Ministry of Health.

Departmental committee on the use of lead and the danger or injury to health arising from dust and other causes in the manufacture of earthenware and china.
Vol.1: Report. June 1910. 1910 Cd.5219 xxix.
Vol.2: Appendices. 1910 Cd.5278 xxix.
Vol.3: Minutes of evidence. 1910 Cd.5385 xxix. Home Office.

Departmental committee on the use of lead compounds in painting.
Vol.1: Report of the danger attendant on the use of lead in the painting of buildings. Nov.1914. 1914/6 Cd.7882 xxiv.
Painting, enamelling and varnishing of coaches and carriages.

HATCH, Ernest Frederick George (continued)
    Vol.2:   Report. Jan.1920. 1920 Cmd.630 xx.
    Vol.3:   Appendices. 1920 Cmd.631 xx.
    Vol.4:   Evidence. 1920 Cmd.632 xx. Home Office.

Report on investigation on the application of the "particulars" section of the Factory and Workshops Act, 1901, to foundries. 7 July 1913. 1913 Cd.6990 xxiii. Home Office.

Report on methods of applying the "particulars" section (of the Factory and Workshops Act, 1901) to sundry industries. 1 March 1909. 1909 Cd.4842 xxi. Home Office.

HATTON, R. G.
Memorandum upon the standardisation of horticultural material by selection and vegetative propagation with special reference to root-stock influence. May 1927. Empire Marketing Board.

HAUGHTON, J. L.
Magnesium and its alloys. July 1937. Department of Scientific and Industrial Research.

HAUSDING, A.
A handbook on the winning and the utilisation of peat, tr. by Hugh Ryan, 1921. 1917. Fuel Research Board. Department of Scientific and Industrial Research.

Haversham, *Lord. SEE:* Hayter, A. D., *1st Baron*

HAWARD, Harry Edwin
Report of proceedings of the conference on electricity supply in rural areas. 12 July 1928. Electricity Commission. Ministry of Transport.

HAWKE, J. A.
Departmental committee on the law relating to the stopping up and diversion of highways.
    Report. 14 July 1926. Ministry of Health.

HAWKINS: Anthony Hope
Why Italy is with the allies. 1917. Ministry of Information.

HAY, David Allan
Commissioner for special areas in Scotland.
    Report. Nov.1937. 1937/8 Cmd.5604 xiii. Scottish Office.

HAY, P. S.
A method of trapping the dust produced by pneumatic rock drills. May 1926. (S.M.R.B. Paper no.23) Mines Department.

HAYCRAFT, Thomas Wagstaff
Commission of inquiry on disturbances of May 1921 in Palestine.
    Reports. 1 July and 10 Aug.1921. 1921 Cmd.1540 xv. Colonial Office.

The system of education in Gibraltar. 15 Nov.1912. (Imperial education conference papers) Board of Education.

HAYDAY, Arthur
Select committee on ministers' remuneration.
    Report, proceedings, evidence, appendices and index. 28 July 1930. 1929/30 (170) vi. House of Commons.

HAYTER, Arthur Divett, *1st Baron Haversham of Bracknell*
Departmental committee on tenant farmers and sales of estates.
    Report. 9 Jan.1912. 1912/3 Cd.6030 xlvii.
    Minutes of evidence, appendices and index. 1912/3 Cd.6031 xlvii. Board of Agriculture and Fisheries.

HEAD, Henry
Sense of stability and balance in the air. April 1919. (Reports of the air medical investigation committee) (S.R.S., no.28) Medical Research Committee.

HEADLAM, James Wycliffe
Belgium and Greece. 1917. Ministry of Information.

The dead lands of Europe. 1917. Ministry of Information.

The peace terms of the Allies. 1917. Ministry of Information.

The starvation of Germany. 1917. Ministry of Information.

The truth about England exposed in a letter to a neutral. 25 Oct.1915. Ministry of Information.

HEARN, Walter Risley
Notes on the openings for British trade in the Bordeaux consular district. 3 July 1901. (Dip.and cons.reports: misc. no.560) 1901 Cd.430-15 lxxx. Foreign Office.

Report on the French mercantile marine law of 1906 and its predecessors. 3 May 1906. (Dip.cons.reports: misc.ser., no.651) 1906 Cd.2683-15 cxxii. Foreign Office.

Report on the French octroi system. 22 Jan.1906. (Dip.cons.reports: misc.ser., no.644) 1906 Cd.2683-8 cxxii. Foreign Office.

Report on the preparation of French plums. 17 Dec.1900. (Dip.cons.reports: misc.ser., no.546) 1900 Cd.430-1 lxxx. Foreign Office.

HEATH, Henry Frank
Departmental committee on the use of the guss in Somerset mines.
    Report. 31 Aug.1928. 1928/9 Cmd.3200 viii. Mines Department.

HEATH, Thomas Little
Departmental committee on the solar physics laboratory.
    Report. 1 June 1911. 1911 Cd.5924 xviii. Board of Education.

Inter-departmental committee on the application of the Whitley report to government establishments.
    Report of the sub-committee on application of the Whitley report to the administrative departments of the Civil Service. 7 March 1919. 1919 Cmd.9 xi. Treasury.

HEDLEY, Gerald W.
Report on the present condition of physical education in Denmark and Sweden. Sept.1935. (Educational pamphlets, no.104) Board of education.

HEDLEY, Walter
Departmental committee on colonies for mental defectives.
    Report. 26 March 1931. Board of Control.

HEGH, Emile
Tsetse-flies; their characteristics, distribution and bionomics with some account of possible methods for their control. July 1922. Imperial Bureau of Entomology.

HELLIWELL, John Percival
Army Advisory Standing Committee.
    Report on maxillo-facial injuries. 6 Oct.1934. War Office.

HELY-HUTCHINSON, R. W. J., *6th Earl of Donomore*
Committee for privileges: Barony of Beauchamp.
    Speeches delivered by counsel and judgment. 29

HELY-HUTCHINSON, R.W.J. *6th Earl of Donomore* (continued)

    July 1924. 1924 (H.L.189) vi. House of Lords.

Committee for privileges: Margaret Haig, *Viscountess Rhondda.*
    Proceedings and evidence. 2 March 1922. 1922 (H.L. 20) v. House of Lords.

Committee on ministers' powers. *SEE:* Scott, L. F.

Joint committee on suspension of bills.
    Report, proceedings, minutes of evidence and appendices. 30 April 1929. 1928/9 (105) iv. House of Commons.

Select committee on compulsory taking of land (insanitary property).
    Report, proceedings, evidence and appendices. 16 June 1913. 1913 (H.L. 66) viii. House of Lords.

Select committee on the peer's war memorial.
    Report and proceedings. 27 May 1925. 1925 (H.L. 133) viii. House of Lords.

Special commission on the constitution of Ceylon.
    Report. 26 June 1928. 1928 Cmd.3131 vii. Colonial Office.

HEMMING, Francis
    East Africa sub-committee of the tsetse-fly committee.
        Report. 4 Feb.1935. 1934/5 Cmd.4951 vii. Economic Advisory Council.

HENDERSON: Alexander, *1st Baron Faringdon*
    Committee on financial facilities for trade.
        Report. 31 Aug.1916. 1916 Cd.8346 xv. Board of Trade.

HENDERSON, Arthur
    Conference on the shops and machinery at Woolwich Arsenal, in order to consider whether any article not now made in the Ordnance factories can appropriately be made there with this machinery.
        Report, proceedings, minutes of evidence and appendices. 25 June 1907. 1907 Cd.3514 xlix. War Office.

    Report on the council of the League of Nations.
        Fifty-sixth and fifty-seventh sessions. 20 Nov.1929. (Misc., no.14, 1929) 1929/30 Cmd.3459 xxxii.
        Fifty-eighth session. 3 Feb.1930. (Misc., no.6, 1930) 1929/30 Cmd.3514 xxxii.
        Fifty-ninth session. 20 June 1930. (Misc., no.12, 1930) 1929/30 Cmd.3632 xxxii.
        Sixty-second session. 5 Feb.1931. (Misc., no.9, 1931) 1930/1 Cmd.3804 xxxv.
        Sixty-third session. 22 June 1931. (Misc., no.12, 1931) 1930/1 Cmd.3901 xxxv. Foreign Office.

HENDERSON, Nevile Meyrick
    Final report on the circumstances leading to the termination of his mission to Berlin. 20 Sept.1939. (Germany, no.1, 1939) 1938/9 Cmd.6115 xxvii. Foreign Office.

HENDERSON: Reginald F. H.
    Inter-departmental conference on the coast guard. 28 Mar.1907. 1908 Cd.4091 xcvi. Admiralty.

HENDERSON, Vivian Leonard
    Committee on approved schools remuneration and conditions of service.
        Report. 29 Jan.1936. Home Office.

    Departmental committee on compensation for silicosis.
        Report dealing with the pottery industry. 27 July

1928. Home Office.

    Departmental committee on factory inspectorate.
        Report. 8 May 1929. Home Office.

    Departmental committee on the use of celluloid in the manufacture of toys, fancy goods, *etc.*
        Report. 12 April 1938. 1937/8 Cmd.5790 ix. Home Office.

HENEAGE, Arthur Pelham
    Central advisory water committee.
        Second report: Consolidation and amendment of the law relating to public water supply. 5 April 1939. 1938/9 Cmd.5986 xv. Ministry of Health.

    Central advisory water committee: underground water. 28 March 1938. (*In* First report of the C.A.W.C.) Ministry of Health.

HENNIKER, Alan Major
    History of the Great War. Transportation on the western front, 1914-1918. Text and maps. 1937. 2 vols. War Office.

HENRIQUES, Philip Gutterez.
    Committee on safeguarding of industries.
        Report on table-wear of translucent pottery. 23 March 1927. 1927 Cmd.2838 xii. Board of Trade.

HENRY, Denis Stanislaus
    Dublin disturbances commission.
        Report. 9 Feb.1914. 1914 Cd.7269 xviii.
        Appendix: evidence and appendices. 1914 Cd.7272 xviii. Irish Secretary's Office.

HENRY, Edward Richard
    Classification and uses of finger prints. 1 June 1900. Home Office.

HENSHAW, A. M.
    Haulage committee.
        Report on haulage accidents in coal mines. 14 Oct.1930. (S.M.R.B. Paper no.66) Mines Department.

HEPBURNE-SCOTT, Walter George, *7th Baron Polworth*
    Enquiry into juvenile delinquency.
        Report by the Scottish National Council of Juvenile Organisations. Jan.1923. Scottish Office.

    Report on the proceedings of the eighth International Penitentiary Congress held at Washington, October 1910. 13 Jan.1911. 1911 Cd.5589 xxxix. Scottish Office.

HEPWORTH, Melville Willis Campbell
    The effect of the Labrador current upon the surface temperature of the north Atlantic.
        Pt.1: Nov.1911. (Geophys.Mem., no.1)
        Pt.2: Aug.1914. (Geophys.Mem., no.10) Meteorological Office.

    The relation between pressure, temperature, and air circulation over the south Atlantic Ocean. Aug.1905. (M.O.177) Meteorological Office.

HERBERT, Sidney, *14th Earl of Pembroke*
    Departmental committee on the Baronetage.
        Report and appendices. 12 Dec.1906. 1907 Cd.3445 lxvii. Home Office.

HERBST, J. F.
    Report on the Rietfontein area, Cape Colony. 12 Feb.1908. 1908 Cd.4323 lxx. (Colonial reports: misc., no.55) Colonial Office.

Hereford, *Lord. SEE:* James, H., *1st Baron James of Hereford*

HERON, Crawford
The handling and transport of fish. 1925. (F.I.B. special rep., no.25) Department of Scientific and Industrial Research.

HERRINGHAM, Wilmot Parker
Memorandum on a visit to the United States, May 1921. Dec.1921. University Grants Committee. Treasury.

HERTSLET, Cecil
Report on the arms industry of Liege. 28 April 1906. (Dip.cons.reports: misc., ser., no.650) 1906 Cd.2683-14 cxxii. Foreign Office.

Report on the canals and other navigable waterways of Belgium. 15 Feb.1904. (Dip.cons.reports: misc.ser., no.604) 1904 Cd.1767-8 xcvi. Foreign Office.

Report on the coal mining industry of Belgium. Sept.1907. (Dip.cons.reports: misc.ser., no.664) 1908 Cd.3728 cviii. Foreign Office and Board of Trade.

Report on the customs tariff of Belgium. 5 May 1904. (Dip.cons.reports: misc.ser., no.612) 1904 Cd.1767-16 xcvi. Foreign Office.

Report on the diamond industry of Antwerp. 17 June 1905. (Dip.cons.reports: misc.ser., no.634) 1905 Cd.2237-15 lxxxvi. Foreign Office.

Report on the new scheme of the Belgian government for the extension of the port of Antwerp. May 1912. (Dip.cons.reports: misc.ser., no.681) 1912/3 Cd.6006 xciv. Foreign Office and Board of Trade.

Report on the precautions taken to combat ankylostomiasis (miners' worm disease) in Belgium. Feb.1907. (Dip.cons.reports: misc.ser., no.656) 1907 Cd.3284 lxxxvii. Foreign Office.

Report on the production of Normandy cider. 6 May 1901. (Dip.cons.reports: misc.ser., no.552) 1901 Cd.430-7 lxxx. Foreign Office.

Report on the scheme of the Belgian Government for the extension of the port of Antwerp. Sept.1905. (Dip.cons.reports: misc.ser., no.640) 1906 Cd.2683-4 cxxii. Foreign Office.

HETHERINGTON, A. L.
British Empire hardwoods from the point of view of turnery. Nov.1931. Empire Marketing Board.

HETHERINGTON, Hector James Wright
Board to consider the making of an order under the Cotton Manufacturing Industry (Temporary Provisions) Act,1934.
        Report. 15 June 1935.
        Report. 2 March 1937. Ministry of Labour.
Royal Commission on workmen's compensation.
        Report. 22 Dec.1944. 1944/5 Cmd.6588 vi.
        Minutes of evidence. 1939-40.

HETHERINGTON, Roger Gaskell
Accidents in sewers.
        Report on the precautions necessary for the safety of persons entering sewers and sewage tanks. 30 April 1934. Ministry of Health.
Commission of inquiry into the Holborn explosions and fires.
        Report. 22 March 1929. 1928/9 Cmd.3306 vi.
        Minutes of evidence. 14 parts. 1929. Home Office.

HEUVEL, J.van den
Slave raids in Belgium; facts about the deportations. 1917. Ministry of Information.

HEW, R. H.
Report on the decline in the agricultural population of Great Britain, 1881-1906. 10 Sept.,1906. 1906 Cd.3273 xcvi. Board of Agriculture and Fisheries.

HEWART, Gordon, *1st Baron Hewart of Bury*
Crown proceedings committee.
        Report. 18 Feb.1927. 1927 Cmd.2842 viii. Lord Chancellor's Office.

HEWETT, John Prescott
Report on Mesopotamia for the Army Council. 10 March 1919. War Office.

Some impressions of Mesopotamia in 1919. May 1920. War Office.

HEWITT, John Theodore
The chemistry of wire making; a report on oenological research. 2 Jan.1928. (E.M.B.7) Empire Marketing Board.

HEWLETT, Hilda Beatrice, *Mrs*.
Our flying men. 1916. Ministry of Information.

HEYWOOD, G. S. P.
An investigation of the lapse rate of temperature in the lowest hundred meters of the atmosphere. Dec.1938. (Geophys.Mem., no.77) Meteorological Office.

HICKS-BEACH, Michael Edward, *1st Viscount St.Aldwyn*
Royal commission on delay in the King's Bench Division.
        First report. April 1913. 1913 Cd.6761 xxx.
        Minutes of evidence with appendix. 1913 Cd.6762 xxx.
        Second and final report. 28 Nov.1913. 1914 Cd.7177 xxxvii.
        Evidence, appendices and index. 1914 Cd.7178 xxxvii.
Royal commission on ecclesiastical discipline.
        Report. 21 June 1906. 1906 Cd.3040 xxxiii.
        Minutes of evidence: Vols.1—4. 1906 Cd.3069, Cd.3070, Cd.3071, Cd.3072 xxxiii, xxxiv.
Royal commission on the Land Transfer Acts.
        First report. 8 Feb.1909. 1909 Cd.4509 xxvii.
        Appendix: minutes of evidence and appendices. 1909 Cd.4510 xxvii.
        Second and final report. 19 Jan.1911. 1911 Cd.5483 xxx.
        Minutes of evidence, January to November 1909, appendices and index. 1911 Cd.5494 xxx.
Select committee on savings banks funds.
        Report, proceedings, minutes of evidence, appendix and index. 17 July 1902. 1902 (282) ix. House of Commons.
Select committee on the church in Wales.
        Report, proceedings, evidence and appendices. 7 Aug.1914. 1914 (H.L.238) House of Lords.
Select committee on the civil list.
        Report, proceedings and appendix. 28 March 1901. 1901 (110) v.
        Special report. 15 March 1901. 1901 (87) v. House of Commons.

HIGGINS, George Herbert
Police pay of new entrants committee.
        Report. 21 Feb.1933. 1932/3 Cmd.4274 xv. Home Office.

HIGGINS, W. F.
Changes of zero in spirit thermometers. Feb.1929. (Prof.Notes, no.51) Meteorological Office.

HIGHTON, John E.
Working-class housing on the continent. 25 June 1935. Department of Health for Scotland.

HILDITCH, J.
Report on the conditions of employment in the manufacture of tinplates with special reference to the process of tinning. 27 Aug.1912. 1912/3 Cd.6394 xxvi. Home Office.

HILDITCH, T. P.
The relative values of codliver oils from various sources. Dec.1930. (E.M.B.35) Empire Marketing Board.

HILL, A. Bradford
The inheritance of resistance to bacterial infection in animal species; a review. 25 July 1934. (S.R.S., no.196) Medical Research Council.

Internal migration and its effects upon the death rates, with special reference to the county of Essex. 9 Jan.1925. (S.R.S., no.95)

An investigation into the sickness experience of London transport workers, with special reference to digestive disturbances. July 1937. (I.H.R.B. Rep., no.79) Medical Research Council.

Investigation into the sickness experience of printers. March 1929. (I.H.R.B. Rep., no.54) Medical Research Council.

Sickness amongst operatives in Lancashire cotton spinning mills. Oct.1930. (I.H.R.B. Rep., no.59) Medical Research Council.

HILL, Arthur Norman
Committee to prepare a draft of a national scheme of training for the sea service.
Report. 10 July 1919. 1919 Cmd.408 xxv. Board of Education.

Merchant shipping advisory committee.
Report on life saving appliances, training and organisation. 13 Dec.1922. Board of Trade.

Report on overloading. 19 Dec.1929. Board of Trade.

Report on the carriage of timber deck cargoes. 23 Nov.1925. Board of Trade.

Report on the deck manning of foreign-going ships. 13 Feb.1936. 1935/5 Cmd.5096 xiii.
Correspondence and instruction to Board of Trade officers. 3 July 1936. 1935/6 Cmd.5242 xvii. Board of Trade.

Report on the statutory regulations as to boats and life-saving appliances and other means of ensuring safety of life at sea, with appendices. 24 July 1912. 1912/3 Cd.6353 xxxviii. Board of Trade.

HILL, Basil Alexander
Ordnance duties. A course of three lectures, 1925. March 1926. War Office.

HILL, J. B.
Geology of Falmouth and Truro and the mining district of Camborne and Redruth. (Sheet 352) 20 Nov.1906. (Mem.Geol.Surv.) Geological Survey.

The geology of mid-Argyll. (Sheet 37) 7 Nov.1905. (Mem.Geol.Surv., Scotl.) Geological Survey, Scotland.

The geology of the country near Oban and Dalmally. (Sheet 45) 27 Feb.1908. (Mem.Geol.Surv., Scotl.) Geological Survey, Scotland.

The geology of the Lizard and Meneage. (Sheet 359) 26 March 1912. (Mem.Geol.Surv.) Geological Survey.

HILL, Leonard Erskine
Investigation of workers' food and suggestions as to dietary. Aug.1916. (Health of munition workers committee memo., no.11) 1916 Cd.8370 xxiii. Ministry of Munitions.

Investigation of workers' food and suggestions as to dietary. Oct.1917. (Health of munition workers committee, memo., no.19) 1917/8 Cd.8789 xx. Ministry of Munitions.

Report on ventilation and the effect of open air and wind on the respiratory metabolism. 30 July 1914. (Rep.Pub.Health & Med.Subj., no.100) Local Government Board.

The science of ventilation and open air treatment.
Part 1. 25 Jan.1919. (S.R.S., no.32)
Part 2. July 1920. (S.R.S., no.52) Medical Research Committee.

HILL, Maurice
Committee on arrestment.
Report. 16 April 1928. 1928 Cmd.3108 vii. Lord Chancellor's Office.

HILLMAN, H. E.
Report on the navigation of the Tung Ting Lake and the Siang and Yuen rivers (upper Yangtse). April 1902. (Hydrographic Publication H.D.182) Admiralty.

HILLS, E. H.
Report on the survey department of the East Africa protectorate. 21 Feb.1907. 1908 Cd.3794 lxx. (Colonial rep: misc., no.44) Colonial Office.

HILLS, John Waller
Commission of enquiry into industrial unrest.
Report of the commissioners for the West Midlands area. SEE: Barnes, G. N.

Credit insurance committee.
Report. March 1926. 1926 Cmd.2619 ix. Department of Overseas Trade.

Departmental committee on the export of horses to the continent.
Report. 31 July 1925. 1924/5 Cmd.2495 xii.
Proceedings and appendices and indices of witnesses and subjects. 1925. Ministry of Agriculture and Fisheries.

Inter-departmental committee on the prices of building materials. SEE: Roberts, S.

Joint select committee on gas authorities (residual products).
Report, proceedings, evidence, appendices and index. 12 Dec.1912. 1912/3 (392) vii. House of Commons.

Women's employment committee.
Report. 28 March 1918. 1918 Cd.9239 xiv. Ministry of Reconstruction.

HILTON, John
Report on an investigation into the personal circumstances and industrial history of 10,000 claimants to unemployment benefit, 5 to 10 November 1923. 14 Feb.1924. Ministry of Labour.

Report on an investigation into the personal characteristics and industrial history of 10,003 claimants to unemployment benefit, 24 to 29 November 1924. 4 June 1925. Ministry of Labour.

Standing committees on prices and trusts. Sub-committee on building materials.

HILTON, John (continued)
Report by a sectional committee on light castings. 12 Feb.1921. 1921 Cmd.1200 xvi. Board of Trade.

Standing committee on trusts.
Report of a sub-committee on dyeing, finishing, bleaching and printing. 10 May 1921. 1921 Cmd.1371 xvi. Board of Trade.

Report by a sub-committee on dyes and dyestuffs. 10 May 1921. 1921 Cmd.1370 xvi. Board of Trade.

Sub-committee on the electric lamp industry. Findings and decisions. 9 March 1920. 1920 Cmd.622 xxiii. Board of Trade.

Sub-committee on the existence of a combine in the farriery trade. Findings. 5 Dec.1919. 1920 Cmd.540 xxiii. Board of Trade.

HINDLEY, Clement D. M.
Inter-departmental committee on cabs and private hire vehicles.
Interim report. 31 Jan.1939. 1938/9 Cmd.5938 ix. (no further reports identified) Home Office *and* Ministry of Transport.

Steel structures research committee.
First report. 6 Oct.1931.
Second report. 1 Jan.1934.
Final report. 21 Feb.1936. Department of Scientific and Industrial Research.

HINTON, C. L.
Fruit pectins; their chemical behaviour and jellying properties. July 1939. (F.I.B., special rep., no.48) Department of Scientific and Industrial Research.

HINTON, H. A.
Report of an inquiry into the teaching of the geography of the British Empire in certain types of schools. Nov.1929. (Educational pamphlets, no.79) Board of Education.

HINXMAN, Lionel Wordsworth
The economic geology of the central coalfield of Scotland. Area 2: Denny and Plean, Banknock, Carron and Grangemouth, Cumbernauld, Castlecary and Bonnybridge, Falkirk and Slamannan. 7 Feb.1917. (Mem.Geol.Surv., Scotl.) Geological Survey, Scotland.

The economic geology of the central coalfield of Scotland. Area 4: Paisley, Barrhead, Renfrew. 22 March 1919. (Mem.Geol.Surv., Scotl.) Geological Survey, Scotland.

The economic geology of the central coalfield of Scotland. Area 9: Carluke, Strathaven and Larkhall. 23 June 1920. (Mem.Geol.Surv., Scotl.) Geological Survey, Scotland.

The geology of Corrour and the Moor of Rannoch. (Sheet 54) 20 Nov.1922. (Mem.Geol.Surv., Scotl.) Geological Survey, Scotland.

The geology of mid-Strathspey and Strathearn. (Sheet 74) 1915. (Mem.Geol.Surv., Scotl.) Geological Survey, Scotland.

The geology of the country around Beauly and Inverness. (Sheet 83) 1914. (Mem.Geol.Surv., Scotl.) Geological Survey, Scotland.

The geology of the lower Strathspey. (Sheet 84) 16 Jan.1902. (Mem.Geol.Surv., Scotl.) Geological Survey, Scotland.

HIPWOOD, Charles
Informal committee on coal-carrying vessels.

Report. 10 April 1924.
Second report. 15 May 1925.
Third report. 28 July 1927. Board of Trade.

HIRD, S.
Committee on the safety of persons working in and about kiers used in paint works and bleaching and dyeing works.
Report. 31 July 1935. Home Office.

Report on the prevention of accidents on combing machines in the cotton spinning trade. 23 May 1940. Home Office.

Rubber trade conference. Committee on the guarding of calenders and extruders.
Interim report. 19 June 1937. 1938.
Final report. 7 Feb.1939. 1940. Home Office.

HIRST, George S.S.
Report on the Cayman Islands, Jamaica. 6 June 1910. (Colonial reports: misc.,no.73) 1910 Cd.5274 lxv. Colonial Office.

HITCHCOCK, Eldred F.
Standing committee on prices.
Report of a sub-committee on the prices, costs and profits of the manufacture of Yorkshire tweed cloths. 16 July 1920. 1920 Cmd.858 xxiii. Board of Trade.

Standing committee on prices and trusts.
Report of a sub-committee on a voluntary scheme for standard clothing. 5 April 1921. 1921 Cmd.1314 xvi. Board of Trade.

HOARE, Samuel
Irish distress committee.
First report. 19 Oct.1922. (No others identified) Colonial Office.

HOARE, Wilson
Report of a formal investigation into the loss of the British steamship "Thistlemor" of Sunderland in or near Barnstapel Bay on 3 December 1901. 13 May 1910. 1910 Cd.5218 lxxxi. Board of Trade.

HOBHOUSE, Charles Edward Henry
Committee on the amalgamation of the Customs and Excise departments.
Report. 3 Aug.1911. 1911 Cd.5830 xv.
Minutes of evidence. 1911 Cd.5834 xv. Treasury.

Committee on the use of cocaine in dentistry.
Report. 20 Feb.1917. 1917/8 Cd.8489 viii. Home Office.

Royal commission upon decentralisation in India.
Vol.1: Report. 25 Feb.1909. 1908 Cd.4360 xliv.
Vol.2: Minutes of evidence taken in Madras. 1908 Cd.4361 xliv.
Vol.3: Minutes of evidence taken in Burma. 1908 Cd.4362 xliv.
Vol.4: Minutes of evidence taken in Bengal. 1908 Cd.4363 xliv.
Vol.5: Minutes of evidence taken in Eastern Bengal and Assam. 1908 Cd.4364 xlv.
Vol.6: Minutes of evidence taken in the Central Provinces. 1908 Cd.4365 xlv.
Vol.7: Minutes of evidence taken in the United Provinces. 1908 Cd.4366 xlv.
Vol.8: Minutes of evidence taken in Bombay. 1908 Cd.4367 xlvi.
Vol.9: Minutes of evidence taken in Baluchistan, Northwest Frontier Province and the Punjab. 1908 Cd.4368 xlvi.

HOBHOUSE, Charles Edward Henry (continued)
Vol.10: Minutes of evidence of witnesses serving directly under the Government of India. 1908 Cd.4369 xlvi.

Select committee on Post Office servants.
Vol.I: Report. 13 Dec.1906. 1906 (380) xii. pt.1.
Vol.II: Minutes of evidence, appendices. 1906 (380) xii. pt.2.
Report and proceedings. 25 July 1907. 1907 (266) vii. House of Commons.

HOBHOUSE, Henry
Departmental committee on land settlement for sailors and soldiers.
Final report. 2 parts. 21 Jan. and 19 June 1916. 1916 Cd.8182, Cd.8277 xii.
Evidence. 1916 Cd.8347 xii. (no others identified) Board of Agriculture and Fisheries.

Departmental committee on motor cars.
Part I: Report. 21 April 1904. 1904 Cd.2069 lxxix.
Part II: Minutes of evidence, appendices and index. 1904 Cd.2070 lxxix. Local Government Board.

Departmental committee on the duties of the police with respect to the preservation of order at public meetings.
Vol.1: Report and appendices. 14 April 1909. 1909 Cd.4673 xxxvi.
Vol.2: Minutes of evidence. 1909 Cd.4674 xxxvi. Home Office.

Housing financial assistance committee.
Interim report on public utility societies. 29 Oct.1918. 1918 Cd.9223 x.
Final report. 5 Feb.1919. 1918 Cd.9238 x. Ministry of Reconstruction.

Military manoeuvres commission.
Report. 1910. 1911 Cd.5478 xlvii. War Office.

Rural education conference.
1st report: county staffs of instructors in agricultural subjects. Nov.1910.
2nd report: qualifications of teachers of rural subjects. 26 May 1911. 1911 Cd.5773 viii.
3rd report: suggested type of agricultural school. 26 May 1911. 1911 Cd. 5774 viii.
5th report: courses in agricultural colleges. 27 Feb.1912. 1912/3 Cd. 6151 xi.
6th report: co-ordination of agricultural education. 13 June 1912. 1912/3 Cd.6273 xi.
7th report: manual instruction in rural elementary schools and the individual examination of children in rural elementary schools. 5 Dec.1912. 1912/3 Cd.6511 xi.
8th report: manual processes of agriculture. 22 May.1913. 1913 Cd.6871 xv. Board of Agriculture and Fisheries and Board of Education.

HODGE, R.E.
Kiln-drying schedules. Oct.1938. (F.P.R. Records, no.26) Department of Scientific and Industrial Research.

HODGES, Frank
National fuel and power committee.
Second report: of the sub-committee on gas. 11 Aug.1928. 1928/9 Cmd.3252 vi. (SEE: Mond, A. for first report) Board of Trade.

HODGSON, C.R.
Sheffield industrial mission to South America.
Report. 26 Jan.1931. Department of Overseas Trade.

HODGSON, E.H.
Temporary staffs cmmmittee.
Report. 24 Aug.1932.
Report. 11 Sept.1934. Treasury.

HODGSON, R. McLeod
Report on the lumber industry in the Russian far east. Nov.1908. (Dip.cons.reports: misc. ser., no.670) 1908 Cd.3728-6 cviii. Foreign Office and Board of Trade.

HOGAN, M.A.
Current meters for use in river guaging. June 1922. Department of Scientific and Industrial Research.

The deterioration of haulage ropes in service. Dec.1934. (S.M.R.B.Paper, no.92) Mines Department.

Measurements of the kinetic loads on colliery winding ropes. Oct.1932. (S.M.R.B.Paper,no.78) Mines Department.

River guaging; report on methods and appliances suitable for use in Great Britain. April 1925. Department of Scientific and Industrial Research.

Tests on pit props. Sept.1931. (S.M.R.B. Paper, no.72) Mines Department.

HOGG, Douglas McGarel, 1st Viscount Hailsham
Select committee on the trial of the Lord de Clifford.
Report and proceedings. 24 Oct.1935. 1934/5 (H.L.153) vi.
Proceedings of the trial. 12 Dec.1935. 1935/6 (H.L.12) vi. House of Lords.

HOLDEN, Henry Capel Lofft
Mechanical transport committee. Experimental sub-committee.
Report on tractor trials at Aldershot, September and October 1903. 5 Jan.1904. War Office.

HOLLAND, Eardley Lancelot
The causation of foetal death; report of an investigation into death in a sample of 300 foetuses of viable age. 24 Feb.1922. (Rep.Pub.Health & Med.Subj.,no.7) Ministry of Health.

A clinical and pathological study of 1,673 cases of dead-births and neonatal births. 14 Aug.1926. (S.R.S.,no.109) Medical Research Council.

HOLLAND, Henry Thurston, 1st Viscount Knutsford
Central British Red Cross Committee.
Report on voluntary organisations in aid of the sick and wounded during the South African War. May 1902. War Office.

HOLLAND, Kenneth G.
Commissioners to administer transitional payments in the County of Durham.
Report. April 1933. 1932/3 Cmd.4339 xv. Ministry of Labour.

HOLLAND, Thomas Henry
Committee on the qualifications and recruitment of officials of mines.
Report. 11 July 1930. Mines Department.
Indian industrial commission.
Report. March 1919. 1919 Cmd.51 xvii.
Evidence, vols. 1-5. 1919 Cmd. 234, Cmd. 235, Cmd. 236, Cmd. 237, Cmd.238, xvii, xviii, xix, xx. India Office.

HOLLINGWORTH, S.E.
The geology of the Brampton district. (Sheet 18) 1 June 1932. (Mem.Geol.Surv.) Geological Survey.

HOLMAN, H.J.
A survey of insecticide materials of vegetable origin. 1940. Imperial Institute.

HOLMES, Edmond Gore Alexander
The Montessori system of education. Oct.1912.
(Educational pamphlets,no.24) Board of Education.

HOLMES, George Charles Vincent
Committee of inquiry into the architects and
surveyors' and engineering divisions of H.M. Office
of Works, London.
Report. 22 Oct.1913. 1914 Cd.7416 xlix.
Treasury.

HOLMES, H.T.
The course system in evening schools. May 1910.
(Educational pamphlets, no.19) Board of
Education.

HOLMES, Joseph Stanley
Committee of the staffing and methods of work of
the Department of Overseas Trade.
Report. 29 Nov.1920. 1921 Cmd.1461 xvii.
Cabinet Office.

Departmental committee on the high cost of
building working-class dwellings.
Report. July 1921. 1921 Cmd.1447 xiii. Ministry
of Health.

HOLT, Richard Durning
Select committee on Post Office servants (wages and
conditions of employment).
Report and proceedings. 5 Feb.1913. 1912/3
(507) ix.
Proceedings. 7 Aug.1913. 1913 (268) x.
Evidence. Vol.1: 8 May - 27 November 1912.
Vol.2: 3 December 1912 to 1 May 1913. 1913
(268) xi, xii.
Appendices and index. 1913 (268) xiii. House of
Commons.

HOOVER, M.M.
Collection of native grass seed in the great plains,
U.S.A. Sept.1937. (Bull.,no.24) Imperial Bureau of
Plant Genetics. Herbage Plants.

Hope, Anthony. SEE. Hawkins, A.H.

HOPE, George Price Webley
Departmental committee on H.M. Coastguard.
Report. 22 July 1931. 1930/1 Cmd.3918 x.
Board of Trade.

HOPE, John Victor Alexander, 2nd Marquess of
Linlithgow
Departmental committee on distribution and prices
of agricultural produce.
Interim report on milk products. 17 April 1923.
1923 Cmd.1854 ix.
Interim report on fruit and vegetables. 14 June
1923. 1923 Cmd.1892 ix.
Interim report on meat, poultry and eggs. 23
July 1923. 1923 Cmd.1927 ix.
Interim report on cereals, flour and bread. 9
Oct.1923. 1923 Cmd.1971 ix.
Final report. 22 Nov.1923. 1924 Cmd.2008 vii.
Ministry of Agriculture and Fisheries.

Joint committee on Indian constitutional reform.
Report and proceedings; evidence; appendices,
records and indices. 16 Nov.1933. 1932/3 (112)
v, vi, vii, viii, ix.
Report, proceedings and records. 31 Oct.1934.
1933/4 (5) vi, vii, viii. House of Commons and
House of Lords.

Royal commision on agriculture in India.
First interim report. 25 April 1927. 1927
Cmd.2878 viii.
Second interim report. 15 May 1927. 1927
Cmd.2887 viii.

Third interim report. 25 May 1927. 1927
Cmd.2905 viii.
Fourth interim report. 7 June 1927. 1927
Cmd.2921 viii.
Fifth interim report. 7 June 1927. 1927
Cmd.2922 viii.
Sixth interim report. 25 May 1927. 1927
Cmd.2924 viii.
Seventh interim report. 30 June 1927. 1927
Cmd.2936 viii.
Eighth interim report. 21 July 1927. 1927
Cmd.2942 viii.
Ninth interim report. 25 July 1927. 1927
Cmd.2944 viii.
Tenth interim report. 25 July 1927. 1927
Cmd.2945 viii.
Eleventh interim report. 2 Aug.1927. 1927
Cmd.2949 viii.
Twelfth interim report. 16 Aug.1927. 1927
Cmd.2957 viii.
Thirteenth interim report. 26 Jan 1928. 1928
Cmd.3105 viii.
Fourteenth interim report. 26 Jan.1928. 1928
Cmd.3117 viii.
Fifteenth interim report. 26 Jan.1928. 1928
Cmd.3139 viii.
Sixteenth interim report. 26 Jan.1928. 1928
Cmd.3105 viii.
Report. 14 April 1928. 1928 Cmd.3132 viii.

Evidence.
Vol.1: Evidence of officers serving under
the Government of India. 3 vols. 1927,
1928.
Vol.2: Evidence taken in the Bombay
Presidency. 2 vols. 1927.
Vol.3: Evidence taken in the Madras
Presidency. 1927.
Vol.4: Evidence taken in Bengal. 1927
Vol.5: Evidence taken in Assam. 1927.
Vol.6: Evidence taken in the Central
Provinces. 1927.
Vol.7: Evidence taken in the United
Provinces. 1927.
Vol.8: Evidence taken in the Punjab. 1927.
Vol.9: Evidence taken in the North-West
Frontier Province. 1927.
Vol.10: Evidence taken in England. 1927.
Vol.11: Evidence taken in Sind. 1928.
Vol.12: Evidence taken in Burma. 1928.
Vol.13: Evidence taken in Bihar and
Orissa. 1928.
Vol.14: Appendix to the report. 1928.

HOPKINS, Frederick Gowland
Committee on accessory food factors (vitamins).
Report on the present state of knowledge. July
1919. (S.R.S.,no.38) Medical Research
Committee.

Committee on cattle diseases.
Report. 16 April 1934. 1933/4 Cmd.4591 ix.
Economic Advisory Council.

Report of a conference between the Advisory
Committee on Nutrition and a committee of the
British Medical Association. May 1934. Ministry of
Health.

HOPKINS, John Wells Wainwright
Select committee on the Great Yarmouth Gas
Special Order.
Report, proceedings and evidence. 16 Dec.1925.
1924/5 (198) vii. House of Commons.

**HOPKINSON, Alfred**
Committee on child adoption.
>    Report. 9 Feb.1921. 1921 Cmd.1254 ix. Home Office.

Departmental committee on the public veterinary services.
Report. 7 Jan.1913. 1912/3 Cd.6575 xlviii.
Minutes of evidence, appendix and index. 1912/3 Cd.6652 xlviii. Board of Agriculture and Fisheries.

**HOPKINSON, B.**
Committee on the horse-power rating of motor cars.
>    Report. Sept.1912. 1912/3 Cd.6414 xlii.
>    Minutes of evidence and appendices. 1912/3 Cd.6415 xlii. Treasury.

**HOPWOOD, Francis John Stephens, *lst Baron Southborough***

Committee of enquiry into "shell-shock".
>    Report. 22 June 1922. 1922 Cmd.1734 xii. War Office.

Committee on disinterested management of public houses.
>    Report. 14 April 1927. 1927 Cmd.2862 x. Home Office.
Committee on the initial salary of "Lytton entrants" and the appointment of ex-servicemen to posts in the civil service.
>    Interim report. 20 June 1923.
>    Second interim report. 30 July 1923.
>    Final report. 5 June 1924. Treasury.

Committee to consider various suggestions which have been made for developing the benefits afforded by the Patent office to inventors.
>    Report. 10 April 1900. 1900 Cd.210 xxvi. Board of Trade.

Committees on constitutional reform in India. Reports.
>    Vol.1: Report of the franchise committee. 22 Feb.1919. 1919 Cmd.141 xvi.
>    Vol.2: Report of the committee on division of functions. 26 Feb.1919. 1919 Cmd.103 xvi.
>    Vol.3: Views of the government of India. 23 April 1919. 1919 Cmd.176 xvi. India Office.

**HORDER, Thomas Jeeves, *1st Baron***
Committee on the conditions of air-raid shelters with special reference to health.
>    Recommendations. Nov.1940. 1939/40 Cmd.6234 iv.
>    Further recommendations. Dec.1940. 1940/1 Cmd.6245 iv. Ministry of Health *and* Home Office.

**HORNE, John**
The geology of the country around Beauly and Inverness. (Sheet 83) (Mem.Geol.Surv.,Scotl.) Geological Survey, Scotland.

The geology of the lower Findhorn and lower Strath Nairn. (Sheet 84 and part of 94) 4 Jan.1923.(Mem.Geol.Surv.,Scotl.) Geological Survey,Scotland.

Guide to the geological model of the Assynt Mountains. 26 May 1914. Geological Survey, Scotland.

**HORRIDGE, T. Gardner.**
Committee on the detention in custody of prisoners committed for trial in England and Wales.
>    Report. 30 Nov.1921. 1922 Cmd.1574 x. Lord Chancellor's Office.

**HORSBRUGH, Florence**
Departmental committee on adoption societies and agencies.
>    Report. 17 June 1937. 1936/7 Cmd.5499 ix. Home Office.

**HORSLEY, J.A.Bernard**
Electric storage battery locomotive competition.
>    Report of judges. 21 April 1926. Mines Department.

**HOSIE, Alexander**
Report on a visit to southern ports of China. Oct.1907. (Dip.cons.reports: misc.ser.,no.665) 1908 Cd.3728-1 cviii. Foreign Office.

**HOTINE, M.**
Calibration of surveying cameras. Jan.1929. (Prof.Papers of the Air Survey Committee, 5) War Office.

Extension of the "Arundel" method. Jan.1929. (Prof.Papers of the Air Survey Committee, 6) War Office.

The fourcade stereogoniometer. 10 Nov.1930.(Prof.Papers of the Air Survey Committee, 7) War Office.

Simple methods of surveying from air photographs. Feb.1927. (Prof.Papers of the Air Survey Committee, 3) War Office.

The stereoscopic examination of air photographs. Aug.1927. (Prof.Paper of the Air Survey Committee, 4) War Office.

**HOUSTON, H.**
Committee on probation officers' superannuation.
>    Report. 1 June 1926. Home Office.

**HOWARD, Edward Stafford**
Advisory committee on forestry.
>    Reports; July to October, 1912. 31 Oct.1912. 1913 Cd.6713 xxv. Board of Agriculture and Fisheries.

Departmental committee on inshore fisheries.
>    Vol.1: Report and appendices. 8 April 1914. 1914 Cd.7373 xxx.
>    Vol.2: Evidence and index. 1914 Cd.7374 xxx. Board of Agriculture and Fisheries.

**HOWARD, Esme**
Report on the institution known as the Initiative in Switzerland. 15 April 1911. (Misc.,no.6, 1911) 1911 Cd.5634 lxiii. Foreign Office.

Report on the municipalisation of bakeries at Catania, Italy. 11 May 1903. (Dip.cons.reports: misc.ser.,no.592) 1903 Cd.1387-5 lxxvi. Foreign Office.

**HOWARD, F.T.**
Memoranda on promotion in elementary schools in London. April 1919. (Elementary School series,no.1. Educational pamphlets,no.35) Board of Education.

Howard, H.F. *SEE*: Fitzalan-Howard, H., *15th Duke of Norfolk.*

**HOWARD, Henry**
Report on the draining of the Zuiderzee. 13 July 1901. (Dip.cons.reports: misc.ser.,no.565) 1902 Cd.787-1 ciii. Foreign Office.

**HOWARD, Keble**
The glory of Zeebrugge and the "Vindictive". 1918. Ministry of Information.

**HOWARTH, Edward Goldie**
Committee on a procedure for the award of

**HOWARTH, Edward Goldie,** (continued)
maintenance allowances in respect of children between the ages of 14 and 15 years.
> Report. May 1930. 1929/30 Cmd.3570 xiii. Board of Education.

**HOWELL, C.E.**
Report on the financial provisions of the Poor Law Superannuation (Ireland) Bill, 1901. 8 Nov.1901. 1902 Cd.925 xxxvii. Irish Secretary's Office.

**HOWELL, J. Pryse**
An agricultural atlas of Wales. 1921. Ministry of Agriculture and Fisheries.

**HOWELL, Walter J.**
Committee on continuous discharge certificates for merchant seamen. *SEE:* Ward, William Humble, *2nd Earl of Dudley.*

**HOWLING, G.E.**
Asbestos. (Rep.Min.Ind.) 1937. Imperial Institute.

Chrome ore and chromium. (Rep.Min.Ind.) 1940. Imperial Institute.

**HUBBARD, John Gellibrand,** *3rd Baron Addington*
Committee on local government and public health consolidation.
> Interim report. 8 March 1933. 1932/3 Cmd.4272 xiii.
> Second interim report. 10 Jan.1936. 1935/6 Cmd.5059.xi.
> Third interim report. 1 Dec.1937. 1937/38 Cmd.5628 xi. Ministry of Health.

**HUBERT, William Henry de Bargue**
Report on the psychological treatment of crime. Dec.1938. Home Office.

**HUCKIN, Victor**
Report on the railways of Colombia. July 1910. (Dip.cons.reports: misc.ser., no.678) 1910 Cd.4963 xcvi. Foreign Office *and* Board of Trade.

**HUDSON, P.S.**
Vernalization, or Lyssenko's method for the pre-treatment of seed. March 1933. (Bull.,no.9) Imperial Bureau of Plant Genetics: Herbage Plants.

**HUDSPETH, Henry Moore**
Explosions in coal mines; a comparison between Great Britain and France. Oct.1937. 1936/7 Cmd.5566 xiii. Mines Department.

**HUGHES, W.E.**
On the electro-deposition of iron. March 1922. Department of Scientific and Industrial Research.

**HUGHES, William Morris**
Royal commission on the Navigation Bill of the Australian commonwealth, 1904. 1906. 1906 Cd.3023 lxxvii.

**HUMBERSTONE, Thomas Lloyd**
An experiment in industrial research. Aug.1915. (Educational pamphlets, no.30) Board of Education.

**HUMPHREYS, George William**
Departmental committee on the construction of flats for the working classes.
> Interim report. 13 May 1935.
> Final report. 20 May 1937. Ministry of Health.

Reinforced concrete structures committee.
> Report. July 1933. Department of Scientific and Industrial Research.

Report on the proposed bridge at Charing Cross. 4 April 1928. Ministry of Transport.

**HUNTER, William,** *Lord*
Committee on the alleged increases in the rental of small dwelling-houses in industrial districts of Scotland.
> Report. 9 Nov.1915. 1914/6 Cd.8111 xxxv.
> Evidence, appendices and index. 1914/6 Cd.8154 xxxv. Scottish Office.
Committee on the disturbances in the Punjab, *etc.*
> Report. 8 March 1920. 1920 Cmd.681 xiv.
> Reports on the Punjab disturbances of April 1919. 1920 Cmd.534 xiv. India Office.
Committee on the increase of rent and mortgage interest (war restrictions) acts.
> Report. 31 Dec.1918. 1918Cd.9235 xiii. Ministry of Reconstruction.

**HUNWICKE, R.F.**
Canned fruit. Nov.1923. (F.I.B. special rep.,no.16) Department of Scientific and Industrial Research.
Studies in sweetened and unsweetened (evaporated) condensed milk. 25 July 1923. (F.I.B. Special Rep.,no.13) Department of Scientific and Industrial Research.

**HURCOMB, Cyril William**
Committee on the valuation for rating of railways situated partly in England and Wales and partly in Scotland.
> Report. 10 Nov.1922. Ministry of Transport.

**HURD, Archibald**
History of the Great War. The merchant navy. Vols. 1-3. 1929. War Office.
Naval prospects in 1917. 1917. Ministry of Information.

**HURD, Percy Angier**
Canada; past,present and future. 1918. Ministry of Information.

**HUTCHINS, D.E.**
Report on the forests of British East Africa. Dec.1908. 1909 Cd.4723 lx. Colonial Office.
Report on the forests of Kenya. June 1907. (Colonial rep: misc.,no.41) 1907 Cd.3561 liv. Colonial Office.

Hutchinson, *Viscount. SEE:* Hely-Hutchinson,R.W.J., *6th Earl of Donomore*

**HUTCHINSON, James Randall**
Report on enteric fever in the Borough of Colne, Lancashire, 1913. 16 Aug. 1913. (Rep. Pub. Health & Med. Subj., no. 84) Local Government Board.

Report on the incidence of scarlet fever and of diptheria in 1922 in the village of Romsbury, Wiltshire. May 1923. (Rep. Publ. Health & Med. Subj., no.16) Ministry of Health.

Report on the sanitary conditions of Chadderton U.D. 31 July 1913. (Rep.Publ.Health & Med.Subj., no.81) Local government Board.

Report on the sanitary conditions of Oakengates U.D., Shropshire. (Rep. Pub. Health & Med. Subj., no. 70) 7 Aug. 1912. Local Government Board.

**HUTCHINSON, Thomas Massie**
Springs research committee.
> Report. 25 Aug.1931. Department of Scientific and Industrial Research.

**HUTTON, James Arthur**
Artificial propagation of salmon: a report by an interdepartmental committee. Dec.1932. (Salmon Fish., 1932, no.7) Fishery Board for Scotland.

**HYAMSON, Albert Montefiore**
Great Britain and the Jews. 1918. Ministry of Information.

HYDE, Clarendon Golding
Departmental committee on engineering trades after the war. 21 March 1917. 1918 Cd.9073 xiii. Board of Trade.

Departmental committee on the method of charging for gas on a thermal basis.
Report. 19 Feb.1923. 1923 Cmd.1825 xi. Board of Trade.

HYDE-JOHNSON, H.J.
The system of education in southern Nigeria. 5 July 1913. (Imperial education conference papers) Board of Education.

HYSLOP, G.P.
Departmental committee on the prevention of dangers in mines from accumulations of water or other liquid matter.
Report. 8 July 1927. Mines Department.

Iddesleigh, *Lord. SEE:* Northcote, W.S., *2nd Earl.*

IDLE, George
The effect of bilge keels on the rolling of lightships. Aug.1924. National Physical Laboratory. Department of Scientific and Industrial Research.

ILES, J.C.
Departmental committee on the playgrounds of public elementary schools.
Report with abstracts of evidence. 17 Oct.1912. 1912/3 Cd.6463 xxi. Board of Education.

Ilkeston, *Lord. SEE:* Foster, W., *1st Baron.*

Inchcape, *Lord. SEE:* MacKay, J.L., *1st Baron*

INGRAMS, William Harold
Report on the social, economic and political condition.of the Hadhramaut, Aden protectorate. 19 July 1936. (Colonial, no.123) Colonial Office.

INMAN, Arthur Conyers
A study of the serological races of the Flexner group of dysentery bacilli. 28 Oct.1919. (S.R.S.,no.42) Medical Research Council.

INNES, Charles Alexander
Ships replacement committee.
Report. 15 March 1937. 1936/7 Cmd.5459 xiii. Board of Trade.

Innes, E.A.M. *SEE:* Mitchell-Innes, E.A.

INSKIP, Thomas Walker Hobart
Chancel repairs committee.
Report. 5 May 1930. 1929/30 Cmd.3571 viii. Lord Chancellor's Office.

Committee of imperial defence.
Report of the sub-committee on the vulnerability of capital ships to air attack. 30 July 1936. 1936/7 Cmd.5301 xii. War Office.

Departmental committee on the employment of women and young persons on the two shift system.
Report. 12 Nov.1920. 1920 Cmd.1037 xix.
Evidence. 1920 Cmd.1038 xix. Home Office.

IRVINE, James Colquhoun
Committee on the training of candidates for appointment as forest officers in the government service. 1 July 1931. (Colonial,no.61) Colonial Office.

IRVINE, James Mercer
Board of inquiry on port labour in Aberdeen and Glasgow.
Report. 18 Oct.1937. Ministry of Labour.

IRVING, E.
The system of education in Hong Kong. June 1914. (Imperial education conference papers) Board of Education.

Islington, *Lord. SEE:* Dickson-Poynder, J.P., *1st Baron*

JACK, Evan Maclean
Report on the work of the British section of the Anglo-German-Belgian boundary commission (for Uganda), 1911. 15 May 1912. Colonial Office.

JACKS, G.V.
Erosion and soil conservation. March 1938. (Bull.,no.25) Imperial Bureau of Plant Genetics: Herbage Plants.

JACKSON, Francis Stanley
Select committee on high prices and profits.
Special report and evidence. 7 Aug.1919. 1919 (166) v.
Report, proceedings and evidence. 17 Dec.1919. 1919 (234) v. House of Commons.

JACKSON, Frederick Huth
Aircraft insurance committee.
Report. 9 July 1915. 1914/6 Cd.7997 xxxvii. Board of Trade.

Sub-committee of the Committee of Imperial Defence on the insurance of British shipping in time of war.
Report. 30 April 1914. 1914 Cd.7560 lxx. War Office.

JACKSON, Henry
London and Home Counties Traffic Advisory Committee. Public inquiry on the provision of a regular passenger service on the River Thames.
Report. 11 Nov.1934.
Minutes of proceedings. 1934. Ministry of Transport.

London and Home Counties Traffic Advisory committee.
Report on Charing Cross bridge. 29 June 1936. Ministry of Transport.

JACKSON, Henry Bradwardine
Committee on trans-atlantic wireless telephony.
Report. 22 March 1927. 1927 Cmd.2858 xii. Post Office.

Radio Research Board. Sub-committee on radio telephone.
Report. July 1922. 1922 Cmd.1707 x. Department of Scientific and Industrial Research.

JACKSON, John
Conferences between employers, operatives and inspectors on fencing of machinery and other safeguards and ventilation in cotton bleaching, dyeing and printing works. 2 June 1914. Home Office.

Departmental committee on artificial humidity in cotton cloth factories.
Report with appendices. 23 Jan.1928. Home Office.

Departmental committee on dust in card rooms in the cotton industry.
Report. 29 Oct. 1931. Home Office.

JACKSON, Richard Hoyle
East African guaranteed loan committee.
Report. 20 Dec.1929. 1929/30 Cmd.3494 viii. Colonial Office.

JACKSON, William Lawies, *1st Baron Allerton*
Royal commission on coal supplies.
Vol.1: Report. 5 Aug.1903. 1903 Cd.1724 xvi.
Vml.2: Minutes of evidence and appendix. 1903 Cd.1725 xvi.
Vol.3: Plans, curves and diagrams. 1903 Cd.1726 xvi.

JACKSON, William Lawies, *1st Baron Allerton* (cont.)
Second report.
Vol.1: Report. 24 Feb.1904. 1904 Cd.1990 xxiii.
Vol.2: Evidence and appendices. 1904 Cd.1991 xxiii.
Vol.3: Plans and diagrams. 1904 Cd.1992 xxiii.
Final report. 7 Jan.1905.
Part I: General report. 1905 Cd.2353 xvi.
Part II: Report on coal resources of district A. 1905 Cd.2354 xvi.
Part III: Report on coal resources of district B. 1905 Cd.2355 xvi.
Part IV: Report on coal resources of district C. 1905 Cd.2356 xvi.
Part V: Report on coal resources of district D. 1905 Cd.2357 xvi.
Part VI: Report on coal resources of district E. 1905 Cd.2358 xvi.
Part VII: Report on coal resources of district F. 1905 Cd.2359 xvi.
Part VIII: Report on coal resources of district G. 1905 Cd.2360 xvi.
Part IX: Report of the geological committee on the resources of the concealed and improved coalfields of the U.K. 1905 Cd.2361 xvi.
Part X: Minutes of evidence. 1905 Cd.2362 xvi.
Part XI: Appendices. 1905 Cd.2363 xvi.
Part XII: Supplement containing maps and diagrams. 1905 Cd.2364 xvi.
Part XIII: Replies of consular officers on the maintenance of the British coal trade in foreign countries. 1905 Cd.2365 xvi.

Select committee on War Office contracts.
Report, proceedings, minutes and appendix. 1 Aug.1900. 1900 (313) ix. House of Commons.

JAGGARD, W.R.
Experimental cottages; a report on the work of the Department at Amesbury, Wiltshire. Jan.1922. Department of Scientific and Industrial Research.

JAGO, Thomas Sampson
Report on the agriculture, horticulture and other natural resources of the vilayet of Tripoli, North Africa. 29 May 1900. (Dip.cons.reports: misc.ser., no.527) 1900 Cd.2-10 xci. Foreign Office.

Report on the trade and economic state of the vilayet of Tripoli, North Africa, during the past 40 years. 13 June 1902. (Dip.cons.reports: misc.ser., no.578) 1902 Cd.787-14 ciii. Foreign Office.

JAMES, H.E.O.
The localisation of sound. 13 Dec.1935. (S.R.S.,no.207) Medical Research Council.

Some factors in auditory location. 1931. (S.R.S.,no.166) Mecical Research Council.

JAMES, Henry, *1st Baron James of Hereford*
Joint select committee of the House of Lords and the House of Commons on charitable agencies for relief of widows and orphans of soldiers and sailors.
Report with the proceedings. 26 July 1901. 1901 (289) v. House of Commons.

Royal commission on accidents to railway servants.
Part I: Report. 1900. 1900 Cd.41 xxvii.
Part II: Minutes of evidence and appendices. 1900 Cd.42 xxvii.

Royal commission on alien immigration.
Report. Vol.1. 10 Aug.1903. 1903 Cd.1741 ix.
Minutes of evidence, appendices, index and analysis of evidence. Vols.2-4. 1903 Cd.1742, Cd.1741-I, Cd.1743 ix.

Royal commission on selection of justices of the peace.
Report. 6 July 1910. 1910 Cd.5250 xxxvii.
Minutes of evidence. 1910 Cd.5358 xxxvii.

Royal commission on whisky and other potable spirits.
Interim report. 24 June 1908. 1908 Cd.4180 lviii.
Minutes of evidence and appendices. Vol.1. 1908 Cd.4181 lviii.
Final report. 28 July 1909. 1909 Cd.4796 xlix.
Appendices. 1909 Cd.4797 xlix.
Index and digests of evidence. 1909 Cd.4876 xlix.

JAMIESON, George
Report on land taxation in the province of Honan, China. 24 July 1905. (Dip.cons.reports: misc.ser., no.641) 1906 Cd.2683-5 cxxii. Foreign OFfice.

JAMIESON, James William
Report on the cotton mills of China. March 1905. (Dip.cons.reports: misc.ser., no.629) 1905 Cd.2237-10 lxxxvi. Foreign Office.

JEE, Edwin C.
Joint committee on damage to fisheries.
Interim report: results of experiments on the influence on inland fisheries of washing from tarred roads. 14 March 1922.
Detailed biological and chemical reports on tars used for roads surfacing. May 1930. Ministry of Transport *and* Ministry of Agriculture and Fisheries.
Standing committee on rivers pollution. Roads dressings sub-committee.
Report on the influence on fish and other forms of stream life of washings from bituminous roads. 14 March 1923. Ministry of Agriculture and Fisheries.

JEFFRAY, R.J.
Report on the conditions and prospects of British trade in Australia by the Advisory Committee on Commercial Intelligence. July 1907. 1907 Cd. 3639 lvi. Board of Trade.
Report on the conditions and prospects of British trade in New Zealand. Dec.1907. 1908 Cd.3867 lxxiii. Board of Trade.

JEFFREY, John
Local government and public health consolidation (Scotland).
Memorandum. 25 Feb.1939. 1938/9 Cmd.5962 xxi. Scottish Office.

JEFFREYS, Arthur Frederick
Select committee on private business.
Report, proceedings, minutes of evidence, appendix and index. 21 Nov.1902. 1902 (378) vii. House of Commons.

JENKIN, Charles Frewen
Earth pressure tables. Aug.1934. (B.R.B.special rep., no.24) Department of Scientific and Industrial Research.
Report on materials of construction used in aircraft and aircraft engines. Dec.1920. Aeronautical Research Committee.
Thermal properties of ethyl chloride. Oct.1923. (F.I.B., special rep., no.14) Department of Scientific and Industrial Research.

JENKINS, Walter St.David
Patents committee.
Reports. 18 March 1930. Civil Service National Whitley Council. Treasury.

JENKINSON, C. Webster
Standing committees on prices and trusts.
Report of a sub-committee on slates. 2 April 1921. 1921 Cmd.1338 xvi. Board of Trade.

JENNINGS, I.R.B.
Explosion at Lord Ashtown's Lodge, Glenahiery, County Waterford.
Reports, 14 Aug., 17 Aug., and 14 Sept. 1907. 1907 Cd.4010 xii.
Copies of report and statements relevant to the explosion. 1907 Cd.3977 xii. Irish Secretary's Office.

JERRAN, Thomas Henry Martyn
Committee on pay, allowances and pensions of the Royal Navy and Royal Marines.
Report. 27 March 1919. 1919 Cmd.149 xxxiii. Admiralty.

Jersey, Earl of. SEE: Villiers, A.G.C.,7th Earl

JESSE, F. Tennyson
The sword of Deborah; first-hand impressions of the British Women's Army in France. 1918. Ministry of Information.

JEUNE, Francis H.
Committee on the mercantile marine.
Vol.I: Report. 7 May 1903. 1903 Cd.1607 lxii.
Vol.II: Minutes of evidence. 1903 Cd.1608 lxii.
Vol.III: Appendices, analysis of evidence and index. 1903 Cd.1609 lxii. Board of Trade.

JEVONS, H. Winifrid
Relation of schools to employment in the United States. April. 1914. (Special reports on education subjects,vol.28) Board of Education.

JOHNSON, Douglas W.
Plain words from America; a letter to a German professor. Feb.1916. Ministry of Information.

JOHNSON, Nelson King
A comparison of the anemometer records for Shoeburyness and Maplin Lighthouse. July 1922. (Prof.Notes,no.28) Meteorological Office.
An investigation of the lapse rate of temperature in the lowest hundred metres of the atmosphere. Dec.1938. (Geophys.Mem., no.77) Meteorological Office.
A study of the vertical gradient of temperature in the atmosphere near the ground. April 1929. (Geophys.Mem., no.46) Meteorological Office.

JOHNSON, W.A.
Back-stays for use in mines. Jan.1940. (S.M.R.B. Paper no.103) Mines Department.

JOHNSTON, Duncan A.
Committee on redistribution of seats at parliamentary elections.
Report and supplementary report. 31 Oct. and 28 Nov.1905. 1906 (79) xcv. Local Government Board.

JOHNSTON, George Lawson
Post Office Advisory Council. Committee on a postal cheque system. 5 March 1928. 1928 Cmd.3151 xii. Post Office.

JOHNSTONE, Hugh
Departmental committee on the use of squibs for the purpose of firing shots in naked light mines.
Report. 20 March 1913. 1913 Cd.6721 xxxiv..
Minutes of evidence and appendices. 1913 Cd.6732 xxxiv. Home Office.

JOHNSTONE, Mary A.
A school week in the country. Bradford, Grange Road Secondary School, Girls Department. Aug.1910. (Educational experiments in secondary schools,2. Education pamphlets,no.21) Board of Education.

JOHNSTONE, Robert William
Report on an outbreak of enteric fever in the U.D's of Pontypool, Panteg and Abersychan and on the sanitary circumstances in these districts. 27 Aug. 1907. (Rep.Med.Insp., no.276) Local Government Board.
Report on epidemic enteric fever in Nuneaton and Chilvers Cotton U.D. 27 Nov. 1900. (Rep.Med.Insp., no.155) Local Government Board.
Report on occurrences of enteric fever in Folkstone U.D. 5 Sept.1910. (Rep.Pub.Health & Med.Subj., no.41) Local Government Board.
Report on outbreaks of enteric fever in Conway R.D. and U.D. and Llandudno U.D. during 1908 and 1909. 28 April 1910. (Rep.Pub.Health & Med.Subj., no.28) Local Government Board.
Report on outbreak of enteric fever in Ormesby U.D. 15 Sept.1909. (Rep.Pub.Health & Med.Subj., no.17) Local Government Board.
Report on the progress and diffusion of plague, cholera and yellow fever throughout the world during 1913 April 1915. (Rep.Pub.Health & Med.Subj., no.104) Local Government Board.
Report on the repeated occurrence of enteric fever at Jennet Hill and Stanford Dingley, in Bradfield R.D. 25 Jan.1910. (Rep.Pub.Health & Med.Subj., no.22) Local Government Board.
Report on the sanitary conditions of Dorchester R.D. 23 Dec.1907. (Rep.Med.Insp., no.296) Local Government Board.
Report on the sanitary conditions of Easington R.D. 23 Nov.1909. (Rep.Med.Health & Med.Subj., no.20) Local Government Board.
Report on the sanitary conditions of West Wickham parish, Bromley R.D. 30 March 1904. (Rep.Med.Insp., no.193) Local Government Board.
Report on the sanitary conditions of Sherborne R.D.,Dorset. 14 Oct.1907. (Rep.Med.Insp., no.285) Local Government Board.
Report on the sanitary conditions of Tyldesley with Shakerley U.D. and on the prevalence of enteric fever there. 13 June 1903. (Rep.Med.Insp., no.186) Local Government Board.
Report on venereal diseases. July 1913. 1913 Cd.7029 xxxii. Local Government Board.

JOHNSTONE, Sydney J.
Potash. 1915. (Mono.Min.Resour.) Imperial Institute.

JOLY, John
British educational mission. Report. Feb.1919. Board of Education.

Jones, C.D.D. SEE: Douglas-Jones, C.D.

JONES, Chester
Committee on objections to the draft regulations under the Dangerous Drugs Act.
Report. 21 May 1921. 1921 Cmd.1307 x. Home Office.
Report on bye-laws made by the London County Council under the Employment of Children Act,1903. 2 Nov.1905. 1906 Cd.2809 xc. Home Office.
Report on bye-laws made by the London County Council under the Employment of Children Act, 1903. Dec.1920. 1921 Cmd.1122 ix. Home Office.
Report on the draft regulations for docks, wharves, quays, etc. 5 Sept.1904. 1905 Cd.2284 lxxii. Home Office.

JONES, Chester (continued)
Report on the draft regulations for factories and workshops in which the process of file-cutting by hand is carried on. 14 May 1903. 1903 Cd.1658 xii. Home Office.

Report on the draft regulations for locomotives and waggons on lines and sidings or in connection with factories,workshops,*etc.* 29 June 1906. 1906 Cd.3167 cx. Home Office.

Report on (the transport workers strike and) certain disturbances at Rotherhithe on 11 June 1912 and complaints against the conduct of the police. 19 July. 1912. 1912/3 Cd.6367 xlvii. Board of Trade.

JONES, D. Rocyn
Report on an outbreak on glanders among the horses and the alleged general insanitary condition of the collieries of the Ebbw Vale Steel, Iron and Coal Co.,Ltd., Monmouthshire. 31 Dec.1910. 1911 Cd.5713 xxxvii. Home Office.

JONES, David Brynmor
Royal commission upon the duties of the metropolitan police.
Vol.1: Report and appendices. 18 June 1908. 1908 Cd.4156 l.
Vol.2: Minutes of evidence, appendices and index. 1908 Cd.4260 l.
Vol.3: Minutes of evidence, appendices and index. 1908 Cd.4261 li.

JONES, Dorothea Pughe
Report of delegates to enquire as to openings in Australia for women from the United Kingdom. 4 June 1920. 1920 Cmd.745 xxii. Colonial Office.

JONES, E.
A method for determination of the velocity of detonation over short lengths of explosive. Oct.1925. (S.M.R.B.Paper no.22) Mines Department.

JONES, Edgar Rees
Welsh consultative council on medical and allied services in Wales.
First Report. May 1920. 1920 Cmd.703 xvii.
Second Report. Aug.1921. 1921 Cmd.1448 xiii. Ministry of Health.

JONES, H.A.
History of the Great War. The war in the air. Vols. 2-6 and appendices. 8 vols. 1928-1937. War Office. *SEE: Raleigh, W. for Vol.1.*

JONES, H.Lewis
Report on the International Congress of Physiotherapy at Paris, 29 March to 2 April 1910. Aug.1910. 1910 Cd.5309 xliii. Privy Council.

JONES, Kennedy
Advisory committe on London traffic.
Report. 20 March 1920. 1920 Cmd.636 xxi.
Select committee on transport. (Metropolitan area)
Report, proceedings, evidence, appendices and index. 25 July 1919. 1919 (147) vii. House of Commons.

JONES, Morgan
Committee on educational problems of the South Wales coalfield.
Report. Nov.1931. Board of Education.

JONES, Owen Thomas
Lead and zinc. The mining district of North Cardiganshire and West Montgomeryshire. May 1920. (Special reports on the mineral resources of Great Britain, vol.20) (Mem.Geol.Surv.) Geological Survey.
Plectambonites and some allied genera. 1 Nov.1928. (Mem.Geol.Surv., Palaeont., vol.1,part5) Geological Survey.

JONES,R.C.B.
Wigan district. (Sheet 84) (Mem.Geol.Surv.) Geological Survey.

JONES, William John
Commission on the conditions of the iron and steel works in Lorraine, in the occupied areas of Germany, in Belgium, and in France.
Report. 18 June 1919. Ministry of Munitions.

JONESCO, Take
The policy of national instinct. 17 Dec.1915. Ministry of Information.

JORDAN, L
The eradication of bovine tuberculosis. 27 July 1933. (S.R.S.,no.184) Medical Research Council.

JOYNSON-HICKS, William
Report on the organisation of the British Empire Exhibition. 31 Jan.1923. 1923 Cmd.1799 x. Colonial Office.

JUBB, A.A.
Report on the occurrence of gastro-intestinal illness in the Sandown U.D., Isle of Wight. 26 July 1921. (Rep.Pub.Health & Med.Subj., no.5) Ministry of Health.

JUKES-BROWNE, A.J.
Cretaceous rocks of Britain. (Mem.Geol.Surv.)
Vol.1: The gault and upper greensand of England. 20 March 1900.
Vol.2: The lower and middle chalk of England. 16 Jan.1903.
Vol.3: The upper chalk of England. 28 Nov.1903. Geological Survey.

The geology around Andover. (Sheet 283) 23 June 1908. (Mem.Geol.Surv.) Geological Survey.

The geology of the country around Henley-on-Thames and Wallingford. (Sheet 254) 5 Aug.1908. (Mem.Geol.Surv.) Geological Survey.

The geology of the country south and east of Devizes. (Sheet 282) 22 Feb.1905. (Mem.Geol.Surv.) Geological Survey.

KATZ, S.H.
Mine rescue apparatus; the S.M.R.B. gas mask. July 1929. (S.M.R.B.Paper no.57) Mines Department.

KAY-SHUTTLEWORTH, Ughtred James, *1st Baron Shuttleworth of Gawthorpe*
Royal commission on canals and inland navigation of the United Kingdom.
Vol.I, Part.I: First report. 31 July 1906. 1906 Cd.3183 xxxii.
Vol.I,Part.II: Minutes of evidence, appendices and index. 1906 Cd.3184 xxxii.
Vol.II, Part I: Second report. 31 July 1907. 1907 Cd.3716 xxxiii.
Vol.II,Part II: Minutes of evidence, and appendices. 1907 Cd.3717 xxxiii.
Vol.III: Minutes of evidence and index. 1907 Cd.3718 xxxiii.
Vol.IV: Returns. 1907 Cd.3719 xxxiii.
Vol.V: Third report. 31 July 1909. 1909 Cd.4839 xiii.
Minutes of evidence and appendices. 1909 Cd.4840 xiii.
Vol.VI: Foreign inquiry. Report on the waterways of France,Belgium, Germany and Holland, by W.H.Lindley. Part.1: reports and appendices. Part.2: maps and tables. 8 Dec.1908. 1909 Cd.4841 xiii.
Vol.VII: Fourth and final report. 4 Dec.1909. 1910 Cd.4979 xii.

**KAY-SHUTTLEWORTH**, Ughtred James, *1st Baron Shuttleworth of Gawthorpe* (continued)

    Vol.VIII: Appendices to fourth report. 1910 Cd.5204 xii.

    Vol.IX: Reports by Sir John Wolfe Barry and Partners on the cost of improving canal routes. 1910 Cd.5083 xii.

    Vol.X: Reports on the water supplies of canal routes by R.B.Dunwoody. 1910 Cd.5447 xiii.

    Vol.XI: Final report on Ireland. 31 March 1911. 1911 Cd.5626 xiii.

    Vol.XII: Appendices to final report on Ireland. 1911 Cd.5653 xiii.

**KAYE**, George William Clarkson

Departmental committee on noise in the operation of mechanically propelled vehicles.

    First interim report. 31 Aug.1935.

    Second interim report. 18 July 1936.

    Third interim report. 13 Aug.1936.

    Final report. 16 Aug.1937. Ministry of Transport.

**KAYE**, W.C.

A comparison of the records of two anemometers at different heights at Southport. Nov.1936. (Prof.Notes, no.74) Meteorological Office.

**KEANE**, Michael

Commission of inquiry on the Cawnpore riots.

    Report and the United Provinces government resolution. 22 May 1931. 1930/1 Cmd.3891 xi. India Office.

**KEARLEY**, Hudson Ewbanke

Committee on the supply and training of boy seamen for the mercantile marine.

    Part I Report. 19 Aug.1907. 1907 Cd.3722 lxxv.

    Part II: Minutes of evidence, appendices, analysis and index. 1907 Cd. 3723 lxxv. Board of Trade.

**KEATING**, J.B.

Report on the agriculture of the State of Maine. 16 Oct.1902. (Dip.cons. reports: misc.ser., no.584) 1902 Cd.787-20 ciii. Foreign Office.

**KEESEY**, Walter Moncton

Industry and art education on the continent. Dec.1934. (Industry series, no.14, Educational pamphlet, no.102) Board of Education.

**KEITH**, James

Departmental committee on poor law in Scotland.

    Report. 7 July 1938. 1937/8 Cmd.5803 xiv. Department of Health for Scotland.

**KEITH**, N.M.

Blood volume changes in wound shock and primary haemorrhage. May 1919. (Special investigation committee on surgical shock and allied conditions, no.9) (S.R.S., no.27) Medical Research Committee.

**KEITH-FALCONER**, Algernon Hawkins Thomond, *10th Earl Kintore*

Joint select committee on government works at Cippenham.

    Report, proceedings, evidence, appendices and index. 3 July 1919. 1919 (131) v. House of Commons.

**KELVIN**, William Thomson, *1st Baron*

Royal commission on arsenical poisoning from the consumption of beer and other articles of food or drink.

    First report. 6 July 1901. 1901 Cd.692 ix.

    First report. Part II: evidence received in 1901, appendices 1 to 15 and index. Nov.1903. 1904 Cd.1845 ix.

    Final report. Part I: 6 Nov.1903. 1904 Cd.1848 ix.

    Part II: evidence, appendices, 16 to 32 and index. 1904 Cd.1869 ix.

**KEMPE**, John Arrow

Departmental committee on local taxation.

    First report. 25 June 1912. 1912/3 Cd.6304 xxxviii.

    Appendix. Vol.1: minutes of evidence, 15 Nov.1911 to 1 May 1912. 1912/3 Cd.6303-I xxxviii.

    Appendix. Vol.2: memoranda submitted to the committee. 1912/3 Cd.6303-II xxxviii.

    Final report. England and Wales. 3 March 1914. 1914 Cd.7315 xl.

    Evidence and memoranda. 1914 Cd.7316 xl. Treasury.

**KENNEDY**, Alexander Blackie William

Electrification of railways advisory committee.

    Interim report. 12 July 1920.

    Final report. 30 June 1921. Ministry of Transport.

**KENNEDY**, John Macfarlane

Investigation committee on fire risks at electricity generating stations.

    Report. March 1938. Electricity Commission. Ministry of Transport.

**KENNEDY**, W.Q.

British sources of alkali-feldspar. May 1940. (Wartime pamphlet, no.2) Geological Survey.

Kennet of the Dene. *SEE:* Young, E.H., *1st Baron.*

**KENRICK**, W.B.

Departmental committee on the hours of employment of young persons in certain unregulated occupations.

    Report. 22 Jan.1937. 1936/7 Cmd.5394 xii. Home Office.

**KENT**, Albert Frank Stanley

Investigation of industrial fatigue by physiological methods.

    Interim report. 17 Aug.1915. 1914/6 Cd.8056 xxiv.

    Second interim report. 16 Aug.1916. 1916 Cd.8335 xi. Home Office.

    (*For others see:* Newman, G.)

**KENYON**, Frederick George

Public libraries in England and Wales committee.

    Report. 24 March 1927. 1927 Cmd.2868 xii. Board of Education.

War graves; how the cemeteries abroad will be designed. 22 Nov.1918. Imperial War Graves Commission.

**KEOGH**, Alfred

Transmission of enteric fever by the "chronic carrier".

    Memorandum. June 1909. 1909 Cd.4609 lii.

    Second report. Dec.1909. 1909 Cd.4712 lii. War Office.

Report on the progress made in constituting the medical service of the Territorial force. 18 July 1908. 1909 Cd.4056 lxiv. War Office.

**KERR**, Helen L.

House planning in Scotland.

    Report of the women's house-planning committee. 3 Oct.1918. Local Government Board for Scotland.

**KERR**, Philip Henry, *11th Marquess of Lothian*

Indian Franchise Committee.

    Vol.1: Report. 1 May 1932. 1931/2 Cmd.4086 viii.

    Vols. 2 and 3: Memoranda submitted by local

KERR, Philip Henry, *11th Marquess of Lothian* (cont.)
governments and provincial franchise committees.
Vols. 4 and 5: Selections from memoranda submitted by individuals and oral evidence. India Office.

KERRIDGE, Phyllis Margaret
Hearing and speech in deaf children. 26 Jan.1937. (S.R.S.,no.221) Medical Research Council.

Kershaw, G.B. *SEE:* Northcote, W.S., *2nd Earl Iddesleigh.*

KIDD, Franklin
Brown heart - a functional disease of apples and pears. 1 July 1923. (F.I.B. special rep.,no.12) Department of Scientific and Industrial Research.

Functional diseases of apples in cold storage. Aug.1925. (F.I.B.special rep., no.23) Department of Scientific and Industrial Research.

The problems of apple transport overseas. Nov.1924. (F.I.B. special rep., no.20) Department of Scientific and Industrial Research.

KIDD, M.N.
The "black spot" of chilled and frozen meat. April 1921. (F.I.B. special rep., no.6) Department of Scientific and Industrial Research.

KIDSTON, George J.
Report on a journey in Mongolia, September to November 1903. 13 Feb.1904. (China no.3, 1904) 1904 Cd.1954 cx. Foreign Office.

KIDSTON, Robert
Fossil plants of the carboniferous rocks of Great Britain. April 1923 to Dec.1925 (Mem.Geol.Surv., Palaeont., vol.2) Geological Survey.

Killanin, *Lord. SEE:* Morris, M.H.P., *2nd Baron*

KING, Alexander F.
Standing committee on trusts.
Report by a sub-committee on the oils, fats and margarine trades. 21 Sept.1920. 1920 Cmd.982 xxiii. Board of Trade.

KING, Charles Albert
Departmental committee on telegraph and telephone accounts.
Report and appendices. 31 Oct.1908. 1909 Cd.4520 xxxvi. Post Office.

KING, George
Report by the actuaries on the preparation of the superannuation scheme for teachers, 1911. 15 March 1911. 1911 Cd.5982 lix. Scotch Education Department.

KING, Henry Douglas
Inter-departmental committee on proposed disciplinary amendments of the Army and Air Force Acts.
Report. 24 Feb.1925. 1924/5 Cmd.2376 ix. War Office.

KING, J.D.
Dental disease in the Island of Lewis. 6 March 1940. (S.R.S., no.241) Medical Research Council.

KING, L.N.F.I.
Graphical methods of plotting from air photographs. 26 May 1925. War Office.

KING, W.B.R.
The geology of the country around Flint, Hawarden and Caergwrle. (Sheet 108) 1 Dec.1923. (Mem.Geol.Surv.) Geological Survey.

KING, William Lyon Mackenzie
Report on a mission to England in connection with the immigration of Asiatics into Canada. 2 May 1908. 1908 Cd.4118 lxxi. Colonial Office.

KINLOCH, John Partane
Maternal mortality; report on maternal mortality in Aberdeen,1918-1927. Nov.1928. Scottish Board of Health.

KINNEAR, Walter Samuel
Departmental committee on approved societies' administration allowance.
Report. 9 May 1921. 1921 Cmd.1291 xv. National Health Insurance Joint Committee.

Report by the delegates to the International Labour Conference, 10th Session, 25 May to 16 June 1927. Nov.1927. 1927 Cmd.2995 xxvi. Ministry of Labour.

Report of the British delegates on the International Labour Conference, 16th Session, 12-30 April 1932. April 1933. Ministry of Labour.

Report of the British delegates on the International Labour Conference, 17th Session, Geneva, 8-30 June 1933. Feb.1934. Ministry of Labour.

Kintore, *Lord. SEE:* Keith-Falconer, A.H.T., *10th Earl.*

KIPLING, Rudyard
The graves of the fallen. 1919. Imperial War Graves Commission.

Kirkley, *Lord. SEE:* Noble, W.J., *1st Baron.*

KIRKUS, A.E.
Committee on the form of the return for tramways and trackless trolley undertakings. Report. 31 May 1923. Ministry of Transport.

KIRSCH, W.
Recent research on forage crop cultivation, fodder, conservation and utilisation at the Animal Breeding Institute of the University, Köningsberg. March 1933. (Bull.,no.8 and Tech.Comm., no.3) Imperial Bureau of Plant Genetics, Herbage Plants.

KITCHIN, F.L.
On the mesozoic rocks in some of the coal explorations in Kent. 16 Nov.1911. (Mem.Geol.Surv.) Geological Survey.

KITSON, Albert Ernest
Geological notes on St.Helena with remarks on the economic geology of that island. 20 April 1931. (Colonial,no.66) Colonial Office.

KLEIN, Joseph
Preliminary report on a new plague prophylactic. 19 Dec.1905. (Rep.Med.Insp., no.223) Local Government Board.

KLINKOWSKI, M.
Lucerne; its ecological position and distribution in the world. Nov.1933. (Bull., no.12) Imperial Bureau of Plant Genetics, Herbage Plants.

KNIGHT, B.C.J.G.
Bacterial nutrition; material for a comparative physiology of bacteria. 3 March 1936. (S.R.S., no.210) Medical Research Council.

KNIGHT, R.A.G.
The determination of the moisture content of timber. Jan.1932. (F.P.R. Bull., no.14) Department of Scientific and Industrial Research.

The moisture content of timber in new buildings. Oct.1935. (F.P.R.records, no.5) Department of Scientific and Industrial Research.

KNOX, Alexander
Notes on the geology of the continent of Africa. Nov.1905. War Office.

KNOX, J.
The economic geology of the Fife coalfields. Area 2: Cowdenbeath and central Fife. 1 March 1933. (Mem.Geol.Surv., Scotl.) Geological Survey, Scotland.

Knutsford, Lord. SEE: Holland, H.T., *1st Viscount*

KOENIG, F.P.
Report on agriculture in the Rheinish province, Germany. 2 May 1906. (Dip.cons.reports: misc.ser., no.652) 1906 Cd.2683-16 cxxii. Foreign Office.

KORENCHEVSKY, V.
The aetiology and pathology of rickets from an experimental point of view. Dec.1922. (S.R.S.,no.71) Medical Research Council.

KYNASTON, H.
The geology of the country near Oban and Dalmally (Sheet 45). 27 Feb.1908. (Mem.Geol.Surv., Scotl.) Geological Survey, Scotland.

LAIDONER, F.
Report on the situation in the locality of the provinsional line of the frontier between Turkey and Irak, fixed at Brussels on October 29,1924. 23 Nov.1925. (Misc., no.15, 1925) 1924/5 Cmd.2557 xxxii. Foreign Office.

LAING, E.V.
Studies on tree roots. Aug.1932. (Bull., no.13) Forestry Commission.

LAMB, J.C.
Inter-departmental committee on injuries to submarine cables.
Report, minutes of evidence, appendices and index. 16 Sept.1908. 1908 Cd.4331 xxv. Post Office *and* Board of Trade.

LAMB, John
Departmental committee on vagrancy in Scotland.
Report. 30 May 1936. 1935/6 Cmd.5194 xiv. Department of Health for Scotland.

LAMB, Joseph Quinton
Departmental committee on the training of rural teachers.
Report. 29 Nov.1928. Board of Education.

LAMBERT, George
Select committee on procedure relating to money resolutions.
Report, proceedings, evidence, appendices and index. 13 July 1936. 1935/6 (149) viii. House of Commons.

LAMBTON, John George, *3rd Earl of Durham*
Select committee of the House of the Lords on betting.
Report, proceedings and minutes of evidence. 17 Aug.1901. 1901 (370)v.
Report, proceedings and minutes of evidence. 8 Dec.1902. 1902 (389) v. House of Commons.

LAMOND, Henry
Some notes on two of the fishes of Loch Lomond: the powan and the lamprey. 1922. (Salmon Fish., 1922,no.2) Fishery Board for Scotland.

LAMPLUGH, George William
The concealed mesozoic rocks in Kent. 12 March 1923. (Mem.Geol.Surv.) Geological Survey.

Economic geology of Isle of Man with special reference to the metalliferous mines. 13 March 1903. (Mem.Geol.Surv.) Geological Survey.

Geology of the country around Nottingham. 16 March 1910. (Mem.Geol.Surv.) Geological Survey.

The geology of the country around Ollerton. (Sheet 113) 10 Oct.1911. (Mem.Geol.Surv.) Geological Survey.

The geology of the country between Newark and Nottingham. (Sheet 126) 23 July 1908. (Mem.Geol.Surv.) Geological Survey.

Geology of the Isle of Man. 22 Sept.1902. (Mem.Geol.Surv.) Geological Survey.

The geology of the Melton Mowbray district and south-east Nottinghamshire. (Sheet 142) 17 Aug.1909. (Mem.Geol.Surv.) Geological Survey.

Iron ores: bedded ores of the lias, oolites and later formations in England. 19 March 1919. (Special reports on the Mineral Resources of Great Britain, vol.12) (Mem.Geol.Surv.) Geological Survey.

On the mesozoic rocks in some of the coal explorations in Kent. 16 Nov.1911. (Mem.Geol.Surv.) Geological Survey.

The water supply of Nottinghamshire from underground sources. 27 March 1914. (Mem.Geol.Surv.) Geological Survey.

LAMPSON-LOCKER, Godfrey
Departmental committee on compensation for silicosis.
Report dealing with the Refractories Industries (Silicosis) Scheme, 1919. 21 Dec.1923. Home Office.

LANE-CLAYPON, Janet Elizabeth
Cancer of the breast and its surgical treatment; a review of the literature. Aug.1924. (Rep.Pub.Health & Med.Subj., no.28).
Further report with special reference to its associated and antecedent conditions. Jan.1926. (Rep.Pub.Health & Med.Subj., no.32) Ministry of Health.

Cancer of the uterus; a statistical enquiry into the results of treatment, being an analysis of the existing literature. May 1927. (Rep.Pub.Health & Med.Subj., no.40) Ministry of Health.

A clinical and pathological study of 1,673 cases of dead-births and neonatal births. 14 Aug.1926. (S.R.S., no.109) Medical Research Council.

Incurable cancer; an investigation of hospital patients in eastern London. Nov.1931. (Rep.Pub.Health & Med.Subj., no.66) Ministry of Health.

Maternity and child welfare. Memorandum on health visiting. Nov.1914. Local Government Board.

Report on the available data on the value of boiled milk as a food for infants and young animals. 24 Feb.1912. (Rep.Pub.Health & Med.Subj., no.63) Local Government Board.

Report on the "biological properties" of milk, both of the human species and of cows, in relation to the feeding of infants. 4 Jan.1913. (Rep.Pub.Health & Med.Subj., no.76) Local Government Board.

Report on cancer of the lip, tongue and skin; an analysis of the literature. May 1930. (Rep.Pub.Health & Med.Subj., no.59) Ministry of Health.

Report on the late results of operation for cancer of the breast. July 1928. (Rep.Pub.Health & Med.Subj., no.51) Ministry of Health.

Report on the provision of midwifery service in the County of London. 24 Jan.1917. (Rep.Pub.Health & Med.Subj., no.111) Local Government Board.

Report on the treatment of cancer of the uterus at the Samaritan Free Hospital. Dec.1927. (Rep.Pub.Health & Med.Subj., no.47) Ministry of Health.

LANE-FOX, George Richard, *1st Baron Bingley*
Re-organisation commission.
> Report on fat stock for England and Wales. 28 March 1934. (Economic Series, no.39) Ministry of Agriculture and Fisheries.
> Report on pigs and pig products. 13 Oct.1932. (Economic Series, no.37) Ministry of Agriculture and Fisheries.

LANGDON, J.N.
An experimental study of certain forms of manual dexterity. Aug.1932. (I.H.R.B.Rep., no.66) Medical Research Council.
Inspection processes in industry; a preliminary report. May 1932. (I.H.R.B.Rep., no.63) Medical Research Council.

LANGLANDS, N.M.S.
Experiments on binocular vision. 18 June 1929. (S.R.S., no.133) Medical Research Council.

Lankester, E.R. *SEE:* Thompson, D.W.

LAPAGE, Geoffrey
The bearing of the physiology of parastic nematodes on their treatment and control. 1935. Imperial Bureau of Agricultural Parasitology.
The effects of some natural factors of the second ecdysis of nematode infective larvae. 1937. Imperial Bureau of Agricultural Parasitology.

LATTER, Oswald Hawkins
Report on science teaching in public schools. June 1909. (Educational pamphlets, no.17) Board of Education.

LAUNDER, W.B.
Report on conferences concerning fencing of machinery and other safety precautions in woolen and worsted factories. 2 March 1936. Home Office.

LAURENCE, Percival Maitland
Royal commission on fire brigades and fire prevention.
> Report. 20 July 1923. 1923 Cmd.1945 xi.
> Minutes of evidence. 1923. Home Office.

LAVISSE, Ernest
German theory and practice of war. 1915. Ministry of Information.

LAW, Andrew Bonar
Committee on the existing provisions of the law...(on seamen's wages, etc.). 8 July 1905. 1905 (334) lxxi. Board of Trade.
Committee on the measurement of the tonnage of steam ships.
> Vol.1: Report. 24 May 1906. 1906 Cd.3045 cix.
> Vol.2: Minutes of evidence, appendices and index. 1906 Cd.3046 cix. Board of Trade.
Select committee on foreign ships (application of statutory powers).
> Report, proceedings, minutes of evidence and appendix. 2 Aug.1904. 1904 (299) vi. House of Commons.
Select committee on foreign ships (statutory requirements).
> Report, proceedings, evidence and appendix. 27 July 1905. 1905 (269) vii. House of Commons.
Select committee on naval and military services (pensions and grants).
> Special report with proceedings. 30 Jan.1915. 1914/6 (53) iv.
> Second special report, proceedings, evidence and appendices. 14 April 1915. 1914/6 (196) iv.
> Third special report with proceedings. 3 Sept.1915. 1914/6 (328) iv. House of Commons.

Select committee on workmen's trains.
> Report, proceedings, evidence and appendix. 30 July 1903. 1903 (297) viii. House of Commons.

LAW, Edward FitzGerald
Committee on the establishment of co-operative credit societies in India.
> Report. 1903. 1903 Cd.1747 xlvi. India Office.

LAW, Hugh Alexander
Why is Ireland at war? 1916. Ministry of Information.

LAWES, Edward Thornton Hill
Report on the draft regulations for factories and workshops in which tinning of metal articles is carried on. 6 May 1909. 1909 Cd.4740 xxi. Home Office.

LAWLEY, Beilby, *3rd Baron Wenlock*
Departmental committee on milk and cream regulaions.
> Report. 16 Jan.1901. 1901 Cd.491 xxx.
> Minutes of evidence, *etc.* 1901 Cd.484 xxx. Board of Agriculture.

LAWRENCE, Alfred Tristram, *1st Baron Trevethin*
Admiralty Transport Arbitration Board.
> Report. 27 July 1927. Admiralty.

Committee of inquiry on venereal disease.
> Report. June 1923. Ministry of Health.

Report of a public inquiry at Carmarthen on the 24th and 25th March 1904. 18 April 1904. 1904 Cd.2041 lxxv. Board of Education.

LAWRENCE, Charles Napier, *1st Baron Lawrence of Kingsgate*
Royal commission on national health insurance.
> Report. 22 Feb.1926. 1926 Cmd.2596 xiv.
> Minutes of evidence. 4 vols. 1925.
> Appendices. 4 parts. 1924-6.
> Index. Feb.1926.

LAWRENCE, Herbert Alexander
Committee on administration of and accounting for army expenditure.
> Report. 23 Oct.1923. 1924 Cmd.2073 vii. War Office.

LAWRENCE, J.D.
The system of education in British Guiana. 23 Dec.1912. (Imperial education conference papers) Board of Education.

LAWRENCE, Maud Agnes
General report on the teaching of domestic subjects in England and Wales. Dec.1911. Board of Education.
Report on the teaching of needlework in public elementary schools. Aug.1912. Board of Education.
Special report on the teaching of cookery to public elementary school children in England and Wales. 30 July 1906. Board of Education.

LAWRENCE, Paul Ogden
Committee on the poor persons rules.
> Report. 29 Oct.1919. 1919 Cmd.430 xxvii. Lord Chancellor's Office.
Poor persons' rules committee.
> Report. 17 Feb.1925. 1924/5 Cmd.2358 xv. Lord Chancellor's Office.
Trustee securities committee.
> Report. 16 April 1928. 1928 Cmd.3107 xii. Lord Chancellor's Office.

LAWRENCE, Robert Daniel
The carbohydrate content of food. 30 April 1929. (S.R.S., no.135) Medical Research Council.

LAWRENCE, S.
   Sub-committee on co-ordination of the vocational training of women.
      Report. Dec.1918. Ministry of Reconstruction.

LAWSON, Harry Lawson Webster, *1st Viscount Burnham*
   Committee on promotion of officers (Not in regular army).
      (For first report *SEE:* Churchill, W.L.S.)
      Second report on promotion and pay of officers of the Royal Army Medical Corps., special reserve and Territorial Force. 1 Sept.1918. 1917/8 Cd.8643 iv.
      Third and final report: promotion of officers in the new armies borne upon the general list. 10 Jan.1918. 1918 Cd.8978 vi. War Office.
   Departmental committee on the training of teachers for public elementary schools.
      Report. April 1925. 1924/5 Cmd.2409 xii. Board of Education.
   Standing joint committee representing local education authorities and the National Union of Teachers.
      Report on a provisional minimum scale of salaries for teachers in public elementary schools. 21 Nov.1919. 1919 Cmd.443 xxi. Board of Education.
   Unemployment insurance advisory committee.
      Report on draft regulations. 5 Oct.1931. 1930/1 (150) xvii. Ministry of Labour.

LAWSON, John A.
   Memories of Deville Wood; South Africa's great battle. 1918. Ministry of Information.

LAWSON, John Grant
   Departmental committee on highway authorities and administration in England and Wales.
      Part I: Report. 11 Aug.1903. 1904 Cd.1793 xxiv.
      Part II: Minutes of evidence, appendix and index. 1904 Cd.1794 xxiv. Local Government Board.
   Departmental committee on the nursing of the sick poor in workhouses.
      Part I: Report and summary of recommendations. 10 Nov.1902. 1902 Cd. 1366 xxxix.
      Part II: Evidence, appendix and index. 1902 Cd.1367 xxxix. Local Government Board.
   Select committee on repayment of loans by local authorities.
      Report, proceedings, minutes of evidence and appendix. 24 June 1902. 1902 (239) viii. House of Commons.

LAWSON, John James
   Report of the British delegates on the International Labour Conference, Geneva, 28 May to 18 June 1931. March 1932. Ministry of Labour.

LAWSON-JOHNSTON, George, *1st Baron Luke of Pavenham*
   Advisory committee on nutrition.
      First report. 5 March 1937. (no other reports identified) Ministry of Health.

LAYLAND-BARRATT, Francis
   Select committee on local legislation.
      Special report and proceedings. 19 Aug.1909. 1909 (260) viii. House of Commons.

LEA, C.H.
   Rancidity in edible fats. June 1937. (F.I.B.special rep., no.46) Department of Scientific and Industrial Research.

LEA, F.M.
   Lightweight concrete aggregates. July 1936. (B.R.B.Bull,no.15) Department of Scientific and Industrial Research.
   The properties of breeze and clinker aggregates and methods of testing their soundness. Aug.1928. (B.R.B.Bull.,no.5) Department of Scientific and Industrial Research.
   Slag, coke, breeze and clinker as aggregates. July 1927. (B.R.B.special rep.,no.10) Department of Scientific and Industrial Research.

LEAF, Walter
   Report on the progress made in discharge of the liabilities of the enemy banks in London. 12 Jan.1917. 1917/8 Cd.8455 v. Treasury.

LEARMOUTH, Frederick Charles
   Committee on the application of the seasonal load-line marks.
      Report. 3 June 1924. Board of Trade.

LEATHES, Stanley Mordaunt
   Committee on civil service class I examination.
      Report. 20 June 1917. 1917/8 Cd.8657 viii. Treasury.
   Committee on the position of modern languages in the educational system of Great Britain.
      Report. 2 April 1918. 1918 Cd.9036 ix. Board of Education.

LEDBURY, W.
   The production of formaldehyde by oxidation of hydrocarbons. July 1927. (Chemistry research special rep.,no.1) Department of Scientific and Industrial Research.

LEDINGHAM, John Charles Grant
   Report on the enteric fever "carrier", being a review of current knowledge on the subject. 5 Oct.1910. (Rep.Pub.Health & Med.Subj., no.43) Local Government Board.

Lee, *Lord. SEE:* Lee, Arthur Hamilton, *1st Viscount*

LEE, A.W.
   Auroral observations at Lerwick observatory, 1924-9. May 1930. (Prof.Notes, no.56) Meteorological Office.
   On the travel of seismic waves from the Baffin Bay earthquake of 20 Nov. 1933. June 1937. (Geophys.Mem.,no.74) Meteorological Office.
   A new relation between atmospheric electricity and terrestrial magnetism. July 1930. (Prof.Notes,no.58) Meteorological Office.
   Seismology at Kew Observatory. Feb.1939. (Geophys.,Mem., no.78) Meteorological Office.
   The three components of micro-seismic disturbance at Kew Observatory; discussion of the records for 1932. April 1935. (Geophys.Mem.,no.66) Meteorological Office.
   The travel-times of the seismic waves P and S; a study of data, 1930 and 1931. Sept.1938. (Geophys.Mem.,no.76) Meteorological Office.
   A world-wide survey of microseismic disturbances recorded during January 1930. Oct.1934. (Geophys.Mem.,no.62) Meteorological Office.

LEE, Arthur Hamilton, *1st Viscount Lee of Fareham*
   Committee on temporary deductions from police pay.
      Report. 9 June 1925. 1924/5 Cmd.2444 xv. Home Office.
   Committee on the humane slaughtering of animals.
      Report with appendices. 1 July 1904. 1904 Cd.2150 xxiv.

LEE, Arthur Hamilton, *1st Viscount Lee of Fareham*
(continued)
> Minutes of evidence. 1904 Cd.2151 xxiv.
> Admiralty.

> Royal Commission on cross-river traffic in London.
> Report. 30 Nov.1926. 1926 Cmd.2772 xiii.
> Minutes of evidence and appendices. 1926.
> Ministry of Transport.

> Royal Commission on police powers and procedure.
> Report. 16 March 1929. 1928/9 Cmd.3297 ix.
> Vols. 2 to 4: evidence, appendices and index.
> 1929.

> Royal Commission on the superior civil services in
> India.
> Report. 27 March 1924. 1924 Cmd.2128 viii.
> India Office.

LEE, Austin
> Report on French colonies. 1 Dec.1899.
> (Dip.cons.reports: misc.ser., no.520) 1900 Cd.2-3
> xci. Foreign Office.

LEE, G.W.
> The British carboniferous trepostomata. 24 May
> 1912. (Mem.Geol.Surv., Palaeont., vol.1 part 3)
> Geological Survey.

> The pre-tertiary geology of Mull, Loch Aline and
> Oban. (Parts of Sheets 35, 43, 44, 45 and 52) 12 June
> 1924. (Mem.Geol.Surv.,Scotl.) Geological Survey,
> Scotland.

LEE, Kenneth
> Inter-departmental committee on the methods of
> dealing with inventions made by workers aided or
> maintained from public funds.
> > Report. 5 Oct.1921. Department of Scientific
> > and Industrial Research.

LEEPER, A.W.A.
> The justice of Rumania's cause. 1917. Ministry of
> Information.

LEGG, V.H.
> The composition of coal: plant cuticles in coal.
> Oct.1925. (S.M.R.B. Paper no.17) Mices
> Department.

LEGGE, J.T.H.
> Committee on assisted wiring and the hiring and
> hire-purchase of electrical apparatus.
> > Report. 30 June 1930. Electricity Commission.
> > Ministry of Transport.

LEGGE, James Granville
> Memorandum giving some account of the
> reformatory and indusrial schools of Great Britain.
> Feb.1904. Home Office.

LEGGE, T.M.
> Report on manufacture of paints and colours
> containing lead, as affecting the health of the
> operatives employed. 8 May 1905. 1905 Cd.2466 x.
> Home Office.

LEGGETT, Frederick William
> Report of the British delegates on the International
> Labour Conference, 16th session, 12-30 April 1932.
> April 1933. Ministry of Labour.

> Report of the British delegates on the International
> Labour Conference, 17th session, Geneva, 8-30 June
> 1933. Feb.1934. Ministry of Labour.

LEGH, Thomas Wodehouse, *2nd Baron Newton*
> Committee on smoke and noxious vapours
> abatement.
> > Interim report. 1 June 1920. 1920 Cmd.755 xxv.
> > Final report. 1 June 1920. Ministry of Health.

> Inter-departmental committee on the Thames and

Lee conservancies.
> Report and appendices. 20 Feb.1923. Ministry
> of Transport *and* Ministry of Health.

LEGROS, Lucien Alphonse
> A note on the legibility of printed matter. April
> 1922. Treasury.

> On the design of machinery in relation to the
> operator. April 1926. (I.H.R.B. Rep., no.36)
> Medical Research Council.

LeGROS CLARK, W.E.
> Anatomical investigation into the routes by which
> infections may pass from the nasal cavities into the
> brain.
> > Report to the committee on vaccination. July
> > 1929. (Rep.Pub.Health & Med.Sub., no.54)
> > Ministry of Health.

LEHMANN, Rudolph C.
> Departmental committee on the establishment of a
> receiving house for alien immigrants at the Port of
> London.
> > Vol.1: Report and appendix. 1 March 1911.
> > 1911 Cd.5575 x.
> > Vol.2: Minutes of evidence. 1911 Cd.5576 x.
> > Home Office.

LEIGHTON, Gerald Rowley
> Milk consumption and the growth of school
> children.
> > Report of an investigation in Lanarkshire
> > schools. Dec.1930. Department of Health for
> > Scotland.

> Milk consumption in Scotland; an inquiry into the
> average amount of liquid milk consumed in Scottish
> households. Oct.1933. Department of Health for
> Scotland.

> Report of an enquiry into a uniform system and
> standard of meat inspection in Scotland. 15
> Nov.1920. Scottish Board of Health.

> Report on the deaths of eight persons from botulism
> at Loch Maree. Oct.1922. Scottish Board of Health.

LEIPER, Robert Thomson
> Report on a parasitic condition (onchocerciasis) met
> with in Australian beef. 22 Dec.1910.
> (Rep.Pub.Health & Med.Subj., no.45) Local
> Government Board.

LEISHMAN, James
> Scottish inter-departmental committee on road
> safety among school children.
> > Report. 23 Dec.1935. Scottish Education
> > Department *and* Ministry of Transport.

LEISHMAN, William Boog
> Foot-and-mouth disease research committee. *SEE:*
> Arkwright, J.A.

> Report on the blood changes following typhoid
> inoculation. May 1905. War Office.

LEITCH, Isabella
> Iodine in nutrition; a review of existing information.
> 14 Dec.1928. (S.R.S.,no.123) Medical Research
> Council.

LEMPFERT, R.G.K.
> The life history of surface air currents; a study of the
> surface trajectories of moving air. March 1906.
> (M.O.174) Meteorological Office.

> Report on observations in connection with the
> London fog inquiry in the winter of 1902-3.
> Nov.1904. (M.O.160) Meteorological Office.

LENTHALL, C.Bertram
> Brief notes on seamanship and navigation for use of
> R.N.V.R. officers under instruction. Feb.1918.
> Admiralty.

**LE QUESNE, Charles Thomas**
Committee on pensions for unmarried women.
> Report. 22 March 1939. 1938/9 Cmd.5991 xiv.
> Minutes of evidence. 1938.
> Appendix and index. 1939. Treasury.

**LEVEAUX, M.V.**
Joint committee of the standing committee on trusts and prices. Sub-committee on the standard boot and shoe scheme.
> Report. 4 Feb.1920. 1920 Cmd.592 xxiii.
> Second report. 22 Feb.1921. 1921 Cmd.1269 xvi. Board of Trade.
Standing committee on trusts.
> Findings and decisions of a sub-committee on the price of fruit in the United Kingdom. 27 July 1920. 1920 Cmd.878 xxiii. Board of Trade.
> Report of a sub-committee on pipes and castings. 8 March 1921. 1921 Cmd. 1217 xvi. Board of Trade.
> Sub-committe on the fish trade. Findings. 5 Nov.1919. 1920 Cmd.514 xxiii. Board of Trade.

**LEVER, Samuel Hardman**
Committee on the inland telegraph service.
> Report. 12 Jan.1928. 1928 Cmd.3058 xii. Post Office.

**LEVESON-GOWER, George Granville Sutherland, *5th Duke of Sutherland***
Civil aviation advisory board.
> Report on aerodrome facilities of London. 29 Jan.1923. 1923 Cmd.1816 ix. Air Ministry.

**LEWIN, Evans**
The Commonwealth of Australia; its development and resources. 1917. Ministry of Information.
German rule in Africa. 1918. Ministry of Information.

**LEWIS, E.O.**
Report on an investigation into the incidence of mental deficiency. 1929. (Pt.4 of the report of the mental deficiency committee) Board of Education *and* Board of Control. *For full report see:* Wood, A.H.

**LEWIS, Frank Charles**
On the destruction of bacteria in milk by electricity. 20 Feb.1920. (S.R.S.,no.49) Medical Research Committee.

**LEWIS, Frederick William**
Departmental committee on co-operative selling in the coal mining industry.
> Report. 30 Nov.1926. 1926 Cmd.2770 xiii. Mines Department.

**LEWIS, John Herbert**
Departmental committee on juvenile education in relation to employment after the war.
> Interim report. 21 Aug.1916. 1916 Cd.8374 viii.
> Final report vol.1: 16 March 1917. 1917/8 Cd.8512 xi.
> Final report, vol.2: summaries of evidence and appendices. 1917/8 Cd.8577 xi. Board of Education.
Juvenile organisations comittee
> Report on juvenile delinquency. Aug.1920. Board of Education.
> Report on the need for youth community centres on new housing estates. Nov.1935.

**LEWIS, Lilian F.**
The frequency of days with specified duration of sunshine. July 1935. (Prof.Notes,no.69) Meteorological Office.
Variations of temperature at Oxford, 1815-1934.

July 1937. (Prof.Notes, no.77) Meteorological Office.

**LEWIS, Thomas**
Report on soldiers returned as cases of "disordered action of the heart" or "valvular disease of the heart". 14 Feb.1917. (S.R.S.,no.8) Supplementary memoranda. 1918. Medical Research Committee.

**LEWIS-FANING, E.**
A comparative study of the seasonal incidence of mortality in England and Wales and in the United States of America. 18 March 1940. (S.R.S.,no.239) Ministry of Health.
A study of the trend of morality rates in urban communities of England and Wales, with special reference to "depressed areas". July 1938. (Rep.Pub.Health & Med.Subj., no.86) Ministry of Health.

**LICHTERVELDE, Louise de**
August the fourth, 1914, in the Belgian Parliament. 27 Sept.1917. Ministry of Information.

**LIDDELL, Lionel C.**
Report on the chemical, metal and other industries of Lyons, France during the year 1904. 19 Aug.1905. (Dip.cons.reports: misc.ser., no.638) 1906 Cd. 2683-2 cxxii. Foreign Office.
Report on the chemical and metal industries of the district of Lyons. 24 Sept.1902. (Dip.cons.reports: misc.ser., no.582) 1902 Cd.787-18 ciii. Foreign Office.

**LINDLEY, W.H.**
Report on the waterways of France, Belgium, Germany and Holland.
> Part 1: reports and appendices. 8 Dec.1908. 1909 Cd.4841 xiii.
> Part 2: maps and tables. 1909 Cd.4841 xiii. Royal Commission on canals and inland navigations of the United Kingdom.

**LINSAY, David Alexander Edward, *27th Earl Crawford***
Broadcasting committee.
> Report. 2 March 1926. 1926 Cmd.2599 viii. Post Office.
Royal commission on wheat supplies.
> First report. 31 Aug.1921. 1921 Cmd.1544 xviii.
> Second report. 4 July 1925. 1924/5 Cmd.2462 xv.

**LINDSAY, R.C.**
Report on liquor traffic legislation in the United States. April 1907. (Dip.cons.reports: misc.ser.,no.657) 1907 Cd.3284-1 lxxxvii. Foreign Office.
Report on migration into the United States. Nov.1906. (Dip.cons.reports: misc.ser.,no.655) 1906 Cd.2683-19 cxxii. Foreign Office.

Linlithgow, *Lord. SEE:* Hope, J.V.A., *2nd Marquess*

**LINTON, Andrew**
Agricultural report on the district between Voi and Kiu, East Africa Protectorate... 20 Jan.1904. 1904 Cd.1953 lxii. Foreign Office.

**LITTLE, H.A.**
Report on the physical, commercial, social and general conditions of Ichang and neighbourhood. Nov.1908. (Dip.cons.reports: misc.ser., no.671) 1908 Cd. 3728-7 cviii. Foreign Office *and* Board of Trade.

**LITTON, G.**
Report on a journey in north-west Yunnan. 6 April 1903. (China, no.3, 1904) 1904 Cd.1836 cx. Foreign Office.

LLANDAFF, Henry Matthews, *1st Viscount*
Royal Commission on water supply within the limits of the Metropolitan water companies.
>Final report. 30 Dec.1899. 1900 Cd.25 xxxviii pt.I.
>Minutes of evidence. Vol.1: 1906 Cd.45 xxxviii pt.I.
>Minutes of evidence. Vol.2: 1900 Cd.198 xxxviii pt.II.
>Appendices. 1900 Cd.108 xxxix.
>Maps, plates, diagrams. 1900 Cd.267 xxxix.

LLEWELLYN, Evan Henry
Departmental committee on vaccination expenses.
>Part I: Report. 25 April 1905. 1905 Cd.2420 xl.
>Part II: Evidence, appendix and index. 1905 Cd.2421 xl. Local Government Board.

LLEWELYN, H.M.
The effect of building materials on paint films. April 1931. (B.R.B.Bull., no.11) Department of Scientific and Industrial Research.

LLEWELLYN, Thomas Lister
Report on miners' "beat knee", "beat hand" and "beat elbow". 15 July 1924. (S.R.S., no.89) Medical Research Council.

LLOYD, F.J.
Report on investigations into cider making. 7 Nov.1903. 1904 Cd.1868 xvi. Board of Agriculture and Fisheries.

LLOYD, H.
An automatic firedamp recorder. April 1934. (S.M.R.B.Paper no.86) Mines Department.

A recording manometer having a low inertia. Jan.1935. (S.M.R.B. Paper no.91) Mines Department.

LLOYD, M.B.
Report on visits to certain explosives factories and testing stations in Belgium, Germany, and Holland. 29 May 1905. 1905 Cd.2650 x. Home Office.

LLOYD-GEORGE, David.
The great war. 19 Sept.1914. Ministry of Information.

Peace proposals and the attitude of the Allies. 19 Dec.1916. Ministry of Information.

Select committee on naval and military services (pensions and grants). *SEE:* Law, A.B.

Select committee on parliamentary elections (Mr.Speaker's seat).
>Report, proceedings and appendices. 4 April 1939. 1938/9 (98) viii. House of Commons.

Select committee on the civil list.
>Report, proceedings and appendices. 5 July 1910. 1910 (211) vi. House of Commons.

The war; its causes and its message. Speeches. Oct.1914. Ministry of Information.

LOCKER-LAMPSON, Godfrey Lampson Tennyson
Departmental committee on accidents in shipbuilding and ship repairing.
>Report. July 1924. Home Office.

LOCKYER, William James Stewart
Discussion of Australian meteorology. Jan. 1909. Solar Physics Committee. Board of Education.

Southern hemisphere surface-air circulation. Sept.1910. Solar Physics Committee. Board of Education.

LÖFGREN, Eliel
Commission on the rights and claims of Moslems and Jews in connection with the Western or Wailing Wall at Jerusalem.
>Report. Dec.1930. Colonial Office.

LOGAN, D.Dale
Mine rescue work on the Western front. July 1920. War Office.

LOGAN, Spencer Henry Metcalfe Login
Committee on canteen and victualling arrangements in H.M.Fleet. 24 Jan. 1907. 1907 Cd.3703 l. Admiralty.

Londonderry, *Lord. SEE:* Vane-Tempest-Stewart, C.S.H., *7th Marquess*

LONG, Amalie E. Weiss
A classification of vocational tests of dexterity. May 1932. (I.H.R.B. Rep., no.64) Medical Research Council.

LONGFORD, J.H.
Notes on the foreign trade and shipping of Japan, 1872 - 1900. 1 Aug.1901. (Dip.cons.reports: misc.ser., no.564) 1902 Cd.787 ciii. Foreign Office.

LONSDALE, T.
The mechanical testing of bituminous road materials, a survey of the literature. Sept.1938. (Road Res.special rep., no.1) Department of Scientific and Industrial Research.

LORDEN, John William
Standing committee on prices and trusts. Building materials sub-committee.
>Findings and decisions of a sectional committee on the prices, costs and profits of timber. 17 Aug.1920. 1920 Cmd.985 xxiii.
>Interim report on the prices, costs and profits of the brick trade. 7 Sept.1920. 1920 Cmd.959 xxiii.
>Final report. 21 Feb.1921. 1921 Cmd.1209 xvi. Board of Trade.

LOSEBY, F.H.
Committee on Mui-tsai in Hong Kong.
>Report. 6 Sept.1935. 1935/6 Cmd.5121 vii. Colonial Office.

Lothian, *Marquess. SEE: Kerr, P.H., 11th Marquess.*

Loti, Pierre. *SEE:* Viaud, L.M.J.

LOUGHNANE, Norma Gerald
Commission on the financial situation of Mauritius.
>Report. 23 Dec.1931. 1931/2 Cmd.4034 vii. Colonial Office.

LOUIS, Henry
Report on the possibility of developing the production of gold and other minerals in Merionethshire. 15 Nov.1930. Mines Department.

Lovat, *Lord. SEE:* Fraser, S.J., *16th Baron*

LOVEDAY, J.
Preliminary notes on the boot and shoe industry. Oct.1920. (I.H.R.B. Rep., no.10) (no other reports identified) Medical Research Council.

LOVEDAY, Thomas
Committee on veterinary education in Great Britain.
>Report. 8 July 1938. Ministry of Agriculture and Fisheries *and* Department of Agriculture for Scotland.

LOVEGROVE, E.J.
Attrition tests of British road-stones. 21 Feb.1929. (Mem.Geol.Surv.) Geological Survey.

LOVETT, Harrington Verney
Committee on medical services in India.
>Report. 22 April 1919. 1920 Cmd.946 xiv. India Office.

LOW, A, Maurice
The law of blockade. 1916. Ministry of Information.

LOW, J. Spencer
Report on an outbreak of enteric fever at Sutton Bonnington in the Leake R.D. Nottinghamshire. 12 Feb.1906. (Rep.Med.Insp., no.227) Local Government Board.

Report on the eight sanitary districts comprised within the Penzance registration district. 24 Oct.1904. (Rep.Med.Insp., no.200) Local Government Board.

Report on the three sanitary districts comprised within the Thetford registration district. 9 July 1907. (Rep.Med.Insp., no.269) Local Government Board.

Report on the three sanitary districts in Knaresborough registration district. 16 Nov.1908. (Rep.Med.Insp., no.321) Local Government Board.

Report on the sanitary conditions of Aberdare U.D., with special reference to continued prevalence of infectious disease. 16 April 1907. (Rep.Med.Insp., no.259) Local Government Board.

Report on the sanitary conditions of Altofts U.D. 30 May 1910. (Rep.Pub. Health & Med.Subj., no.33) Local Government Board.

Report on the sanitary conditions of the Batley Borough. 4 Sept.1906. (Rep.Med.Insp., no.242) Local Government Board.

Report on the sanitary conditions of Bedwellty U.D. 9 Feb.1910. (Rep.Pub. Health & Med.Subj., no.23) Local Government Board.

Report on the sanitary conditions of Bridport R.D. 29 Nov.1906. (Rep.Med.Insp., no.249) Local Government Board.

Report on the sanitary conditions of Denton U.D. 19 June 1907. (Rep.Med.Insp., no.264) Local Government Board.

Report on the sanitary conditions of Droylsden U.D. 19 June 1907. (Rep.Med.Insp., no.263) Local Government Board.

Report on the sanitary conditions of Failsworth U.D. 1 July 1907. (Rep.Med.Insp., no.266) Local Government Board.

Report on the sanitary conditions of Featherstone U.D. 30 May 1910. (Rep.Pub.Health & Med.Subj., no.34) Local Government Board.

Report on the sanitary conditions of Hartley Witney R.D. 17 Oct.1907. (Rep.Med.Insp., no.288) Local Government Board.

Report on the sanitary conditions of Haverfordwest R.D. 17 Feb.1905. (Rep.Med.Insp., no.209) Local Government Board.

Report on the sanitary conditions of Hawarden R.D. 13 Nov.1907. (Rep.Med.Subj., no.295) Local Government Board.

Report on the sanitary conditions of Heckmonwike U.D., with a memorandum on the occurrence of lead poisoning. 16 Sept.1908. (Rep.Med.Insp., no.311) Local Government Board.

Report on the sanitary conditions of Hurst U.D. 1 July 1907. (Rep.Med.Insp., no.268) Local Government Board.

Report on the sanitary conditions of Lees U.D. 1 July 1907. (Rep.Med.Insp., no.267) Local Government Board.

Report on the sanitary conditions of Limehurst R.D. 24 July 1907. (Rep.Med.Insp., no.273) Local Government Board.

Report on the sanitary conditions of Merthyr Tydfil U.D. 31 March 1906. (Rep.Med.Insp., no.231.) Local Government Board.

Report on the sanitary conditions of Mitford and Launditch R.D., and on the prevalence of diphtheria in the Parish of Guist. 16 March 1907. (Rep.Med.Insp., no.256) Local Government Board.

Report on the sanitary conditions of the Morley Borough, with special reference to the prevalence of infectious disease. 19 Aug.1907. (Rep.Med.Insp., no.275) Local Government Board.

Report on the sanitary conditions of Normanton U.D. 30 May 1910. (Rep.Pub.Health & Med.Subj., no.32) Local Government Board.

Report on the sanitary conditions of Patrington R.D., with special reference to the prevalence of diphtheria therein. 24 Jan.1911. (Rep.Pub.Health & Med.Subj., no.48) Local Government Board.

Report on the sanitary conditions of Preesall-with-Hackinsall U.D. 1 Sept. 1904. (Rep.Med.Insp., no.198) Local Government Board.

Report on the sanitary conditions of Tredegar U.D. 1 June 1909. (Rep.Pub.Health & Med.Subj., no.8) Local Government Board.

Report on the sanitary conditions of Winterton U.D. 11 Nov.1908. (Rep.Med.Insp., no.317) Local Government Board.

LOW, Robert Bruce
The incidence of smallpox throughout the world in recent years. 23 May 1918. (Rep.Pub.Health & Med.Subj., no.117) Local Government Board

The progress and diffusion of plague, cholera and yellow-fever throughout the world, 1914-1917. Oct.1920. (Rep.Pub.Health & Med.Subj., no.3) Ministry of Health.

Report on arrangements made in Germany for the isolation of smallpox cases. 10 March 1904. (Rep.Med.Insp., no.192) Local Government Board.

Reports and papers on bubonic plague, 1901. 1901 Cd.748 xxvii. Local Government Board.

LOWNDES, George Rivers
Safeguarding of industries.
Report of the committee on buttons, pins, hooks and eyes, and snap fasteners. 3 April 1928. 1928 Cmd.3080 xii. Board of Trade.

LOWRY, Arthur Belmore
Departmental committe on machinery and engineering staffs at poor law institutions.
Report. 9 Jan.1909. 1909 Cd.4502 xxxvi.
Minutes of evidence, appendices and index. 1909 Cd.4503 xxxvi. Local Government Board.

Report on a public inquiry into the administration of relief in the Sheffield Union. 5 Feb.1923. Ministry of Health.

Report on investigation in the coalfield of south Wales and Monmouthshire. 28 Jan.1929. 1928/9 Cmd.3272 viii. Ministry of Health.

Report on municipal labour bureaux. Nov.1905. 1906 (86) cii. Local Government Board.

Royal commission on Merthyr Tydfil.
Report. 12 Nov.1935. 1935/6 Cmd.5039 xiv.

LOWTHER, Gerard
Report on the purchase and holding of lands by aliens. 15 Aug.1901. (Dip.cons.reports: misc.,ser., no.567) 1902 Cd.787-3 ciii. Foreign Office.

LOWTHER, Henry C.
Report on the railway systems of Brazil. 27 May 1904. (Dip.cons.reports: misc.ser., no.617) 1904 Cd.1767-21 cxvi. Foreign Office.

LOWTHER, James William, *1st Viscount Ullswater*
Boundary commission for England and Wales.
Report and appendics. Vol.1. 27 Sept.1917.

LOWTHER, James William, *1st Viscount Ullswater* (continued)
　　1917/8 Cd.8756 xiii.
　　Vols. 2 and 3. Schedules. 1917/8 Cd.8757, Cd.8758 xiii. Home Office.
　Boundary commission for Ireland.
　　Report. 27 Nov.1917. 1917/8 Cd.8830 xiv. Irish Secretary's Office.
　Boundary commission for Scotland.
　　Report. 28 Sept.1917. 1917/8 Cd.8759 xiv. Scottish Office.
　Broadcasting committee.
　　Report. 31 Dec.1935. 1935/6 Cmd.5091 vii. Post Office.
　Conference on devolution.
　　Report to the Prime Minister. 27 April 1920. 1920 Cmd.692 xiii. Prime Minister's Office.
　Conference on electoral reform.
　　Letter to the Prime Minister. 27 Jan.1917. 1917/8 Cd.8463 xxv. Prime Minister's Office.
　Conference on electoral reform.
　　Report. 17 July 1930. 1929/30 Cmd.3636 xiii. Cabinet Office.
　Joint select committee on the sittings of Parliament.
　　Report, proceedings, and evidence. 14 Nov.1923. 1923(135) viii. House of Commons.
　Report of the international conference on the protection of migratory wildfowl, London, 12th to 14th October 1927. 14 Nov.1927. Home Office.
　Royal commission on local government of Greater London.
　　Report. 27 Feb.1923. 1923 Cmd.1830 xii pt.1.
　　Evidence, 7 parts. 1922-3.
　　Index. Sept.1924.
　Royal commission on proportional representation.
　　Report and scheme. 30 April 1918. 1918 Cd.9044 viii.

LUBBOCK, Cecil
　Committee on the maturity of savings certificates of the first issue.
　　Interim and final reports. 12 Nov.1925 and 3 Feb.1926. 1926 Cmd.2610 xv. Treasury.

LUBBOCK, John, *1st Baron Avebury*
　Joint select committe on Sunday trading.
　　Report, proceedings, evidence, appendix and index. 19 July 1906. 1906 (275) xiii. House of Commons.
　Select committee of the House of Lords on early closing of shops.
　　Report, proceedings, and minues of evidence. 17 Aug.1901. 1901 (369) vi. House of Commons.

LUCAS, Alfred George
　Report of the deputy adjutant-general of the Imperial Yeomanry regarding its home organisation...and proposals for future organisation. 15 May 1901. 1902 Cd.803 lvi. War Office.

LUCAS, Charles
　Note on a visit to Australia, New Zealand and Fiji in 1909. March 1910. 1910 Cd.5100 lxv. Colonial Office.

LUGARD, Frederick Dealtry
　Memorandum on the taxation of natives in northern Nigeria. 22 Nov.1906. (Colonial reports: misc., no.40) 1907 Cd.3309 liv. Colonial Office.
　Report on the amalgamation of Northern and Southern Nigeria and adminstration, 1912-1919. 9 April 1919. 1919 Cmd.468 xxxvi. Colonial Office.

*Luke of Pavenham. SEE:* Lawson-Johnston, G., *1st Baron Luke of Pavenham.*

LUMB, A.D.
　The platinum metals. July 1920. (Mono.Min.Resour.) Imperial Institute.

LUMSDEN, J.
　Magnesium, magnesite and dolomite. 1939. (Rep.Min.Ind.) Imperial Institute.

LUSH, Alfred Herbert
　Report on the draft regulations for factories in which the grinding of metals and racing of grindstones is carried on. 16 Sept.1909. 1909 Cd.4913 xxi. Home Office.
　Report on draft regulations for the manufacture of patent fuel (briquettes) with the addition of pitch. 15 Aug.1911. 1911 Cd.5878 xxii.
　　Second report. 12 Aug.1913. 1914 Cd.7051 xliv. Home Office.

LYLE, Thomas Harold
　Report on the commercial situation in Siam, 1920. April 1921. Board of Trade.

LYNE, R.N.
　Report on the agricultural prospects of the plateaux of the Uganda railway. May 1902. (Dip.cons.reports: Misc.ser., no.577) 1902 Cd.787-13 ciii. Foreign Office.

LYON, Percy Comyn
　Inter-departmental committee on research and development in the dependencies of the Falkland Islands.
　　Report, appendices, maps, *etc.* 27 Aug.1919. 1920 Cmd.657 xvi. Colonial Office.

LYTHGOE, R.J.
　Adaptation of the eye: its relation to the critical frequency of flicker. 18 June 1929. (S.R.S., no.134) Medical Research Council.
　Illumination and visual capacities; a review of recent literature. 10 May 1926. (S.R.S., no.104) Medical Research Council.
　The measurement of visual acuity. 11 Oct.1932. (S.R.S., no.173) Medical Research Council.

LYTTELTON, Alfred
　Transvaal concessions commission.
　　Report. 19 April 1901. Cd.623 xxxv.
　　Part II: Minutes of evidence. 1901 Cd.624 xxxv.
　　Part III: Appendix. 1901 Cd.625 xxxv. Colonial Office.

LYTTELTON, Neville Gerald
　Report of the military court of inquiry on certain matters connected with the British Empire committee. 2 July 1915. 1914/6 Cd.7681 xxxix. War Office.

LYTTON, Alexander George Robert, *2nd Earl of Lytton*
　His Majesty's commissioners for the international exhibitions at Brussels, Rome and Turin, 1910 and 1911.
　　Report. 1912. 1912/3 Cd.6609 xxii.
　Committee on the appointment of ex-servicemen to posts in the civil service.
　　Report. 19 Aug.1920.
　　Second interim report. 29 March 1921.
　　Third interim report. 13 June 1921. (no further identified) Treasury.
　Commission of enquiry on conditions in Manchuria.
　　Preliminary report. 30 April 1932. (China, no.2, 1932) 1931/2 Cmd. 4078 xxvii. (no further identified) Foreign Office.

MACALISTER, D.A.
　Geology of Falmouth and Truro and the mining district of Camborne and Rudruth. (Sheet 352) 20 Nov.1906. (Mem.Geol.Surv.) Geological Survey.

MACALISTER, Donald
Belfast commissioners appointed by the Irish Universities Act, 1908.
> Report. 31 July 1911. 1911 Cd.5929 xxi.
> Report and appendices. 1911. Royal Commission on Belfast University.

Consultative council on medical and allied services.
> Interim report on a scheme of medical service for Scotland. 8 Nov.1920. 1920 Cmd.1039 xvii. (no further reports identified) Scottish Board of Health.

McCANCE, John Stouppe F.
Departmental committee on fixing of charges for scutching flax and tow.
> Report. 28 Oct.1918. 1918 Cd.9196 x. Department of Agriculture and Technical Instruction for Ireland.

McCANCE, Robert Alexander
The carbohydrate content of food. 30 April 1929. (S.R.S., no.135) Medical Research Council.

The chemical composition Of foods. 8 Nov.1939. (S.R.S., no.235) Medical Research Council.

The chemistry of flesh foods and their losses on cooking. 12 Oct.1933. (S.R.S., no.187) Medical Research Council.

McCARDIE, Henry A.
Committee on labour embargoes.
> Interim report. Sept.1918. (no further reports identified) Ministry of Munitions.

McCLEARY, G.F.
Memorandum on the English scheme of national health insurance with special reference to its medical aspects. 1929. Ministry of Health.

McCONKEY, O.
Recent advances in pasture management. July 1931. (E.M.B.43) Empire Marketing Board.

McCORMICK, William Symington.
Advisory committee on the distribution of Exchequer grants to universities and colleges in England.
> Report. 28 March 1912. 1912/3 Cd.6140 xxii.
> Second report. 4 Feb.1913. 1912/3 Cd.6617 xxii.
> Third report. 11 June 1913. 1913 Cd.6869 xxi. Board of Education.

Departmental committee on a national medical school for Wales and Cardiff.
> Report. 9 Dec.1914. 1916 (62) viii. Treasury.

MACCULLAGH, James Acheson
Typhoid fever in Limerick city and prisons.
> Report. 6 Oct.1902. 1902 Cd.1331 xlvii. Irish Secretary's Office.

McCULLAGH, William McKim Herbert
Report on the treatment of cancer of the uterus at the Samaritan Free Hospital. Dec.1927. (Rep.Publ.Health & Med.Subj., no.47) Ministry of Health.

McCURDY, Charles A.
Committee on trusts.
> Report. 24 April 1919. 1918 Cd.9236 xiii. Ministry of Reconstruction.

Departmental committee on wholesale food markets of London. SEE: Strange, E.F.

Joint committee of the standing committees on trusts and prices. Sub-committee on the standard boot and shoe scheme. SEE: Leveaux, M.V.

Standing committee on prices.
> Findings of a committee on worsted yarns. 22 Jan.1920. 1920 Cmd.550 xxiii. Board of Trade.

Report on costings in government departments. 4 Feb.1920. 1920 Cmd.1047 xxiii. Board of Trade.

Report on metal bedsteads. 27 Feb.1920. 1920 Cmd.607 xxiii. Board of Trade.

To restore the ten commandments; the basis of a permanent peace for Europe. 1917. Ministry of Information.

MACDERMOT, Charles Edward
Inquiry into the facts and circumstances connected with or relating to the treatment while in Limerick prison and the nature and cause of the illness of Mr. Timothy Flanagan.
> Report and appendices. 26 Nov.1902. 1902 Cd.1315 xlvii. Irish Secretary's Office.

MACDONALD, J.
Forest gardens. March 1931. (Bull., no.12) Forestry Commission.

Growth and yield of conifers in Great Britain. July 1928. (Bull., no.10) Forestry Commission.

MACDONALD, James Ramsay
Committee on privileges.
> Report. 30 May 1924. 1924 (98) vi. House of Commons.

Indian round table conference, 12 Nov. 1930 to 19 Jan. 1931.
> Proceedings 12 Nov.1930 to 19 Jan.1931. 1930/1 Cmd.3778 xii.
> Proceedings of sub-committees. 2 parts. 1931.
> Sub-committees' reports; conference resolution and Prime Minister's statement. 22 Jan.1931. 1930/1 Cmd.3772 xii.
> Proceedings; second session, 7 Sept.1931 to 1 Dec.1931. Jan.1932. 1931/2 Cmd.3997 viii.
> Third session, 17 Nov. to 24 Dec.1932. Jan.1933. 1932/3 Cmd.4238 xi. India Office.

Select committee of privileges.
> Report and evidence. 30 July 1930. 1929/30 (178) vii. House of Commons.

MACDONALD, Malcolm
Inter-departmental committee on migration policy.
> Report. Aug.1934. 1933/4 Cmd.4689 x. Dominion Affairs Office.

Report of the United Kingdom delegates on the League of Nations, 18th assembly. 1 Dec.1937. (Misc., no.9. 1937) 1937/8 Cmd.5625 xxx. Foreign Office.

MACDONNELL, Anthony Patrick, *1st Baron Macdonnell of Swinford*
Departmental committee on the constitution, *etc.*, of the Isle of Man.
> Report. 31 Aug.1911. 1911 Cd.5950 xxix, pt.1.
> Minutes of evidence and appendices. 1912/3 Cd.6026 xxxiv. Home Office.

Indian famine commission, 1901.
> Report and papers. 8 May 1901. 1902 Cd.876 lxx. India Office.

Joint committee of the House of Lords and the House of Commons on the organisation and methods of the central prisoners of war committee.
> Report. 20 June 1917. 1917/8 Cd.8615 xviii. House of Commons.

Royal commission on the civil service.
> First report. 2 May 1912. 1912/3 Cd.6209 xv.
> Appendix: minutes of evidence. 26 March to 19 April 1912. 1912/3 Cd. 6210 xv.
> Second report. 21 Nov.1912. 1912/3 Cd.6534 xv.
> Appendix: minutes of evidence 25 April to 2 Aug.1912, with appendices. 1912/3 Cd.6535 xv.

MACDONNELL, Anthony Patrick, *1st Baron Macdonnell of Swinford* (continued)

> Third report. 14 March 1913. 1913 Cd.6739 xviii.
>
> Appendix: minutes of evidence, 10 Oct. to 13 Dec.1912. 1913 Cd.6740 xviii.
>
> Fourth report. 20 April 1914. 1914 Cd.7338 xvi.
>
> First appendix. 1914 Cd.7339 xvi.
>
> Second appendix: evidence 9 Jan. to 20 June 1913. 1914 Cd.7340 xvi.
>
> Fifth report. 18 Dec.1914. 1914/6 Cd.7748 xi.
>
> Appendix: evidence 29 April to 16 July 1914. 1914/6 Cd.7749 xi.
>
> Sixth report, (and final). 18 Nov.1915. 1914/6 Cd.7832 xii.
>
> Appendix: evidence, 11 Feb. to 8 July 1915. 1914/6 Cd.8130 xii.

McDONNEL, Michael F.J.

The system of education in the Gambia. April 1914. (Imperial education conference papers) Board of Education.

McDONNELL, Randal Mark Kerr, *Viscount Dunluce*

An inquiry into the composition of dietaries with special reference to munition workers. 31 Dec.1917. (S.R.S., no.13) Medical Research Committee.

McDOUGALL, Frank Lidgett

The growing dependence of British industry upon Empire markets. Dec.1929. (E.M.B.23) Empire Marketing Board.

MACDOUGALL, J.Patten

Departmental committee on poor law medical relief (Scotland).

> Vol.1: Report with supplement. 17 March 1904. 1904 Cd.2008 xxxiii.
>
> Vol.2: Minutes of evidence, appendices and index. 1904 Cd.2022 xxxiii.
>
> Local Government Board for Scotland.

McDOUGALL, William

The effects of alcohol and some other drugs during normal and fatigued conditions. 1 Sept.1920. (S.R.S., no.56) Medical Research Council.

MACE, G.A.

Incentives; some experimental studies. Oct.1935. (I.H.R.B.Rep., no.72) Medical Research Council.

McEWAN, J.R.

Report on fishing boat motor engines exhibited at the Fisheries and Marine Motor Exhibition, Copenhagen, July and August 1912. 30 Sept.1912. Fishery Board for Scotland.

Report on fishing boat engines exhibited at the North Sea Fisheries Exhibition, Yarmouth, November 1910. 30 Nov.1910. Fishery Board for Scotland.

MacEWEN, Hugh Allen

Report on an outbreak of enteric fever in Ringwood, 1912. 6 Dec.1912. 6 Dec.1912. (Rep.Pub.Health & Med.Subj., no.74) Local Government Board.

Report on diphtheria in south London attributable to milk infection. 8 April 1914. (Rep.Pub.Health & Med.Subj., no.94) Ministry of Health.

MACFADDEN, Arthur William Janes

Lead and arsenic in tartaric acid, citric acid and cream of tartar. 16 March 1907. (Rep.Insp.Food, no.2) Local Government Board.

Report on a parasitic condition (onchocerciasis) met with in Australian beef. 22 Dec.1910. (Rep.Pub.Health & Med.Subj., no.45) Local Government Board.

Report on inquiries with regard to the wholesomeness of tripe of home and foreign origin. 29 Jan.1908. (Rep.Insp.Food, no.4) Local Government Board.

Report on preservatives in canned and glass-packed meets of home and foreign origins, with observations on the manufacture of such meats. 26 May 1908. (Rep.Insp.Food, no.6) Local Government Board.

McFADYEAN, John

Departmental committee on epizootic abortion.

> Part 1: epizootic abortion in cattle. Aug.1909. 1909 Cd.4742 xvi.
>
> Appendix, by J.McFadyean and Stewart Stockman. 1909 Cd.4863 xvi.
>
> Report, Part 2: epizootic abortion in cattle with minutes of evidence and appendices. 25 June 1910. 1910 Cd.5279 xxii.
>
> Report, Part 3: abortion in sheep. 20 Oct.1913. 1914 Cd.7156 xii.
>
> Appendix to Part 3: 1914 Cd.7157 xii. Board of Agriculture and Fisheries.

MacFARLANE, George Lewis, *Lord Ormidale*

Committee on police consolidation in Scotland.

> Report. 25 Nov.1933. 1933/4 Cmd.4463 xiv. Scottish Office.

MacFARLANE, P.R.C.

Salmon of the River Dee, 1924. 1927. (Salmon Fish., 1927, no.3) Fishery Board for Scotland.

Salmon of the River Dee in 1925. 1931. (Salmon Fish., 1931, no.4) Fishery Board for Scotland.

Salmon of the River Dee, 1928 and 1929. 1931 (Salmon Fish., 1931, no.2) Fishery Board for Scotland.

Salmon of the River Nith, 1935. 1936 (Salmon Fish., 1936, no.3) Fishery Board for Scotland.

Salmon investigations in Scotland. 1922.

> 1: Salmon in the River Spey. 1924. (Salmon Fish., 1924, no.1)
>
> 2: Salmon of the River Dee. 1924. (Salmon Fish., no.3) Fishery Board for Scotland.

Salmon investigations in Scotland, 1923.

> 1: Salmon of the River Dee. 1926. (Salmon Fish., 1926, no.4)
>
> 2: Salmon of the River Spey. 1926. (Salmon Fish., 1926, no.5) Fishery Board for Scotland.

Salmon of the River Spey, 1924. 1928. (Salmon Fish., 1928, no.1) Fishery Board for Scotland.

Salmon of the River Spey, 1925. 1928. (Salmon Fish., 1928, no.3) Fishery Board for Scotland.

Salmon of the River Tay, 1930. (Salmon Fish., 1931, no.5) Fishery Board for Scotland.

Salmon of the River Tay, 1934. 1935. (Salmon Fish., 1935, no.5) Fishery Board for Scotland.

Salmon of the River Tweed, 1929. 1932. (Salmon Fish., 1932, no.3) Fishery Board for Scotland.

Salmon of the River Tweed, 1930. 1933. (Salmon Fish., 1933, no.3) Fishery Board for Scotland.

Salmon of the upper Solway district, 1934. 1938. (Salmon Fish., 1938, no.3) Fishery Board for Scotland.

McGEE, George

Aircraft experiments for the location of herring shoals in Scottish waters, 1924. 1925. (Sci.Invest., 1925, no.1) Fishery Board for Scotland.

McGOWAN, H.

Committe on electricity distribution.

> Report. 8 May 1936. Ministry of Transport.

McGOWAN, John Pool
Report of an enquiry into a series of outbreaks of febrile illness affecting boys in St.Joseph's Industrial School, Tranent. Nov.1912. Scottish Office.

MACGREGOR, A.G.
British regional geology. The midland valley of Scotland. 1936. Geological Survey, Scotland.

The economic geology of the Ayrsnire coalfields. Area 4: Dailly, Patna, Rankinston, Dalmellington and New Cumnock. 12 Feb.1932. (Mem.Geol.Surv., Scotl.) Geological Survey, Scotland.

MACGREGOR, Alexander Stuart Murray
Puerperal infection in maternity hospitals. 31 Aug.1929. Department of Health for Scotland.

MACGREGOR, David Sliman
Commission on the financial situation of British Guiana.
Report. 1 June 1931. 1930/1 Cmd.3938 x. Colonial Office.

MACGREGOR, M.
British regional geology. The midland valley of Scotland. 1936. Geological Survey, Scotland.

The economic geology of the central coalfield. Area 3: Boñess and Linlithgow. 2 Aug.1932. (Mem.Geol.Surv., Scotl.) Geological Survey, Scotland.

Economic geology of the central coalfield of Scotland. Area 6: Bathgate, Wilsontown and Shotts. 7 May 1923. (Mem.Geol.Surv., Scotl.) Geological Survey, Scotland.

The iron ores of Scotland. 31 Jan.1919. (Special reports on the mineral resources of Great Britain, vol.11) (Mem.Geol.Surv., Scotl.) Geological Survey, Scotland.

Synopsis of the mineral resources of Scotland. 10 July 1940. (Special reports on the mineral resources of Great Britain, vol.33) (Mem.Geol.Surv.) Geological Survey.

MACGREGOR, William
Report on a visit to the Micmac Indians at Bay D'espoir, Newfoundland. 8 July 1908. 1908 Cd.4197 lxx. (Colonial reports, misc., no.54) Colonial Office.

McGUIRE, Laurence P.
Banana storage; an account of recent investigations into the storage behaviour of several varieties. Sept.1933. (E.M.B.72) Empire Marketing Board.

The behaviour and distress of the banana in storage and transport. Jan.1931. (E.M.B.36) Empire Marketing Board.

Control of wastage in bananas; with special reference to time and temperature factors. Sept.1932. (E.M.B.60) Empire Marketing Board.

Panama disease of bananas. July 1929. (E.M.B.20) Empire Marketing Board.

The storage of tropically-grown tomatoes. Sept.1932. (E.M.B.59) Empire Marketing Board.

Transport and storage of bananas with special reference to chilling. Nov. 1931. (E.M.B.45) Empire Marketing Board.

McINTOSH, James
The classification and study of the anaerobic bacteria of war wounds. 15 Nov.1917. (S.R.S., no.12) Medical Research Committee.

Studies in the aetiology of epidemic influenza. 27 May 1922. (S.R.S., no.63) Medical Research Council.

MACINTYRE, W.A.
Economic and manufacturing aspects of the building brick industries. July 1933. (B.R.B.special rep., no.20) Department of Scientific and Industrial Research.

Investigations into the durability of architectural terra-cotta and faience. Feb.1929. (B.R.B.,special rep., no.12) Department of Scientific and Industrial Research.

The manufacture of clay roofing tiles in France, Belgium and Holland. April 1928. (B.R.B.Bull., no.4) Department of Scientific and Industrial Research.

MACKAY, Alexander Morrice,
Royal commission on licensing in Scotland.
Report. 25 May 1931. 1930/1 Cmd.3894 xv. Minutes of evidence. 1931.

Mackay, Donald James, 11th Baron Reay
Committee on the organisation of oriental studies in London.
Report and appendices. 28 Dec.1908. 1909 Cd.4560 xxxv.
Minutes of evidence, list of witnesses and index. 1909 Cd.4561 xxxv. Treasury.

Departmental committee on agricultural education in England and Wales.
Report and appendices. 14 July 1908. 1908 Cd.4206 xxi.
Minutes of evidence and index. 1908 Cd.4207 xxi. Board of Agriculture and Fisheries.

MACKAY, George
The system of education in the Seychelles. Nov.1912. (Imperial education conference papers) Board of Education.

MACKAY, Helen Marion Macpherson
Nutritional anaemia in infancy, with special reference to iron deficiency. 15 May 1931. (S.R.S., no.157) Medical Research Council.

MACKAY, James Lyle, 1st Baron Inchcape of Strathnaver
Gold production committee.
Report. 29 Nov.1918. 1919 Cmd.11 xxii. Treasury.

Indian retrenchment committee.
Report. 1 March 1923. India Office.

McKENNA, Reginald
Select committee on naval and military services (pensions and grants). SEE: Low, A.B.

Committee on retrenchment in the public expenditure.
First report. 20 Sept.1916. 1914/6 Cd.8068 xxxiii.
Second report. 6 Dec.1915. 1914/6 Cd.8139 xxxiii.
Third report. 5 Jan.1916. 1916 Cd.8180 xv.
Final report. 21 Feb.1916. 1916 Cd.8200 xv. Treasury.

Royal commission on the sugar supply. SEE: Primrose, H.W.

MACKENZIE, Charles Kincaid, Lord
Committee on criminal appeal in Scotland.
Report. 30 June 1925. 1924/5 Cmd.2456 ix. Scottish Office.

Committee on hospital services, Scotland.
Report on the hospital services of Scotland. Dec.1925. Scottish Board of Health.

MACKENZIE, Charles Kincaid, *Lord* (Continued)
Departmental committee on educational endowments in Scotland.
Report. 4 Aug.1927. Scottish Education Department.
Departmental committee on trawling and policing of Scottish sea fisheries.
Report. 10 Dec.1923. Scottish Office.

McKENZIE, F.A.
Americans at the front. 1917. Ministry of Information.

British railways and the war. 1917. Ministry of Information.

Serving the King's men. How the Salvation Army is helping the nation. 1918. Ministry of Information.

MacKenzie, M.J.M. *SEE:* Muir-MacKenzie, M.J.

MACKENZIE, Sholto
Cancer; an inquiry into the extent to which patients receive treatment. Dec.1938. (Rep.Pub.Health & Med.Subj., no.89) Ministry of Health.

MACKENZIE, William Leslie
Committee on claims of the men dismissed from the police and prison services on account of the strike of 1919.
Report. 21 Nov.1924. 1924/5 Cmd.2297 xv. Home Office.

Inter-departmental committee on the sale of milk in Scotland.
Report. Aug.1922. 1922, session 2, Cmd.1749 ii.
Minutes of evidence with appendices. 1922. Scottish Board of Health.

Physical condition of children attending the public schools of the school board for Glasgow, with relative tables and diagrams.
Report by W.L.MacKenzie and A.Foster. 18 July 1907. 1907 Cd.3637 lxv. Scottish Education Department.

The teaching of school and personal hygiene to students in training as teachers in Scotland.
Report. March 1907. 1907 Cd.3443 lxv. Scotch Education Department.

MACKENZIE, William Lyon
Committee on the Scotish whaling industry.
Report. 12 Dec.1919. Fishery Board for Scotland.

Report of inquiry on the dismissal of constables Hill and Moore from the Kilmarnock Police Force. 22 April 1926. 1926 Cmd.2659 xv. Scottish Office.

MACKENZIE, William Warender, *1st Baron Amulree of Strathbraan*
Commission of enquiry into industrial unrest.
Report of the commissioners for the south-western area. *SEE:* Barnes, G.N.

Committee of inquiry into London motor coach services.
First report. 18 June 1932.
Final report. 2 Aug.1932.
Proceedings. 1932.
Documents. 1932. Ministry of Transport.

Committee of inquiry into night work in the bread baking and flour confectionery trade.
Report. 9 July 1919. 1919 Cmd.482 xxvi. Ministry of Labour.

Committee on holidays with pay.
Report. 6 April 1938. 1937/8 Cmd.5724 xii.

Minutes of evidence, 1-14th days. 1937-38.
Appendix. 1938.
Index. 1938. Ministry of Labour

Departmental committee on the Shops (Early Closing) Acts, 1920 and 1921.
Report. 22 Nov.1927. 1927 Cmd.3000 xii. Home Office.

National wages board. Conclusions respecting claims relating to the railways of Great Britain, referred on 6 May 1920. 3 June 1920. Ministry of Labour.

Newfoundland Royal Commission.
Report. 4 Oct.1933. 1933/4 Cmd.4480 xiv.
Papers relating to the report. Nov.1933. 1933/4 Cmd.4479 xiv. Dominion Affiairs Office.

Report by a court of inquiry concerning the engineering trades dispute, 1922. 10 May 1922. 1922 Cmd.1653 viii. Ministry of Labour.

Report of the delegation to study the industrial conditions in Canada and the United States of America. 18 March 1927. 1927 Cmd.2833 x. Ministry of Labour.

Report on the draft regulations for preventing danger from lead paint to persons employed in or in connection with the painting of buildings. 29 Aug.1927. Home Office.

Royal Commission on licensing in England and Wales.
Report. 17 Dec.1931. 1931/2 Cmd.3988 xi.
Minutes of evidence. 70 parts. 1931.
Index. 1932.
Extracts from written statements. 1932.

MACKIE, Horatio George Arthur
Report on the wine and fruit industries of Argentina. March 1914. (Dip.cons.reports; misc.ser., no.687) 1914 Cd.7049-2 lxxxix. Foreign Office *and* Board of Trade.

MACKIE, Thomas Jones
Furunculosis committee.
Interim report. Dec.1929.
Second interim report. June 1933.
Final report. July 1935. Scottish Office *and* Ministry of Agriculture and Fisheries.

An inquiry into post-operative tetanus. May 1928. Scottish Board of Health.

Some factors that promote the development of the tetanus bacillus in the tissues. Nov.1929. Department of Health for Scotland.

MACKINDER, Halford John
Imperial Economic Committee. Report on marketing and preparing for market foodstuffs produced in the overseas parts of the Empire.

First report: general. Aug.1925. 1924/5 Cmd.2493 xiii.
Second report: Meat. 29 July 1925. 1924/5 Cmd.2499 xiii.
Third report: Fruit. 31 March 1926. 1926 Cmd.2658 xii.
Fourth report: Diary produce. 5 Aug.1926. 1926 Cmd.2725 xii.
Fifth report: Fish. 4 Aug.1927. 1927 Cmd.2934 x.
Sixth report: Poultry and eggs. 13 Dec.1927. 1928 Cmd.3015 x.
Seventh report: Honey. 13 Dec.1927. 1928 Cmd.3015 x.
Eighth report: Functions and work of the Committee. 13 Dec.1927. 1928 Cmd.3018 x.

MACKINDER, Halford John (Continued)
Ninth report: Tobacco. 10 July 1928. 1928 Cmd.3168 x.
Tenth report: Timber. 27 July 1928. 1928 Cmd.3175 x. Colonial Office.

Imperial Shipping Committee
British shipping in the orient. 9 Dec.1938. Board of Trade.

Canadian cattle trade. Report on certain aspects. 31 Jan.1926. 1926 Cmd.2609 xii. Board of Trade.

Deferred rebate system for trade between the United Kingdom and Australia.

Interim report. 5 Aug.1921. 1921 Cmd.1486 xv.

Final report. 9 Dec.1922. 1923 Cmd.1802 xii, pt.1. Board of Trade.

East African shipping services. Interim report. 27 Oct.1924. (no other reports identified) Board of Trade.

Economic size and speed of vessels trading between the United Kingdom and Australia and on the subisides necessary. Report. 6 June 1923. 1923 Cmd.1917 xii, pt.1. Board of Trade.

Functions and constitution of a permanent imperial body for shipping questions. Report. 3 June 1921. 1921 Cmd.1483 xv. Board of Trade.

The harbour of Dar-es-Salaam, Tanganyika Territory. Report. 10 June 1927. 1927 Cmd.2917 x. Board of Trade.

The harbour of Singapore. Report. 15 March 1929. 1928/9 Cmd.3328 vii. Board of Trade.

The harbour of Port Louis, Mauritius. Report. 24 July 1931. 1931/2 Cmd.3975 x. Board of Trade.

The harbour of Port of Spain, Trinidad. Report. 21 Aug.1930. 1930/1 Cmd.3665 xiv. Board of Trade.

The harbours of Nigeria. Report. 20 July 1928. 1929/9 Cmd.3205 vii. Board of Trade.

Limitation of shipowners' liability by clauses in bills of lading. Report. 25 Feb.1921. 1921 Cmd.1205 xv. Board of Trade.

Methods of assessment of shipping to income tax within the Empire. Report. 19 Oct.1923. 1923 Cmd.1979 xii, pt.1. Board of Trade.

Mombassa (Kilindini) Harbour, Kenya Colony. Report on its control and working. 17 July 1926. 1926 Cmd.2713 xii. Board of Trade.

The possibilities of a British passenger and cargo service between western Canada and Australia-New Zealand. 16 Oct.1936. Board of Trade.

Port Swettenham, Federated Malay States. Report. 24 July 1931. 1930/1 Cmd.3953 xiv. Board of Trade.

Prai River railway wharves (Penang harbour) with certain observations on the relation of ocean traffic to the development of new ports. Report. 3 June 1926. 1926 Cmd.2703 xii. Board of Trade.

Prospective sizes of vessels in the eastern and Australian trades *via* Suez in relation to proposals for the deepening of Colombo harbour. Report. 28 July 1924. Board of Trade.

Rates of freight on Canadian flour in the North Atlantic. Interim report. 13 June 1924. 1924 Cmd.2248 xi. (no further reports identified) Board of Trade.

Rates of freight in the New Zealand trade. Report. Dec.1921. 1922 Cmd.1564 viii. Board of Trade.

Rates of freight in the trade from the United Kingdom to New Zealand. Report. 30 Aug.1935. Board of Trade.

Shipment of grain through the Canadian ports of Halifax, N.S., and St.John, N.B. Report. 14 May 1929. 1929/30 Cmd.3345 xiv. Board of Trade.

Inter-departmental committee to survey the prices of building materials. *SEE:* Roberts, S.

McKINLAY, Peter Laird.
Milk consumption and the growth of school children.
Report of an investigation in Lanarkshire schools. Dec.1930. Department of Health for Scotland.

Milk consumption in Scotland; an inquiry into the average amount of liquid milk consumed in Scottish households. Oct.1933. Department of Health for Scotland.

Report on maternal morbidity and mortality in Scotland. June 1935. Department of Health for Scotland.

MACKINNON, Doris L.
A contribution to the study of chronicity in dysentery carriers. May 1919. (S.R.S., no.29) Medical Research Committee.

MACKINNON, Frank Douglas
Committee on the law of arbitration.
Report. 10 Jan.1927. 1927 Cmd.2817 vii. Lord Chancellor's Office.

MACKLIN, E.L.
Report on the grinding of metals and cleaning of castings with special reference to the effects of dust inhalation upon the workers. 10 March 1923. Home Office.

McLAREN, Charles Benjamin Bright, *1st Baron Aberconway*
Departmental committee on a scheme of out-of-work donation.
Interim report. June 1919. 1919 Cmd.196 xxx.
Final report. 25 July 1919. 1919 Cmd.305 xxx. Ministry of Labour.

McLAREN, Henry D.
Engineering trades (new industries) committee.
Report. Dec.1918. 1918 Cd.9226 viii. Ministry of Reconstruction.

MACLEAN, Donald
Committee of enquiry on port labour.
Report. 26 March 1931. Ministry of Labour.

Inter-departmental committee on the effect of migration on schemes of social insurance.
Report. 12 Feb.1926. 1926 Cmd.2608 x. Colonial Office.

Local government committee.
Report on transfer of functions of poor law authorities in England and Wales. 19 Dec.1917. 1917/8 Cd.8917 xviii. Ministry of Reconstruction.

Select committee on the procedure governing bills which involves charges.

MACLEAN, Donald (continued)
Report, proceedings, evidence and appendices. 23 Dec.1920. 1920 (257) viii. House of Commons.

MACLEAN, Frank
Germany's colonial failure; her rule in Africa condemned on German evidence. 1918. Ministry of Information.
Towards extermination; Germany's treatment of the African native. 1918. Ministry of Information.

MACLEAN, H.W.
Report on British trade in Persia. June 1904. 1904 Cd.2146 xcv. Board of Trade.
Report on the condition and prospects of British trade with the Muscat region. Sept.1904. 1905 Cd.2281 lxxxv. Board of Trade.

MACLEAN, Hugh
Albuminuria and war nephritis among British troops in France. 5 Nov.1919. (S.R.S., no.43) Medical Research Committee.

McLEAN, William Hannah
Commission on higher education in Malaya.
Report. 17 June 1939. (Colonial,no.173) Colonial Office.

MACLEAY, J.Ronald
Report on the mining and metallurgical industries of Spain for the year 1903. Dec.1904. (Dip.cons.reports: mis.ser., no.623) 1905 Cd.2237-4 lxxxvi. Foreign Office.

McLEOD, Charles Campbell
Indian trade enquiry.
Reports on jute and silk. 18 May 1918. Imperial Institute.

McLEOD, F.H.
Report of an enquiry into working-class rents and retail prices together with rates of wages in the United Kingdom in 1912. July 1913. 1913 Cd.6955 lxvi. Board of Trade.

McLINTOCK, W.F.P.
Guide to the collection of gemstones in the Museum of Practical Geology. 29 March 1912. Geological Survey.

MACMILLAN, Hugh Pattison, *Baron Macmillan of Aberfeldy*
Committee of civil research.
Report of the sub-committee on the British Pharmacopoeia. 12 March 1928. 1928 Cmd.3101 vii. Treasury.
Committee on finance and industry.
Report. 23 June 1931. 1930/1 Cmd.3897 xiii.
Minutes of evidence. 2 vols. 1931. Treasury.
Court of inquiry concerning the coal mining industry dispute, 1925.
Report. 28 July 1925. 1924/5 Cmd.2478 xiii. Ministry of Labour.
Court of inquiry on the dispute regarding wages in the northern counties wool textile industry.
Report. 28 Feb.1930. 1929/30 Cmd.3505 xv. Ministry of Labour.
Income tax codification committee.
Vol.1: Report and appendices. 12 March 1936. 1935/6 Cmd.5131 xii.
Vol.2: Draft of an income tax bill. April 1936. 1935/6 Cmd.5132 xii. Treasury.
Royal commission on lunacy and mental disorder.
Report. 7 July 1926. 1926 Cmd.2700 xiii.
Evidence, appendices and index. 3 parts. 1926.

Street offences committee.
Report. 21 Nov.1928. 1928/9 Cmd.3231 Ix. Home Office.

MACNALTY, Arthur Salusbury
An investigation of lymphadenoma with relapsing pyrexia. Feb.1928. (Rep.Pub.Health & Med.Subj., no.50) Ministry of Health.
Report on artificial pneumothorax. 21 June 1922. (S.R.S., no.67) Medical Research Council.
Report on the prevention of mortality and disablement due to measles and pneumonia in children. Dec.1917. (Rep.Pub.Health & Med.Subj., no.115) Local Government Board.
A report on tuberculosis including an examination of the results of sanitorium treatment. Dec.1931. (Rep.Pub.Health & Med.Subj., no.64) Ministry of Health.

MACNAMARA, Thomas James
Report on children under the poor law. 10 Dec.1907. 1908 Cd.3899 xcii. Local Government Board.

MACNAUGHTEN, Malcolm Martin
Committee on county court fees.
Report. 20 March 1923. 1923 Cmd.1856 x. Lord Chancellor's Office.
Supreme court fee committee.
Report. 3 Nov.1921. 1927 Cmd.1565 x. Lord Chancellor's Office.

MACNAUGHTEN, Terence Charles
Report on visit to Canada in connection with British settlement. Oct.1926. 1926 Cmd.2760 xv. Colonial Office.

MACNAUGHTON, D.A.
Memorandum on the present position of Latin and Greek in grant-aided secondary schools in England. March 1929. (Educational pamphlets, no.71) Board of Education.

McNEIL, Charles P.
Report of an inquiry into a series of outbreaks of febrile illness affecting boys in St.Joseph's Industrial School, Tranent. Nov.1912. Scottish Office.

McNEILL, James
Report on the conditions of Indian immigrants in four British colonies and Surinam.
Part 1: Trinidad and British Guiana. 1914. 1914/6 Cd.7744 xlvii.
Part 2: Surinam, Jamaica, Fiji and general remarks. 9 June 1914. 1914/6 Cd.7745 xlvii. India Office.

McNEILL, Ronald John, *1st Baron Cushendun*
Report of the British delegates on the League of Nations, ninth assembly. 21 Nov.1928. (Misc., no.8, 1928) 1928/9 Cmd.3242 xxiii. Foreign Office.
Report on the 51st and 52nd sessions of the Council of the League of Nations. 26 Nov.1928. (Misc., no.9, 1928) 1928/9 Cmd.3243 xxiii. Foreign Ofice.

MACPHERSON, William Grant
History of the Great War. Medical services. General history. 4 vols. 1921-1924. War Office.

MACRAE, A.E.
Overstrain of metals and its application to the auto-frettage process of cylinder and gun construction. June 1930. War Office.

MACROSTY, Henry W
Standing committee on trusts. Sub-committee on meat.
Interim report. 9 Nov.1920. 1920 Cmd.1057 xxiii.
Final report. 18 March 1921. 1921 Cmd.1356 xvi. Board of Trade.

McWEENEY, Edmond Joseph
Report on shell-fish layings on the Irish coast, as respects their liability to contamination. Aug.1903. 1904 Cd.1900 xxvii. Local Government Board for Ireland.

MADDOCKS, Henry
Report of inquiry on the St.Helen's County Borough police force held in November 1927. 15 Nov.1927 1928 Cmd.3103 xii. Home Office.

MAGRO, E.
The system of education in Malta. July 1914. (Imperial education conference papers) Board of Education.

MAHAFFY, Arthur
Report on a visit to the Gilbert and Ellice Islands, 1909. 11 March 1909. 1910 Cd.4992 lxvi. Colonial Office.

MAHON, J
Report on exotic plants of economic interest in the botanic gardens at Entebbe, Uganda. 1 Dec.1902. (Dip.cons.reports: misc.ser., no.588) 1903 Cd.1387-1 lxxvi. Foreign Office.

MAIR, Ludovic William Darra
Back-to-back houses; a report on relative morality in through and back-to-back houses in certain towns of the West Riding of Yorkshire. 20 July 1910. 1910 Cd.5314 xxxviii. Local Government Board.

Departmental committee on intercepting traps in house drains.
    Report. 22 Dec.1911. 1912/3 Cd.6359 xxix.
    Minutes of evidence. 1912. Local Government Board.

Report on a localised outbreak of enteric fever at Coventry. 26 March 1902. (Rep.Med.Insp., no.174) Local Government Board.

Report on a prevalence of throat illness in and near Ditcham Park Estate in the Catherington and Petersfield R.D's, Hampshire. 10 May 1902. (Rep.Med.Insp., no.175) Local Government Board.

Report on the prevalence of diphtheria in Chard R.D. 2 Sept.1902. (Rep.Med.Insp., no.179) Local Government Board.

Report on the sanitary conditions of Ashington U.D. and on recent enteric fever there. 18 March 1903. (Rep.Med.Insp., no.183) Local Government Board.

Report on the sanitary conditions of Bedlingtonshire U.D. and on recent enteric fever there. 23 Aug.1902. (Rep.Med.Insp., no 178) Local Government Board.

Report on the sanitary conditions of Bilston and Coseley U.D's and on a prevalence of enteric fever therein. 23 Jan.1900. (Rep.Med.Insp., no.147) Local Government Board.

Report on the sanitary conditions of Dartford R.D. 24 Aug.1908. (Rep.Med.Insp., no.310) Local Government Board.

Report on the sanitary conditions of Pocklington R.D. 17 May 1906.(Rep.Med.Insp., no.236) Local Government Board.

Report on the sanitary conditions of Sleatford R.D. 2 Jan.1906. (Rep.Med.Insp., no.224) Local Government Board.

Report on the sanitary conditions of Whickam U.D; on its housing, accommodation generally and on certain back-to-back houses at Marley Hill in particular. 3 May 1907. (Rep.Med.Insp., no.262) Local Government Board.

Report on the sanitary conditions of Wrexham R.D. 6 March 1905. (Rep.Med.Insp., no.210) Local Government Board.

MAITLAND, Adam
Departmental committee on the cost of hospitals and other public buildings.
    First report: the acute general hospital. 16 Dec.1936.
    Final report. 2 Feb.1938. Ministry of Health.

MAITLAND, Alexander
Committee on Scottish barley for use by Scottish distilleries. 31 March 1934. Scottish Office.

MAITLAND, J.S.
Special report on the causes and prevention of accidents at docks, wharves and quays. 1900. Home Office.

MALCOLM, Dugal Orme
Committee on education and industry (England and Wales).
    Report. First part. 3 Nov.1926.
    Report. Second part. 23 April 1928. Ministry of Labour.

MALLET, Bernard
Safeguarding of industries committee.
    Report on gas mantles. 2 Sept.1922. Board of Trade.

    Report on vulcanized fibre. 25 Oct.1922. Board of Trade.

MALLON, James Joseph
Standing committee on trusts.
    Findings and decisions of a sub-committee on combines of laundries. 20 July 1920. 1920 Cmd.903 xxiii. Board of Trade.

MANBY, Edward Petronell
Report on an outbreak of typhus fever in Hexham U.D. 23 April 1901. (Rep.Med.Insp., no.159) Local Government Board.

Report on enteric fever in Kenilworth U.D. 5 March 1914. (Rep.Pub.Health & Med.Subj., no.92) Local Government Board.

Report on the four sanitary districts within the Staines registration district. 29 Oct.1907. (Rep.Med.Insp., no.292) Local Government Board.

Report on the prevalence of diphtheria in the Risborough registration sub-district, forming part of the Wycombe R.D. 13 Jan.1903. (Rep.Med.Insp., no.181) Local Government Board.

Report on the sanitary conditions of Barnard Castle and Startforth R.D's., comprised within the Teesdale Union. 19 Oct.1905. (Rep.Med.Insp., no.220) Local Government Board.

Report on the sanitary conditions of Brecknock R.D. 5 April 1907. (Rep.Med.Insp., no.258) Local Government Board.

Report on the sanitary conditions of Brentford U.D. 22 May 1907. (Rep.Med.Insp., no.261) Local Government Board.

Report on the sanitary conditions of Holywell registration district. 29 April 1910. (Rep.Pub.Health & Med.Subj., no.29) Local Government Board.

Report on the sanitary conditions of Ince-in-Makerfield U.D. 2 April 1912. (Rep.Pub.Health & Med.Subj., no.65) Local Government Board.

Report on the sanitary conditions of West Hartlepool C.B. 5 Aug.1912. (Rep.Pub.Health & Med.Subj., no.71) Local Government Board.

Report on the sanitary conditions of Windsor R.D.,

MANBY, Edward Petronell (Continued)
with special reference to the need for a drainage system in the Parishes of Sunninghill and Sunningdale. 27 Aug.1906. (Rep.Med.Insp., no.241) Local Government Board.

MANN, Harold Charles Corry
Diets for school boys during the school age. 14 May 1926. (S.R.S., no.105) Medical Research Council.

Rickets; the relative importance of environment and diet as factors of causation: an investigation in London. Nov.1922. (S.R.S., no.68) Medical Research Council.

MANN, W.L.
Statistical reports from the British forces in France on penetrating wounds of the chest. 24 June 1919. (Stat.Rep., no.5) Medical Research Committee.

Mansfield, *Earl. SEE:* Murray, W.D., *5th Earl of Mansfield*

MARKS, George Croydon, *1st Baron*
Commission of enquiry into industrial unrest.
Report for the Yorkshire and east Midlands area. *SEE:* Barnes, G.N.

Joint select committee of both Houses on gas undertakings (powers of investment).
Report, proceedings, evidence and appendices. 12 May 1932. 1931/2 (73) v. House of Commons.

Marley, *Lord. SEE:* Aman, D.L., *1st Baron*

MARRACK, John Richardson
The chemistry of antigens and antibodies. 15 Jan.1934. (S.R.S., no.194) Medical Research Council.

The chemistry of antigens and antibodies. 9 Feb.1938. (S.R.S., no.230) Medical Research Council.

MARRIOTT, F.C.
Commission on secondary and primary education in Trinidad, Barbados, Leeward and Windward Islands. 26 Sept.1932. (Colonial, no.79) 1933. Colonial Office.

MARRIS, Henry Fairley
Report on the use of antropine as a diagnostic agent in typhoid infections. 15 Aug.1917. (S.R.S., no.9) Medical Research Committee.

MARSHALL, Alfred
Memorandum on the fiscal policy of foreign trade. 11 Nov.1908. 1908 (321) cvii. Treasury.

MARSHALL, C.F.Dendy
Notes on the variation of atmospheric conditions with altitude. July 1919. Ministry of Munitions.

MARSHALL, Francis Hugh Adam
Report on Dr.Serge Voronoff's experiments on the improvement of livestock. Jan.1928. Ministry of Agriculture and Fisheries *and* Board of Agriculture for Scotland.

MARSHALL, G.A.K.
Committee on locust control. *SEE:* Miers, H.A.

MARTIN, Charles James
Anti-typhoid committee.
Interim report. 8 July 1904. 1906 Cd.2698 lxvii.
Report. 28 Oct.1912. War Office. (*See also:* Leishman, W.B.)

Departmental committee on the reconstruction of the Royal Veterinary College.
Report. 8 Aug.1929. Ministry of Agriculture and Fisheries.

Foot-and-mouth disease research committee. *SEE:* Arkwright, J.A.

MARTIN, L.C.
A study of the performance of "night-glasses". March 1919. Department of Scientific and Industrial Research.

MARTIN, T. Carlaw
Committee on rural transport in Scotland.
Report. 17 April 1920. 1919 Cmd.227 xxx.
Supplementary report. 26 March 1920. 1920 Cmd.987 xxiv. Scottish Office.

MARVIN, Francis Sydney
Committee on the teaching of history in grant aided schools in England.
Report. 25 Nov.1922. (Educational pamphlets, no.37) Board of Education.

MARWICK, A.H.D.
The shape of road aggregate and its measurement. June 1936. (Road Res.Bull., no.2) Department of Scientific and Industrial Research.

MARWOOD, William Francis.
Report of an inquiry on Edinburgh Corporation tramways. 5 April 1922. Ministry of Transport.

MASCART, E.
Report of the International Meteorological Committee, Southport, 1903. Oct.1904. (M.O.164) Meteorological Office.

MASON, E.W.
Annotated account of fungi received at the Imperial Bureau of Mycology. List 2, fascicles 1 to 3. Imperial Bureau of Mycology.

MASON, Robert
Newport (Mon). harbour extension committee.
Report. 10 March 1921. Ministry of Transport.

MASON, T.N.
Gob fires.
Part 1: Explosions in sealed off areas in non-gassy seams. Aug.1932. (S.M.R.B.Paper no.75)
Part 2: The revival of heatings by inleakage of air. Aug.1932. (S.M.R.B.Paper no.76) Mines Department.

The inflammation of coal dusts: the effect of the chemical composition of the dust. March 1927. (S.M.R.B.Paper no.33) Mines Department.

The inflammation of coal dusts: the effect of the fineness of the dust. Jan.1936. (S.M.R.B.Paper no.95) Mines Department.

The inflammation of coal dusts: the effect of the nature of added incombustible dust. June 1933. (S.M.R.B.Paper no.79) Mines Department.

The inflammation of coal dusts: the effect of the presence of firedamp. Sept.1930. (S.M.R.B.Paper no.64) Mines Department.

The inflammation of coal dusts: the value of the presence of carbon dioxide and combined water in the dusts. Jan.1936. (S.M.R.B.Paper no.96) Mines Department.

The relative inflammability and explosibility of coal dusts. Sept.1928. (S.M.R.B.Paper no.48) Mines Department.

MASSEY, Marion E.
Some factors in auditory location. 1931. (S.R.S., no.166) Medical Research Council.

MASSEY, P.H.H.
Suggestions for British traders with Turkey in Asia. 27 Sept.1901. (Dip.cons.reports: misc.ser., no.568) 1902 Cd.787-4 ciii. Foreign Office.

MASTERMAN, Charles Frederick George
After twelve months of war. Aug.1915. Ministry of Information.

Departmental committee on rescue and aid in the case of accidents in mines.
Report. 8 Feb.1911. 1911 Cd.5550 xxxvii. Home Office.

Report of inquiry into charges made concerning the management of the Heswall Nautical School. Feb.1911. 1911 Cd.5541 lxii. Home Office.

Select committee on the application of sinking funds in the exercise of Borrowing powers, 1908.
Report, proceedings, evidence and appendix. 16 Dec.1908. 1908 (372) vi.
Report, proceedings, evidence, appendices and index. 16 June 1909. 1909 (193) vi. House of Commons.

MASTERMAN, E.W.G.
The deliverance of Jerusalem. 1918. Ministry of Information.

MATHESON, M.Cecile
School training for the home duties of women.
Part III: Domestic training of girls in Germany and Austria. Dec.1907. 1908 Cd.3860 xxvii. (special reports on education subjects, vol.19) Board of Education.

MATHESON, Robert E.
Special report on cancer in Ireland. (Supplement to 28th annual report of the Registrar-General, Ireland). Feb.1903. 1903 Cd.1450 xvi. Registrar General, Ireland.

MATHEWS, Basil
The freedom of Jerusalem. 1918. Ministry of Information.

MATTHEWS, D.J.
Tables of the velocity of sound in pure water and sea water for use in echo-sounding and sound-ranging. Jan.1927. 2nd ed. Aug.1939. (Hydrographic publication H.D.282) Admiralty.

MATTHEWS, William, *Sir*
Report of an inspection of the Cromford canal. 13 June 1907. 1907 Cd.3595 lxxiv. Board of Trade.

MAUDE, Evelyn John
Town and country planning advisory committee.
Report on the preservation of the countryside. 23 July 1938. Ministry of Health.

MAUGHAM, Frederick Herbert, *1st Viscount*
Committee on correspondence between Sir Henry McMahon, H.M. High Commissioner in Egypt and the Sharif of Mecca in 1915 and 1916.
Report. 16 March 1939. 1938/9 Cmd.5974 xiv. Colonial Office.

North Charterland concession, Northern Rhodesia, inquiry.
Report. 12 July 1932. (Colonial no.73).
Report. 30 May 1933. (Colonial no.85) Colonial Office.

MAURICE, Henry G.
Advisory committee on fishery research.
Report and appendices. Sept.1913. 1914 Cd.7200 xxx. Board of Agriculture and Fisheries.

Fish preservation committee.
Interim report: methods of freezing fish, with special reference to handling of large quantities in gluts. Nov.1920. (F.I.B.Special rep., no.4) (no further reports identified) Department of Scientific and Industrial Research.

MAVOR, James
Report on the north-west of Canada, with special reference to wheat production for export. 31 Dec.1904. 1905 Cd.2628 liv. Board of Trade.

MAXIMOV, N.A.
The theoretical significance of vernalization. Dec.1934. (Bull., no.16) Imperial Bureau of Plant Genetics: Herbages.

MAXTON, J.P.
The survey method of research in farm economics. Jan.1929. (E.M.B.14) Empire Marketing Board.

MAXWELL, Alexander
Departmental committee on courts of summary jurisdiction in the Metropolitan area.
Report. 28 June 1937. Home Office.

MAXWELL, G.B.
Firedamp explosions within closed vessels; the effects of turbulence. July 1925. (S.M.R.B.Paper no.10) Mines Department.

MAXWELL, Herbert Eustance, *6th baron Monreith*
Departmental committee on poisons.
Part I: Reports, supplementary and minority reports. 10 Dec.1902. 1903 Cd.1442 xxxiii.
Part II: Minutes of evidence, appendices and index. 1903 Cd.1443 xxxiii. Privy Council Office.
Departmental committee on the use of preservatives and colouring matters on preservation and colouring of food.
Report, evidence, appendices and index. 1901. 1902 Cd.833 xxxiv. Local Government Board.
Meteorological grant committee.
Vol.I: Report. 16 May 1904. 1904 Cd.2123 xviii.
Vol.II: Evidence and appendices. 1904 Cd.2124 xviii. Treasury.

Maxwell, J.S. *SEE:* Stirling-Maxwell, J.

MAXWELL, John T.
Burden of the existing rates and the general financial position of the Outer Hebrides.
Report on the Lews Parishes. 25 May 1906. 1906 Cd.3014 civ. Local Government Board for Scotland.

MAY, Eliot F.
Report on conferences between employers, operatives and inspectors concerning fencing of machinery, first aid, and other safeguards in cotton weaving factories. 29 May 1929. Home Office.
Report on conferences between employers, operatives and inspectors concerning fencing of machinery, prevention of accidents, first aid and temperature in cotton spinning mills. 24 April 1929. Home Office.

MAY, George Ernest, *1st Baron*
Committee on national expenditure.
First interim report. 14 Dec.1921. 1922 Cmd.1581 ix.
Second interim report. 28 Jan.1922. 1922 Cmd.1582 ix.
Third report. 21 Feb.1922. 1922 Cmd.1589 ix.
Report. 24 July 1931. 1930/1 Cmd.3920 xvi. Treasury.
Import Duties Advisory Committee.
Report on the position that will arise on the expiry of the Dyestuffs (Import Regulation) Act, 1920. 10 July 1933. 1932/3 Cmd.4411 xi. Treasury.
Report on the present position and future development on the iron and steel industry. 21 June 1937. 1936/7 Cmd.5507 xii. Board of Trade.

## MAY. M.G.
Provision made for children under compulsory school age in Belgium, France, Germay and Switzerland. Dec.1908. (Special reports on educational subjects, vol.22) Board of Education.

## MAYALL, P.
The system of education in the Gold Coast Colony, Ashanti and the Northern Territories. Sept.1914. (Imperial education conference papers) Board of Education.

## MAYBURY, Henry Percy
Committee on the development of civil aviation in the United Kingdom.
> Report and appendices. 9 Dec.1936. 1936/7 Cmd.5351 xvii. Air Ministry.

Departmental committee on lights on vehicles.
> First interim report. 11 Feb.1920. 1920 Cmd.659 xxv.
> Second interim report. 31 March 1920. 1920 Cmd.659 xxv.
> Third interim report: dazzle. 30 Sept.1921. (no further reports identified) Ministry of Transport.

Departmental committee on the licensing and regulation of public service vehicles.
> First interim report. 25 May 1925. (no further reports identified) Ministry of Transport.

Departmental committee on the taxation and regulation of road vehicles.
> Interim report. 31 March 1920. 1920 Cmd.660 xxv.
> Second interim report. 17 March 1922.
> Proceedings of meetings. 1923-4.
> Evidence. 1924.
> Third interim report. 27 June 1924. (no further reports identified) Ministry of Transport.

Departmental committee on traffic signs.
> Report. May 1933. Ministry of Transport.

Report on direction indicators on motor vehicles. 28 Nov.1932. Ministry of Transport.

London and home counties traffic advisory committee.
> Public inquiry on travelling facilities in East London.
>> Report. 7 Aug.1926.
>> Minutes of evidence and appendices. 1926. Ministry of Transport.
> Public inquiry on travelling facilities in North and North-east London.
>> Report. 17 March 1926.
>> Minutes of evidence. 1925. Ministry of Transport.
> Public inquiry on the travelling facilities in South-east London.
>> Report. 31 Jan.1927.
>> Minutes of evidence. 1926. Ministry of Transport.

Report of conference on road traffic noises and priority of traffic and crossroads. 20 Feb.1929. Ministry of Transport.

Report on "cruising" cabs. June 1927. Ministry of Transport.

Report on London bridges. 1 April 1926. Ministry of Transport.

Report on omnibus competition with tramways. 9 Feb.1926. Ministry of Transport.

Report on parking places. Nov.1927. Ministry of Transport.

Report on a scheme for the co-ordination of passenger transport facilities in the London traffic area. 27 July 1927. Ministry of Transport.

Report on street accidents to children in greater London. 16 July 1929. Ministry of Transport.

Slippery road surfaces. 26 Oct.1921. Ministry of Transport.

Street accidents in great London.
> Report. 10 March 1927.
> Second report. 10 July 1929. Ministry of Transport.

## MAYHEW, Arthur Innes
Commission on secondary and primary education in Trinidad, Barbados, Leeward and Windward Islands. 26 Sept.1932. (Colonial, no.79) Colonial Office.

## MAYNE, J.E.O.
The effect of fibre cores on internal corrosion in colliery winding ropes. March 1937. (S.M.R.B.Paper no. 97) Mines Department.

Fibre cores for colliery winding ropes. Dec.1938. (S.M.R.B.Paper no.102) Mines Department.

## MAYOR, R.G.
Committee on universities and training colleges.
> Report. April 1928. Board of Education.

## MEAGHER, E.T.
General paralysis and its treatment by induced malaria. 1929. Board of Control.

## MEARS, Grimwood
Committee on the Bombay Back Bay reclamation scheme.
> Report. 1 Dec.1926.
> Evidence, oral and documentary.
>> Part 1: evidence recorded in India. 1926.
>> Part 2: evidence recorded in England. 1927. India Office.

The destruction of Belgium; Germany's confession and avoidance. 1916. Ministry of Information.

Judgement of the High Court of Judicature at Allahabad in the revolutionary conspiracy case. 10 Nov.1924. 1924/5 Cmd.2309 xi. India Office.

## MEDD, J.C.
A short account of education in the Netherlands. 1902. (Special reports on educational subjects, supplement to vol.8) 1902 Cd.1157 xxvii. Board of Education.

## MEGAW, William J.
Departmental committee on charges for scutching flax and the disposal of tow.
> Report. 30 March 1918. 1918 Cd.9029 x.
> Minutes of evidence and index. 1918 Cd.9207 x. Department of Agriculture and Technical Instruction for Ireland.

## MEIKLEJOHN, Roderick Sinclair
Cost of living committee.
> Report. 8 May 1920. 1921 Cmd.1107 ix. Treasury. Civil Service National Whitley Council.

Melchett, *Lord. SEE:* Mond, A.M., *1st Baron Melchett.*

## MELGAR, Francisco
A Spanish Catholic's visit to England. 1917. Ministry of Information.

## MELLANBY, Edward
Alcohol: its absorption into and disappearance from

MELLANBY, Edward (continued)
the blood under different conditions. 7 Feb.1919. (S.R.S., no.31) Medical Research Committee.

Cmmmittee on accessory food factors (vitamins).
Report: vitamins, a survey of present knowledge. 10 May 1932. (S.R.S., no.167) Medical Research Council.

Experimental rickets. Oct.1921. (S.R.S., no.61) Medical Research Council.

Experimental rickets: the effect of cereals and their interaction with other factors of diet and environment in producing rickets. March 1925. (S.R.S., no.93) Medical Research Council.

MELLANBY, May
Diet and the teeth: an experimental study.
Part 1: dental structure in dogs. 28 Nov.1929. (S.R.S., no.140)
Part 2: diet and dental disease, and diet and dental structure in mammals other than dogs. 28 Nov.1930. (S.R.S., no.153)
Part 3: the effect of diet on dental structure and disease in man. 15 Dec.1933. (S.R.S., no.191) Medical Research Council.

MELLOR, John W.
Advisory Committee on University Colleges, Great Britain. Grant in aid.
Report. 10 June 1902. 1902 (252) lxxx. Treasury.

MENDONÇA, Henrique Lopes de
Moral aspects of the European war; a lecture. 13 May 1917. Ministry of Information.

MENZIES, W.J.M. *jr.*
The common eel and its capture. 1932. (Salmon Fish., 1932, no.6) Fishery Board for Scotland.

Difficulties of age determination and length calculations from the scales of sea trout. 1931. (Salmon Fish., 1931, no.5) Fishery Board for Scotland.

Further notes on the percentage of previously spawned salmon. 1914. (Salmon Fish., 1914, no.2) Fishery Board for Scotland.

The frequency of spawning in salmon. 1911. (Salmon Fish., 1911, no.1) Fishery Board for Scotland.

The movements of salmon marked in the sea.
1. North-west coast of Scotland in 1936. (Salmon Fish., 1937, no.1) 1937.
2. West coast of Sutherland in 1937. (Salmon Fish., 1938, no.1) 1938.
3. Island of Soay and Ardnamurchan in 1938. (Salmon Fish., 1938, no.7) 1938. Fishery Board for Scotland.

Salmon of the east coast of Sutherland. 1915. (Salmon Fish., 1915, no.2) Fishery Board for Scotland.

Salmon of the Grimersta district, Lewis, 1925. 1926. (Salmon Fish., 1926, no.6) Fishery Board for Scotland.

Salmon investigations in Scotland. 1921.
1. Salmon of the River Dee. (Salmon Fish., 1921, no.1) 1922.
2. Salmon of the River Spey. (Salmon Fish., 1921, no.2) 1923.
3. Salmon of the River Don, Findhorn, Forth and Tweed. (Salmon Fish., 1921, no.3) 1923.
4. Summary of results. (Salmon Fish., 1921, no.4) 1923. Fishery Board for Scotland.

Salmon investigations in Scotland, 1922.
1. Salmon of the River Spey. (Salmon Fish., 1924,no.1) 1924.
2. Salmon of the River Dee. (Salmon Fish., 1924, no.3) 1924. Fishery Board for Scotland.

Salmon investigations in Scotland, 1923.
1. Salmon of the River Dee. (Salmon Fish., 1926, no.4) 1926.
2. Salmon of the River Spey. (Salmon Fish., 1926, no.5) 1926. Fishery Board for Scotland.

Salmon of the River Conon, 1927. 1928. (Salmon Fish., 1928, no.8) Fishery Board for Scotland.

Salmon of the River Dee, 1924. 1927. (Salmon Fish., 1927, no.3) Fishery Board for Scotland.

Salmon of the River Dee, 1925. 1931. Salmon Fish., 1931, no.4) Fishery Board for Scotland.

Salmon of the River Spey, 1924. 1928. (Salmon Fish., 1928, no.1) Fishery Board for Scotland.

Salmon of the River Spey, 1925. 1928. (Salmon Fish., 1928, no.3) Fishery Board for Scotland.

Salmon passes; their design and construction.
1. At smaller obstructions. 1934. (Salmon Fish., 1934, no.1) (no others identified) Fishery Board for Scotland.

Scales of salmon of the River Add. June 1913. (Salmon Fish., 1912, no.1) Fishery Board for Scotland.

Sea trout of the River Forth. 1919. (Salmon Fish., 1919, no.1) Fishery Board for Scotland.

Some aspects of the growth of salmon in river and sea as observed from scale examination of Dee and Spey salmon 1921 to 1923 inclusive. 1927. (Salmon Fish., 1927, no.1) Fishery Board xor Scotland.

Study of the salmon of the Moray Firth. 1914. (Salmon Fish., 1914, no.4) Fishery Board for Scotland.

MERCIER, Desiré J. *Archbishop of Mechlin, 1906-1926.*
Charity towards our enemies; from a pastoral letter. Jan.1917. Ministry of Information.

For our soldiers; an address. 21 July 1916. Ministry of Information.

For those in captivity; a sermon. 26 Nov.1917. Ministry of Information.

The seizure of church bells and organs in occupied Belgium; a letter. 2 March 1918. Ministry of Information.

The voice of God. 1916. Ministry of Information.

MERRIMAN, Frank Boyd
Committee on the Optical Practitioners' (Registration) Bill, 1927.
Report. 17 Dec.1927. 1927 Cmd.2999 xi. Ministry of Health *and* Scottish Office.

Poor persons procedure committee.
Report. 30 July 1934. Lord Chancellor's Department.

Mersey, *Lord. SEE:* Bigham, J.C., *1st Viscount*
       *SEE ALSO:* Bigham, C.C., *2nd Viscount.*

MESTON, James Scorgie, *1st Baron Meston*
Committee on the financial relations between the central and provincial goverments in India.
Report. 31 March 1920. 1920 Cmd.724 xiv. India Office.

Joint select committee on gas undertakings (basic prices).

MESTON, James Scorgie, *1st Baron Meston* (continued)
Report, proceedings and evidence. 20 Dec.1932. 1932/3 (19) v. House of Commons.

METCALFE, Charles
Advisory council.
Report on the standardisation of railway equipment. 4 July 1918. 1918 Cd.9193 xiii. Ministry of Reconstruction.

MEUX, Hedworth
Committee on export of cement from the United Kingdom to Holland.
Report. 27 March 1918. 1918 Cd.9032 xxvi. Foreign Office.

MEYER, William Stevenson
Lecture on the position of India in the Empire delivered to the Working Men's Club, Mornington Crescent, London. 4 Feb.1922. India Office.

MICKLETHWAIT, St.John Gore
Standing committee on merchandise marks.
Report on bacon and ham. 23 Mar.1933. 1932/3 Cmd.4337 xiv. Ministry of Agriculture and Fisheries.

Report on grapes. 3 March 1936. 1935/6 Cmd.5147 xiii. Ministry of Agriculture and Fisheries.

Report on margarine. 25 Oct.1938. 1938/9 Cmd.5097 xiii. Ministry of Agriculture and Fisheries.

Report on meat. 10 Nov.1933. 1933/4 Cmd.4470 xiv. Ministry of Agriculture and Fisheries.

Report on meat. 31 May 1935. 1934/5 Cmd.4926 x. Ministry of Agriculture and Fisheries.

Report on poultry. 22 Sept.1933. 1932/3 Cmd.4439 xiv. Board of Trade.

MICKS, William Lawson
Commission on poor law reform in Ireland.
Vol.I: Report. 10 Oct.1906. 1906 Cd.3202 li.
Vol.II: Appendix. 1906 Cd.3203 li.
Vol.III: Minutes of evidence and index. 1906 Cd.3204 lii. Irish Secretary's Office.

MIDDLEBROOK, William
Committee on the hours, pay and conditions of service of firemen in professional fire brigades in Great Britain.
Report. 15 May 1920. 1920 Cmd.710 xvi.
Evidence. 1920 Cmd.876 xvi. Home Office.

Departmental committee on disinfection of horsehair.
Report. 2 April 1921. 1921 Cmd.1365 xiii. Home Office.

Departmental committee on preventing danger of infection by anthrax.
Vol.1: Report of the disinfection sub-committee. 23 April 1918. 1918 Cd.9057 vi.
Vol.2: Report of the committee. 22 Aug.1918. 1918 Cd.9171 vi.
Vol.3: Summary of evidence and appendices. 1918 Cd.9172 vi. Home Office.

Select committee on gas undertakings (statutory prices).
Report, proceedings, evidence, and appendices. 11 June 1918. 1918 (74) iii. House of Commons.

Middleton, *Lord. SEE:* Willoughby, D.W.B., *9th Baron*

MIDDLETON, Edward Loggie
Report on grinding of metals and cleaning of castings with special reference to the effects of dust inhalation upon the workers. 10 March 1923. Home Office.

Report on the international conference on silicosis, Johannesburg, August 1930. 17 Dec.1930. Home Office.

MIDDLETON, Thomas H.
Recent development of German agriculture. 1 June 1916. 1916 Cd.8305 iv. Board of Agriculture and Fisheries.

Scheme for establishing scholarships and maintenance grants for the sons and daughters of agricultural workmen and others.
Report of the Central Committee. 28 Aug.1926. Ministry of Agriculture and Fisheries.

MIERS, Henry Alexander
Committee on locust control.
First and second interim reports. 31 May 1929. 1929/30 Cmd.3367 viii.
Third report. 8 July 1930. 1929/30 Cmd.3642 xii.
Fourth report. 15 April 1932. 1931/2 Cmd.4124 xi.
Fifth report: Proposals for the use of aircraft against locusts. 26 Aug. 1932. 1932/3 Cmd.4321 xiv.
Sixth report: Review of the present locust outbreak in Africa and Western Asia and of investigations since 1929 and general programme of further investigations. 12 July 1934. 1933/4 Cmd.4692 xiii. Treasury. Economic Advisory Council.

MILES, Wilfred
History of the great war; military operations. France and Belgium, 1916. Text and maps. 4 vols. 1932 and 1938. War Office.

MILLAR, Alexander B.
Burden of the existing rates and the general financial position of the Outer Hebrides.
Report on the Lews Parishes. 25 May 1906. 1906 Cd.3014 civ. Local Government Board for Scotland.

Report on the sanitary conditions of the Lews. 10 April 1905. 1905 Cd.2616 xxxiv. Local Government Board for Scotland.

MILLER, Alexander Thomas
Committee on insurance of ships.
Report. 23 Dec.1936. 1936/7 Cmd.5349 xiii. Board of Trade.

MILLIGAN, John C.
Report on British trade with Switzerland for the year 1899. 7 Nov.1900. (Dip.cons.reports: misc.ser., no.542) 1900 Cd.353-7 xci. Foreign Office.

MILLOY, L.
Inquiry as to herring industry in the Firth of Clyde.
Report. 1903. 1903 Cd.1674 xiv. Fisheries Board for Scotland.

MILLS, Frederick
Safeguarding of industries.
Report of the committee on gas mantles. 29 July 1925. 1924/5 Cmd.2533 xv. Board of Trade.

MILLS, J. Saxon
The gathering of the clans. 1917. Ministry of Information.

MILNE, G.T.
Reports on the conditions and prospects of British trade in Central America, Colombia and Venezuela. June 1913. 1913 Cd.6969 lxviii. Board of Trade.

MILNE, George Francis, *1st Baron Milne*
Central advisory water committee.
First report: underground water. Planning of water resources and supplies. March 1928.
Second report: consolidation and amendment of the law relating to public water supply. 5 April 1939. 1938/9 Cmd.5986 xv.
Third report: river boards. 12 July 1943. 1942/3 Cmd.6465 vi. Ministry of Health.

MILNER, Alfred, *1st Viscount Milner*
Cotton contraband. 21 Aug.1915. Ministry of Information.

Departmental committee on the production of food in England and Wales.
Interim report. 17 July 1915. 1914/6 Cd.8048 v.
Final report. 15 Oct.1915. 1914/6 Cd.8095 v.
Board of Agriculture and Fisheries.

Report of the special mission to Egypt. 9 Dec.1920. (Egypt, no.1, 1921) 1921 Cmd.1131 xlii. Foreign Office.

Milnes, R.O.A.C. *SEE:* Crewe-Milnes, R.O.A., *1st Earl of Crewe.*

MINETT, E.P.
Further report on the nastin and benzoyl chloride treatment for leprosy at the Mahaica Leper Asylum, British Guiana, 1910-11. 30 Nov.1911. 1912/3 Cd.6023 lx. Colonial Office.

MIRRLEES, S.T.A.
Meteorological results of the British Arctic air-route expedition, 1930-1. June 1934. (Geophys.Mem., no.61) Meteorological Office.

A study of the atmospheric circulation over tropical Africa. Oct.1932. (Geophys.Mem., no.55) Meteorological Office.

MITCHELL, George A.
Committee on obsolete tonnage.
Report. 16 April 1931. Board of Trade.

MITCHELL, Peter Chalmers
Report on the German propaganda library attached to the War Office. Aug.1917. War Office.

MITCHELL, T. J.
History of the Great War; medical services. Casualties and medical statistics of the Great War. March 1931. War Office.

MITCHELL-INNES, Edward A.
Departmental committee on the Poisons and Pharmacy Acts.
Report. 14 Jan.1930. 1929/30 Cmd.3512 xvi. Privy Council.

Standing committee on merchandise marks.
Report on apples and pears. 23 Feb.1928. 1928 Cmd.3062 ix. Ministry of Agriculture and Fisheries.

Report on butter. 22 May 1931. 1930/1 Cmd.3878 xv. Ministry of Agriculture and Fisheries.

Report on currants, sultanas and raisins. 14 Oct.1927. 1928 Cmd.3026 ix. Ministry of Agriculture and Fisheries.

Report on frozen or chilled salmon and trout. 25 July 1930. 1930/1 Cmd.3606 xv. Ministry of Agriculture and Fisheries.

Report on eggs. 14 Oct.1927. 1927 Cmd.2969 xi.
Second report on eggs. 1 June 1928. 1928 Cmd.3145 ix. Ministry of Agriculture and Fisheries.

Report on honey. 25 Nov.1927. 1928 Cmd.3012 ix. Ministry of Agriculture and Fisheries.

Report on malt products. 13 Dec.1929. 1929/30 Cmd.3474 xvi. Ministry of Agruclture and Fisheries, Home Office *and* Scottish Office.

Report on oats and oat products. 14 May 1928. 1928 Cmd.3118 ix. Ministry of Agriculture and Fisheries.

Report on rose trees. 28 Nov.1928. 1928/9 Cmd.3245 viii. Ministry of Agriculture and Fisheries.

Report on tomatoes. 10 May 1929. 1929/30 Cmd.3344 xvi. Ministry of Agriculture and Fisheries, Home Office *and* Scottish Office.

MITCHELL-THOMSON, William, *1st Baron Selsdon*
Inter-departmental committee on the civil duties of the coast guard.
Report. 18 July 1927. 1922 Session 2 Cmd.1753 ii. Treasury.

Television committee.
Report. 14 Jan.1935. 1934/5 Cmd.4793 xi. Post Office.

Wireless telegraphy commission.
Report. 5 Dec.1921. 1922 Cmd.1572 x.
Second report. 7 July 1926. 1926 Cmd.2781 xv. Cabinet Office.

MITRANY, D.
Greater Rumania: a study in national ideals. 1917. Ministry of Information.

MIVART, F. St.George
Report on the sanitary conditions of Bedale R.D. and on a prevalence of diphtheria. 13 Feb.1908. (Rep.Med.Insp., no.302) Local Government Board.

Report on the sanitary conditions of Borough of Blanford Forum. 9 June 1909. (Rep.Pub.Health & Med.Subj., no.9) Local Government Board.

Report on the sanitary conditions of Borough and R.D. of Bridgnorth. 17 March 1910. (Rep.Pub.Health & Med.Subj., no.25) Local Government Board.

Report on the sanitary conditions of the Borough of Dartmouth. 30 Jan.1914. (Rep.Pub.Health & Med.Subj., no.90) Local Government Board.

Report on the sanitary conditions of the Borough of King's Lynn. 26 Oct.1909. (Rep.Pub.Health & Med.Subj., no.18) Local Government Board.

Report on the sanitary conditions of Bourne R.D. and the prevalence of scarlatina and diphtheria during 1905. 17 Oct.1906. (Rep.Med.Insp., no.247) Local Government Board.

Report on the sanitary conditions of Bourne U.D. 18 Oct.1907. (Rep.Med.Insp., no.289) Local Government Board.

Report on the sanitary conditions of Hollingburn R.D. 11 June 1908. (Rep.Med.Insp., no.304) Local Government Board.

Report on the sanitary conditions of Lancaster R.D. 1 April 1902. (Rep.Med.Insp., no.172) Local Government Board.

Report on the sanitary conditions of Romford R.D.

**MIVART, F. St.George** (Continued)
and on the prevalence of diphtheria in certain localities therein. 15 April 1904. (Rep.Med.Insp., no.195) Local Government Board.

Report on the sanitary conditions of Royston U.D. and on the prevalence of certain infectious diseases therein. 5 May 1906. (Rep.Med.Insp., no.234) Local Government Board.

Report on the sanitary conditions of Shaftesbury R.D. and Borough. 4 April 1912. (Rep.Pub.Health & Med.Subj., no.67) Local Government Board.

Report on the sanitary conditions of Stroud R.D. and Nailsworth U.D. 2 Oct.1900. (Rep.Med.Insp., 153) Local Government Board.

Report on the sanitary condptions of Thingoe R.D. 17 Oct.1907. (Rep.Med.Insp., no.286) Local Government Board.

Report on the sanitary conditions of Westhampnett R.D. 16 Oct.1908. (Rep.Med.Insp., no.313) Local Government Board.

**MOBERLY, Frederick James**
History of the Great War. (Military operations.) The campaign in Mesopotamia, 1914-1918. 4 vols. 1923-1927. War Office.

History of the Great War. (Military operations.) Togoland and the Cameroons, 1914-1916. 1931. War Office.

**MOIR, Ernest William**
Committee on new methods of house construction.
Interim report. 4 Nov.1924.
Second interim report. 7 Jan.1925. 1924/5 Cmd.2310 xiii.
Third interim report. 29 Jan.1925. 1924/5 Cmd.2334 xiii.
Fourth interim report. 28 Sept.1925. (no other reports identified) Ministry of Health.

**MOLONY, Thomas Francis**
Departmental committee on the treatment of young offenders.
Report. 17 March 1927. 1927 Cmd.2831 xii. Home Office.

Vice-regal committee on intermediate education in Ireland.
Repmrt. 4 March 1919. 1919 Cmd.66 xxi. Irish Secretary's Office.

**MOLYNEUX, Osbert Cecil, *6th Earl of Sefton***
Royal commission on horse breeding. *SEE:* Cavendish-Bentinck, W.J.A.C.J., *6th Duke Portland.*

**MONCKTON, Walter**
Departmental committee on the distribution of coal, coke and manufactured fuel.
(No report identified.)
Minutes of evidence, 1st to 7th days. 1938-9. Mines Department.

**MONCRIEFF, Alan Aird**
Tests for respiratory efficiency. 1 Oct.1934. (S.R.S., no.198) Medical Research Council.

**MOND, Alfred Moritz, *1st Baron Melchett***
Committee on audit of unemployment benefit.
Report. 26 Oct.1916. 1916 Cd.8412 xiv. Treasury.

National fuel and power committee.
Report. 4 Sept.1928. 1928/9 Cmd.3201 vi.
Second report. 27 Nov.1928. 1928/9 Cmd.3252 vi. Board of Trade.

Report on the cultivation of certain areas in the

Royal parks. 26 Feb. 1918. 1918 Cd.8996 xii.

Report on the cultivation of certain areas in the Royal parks. 28 March 1919. 1919 Cmd.114 xxvii. Board of Works.

**MONIER-WILLIAMS, G.W.**
Aluminium in food. Oct.1935. (Rep.Pub.Health & Med.Subj., no.78) Ministry of Health.

Antimony in enamelled hollow-ware. March 1934. (Rep.Pub.Health & Med.Subj., no.73) Ministry of Health.

Committee on the eradication of bed-bugs.
Report 22 Dec.1933. (Rep.Pub.Health & Med.Subj., no.72) Ministry of Health.

The determination of benzoic acid in foodstuffs. Jan.1927. (Rep.Pub.Health & Med.Subj., no.39) Ministry of Health.

The determination of sulphur dioxide in foods. May 1927. (Rep.Pub.Health & Med.Subj., no.43) Ministry of Health.

Lead in food. Oct.1938. (Rep.Pub.Health & Med.Subj., no.88) Ministry of Health.

Report on analyses and methods of detection of certain proprietary substances sold as preservatives for milk, cream, *etc.* 19 Jan.1912. (Rep.Pub.Health & Med.Subj., no.60) Local Government Board.

Report on the chemical changes produced in flour bleaching. 3 April 1911. (Rep.Pub.Health & Med.Subj., new series, no.49) (Food reports, no.12) 1911 Cd.5613 xxxii. Local Government Board.

Report on the determination of sucrose, lactose and invert sugar in sweetened condensed milk. April 1930. (Rep.Pub.Health & Med.Subj., no.57) Ministry of Health.

Report on the freezing point of milk in relation to the detection of added water. 11 Jan.1915. (Rep.Pub.Health & Med.Subj., no.103) Local Goverment Board.

Report on the nature of the colouring matter of flour and its relation to processes of natural and artificial bleaching. 8 Oct.1912. (Rep.Pub.Health & Med.Subj., no.73) Local Government Board

The solubility of glazes and enamels used in cooking utensils. Dec.1924. (Rep.Pub.Health & Med.Subj., no.29) Ministry of Health.

Use of hydrogen cyanide for fumigation purposes.
Preliminary report. Aug.1923. (Rep.Pub.Health & Med.Subj., no.19)
The effect on foods of fumigation with hydrogen cyanide. Sept.1930. (Rep.Pub.Health & Med.Subj., no.60) Ministry of Health.

**MONKHOUSE, Cosmo**
Committee appointed to examine the claims and suggestions for exemption from light dues.
Vol.1: Report. 26 Oct.1900. 1900 Cd.413 lxxvii.
Vol.2: Appendix. 1901 Cd.446 lxxviii. Board of Trade.

**MONKSWELL, Robert Collier, *2nd Baron***
Royal commission on mines.
First report. 30 May 1907. 1907 Cd.3548 xiv.
Minutes of evidence.
Volume I: 1907 Cd.3549 xiv.
Volume II: 1908 Cd.3873 xx.
Volume III: 1908 Cd.4349 xx.
Volume IV: 1909 Cd.4667 xxxiv.
Volume V: 1911 Cd.5642 xxxvi.
Second report. July 1909. 1909 Cd.4820 xxxiv.
Enquiry into ventilation of coal mines and the

MONKSWELL, Robert Collier, *2nd Baron* (continued)
methods of examination for fire damp. Reports by John Cadman and E.B. Whalley. 1090 Cd. 4551 xxxiv.
Third report. Feb.1911. 1911 Cd.5561 xxxvi.

MONRO, Horace Cecil
Comission on mining and drainage around the county borough of Doncaster.
Report. 10 Feb.1928.
Minutes of evidence and index. 1927. Home Office.

Commission on the Ouse Drainage District.
Report. 21 Dec. 1925. 1926 Cmd.2572 xv. Ministry of Agriculture and Fisheries.

Departmental committee on meat inspection.
Report. 16 July 1921. Ministry of Health.

Departmental committee on the provisions and effect of the Metropolis Water Act, 1902.
Report. June 1920. 1920 Cmd.845 xxi.
Minutes of evidence. 1920. Ministry of Health.

Departmental committee on the treatment of flour with chemical substances.
Report. 14 Feb.1927. Ministry of Health.

Food preservatives committee.
Interim report on the treatment of chilled beef and other foods with formaldehyde. 12 June 1924.
Final report. 30 Sept.1924. Ministry of Health.

Joint advisory committee on river pollution. *SEE:* Atkey, A.R.

MONSON, W.J.
Report on slavery and labour in the British East African Protectorate. April 1903. 1903 Cd.1631 xlv. Foreign Office.

MONTAGU, Edwin Samuel
Committee of inquiry into savings certificates and local loans.
Report. 30 April 1923. 1923 Cmd.1865 xii pt.2. Treasury.

Committee on retrenchment in the public expenditure. *SEE:* McKenna, R.

Committee on war loans for the small investor.
Interim report. 28 Dec.1915. 1914/6 Cd.8146 xxxvii.
Report. 26 Jan.1916. 1916 Cd.8179 xv. Treasury.

Departmental committee on the protection of wild birds.
Report. 4 July 1919. 1919 Cmd.295 xxxi.
Evidence and appendices. 1919. Cmd.189 xxxi. Home Office.

The means of victory; a speech. 15 Aug.1916. Ministry of Information.

Report on Indian Constitutional reforms. 22 April 1918. 1918 Cd.9109 viii. India Office.

Montagu-Douglas-Scott, J.C. *SEE:* Scott, J.C.M.D., *7th Duke of Buccleuch*

MONTAGUE, C.E.
Notes from Calais base. 1918. Ministry of Information.

MOODIE, P.B.
Sub-committee of the Scottish Police Council on rent allowances of police and pay of new entrants.
Report. 19 Dec.1924. Scottish Office.

MOON, Ernest
Committee on trading with the enemy.
Report. 16 April 1918. 1918 Cd.9059 xiii. Board of Trade.

MOONEY, F.M.
Tests of some home-grown timbers in their green and seasoned conditions. Sept.1929. Department of Scientific and Industrial Research.

MOORE, Benjamin
The causation and prevention of T.N.T. poisoning. 30 Oct.1917. (S.R.S., no.11) Medical Research Committee.

MOORE-BRABAZON, John Theodore Cuthbert
Air mails committee.
Interim report. 19 Jan.1924. 1924 Cmd.2038 vii. Post Office *and* Board of Trade. *SEE ALSO:* Barnes, R.G.

Severn Barrage committee.
Report. 19 Jan.1933.
Appendix: report of expert co-ordinating sub-committee. 7 July 1932.
Plans, diagrams, *etc.* 1933. Economic Advisory Council. Treasury.

MOORHOUSE, Henry Claude
Report on murderous attacks in 1927 on government officials on Guadal canal and Malaita, British Solomon Islands Protectorate. 22 Sept.1928. 1928/9 Cmd.3248 v. Colonial Office.

MORAN, T.
Postmortem changes in animal tissues: the conditioning or ripening of beef. June 1929. (F.I.B.special rep., no.36) Department of Scientific and Industrial Research.

The storage of eggs. Dec.1925. (F.I.B.special rep., no.26) Department of Scientific and Industrial Research.

MORGAN, Montague Travers
Epidemic catarrhal jaundice. May 1927. (Rep.Pub.Health & Med.Subj., no.42) Ministry of Health.

MORISON, Theodore
Committee on the system of state technical scholarships established by the government of India in 1904.
Report with appendices. 8 Oct.1912. 1913 Cd.6867 xlvii. India Office.

MORISON, Thomas Brash, *Lord*
Departmental committee on the law of Scotland relating to the constitution of marriage.
Report. 17 Dec.1935. 1936/7 Cmd.5354 xiii. Scottish Office.

MORISON, William Thomson
Indian factory labour commission.
Vol.1: Report and appendix. 1908. 1908 Cd.4292 lxxiv.
Vol.2: Evidence. 1909 Cd.4519 lxiii. India Office.

MORLEY, Robert
Standing committee on trusts.
Findings and decisions of a sub-committee on the existence and effect of a ring in the salt trade. 26 May 1920. 1920 Cmd.832 xxiii. Board of Trade.

MORREAU, C.J.
The reduction of noise in buildings. June 1939. (B.R.B.special rep., no.26) Department of Scientific and Industrial Research.

MORRIS, Daniel
Imperial Department of Agriculture in the West Indies: a summary. 16 Jan. 1911. (Colonial rep.misc., no.75) 1911 Cd.5515 lii. Colonial Office.

Report on the agricultural resources of St.Helena. (Reprint) 1884. (Colonial rep.misc., no.38) 1906 Cd.3248 lxxvi. Colonial Office.

MORRIS, Harold S.
Committee on procedure and evidence for the determination of claims for unemployment insurance benefit.
    Report. 16 Oct.1929. 1929/30 Cmd.3415 xvii.
    Minutes of evidence. 1929. Ministry of Labour.

Report on the draft clay works welfare order. 9 Nov.1932. Home Office.
Report on the draft tanning welfare order, 1929. 2 April 1930. Home Office.

MORRIS, Malcolm
Report of the British delegates to the international scientific conference on leprosy, held at Bergen, 15-19 August 1909. 14 Sept.1909. 1909 Cd.4916 lxxi. Privy Council.

MORRIS, Martin Henry Fitzpatrick, *2nd Baron Killanin*
Vice-regal committee of enquiry into primary education in Ireland.
    Vol.1: Report. 26 Feb.1919. 1919 Cmd.60 xxi.
    Vol.2: Summaries of evidence, memoranda and returns. 1919 Cmd.178 xxi. Irish Secretary's Office.

MORRIS, T.N.
The corrosion of the tin-plate container by food products. Feb.1936. (F.I.B.special rep., no.40).
    Second report. Nov.1936. (F.I.B.special rep., no.44) Department of Scientific and Industrial Research.

MORTON, George
Committee on poor persons' representation in Scotland.
    Report. 25 March 1937. 1936/7 Cmd.5435 xiv. Scottish Office.

Protection and training.
    Report of the Departmental Committee on the treatment of young offenders. 9 April 1928. Scottish Office.

MOTTRAM, Thomas Harry
Departmental committee mn the provision and maintenance of rescue appliances and for the formation and training of rescue corps and brigades.
    Report. 27 March 1926. Mines Department.

Support of working in mines committee.
    The support of underground workings in the east Midland coalfield. Jan.1927. (S.M.R.B.Paper no.30).
    The support of underground workings in the coalfields of Lancashire, Cheshire and north Wales. July 1929. (S.M.R.B.Paper no.55)
    The support of underground workings in the coalfields of the north of England. July 1930. (S.M.R.B.Paper no.61).
    The support of underground workings in the coalfields of Scotland. Oct.1925. (S.M.R.B.Paper no.12)
    The support of unerground workings in the coalfields of the south Midlands and and the south of England. Sept.1928. (S.M.R.B.Paper no.45).
    The support of underground workings in the south Wales coalfield. 14 Oct.1924.

(S.M.R.B.Paper no.6) Mines Department.

Mount Temple, *Lord. SEE:* Ashley, W.W., *1st Baron.*

MOWATT, Francis
Inter-departmental committee on outdoor staff (to be appointed under the National Insurance Act).
    Report. 16 May 1912. 1912/3 Cd.6231 xlii. Treasury.

Royal commission on the finances, economic position and judicial procedure of Malta.
    Report. 22 April 1912. 1912/3 Cd.6090 xl.
    Minutes of evidence. 1912/3 Cd.6280 xl.
    Appendix B: documents. 1912/3 Cd.6281 xl.

Moyne, *Baron. SEE:* Guinness, W.E., *1st Baron Moyne.*

MUDIMAN, Alexander Phillips
India reforms enquiry committee.
    Report and connected papers. 3 Dec.1924. 1924/5 Cmd.2360 x.
    Appendix 5: Written evidence, 1925.
    Appendix 6: Oral evidence. 2 vols. 1925.
    Views of local governments on the working of the reforms:
        Dated 1923. 1924/5 Cmd.2361 x.
        Dated 1924. 1924/5 Cmd.2362 x.
        Dated 1927. India Office.

MÜLLER, W. Max.
Report on the Mexican isthmus (Tehuantepec) railway. April 1907. (Dip.cons.reports: misc.ser., no.658) 1907 Cd. 3284-2 lxxxvii. Foreign Office.

MUFF, H.Brantwood
Report relating to the geology of the East Africa Protectorate. 20 Dec.1907. 1908 Cd.3828 lxx. (Colonial rep.misc., no.45) Colonial Office.

MUGERDITCHIAN, Ester
From Turkish toils; the narrative of an Armenian family's escape. 1918. Ministry of Information.

MUIR, Ramsay
The character of the British Empire. 1917. Ministry of Information.

MUIR-MACKENZIE, Montgue J.
Committee on the bankruptcy law and its administration.
    Report. 8 April 1908. 1908 Cd.4068 xxxiv.
    Minutes of evidence, appendices and index. 1908 Cd.4069 xxxiv. Board of Trade.

MUIR-WOOD, Helen Marguerite
The British carboniferous producti: II: Productus, Semireticulatus and Longispinus groups. 22 Dec.1928. (Mem.Geol.Surv., Palaeont, vol.3, pt.1.) Geological Survey.

MUIRHEAD, W.
Standing committees on investigation of prices and trusts. Sectional committee on the sub-committee on building materials.
    Report on cement and mortar. 20 Nov.1920. 1920 Cmd.1091 xxiii. Board of Trade.

MULLER, H.J.
Bibliography on the genetics of drosophila. 20 July 1939. Imperial Bureau of Animal Breeding and Genetics.

MULVANY, T.R.
Reports on the epidemic of ankylostomiasis in the Westphalian colliery district. 6 July 1903. 1903 Cd.1671 xv. Home Office.

MUMMERY, John Howard
The structure of teeth in relation to dental disease. Nov.1922. (S.R.S., no.70) Medical Research Council.

MUNCH-PETERSEN, E.
Bovine mastitis; a survey of the literature to the end of 1935. 1938. Imperial Bureau of Animal Health.

MUNRO, A.M.
Report of a conference on the outbreak of foot-and-mouth disease at Birkenhead. April 1914. 1914 Cd.7326 xii. Board of Agriculture and Fisheries *and* Department of Technial Instruction for Ireland.

MUNRO, H.C.
Report on special work of the Local Government Board arising out of the war. 31 Dec.1914. 1914/6 Cd.7763 xxv. Local Government Board.

MUNRO, James Watson
Beetles injurious to timber. Jan.1928. (Bull., no.9) Forestry Commission.

British bark-beetles. Aug.1926. (Bull., no.8) Forestry Commission.

Report on insect infestation of stored cacao. Dec.1929. (E.M.B.24) Empire Marketing Board.

Survey of forest insect conditions in the British Isles, 1919. 24 Feb.1920. (Bull., no.2) Forestry Commission.

MUNRO, Robert, *1st Baron Alness*
Departmental committee on night baking.
Report. 13 July 1937. 1936/7 Cmd.5525 xiv. Home Office.

Scottish departmental committee on nursing.
Report. 29 Sept.1938. 1937/8 Cmd.5866 xii. Department of Health for Scotland.

Special committee on an application by the university courts of the universities of Scotland for a grant from the Education (Scotland) Fund.
Report. 28 April 1938. 1937/8 Cmd.5735 xv. Scottish Office.

Select committee on the prevention of road accidents.
Report, proceedings, evidence and index. 29 July 1938. 1937/8 (H.L.192) iv.
Report, proceedings, evidence and index. 29 March 1939. 1938/9 (H.L.52) v. House of Lords.

MUNRO, Thomas
Commission of enquiry into industrial unrest.
Report of the commissioners for the north-eastern area. *SEE:* Barnes, G.N.

Consultative council on local health administration and general health questions.
Report on a reformed local authority for health and public assistance. April 1923. Scottish Board of Health.

Provisional joint committee on industrial conference.
Report to meeting of 4 April 1919. 1919 Cmd.139, Cmd.501 xxiv. Home Office.

MUNRO-FERGUSON, Ronald Crauford
Departmental committee on British forestry.
Report. 29 Nov.1902. 1902 Cd.1319 xx.
Minutes of evidence, appendices and index. April 1903. 1903 Cd.1565 xvii. Board of Agriculture.

Select committee on protection of life from fire.
Report and proceedings. 20 July 1905. 1905 (254) vii. House of Commons

MURNAGHAN, George
Departmental committee on agricultural credit in Ireland.
Report. 9 April 1914. 1914 Cd.7375 xiii.

Evidence, apendices and index. 1914.Cd.7376 xiii. Department of Agriculture and Technical Instruction for Ireland.

MURPHY, Harold Lawson
Report on a public local inquiry into an outbreak of typhoid fever at Croydon, in October and November 1937. 8 Feb.1938. 1937/8 Cmd.5664 xi. Ministry of Health.

MURRAY, A.M.T.
A dietary survey in terms of the actual foodstuffs consumed. 15 Dec.1936. (S.R.S., no.218) Medical Research Council.

A study in nutrition; an inquiry into the diet of 154 families of St.Andrews. 1 Dec.1930. (S.R.S., no.151) Medical Research Council.

MURRAY, Andrew Graham *1st Baron Dunedin of Stenton*
Departmental commitee on local taxation in Scotland.
Report. 11 May 1922. 1922 Cmd.1674 viii. Scottish Office.

Irish Free State compensation.
Report of a committee. 1 July 1926. 1926 Cmd.2748 ix. Colonial Office.

Judicial committee of the Privy Council on questions connected with the Irish boundary commission.
Report. 31 July 1924. 1924 Cmd.2214 xi. Privy Council.

Royal commission on honours.
Report. 22 Dec.1922. 1923 Cmd.1789 xi.

Royal commission on registration of title in Scotland.
Report. 25 July 1910. 1910 Cd.5316 lviii.
Minutes of evidence and appendices. 1910 Cd.5357 lviii.

Royal commission on trade disputes and trade combinations.
Report. 15 Jan.1906. 1906 Cd.2825 lvi.
Minutes of evidence, index and appendices. 1906 Cd.2826 lvi.

Select committee on Irish Valuation Acts.
Report, proceedings, minutes of evidence, appendix and index. 12 Nov.1902. 1902 (390) vi.
Report, proceedings, evidence and appendix. 11 Aug.1903. 1903 (337) vi. House of Commons.

MURRAY, Charles Gideon
Report on the administration of the Roads and Land Settlement Fund, St. Vincent. 13 March 1911. (Colonial rep.misc., no.77) 1911 Cd.5742 lii. Colonial Office.

MURRAY, Everett George Dunne
The meningococcus. 11 Dec.1928. (S.R.S., no.124) Medical Research Council.

MURRAY, George Evelyn Pemberton
Board of enquiry on certain discussions engaged in by the permanent secretary to the Air Ministry.
Report. 25 July 1936. 1935/6 Cmd.5254 vii. Cabinet Office.

Departmental committee on telephone rates.
Report and appendices. 30 June 1920. 1920 Cmd.804 xxv. Post Office.

MURRAY, George Herbert
Committee on organisation of the Office of the Public Trustee.
Interim report. 8 July 1919. 1919 Cmd.421 xxviii.
Final report. Oct.1919. 1919 Cmd.422 xxviii. Lord Chancellor's Office.

MURRAY, George Herbert (Continued)
Committee on the provision of employment for sailors and soldiers disabled in the war.
Report. 4 May 1915. 1914/6 Cd.7915 xl. Local Government Board.

Fair wages committee.
Report with appendices. 18 Nov.1908. 1908 Cd.4422 xxxiv.
Minutes of evidence and index. 1908 Cd.4423 xxxiv. Treasury.

Government factories and workshops committee.
Report. 13 March 1907. 1907 Cd.3626 x. Treasury.

Investiments advisory committee
Report. 20 May 1914. 1914 Cd.4498 lxxii. National Health Insurance Joint Committee.

Reconstruction committee. Acquisition of powers sub-committee.
Report. 6 Feb.1918. 1918 Cd.8982 xii. Ministry of Reconstruction.

MURRAY, Gerald W.
Report on the present condition of physical education in Denmark and Sweden. Sept.1935. (Educational pamphlets, no.104) Board of Education.

MURRAY, Gilbert
The pale shade. 1917. Ministry of Information.

MURRAY, Graham
Select committee on the Irish Valuation Acts.
Report, proceedings and appendix. 18 April 1904. 1904 (130) vi.
Minutes of evidence, etc. 1902 (370) vi, 1903 (33) vi. House of Commons.

MURRAY, James
Departmental committee on poultry breeding in Scotland.
Report. 13 April 1909. 1909 Cd.4616 xxxvi.
Minutes of evidence and index. 1909 Cd.4617 xxxvi. Scottish Office.

MURRAY, John
Standing committee on prices. Sub-committee on wool, tops and yarns.
Report on the top making trade. 10 Feb.1921. 1921 Cmd.1192 xvi. Board of Trade.

MURRAY, M.Bruce
The effect of maternal social conditions and nutrition upon birth-weight and birth-length. 25 Dec.1923. (S.R.S., no.81) Medical Research Council.

MURRAY, O.
Committee on promotion of minor and manipulative grades.
Report. 29 March 1927. Civil Service National Whitley Council. Treasury.

MURRAY, William David, 5th Earl of Mansfield
Departmental committee on sea fisheries of Sutherland and Caithness.
Report. 7 June 1905. 1905 Cd.2557 xiii.
Minutes of evidence, etc. 1905 Cd.2608 xiii. Scottish Office.

Departmental committee on the prices of agricultural products in Scotland.
Report. 30 Aug.1901. 1902 Cd.805 xxi.
Evidence, appendices and index. 1902 Cd.828 xxi. Board of Agriculture.

Royal commission on physical training (Scotland).
Vol.I: Report. 14 March 1903. 1903 Cd.1507 xxx.

Vol.II: Minutes of evidence and index. 1903 Cd.1508 xxx.

MUSCIO, B.
Vocational guidance; a review of the literature. Nov.1921. (I.H.R.B. Rep., no.12) Medical Research Council.

MYERS, Charles Samuel
A study of improved methods in an iron foundry June 1919. (I.H.R.B. Rep., no.3) Medical Research Council.

MYERS, J.G.
A preliminary report on an investigation into the biological control of West Indian insect pests. July 1931. (E.M.B.42) Empire Marketing Board.

Report on insect infestation of dried fruit. Nov.1928. (E.M.B.12) Empire Marketing Board.

MYRES, John Linton.
Saving through the ages. 1937. National Savings Committee.

Nair, C.S. SEE: Sarkaran Nair, Chettur

NAIRNE, John Gordon, 1st Baron.
Committee on land settlement in Scotland.
Report. 5 May 1927. 1928 Cmd.3110 xi. Scottish Office.

NALL, G. Herbert
Difficulties of age determination and length calculations from the scales of sea trout. 1931. (Salmon Fish., 1931, no.5) Fishery Board for Scotland.

Notes on sea trout from the Dee tidal nets, Aberdeen, 1935. 1936 (Salmon Fish., 1936, no.4) Fishery Board for Scotland.

Notes on collections of sea trout scales from Lewis and Harris and from North Uist. 1932. (Salmon Fish., 1932, no.1) Further notes. 1934. (Salmon Fish., 1934, no.4) Fishery Board for Scotland.

Orkney sea trout. 1932. (Salmon Fish., 1932, no.8) Fishery Board for Scotland.

Report on a collection of salmon scales from the River Hope and Loch Hope in Sutherland. 1926. (Salmon Fish., 1926, no.7) Fishery Board for Scotland.

Report on a collection of sea trout scales from the River Carron and Loch Dhughaill (Doule), Western Ross-shire. 1928. (Salmon Fish., 1928, no.4) Fishery Board for Scotland.

Report on a collection of sea trout scales from the River Hope and Loch Hope in Sutherland. 1925. (Salmon Fish., 1925, no.1) Fishery Board for Scotland.

Salmon of the River Ewe and Loch Maree. 1932. (Salmon Fish., 1932, no.5) Fishery Board for Scotland.

Sea trout from the Broom of Moy waters of the Findhorn and from the tidal water of the Ugie. 1928. (Salmon Fish., 1928, no.6) Fishery Board for Scotland.

Sea trout from the tidal waters of the Don and Ython. 1927. (Salmon Fish., 1927, no.2) Fishery Board for Scotland.

Sea trout of Mull. 1935. (Salmon Fish., 1935, no.1) Fishery Board for Scotland.

Sea trout of the Ayrshire rivers Doon, Girvan and Stinchar. 1933. (Salmon Fish., 1933, no.2) Fishery Board for Scotland.

NALL, G. Herbert (Continued)
Sea trout from the Beauly Firth and from the tidal waters of the Beauly and Ness rivers. 1929. (Salmon Fish., 1929, no.3) Fishery Board for Scotland.

Sea trout of the Kyle of Sutherland district, 1934-35. 1936. (Salmon Fish., 1936, no.1) Fishery Board for Scotland.

Sea trout of the Laxford system. 1936. (Salmon Fish., 1936, no.2) Fishery Board for Scotland.

Sea trout of the Montrose district.
    Part 1: The district and its sea trout. 1934. (Salmon Fish., 1934, no.3)
    Part 2: Growth on the scales of recaptured fish. 1935. (Salmon Fish., 1935, no.2)
    Part 3: Migrations of sea trout. 1935. (Salmon Fish., 1935, no.3) Fishery Board for Scotland.

Sea trout of the Solway rivers. 1931. (Salmon Fish., 1931, no.3) Fishery Board for Scotland.

Sea trout of South Uist. 1928. (Salmon Fish., 1928, no.7)
    Part 2: 1929. (Salmon Fish., 1929, no.4). Fishery Board for Scotland.

Sea trout of the River Ailort and Loch Eilt. 1928. (Salmon Fish., 1926, no.3)
    Part 2: 1920 and 1925-27. 1928. (Salmon Fish., 1928, no.9) Fishery Board for Scotland.

Sea trout of the River Ewe and Loch Maree. 1926. (Salmon Fish., 1926, no.1)
    Part 2: 1926-27. (Salmon Fish., 1928, no.2) Fishery Board for Scotland.

Sea trout of the River Conon. 1937. (Salmon Fish., 1937, no.4) Fishery Board for Scotland.

Sea trout of the River Carron and Loch Doule (Dhughaill), Western Ross-shire. 1938. (Salmon Fish., 1938, no.4) Fishery Board for Scotland.

Sea trout of the River Leven and Loch Lomond. 1932. (Salmon Fish., 1932, no.4) Fishery Board for Scotland.

Sea trout of the River Spey. 1928. (Salmon Fish., 1928, no.10) Fishery Board for Scotland.

Sea trout of the River Tay. 1931. (Salmon Fish., 1931, no.1) Fishery Board for Scotland.

Sea trout of the River Tweed. 1929. (Salmon Fish., 1929, no.5) Fishery Board for Scotland.

NAMIER, Lewis B.
The Czecho-slovaks; an oppressed nationality. 1917. Ministry of Information.

NASH, Vaughan
Committee on the causes of the present rise in the retail price of coal sold for domestic use.
    Report. 24 March 1915. 1914/6 Cd.7866 xxix.
    Evidence and appendix. 1914/6 Cd.7923 xxix. Board of Trade.

NATHAN, Frederick L.
Explosives in mines research committee.
    Memorandum on explosives for use in fiery and dusty mines and the methods of testing them. 13 Dec.1922. (S.M.R.B.Paper, no.1).
    Report of sub-committee for research on electrical shot-firing apparatus: electrical exploders for shot-firing in coal mines. 1925. (S.M.R.B.Paper no.11). Mines Department.

Fuel for motor transport
    Interim memorandum. July 1920.
    Second memorandum. Dec.1921.
    Third memorandum: power alcohol from tuber

and root crops in Great Britain. Jan.1925.
    Fourth memorandum: power alcohol from grasses, staws and waste vegetable products. July 1927. Department of Scientific and Industrial Research.

Inter-departmental committee on alcohol motor-fuel.
    Report. 23 June 1919. 1919 Cmd.218 x. H.M.Petroleum Executive.

NATHAN, Matthew
Committee of Civil Research, sub-committee on geophysical surveying.
    Report. 14 July 1927. (E.M.B.6) Empire Marketing Board.

Inter-departmental committee on employment under the Crown as affected by part 1 of the National Insurance Act.
    First report. 30 May 1912. 1912/3 Cd.6234 xlii.
    Second report. 26 June 1912. 1912/3 Cd.6234 xlii.
    Third report. 23 Oct.1913. 1914 Cd.7176 lxxii. Treasury.

NAYLOR, C.A.
The lag on ignition of firedamp. July 1925. (S.M.R.B.Paper no.9) Mines Department.

NEILL, J.S.
General administrative report on Pitcairn Island. 1938. (Colonial, no.155) Colonial Office.

NELSON, Ian T.
Hatchery results at Glen Etive. 1914. (Salmon Fish., 1914, no.1) Fishery Board for Scotland.

NEVILLE-ROLFE, Eustace
Report on the agriculture of southern Italy. Jan.1909. (Dip.cons.reports: misc.ser., no.673) 1909 Cd.4447-1 xcii. Foreign Office and Board of Trade.

NEWALL, H.E.
The propagation of combustion in powdered coal. Dec.1930. (S.M.R.B.Paper no.63) Mines Department.

NEWBOLD, E.M.
A contribution to the study of the human factor in the causation of accidents. Feb.1926. (I.H.R.B. Rep., no.34) Medical Research Council.

NEWBOLT, Henry
Departmental committee on the position of English in the educational system of England.
    Report. 2 May 1919.
    Report: the teaching of English in England. 23 April 1921. Board of Education.

NEWBOLT, Henry John
History of the Great War. Naval operations. Vols.4-5 and maps. 4 vols. 1928-1931. War Office. For vols.1-3 see: Corbett, J.S.

NEWMAN, George
Committee on defective vision in school children.
    Report. Oct.1931. Board of Edcuation.

Departmental committee on maternal mortality and morbidity.
    Interim report. June 1930.
    Final report. July 1932. Ministry of Health.

The foundations of national health. July 1928. Ministry of Health.

Health of munitions workers committee.
    Report on industrial canteens. Nov.1915. (memo, no.1) 1914/6 Cd.8133 xxix.
    Report on welfare supervision. Dec.1915.

NEWMAN. George (Continued)
(memo, no.2) 1914/6 Cd.8151 lv.
Report on Sunday labour. Nov.1915. (memo, no.3) 1914/6 Cd.8132 xxix.
Employment of women. Jan.1916. (memo, no.4) 1916 Cd.8185 xxiii.
Hours of work. Jan.1916. (memo, no.5) 1916 Cd.8186 xxiii.
Canten construction and equipment. Jan.1916. (memo, no.6, appendix to memo, no.3) 1916 Cd.8199 xxiii.
Industrial fatigue and its causes. Jan.1916. (memo, no.7) 1916 Cd.8213 xxiii.
Special industrial diseases. Feb.1916. (memo, no.8) 1916 Cd.8214 xxiii.
Ventilation and lighting of munition factories and workshops. Jan.1916. (memo, no.9) 1916 Cd.8215 xxiii.
Sickness and injury. Jan.1916. (memo. no.10) 1916 Cd.8216 xxiii.
Investigation of workers' food and suggestions as to dietary, by Leonard E.Hill. August, 1916. (memo, no.11) 1916 Cd.8370 xxiii.
Statistical information concerning output in relation to hours of work, by H.M. Vernon. July 1916. (memo, no.12) 1916 Cd.8344 xxiii.
Juvenile employment. Aug.1916. (memo, no.13) 1916 Cd.8362 xxiii.
Washing facilities and baths. Aug.1916. (memo, no.14) 1916 Cd.8387 xxiii.
Effect of industrial conditions on eyesight. Oct.1916. (memo, no.15) 1916 Cd.8409 xxiii.
Medical certificates for munition workers, Feb.1917. (memo, no.16) 1917/8 Cd.8522 xxi.
Further statistical information concerning output in relation to hours of work with special reference to the influence of Sunday labour. April 1917. (memo, no.18; appendix to memo, no.5) 1917/8 Cd.8628 xx.
Investigation of workers' food and suggestions as to dietary, by Leonard E.Hill. Oct.1917. (memo, no.19; second appendix to memo, no.3) 1917/8 Cd.8798 xx.
Weekly hours of employment. Oct.1917. (memo, no.20; supplementary to memo, no.5) 1917/8 Cd.8801 xx.
Investigation into the factors concerned in the causation of industrial accidents, by H.M.Vernon. Feb.1918. (memo, no.21) 1918 Cd.9046 xv.
Interim report: Industrial efficiency and fatigue. Feb.1917. 1917/8 Cd.8511 xvi.
Final report: Industrial health and efficiency. April 1918. 1918 Cd. 9065 xii. Ministry of Munitions.

Medical committee on adenoids and enlarged tonsils.
Interim report. Nov.1928.
Second interim report. Jan.1931. (no further reports identified) Board of Education.

Memorandum on closure and exclusion from school. Sept.1909. Local Government Board.

Minutes of discussion at an informal conference on "pediatrics". 6 March 1919. Local Government Board.

Outline of the practice of preventive medicine. Aug.1919. 1919 Cmd.363 xxxix. (Non-parliamentary edition: April 1926) Ministry of Health.

Public education in health; a memorandum. July 1924. Ministry of Health.

Recent advances in medical education. April 1923. Ministry of Health.

School epidemics committee.
Epidemics in schools; an analysis of data. 3 Feb.1938. (S.R.S., no.227) Medical Research Council.

Some notes on medical education in England. June 1918. 1918 Cd.9124 xix. Board of Education.

NEWNHAM, E.V.
Classification of synoptic charts for the north Atlantic for 1896-1910. March 1925. (Geophys.Mem., no.26) Meteorological Office.

Hurricanes and tropical revolving storms. July 1922. (Geophys.Mem., no.19) Meteorological Office.

Report on the thunderstorm which caused disasterous floods at Louth on 29 May 1920. March 1921. (Prof.Notes, no.17) Meteorological Office.

Upper air temperatures in Egypt. May 1925. (Prof.Notes, no.41) Meteorological Office.

NEWSHOLME, Arthur
Infant and child mortality.
Report. 18 July 1910. 1910 Cd.5263 xxxix.
Second report. July 1913. 1913 Cd.6909 xxxii.
Third report, dealing with infant mortality in Lancashire. July 1914. 1914 Cd.7511 xxxix.
Local Government Board.

Memorandum on administrative measures against tuberculosis. Feb.1909. Local Government Board.

Memorandum on cerebro-spinal fever. Aug.1918. Local Government Board.

Memorandum on closure and exclusion from school. Sept.1909. Local Government Bord.

Memorandum on epidemic catarrhs and influenza. Oct.1918. Local Government Board.

Memorandum on health visiting and maternity and child welfare centres. Nov.1915. Local Government Board.

Memorandum on measles. March 1911. Local Government Board.

Memorandum on pneumonia. Jan.1919. Local Government Board.

Report of the British delegates to the International Congress on Tuberculosis, held at Washington from 21 September to 3 October 1908. 9 Dec.1908. 1909 Cd. 4508 lxxi. Privy Council.

Report of the British delegates to the International Scientific conference on leprosy, held at Bergen from 15 to 19 August 1909. 14 Sept.1909. 1909 Cd.4916 lxxi. Privy Council.

Venereal diseases
Memorandum on the organisation of medical measures. July 1916. Local Government Board.

Newton, *Lord. SEE:* Legh, T.W., *2nd Baron*

NEWTON, George Douglas Cochrane, *1st Baron Eltisley of Croxton*
Committee on tobacco growing in Great Britain.
Report. 2 Nov.1923. 1923 Cmd.1983 xii pt.2. Treasury.

Departmental committee on agricultural machinery.
Report, appendix and summaries of evidence. March 1920. 1919 Cmd.506 viii. Ministry of Agriculture and Fisheries.

Joint committee on water resources and supplies.
Vol.1: Proceedings 3 to 25 July 1935. 1934/5

NEWTON, George Douglas Cochrane, *1st Baron Eltisley of Croxton* (continued)
>(121) vi.
>Vol.2: Evidence and appendix. 25 July 1935. 1934/5 (121) vi.
>Report, proceedings, evidence and an appendix. 29 July 1936. 1935/6 (159) vi. House of Commons.

NICHOLLS, William H.
>Report on the present position in the building industry, with regard to the carrying out of a full housing programme. 10 April 1924. 1924 Cmd.2104 vii. Ministry of Health.

NICHOLSON, William Gustavus, *1st Baron Nicholson of Roundhay*
>Court of inquiry constituted by the Army Council under the Army (Courts of Inquiry) Act, 1916.
>>Reports. 2 Jan. 1917. 1917/8 Cd.8435 iv. War Office.

NICOLAU, S.
>Borna disease and enzootic encaphalo-myelitis of sheep and cattle. 28 July 1928. (S.R.S., no.121) Medical Research Council.

NICOLSON, Frederick Archibald, *2nd Baron Carnock*
>Joint committee on the breaking up of streets by statutory undertakers.
>>Report, proceedings, evidence, speeches by counsel and appendices. 20 June 1939. 1938/9 (134) vii. House of Commons.

NIEMEYER, Otto Ernst
>Committee on the administration of the Export Credits Guarantee Scheme.
>>Report. 31 July 1929. 1929/30 Cmd.3450 xiii. Department of Overseas Trade.

>Indian financial enquiry.
>>Report. 6 April 1936. 1935/6 Cmd.5163 ix. India Office.

NIEPAGE, Martin
>The horrors of Aleppo...seen by an eyewitness. 1916. Ministry of Information.

NIESSEN, C.A.
>Report on the vine culture and wine trade of Germany. 1907. (Dip.cons.reports: misc.ser., no.661) 1907 Cd.3284-5 lxxxvii. Foreign Office *and* Board of Trade.

>Report on the vine culture and wine trade of Germany for the years 1898-1900. 8 June 1901. (Dip.cons.reports: misc.ser., no.559) 1901 Cd.430-14 lxxx. Foreign Office.

NIMMO, Adam
>Committee on coal trade after the war.
>>Report. 25 April 1917. 1918 Cd.9093 xiii. Board of Trade.

NIMMO, Henry
>Report on an electricity breakdown which occurred at Blackpool, Lytham St.Annes and Fleetwood on 6 January 1939. March 1939. Ministry of Transport.

>Report on an electricity breakdown which occurred at Bradford, February 1936. 26 May 1936. Electricity Commission. Ministry of Transport.

>Report on a failure of supply of electricity at the Kingston-upon-Thames generating station on 14 December 1938. April 1939. Electricity Commission. Ministry of Transport.

NIPPOLD, Otfried
>The awakening of the German people. 1918. Minsitry of Information.

Dangerous optimism. Nov.1917. Ministry of Information.

NIVEN, A. Mackie
>Transvaal labour commission.
>>Reports. 19 Nov.1903. 1904 Cd.1896 xxxix.
>>Reports. 11 Nov.1903. 1904 Cd.1894 xxxix.
>>Minutes of proceedings and evidence. 1904 Cd.1897 xxxix. Colonial Office.

NOBLE, A,H.
>The geology of the country around Beaconsfield. (Sheet 255) 23 June 1922. (Mem.Geol.Surv.) Geological Survey.

NOBLE, William Joseph, *1st Baron Kirkley*
>Inter-departmental committee on the grading and marking of beef.
>>Report. Feb.1932. 1931/2 Cmd.4047 vi. Ministry of Agriculture and Fisheries *and* Scottish Office.

>United Kingdom trade mission to the Union of South Africa, Southern Rhodesia and Northern Rhodesia.
>>Report. Jan.1931. Department of Overseas Trade.

Norfolk, *Lord. SEE:* Fitzallan-Howard, H., *15th Duke of Norfolk.*

NORMAN, Henry
>Departmental committee on the Increase of Rent and Mortgage Interest (Restrictions) Act,1920. *SEE:* Onslow, R.W.A., *5th Earl*

>Departmental committee on industrial paints.
>>Report. Feb.1923.
>>Minutes of evidence. 1923. Home Office.

>Imperial wireless telegraphy committee.
>>Report 28 May 1920. 1920 Cmd.777 xviii. Colonial Office.

>Report on the treatment and training of disabled and discharged soldiers in France. Oct.1916. War Office.

>Select committee on cabs and omnibuses (metropolis).
>>Report, proceedings, minutes, appendix and index. 31 July 1906. 1905 (295) vii. House of Commons.

>Select committee on patent medicines.
>>Report and proceedings. 6 Feb.1913. 1912/3 (508) ix.
>>Report. 6 Aug 1913. 1913 (258) x.
>>Report, proceedings, evidence and appendices. 4 Aug.1914. 1914 (414) ix. House of Commons.

NORMAN, Ronald C.
>Departmental committee on the superannuation of persons employed by local authorities in England and Wales.
>>Report. 30 July 1919. 1919 Cmd.329 xxiv. Local Government Board.

Northbrook, *Lord. SEE:* Baring, F.G., *2nd Earl*

NORTHCOTE, Walter Stafford, *2nd Earl Iddesleigh*
>Royal commission on sewage disposal.
>>Vol.1: Interim report. 12 July 1901. 1901 Cd.685 xxxiv, pt.I.
>>Vol.2: Evidence. 1901 Cd.686 xxxiv, pt.I.
>>Vol.3: Appendices. 1901 Cd.686-I xxxiv, pt.II.
>>Second report. 7 July 1902. 1902 Cd.1178 xlix.
>>Third report. Vol.I: Report. 2 March 1903. 1903 Cd.1486 xxxi.
>>Third report. Vol.II: Minutes of evidence. 1903 Cd.1487 xxxi.

**NORTHCOTE, Walter Stafford,** *2nd Earl Iddesleigh* (continued)

    Fourth report. Vol.I: Report. 28 Dec.1904. 1904 Cd.1883 xxxvii.

    Fourth report. Vol.II: Minutes of evidence. 1904 Cd.1884 xxxvii.

    Fourth report. Vol.III: Reports on bacteriological investigations by Dr.Houston and correspondence with foreign countries. 1904 Cd.1885 xxxvii.

    Fourth report. Vol.IV: Supplementary volumes.

        Part I: General report. 1904. 1904 Cd.1886 xxxviii.

        Part II: Chemical report by Dr. G.McGowan. 1904 Cd.1886-I xxxviii.

        Part III: Bacteriological report by Dr. A.C. Houston. 1904 Cd.1886-II xxxviii.

        Part IV: Engineering and practical report by G.B.Kershaw. 1904 Cd.1886-III xxxviii.

        Part V: Report on chemical analysis. 1904 Cd.1886-IV xxxviii.

    Fifth report. 7 Aug.1908. 1908 Cd.4278 liii.

    Fifth report. Appendix 1: Minutes of evidence. 1908 Cd.4279 liv.

    Fifth report. Appendix 2: Summary of evidence. 1908 Cd.4280 liv.

    Fifth report. Appendix 3: Memoranda giving results of observations. 1908 Cd.4281 lv.

    Fifth report. Appendix 4: Memoranda on special investigations and experiments. 1908 Cd.4282 lv.

    Fifth report. Appendix 5: Reports on the effects of rainfall on the flow of sewage. 1908 Cd.4283 lvi.

    Fifth report. Appendix 6: Report on the pollution of estuaries and tidal waters. 1908 Cd.4284 lvi.

    Fifth report. Appendix 7: Standards for sewage effluents: replies to circular letter. 1908 Cd.4285 lvi.

    Fifth report. Appendix 8: Manurial value of sewage sludge. 1908 Cd.4286 lvi.

    Sixth report. Disposal of liquid refuse from distilleries. 9 Feb.1909. 1909 Cd.4511 xlvi.

    Seventh report. Vol.1: Report. 16 Feb.1911. 1911 Cd.5542 xli.

    Seventh report. Vol.2: Appendices, part. 1. 1911 Cd.5543 xli.

    Seventh report. Vol.3: Appendices, part 2. 1911 Cd.5543-I xli.

    Eighth report. Vol.1: Report. 4 Nov.1912. 1912/3 Cd.6464 xlvi.

    Eighth report. Standards and tests for sewage and sewage effluents discharging into rivers and streams. Vol.2: Appendix. 1913 Cd.6943 xxxix.

    Ninth report. Vol.1: Report. 11 Feb.1915. 1914/6 Cd.7819 xxxv.

    Ninth report. Vol.2: Evidence and appendices. 1914/6 Cd.7820 xxxv.

    Final report. 11 Feb.1915. 1914/6 Cd.7821 xxxv.

**NORTON, Cecil William,** *1st Baron Rathcreedan*

    Committee on high-speed telegraphy.

        Report. 19 Jan.1916. 1916 Cd.8413 xiv. Post Office.

    Departmental committee on Post Office factories.

        Report. 10 Oct.1911. 1912/3 Cd.6027 xliii. Post Office.

    Inter-departmental committee on the sale of bread by weight.

        Report. 14 June 1921. 1921 Cmd.1400 xvii. Board of Trade.

**NORWOOD, Cyril**

    Secondary school examinations council.

        Reports of the investigators on the first examinations held in July 1918. Subject reports.

            Group 1: English subjects, history, and geography. 11 April 1919.

            Group 2: Classics and modern languages. 11 April 1919.

            Group 3: Mathematics and science. 12 April 1919. Board of Education.

    Reports of investigators on the second examinations held in July 1920. 19 Sept.1921. Board of Education.

**NOWELL, William**

    Commission on the marketing of West African cocoa.

        Report. 5 Sept.1938. 1937/8 Cmd.5845 ix. Colonial Office.

**NOYES, Alfred**

    What is England doing? 1916. Ministry of Information.

**OAKLEY, K.P.**

    British regional geology: the central England district. 1936. Geological Survey.

**OATES, Francis Hamer**

    Committee on licences to children to take part in entertainments.

        Report. 28 July 1919. 1919 Cmd.484 xxx. Board of Education.

**O'CONNOR, Arthur**

    Commission of enquiry into industrial unrest.

        Report of the commissioners for the London and south-east areas. *SEE:* Barnes, G.N.

**O'CONNOR, James**

    Irish coal industry committee.

        Report. 23 Feb.1920. 1920 Cmd.650 xiii. Irish Secretary's Office.

**O'CONOR, Charles H.**

    Departmental committee on the housing conditions of the working classes in Dublin.

        Report. 7 Feb.1914. 1914 Cd.7273 xix.

        Appendix: evidence and appendices. 1914 Cd.7317 xix. Local Government Board for Ireland.

**O'DONOGHUE, Charles H.**

    A preliminary investigation of the food of the sea trout. 1930. (Salmon Fish., 1930, no.3) Fishery Board for Scotland.

    A second investigation of the food of the sea trout. 1932. (Salmon Fish., 1932, no.2) Fishery Board for Scotland.

    A third investigation of the food of the sea trout, with a note on the food of the perch. 1934. (Salmon Fish., 1934, no.2) Fishery Board for Scotland.

**OGILVIE, Francis Grant**

    Report on Sheffield City museums. Jan.1919. (Educational pamphlets, no.34) Board of Education.

**OGILVIE, Helen S.**

    Observations on the food of post-larval herring from the Scottish coast. 1927. (Sci.invest., 1927, no.1) Fishery Board for Scotland.

**O'GORMAN, Mervyn**

    Adhesives research committee.

        First report. June 1922.

        Second report. Dec.1925.

        Third and final report. Oct.1931. Department of Scientific and Industrial Research.

**OLDHAM, J.N.**
The helminth parasites of common rats. 1931. Imperial Bureau of Agricultural Parasitology.

Helminths in the biological control of insect pests. 1933. (Notes and Memo., no.9) Imperial Bureau of Agricultural Parasitology.

**OLIVER, Francis A.**
Report on the fishing trade of the Weser seaports. 28 June 1904. (Dip.cons.reports: misc.ser., no.616) 1904 Cd.1767-20 xcvi. Foreign Office.

Report on German sea fishing industry and trade. 26 July 1905. (Dip.cons.reports: misc.ser., no.636) 1906 Cd.2683 cxxii. Foreign Office.

**OLIVER, Henry Francis**
Departmental committee on kapok.
　　Report. 29 July 1929. Board of Trade.

International load line conference, 1930.
　　Report of the British delegation. 5 July 1930. 1930/1 Cmd.3669 xxxvi.Foreign Office.

**OLIVER, Roland Gifford**
Army and airforce courts-martial committee.
　　Report. 28 July 1938. 1939/40 Cmd.6200 iv. War Office *and* Air Ministry.

**OLIVER, Sidney,** *1st Baron Olivier of Ramsden*
West Indian sugar commission.
　　Report. 1 Feb.1930. 1929/30 Cmd.3517 viii.
　　Part 4: (Continuation of report.) 12 March 1930. (Colonial no.42) Colonial Office.

**OMAN, Charles William Chadwick**
The outbreak of the war of 1914-18; a narrative based mainly on British official documents. 1919. War Office.

**O'NEILL, Patrick J.**
Irish milk commission.
　　First report. 18 Feb 1913. 1913 Cd.6683 xxix.
　　Appendix: minutes of evidence, 29 Nov.1911 to 1 March 1912, with index. 1913 Cd.6684 xxix.
　　Second report. 15 May 1913. 1913 Cd.6936 xxix.
　　Appendix: minutes of evidence, 19 march to 15 July 1912, with index. 1913 Cd.6937 xxix.
　　Final report. 23 Oct.1913. 1914 Cd.7129 xxxvi.
　　Appendix. 1914 Cd.7134 xxxvi. Irish Secretary's Office.

**O'NEILL, Robert William Hugh**
Select committee on private bill procedure (local legislation clauses).
　　Report, proceedings, evidence and index. 22 April 1937. 1936/7 (112) viii. House of Commons.

Select committee on police forces amalgamation.
　　Report, proceedings, evidence, appendices and index. 5 July 1932. 1931/2 (106) v. House of Commons.

**ONSLOW, Richard William Alan,** *5th Earl*
Committee for privileges. Barony of Vaux of Harrowden.
　　Proceedings and evidence. 13 April 1938. 1937/8 (H.L.83) iv. House of Lords.

Departmental committee on the Increase of Rent and Mortgage Interest (Restrictions) Act, 1920.
　　Interim report. 19 Oct.1922.
　　Final report. 5 Feb.1923. 1923 Cmd.1803 xii, pt.2. Ministry of Health.

Joint committee on closer union in East Africa.
　　Vol.1: Report. 6 Oct.1931. 1930/1 (156) vii.
　　Vol.2: Minutes of evidence and index. 1930/1 (156) vii.

Vol.3: Appendices. 1930/1 (156) vii. House of Commons.

Joint committee on public sewers (contributions by frontagers).
　　Report, proceedings, evidence and speeches by counsel. 17 June 1936. 1935/6 (122) vi. House of Commons.

Joint committee on refreshment rooms and lavatories in the Palace of Westminster.
　　Minutes of evidence and proceedings. 25 Oct.1935. 1934/5 (135) vi.
　　Report and proceedings. 16 July 1936. 1935/6 (149) vi. House of Commons.

Report of the British delegates on the 8th assembly of the League of Nations. 25 Nov.1927. (Misc., no.1, 1928) 1928 Cmd.3008 xxvi. Foreign Office.

Royal commission on local government.
　　First report. Constitution and extension of county boroughs. 7 Aug.1925. 1924/5 Cmd.2506 xiv.
　　Second report. 9 Oct.1928. 1928/9 Cmd.3213 viii.
　　Final report. 12 Nov.1929. 1929/30 Cmd.3436 xv.
　　Minutes of evidence. 14 parts. 1923-1929.
　　Index to evidence. 1930.

Select committee on proceedings in relation to special orders.
　　Report, proceedings and appendix. 18 Dec.1933. 1933/4 (H.L.13) iv.
　　Report on further consideration. 12 June 1934. 1933/4 (H.L.117) iv. House of Lords.

Select committee on the Official Secrets Act.
　　Report and proceedings. 17 July 1939. 1938/9 (H.L.158) v. House of Lords.

Voluntary hospitals commission.
　　Interim report. Feb.1923.
　　Second interim report. 22 Aug.1924.
　　Final report. March 1928. Ministry of Health.

Report on voluntary hospital accommodation in England and Wales. 13 July 1925. 1924/5 Cmd.2486 xv. Ministry of Health.

**ONSLOW, William Hillier,** *4th Earl*
Committee for privileges on the Graves peerage (claim to vote).
　　Minutes of evidence. 2 July 1906. 1906 (H.L.148) ix. House of Lords.

Departmental committee appointed to inquire into the conditions under which agricultural seeds are at present sold.
　　Report. 18 Oct.1900. 1901 Cd.489 ix.
　　Minutes of evidence, appendices and index. 1901 Cd.493 ix. Board of Agriculture.

Departmental committee on small holdings in Great Britain.
　　Report. 10 Dec.1906. 1906 Cd.3277 lv.
　　Minutes of evidence, appendices and index. 1906 Cd.3278 lx. Board of Agriculture.

Select committee on the House of Lords on the Office of the Gentleman Usher of the Black Rod.
　　Report, proceedings, and appendix. 26 June 1906. 1906 (H.L.140) ix. House of Lords.

**OPPENHEIMER, Francis**
Report on the German law of 1909 against unfair competition. Jan.1913. (Dip.cons.reports: misc.ser., no.683) 1912/3 Cd.6006-2 xciv. Foreign Office *and* Board of Trade.

OPPENHEIMER, Francis (continued)
Report on the supply of electricity in Germany by the chief works in which private concerns and public bodies are jointly interested. Oct.1913. (Dip.cons.reports: misc.ser., no.685) 1914 Cd.7049 lxxxix. Foreign Office *and* Board of Trade.

ORDE-BROWNE, Granville St.John
Labour conditions in Northern Rhodesia.
Report. 14 May 1938. (Colonial, no.150) Colonial Office.

Labour in the Tanganyika territory.
Report. 6 Jan.1916. (Colonial, no.19) Colonial Office.

Labour conditions in West Africa.
Report. July 1940. 1940/1 Cmd.6277 iv. Colonial Office.

Labour conditions in the West Indies.
Report. 26 May 1939. 1938/9 Cmd.6070 xv. Colonial Office.

Ormidale, *Lord. SEE:* MacFarlane, G.L.

ORMOND, Arthur William
An analysis of 15,584 ophthalmic cases treated at a home hospital. 13 Jan.1919. (Stat.Rep., no.6) Medical Research Committee.

ORMSBY-GORE, William George Arthur
Advisory committee on social hygiene.
First report; proposed regulation of prostitution in Singapore. 18 June 1925. 1924/5 Cmd.2501 xv. (no further reports identified) Colonial Office.

East Africa commission.
Report. 17 April 1925. 1924/5 Cmd.2387 ix. Colonial Office.

Education policy in British tropical Africa.
Memorandum submitted by the Advisory Committee on native education in the British tropical and African dependencies. 13 March 1925. 1924/5 Cmd.2374 xxi. Colonial Office.

Imperial Institute committee of inquiry.
Report with resolutions of the Imperial Economic Conference on the subject. Aug.1923. 1923 Cmd.1997 xii, pt.1. Colonial Office.

Report of the United Kingdom delegates on the League of Nations, 14th assembly. 30 Nov.1933. (Misc., no.1, 1934) 1933/4 Cmd.4490 xxvii. Foreign Office.

Report on visit to Malaya, Ceylon, and Java during the year 1928. Nov.1928. 1928/9 Cmd.3235 v. Colonial Office.

Report on visit to West Africa during the year 1926. Sept.1926. 1927 Cmd.2744 ix. Colonial Office.

West Indian currency committee.
Report. June 1923. 1923 Cmd.1894 xii, pt.2. Colonial Office.

ORR, John Boyd
Committee on iodine deficiency and thyroid disease.
Report on the relationship of the iodine contents of water, milk and pasture to the occurrence of endemic goitre in two districts of England. 24 July 1936. (S.R.S., no.217) Medical Research Council.

The composition of pastures. June 1929. (E.M.B.18) Empire Marketing Board.

The energy expenditure of the infantry recruit in training. Dec.1919. War Office.

Iodine in nutrition; a review of existing information. 14 Dec.1928. (S.R.S., no.123) Medical Research Council.

Iodine supply and the incidence of endemic goitre. 23 Oct.1930. (S.R.S., no.154) Medical Research Couuncil.

The physique and health of two African tribes. 9 March 1931. (S.R.S., no.155) Medical Research Council.

OSBORN, Edward H.
Departmental committee on ventilation of factories and workshops.
First report. 15 Aug.1902. 1902 Cd.1302 xii.
Second report. 2 pts. May 1907. 1907 Cd.3552, Cd.3553 x. Home Office.

OSBORNE, Ethel E.
The output of women workers in relation to hours of work in shell-making. June 1919. (I.H.R.B.Rep., no.2) Medical Research Council.

Two contributions to the study of accident causation. Nov.1922. (I.H.R.B. Rep., no.19) Medical Research Council.

Osborne-White, H.J. *SEE:* White, H.J.O.

O'SHAUGHNESSY, Thomas Lopdell
Committee of inquiry on under sheriffs and bailiffs in Ireland.
Report. 6 May 1919. 1919 Cmd. 190 xxx. Irish Secretary's Office.

OSSIANNILSSON, K.G.
Militarism at work in Belgium and Germany. 1917. Ministry of Information.

OSWALD, Richard Alexander
Military manoeuvres commission, Ayr.
Report. 1911. 1911 Cd.5999 xlvii. War Office.

OWEN, B.J.
Investigations into the desiccation (De Vecchis) process for producing sugar from sugar beet.
Progress report. 8 Aug.1926.
Report with a note on the treatment of sugar beet effluents. June 1927. Ministry of Agriculture and Fisheries.

OWEN, David John
Planning of water resources and supplies. 28 March 1938. (*In* First report of the Central Advisory Water Committee) Ministry of Health.

OWEN, Hugh
Report of the proceedings of the commissioners under the London Government Act, 1899. 15 July 1907. Privy Council.

OXLEY, J.S.
Metropolitan poor law inspectors' advisory committee on the homeless poor.
Report to 31 Dec.1913. 12 Feb.1914. 1914 Cd.7307 xliv.
Report. 19 Feb.1915. 1914/6 Cd.7840 xxxii. Local Government Board.

PAGE, Walter Hines
The union of two great peoples; a speech. 4 Aug.1917. Ministry of Information.

PAILTHORPE, Grace Winifred
Studies in the psychology of delinquency. 29 March 1932. (S.R.S., no.170) Medical Research Council.

PALLES, Christopher
Commissioners appointed under the Irish Universities Act, 1908.
Report to accompany statutes made by the

PALLES, Christopher (continued)
Dublin commissioners. 18 May 1909. 1909 Cd.4726 xx.
Final report. 25 July 1911. 1911 Cd.5877 xxi.
Appendix. 1911. Royal Commission on Dublin University.

PALMER, Alexander Croydon
The cause of foetal death in 144 cases. 30 Nov.1927. (S.R.S., no.118) Medical Research Council.

PALMER, T.H.
The development of cardiac enlargement in disease of the heart: a radiological study. 5 May 1937. (S.R.S., no.222) Medical Research Council.

PALMER, William Waldegrave, *2nd Earl Selbourne*
Joint select committee on the Government of India Act, 1919, draft rules.
First report. 6 July 1920. 1920 (140) vi.
Second report. 10 Aug.1920. 1920 (189) vi.
Minutes of proceedings. 1920 (189) vi. House of Commons.

Reconstruction committee. Agricultural policy sub-committee.
First report. 30 Jan.1917. 1917/8 Cd.8056 xviii.
Second report. 30 Jan.1918. 1918 Cd.9079 v.
Summaries of evidence. 1918 Cd.9080 v.
Ministry of Reconstruction.

PARFIT, J.T.
Mesopotania; the key to the future. 1917. Ministry of Information.

PARKER, Gilbert
Two years of war. 1916. Ministry of Information.

What is the matter with England? Criticism and a reply. 1915. Ministry of Informatimn.

PARKER, Robert John, *Lord Parker of Waddington.*
Advisory committee on wireless telegraphy.
Report. 30 April 1913. 1913 Cd.6781 xxxiii. Post Office.

Committee on wireless telegraphy research.
Report. June 1914. 1914 Cd.7428 xliv. Post Office.

PARKINSON, John
Report on the geology and geography of the northern part of the East Africa Protectorate. March 1920. (Colonial reports, misc., no.91) 1920 Cmd.729 xxxiii. Colonial Office.

PARLETT, H.G.
Report on the mining industry in the Hokkaido, Japan. March 1909. (Dip.cons.reports: misc.ser., no.676) 1909 Cd.4447-4 xcii. Foreign Office *and* Board of Trade.

Parmoor, *1st Baron. SEE:* Cripps, Charles Alfred, *1st Baron Parmoor*

PARNELL, Roderick Joseph Graham
An analysis of the results of Wassermann reactions in 1,435 cases of syphilis or suspected syphilis. 30 Dec.1918. (S.R.S., no.23) Medical Research Committee.

PARRY, Charles De Courcy
Report of inquiry on St.Helen's County Borough police force held in March and April 1928. 27 April 1928. 1928 Cmd.3103 xii. Home Office.

PARRY, Edward A.
Commission of enquiry into industrial unrest.
Report of the commissioners for the north-western area. *SEE:* Barnes, G.N.

PARSONS, Allan Chilcott
Fur dermatitis. Sept.1924. (Rep.Pub.Health & Med.Subj., no.27) Ministry of Health.
Report of an inquiry into the after histories of persons attacked by *encephalitis lethargica*. April 1928. (Rep.Pub.Health & Med.Subj., no.49) Ministry of Health.
Report on *encephalitis lethargica*. Aug.1922. (Rep.Pub.Health & Med.Subj., no.11) Ministry of Health.
Some administrative aspects of scarlet fever. April 1927. (Rep.Pub.Health & Med.Subj., no.35) Ministry of Health.

PARSONS, Charles Algernon
Departmental committee on electrical trades after the war.
Report. 18 April 1917. 1918 Cd.9072 xiii. Board of Trade.

PARSONS, John Herbert
Committee on the physiology of vision. Reports.
1: Illumination and visual capacities; a review of recent literature. 10 May 1926. (S.R.S., no.104)
2: Dark adaptation; a review of the literature. 20 April 1929. (S.R.S., no.127)
3: Studies in the psychology of reading. 2 April 1929. (S.R.S., no.130)
4: Experiments on binocular vision. 18 June 1929. (S.R.S., no.133)
5: Adaptation of the eye; its relation to the critical frequency of flicker. 18 June 1929. (S.R.S., no.134)
6: Some experiments on peripheral vision. 2 Aug.1929. (S.R.S., no.136)
7: A redetermination of the trichromatic mixture data. 18 Oct.1929. (S.R.S., no.139)
8: The movements of the eyes in reading. 25 July 1930. (S.R.S., no.148)
9: Psychological factors in peripheral vision. 31 Oct.1931. (S.R.S., no.163)
10: The measurement of visual acuity. 11 Oct.1932. (S.R.S., no.173)
11: Individual differences in normal colour vision; a survey of recent experimental work. 29 April 1933. (S.R.S., no.181)
12: Colour vision requirements in the Royal Navy. 6 July 1933. (S.R.S., no.185)
13: Determination of the sensitiveness of the eye to differences in the saturation of colours. 28 Sept.1934. (S.R.S., no.188)
14: Characterisitcs of dichromatic vision. 30 April 1935. (S.R.S., no.200) Medical Research Council.

PASSELECQ, Fernand
Truth and travesty. An analytical study of the reply of the Belgian government to the German white book. 1916. Ministry of Information.
Unemployment in Belgium during the German occupation and its general causes. 1917. Ministry of Information.

Passfield, *Baron. SEE:* Webb, S.J., *1st Baron Passfield*

PATERSON, Clifford C.
Departmental committee on ships' navigation lights.
Report. 22 March 1922. Board of Trade.

PATON, Dairmid Noël
Poverty, nutrition and growth. Studies of child life in cities and rural districts of Scotland. 4 May 1926. (S.R.S., no.101) Medical Research Council.
A study of three fish received as "mended male kelts". 1910. (Salmon Fish., 1910 no.3) Fishery Board for Scotland.

PATON, G.P.
Report on the organisation of foreign trade of the Union of Soviet Socialist Republics. May 1931. 1930/1 Cmd.3904 xvii. Department of Overseas Trade.

Report on the raw silk industry of Japan. Jan.1909. (Dip.cons.reports: misc.ser., no.672) 1909 Cd.4447 xcii. Fogeign Office *and* Board of Trade.

PATTERSON, J.Hume
The cause of salmon disease: a bacteriological investigation. 1903. 1903 Cd.1544 xiv. Fishery Board for Scotland.

PAUL, George Morrison
Departmental committee on the conditions of employment of the present members of the engrossing staff in the General Register of Sasines, Edinburgh.
Vol.1: Report. 6 Dec.1912. 1913 Cd.6789 xxxix.
Vol.2: Minutes of evidence and appendices. 1913 Cd.6790 xxxix. Scottish Office.

PAULTON, James Mellor
Select committee on employment of military in cases of disturbances.
Report, proceedings, evidence and appendix. 16 July 1908. 1908 (236) vii. House of Commons.

PAVY, F.W.
Report on the International Congress of Medicine at Budapest, 29 August to 4 September 1909. Feb.1910. 1910 Cd.5047 xliii. Privy Council.

PAYMAN, W.
The ingnition of firedamp by coalmining explosives.
1: Gallery experiments. Jan.1931. (S.M.R.B.Paper, no.69)
2: Sheathed explosives. Oct.1934. (S.M.R.B.Paper, no.90) Mines Department.

The pressure wave sent out by an explosion.
Part 1: Dec.1925. (S.M.R.B.Paper, no.18)
Part 2: July 1926. (S.M.R.B.Paper, no.29)
Part 3: Spark photographs with permitted explosives. March 1934. (S.M.R.B.Paper, no.88) Mines Department.

PEACE, T.R.
Spring frosts; with special reference to the frosts of May 1935. May 1937. (Bull., no.18) Forestry Commission.

PEACEY, E.
Report on the condition of horses shipped to the continent. March 1921. 1921 Cmd.1249 xiii. Ministry of Agriculture and Fisheries.

PEACH, Benjavin Neeve.
Description of Arthur's Seat volcano. 15 March 1911. (Mem.Geol.Surv., Scotl.) Geological Survey, Scotland.

Guide to the geological model of the Assynt Mountains. 26 May 1914. Geological Survey, Scotland.

The geology of Ben Wyvis, Carn Chuinneag, Inchbae and the surrounding country. (Sheet 93) 13 Jan.1912. (Mem.Geol.Surv., Scotl.) Geological Survey, Scotland.

The geology of central Ross-shire. (Sheet 82) 29 May 1912. (Mem.Geol. Surv., Scotl.) Geological Survey, Scotland.

The geology of the Fannich Mountains and the country around upper Loch Maree and Strath Broom. (Sheet 92) 21 Nov.1912. (Mem.Geol.Surv., Scotl.) Geological Survey, Scotland.

The geology of Knapdale, Jura and North Kintyre. (Sheet 28 and parts of 27 and 29) 13 Oct.1910. (Mem.Geol.Surv., Scotl.) Geological Survey, Scotland.

The geology of the neighbourhood of Edinburgh. (Sheet 32 with part of 31) 17 Nov.1910. (Mem.Geol.Surv., Scotl.) Geological Survey, Scotland.

The geology of the seaboard of mid-Argyll. (Sheet 36) 12 Jan.1909. (Mem.Geol.Surv., Scotl.) Geological Survey, Scotland.

The geological structure of the north-west Highlands of Scotland. 29 June 1907. (Mem.Geol.Surv., Scotl.) Geological Survey, Scotland.

Monograph on the higher crustacea of the carboniferous rocks of Scotland. 28 Oct.1908. (Mem.Geol.Surv., Palaeont.) Geological Survey.

PEACOCK, Edward Robert
Channel tunnel committee.
Report. 28 Feb.1930. 1929/30 Cmd.3513 xii. Treasury. Economic Advisory Council.

PEAR, Tom Hatherley
A classification of vocational tests of dexterity. May 1932. (I.H.R.B. Rep., no.64) Medical Research Council.

PEARCE, Harold V.
Report on the mining and metallurgical industry of the Butte district, in the State of Montana. 9 Nov.1900. (Dip.Cons.report: Misc.ser., no.541) 1900 Cd.353-6 xci. Foreign Office.

Report on the mining industry of Colorado. 19 June 1900. (Dip.cons.reports: misc.ser., no.532) 1900 Cd.2-15 xci. Foreign Office.

PEARCE, William
Departmental committee on carbon monoxide.
Report. 1 July 1921. 1921 Cmd.1422 xii. Board of Trade.

Select committee on increase of wealth (war).
Report, proceedings, evidence and appendices. 13 May 1920. 1920 (102) vii. House of Commons.

Select committee on tramways, *etc*. (statutory requirements)
Report, proceedings and minutes of evidence. 5 June 1918. 1918 (72) iv. House of Commons.

PEARSE, James
The co-ordination of the public health services in the counties of Essex, Hampshire, Gloucester and West Sussex. Oct.1927. (Rep.Pub.Health & Med.Subj., no.45) Ministry of Health.

Report of an inquiry into the effects of existing economic circumstances on the health of the community in the county borough of Sutherland and certain districts of County Durham. Feb.1935. 1934/5 Cmd.4886 ix. Ministry of Health.

Report on investigation in the coalfield of south Wales and Monmouthshire. 28 Jan.1929. 1928/9 Cmd.3272 viii. Ministry of Health.

PEARSON, C.H.
Report on railways in Austria and Hungary. Aug.1909. 1909 Cd.4878 lxxvii. Board of Trade.

PEARSON, Edward Ernest
Committee of inquiry into the future of His Majesty's factories at Gretna and Waltham Abbey.
Report. June 1919. 1920 Cmd.667 xvi. Ministry of Munitions.

PEAT, Harry William Henry
Agricultural costing committee.
Interim report on the cost of milk production, October 1919 to April 1920. Nov.1920. 1920 Cmd.1028 ix.
Final report on the cost of milk production, 1 October 1919 to 30 September 1920. May 1921. 1921 Cmd.1305 xv. Minsitry of Food.

PEAT, William Barclay
Royal commission on agriculture.
Interim report. 10 Dec.1919. 1919 Cmd.473 viii.
Evidence, vols.1-4. 1919 Cmd.345, Cmd.365, Cmd.391, Cmd.445. viii.
Evidence, vol.5. 1920 Cmd.665 ix. (no final report)

PECK, James Wallace
Standing committees on prices and trusts.
Report of a sub-committee on a scheme for maximum retail prices for coal in London. 25 Jan.1921. 1921 Cmd.1161 xvi. Board of Trade.

PEEL, Arthur Wellesley, *1st Viscount*
Royal commission for the St. Louis International Exhibition for 1904.
Report. 1906. 1906 Cd.2800 liv.

PEEL, Sidney
Committee on the staffing and methods of work of the Ministry of Labour.
Report. 11 Aug.1920. 1920 Cmd.1069 xxv.Cabinet Office.

PEEL, William Robert Wellesley, *1st Earl*
Burma round table conference, 27 November 1931 to 12 January 1932.
Proceedings. Jan.1932. 1931/2 Cmd.4004 vi.
Proceedings of the committee of the whole conference. 1932. India Office.

Committee on compensation for disabled sailors and soldiers.
Report. 26 Aprol 1918. 1919 Cmd.49 xxxi. Home Office.

Departmental committee on compensation for disabled sailors and solders under the Workmen's Compensation Act, 1906.
Report. 26 April 1918. Home Office.

Royal commission on Palestine.
Report. 22 June 1937. 1936/7 Cmd.5479 xiv.
Summary of report. (Colonial, no.135) 1937.
Memoranda prepared by the government of Palestine. (Colonial, no.133). 1937.
Minutes of evidence heard at public sessions, with index. (Colonial, no.134) 1937. Colonial Office.

Royal commission on the despatch of business at common law.
Report. 20 Jan.1936. 1935/6 Cmd.5065 viii.
Minutes of evidence, 1st to 26th days. 1935.
Appendix. 1935.
Index. 1935.

PEERS, Edgar Allison
Report on the teaching of Spanish in evening and part-time day courses, school year 1928-29. May 1929. (Educational pamphlet, no.76) Board of Education.

PEET, J.O.
Training in farm and garden work in reformatory and industrial schools. March 1919. Home Office.

PELHAM, Thomas Henry William
Inter-departmental committee on collecting fishery statistics.

Report, minutes of evidence, appendix and index. 2 April 1901. 1902 Cd.1063 xv. Board of Trade.

Pembroke, *Lord. SEE:* Herbert, S., *14th Earl.*

PENN, John
Select committee on boilers registration and inspection.
Report, proceedings, minutes of evidence.... 20 July 1900. 1900 (294) vi. House of Commons.

PENNEFATHER, John de Fonblanque
Select committee on the Barnsley Gas Special Order.
Report. 5 July 1923. 1923 (105) iv. House of Commons.

PENROSE, Lionel Sharples
A clinical and genetic study of 1280 cases of mental defect. 31 Jan.1938. (S.R.S., no.229) Medical Research Council.

PERCY, Eustace, *Lord*
Committee on land purchase in Northern Ireland.
Report. 20 July 1923. 1923 Cmd.1967 xii pt.l. Treasury.

Indian federal finance committee.
Report. 28 March 1932. 1931/2 Cmd.4069 viii. India Office.

Irish grants committee.
(First interim report not published.)
Second interim report. 16 Jan.1924. 1924 Cmd.2032 xi. (No other reports identified.) Colonial Office.

Select committee on witnesses.
Report, proceedings, evidence, appendices and index. 9 May 1935. 1934/5 (84) vi. House of Commons.

PEREIRA, Horace Alvarey de Courcy
Committee on documents and records in the principal Probate Registry and district Probate Registries.
First report: Principal registry documents. 18 May 1926.
Second report: District registry documents. 9 Feb.1927. Lord Chancellor's Office.

PERNTER, J.M.
International Meteorological Conference, Innsbruck, September 1905.
Report. Sept.1908. (M.O.195) Meteorological Office.

PERRIN, William Gordan
Nelson's signals. The evolution of the signal flags. Oct.1908. (N.D.Historical, no.1) Admiralty.

PERRING, John
Standing committee on prices.
Findings and decisions of a sub-committee on costs, profits and prices of furniture. 13 Sept.1920. 1920 Cmd.983 xxiii. Board of Trade.

PERRY, H. Marrian
Report on the investigation of an epidemic caused by *bacillus aertryke*.
14 Nov.1918. (S.R.S., no.24) Medical Research Committee.

PETERS, Robert James
An analysis of the results of treatment of early, latent and muco-cutaneous tertiary syphili. 21 July 1937. (S.R.S., no.224) Medical Research Council.

PETERS, S.P.
Sea breezes at Worthy Down, Winchester. March 1939. (Prof.Notes, no.86) Meteorological Office.

PETERS, S. P. (continued)
Some observations of upper air temperatures in Iraq. Nov.1930. (Prof.Notes, no.59) Meteorlogical Office.

Some upper-air observations over lower Egypt. Dec.1932. (Geophys.Mem., no.56) Meteorological Office.

The vertical extent of north-westerly winds over Iraq in summer. April 1933. (Prof.Notes, no.64) Meteorological Office.

PETO, Basil Edward
Committee on two-seater cabs
Report. 17 June 1925. 1924/5 Cmd.2466 xv. Home Office.

PETO, Geoffrey Kelsall
Committee on gift coupons and trading stamps.
Report. 10 July 1933. 1932/3 Cmd.4385 xii. Board of Trade.

Departmental committee on international copyright.
Report. 21 Nov.1935. Board of Trade.

Food council.
Report on costs and profits of retail milk distribution in Great Britain. 24 Sept.1937. Board of Trade.

PHELPS, Lancelot Ridley
Departmental committee on the relief of the casual poor.
Report. 18 June 1930. 1929/30 Cmd.3640 xvii. Ministry of Health.

PHEMISTER, James
British regional geology, Scotland. The northern highlands. 1936. Geological Survey, Scotland.

The geology of the country around Golspie, Sutherland-shire. (Sheet 103) 9 Feb.1925. (Mem.Geol.Surv., Scotl.) Geological Survey, Scotland.

PHILIPPS, John Wynford, 1st Viscount St.Davids
Unemployment grants committee.
Report to 30 Aug.1930. 3 Nov.1930. 1930/1 Cmd.3744 xvii.
Report, 1 Sept.1930 to 31 Dec.1931. March 1932. 1931/2 Cmd.4029 xiii.
Final report, 20 Dec.1930 to 31 Aug.1932. 18 May 1933. 1932/3 Cmd.4354 xv. Ministry of Labour.

PHILIPPS, Owen
Committee on distressed colonial and Indian subjects.
Report. 14 April 1910. 1910 Cd.5133 xxii.
Minutes of evidence and appendices. 1910 Cd.5134 xxii. Colonial Office.

PHILLIPS, D.W.
Coal measure rocks.
Part 1: Classification, nomenclature and relative strengths. March 1937. (S.M.R.B.Paper, no.98) Mines Department.

PHILLIPS, Lionel, Baron
Mineral resources in the U.K. 12 March 1918. 1918 Cd.9184 xii. Ministry of Munitions.

PHILLIPS, T.W.
Committee on re-employment of ex-servicemen.
Interim report. 12 Aug.1920. 1920 Cmd.951 xix. Ministry of Labour.

PHILPOT, J. St.L.
Apparatus for the rapid study of ultra violet absorption spectra. 6 Dec.1933. (S.R.S., no.177) Medical Research Council.

PHIPPS, G.H.
Report on tea culture in Japan. 31 July 1905. (Dip.cons.reports: misc.ser., no.637) 1906 Cd.2683-1 cxxii. Foreign Office.

Report on the matting industry in Japan. Jan.1909. (Dip.cons.reports: misc.ser., no.674) 1909 Cd.4447-2 xcii. Foreign Office and Board of Trade.

PICCOLI, Raffaello
Italy and the war; an address. 10 June 1915. Ministry of Information.

PICK, Frank
Council on art and industry.
Report on design and the designer in industry. 10 Dec.1936. Board of Trade.

Report on design in the jewellery and silver smithing and allied trades. 8 Dec.1936. Board of Trade.

Report on education for the consumer; art in elementary and secondary education. 26 July 1935. Board of Trade.

Report on the working class home; its furnishings and equipment. 24 March 1937. Board of Trade.

PICK, W.H.
The ground day visibility at Cranwell, Lincolnshire, April 1920 to December 1923. March 1925. (Prof.Notes, no.40) Meteorological Office.

A note on the bumpiness at Cranwell, Lincolnshire, December 1925 to April 1926. March 1927. (Prof.Notes, no.46) Meteorological Office.

Note on the upper air observations taken in north Russia in 1919. June 1923. (Prof.Notes, no.32) Meteorological Office.

A short course in elementary meteorology. Aug.1921. (M.O.247) Meteorological Office.

PICKARD, Robert Howson
Fabrics co-ordinating research committee.
First report. March 1925.
Second report. Oct.1929. Department of Scientific and Industrial Research.

Fabrics research commmittee.
Report on the viscosity of cellulose solutions. March 1932. Department of Scientific and Industrial Research.

PICKARD-CAMBRIDGE, Arthur Wallace
Commission on Fourah Bay College, Freetown.
Report. 1939. (Colonial, no.169) Colonial Office.

PICKERSGILL, Edward Hare
Select committee on debtors (imprisonment).
Report and proceedings. 22 Dec.1908. 1908 (344) vii. House of Commons.
Report, proceedings, evidence, appendices and index. 28 July 1909. 1909 (239) vii. House of Commons.

PICKFORD, W.
Royal commission on the Dardanelles. SEE: Baring, R.T.

PIERCE, W. O'D.
Individual differences in normal colour vision; a survey of recent experimental work. 29 April 1933. (S.R.S., no.181) Medical Research Council.

PILLING, H.G.
Report on a visit to Pitcairn Island. 9 Dec.1929. (Colonial, no.53) Colonial Office.

PIM, Alan William
Commission on the financial and economic position of Basutoland.
Report. Jan.1935. 1934/5 Cmd.4907 vii. Dominion Affairs Office.

Commission on the financial and economic position of Bechuanaland Protectorate.
Report. March 1933. 1932/3 Cmd.4368 x. Colonial Office.

Report on the financial and economic position of British Honduras. March 1934. 1933/4 Cmd.4586 x. Colonial Office.

Commission on the financial and economic position of Northern Rhodesia. 29 Jan.1938. (Colonial, no.145) Colonial Office.

Commission on the financial and economic position of Swaziland.
Report. Jan.1932. 1931/2 Cmd.4114 vii. Colonial Office.

Commission on the financial position and system of taxation of Kenya. 25 May 1936. (Colonial, no.116) Colonial Office.

PIPPARD, W.R.
Calcium sulphate plasters. Aug.1938. (B.R.B.Bull., no.13) Department of Scientific and Industrial Research.

PIQUÉ, J.
The storage of eggs. Dec.1925. (F.I.B.special rep., no.26) Department of Scientific and Industrial Research.

PITT, F.H.G.
Characterisitics of dichromatic vision. 30 April 1935. (S.R.S., no.200) Medical Research Council.

PLATT, C.B.M.
Report on experiments on miners' flame safety lamps fitted with pyrophor internal relighters. 12 March 1925. Mines Department.

Report on tests of miners' flame safety lamps fitted with open mesh gauzes. 28 May 1924. Mines Department.

Report on the safety of certified mine signalling bells when connected in parallel. 23 Oct.1928. Mines Department.

Report on the safety of miners' electric cap lamps when the battery is short-circuited. 9 April 1929. Mines Department.

Report on the safety of mining telephones of the magneto ringing type. July 1933. Mines Department.

PLENDER, William
Report on British establishments of German and Austrian banks. 16 Dec.1916. 1916 Cd.8430 v.
Second report. 13 Dec.1917. 1917/8 Cd.8889 v. Treasury.

Report on investigation into existing conditions in respect of medical attendance and remuneration in certain towns. 11 July 1912. 1912/3 Cd.6305 lxxviii. Treasury.

War service canteens; disposal of surplus funds.
Accounts and report. 14 July 1922. 1922 Cmd.1717 xii. War Office.

PLEYDELL-BOUVERIE, Jacaob, 6th Earl of Radnor
Royal commission on the care and control of the feeble-minded.
Minutes of evidence.
Vol.1: England and Wales. 1908 Cd.4215 xxxv.

Vol.2: England and Wales. 1908 Cd.4216 xxxvi.
Vol.3: Scotland and Ireland. 1908 Cd.4217 xxxvii.
Vol.4: England and Wales. 1908 Cd.4218 xxxvii.
Vol.5: Appendices. 1908 Cd.4219 xxxviii.
Vol.6: Reports of medical investigators, with memorandum. 1908 Cd.4220 xxxviii.
Vol.7: Report on visit to American institutions. 1908 Cd.4221 xxxix.
Vol.8: Report of the Royal Commission. 10 July 1908. 1908 Cd.4202 xxxix.

PLIMMER, Robert Henry Aders.
Analyses and energy values of foods. May 1921. War Office.

PLUNKETT, Horace Curzon
Departmental committee on regulations for butter.
Interim report. 24 Jan.1902. 1902 Cd.944 xx.
Evidence, digest and appendices. 1902 Cd.1039 xx.
Final report. 1903. 1903 Cd.1749 xvii.
Minutes of evidence with a digest of the evidence, appendices, diagrams and index. 1903 Cd.1750 xvii. Board of Trade.

Report of the proceedings of the Irish convention. 8 April 1918. 1918 Cd.9019 x. Prime Minister's Office.

Plymouth, Lord. SEE: Windsor-Clive, R.G., 1st Earl
Windsor-Clive, I.M., 2nd Earl

POCOCK, R.W.
British regional geology; the Welsh borderland. 1935. Geological Survey.

The geology of the country around Hertford. (Sheet 239) 4 July 1924. (Mem.Geol.Surv.) Geological Survey.

The geology of the country around Wem. (Sheet 138) 7 Aug.1924. (Mem.Geol.Surv.) Geological Survey.

Shrewsbury district including the Hanwood coalfield. (Sheet 152) 29 Oct. 1937. (Mem.Geol.Surv.) Geological Survey.

POCOCK, T.I.
The geology of the country around Macclesfield, Congleton, Crewe and Middlewich. (Sheet 110) 12 May 1906. (Mem.Geol.Surv.) Geological Survey.

The geology of the country around Oxford. 5 Nov.1907. (Mem.Geol.Surv.) Geological Survey.

POLLARD, W.
The coal of south Wales; with special reference to the origin and distribution of anthracite. 17 Feb.1908. (Mem.Geol.Surv.) Geological Survey.

POLLOCK, Ernest Murray, 1st Baron Hanworth
Business of courts committee.
Interim report. 24 Feb.1933. 1932/3 Cmd.4265 x.
Second interim report. 13 Dec.1933. 1933/4 Cmd.4471 xi.
Third and final report. 17 Jan.1936. 1935/6 Cmd.5066 viii. Lord Chancellor's Office.

Law Revision committee.
Interim report: Actio personalis moritur cum persona. 7 March 1934. 1933/4 Cmd.4540 xi.
Second interim report: Recovery of interest in civil proceedings. March 1934. 1933/4 Cmd.4546 xi.
Third interim report: Doctrine of no contribution between tort-feasors. July 1934. 1933/4 Cmd. 4637 xi.

POLLOCK, Ernest Murray, *1st Baron Hanworth* (continued)

Fourth interim report: Liability of husband for torts of the wife and of the wife in tort and contract. Dec.1934. 1934/5 Cmd.4770 x. Lord Chancellor's Office. *For further reports see,* Wright, R.A.

POLLOCK, Frederick
Royal commission on public records of England and Wales.
Vol.1,part 1: First report. Sept.1912. 1912/3 Cd.6361 xliv.
Vol.1,part 2: Appendices. 1912/3 Cd.6395 xliv.
Vol.1,part 3: Evidence, appendices and index. 1912/3 Cd.6396 xliv.
Vol.2,part 1: Second report. 18 June 1914. 1914 Cd.7544 xlvi.
Vol.2,part 2: Appendices. 1914 Cd.7545 xlvi.
Vol.2,part 3: Evidence and index. 1914 Cd.7546 xlvi.
Vol.3,part 1: Third report. 11 April 1918. 1919 Cmd.367 xxviii.
Vol.3,part 2: Appendices. 1919 Cmd.368 xxviii.
Vol.3,part 3: Evidence and appendix. 1919 Cmd.369 xxviii. (no further reports identified)

Polwarth, *Master of SEE:* Hepburne-Scott, W.G., *Master of Polwarth*

POPE, Samuel
Report on objections against the draft special order including married women outworkers within the provisions of part 1 of the National Insurance Act. 7 Jan.1913. 1912/3 Cd.6600 lxxviii. National Health Insurance Commission.

Report on the byelaw made by the Devon County Council under the Employment of Children Act, 1903 and on the objections. 3 June 1913. 1913 Cd.6988 xxiii. Home Office.

Report on the proposed general early closing order for the Borough of Blackpool. 28 July 1913. 1914 Cd.7082 lxxi. Home Office.

Report on the proposed general early closing order for the Borough of Nelson. 18 Jan.1915. 1914/6 Cd.7868 xxxv. Home Office.

PORTAL, Wyndham
Report of investigation into the industrial conditions in certain depressed areas. 3: South Wales and Monmouthshire. 2 July 1934. 1933/4 Cmd.4728 xiii. Ministry of Labour.

PORTER, Samuel Loury, *Baron.*
Budget disclosure inquiry.
Report. 27 May 1936. 1935/6 Cmd.5184 vii.
Minutes of evidence. 1936. Home Office.

Portland, *Lord. SEE:* Cavendish-Bentinck, W.J.A.C.J.

POTT, Gladys S.
Report of delegates to enquire as to openings in Canada for women from the United Kingdom. Nov.1919. 1919 Cmd.403 xxxi. Colonial Office.

POWELL, H. Clark
Grapefruit culture in the British West Indies and British Honduras. Dec.1928. (E.M.B.13) Empire Marketing Board.

POWER, William Henry
Memorandum on the circumstances under which the closing of public elementary schools or the exclusion of particular children may be required to prevent the spread of disease. Sept.1901. Local Government Board.

Royal commission on human and animal tuberculosis.
Interim report. 16 May 1904. 1904 Cd.2092 xxxix.
Second interim report.
Part 1: Report. Jan.1907. 1907 Cd.3322 xxxviii.
Part 2: Appendix.
Vol.1: The pathogenic effects of bovine viruses, by A.Stanley Griffiths. 1907 Cd.3584 xxxviii.
Vol.2. The pathogenic effects of human viruses, by L. Cobbett. 1907 Cd.3660 xxxix, and 1907 Cd.3661 xl.
Vol.3: Additional investigations of bovine and human viruses. 1908 Cd.3758 lvii.
Vol.4. Comparative histological and bacteriological investigations on the relationship of human and bovine tuberculosis by Arthur Eastwood. 1907 Cd.3378 xl.
Third interim report and appendix. Jan.1909. 1909 Cd.4483 xlix.
Final report.
Part 1: Report. June 1911. 1911 Cd.5761 xlii.
Part 2: Appendix. Vol.1. Investigation of viruses obtained from cases of human tuberculosis (other than lupus), by A.S.Griffith. 1911 Cd.5790 xlii.
Part 2: Appendix. Vol.2. Investigation of viruses obtained from cases of lupus, by A.Stanley Griffith. 1911 Cd.5791 xliii.
Part 2: Appendix. Vol.3. Reports on investigations dealing with (various topics). 1911 Cd.5893 xliii.
Part 2: Appendix. Vol.4. Investigations into the tuberculosis occurring naturally in certain animals other than man: and modification experiments, by F.Griffith. 1911 Cd.5894 xliv.
Part 2: Appendix. Vol.5. Comparative histological and bacteriological investigations, by A.Eastwood. 1911 Cd.5975 xliv.
Part 2: Appendix. Vol.6. Report on the results of a chemical investigation, by A.Harden. 1913 Cd.6904 xl.
Part 2: Appendix. Vol.6. Supplemental volume. Report on tuberculin tests. 1913 Cd. 6796 xl.
Part 2: Appendix. Vol.7. Graphic charts. 1914/6 Cd.7941 xxvii.

POWNALL, Assheton
Committee on the valuation of navy, army and air force stocks.
Report. 11 March 1927. 1927 Cmd.2839 xii. Treasury.

Poynder, J.P.D. *SEE:* Dickson-Poynder, J.P., *1st Baron Islington*

PRAIN, David
Advisory committee on research into diseases in animals.
Report. 15 Feb.1922. Development Commission.

PRATT, D.D.
An investigation into the causes and prevention of the corrosion of tar stills. Jan.1938. (Chemistry research special rep., no.4) Department of Scientific and Industrial Research.

PRAUSNITZ, Oto Carl Willy
Investivations on respiratory dust disease in operatives in the cotton industry. 25 June 1936. (S.R.S., no.212) Medical Research Council.

PRESTON, K.
Report on a breakdown of a turbo-alternator at the Ifor power station, Dowlais, of the South Wales Electric Power Co. 14 July 1933. Home Office.

PRESTON, Sidney
Report on the application of the Lower Muse Drainage Board for approval of certain works on the River Ouse. 21 Oct.1918. Board of Agriculture and Fisheries.

PRESTON-THOMAS, H
Report on methods of dealing with vagrancy in Switzerland. 25 June 1904. 1904 Cd.2235 lxxxii. Local Government Board.

PRETYMAN, Ernest George
Committee on berthing accommodation for H.M. ships.
Report. 31 Jan.1902. 1903 Cd.1649 xl. Admiralty.

Departmental committee on foot-and-mouth disease.
Report. 7 Dec.1922. 1922 Session 2 Cmd.1784 ii. Ministry of Agciculture and Fisheries.

Departmental committee on the outbreak of foot-and-mouth disease in 1923-4.
Report. 2 Feb.1925. 1924/5 Cmd.2350 xiii. Ministry of Agriculture and Fisheries.

PRICE, C.W.
Report on a breakdown of a turbo-alternator at the Ifor power station, Dowlais of the South Wales Electric Power Co. 14 July 1933. Home Office.

PRICE, Crawford
The dawn of Armageddon; or, the provocation by Serbia (*vide* German note for neutrals, Jan.11, 1917) 1917. Ministry of Information.

PRICE, E.S.
The experiment in geography teaching at Ruabon county school. June 1924. Board of Education. Welsh Department.

PRICE, Keith W.
Committee on the chemical trade.
Report. 1 Nov.1917. 1917/8 Cd.8882 xviii. Ministry of Reconstruction.

PRIESTLEY, Joseph Child
Departmental committee on sexual offences against young persons.
Report. 2 Dec.1925. 1924/5 Cmd.2561 xv. Home Office.

PRIMROSE, Archibald Philip, *5th Earl Rosebery*
Select committee on the House of Lords.
Report, proceedings and Appendices. Dec.1908. 1908 (H.L.234) x. House of Lords.

PRIMROSE, Henry W.
Committee on Irish finance.
Report. 17 Oct.1911. 1912/3 Cd.6153 xxxiv. Minutes of evidence with appendices. 1913 Cd.6799 xxx. Treasury.

Departmental committee on education rates.
Report and appendices. 31 Aug.1906. 1907 Cd.3313 xxi. Treasury.

Departmental committee on industrial alcohol.
Report. 23 Mar.1905. 1905 Cd.2472 lxiv. Minutes of evidence with appendices. 1905 Cd.2477 lxiv.Treasury.

Royal commission on the sugar supply.
First report. 22 Dec.1916. 1917/8 Cd.8728 xviii. Second report. April 1921. 1921 Cmd.1300 xviii.

PRINGLE, J
British regional geology. The south of Scotland. July 1935. Geological Survey, Scotland.

British regional geology. South Wales. 1937. Geological Survey.

PRINGLE, John Wallace
Advisory committee for revision of the requirements for the opening of railways.
Report on tests on railway bridges in respect of impact effect. 21 Dec.1920. Ministry of Transport.

Automatic train control committee.
Report. 20 April 1922.
Report. 3 Nov.1930. Ministry of Transport.

Railway electrification committee.
Report. 23 July 1928. Ministry of Transport.

Report of an inquiry on Edinburgh Corporation tramways. 5 April 1922. Ministry of Transport.

PROTHERO, George Walter
A lasting peace; a conversation between a neutral and an Englishman. 1917. Ministry of Information.

PROUD, S.
Upper winds at Kingston, Jamaica. Oct.1937. (Prof.Notes, no.78) Meteorological Office.

PROVIS, Samuel Butler
Departmental committee on orders relating to the administration of outdoor relief.
Report. 28 Dec.1910. 1911 Cd.5525 xxxix. Local Government Board.

Departmental committee on poor law orders.
First report. 14 July 1913. 1913 Cd.6968 xxxviii. (No further reports identified) Local Government Board.

PRYTHERCH, W.E.
Magnesium and its alloys. July 1937. Department of Scientific and Industrial Research.

PUAUX, René
The German colonies: what is to become of them. 1918. Ministry of Information.

PURCELL, Pierce Francis
The peat resources of Ireland; a lecture. 5 March 1919. (F.R.B.special rep., no.2) Department of Scientific and Industrial Research.

PUREY-CUST, H.E.
Report on the undercurrents in the River Congo, West Africa from observations, 1899. Jan.1900. Hydrographic Department. Admiralty.

PYKE, R.L.
The legibility of print. 30 Sept.1926. (S.R.S., no.110) Medical Research Council.

QUENNELL, Winifred A.
Classification of monthly charts of pressure anomaly over the northern hemisphere. 1926. (Gemphys.Mem., no.31) Meteorological Office.

The influence of the Arctic ice on the subsequent distribution of pressure over the eastern north Atlantic and western Europe. July 1928. (Geophys.Mem., no.41) Meteorological Office.

Variations of pressure distribution in the northern hemisphere during the period 1904-13. Dec.1929. (Prof.Notes, no.54) Meteorolmgical Office.

RABINO, H.L.
Report on the trade and general condition of the city and province of Kermanshah, Persia. 26 Feb.1903. (Dip.cons.reports: misc.ser., no.590) 1903 Cd.1387-3 lxxvi. Foreign Office.

RADCLIFFE, Francis Reynolds Yonge
Committee on county courts.
Report. 20 Oct.1919. 1919 Cmd.431 xiii, pt.1. Lord Chancellor's Office.

Radnor, *Lord. SEE:* Pleydell-Bouverie, J., *6th Earl.*

RAE, Bennet B.
Age and growth of lemon soles in Scottish waters. 1939. (Sci.invest., 1939 no.1) Fishery Board for Scotland.

Factors in the growth of lemon soles. 1939. (Sci.invest., 1939 no.3) Scottish Home Department. Fisheries Division.

RAE, James
Committee of inquiry into the working of the Directorate of Operational Service and Intelligence of the Department of Civil Aviation.
Report. 30 Sept.1938. 1937/8 Cmd.5864 viii. Air Ministry.
Superannuation committee.
Report. 24 Oct.1934. Treasury.

RAE, James Stanley
Commission on conditions in the Carib Reserve and the disturbance of 19 September 1930, Dominica. 30 July 1931. 1931/2 Cmd.3990 vi. Colonial Office.

RAEBURN, William Norman
Committee on the present position of co-operative societies in relation to income tax.
Report. 24 Dec.1932. 1932/3 Cmd.4260 x. Evidence. 1933. Treasury.
Crinan canal committee.
Report. 15 July 1921. Ministry of Transport.

RAHIMTOOLA, Ibrahim
Indian fiscal commission.
Report. 6 July 1922. 1922 Session 2 Cmd.1764 ii. India Office.

RAINEY, J.W.
History of the Great War. Veterinary services. 21 April 1924. War Office.

RAINFORD, H.
Flame-proof electrical apparatus for use in coal mines.
Third report: Ring-relief protection. Feb.1927. (S.M.R.B.Paper, no.35) Mines Deparmtent.

RAITT, D.S.
The fecundity of the haddock. 1932. (Sci.invest., 1932, no.1) Fishery Board for Scotland.
The haddock stocks of the north-east Atlantic, 1916-1935. 1936. (Sci.invest., 1936, no.1) Fishery Board for Scotland.

RAJCHMAN, L.
Report upon 878 cases of bacillary enteritis received from the eastern Mediterranean. 2 Feb.1917. (S.R.S., no.5) Medical Research Committee.

RALEIGH, Thomas
Committee on the University of Wales and the Welsh university colleges.
Report. 25 June 1909. 1909 Cd.4571 xix.
Minutes of evidence and appendices. 1909 Cd.4572 xix. Treasury.

RALEIGH, Walter
History of the Great War. The war in the air. 1922. War Office. *SEE:* Jones, H.A. for further vols.

RAM, Abel John
Royal commission on vivisection. *SEE:* Gully, W.C., *1st Viscount Selby.*

RAMSAY, Malcolm Graham
Civil service reorganisation committee.
Final report. 28 Jan.1921. Civil Service National Whitley Council. Treasury.

Committee on the principles on which charges for certain services rendered by government departments should be assessed.
Report. 14 July 1927. 1927 Cmd.2950 ix. Treasury.

Joint committee on the organisation, *etc.* of the civil service.
Report. 17 Feb.1920. Civil Service National Whitley Council. Treasury.

Nursing homes committee.
First report. 19 April 1928.
Second report. Jan.1929. Civil Service National Whitley Council. Treasury.

Report of the national provisional joint committee on the application of the Whitley report to the administrative departments of the civil service. 28 May 1919. 1919 Cmd.198 xi. Treasury.

RANKIN, G.C.
Enquiry into the administration and discipline of Barlinnie Prison, and existing arrangements for the inspection of Scottish prisons.
Report. 12 March 1935. 1934/5 Cmd.4860 xi. Scottish Office.

RASON, Ernest
Report on the trade of the New Hebrides. Aug.1905. 1906 Cd.2714 lxxviii. Colonial Office.

RASTALL, Robert Heron
Molybdenum ores. July 1922. (Mono.Min.Resour.) Imperial Institute.

Tungsten ores. Dec.1919. (Mono.Min.Resour.) Imperial Institute.

Rathcreedan, *Lord. SEE:* Norton, C.W., *1st Baron Rathcreedan*

RAVEN, Edward
Committee on women's questions.
Report. 23 March 1934. Treasury.

RAVEN, R.W.
Radium treatment in cancer of certain sites.
Preliminary report. Nov.1934. (no further identified) National Radium Commission. Treasury.

RAVENHILL, Alice
School training for the home duties of women.
Part.I: Teaching of 'domestic science' in the United States of America. May 1903. (Special reports on educational subjects, vol.15) 1905 Cd.2498 xxvi. Board of Education.

RAWLINSON, John Frederick Peel
Report of an enquiry on the arrest of Major R.O. Sheppard. 6 Aug.1925. 1924/5 Cmd.2497 xv. Home Office.

RAY, William
Committee on local expenditure in England and Wales.
Report. 28 Oct.1932. 1932/3 Cmd.4200 **xiv.** Ministry of Health.

Rayleigh, *Lord. SEE:* Strutt, J., *3rd Baron*
Strutt, R.J., *4th Baron*

REA, Russell
Departmental committee on railway agreements and amalgamations.
Report. 11 April 1911. 1911 Cd.5631 xxix.
Minutes of evidence, appendices and index. 1911 Cd.5927 xxix. Board of Trade.

Departmental committee on the probable economic effect of a limit of eight hours to the working day of a coal miner.
First report.
Part I: Report. 23 March 1907. 1907 Cd.3426 xiv.
Part II: Minutes of evidence; 1st day. 1907 Cd.3427 xiv.
Part III: Minutes of evidence; 2nd to 11th days. 1907 Cd.3428 xv.
Final report.
Part I: Report and appendices. 15 May 1907. 1907 Cd.3505 xv.
Part II: Minutes of evidence; 12th to 27th days and index. 1907 Cd.3506 xv. Board of Trade.

READ, Herbert Harold
British regional geology. The Grampian highlands. 1935. Geological Survey, Scotland.

The geology of central Sutherland. (Sheets 108 and 109) 5 May 1930. (Mem.Geol.Surv., Scotl.) Geological Survey, Scotland.

The geology of Strath Oykell and lower Loch Shin. (Sheet 102) 10 Feb.1925. (Mem.Geol.Surv., Scotl.) Geological Survey, Scotland.

The geology of the country around Banff, Huntly and Turriff. (Sheets 86 and 96) 10 May 1923. (Mem.Geol.Surv., Scotl.) Geological Survey, Scotland.

The geology of the country around Golspie, Sutherlandshire. (Sheet 103) 9 Feb.1925. (Mem.Geol.Surv., Scotl.) Geological Survey, Scotland.

READ, Herbert James
Committee on the staffing of the agricultural departments in the Colonies.
Report. May 1920. 1920 Cmd.730 xiii. Colonial Office.

Committee on the staffing of the veterinary departments in the Colonies and Protectorates.
Report. 18 Aug.1920. 1920 Cmd.922 xiii. Colonial Office.

Departmental committee on the West African medical staff.
Report. 23 Feb.1909. 1909 Cmd.4720 lxi. Colonial Office.

READE, Arthur
Russia under Nicholas II. Aug.1915. Ministry of Information.

Reay, Lord. SEE: MacKay, D.J., 11th Baron

REDMAN, Arthur Stanley
Transportation in war. A course of five lectures, 1925. Dec.1925. War Office.

REDMAYNE, Richard Augustine Studdert
Committee on the drainage of the mines in the south Staffordshire coalfield.
Report. 21 Sept.1920. 1920 Cmd.969 xxi. Board of Trade.

Committee to inquire into the causes of and means of preventing accidents from fall of ground, underground haulage and shafts.

Report. Oct.1909. 1909 Cd.4821 xxxiv. Home Office.

Departmental committee on conditions prevailing in the coal mining industry due to the war.
Part 1: Report. 27 May 1916. 1914/6 Cd.7939 xxviii.
Part 2: Evidence and index. 1914/6 Cd.8009 xxviii.
Second general report. 10 Dec.1915. 1914/6 Cd.8147 xxviii.
Third general report. 1 Sept.1916. 1916 Cd.8345 vi. Home Office.

Departmental committee on electricity in mines.
Report. 28 Dec.1910. 1911 Cd.5498 xxxvii.
Minutes of evidence and index. 1911 Cd.5533 xxxvii. Home Office.

Departmental committee on spontaneous combustion of coal in mines.
First report. 1 Dec.1913. 1914 Cd.7218 xlii.
Final report. Aug.1921. 1921 Cmd.1417 xv.
Minutes of evidence, with index. 3 Parts. 1916, 1920 and 1921. Home Office.

Departmental committee on the Home Office experimental station at Eskmeals, Cumberland.
Report. 31 July 1920. Home Office.

Departmental committee on the testing of miners' safety lamps.
Report. 5 Aug.1912. 1912/3 Cd.6387 xlvii. Home Office.

REDWOOD, Boverton, Bt.
Gas traction committee.
Interim report. 11 April 1918. (No further reports identified) H.M. Petroleum Executive.

Inter-departmental committee on alcohol motor fuel.
Report. 23 June 1919. 1919 Cmd.218 x. H.M.Petroleum Executive.

REECE, Richard James
Report on the appointment of the medical officer of health and on the sanitary conditions of the Borough of Gravesend. 27 Aug.1909. (Rep.Pub.Health & Med.Subj., no.15) Local Government Board.

Report on the epidemic of enteric fever in the City of Lincoln, 1904-5. 3 Feb.1906. (Rep.Med.Insp., no.226) Local Government Board.

Report on the influence of the Brynmawr U.D. Council's sewage works on the health of the parish of Llanelly through pollution of the local water supplies. Nov.1901. Local Government Board.

Report on the prevalence of diphtheria at the village of Ringmer in Chailey R.D., Sussex. 30 Oct.1907. (Rep.Med.Insp., no.290) Local Government Board.

Report on a recent epidemic of scarlatina in Sidmouth U.D. 22 May 1909. (Rep.Pub.Health & Med.Subj., no.6) Local Government Board.

Report on the sanitary conditions of Braintree U.D. 14 Sept.1907. (Rep.Med.Insp., no.282) Local Government Board.

Report on the sanitary conditons of Clutton. R.D. and Peasedown St.John situated in Bath. R.D. 26 May 1910. (Rep.Pub.Health & Med.Subj., no.31) Local Government Board.

Report on the sanitary conditions of Hebburn U.D., with reference to its housing accommodation generally. 13 Nov.1908. (Rep.Med.Insp., no.318) Local Government Board.

REECE, Richard James (Continued)
Report on the sanitary conditions of Northam U.D., Devonshire. 14 Dec. 1900. (Rep.Med.Insp., no.156) Local Government Board.

Report on the sanitary conditions of Trowbridge U.D., with special refeence to the appointment of an inspector of nuisances. 19 Feb.1907. (Rep.Med.Insp., no.251) Local Government Board.

Report on the sanitary conditions of Williton R.D., with reference to the appointment of medical officer of health. 30 July 1910. (Rep.Pub.Health & Med.Subj., no.36) Local Govenment Board.

Report on the sanitary conditions of Witham U.D. 10 Sept.1907. (Rep.Med.Insp., no.281) Local Government Board.

Report on smallpox and smallpox hospitals at Liverpool, 1902-3. 3 Feb.1905. (Rep.Med.Insp., no.208) Local Government Board.

Report on water supply, *etc,* of Thorne R.D. 20 Aug.1903. (Rep.Med.Insp., no.188) Local Government Board.

REES, Morgan James
Report on conditions of housing and other sanitary circumstances in St.Dogmells R.D. 5 Sept.1913. (Rep.Pub.Health & Med.Subj., no.82) Local Government Board.

Report on diarrhoea in the parishes of Blackwell and South Normanton in Blackwell R.D., associated with pollution of the public water supply. 30 Sept.1915. (Rep.Pub.Health & Med.Subj., no.108) Local Government Board.

Report on the sanitary conditions of Blaenavon U.D. 23 Dec.1911. (Rep.Pub.Health & Med.Subj., no.62) Local Government Board.

Report on the sanitary conditions of Mallwyd U.D. 8 May 1912. (Rep.Pub.Health & Med.Subj., no.68) Local Government Board.

REES-THOMAS, William
Report on cardiazol treatment and on the present application of hypoglycaemic shock treatment in schizophrenia. June 1938. Board of Control.

REEVES, F.W.
The system of education in St.Vincent. March 1914. (Imperial education conference papers) Board of Education.

REGAN, Charles Tate
Report on the fishes of the colonies. Sept.1920. (Colonial reports; misc., no.92) 1920 Cmd.958 xxxiii. Colonial Office.

REID, Clement
The geology of Dartmoor. (Sheet 338) 8 May 1912. (Mem.Geol.Surv.) Geological Survey.

The geology of the country around Mevagissey. (Sheet 353) 12 July 1907. (Mem.Geol.Surv.) Geological Survey.

The geology of the country around Padstow and Camelford. (Sheets 335 and 336) 12 Sept.1910. (Mem.Geol.Surv.) Geological Survey.

The geology of the country around Ringwood. (Sheet 314) 2 Dec.1901. (Mem.Geol.Surv.) Geological Survey.

The geology of the country around Salisbury. (Sheet 298) 18 Oct.1901. (Mem.Geol.Surv.) Geological Survey.

The geology of the country around Southampton. (Sheet 315) 19 June 1901. (Mem.Geol.Surv.)

Geological Survey.

The geology of the country around Tavistock and Launceston. (Sheet 337) 30 Sept.1911. (Mem.Geol.Surv.) Geological Survey.

The geology of the country near Chichester. (Sheet 317) 25 March 1903. (Mem.Geol.Surv.) Geological Survey.

The geology of the country near Newquay. (Sheet 346) 10 Nov.1906. (Mem.Geol.Surv.) Geological Survey.

The geology of the Land's End district. (Sheet 351 and 358) 11 May 1907. (Mem.Geol.Surv.) Geological Survey.

The water supply of Sussex from underground sources. 1899 and 31 Oct.1918.
Supplement. 2 Oct.1910. (Mem.Geol.Surv.) Geological Survey.

REID, David Douglas
Select committee on the Marple Gas Special Order.
Report, proceedings and evidence. 2 April 1924. 1924 (51) vi. House of Commons.

REID, Marshall Frederick
Indian trade enquiry.
Reports on rice. 12 Dec.1917. Imperial Institute.

REID, Thomas
Report on the financial situation of the Seychelles. July 1933. (Colonail, no.90) Colonial Office.

RENDLE, B.J.
British hardwoods; their structure and identification. Aug.1929. (F.P.R. Bull., no.3) Department of Scientific and Industrial Research.

Commercial mahoganies and allied timbers. March 1938. (F.P.R. Bull., no.18) Department of Scientific and Industrial Research.

The growth and structure of wood. Aug.1937. (F.P.R. Records, no.21) Department of Scientific and Industrial Research.

Seraya, meranti and lauan. Sept.1936. (F.P.R. Records, no.12) Department of Scientific and Industrial Research.

Rennel, *Baron, SEE:* Rodd, J.R., *1st Baron*

Revelstoke, *Lord. SEE:* Baring, J., *2nd Baron*

REW, R. Henry
Agricultural output of Great Britain.
Report and memorandum. Oct.1911. 1912/3 Cd.6277 x. Board of Agriculture and Fisheries.

Committee on the financial results of the occupation of agricultural land and the costs of living of rural workers.
Report. 5 March 1919. 1919 Cmd.76 viii. Agricultural Wages Board.

Committee on unemployment insurance in agriculture.
Report. 21 April 1921. 1921 Cmd.1344 xviii. Agricultural Wages Board.

Decline in the agricultural population of Great Britain, 1881-1906.
Report. 10 Sept.1906. 1906 Cd.3273 xcvi. Board of Agriculture and Fisheries.

Inter-departmental committee on agricultural unemployment insurance.
Report. 17 Aug.1926. Ministry of Agriculture and Fisheries *and* Scottish Office.

Safeguarding of industries committee.

REW, R. Henry (continued)
Report on fabric gloves and glove fabric for the manufacture of fabric gloves. 26 Jan.1922. Board of Trade.

Report on fabric gloves and glove fabrics manufactured in Germany. 25 July 1922. Board of Traxe.

Report on optical elements and optical and other scientific instruments. 3 Aug.1922. Board of Trade.

REYNTIENS, N.S.
Report on railways in Austria and Hungary. Aug.1909. 1909 Cd.4878 lxxvii. Board of Trade.

RHIND, C.B.
Report on the financial and economic situation in Brazil. 4 June 1901. (Dip.and cons.reports: misc.ser., no.558) 1901 Cd.430-13 lxxx. Foreign Office.

RICE, Ernest
Committee on navy rations, meal hours, the prices paid for "savings" and the management of canteens.
Report and appendices. 1901. 1901 Cd.782 xlii. Admiralty.

RICE, G.S.
Stonedust as a preventative of coal dust explosions; comparative tests. Sept.1925. (S.M.R.B.Paper no.13) Mines Department.

RICH, T.
Notes on electric light and power work of the German Army. 30 Sept.1919. War Office.

RICHARDSON, Albion Henry Herbert
Report of an inquiry into allegations against the acting governor of Wandsworth prison concerning his action against disorderly prisoners. 2 April 1919. 1919 Cmd.131 xxvii. Home Office.

RICHARDSON, Lewis Fry
Cracker balloons for signalling temperature. June 1921. (Prof.Notes, no.9) Meteorological Office.

How to observe the wind by shooting spheres upward. June 1924. (Prof.Notes, no.34) Meteorological Office.

Lizard balloons for signalling the ratio of pressure to temperature. June 1921. (Prof.Notes, no.17) Meteorological Office.

RICHARDSON, Linsdall
The geology of the country around Cirencester. (Sheet 235) 31 Aug.1932. (Mem.Geol.Surv.) Geological Survey.

The geology of the country around Moreton-in-Marsh. (Sheet 217) 22 May 1929. (Mem.Geol.Surv.) Geological Survey.

Wells and springs of Gloucestershire. 4 March 1930. (Mem.Geol.Surv.) Geological Survey.

Wells and springs of Herefordshire. Dec.1934. (Mem.Geol.Surv.) Geological Survey.

Wells and springs of Leicestershire. 23 Feb.1931. (Mem.Geol.Surv.) Geological Survey.

Wells and springs of Somerset. 6 Feb.1928. (Mem.Geol.Surv.) Geological Survey.

Wells and springs of Warwickshire. 30 April 1928. (Mem.Geol.Surv.) Geological Survey.

Wells and springs of Worcestershire. 11 Dec.1929. (Mem.Geol.Surv.) Geological Survey.

RICHARDSON, N.A.
Experiments on the preservation of mine timber.

Aug.1935. (F.P.R.records, no.3) Department of Scientific and Industrial Research.

Wood preservatives. May 1937. (F.P.R. records, no.17) Department of Scientific and Industrial Research.

RICHEY, J.E.
British regional geology, Scotland. The teritiary volcanic districts. 1935. Geological Survey, Scotland.

The economic geology of the Ayrshire coalfield. Area 1: Kilbirnie, Dalry and Kilmaurs. 6 May 1925. (Mem.Geol.Surv., Scotl.) Geological Survey, Scotland.

The geology of Ardnamurchan, north-west Mull and Coll. (Sheet 51 and part of 52) 15 May 1930. (Mem.Geol.Surv., Scotl.) Geological Survey, Scotland.

The geology of north Ayrshire. (Sheet 22) 10 Oct.1929. (Mem.Geol.Surv., Scotl.) Geological Survey, Scotland.

The geology of the Sanquair coalfield and the adjacent basin of Thornhill. 6 March 1936. (Mem.Geol.Surv., Scot.) Geological Survey, Scotland.

Guide to the geological model of Ardnamurchan. 1934. Geological Survey, Scotland.

RICHMOND, Frederick
Standing committee on trusts. Findings and decisions of a committee on a combine among the manufactures of sewing cotton.
1st report. 3 Feb.1920. 1920 Cmd.563 xxiii.
2nd report. 14 May 1920. 1920 Cmd.930 xxiii.
3rd report. 8 Feb.1921. 1921 Cmd.1173 xvi. Board of Trade.

RICHMOND, H.S.
Report on safeguards for the prevention of accidents in the manufacture of cotton. 18 June 1906. 1906 Cd.3168 cx. Home Office.

RICHMOND, John Ritchie
Scottish architectural advisory committee.
Report on the incorporation of architectural quality in houses for the working classes; and on the erection of high tenements. 18 March 1935. Department of Health for Scotland.

RICHMOND, T.J.
Notes on the determination of the value to be accepted from observations for latitude and longitude with the prismatic astrolabe. 12 Nov.1926. (H.D.281 and H.D. 285 of 1928) Admiralty.

Rider-Haggard, H. SEE: Haggard, H.R.

RIDLEY, Matthew White, 3rd Viscount Ridley
Inter-departmental committee on the Rent Restriction Acts.
Report. 6 Dec.1937. 1937/8 Cmd.5621 xv. Ministry of Health.

RITCHIE, Alfred
The food and feeding habits of the haddock in Scottish waters. 1937. (Sci.invest., 1937, no.2) Fishery Board for Scotland.

RITCHIE, Charles T.
Departmental committee on income tax.
Report. June 1905. 1905 Cd.2575 xliv.
Appendix with minutes of evidence. 1905 Cd.2576 xliv. Treasury.

RITCHIE, R.L. Graeme
Report on the position of French in the first school

RITCHIE, R. L. Graeme (continued)
certificate examinations, 1928. May 1929. (Educational pamphlets, no.70) Board for Education.

RITSON, John Anthony Sydney
Simultaneous shot-firing; a report by the shot-firing committee. April 1934. (S.M.R.B. Paper no.85) Mines Department.

Stemming materials. Jan.1934. (S.M.R.B. Paper no.84) Mines Department.

Riverdale, *Baron. SEE:* Balfour, A., *1st Baron*

ROBERTS, Charles Henry
Select committee on emergency legislation.
First report. 5 Aug.1918. 1918 (108) iii.
Second report. 18 Nov.1918. 1918 (141) iii. House of Commons.

Select committee on Putumayo, Peru, atrocities.
Special report. 30 Oct.1912. 1912/3 (354) ix.
Report. 6 Feb.1913. 1912/3 (509) ix.
Report and special report, proceedings, evidence, appendices and index. 5 June 1913. 1913 (148) xiv. House of Commons.

ROBERTS, George H.
Departmental committee on the causes and prevention of blindness.
Interim report: alleged dangerous lights in Kinema studios. 27 May 1921.
Final report. Sept.1922. Ministry of Health.

ROBERTS, Samuel
Committee on canteen profits.
Report. 4 May 1921. 1921 Cmd.1280 xx. War Office.

Inter-departmental committee to survey the prices of building materials.
Interim report. 27 June 1923. 1923 Cmd.1908 x.
Second interim report. 25 July 1923. 1923 Cmd.1935 x.
Third interim report. 10 Nov.1923. 1923 Cmd.2003 x.
Fourth interim report. 29 May 1924. Cmd.2153 vii.
Fifth interim report. July 1926. 1926 Cmd.2719 viii.
Sixth interim report. April 1934. 1933/4 Cmd.4750 ix. (No further identified) Ministry of Health.

ROBERTSON, Benjamin
Report on the proposed settlement of Indian agriculturalists in Tanganyika Territory. 4 Aug.1920. 1921 Cmd.1312 x. Indian Office.

ROBERTSON, J.M.
The effect of the rate of cooling on the structure and constitution of steel. Dec.1929. (S.M.R.B. Paper no.59) Mines Department.

ROBERTSON, James Patrick Bannerman, *Baron Robertson of Forteviot*
Royal commission on university education in Ireland.
First report. 28 Sept.1901. 1902 Cd.825 xxxi.
Evidence. 1902 Cd.826 xxxi.
Second report. 21 Dec.1901. 1902 Cd.899 xxxi.
Evidence. 1902 Cd.900 xxxi.
Third report. 28 July 1902. 1902 Cd.1228 xxxii.
Evidence. 1902 Cd.1229 xxxii.
Final report. 28 Feb.1903. 1903 Cd.1483 xxxii.
Appendix: documents. 1903 Cd.1484 xxxii.

ROBERTSON, John Mackinnon
Departmental committee on the increase of prices since the beginning of the War.
Interim report on meat, milk, and bacon. 22 Sept.1916. 1916 Cd.8358 xiv.
Second interim report: Bread, flour and wheat prices. 15 Nov. 1916. 1917/8 Cd. 8483 xviii.
Third interim report: Potato, tea and sugar prices. 30 Dec.1916. 1917/8 Cd.8483 xviii. Board of Trade.

German truth and a matter of fact. 1917. Ministry of Information.

Neutrals and the war; an open letter to *heer* L.Simons. 1917. Ministry of Information.

ROBERTSON, Robert
Departmental committee on the manufacture of alcohol for power purposes from sugar beet.
Report: Power alcohol production. 14 April 1926. Ministry of Agriculture and Fisheries.

Committee on treatment of chimney gases at the Townmead Road power station of the Fulham Borough Council.
Report. 13 Feb.1935. 1934/5 Cmd.4885 ix. Ministry of Transport.

Committee on the treatment of flue gases at the Battersea electric power station.
Interim report on tests of proposed treatment. 9 Aug.1929. 1929/30 Cmd. 3442 xvii.
Interim report. 30 Oct.1929 1929/30 Cmd.3442 xvii.
Second report. 22 July 1930. 1930/1 Cmd.3714 xvii.
Further report. 15 Oct.1934. 1934/5 Cmd.4771 ix.
Further report. 21 Jan.1937. 1936/7 Cmd.5572 xv. Ministry of Transport.

ROBERTSON, T.
The economic geology of the central coalfield. Area 1: Kilsyth and Kirkintilloch. 27 July 1937. (Mem.Geol.Surv., Scotl.) Geological Survey, Scotland.

ROBERTSON, Thomas
Report on the administration and working of Indian railways. 5 March 1903. 1903 Cd.1713. xlvii. India Office.

ROBINSON, H.
The pressure wave sent out by an explosion. Part 1. Dec.1925. (S.M.R.B. Paper, no.18) Mines Department.

Spontaneous electrification in coal-dust clouds. March 1931. (S.M.R.B. Paper, no.71) Mines Department.

ROBINSON, Hugh Malcolm
Report on accidents occurring in shipbuilding yards. 1 Aug.1913. 1913 Cd.7046 lx. Home Office.

ROBINSON, Oliver Long
Committee on the employment of pharmacists in the army.
Report. 30 Dec.1921. War Office.

ROBINSON, Roy Lister
Afforestation in the Lake District.
Report by the Joint Informal Committee of the Forestry Commission and the Council for the Preservation of Rural England. July 1936. Forestry Commission.

Protection of the New Forest.
Report of the Committee of planning officers, 1938-9. May 1939. Forestry Commission.

ROBINSON, Thomas Bilbe
Committee on the utilisation of British cattle.
Report, part 1. May 1918; Part 2. October 1919.
Board of Agriculture and Fisheries.

ROBINSON, William Arthur
National council for the administrative and legal
departments of the Civil Service. Committee "A".
Report: Professional and technical grades. 22
June 1925. Civil Service National Whitley
Council. Treasury.

Rockley, *Lord. SEE:* Cecil, Evelyn, *1st Baron*

RODD, James Rennell, *1st Baron Rennell*
Joint committee on the measurement of gas.
Report, proceedings and evidence. 7 July 1936.
1935/6 (140) vi. House of Commons.

RODGER, Alec
A borstal experiment in vocational guidance.
Feb.1937. (I.H.R.B.Rep., no.78) Medical Research
Council.

RODWELL, Cecil
Report on a visit to Pitcairn Island. 25 June 1921.
(Colonial reports, misc., no.93) Colonial Office.

RÖSEMEIER, Herman
A german to Germans; an open letter. April 1916.
Ministry of Information.

ROGERS, James H.
Report on conferences between employers,
operatives and inspectors concerning precautions
necessary for health and safety in tinplate factories.
May 1914. Home Office.

ROGERS, Leonard
Smallpox and climate in India; forecasting of
epidemics. June 1926. (S.R.S., no.106) Medical
Research Council.

Rolfe, Eustace Neville. *SEE:* Neville-Rolfe, E.

ROLLESTON, Humphrey Davy
Committee on manufacture, testing and clinical
administration of salvarsan and its substitutes.
First report. Dec.1919. (S.R.S., no.44)
Second report. June 1922. (S.R.S., no.66)
Medical Research Council.

Committee on vaccination.
Report. 4 Feb.1928. 1928 Cmd.3148 xii.
Further report: observations on the
epidemiology and clinical and pathological
character of post-vaccinal nervous disease. 5
Sept.1930. 1930/1 Cmd.3738 xvii. Ministry of
Health.

Departmental committee on compensation for
industrial diseases.
Report. 16 Nov.1931.
Second report. 12 June 1933.
Third report: Spirochaetal jaundice (Weil's
disease). July 1936. Ministry of Health.

Departmental committee on morphine and heroin
addiction.
Report. 21 Jan.1926. Ministry of Health.

Inter-departmental committee on insurance medical
records.
Report. June 1920. 1920 Cmd.836 xxii. Ministry
of Health.

ROLLESTON, Thomas William
Ireland and Poland; a comparison. 1917. Ministry of
Information.

ROMER, Mark Lemon
Committee on the law of property consolidation
bills.

Report. May 1924. 1924 Cmd.2271 xi. Lord
Chancellor's Office.

ROMER, Robert
Report of an inquiry upon certain byelaws made by
the Port of London Authority as to the licensing of
lightermen and watermen in the Port of London. 15
Jan.1913. 1913 Cd.6700 lx. Board of Trade.

Royal commission on the care and treatment of the
sick and wounded during the South African
campaign.
Report. Jan.1901. 1901 Cd.453 xxix.
Minutes of evidence. 1901 Cd.454 xxix.
Appendix. 1901 Cd.455 xxx.

Ronaldshay, *Earl. SEE:* Dundas, L.J.L., *Earl of
Ronaldshay*

RONALDSON, J.H.
Coal. Sept.1920. (Mono.Min.Resour.) Imperial
Institute.

ROSE, Arthur H.
Commissioner for special areas in Scotland.
Report. July 1935. 1934/5 Cmd.4958 x.
Report. Feb.1935. 1935/6 Cmd.5089 xiii.
Final report. July 1936. 1935/6 Cmd.5245 xiii.
Fourth report. Nov.1937. 1937/8 Cmd.5604 xiii.

Report of investigation into the industrial conditions
in certain depressed areas. 4: Scotland. 17 July 1934.
1933/4 Cmd.4728 xiii. Ministry of Labour.

ROSE, Frederick
Chemical instruction in Germany and the growth
and present conditions of the German chemical
industries.
Report. 10 July 1901. (Dip.cons.reports:
misc.ser., no.561) 1901 Cd. 430-16 lxxx.

Supplementary report. 25 Jan.1902.
(Dip.cons.reports: misc.ser., no.573) 1902
Cd.787-9 ciii. Foreign Office.

Report on agricultural instruction in Germany and
the development of German agriculture and
agricultural industries. 28 May 1903.
(Dip.cons.reports; misc.ser., no.594) 1903 Cd.1387-
7 lxxvi. Foreign Office.

Report on art-trade schools in Germany. Dec.1904.
(Dip.cons.reports: misc.ser., no.621) 1905 Cd.2237-
2 lxxxvi. Foreign Office.

Report on commercial instruction in Germany. 22
Aug.1904. (Dip.cons.reports: misc.ser., no.619)
1905 Cd.2237 lxxxvi. Foreign Office.

Report on instruction in forestry and the present
condition of forest economy in Germany. 31 July
1903. (Dip.cons.reports: misc.ser., no.596) 1904
Cd.1767 xcvi. Foreign Office.

Report on instruction in mining and metallurgy in
Germany and the German mining and metallurgical
industries. 14 Sept.1903. (Dip.cons.reports:
misc.ser., no.597) 1904 Cd.1767-1 xcvi. Foreign
Office.

Report on the German technical high schools. 1 May
1903. (Dip.cons.reports: misc.ser., no.591) 1903
Cd.1387-4 lxxvi. Foreign Office.

Report on the German veterinary high schools. 19
June 1903. (Dip.cons.reports: misc.ser., no.595)
1903 Cd.1387-8 lxxvi. Foreign Office.

Report on the higher, middle and lower schools of
Würtemberg. 1902. (Dip.cons.reports: misc.ser.,
no.572) 1902 Cd.787-8 ciii. Foreign Office.

ROSE, Frederick (Continued)
Report on the projected Rhine-Neckar-Danube ship canal. 9 May 1904. (Dip.cons.reports: misc.ser., no.613) 1904 Cd.1767-17 xcvi. Foreign Office.

Report on the rise, progress and present condition of the carbide and acetylene industries in Germany. 25 Oct.1900. (Dip.cons.reports: misc.ser., no.540) 1900 Cd.353-5 xci. Foreign Office.

Report on the technical agricultural, industrial, commercial and art schools of Würtemberg. 2 Sept.1901. (Dip.cons.reports: misc.ser., no.566) 1902 Cd.787-22 ciii. Foreign Office.

Report on the technical instruction in Germay: the building and engineering trades' schools. 8 Oct.1903. (Dip.cons.reports: misc.ser., no.600) 1904 Cd.1767-4 xcvi. Foreign Office.

Report on technical instruction in Germany: navigation schools in Germay. 4 May 1904. (Dip.cons. reports: misc.ser., no.611) 1904 Cd.1767-15 xcvi. Foreign Office.

Report on technical instruction in Germany: special schools and courses for mechanical engineering and electro-technics. 15 Nov.1903. (Dip.cons.reports: reports: misc.ser., no.601) 1904 Cd.1767-5 xcvi. Foreign Office.

Report on technical instruction in Germany: special schools for ship engineers. 28 March 1904. (Dip. cons.reports: misc.ser., no.608) 1904 Cd.1767-12 xcvi. Foreign Office.

Report on technical instruction in Germany: special technical schools for the ceramic industries. 21 June 1904. (Dip.cons.reports: misc.ser., no.615) 1904 Cd.1767-19 xcvi. Foreign Office.

Report on technical instruction in Germany: special technical schools for the woodworking industries. 21 July 1904. (Dip.cons.reports: misc.ser., no.618) 1904 Cd.1767-22 xcvi. Foreign Office.

Report on technical education in Germany: supplementary and miscellaneous. (Dip.cons. reports: misc.ser., no.630) 1905 Cd.2237-11 lxxxvi. Foreign Office.

Report on technical instruction in naval architecture and engineering in Germany. 9 April 1904. (Dip.cons.reports: misc.ser., no.609) 1904 Cd.1767-13 xcvi. Foreign Office.

Report on technical schools for special branches of the metal industries. 22 Feb.1904. (Dip.cons.reports: misc.ser., no.603) 1904 Cd.1767-7 xcvi. Foreign Office.

Report on the textile technical schools and the development of the textile industries. 23 Jan.1904. (Dip.cons. reports: misc.ser., no.602) 1904 Cd.1767-6 xcvi. Foreign Office.

ROSE, Hugh Aurthur
Advisory council report on the organisation of day schools and of continuation schools and classes under the Education (Scotland) Act, 1918. 22 Dec.1922. Scottish Education Department.

Commissioner for special areas in Scotland.
Report. July 1935. 1934/5 Cmd.4958 x.
Report. Feb.1936. 1935/6 Cmd.5089 xiii.
Final report. July 1936. 1935/6 Cmd.5245 xiii.
Ministry of Labour.

ROSE, John Holland
Why we carry on. 1918. Ministry of Information.

ROSE, Thomas Kirke
Tin and tungsten research board.
Report. 21 March 1922. Department of Scientific and Industrial Research.

Rosebery, *Lord. SEE:* Primrose, A.P., *5th Earl*

ROSS, Alexander C.
Report on quebracho and cotton in the Argentine Chaco. 12 July 1905. (Dip.cons.reports: misc.ser., no.639) 1906 Cd.2683-3 cxxii. Foreign Office.

ROSS, John, *1st Bt.*
Vice-regal commission on the re-organisation and pay of the Irish police forces.
Report. 2 Dec.1919. 1920 Cmd.603 xxii. Irish Secretary's Office.

ROSS, Ronald
Report on the prevention of malaria in Cyprus. 4 June 1913. 1914 Cd.7174 lx. Colonial Office.

ROSS, William David.
Board of inquiry into the wages and hours of work in the wool textile industry in Yorkshire.
Report. 27 Nov.1936. Ministry of Labour.

Departmental committee on compensation for card room workers.
Report. 15 Dec.1938. Home Office.

ROSS-TAYLOR, Joshua P.
Scottish housing advisory committee.
Report on rural housing in Scotland. 27 Feb.1937. 1936/7 Cmd.5462 xi. Scottish Office.

ROSSE, Lawrence Parsons, *4th Earl of Rosse*
Committee on the working of the London County Council generating station at Greenwich in its relation to the Royal Observatory.
Report. 17 Dec.1906. 1907 Cd.3290 xxi. Royal Greenwich Observatory.

Roundhay, *1st Baron Nicholson of SEE:* Nicholson, W.G. 1st Baron Nicholson

ROWE, H.V.
Enquiry respecting escapes of patients from London County Council asylums situate upon the Horton Estate at Epsom.
Report by the Commissioners in Lunacy. 3 Feb.1908. 1909 Cd.4591 xxxi. Home Office.

ROWLATT, Sidney Arthur Taylor
Committee on revolutionary conspiracies in India.
Report. Oct.1918. 1918 Cd.9190 viii. India Office.

Departmental committee on the simplification of income tax and super-tax forms.
Report. 23 July 1923. 1924 Cmd.2019 xi. Treasury.

Royal commission on lotteries and betting.
Interim report. 5 Jan.1933. 1932/3 Cmd.4234 xiv.
Final report. 1 June 1933. 1932/3 Cmd.4341 xiv.
Minutes of evidence 1932-3.
Selection from statements. 1933.
Index. 1933.

ROWSELL, Philip F.
Standing committee on trusts. Sub-committee on glass bottles and jars and scientific glassware.
Interim report. 22 Nov.1920. 1920 Cmd.1066 xxiii.
Final report. 12 May 1921. 1921 Cmd.1385 xvi. Board of Trade.

RUDLER, F.W.
Handbook to the collection of the minerals of the British Islands. 21 Dec.1904. Geological Survey.

RUDOLF, Robert de Montjoie
Short histories of the territorial regiments of the British Army. May 1905. War Office.

RUEGG, Alfred Henry
Report on the application of the Factory and Workshop Act, 1901, to florists' workshops. Nov.1909. 1909 Cd.4932 xxi. Home Office.

Report on the draft regulations for the hours of employment of winding enginemen. 9 March 1913. 1913 Cd.6568 xxvi. Home Office.

Report on the draft regulations for the manufacture and decoration of pottery. 31 Dec.1912. 1912/3 Cd.6710 xxxv. Home Office.

RUFFIN, Henry
Brother Tommy; the British offensives on the western front, January to June 1917. 1917. Ministry of Information.

RUGGLES-BRISE, Evelyn John
Report on the proceedings of the fifth and sixth International Penitentiary Congresses. 1901. 1901 Cd.573 xxxiii. Home Office.

Report on the proceedings of the seventh International Penitentiary Congress held at Budapesth. Feb.1906. 1906 Cd.2849 li. Home Office.

Report on the proceedings of the eighth International Penitentiary Congress held at Washington, October, 1910. 1911. 1911 Cd.5593 xxxix. Home Office.

RULE, Frank Gordon
Report on a journey made fron Chinde to Tete (Angola). Jan.1914. (Dip.cons.reports: misc.ser., no.686) 1914 Cd.7049-1 lxxxix. Foreign Office *and* Board of Trade.

RUMBOLD, Horace
Report on British trade with Egypt during the years 1895-1900. 5 June 1901. (Dip.cons.reports: misc.ser., no.557) 1901 Cd.430-12 lxxx. Foreign Office.

RUMBOLD, W.G.
Nickel ores. 1923. (Mono.Min.Resour.) Imperial Institute.

Bauxite and aluminium. 1925. (Mono.Min.Resour.) Imperial Institute.

RUNCIMAN, Walter
Departmental committee on examinations of masters and mates.
Report. 1 Aug.1928. Board of Trade.

Departmental committee on Irish land purchase finance.
Report. 18 Feb.1908. 1908 Cd.4005 xxiii. Treasury.

Departmental committee on the accounts of local authorities.
Vol.1: Report. 8 July 1907. 1907 Cd.3614 xxxvii.
Vol.2: Minutes of evidence, digest and index. 1907 Cd.3615 xxxvii. Local Government Board.

Memorandum on agricultural education in England and Wales. 22 Sept.1909. 1909 Cd.4886 xlvii.
Revised arrangements. 19 Jan.1912. 1912/3 Cd.6039 lxv. Board of Agriculture and Fisheries.

RUSSELL, Alison
Commission on the disturbances in the Copperbelt,

Northern Rhodesia.
Report. Oct.1935. 1934/5 Cmd.5009 vii. Colonial Office.

RUSSELL, Charles Alfred
Safeguarding of industries committee.
Report on glass bottles. 1 Aug.1922. Board of Trade.

RUSSELL, Charles E.B.
Libraries for reformatory and industrial schools. 1 May 1916. Home Office.

Report on the school training and early employment of Lancashire children. Nov.1903. (Special reports on educational subjects) Board of Education.

RUSSELL, Dorothy Stuart
A classification of Bright's disease. 30 Nov.1929. (S.R.S., no.142) Medical Research Council.

RUSSELL, E.S.
Report on the cephalopoda collected by the research steamer S.S. "Goldseeker" during the years 1903-1908. 1921. (Sci.invest., no.3, 1921) Fishery Board of Scotland.

RUSSELL, Thomas Wallace
Departmental committee on food production in Ireland.
Report. 14 Aug.1915. 1914/6 Cd.8046 v.
Evidence, deliberative conferences and appendices. 1914/6 Cd.8158 v. Department of Agriculture and Technical Instruction for Ireland.

Select committee on hospitals (exemption from rates).
Report, proceedings, minutes of evidence, appendix and index. 13 July 1900. 1900 (273) vii. House of Commons.

RUSSELL, W.T.
Appendicitis; a statistical study. 10 Feb.1939. (S.R.S., no.233) Medical Research Council.

RYAN, Gerald Hemmington
Departmental committee on approved society finance and administration.
Interim report. 11 May 1916. 1916 Cd.8251 xiv.
Further report. 27 Oct.1916. 1916 Cd.8396 xiv.
Final report. 14 Dec.1916. 1917/8 Cd.8451 xvii. Treasury.

RYKATCHEFF, M.
Commission for terrestrial magnetism and atmospheric electricity.
Report of the sixth meeting, Berlin, 23-24 September, 1910. 1912. (M.O. 208) Meteorological Office.

SACKVILLE, Herbrand Edward Dundonald Brassey, *9th Earl De La Warr*.
Commission on higher education in East Africa.
Report. 23 Sept.1937. (Colonial, no.142) Colonial Office.

Committee on nutrition in the colonial Empire.
First report. Part 1: Nutrition in the colonial Empire. 12 June 1939. 1938/9 Cmd.6050 x.
First report. Part 2: Summary of information. July 1939. 1938/9 Cmd. 6051 x. (No other reports identified) Economic Advisory Council. Treasury.

Committee on the slaughtering of livestock.
Report. 15 July 1932. Economic Advisory Council. Treasury.

SACKVILLE: Herbrand Edward Dundonald Brassey, *9th Earl de La Warr.* (Continued)
> Report of the United Kingdom delegates to the League of Nations, 19th assembly. 1 Dec.1938. (Misc., no.10, 1938) 1938/9 Cmd.5899 xxvii. Foreign Office.

SACKVILLE, Sackville George Stafford
Military Manoeuvres Commission, 1913.
> Report. Dec.1913. 1914 Cd.7183 li. War Office.

SADLER, Michael Ernest
Commission on the University of Calcutta.
> Report.
>> Vol.1-3, part 1: Analysis of present conditions. 1919 Cmd.386, Cmd.387, Cmd.388 xiv, xv.
>> Vol.4-5, part 2: Recommendations. 18 March 1919. 1919 Cmd.389, Cmd.390 xv, xvi. India Office.

St. Aldwyn, *Lord. SEE:* Hicks-Beach, M.E., *1st Viscount.*

St. Ledgers, *Lord Ashby. SEE:* Guest, I.C., *1st Baron Ashby St.Ledgers.*

SALAMAN, Meyer
Some experiments on peripheral vision. 2 Aug.1929. (S.R.S., no.136) Medical Research Council.

Salisbury, *Lord. SEE:* Cecil, J.E.H.G., *4th Marquess of Salisbury.*

SALMON, Isidore
Departmental committee on the employment of prisoners.
> Report.
>> Part 1: Employment of prisoners. Nov.1933. 1933/4 Cmd.4462 xv.
>> Part 2: Employment on discharge. 29 April 1935. 1934/5 Cmd.4897 xi. Home Office.

SALT, J.S.A.
A simple method of surveying from air photographs. 8 June 1932. (Prof. Papers of the Air Survey Committee, no.8)
Parallax tables, supplement to no.8. War Office.

SALTER, Arthur Clavell
Certificates of naturalisation (revocation) committee.
> Report on the case of Sir Edgar Speyer. 28 Nov.1921. 1922 Cmd.1569 vii. Home Office.

SALTER, James Arthur
Conference on rail and road transport.
> Report. 29 July 1932. Ministry of Transport.

SALVESEN, Edward Theodore
Committee on education and industry in Scotland.
> First report. 24 Jan.1927.
> Second report. March 1928. Ministry of Labour.
Departmental committee on minor legal appointments in Scotland.
>> Vol.1: report. 11 March 1911. 1911 Cd.5602 xxxv.
>> Vol.2: minutes of evidence and index. 1911 Cd.5603 xxxv. Scottish Office.
Departmental committee on puerperal morbidity and mortality.
> Report. April 1924. Scottish Office.

SAMBON, Louis Westeura
Reports on pellagra in the West Indies. 9 Feb.1915 and 17 March 1917. 1917/8 Cd.8796 xviii. Colonial Office.

SAMPSON, Hugh Charles
Report on development of agriculture in the Bahamas. June 1931. (E.M.B. 40) Empire Marketing Board.

Report on development of agriculture in British Guiana. Nov.1927. (E.M.B. 4) Empire Marketing Board.

Report on development of agriculture in British Honduras. May 1929. (E.M.B. 16) Empire Marketing Board.

Report on development of agriculture in the Leeward and Windward Islands and Barbados. Nov.1927. (E.M.B. 5) Empire Marketing Board.

Report on development of agriculture in Trinidad. Nov.1927. (E.M.B. 3) Empire Marketing Board.

SAMSON, Edward Marlay
Report of the public inquiry into the conduct of the East Ham Local War Pensions Committee. 19 Jan.1920. 1920 Cmd.575 xxx. Ministry of Pensions.

SAMUEL, Herbert Louis
Advisory committee on liquor trade finance, England and Wales.
> Report on proposals for the state purchase of the licensed liquor trade. April 1916. 1916 Cd.8283 xii. Home Office.
Departmental committee on compensation for industrial diseases.
> Report. 15 May 1907. 1907 Cd.3495 xxxiv.
> Minutes of evidence, appendices and index. 1907 Cd.3496 xxxiv.
> Second report. 12 Oct.1908. 1908 Cd.4386 xxxv.
> Minutes of evidence and appendix. 1908 Cd.4387 xxxv. Home Office.
Departmental committee on the Probation of Offenders Act, 1907.
> Report. 23 Dec.1909. 1910 Cd.5001 xlv.
> Minutes of evidence and appendices. 1910 Cd.5002 xlv. Home Office.
Joint select committee on the stage plays (censorship).
> Report, proceedings, evidence, appendices, and index. 2 Nov.1909. 1909 (303) viii. House of Commons.
Memorandum on steps taken for the prevention and relief of distress due to the war. Aug.1914. 1914 Cd.7603 lxxi.
Royal commission on the coal industry.
> Report. 6 March 1926. 1926 Cmd.2600 xiv.
> Vol.2: Evidence. 2 vols. 1926.
> Vol.3: Appendices and index. 1926. Mines Department.
Select committee on national expenditure.
> Special report. 1 Aug.1917. 1917/8 (125) iii.
> First report. 24 Aug.1917. 1917/8 (151) iii.
> Second report. 13 Dec.1917. 1917/8 (167) iii.
> Third report and proceedings. 5 Feb.1918. 1917/8 (188) iii.
Select committee on national expenditure. (Continued)
> Reports, proceedings and evidence before the sub-committee on the form of public accounts. 6 March to 13 Nov.1918. 1918 (132) iv. House of Commons.

SAMUEL, Stuart
Report on mission to Poland. 2 June 1920. (Misc., no.10, 1920) 1920 Cmd. 647 li. Foreign Office.

SANDAY, William
When should the war end? 1917. Ministry of Information.

SANDBACH, Arthur Edmund
Advisory council committee.
Report on local reconstruction organisations. 31 March 1919. 1919 Cmd. 136 xxix. Ministry of Reconstruction.

SANDERS, Charles John Ough
Committee on load lines.
Report. 13 Aug.1929. Board of Trade.

SANDERS, Robert
Select committee on the election of a member (unemployment insurance umpire).
Report and proceedings. 25 June 1925. 1924/5 (131) vii. House of Commons.

SANDERSON, Thomas Henry, *1st Baron Sanderson*
Committee on emigration from India to the Crown Colonies and Protectorates.
Part 1: Report. 26 April 1910. 1910 Cd.5192 xxvii.
Part 2: Minutes of evidence. 1910 Cd.5193 xxvii.
Part 3: Papers laid before the committee. 1910 Cd.5194 xxvii. Colonial Office.

SANGER, Ernest
Departmental committee on London cleansing.
Report. May 1930. 1929/30 Cmd.3613 xv. Ministry of Health.

SANKARAN NAIR, Chettur
Indian constitutional reforms central committee.
Report. 18 Oct.1929. 1929/30 Cmd.3451 x.
Supplementary note by A.A. Suhrawardy. 18 Feb.1930. 1929/30 Cmd.3525 x. India Office.

SANKEY, John, *1st Viscount*
Coal industry commission (Royal).
Interim report. 20 March 1919. 1919 Cmd. 84 xi.
Report by R. Smillie (and others). 20 March 1919. 1919 Cmd. 85 xi.
Interim report by R.W. Cooper (and others). 20 March 1919. 1919 Cmd. 86 xi.
Second stage reports. 20 June 1919. 1919 Cmd. 210 xi.
Vol.1: Reports and evidence on the first stage of the inquiry. 20 March 1919. 1919 Cd. 359 xi.
Vol.2: Reports and evidence on the second stage of the inquiry. 20 June 1919. 1919 Cmd. 360 xii.
Vol.3: Appendices, charts and index. 1919 Cmd. 361 xiii, pt.1.
Select committee on gas, electricity and water undertakings.
Proceedings, evidence, speeches and appendices, 9-19 May 1939. 27 Sept.1939. 1938/9 (H.L. 216) v. House of Lords.

SAPRU, Tej Bahadur
Committee on the Press and Registration of Books Act, 1867, the Indian Press Act, 1910 and the Newspaper (Incitement to Offences) Act, 1908 (the Press Acts).
Report. Aug.1921. 1921 Cmd.1489 x. India Office.

Committee on racial distinctions in Indian criminal procedure.
Report. 14 June 1922. 1923 Cmd.1823 x. India Office.

SARGANT, Charles
Departmental committee on the Patents and Designs Acts and the practice of the Patent Office.
Report. 14 March 1931. 1930/1 Cmd.3829 xvi.
Minutes of evidence. 1931. Board of Trade.

SARGENT, Arthur J.
British industries and Empire markets. March 1930.

(E.M.B. 26) Empire Marketing Board.

SARGENT, E.B.
Report on native education in South Africa. Part III: Education in the protectorates. March 1908. 1908 Cd.4119 lxx. (Colonial reports, misc., no.62) Colonial Office.

SAUNDERS, Owen A.
The calculation of heat transmission. July 1931. Department of Scientific and Industrial Research.

SAVAGE, Edward Graham
Physical education in Germany. June 1937. (Educational pamphlets, no.104) Board of Education.

Secondary education in the states of New York and Indiana. Jan.1928. (Educational pamphlets, no.56) Board of Education.

SAVAGE, George
Report on the treatment of William Ball in Pentonville Prison and the circumstances connected with his removal to Colney Hatch Asylum. 23 April 1912. 1912/3 Cd.6175 lxix. Home Office.

SAVAGE, William George
Canned fruit. Nov.1923. (F.I.B. special rep., no.16) Department of Scientific and Industrial Research.
Food poisoning; a study of 100 recent outbreaks. 30 Jan.1925. (S.R.S., no.92) Medical Research Council.
An investigation of the salmonella group with special reference to food poisoning. 15 Dec.1924. (S.R.S., no.91) Medical Research Council.
Report on bacterial food poisoning and food infections. July 1913. (Rep.Pub.Health & Med.Subj., no.77) Local Government Board.
Report on the methods used for the inspection of canned foods and their reliability. Sept.1920. (F.I.B. special rep., no.3)
Part 2: Canned marine products. March 1922. (F.I.B. special rep., no.10) Department of Scientific and Industrial Research.
Studies in sweetened and unsweetened (evaporated) condensed milk. 25 July 1923. (F.I.B. special rep., no.13) Department of Scientific & Industrial Research.

SAWYER, L. Doris
Some regions of formation of depressions in the North Atlantic. Sept.1928. (Prof.Notes, no.50) Meteorological Office.

SCHAFFER, R.J.
The weathering of natural stones. Sept.1931. (B.R.B. special rep., no.18) Department of Scientific and Industrial Research.

SCHLOSS, David F.
Report on agencies and methods for dealing with the unemployed in certain foreign countries. Oct.1904. 1905 Cd.2304 lxxiii. Board of Trade.

Report on collective agreements between employers and work people in the United Kingdom. Sept.1910. 1910 Cd.5366 xx. Board of Trade.

Report on profit-sharing and co-partnership in the United Kingdom. Nov.1912. 1912/3 Cd.6496 xliii. Board of Trade.

SCHOLEFIELD, G.H.
New Zealand. 1917. Ministry of Information.

SCHRYVER, G.S.
Report on the presence of tin in certain canned foods. 18 Dec.1908. (Rep.Insp.Foods, no.7) Local Government Board.

SCHRYVER, S.B.
Report on the changes in certain meat essences kept for several years in tins. 4 Dec.1906. (Rep.Insp. Foods, no.1) Local Government Board.

Report on the application of formaldehyde to meat. 28 July 1909. (Rep.Pub.Health & Med.Subj., no.12) Local Government Board.

SCHUSTER, Claud
Committee on fees and duties payable to public funds on the grant of honours and dignities.
Interim report. 19 April 1937. 1936/7 Cmd.5450 xi.
Final report. 31 May 1938. 1937/8 Cmd.5676 xii. Treasury.

Departmental committee on the effect of the law against perpetuities in its application to certain superannuation funds and funds with analogous purposes.
Report. 19 July 1927. 1927 Cmd.2918 xi. Treasury.

Departmental committee on sickness benefit claims under the National Insurance Act.
Report. 24 July 1914. 1914/6 Cd.7687 xxx.
Appendix.
Vol.1: Evidence, 15 October to 18 December 1913. 1914/6 Cd. 7688 xxx.
Vol.2: Evidence, 31 December 1913 to 5 March 1914. 1914/6 Cd.7689 xxx.
Vol.3: Evidence, 11 March to 22 May 1914. 1914/6 Cd.7690 xxxi.
Vol.4: Index to the evidence. 1914/6 Cd.7691 xxxi. National Health Insurance Joint Committee.

Inter-departmental committee on admission of women to the diplomatic and consular services.
Report and government statement. 30 July 1934. 1935/6 Cmd.5166 xxvii. Foreign Office.

Poor persons (divorce jurisdication) committee.
Report. 25 July 1929. 1929/30 Cmd.3375 xvii. Lord Chancellor's Office.

SCHUSTER, E.H.J.
Apparatus for the rapid study of ultra violet absorption spectra. 6 Dec.1933. (S.R.S., no.177) Medical Research Council.

SCHUSTER, George
Joint committee of enquiry into the Anglo-Argentine meat trade.
Report. 25 April 1938. 1937/8 Cmd.5839 viii. Board of Trade.

SCHWABACH, Paul
Report on agriculture in Germany. 1 Feb.1906. (Dip.cons.reports: misc.ser, no.645) 1906 Cd.2683-9 cxxii. Foreign Office.

Report on the new imperial German mortgage bank law. Jan.1900. (Dip.cons.reports: misc.ser., no.521) 1900 Cd.2-4 xci. Foreign Office.

SCOBY-SMITH, G.
Departmental committee on the iron and steel trades after the war.
Report. 13 June 1917. 1918 Cd.9071 xiii. Board of Trade.

SCOTT, Alexander
Ball clays. 1 March 1929. (Special reports on the mineral resources of Great Britain, vol.31) (Mem.Geol. Surv.) Geological Survey.

Refractory materials: fireclays.
Analyses and physical tests. 8 May 1924. (Special reports on the mineral resources of Great Britain, vol.28) (Mem.Geol.Surv.) Geological Survey.

SCOTT, Angus Newton
Royal commission on local government in the Tyneside area.
Report. 23 Feb.1937. 1936/7 Cmd.5402 xiii. Home Office.

SCOTT, Charles Mervyn
Some quantitative aspects of the biological action of X and Y (gamma) rays. 18 June 1937. (S.R.S., no.223) Medical Research Council.

SCOTT, Harold
Russian banks and communist funds.
Report of an enquiry into certain transactions of the Bank for Russian Trade, Ltd., and the Moscow Narodny Bank, Ltd., with a memorandum by the Moscow Norodny Bank. 1 June 1928. 1928 Cmd.3125 xii. Home Office.

SCOTT, Harold Claughton
Committee on copyright royalty (mechanical musical instruments).
Report. 19 May 1928. 1928 Cmd.3122 vii. Board of Trade.

SCOTT. Henry Harold
Tuberculosis in man and lower animals. 25 Sept.1930. (S.R.S., no.149) Medical Research Council.

SCOTT, John Charles Montagu-Douglas, *7th Duke of Buccleuch*
Committee on game and heather-burning in Scotland.
Report. 4 July 1921. 1921 Cmd.1401 xii. Scottish Office.

SCOTT, Leslie Frederick
Advisory council (section iv).
Report on the employment on the land of returned sailors and solders. 20 Dec.1918. Ministry of Reconstruction.

Committee on ministers' powers.
Report. 17 March 1932. 1931/2 Cmd.4060 xii.
Memoranda submitted by government departments and minutes of evidence.
Vol.1: Memoranda. 1932.
Vol.2: Minutes of evidence. 1932. Lord Chancellor's Office.

Committee on the law and practice of acquisition and valuation of land for public purposes.
First report. 9 Jan.1918. 1918 Cd.8998 xi.
Second report. 20 Nov.1918. 1918 Cd.9229 xi.
Third report: Acquisition, for public purposes, of rights and powers in connection with mines and minerals. 18 March 1919. 1919 Cmd.156 xxix.
Fourth report: Transfer of land in England and Wales. 6 Nov.1919. 1919 Cmd.424 xxix. Ministry of Reconstruction.

Great Britain and neutral commerce. 1915. Ministry of Information.

Report of British delegates at the International Maritime Conference, Brussels, 17-26 October 1922. 13 Dec.1922. Board of Trade.

SCOTT, Robert Russell.
Reorganisation committee. Civil Service National Whitley Council. Sub-committee on temporary staffs.
Report. 24 Feb.1920. Treasury.

SCOTT, Thomas
Notes on small crustacea from the "Goldseeker" collections. 1911. (Sci.Invest., 1911, no.1) Fishery Board for Scotland.

Scott, W.G.H., *Master of Polwarth. SEE:* Hepburne-Scott, W.G., *Master of Polwarth.*

SCOTT, W.R.
Economics of small farms and small-holdings in Scotland.
Interim report. Dec.1919. (no further identified) Report on agricultural credit and organisation in France, with suggestions for a Scottish scheme of agricultural credit. June 1920. Board of Agriculture for Scotland.

Fishing industry committee.
Report. 27 Dec.1931. 1931/2 Cmd.4012 ix. Economic Advisory Council. Treasury.

Report on home industries in the highlands and islands of Scotland. 13 Oct.1913. 1914 Cd.7564 xxxii. Board of Agriculture for Scotland.

SCOTT-MONCRIEFF, Colin Campbell
Committee on fisheries of Great Britain and Ireland (ichthylogical research).
Report, evidence, etc. Sept.1902. 1902 Cd.1312 xv. Board of Agriculture and Fisheries.

India irrigation commission, 1901-1903. Report. 11 April 1903.
Part I: General. 1904 Cd.1851 lxvi.
Part II: Provincial. 1904 Cd.1852 lxvi.
Part III: Maps. 1904 Cd.1853 lxvi.
Part IV: Appendix. 1904 Cd.1854 lxvi. India Office.

SCOTTER, Charles
Royal commission on Irish railways.
First report. 9 July 1907. 1907 Cd.3632 xxxvii.
Appendix, minutes of evidence and documents. 1907 Cd.3633 xxxvii.
Second report. 13 Jan.1908. 1908 Cd.3895 xlvii.
Appendix, minutes of evidence and documents. 1908 Cd.3896 xlvii.
Third report. 25 April 1908. 1908 Cd.4053 xlviii.
Appendix, minutes of evidence and documents. 1908 Cd.4054 xlviii.
Fourth report. 4 July 1908. 1908 Cd.4204 xlviii.
Appendix, minutes of evidence and documents. 1908 Cd.4205 xlviii.
Vol.5: Fourth report. Second appendix: minutes of evidence and documents. 1909 Cd.4481 xxvii.
Vol.6: Fifth and final report.4 July 1910. 1910 Cd.5247 xxxvii.
Vol.7: Appendix to the final report, minutes of evidence and documents relating thereto. 1910 Cd.5248 xxxvii. Irish Secretary's Office.

SCRASE, F.J.
The air-earth current at Kew Observatory. Jan.1933. (Geophys.Mem., no.58) Meteorological Office.

The charged and uncharged nuclei in the atmosphere and their part in atmospheric ionisation. Feb.1935. (Geophys.Mem., no.64) Meteorological Office.

Electricity on rain; a discussion of records obtained at Kew Observatory, 1935-6. Aug.1938. (Geophys.Mem., no.75) Meteorological Office.

Observations of atmospheric electricity at Kew Observatory, 1843-1931. April 1934. (Geophys.Mem., no.60) Meteorological Office.

Point discharge in the electric field of the earth. May 1936. (Geophys. Mem., no.68) Meteorological Office.

Some characterisitics of Eddy motion in the atmosphers. Nov.1930. (Geophys.Mem., no.52) Meteorological Office.

Some measurements of the variation of potential gradient with height near the ground at Kew Observatory. July 1935. (Geophys.Mem., no.67) Meteorological Office.

Two notes on the operation of Galitzin seismographs. Feb.1930. (Geophys.Mem., no.49) Meteorological Office.

SCRIVENOR, J.B.
The geology of the country near Newquay. (Sheet 346) 10 Nov.1906. (Mem.Geol.Surv.) Geological Survey.

SCUDDER, Frank
Report on air tests in humid cotton weaving sheds. 20 May 1904. 1904 Cd. 2135 x. Home Office.

SEAGER, William Henry
South Wales regional survey committee.
Report. 28 Sept.1920. Ministry of Health.

SEARS, John Edward
Report on the comparisons of the Parliamentary copies of the Imperial Standards with the Imperial Standard yard and pound and with each other. March 1929. 1929/30 Cmd.3507 xiv. Board of Trade.

SEELY, John Edward Bernard
Committee of inquiry into the organisation of the Crown Agents' Office.
Report. 10 Dec.1908. 1909 Cd.4473 xvi.
Minutes of evidence and appendices. 1909 Cd.4474 xvi. Colonial Office.

SEELY, John Edward Bernard
Report of the military manoeuvres commission, 1925. 12 Oct.1925. 1924/5 Cmd.2569 xvii. War Office.

Select committee on the Expiring Laws Continuance Act.
Report, proceedings, evidence and appendices. 21 July 1922. 1922 (152) v. House of Commons.

SELBIE, William Boothby
Christian nationalism. 1917. Ministry of Information.

Selborne, *Lord. SEE:* Palmer, W.W., *2nd Earl Selborne*

Selby, *Lord. SEE:* Gully, W.C., *1st Viscount Selby.*

SELBY-BIGGE, Lewis Amherst
Departmental committee on the cost of school buildings.
Report and abstracts of evidence. 6 Dec.1910. 1911 Cd.5534 xvii. Board of Education.

Departmental committee on the superannuation of local government employees.
Report. 19 Dec.1927. Ministry of Health.

Report of the Imperial Education Conference, 1923. Sept.1924. Board of Education.

Selsdon, *Baron. SEE:* Mitchell-Thomson, W.

SEN, Sachindra Nath
A comparison of the anemometer records for Shoeburyness and Maplin lighthouse. July 1922. (Prof.Notes, no.28) Meteorological Office.

On the design of the Kew pattern barometer. Nov.1925. (Geophys. Mem., no.27) Meteorological Office.

SEN, Sachindra Nath (continued)
Surface and geostrophic wind components at Deerness, Holyhead, Great Yarmouth and Scilly. March 1925. (Geophys.Mem., no.25) Meteorological Office.

SEYMOUR, Frank
Report on lead poisoning in Guisborough U.D. and its relation to the public water supply. 9 Dec.1913. (Rep.Pub.Health & Med.Subj., no.86) Local Government Board.

SHACKLETON, David James.
Departmental committee on out-workers in relation to unemployment insurance.
Report. May 1923. Ministry of Labour.

Shaftsbury, *Lord. SEE:* Ashley-Cooper, A., *9th Earl Shaftesbury.*

SHAKESPEARE, Geoffrey Hithersay
Inter-departmental committee on the reception of children overseas.
Report. June 1940. 1939/40 Cmd.6213 v. Dominion Affairs Office *and* Ministry of Health.

SHAKESPEARE, John Howard
Two republics. 1918. Ministry of Information.

SHAW, Alexander
Great Britain and neutral commerce. 1915. Ministry of Information.

SHAW, James J.
Commission on the loss of the regalia of the order of Saint Patrick.
Report. 25 Jan.1908. 1908 Cd.3906 xi. Appendix: minutes of evidence. 1908 Cd.3936 xi. Irish Secretary's Office.

SHAW, Thomas, *Baron Shaw of Dunfermline*
Departmental committee on state purchase and control of the liquor trade in Scotland.
Report. 24 Dec.1917. 1918 Cd.9042 xi. Scottish Office.

Departmental committee on the Truck Acts.
Vol.1: Report and appendices. 14 Dec.1908. 1908 Cd.4442 lix.
Vol.2: Minutes of evidence. 1908 Cd.4443 lix.
Vol.3: Minutes of evidence and index. 1908 Cd.4444 lix.
Vol.4: Precis and appendices. 1909 Cd.4568 xlix. Home Office.

Report of a court of inquiry concerning transport workers' wages and conditions of employment of dock labour. 30 March 1920. 1920 (55) xxiv.
Vol.1: Report and minutes of evidence. 30 March 1920. 1920 Cmd.936 xxiv.
Vol.2: Appendices, documents and indexes. 1920 Cmd.937 xxiv. Ministry of Labour.

Royal commission of the landing of arms at Howth (Ireland) on 26 July 1914.
Report. 4 Sept.1914. 1914/6 Cd.7631 xxiv. Minutes of evidence, appendices and index. 1914/6 Cd.7649 xxiv.

SHAW, Walter Sidney
Commission on the Palestine disturbances of August, 1929.
Report. 12 March 1930. 1929/30 Cmd.3530 xvi. Evidence and a selection of exhibits with an index. 3 vols. (Colonial, no.48) 1930. Colonial Office.

SHAW, William Napier
Commission for the exploration of the upper air.

Report of the Leipzig meeting, 29 August to 3 September 1927. April 1928. (M.O.300) Meteorological Office.

Report of the London meeting, 16 to 22 April 1925. Dec.1925. (M.O.281) Meteorological Office.

The life history of surface air currents; a study of the surface trajectories of moving air. March 1906. (M.O.174) Meteorological Office.

International meteorological committee.
Report of the eighth meeting, Paris, September 1907. Dec.1908. (M.O.197) Meteorological Office.
Report of the ninth meeting, Berlin, 1910. Feb.1912. (M.O.208) Meteorological Office.
Report of the tenth meeting, Rome, 1913. April 1914. (M.O.216) Meteorological Office.

Report on proceedings of the commission for weather telegraphy, 17 to 20 September 1912. Jan.1913. (M.O.211) Meteorological Office.

The travel of circular depressions and tornadoes. April 1918. (Geophys. Mem., no.12) Meteorological Office.

SHAW, William Vernon
Report on an epidemic of enteric fever at Bolton-upon Dearne. April 1922. (Rep.Pub.Health & Med.Subj., no.12) Ministry of Health.

Report of an outbreak of enteric fever in the county borough of Bournemouth and in the boroughs of Poole and Christchurch. April 1937. (Rep.Pub.Health & Med.Subj., no.81) Ministry of Health.

Report on an outbreak of enteric fever in the Malton U.D. Dec.1932. (Rep.Pub.Health & Med.Subj., no.69) Ministry of Health.

Report on an outbreak of paratyphoid fever in Hertfordshire. May 1928. (Rep.Pub.Health & Med.Subj., no.53) Ministry of Health.

Report on an outbreak of paratyphoid fever in the borough of Chorley. Jan.1925. (Rep.Pub.Health & Med.Subj., no.30) Ministry of Health.

SHAXBY, J. H.
Localisation of sounds in the median plane. 1931. (S.R.S., no.166) Medical Research Council.

SHEARMAN, Montagu
Army council (Halakite) enquiry.
Interim and final reports. 29 March and 10 May 1917. 1917/8 Cd.8446 iv. War Office.

SHELLEY, A. N. C.
Committee on the standardisation and simplification of the requirements of local authorities.
Report. 29 March 1934.
Second report. 4 May 1935. Ministry of Health.

SHENNAN, Timothy
Dissecting aneurysms. 19 Dec.1933. (S.R.S., no.193) Medical Research Council.

SHEPHERD, W. C. F.
The ignition of gases by hot wires. June 1927. (S.M.R.B. Paper, no.36) Mines Department.

The pressure wave sent out by an explosive.
Part 2. July 1926. (S.M.R.B. Paper, no.29) Mines Department. *For part 1. SEE:* Robinson, H. *and* Payman, W.

SHERLOCK, R. L.
British regional geology: London and Thames Valley. 1935. Geological Survey.

The geology of the country around Aylesbury and Hemel Hempstead. (Sheet 238) 28 Sept.1922. (Mem.Geol.Surv.) Geological Survey.

The geology of the country around Beaconsfield. (Sheet 255) 23 June 1922. (Mem.Geol.Surv.) Geological Survey.

The geology of the country around Hertford. (Sheet 239) 4 July 1924. (Mem.Geol.Surv.) Geological Survey.

Guide to the geological column exhibited in the Museum of Practical Geology. Oct.1938. Geological Survey.

Gypsum and anhydrite and celestine and strontionite. 5 Dec.1915. (Special reports on the mineral resources of Great Britain, vol.3) (Mem.Geol,Surv.) Geological Survey.

Rock-salt and brine. 7 March 1921. (Special reports on the mineral resources of Great Britain, vol.17) (Mem.Geol.Surv.) Geological Survey.

SHERRIFF, Catherine W. M.
Herring investigations.
Report on the mathematical analysis of random samples. 1922. (Sci. Invest., no.1, 1922) Fishery Board for Scotland.

SHINWELL, Emanuel
Report of the British coal delegation to Sweden, Norway and Denmark, 13 to 25 September 1930. 29 Oct.1930. 1930/1 Cmd.3702 xv. Mines Department.

Report by the British delegates on the International Labour Conference, 14th Session, 10-28 June 1930. Jan.1931. 1930/1 Cmd.3774 xxxv. Ministry of Labour.

Report of the British delegates on the International Labour Conference, 15th Session, Geneva, 28 May to 18 June 1931. March 1932. Ministry of Labour.

SHIPLEY, Arthur Everett
Committee on a tropical agriculture college in the West Indies.
Report. 22 Oct.1919. 1920 Cmd.562 xxv. Colonial Office.

SHIPP, H. L.
The chemistry of flesh foods and their losses on cooking. 12 Oct.1933. (S.R.S., no.187) Medical Research Council.

SHORTHOSE, D. N.
Thermal properties of ethyl chloride. Oct. 1923. (F.I.B., special rep., no.14) Department of Scientific and Industrial Research.

The thermal properties of methyl chloride. March 1924. (F.I.B., special rep., no.19) Department of Scientific and Industrial Research.

SHORTT, Charles S.
Board of guardians of the Chester-le-le-Street union.
Report on administration, 30 August 1926 to 31 December 1926. Feb.1927. 1927 Cmd.2818 xi.
Second report, 1 January 1927 to 30 June 1927. Aug.1927. 1927 Cmd.2937 xii.
Third report, 1 July 1927 to 31 December 1927. 6 March 1928. 1928 Cmd.3072 xii. Ministry of Health.

SHORTT, Edward
Committee on rating of machinery.
Report. 30 Nov.1926. Ministry of Health.

Departmental committee on crowds.
Report. 13 March 1924. 1924 Cmd.2088 viii. Home Office.

Departmental committee on road locomotives and heavy motor cars in Great Britain.
Part 1. Report. 21 Oct.1918. 1919 Cmd.5 xxix.
Part 2. Evidence, appendices and index. 1919 Cmd.6 xxix. Local Government Board.

Departmental committee on sulphuric acid and fertiliser trades.
Report. Feb.1919. 1919 Cmd.23 xxix. Ministry of Munitions.

Departmental committee on the post-war position of the sulphuric acid and fertiliser trades.
Report. Feb.1918. 1918 Cd.8994 xiii. Ministry of Munitions.

Inter-departmental committee on the rating of machinery and plant in England and Scotland.
Report. 6 Feb.1925. 1924/5 Cmd.2340 xv. Ministry of Health *and* Scottish Office.

Select committee on Military Service (Review of Exceptions) Act, 1917.
Special report. 2 Aug.1917. 1917/8 (126) iii.
Report, proceedings, evidence and appendices. 31 Jan.1918. 1917/8 (185) iii. House of Commons.

SHUTE, P. G.
A report on the longevity of mosquitoes in relation to the transmission of malaria in nature. May 1938. (Rep.Pub.Health & Med.Subj., no.85) Ministry of Health.

Shuttleworth, *Lord. SEE:* Kay-Shuttleworth, U. J., *1st Baron Shuttleworth*

SIBLY, T. Franklin
Iron ores; the haematites of the forest of Dean and South Wales. 23 Jan.1919. (Special reports on the mineral resources of Great Britain, vol.10) (Mem.Geol.Surv.) Geological Survey.

SIMON, John Allsebrook
Departmental committee on the Employment of Children Act, 1903.
Report. 30 April 1910. 1910 Cd.5229 xxviii.
Minutes of evidence, appendices and index. 1910 Cd.5230 xxviii. Home Office.

Indian statutory commission.
Interim report. 25 Sept.1929. 1929/30 Cmd.3407 x.
Report:
Vol.1. Survey. 12 May 1930. 1929/30 Cmd.3568 xi.
Vol.2. Recommendations. 27 May 1930. 1929/30 Cmd.2569 xi.
Vol. 3. Reports of the committees appointed by the provincial legislative councils. 1930. 1929/30 Cmd.3572 xii.
Memoranda:
Vols. 4 and 5. The Government of India and the India Office. 1930.
Vol.6. Government of Madras. 1930.
Vol.7. Government of Bombay. 1930.
Vol.8. Government of Bengal. 1930.
Vol.9. Government of the United Provinces. 1930.
Vol.10. Government of the Punjab. 1930.
Vol.11. Government of Burma. 1930.
Vol.12. Government of Bihar and Orissa. 1930.
Vol.13. Government of the Central Provinces. 1930.

SIMON, John Allsebrook (continued)
Vol.14.   Government of Assam. 1930.
Vol.15   Extracts from oral evidence. 1930.
Vols. 16 and 17. Selections from memoranda and oral evidence by non-officials. 1930. India Office.

Report of the (air ship) R.101 inquiry. 27 March 1931. 1930/1 Cmd.3825 x. Air Ministry.

Royal commission on the arrest and subsequent behaviour of Mr. Francis Sheehy Skeffington, Mr. Thomas Dickson and Mr. Patrick James McIntyre.
Report. 29 Sept.1916. 1916 Cd.8376 xi.

SIMON, Shena D.
Committee on the conditions of service of women staff employed in the Navy, Army and Air Force Institutes.
Report. 9 Jan.1931. 1930/1 Cmd.3769 xvii. Ministry of Labour.

SIMONS, R. T.
Report on Pitcairn Island. 1905. 1905 Cd.2342 liii. (Colonial Rep., misc., no.30) Colonial Office.

SIMPKINSON, Henry Walrond
Inter-departmental committee on medical inspection and feeding of children attending public elementary schools.
Vol.I: Report and appendices. 9 Nov.1905. 1906 Cd.2779 xlvii.
Vol.II: Minutes of evidence, appendices and index. 1906 Cd.2784 xlvii. Board of Education.

SIMPSON, George
The system of education in Bermuda. 18 Oct.1912. (Imperial education conference papers) Board of Education.

SIMPSON, George Clark
Commission for the Riseau mondial.
Report of meetings, September 1926. June 1927. (M.O.296) Meteorological Office.

Ice accretion on aircraft; notes for pilots. Oct.1937. (Prof.Notes, no.82) Meteorological Office.

Lightning and aircraft. Aug.1934. (Prof.Notes, no.66) Meteorological Office.

Report on the relation between the estimates of wind-force according to the Beaufort scale and the velocities recorded by anemometers. Feb.1906. (M.O. 180) Meteorological Office.

The velocity equivalents of the Beaufort scale. June 1926. (Prof. Notes, no.44) Meteorological Office.

SIMPSON, J. B.
Barium minerals. 1937. (Rep.Min.Ind.) Imperial Institute.

The economic geology of the Ayrshire coalfields. Area 4: Dailly, Patna, Rankinston, Dalmellington and New Cumnock. 12 Feb.1932. (Mem.Geol.Surv., Scotl.) Geological Survey, Scotland.

The geology of the Sanquhar coalfield and the adjacent basin of Thornhill. 6 March 1936. (Mem.Geol.Surv., Scotl.) Geological Survey, Scotland.

SIMPSON, John Hope
Report on immigration, land settlement and development in Palestine. Oct.1930. 1930/1 Cmd.3686 xvi.
Appendix. 1930/1 Cmd.3687 xvi. Colonial Office.

SIMPSON, Robert John Shaw
Medical history of the war in South Africa; an epidemiological essay. 1911. War Office.

SIMPSON, W. J.
Report on sanitary matters in various West African colonies and the outbreak of plague in the Gold Coast. Aug.1909. 1909 Cd.4718 lxi. Colonial Office.

SINHA, Satyendra Prassano
The future of India; Presidential Address to the Indian National Congress. 27 Dec.1915. Ministry of Information.

SINNATT, Frank Sturdy
The propogation of combustion in powdered coal. Dec.1930. (S.M.R.B. Paper, no.63) Mines Department.

Report of test on the plant of the British Coal Distillation Co. Ltd., Newbold, Leicestershire. Nov.1934. Department of Scientific and Industrial Research.

Report of tests on the Turner retort installed at Comac Oil Co. Ltd., Coalburn, Lanarkshire. Aug.1932. Department of Scientific and Industrial Research.

Report of tests on a retort of the Coal Research Syndicate Ltd., Mansfield Colliery, Mansfield, Nottinghamshire. March 1936. Department of Scientific and Industrial Research.

Report of test on the carbonising plant of Coal and Allied Industries Ltd., at Seaham Harbour, County Durham. Feb.1937. Department of Scientific and Industrial Research.

Report of test on the plant of the National Coke and Oil Co. Ltd., Erith, Kent. June 1937. Department of Scientific and Industrial Research.

Report on a demonstration of the Freeman assay for coal and carbonaceous materials. July 1938. Department of Scientific and Industrial Research.

Report of test on the Morgan rotary retort installed at Rodridge Hall, near Wingate, County Durham. Feb.1938. Department of Scientific and Industrial Research.

SINTON, John Alexander
A report on the longevity of mosquitoes in relation to the transmission of malaria in nature. May 1938. (Rep.Pub.Health & Med.Subj., No.85) Ministry of Health.

A report on the provision and distribution of infective material for the practice of malaria-therapy in England and Wales. May 1938. (Rep.Pub.Health & Med.Subj., no.84) Ministry of Health.

SKEEN, Andrew
Indian Sandhurst committee.
Report. 14 Nov.1926. India Office.

SKELTON, Oscar Douglas
Imperial committee on economic consultation and co-operation.
Report. 11 April 1933. 1932/3 Cmd.4335 xi. Colonial Office.

SKINNER, W.
The system of education in the Leeward Islands. 22 April 1913. (Imperial Education Conference papers) Board of Education.

SLADER, C. H. Yorke
Report on the Cayman Islands. 16 Nov.1906. (Colonial reports: misc., no.39) 1907 Cd.3307 liv. Colonial Office.

SLOSS, Robert
An American's view of the British mail censorship. 1916. Ministry of Information.

SMAIL, James Cameron
    Council for art and industry, Scottish Committee.
        Report on printing and allied trades in
        Scotland. July 1936. Board of Trade.

SMALLMAN, Arthur Briton
    Cancer; memorandum on provision of radio-
    therapeutic departments in general hospitals. March
    1937. (Rep.Pub.Health & Med.Subj., no.79)
    Ministry of Health.

SMITH, A. J. M.
    Bitter pit in apples; a review of the problem.
    Nov.1926. (F.I.B. special rep., no.28) Department
    of Scientific and Industrial Research.

    Experiments on the leakage of carbon dioxide gas
    from "unventilated" holds of ships. Sept.1925.
    (F.I.B. special rep., no.24) Department of Scientific
    and Industrial Research.

    Temperature conditions in refrigerated holds
    carrying apples. Oct.1926. (F.I.B. special rep.,
    no.27) Department of Scientific and Industrial
    Research.

    Temperature conditions in small cold storage
    chambers containing fruit. Nov.1926. (F.I.B.
    special rep., no.29) Department of Scientific and
    Industrial Research.

SMITH, Arthur Lionel
    Committee on adult education.
        Interim report: Industrial and social conditions
        in relation to adult education. 14 March 1918.
        1918 Cd.9107 ix
        Second interim report: Education in the Army.
        3 July 1918. 1918 Cd.9225 ix.
        Third interim report: Libraries and museums. 1
        May 1919. 1918 Cd.9237 ix.
        Final report, appendices and index. 29 July
        1919. 1919 Cmd.321 xxviii. Ministry of
        Reconstruction.

SMITH, Bernard
    British regional geology: North Wales. 1935.
    Geological Survey.

    Gypsum and anhydrite and celestine and
    strontianite. 5 Dec.1915. (special reports on the
    mineral resources of Great Britain, vol.3)
    (Mem.Geol.Surv.) Geological Survey.

    Iron ores: haematites of west Cumberland,
    Lancashire and the Lake District. 18 Nov.1918.
    (Special reports on the mineral resources of Great
    Britain, vol.8) (Mem.Geol.Surv.) Geological Survey.

    Lead and zinc ores in the carboniferous rocks of
    north Wales. 16 March 1921. (Special reports on the
    mineral resources of Great Britain, vol.19)
    (Mem.Geol.Surv.) Geological Survey.

    Lead and zinc ores in the pre-carboniferous rocks of
    Shropshire and north Wales. 1 July 1921. (Special
    reports on the mineral resources of Great Britain,
    vol.23) (Mem.Geol.Surv.) Geological Survey.

    The water supply of Nottinghamshire from
    underground sources. 27 March 1914. (Mem.Geol.
    Surv.) Geological Survey.

SMITH, Cecil Clementi
    Commission of inquiry into the recent disturbances
    at Port of Spain, Trinidad.
        Report. 2 July 1903. 1903 Cd.1662 xliv. colonial
        Office.

SMITH, Cecil H.
    Committee on re-arrangement of the Victoria and
    Albert Museum art division.

Report. 29 July 1908. 1908 Cd.4389 xxix. Board
of Education.

SMITH, Charles Milliken
    Housing conditions and respiratory disease;
    morbidity in a poor-class quarter and in a rehousing
    area in Glasgow. 12 Jan.1934. (S.R.S., no.192)
    Medical Research Council.

SMITH: E. C.
    Post mortem changes in animal tissues; the
    conditioning or ripening of beef. June 1929. (F.I.B.
    special rep., no.36) Department of Scientific and
    Industrial Research.

    The storage of meat in small refrigerators.
    Aug.1933. (F.I.B. special rep., no.43) Department
    of Scientific and Industrial Research.

SMITH, Frederick Henry, *1st Baron Colwyn*
    Committee on national debt and taxation.
        Report. 15 Nov.1926. 1927 Cmd.2800 xi.
        Minutes of evidence. 2 vols. 1927.
        Appendices. 1927. Treasury.

    Committee on bank amalgamations.
        Report. 1 May 1918. 1918 Cd.9052 vi. Treasury.

    Committee on the use of the Royal dockyards for the
    construction of merchant ships.
        Report. 4 Dec.1919. 1920 Cmd.581 xxi. Board
        of Trade.

    Departmental committee on railway agreements.
        Report and appendices. 8 Feb.1921. 1921
        Cmd.1132 xvii.
        Minutes of evidence. 1921. Ministry of
        Transport.

    Empire flax growing committee.
        Interim report on the general situation and
        immediate prospects of supply in April, 1919. 7
        May 1919. 1919 Cmd.281 xxii.
        Report on substitutes for flax. 27 April 1920.
        1920 Cmd.762 xvi. Board of Trade.

    Northern Ireland special arbitration committee.
        First report. 4 Sept.1923. 1924 Cmd.2072 xi.
        Final report. 2 March 1925. 1924/5 Cmd.2389
        xiv. Treasury.

    Royal commission on income tax.
        Report. 11 March 1920. 1920 Cmd.615 xviii.
        Evidence, 1st to 7th instalments and index. 1919
        Cmd.288 xxiii, parts 1 and 2 (also published by
        the Inland Revenue in 1920).

    Standing committee on co-ordination of
    departmental action in regard to contracts.
        First report. 2 Aug.1918. 1918 Cd.9179 vii. (no
        other reports identified) Treasury.

SMITH, G. M.
    History of the Great War. Medical services.
    Casualties and medical statistics of the Great War.
    March 1931. War Office.

Smith, G. S. *SEE:* Graham-Smith, G. S.

SMITH, Hamilton P.
    Report on conditions of work in flax and linen mills
    as affecting the health of the operatives employed.
    Jan.1904. 1904 Cd.1997 x. Home Office.

SMITH, Henry Babbington
    Committee on Indian exchange and currency.
        Vol.1: Report. 22 Dec.1919. 1920 Cmd.527
        xiv.
        Vol.2: Evidence. 1920 Cmd.528 xiv.
        Vol.3: Appendices. 1920 Cmd.529 xiv.
        Vol.4: Index. 1920 Cmd.530 xiv. India Office.

SMITH, Henry Babbington (continued)
Royal commission on the civil service. *SEE:* MacDonnell, A. P., *1st Baron.*

SMITH, Hubert Llewellyn
Memorandum summarising the regulations in force in foreign countries with regard to British commercial travellers. Jan.1904. 1904 Cd.1961 xcv. Board of Trade.

Report on the system of British commercial attaches and commercial agents. 6 July 1907. (Commercial, no.8, 1907) 1907 Cd.3610 lxxxvii. Foreign Office.

Safeguarding of industries. Report of the woollen and worsted committee. 30 April 1929. 1929/30 Cmd.3355 xvii. Board of Trade.

Special committee on public departments and industrial art.
Report. 23 Feb.1923. board of Trade.

Standing committee on merchandise marks.
Report on abrasive cloth and paper. 7 March 1932. 1931/2 Cmd.4049 xii. Board of Trade.

Report on abrasive wheels, cylinders, blocks, stones, sticks, etc. 12 Jan.1932. 1931/2 Cmd.4011 xii. Board of Trade.

Report on adhesive insulating tape for electrical purposes. 3 June 1931. 1930/1 Cmd.3917 xv. Board of Trade.

Report on air and gas compressors and exhausters; pneumatic tools and appliances and parts thereof. 22 Dec.1930. 1930/1 Cmd.3783 xv. Board of Trade.

Report on artists' and drawing materials, etc. 2 June 1930. 1929/30 Cmd.3625 xvi.
Addendum: letter respecting prepared wood panels. 17 Nov.1930. 1930/1 Cmd.3721 xv. Board of Trade.

Report on asbestos cement products. 23 July 1929. 1929/30 Cmd.3382 xvi. Board of Trade.

Report on ball and roller bearings and parts thereof. 18 July 1928. 1928/9 Cmd.3184 viii. Board of Trade.

Report on basketware. 11 April 1938. 1937/8 Cmd.5796 xiii. Board of Trade.

Report on bifurcated and tubular rivets of metal. 25 Nov.1932. 1932/3 Cmd.4221 xiv. Board of Trade.

Report on bolts, nuts, rivets, set screws, coach screws and studs. 18 Feb.1930. 1929/30 Cmd.3531 xvi. Board of Trade.

Report on bone meal and flour; hoof meal, meat meal, meat and bone meal and carcase meal; dried blood. 3 Nov.1930. 1930/1 Cmd.3729 xv. Board of Trade.

Report on boots, shoes and slippers. 17 Jan.1928. 1928 Cmd.3024 ix. Board of Trade.

Report on boxes, cartons, *etc.,* and flats therefor. 31 March 1930. 1929/30 Cmd.3562 xvi. Board of Trade.

Report on brass water taps and fittings; electrical accessories, *etc.* 4 Aug.1927. 1927 Cmd.2959 xi. Board of Trade.

Report on briar pipes and briar bowls. 25 April 1928. 1928 Cmd.3128 ix. Board of Trade.

Report on bricks, tiles and refractory bricks, *etc.* 19 Dec.1929. 1929/30 Cmd.3482 xvi. Board of Trade.

Report on brooms and brushes. 7 April 1930. 1929/30 Cmd.3557 xvi. Board of Trade.

Report on buckles, slides, clasps and buttons. 4 July 1939. 1938/9 Cmd.6080 xiii. Board of Trade.

Report on carbon papers. 30 July 1928. 1928/9 Cmd.3190 viii. Board of Trade.

Report on carpets, rugs and mats. 6 Oct.1928. 1928/9 Cmd.3228 viii. Board of Trade.

Report on cased tubes. 24 July 1939. 1938/9 Cmd.6094 xiii. Board of Trade.

Report on cast iron enamel baths. 12 March 1928. 1928 Cmd.3081 ix. Board of Trade.

Report on chain blocks. 26 March 1934. 1933/4 Cmd.4565 xiv. Board of Trade.

Report on chucks for lathes and other machine tools. 15 Nov.1932. 1932/3 Cmd.4214 xiv. Board of Trade.

Report on clocks, movements, escapements and synchronous motors. 4 Sept.1933. 1932/3 Cmd.4417 xiv. Board of Trade.

Report on coat hangers. 15 April 1930. 1929/30 Cmd.3566 xvi. Board of Trade.

Report on compasses, ruling and dotting pens, *etc.* 9 Sept.1932. 1931/32 Cmd.4169 xii. Board of Trade.

Report on copper plates, sheets, strips, rods, wire and tubes. 24 Aug.1928. 1928/9 Cmd.3199 viii. Board of Trade.

Report on cordage, cables, ropes and twine. 10 April 1933. 1932/3 Cmd.4304 xiv. Board of Trade.

Report on cotton wool, gauze tissues and sanitary towels. 22 Aug.1928. 1928/9 Cmd.3197 viii. Board of Trade.

Report on crepe bandages and binders. 9 Feb.1931. 1930/1 Cmd.3810 xv. Board of Trade.

Report on cutlery. 2 July 1928. 1928/9 Cmd.3180 viii. Board of Trade.

Report on domestic, fancy and illuminating glassware and glass bottles. July 1929. 1929/30 Cmd.3380 xvi. Board of Trade.

Report on door bolts of iron or steel. 13 Nov.1937. 1937/8 Cmd.5619 xiii. Board of Trade.

Report on drawing pins; fittings for letter files and folders; perforators; pencil sharpeners; stapling machines and staples. 31 March 1933. 1932/3 Cmd.4305 xiv. Board of Trade.

Report on elastic and articles made therefrom. 14 Jan.1929. 1928/9 Cmd.3280 viii. Board of Trade.

Report on electric incandescent lamps. 14 March 1928. 1928 Cmd.3083 ix. Board of Trade.

Report on electrical accessories. 15 May 1933. 1932/3 Cmd.4344 xiv. Board of Trade.

Report on electricity meters and parts thereof. 1 Dec.1930. 1930/1 Cmd.3759 xv. Board of Trade.

Report on enamel zinc sheets. 28 Feb.1928. 1928 Cmd.3067 ix. Board of Trade.

SMITH, Hubert Llewellyn (Continued)
Standing committee on merchandise marks. (Continued)

Report on felt hats and felt hoods. 18 Aug.1927. 1927 Cmd.2956 xi. Board of Trade.

Report on firearms and parts thereof. 20 Feb.1929. 1928/9 Cmd.3289 viii. Board of Trade.

Report on flooring blocks and strips. 12 Dec.1934. 1934/5 Cmd.4777 x. Board of Trade.

Report on flush pipes of iron and steel. 26 Oct.1931. 1931/2 Cmd.3968 xii. Board of Trade.

Report on fountain pens, stylographic pens, propelling pencils and gold pen nibs. 5 May 1930. 1929/30 Cmd.3587 xvi. Board of Trade.

Report on furniture and cabinet ware. 3 Nov.1927. 1927 Cmd.2980 xi. Board of Trade.

Report on geographical globes. 24 July 1939. 1938/9 Cmd.6086 xiii. Board of Trade.

Report on glue and gelatine. 1 March 1928. 1928 Cmd.3068 ix. Board of Trade.

Report on gold and silver leaf. 21 June 1927. 1927 Cmd.2907 xi. Board of Trade.

Report on hair combs and blanks therefor. 16 July 1934. 1933/4 Cmd.4675 xiv. Board of Trade.

Report on hand riven or split nails. 10 May 1932. 1931/2 Cmd.4087 xii. Board of Trade.

Report on hollow-ware. 15 July 1930. 1930/1 Cmd.3656 xv. Board of Trade.

Report on hosiery and knitted goods. 3 Nov.1930. 1930/1 Cmd.3725 xv. Board of Trade.

Report on hosiery, knitted goods and fabrics. 23 Aug.1929. 1929/30 Cmd.3405 xvi. Board of Trade.

Report on ice skates. 15 July 1930. 1930/1 Cmd.3652 xv. Board of Trade.

Report on incandescent lamps. 3 Nov.1930. 1930/1 Cmd.3724 xv. Board of Trade.

Report on insulated electric cables and wires. 1 Feb.1928. 1928 Cmd.3040 ix. Board of Trade.

Report on iron and steel. 4 July 1927. 1927 Cmd.2908 xi. Board of Trade.

Report on iron and steel wire, nails and staples. 18 Aug.1927. 1927 Cmd.2955 xi. Board of Trade.

Report on jewellery and imitation jewellery; vanity and compact cases, cosmetic boxes and containers, etc. 18 March 1935. 1934/5 Cmd.4879 x. Board of Trade.

Report on leather, fur and fabric gloves. 25 Oct.1927. 1927 Cmd.2978 xi. Board of Trade.

Report on machinery belting. 21 Dec.1929. 1929/30 Cmd.3475 xvi. Board of Trade.

Report on maize starch including maize starch cornflour. 16 Jan.1934. 1933/4 Cmd.4511 xiv. Board of Trade.

Report on measuring tapes made of cotton or linen. 20 Dec.1932. 1932/3 Cmd.4240 xiv. Board of Trade.

Report on metal spools for typewriter, etc., ribbons, and flanges therefor. 23 April 1934. 1933/4 Cmd.4581 xiv. Board of Trade.

Report on mill bobbins. 11 July 1927. 1927 Cmd.2929 xi. Board of Trade.

Report on mounted thermometers. 9 Nov.1933. 1933/4 Cmd.4466 xiv. Board of Trade.

Report on mowing machines of the rotary blade type. 22 Oct.1927. 1927 Cmd.2977 xi. Board of Trade.

Report on needles, etc, and fishing tackle. 15 May 1935. 1934/5 Cmd.4909 x. Board of Trade.

Report on pencils and pencil strips. 24 Feb.1933. 1932/3 Cmd.4278 xiv. Board of Trade.

Report on picture and greeting postcards. 28 April 1937. 1936/7 Cmd.5472 xiii. Board of Trade.

Report on polishing wheels or discs of felt. 26 Feb.1931. 1930/1 Cmd.3827 xv. Board of Trade.

Report on portland cement. 23 Aug.1929. 1929/30 Cmd.3408 xvi. Board of Trade.

Report on portable electric lamp casings. 10 May 1932. 1931/2 Cmd.4088 xii. Board of Trade.

Report on pottery. 11 Jan.1928. 1928 Cmd.3028 ix. Board of Trade.

Report on printing blocks. 11 Nov.1932. 1932/3 Cmd.4228 xiv. Board of Trade.

Report on pumps. 14 Aug.1928. 1928/9 Cmd.3195 viii. Board of Trade.

Report on radio goods. 17 Aug.1934. 1933/4 Cmd.4698 xiv. Board of Trade.

Report on refractory bricks. 6 May 1937. 1936/7 Cmd.5473 xiii. Board of Trade.

Report on rims for motor and other cycles, and cycle parts. 6 June 1928. 1928/9 Cmd.3183 viii. Board of Trade.

Report on roofing slates. 2 Dec.1929. 1929/30 Cmd.3461 xvi. Board of Trade.

Report on rubber boots, shoes and slippers. 3 Sept.1931. 1931/2 Cmd.3964 xii. Board of Trade.

Report on rubber boots, shoes and slippers: merchandise marks(imported goods) exemption direction (no.1), 1933. 3 July 1933. 1932/3 Cmd.4395 xiv. Board of Trade.

Report on rubber manufactures. 1 Feb.1929. 1928/9 Cmd.3281 viii. Board of Trade.

Report on rubber tyres and tubes. 12 Aug.1927. 1927 Cmd.2962 xi. Board of Trade.

Report on sacks and bags. 12 Feb.1935. 1934/5 Cmd.4826 x. Board of Trade.

Report on safety flame lamps and parts thereof. 1 June 1928. 1928 Cmd.3154 ix. Board of Trade.

Report on salt. 11 Feb.1935. 1934/5 Cmd.4833 x. Board of Trade.

Report on sanitary ware of pottery. 21 March 1938. 1937/8 Cmd.5753 xiii. Board of Trade.

Report on school rules. 14 Nov.1928. 1928/9 Cmd.3239 viii. Board of Trade.

Report on scientific glassware. 8 July 1929. 1929/30 Cmd.3381 xvi. Board of Trade.

SMITH, Hubert Llewellyn (Continued)
Standing committee on merchandise marks. (Continued)

Report on screw bottle stoppers. 12 July 1927. 1927 Cmd.2958 xi. Board of Trade.

Report on sheet lead and lead pipes. 21 May 1928. 1928 Cmd.3137 ix. Board of Trade.

Report on shuttles. 4 Jan.1928. 1928 Cmd.3019 ix. Board of Trade.

Report on slider fasteners. 24 Nov.1931. 1931/2 Cmd.3981 xii. Board of Trade.

Report on solid-headed pins of brass, iron or steel. 25 July 1938. 1937/8 Cmd.5835 xiii. Board of Trade.

Report on spectacle frames, fronts, sides and bridges; and eyeglass frames and bridges. 19 Aug.1939. 1939/40 Cmd.6147 v. Board of Trade.

Report on spoons, forks and knives; gold and silversmiths' wares; watch and clock cases. 20 June 1932. 1931/2 Cmd.4138 xii. Board of Trade.

Report on sporting cartridge cases. 3 March 1938. 1937/8 Cmd.5729 xiii. Board of Trade.

Report on steel nails. 1 July 1929. 1929/30 Cmd.3373 xvi. Board of Trade.

Report on steel shafts for golf clubs. 12 Aug.1930. 1930/1 Cmd.3664 xv. Board of Trade.

Report on strap butts. 2 Dec.1929. 1929/30 Cmd.3466 xvi. Board of Trade.

Report on surgical, medical, dental and veterinary instruments and appliances; aseptic hospital and dental furniture and dental supplies. 12 June 1928. 1928/9 Cmd.3178 viii. Board of Trade.

Report on tea. 14 Feb.1929. 1928/9 Cmd.3288 viii. Board of Trade.

Report on textile smallwares. 19 Nov.1937. 1937/8 Cmd.5638 xiii. Board of Trade.

Report on tools. 6 Sept.1929. 1929/30 Cmd.3406 xvi. Board of Trade.

Report on tools. 4 March 1931. 1930/1 Cmd.3826 xv. Board of Trade.

Report on tooth brushes and shaving brushes. 12 March 1928. 1928 Cmd.3082 ix. Board of Trade.

Report on toys, sports and games requisites, gymnastic and athletic requisites, *etc.*, 14 March 1932. 1931/2 Cmd.4059 xii. Board of Trade.

Report on umbrella parts and on wire netting and woven wire, wire, and wire nails and staples. 28 Nov.1932. 1932/3 Cmd.4245 xiv. Board of Trade.

Report on wallpapers, ceiling papers, *etc* 18 Feb.1930. 1929/30 Cmd.3549 xvi. Board of Trade.

Report on wallboard. 11 June 1930. 1929/30 Cmd.3626 xvi. Board of Trade.

Report on watch straps, *etc*, 5 July 1938. 1937/8 Cmd.5819 xiii. Board of Trade.

Report on wire netting and woven wire. 20 July 1927. 1927 Cmd.2930 xi. Board of Trade.

Report on wireless valves and rectifying valves. 19 July 1933. 1932/3 Cmd.4410 xiv. Board of Trade.

Report on women's and girls' garments of woven fabrics. 16 April 1935. 1934/5 Cmd.4893 x. Board of Trade.

Report on wood split pulleys. 1 July 1929. 1929/30 Cmd.3374 xvi. Board of Trade.

Report on wood wool and wood wool rope. 19 Dec.1932. 1932/3 Cmd.4239 xiv. Board of Trade.

Report on wooden tobacco pipes and bowls. 12 Aug.1933. 1932/3 Cmd.4412 xiv. Board of Trade.

Report on woven labels. 5 July 1927. 1927 Cmd.2909 xi. Board of Trade.

Report on woven piece goods, ribbons and certain articles therefrom. 12 June 1934. 1933/4 Cmd.4624 xiv. Board of Trade.

Report on wrought hollow-ware of iron or steel, self colour, galvanised, tinned, Japanned, *etc.* 10 Aug.1932. 1931/2 Cmd.4162 xii. Board of Trade.

State of employment in the United Kingdom in:
October 1914. 1914/6 Cd.7703 xxi.
December 1914. 1914/6 Cd.7755 xxi.
February 1915. 1914/6 Cd.7850 xxi. Board of Trade.

SMITH, J.
Causation and source of infection in puerperal fever. Dec.1930. Department of Health for Scotland.

SMITH, L.A. Brooke
Weather forecasting in the eastern north Atlantic and home waters for seamen. July 1921. (M.O. 246) Meteorological Office.

SMITH, May Penelope
The effects of alcohol and some other drugs during normal and fatigued conditions. 1 September 1920. (S.R.S., no.50) Medical Research Council.

The nervous temperament. Dec.1930. (I.H.R.B. Rep., no.61) Medical Research Council.

Some studies in the laundry trade. Dec.1922. (I.H.R.B. Rep., no.22) Medical Research Council.

SMITH, Morton William
Report on the trial of a petition against the election (on 1 November 1902) of a town councillor for the Castle Fields ward of the Borough of Shrewsbury. 7 Feb.1903. 1903 Cd.1541 lv. Home Office.

SMITH, P.B.
The pressures produced on blowing electric fuse links: the effect of the surrounding atmosphere. Feb.1930. (S.M.R.B. Paper no.67) Mines Department.

SMITH, Stanley
Lead and zinc ores of Northumberland and Alston Moor. 8 Nov.1922. (Special reports on the mineral resources of Great Britain, vol.25) (Mem.Geol.Surv.) Geological Survey.

SMITH, T.
Constructional data of small telescope objectives. 1915. National Physical Laboratory.

SMITH, T.J.
Report of the county inspector, Royal Irish Constabulary, on the state of Galway East Riding, October 1907. 4 Nov.1907. 1908 Cd.3949 xc. Irish Secretary's Office.

SMITH, Walter R.
Conference on standardisation.
Report, including resolutions adopted by the Imperial Conference. 30 Oct.1930. 1930/1 Cmd.3716 xiv. Colonial Office.

Editorial committee on the international code of signals.
Report. 12 Dec.1930. Board of Trade.

Report of the British delegates on the International Labour Conference, 13th session, Geneva, 10 to 26 October 1929. April 1930. 1929/30 Cmd.3559 xxxii. Ministry of Labour.

SMITH, William Frederick Danvers, *2nd Viscount Hambleden*
Central tribunal appointed under the Military Service Act, 1916.
Report. 4 Feb.1919. Local Government Board *and* Scottish Office.

Committee on advanced art education in London.
Report. 24 June 1936. Board of Education.

SMITH, William R.
Inter-departmental committee on agricultural tied cottages.
Report. 24 May 1932. 1931/2 Cmd.4148 vi. Ministry of Health *and* Ministry of Agriculture and Fisheries.

SMITH, William Sydney
Report on the construction, arrangement and fencing of hoists and teagles. 16 Feb.1904. 1904 Cd.2051 x. Home Office.

Report on the manufacture of silica bricks and other refractory materials used in furnaces. 14 Aug.1917. Home Office.

SMITH-ROSE, R.L.
A discussion of the practical systems of direction-finding by reception. May 1923. (R.R.B. special rep., no.1) Department of Scientific and Industrial Research.

An investigation of a rotating radio beacon. Dec.1927. (R.R.B. special rep., no.6) Department of Scientific and Industrial Research.

An investigation of the interference caused by transmissions from radio stations. Nov.1928. (R.R.B.special rep., no.8) Department of Scientific and Industrial Research.

The Orfordness rotating beacon and marine navigation. March 1931. (R.R.B. special rep., no.10) Department of Scientific and Industrial Research.

A study of radio direction-finding. May 1927. (R.R.B. special rep., no.5) Department of Scientific and Industrial Research.

Variations of apparent bearings of radio transmitting stations.
Part 1: observations on fixed stations, Feb.1921-March 1922. Oct.1924. (R.R.B. special rep., no.2)
Part 2: observations on fixed stations, March 1922 - April 1924. Aug.1925. (R.R.B. special rep., no.3)
Part 3: observations on ship and shore stations, November 1922 - March 1924. April 1926. Department of Scientific and Industrial Research.

SMUTS, Jan Christiaan
The British commonwealth of nations; a speech. 15 May 1917. Ministry of Information.

SMYTH, Corisande
Facial growth in children, with special reference to dentition. 29 Sept.1932. (S.R.S., no.171) Medical Research Council.

SNAGG, Thomas Mordaunt
Report on the constitution, jurisdiction, procedure and work of the County of London Appeal Tribunal under the Profiteering Acts. 12 May 1921. 1921 Cmd. 1384 xvi. Board of Trade.

SNAGGE, Harold Edward
Safeguarding of industries.
Report of the committee on monumental and architectural granite, wholly or mainly manufactured. 30 March 1928. 1928 Cmd.3079 xii. Board of Trade.

SNELL, Henry, *1st Baron*
Colonial films committee.
Report. 30 June 1930. 1929/30 Cmd.3630 viii. Colonial Office.

Arandora Star inquiry.
Summary. Dec.1940. 1940/1 Cmd.6238 v. Privy Council Office.

SNELL, John Francis Cleverton
Report of expert co-ordinating sub-committee of the Severn Barrage Committee. 7 July 1932. Economic Advisory Council. Treasury. *SEE ALSO:* Moore-Brabazon, J.I.C.

Water power resources committee.
Interim report: Scotland. 25 Jan.1919. 1919 Cmd.79 xxx.
Second interim report. 5 June 1920. 1920 Cmd.776 xxv.
Third interim report: Tidal power. 1 Dec.1920. 1920 Cmd.1079 xxv.
Final report. 17 Nov.1921. Board of Trade.

SNODGRASS, William Robertson
An analysis of the results of treatment of early, latent, and muco-cutaneous teritiary syphilis. 21 July 1937. (S.R.S., no.224) Medical Research Council.

SNOWDEN, G.R.
Report on guilds of help in England. Jan.1911. 1911 Cd.5664 xxxii. Local Government Board.

SOLOMON, William Henry
Indian enquiry commission, Union of South Africa.
Report. 7 March 1914. 1914 Cd.7265 xliv. Colonial Office.

SOMERSET, Henry Adelbert Wellington Fitzroy, *9th Duke of Beaufort.*
Military manoeuvres commission, 1909.
Report. 1909. 1910 Cd.5014 lx. War Office.

SOMERVILLE, Boyle T.
Ocean passages for the world: winds and currents. 1923. Admiralty.

Report on sounding cruise of HMS Egeria on the proposed pacific cable route, North Pacific Ocean, 1899. June 1900. (H.D. no.173) Admiralty, Hydrographic Department.

SOMERVILLE, H.C.
Report on the navigability of the Kialing Kiang and the Fu Ho, two tributaries of the upper Yangtse Kiang. Feb.1903. (Hydrographic Publication, H.D. 191) Admiralty.

Southborough, *Lord. SEE:* Hopwood, F.J.S., *1st Baron Southborough.*

SOUTHERN, R.M.
Admiralty manual of hydrographic surveying. 1938. Admiralty.

Southwark, *Lord. SEE:* Causton, R.K., *1st Baron Southwark.*

SPARKES, F.N.
Machinery and its uses in concrete road construction. Dec.1938. (Road Res., special rep., no.2) Department of Scientific and Industrial Research.

SPAULDING, Ethel H.
The problem of rural schools and teachers in North America. Sept.1908. (Educational pamphlets, no.13) Board of Education.

SPENCE, M.T.
A minor line-squall. Sept.1921. (Prof.Note, no.25) Meteorological Office.

SPENCER, Frederick
Position of French in grant-aided secondary schools in England. April 1926. (Educational pamphlets, no.47) Board of Education.

SPENCER, J. Poyntz, *5th Earl Spencer*
Joint select committee on the presence of the sovereign in Parliament.
Report, proceedings, minutes of evidence, appendix. 14 June 1901. 1901 (212) vii. House of Commons.

Select committee of the House of Lords on light load line.
Report, procedings, evidence and appendix. 14 Aug.1903. 1903 (356) vi. House of Commons.

SPENCER, Thomas
Merchant shipping advisory committee.
Report on the efficiency of wireless watchers. 13 Feb.1922. Board of Trade.

SPENS, Will
Consultative committee of the Board of Education.
Report on secondary education with special reference to grammer schools and technical high schools. Report. 13 Oct.1938. Board of Education.

SPICER, Albert
Select committee on Marconi's Wireless Telegraph Co.,Ltd., Agreement.
Report, proceedings, evidence, appendices and index. 28 Oct.1912, 14 Jan. and 12 Feb.1913. 1912/3 (351, 430, 515 and 515-I) viii.
Report, proceedings, evidence and appendices with an index. 13 June 1913. 1913 (152) vii.
Report, proceedings and appendix. 2 July 1913. 1913 (185) vii. House of Commons.

SPIELMANN, Percy Edwin
Tables of chemical and physical constants. July 1918. Ministry of Munitions.

SPRIGGS, Edmund Ivens
Food and how to save it. Jan.1917. Ministry of Food.

SPROT, Mark
Agricultural marketing reorganisation commission for eggs and poultry for Scotland.
Report. 24 Jan.1935. Department of Agriculture for Scotland.

Committee on agricultural co-operation in Scotland.
Report. 3 April 1930. 1929/30 Cmd.3567 viii. Scottish Office.

Scottish fat stock marketing reorganisation commission.
Report. 26 March 1934. Department of Agriculture for Scotland.

STAFFORD, E.H.
Linear perspective projection; a text-book for the use of the Royal Military Academy, Woowich. Oct.1904. 2 parts. War Office.

STAFFORD, H.
Stemming materials. Jan.1934. (S.M.R.B. Paper, no.84) Mines Department.

STAGG, J.M.
The absolute daily range of magnetic declination at Kew Observatory, 1901 to 1910. Feb.1926. (Geophys.Mem., no.29) Meteorological Office.

Hourly character figures of magnetic disturbance at Kew Oberservatory, 1913-23. Dec.1926. (Geophys.Mem., no.32) Meteorological Office.

On magnetic fluctuations and sunspot frequency. July 1927. (Geophys.Mem., no.36) Meteorological Office.

Some effects produced by protective shields on the readings of Grass minimum thermometers. Nov.1925. (Prof.Notes, no.43) Meteorological Office.

The time interval between magnetic disturbance and associated sunspot changes. July 1928. (Geophys.Mem., no.42) Meteorological Office.

The twenty-seven-day recurrence interval in magnetic disturbance. Dec.1927. (Geophys.Mem., no.40) Meteorological Office.

STALKER, James
The Luther celebrations of 1917. Ministry of Information.

STAMP, Josiah Charles, *1st Baron*
Special board of inquiry on certain statements made in the course of the recent case of Lambert *v.* Levita, affecting the British Broadcasting Corporation.
Report. 15 Dec.1936. 1936/7 Cmd.5337 ix. Cabinet Office.

STANHOPE, James Richard, *7th Earl*
Committee on prison officers' pay and conditions of service.
Report. 27 July 1923. 1923 Cmd.1959 xii, pt.2. Home Office.

STANLEY, Arthur
Joint War Committee on the British Red Cross Society and the Order of St.John of Jerusalem in England.
Report on voluntary aid rendered to the sick and wounded at home and abroad and to British prisoners of war, 1914-1919, with appendices. 5 May 1921. Prime Minister's Office.

STANLEY, Edward George Villers, *17th Earl Derby*
Report on recruiting. 12 and 20 Dec.1915. 1914/6 Cd.8149 xxxix. War Office.

STANLEY, George J.
Report on anti-trust legislation in the British self-governing dominions. Sept.1912. 1912/3 Cd.6439 lx. Board of Trade.

STANLEY, Henry John, *3rd Baron Stanley of Alderley*
Committee on expenses incurred by officers of the army and to suggest measures for bringing commissions within reach of men of moderate means.
Report with appendices *etc.* 21 July 1902. 1903 Cd.1421 x. War Office.

Stanmore, *Lord. SEE:* Gordon, A. H. *1st Baron*

STANNIER, Beville
Committee on the staffing and methods of work of

STANNIER, Beville (continued)
the Ministry of Agriculture and Fisheries.
Report. 18 Sept.1920. 1920 Cmd.1069 xxv.
Prime Minister's Office.

STANSFELD, Ina
Report on industrial training of girls in the separate
and district schools in the Metropolitan district. 1
Dec.1898. 1900 Cd.237 lxxiii. Local Government
Board.

STATHAM, Ira Cyril
Flame-proof electrical apparatus for use in coal
mines.
First report: Flange protection. Sept.1924.
(S.M.R.B. Paper, no.5)
Summarising report. April 1929. (S.M.R.B.
Paper, no.60) Mines Department.

STEEL-MAITLAND, Arthur Herbert Drummond
Ramsay
Committee on edible and oil-producing nuts and
seeds.
Report. 5 May 1916. 1916 Cd.8247 iv.
Minutes of evidence. 1916 Cd.8248 iv. Colonial
Office.
Select committee on sky-writing.
Report, proceedings, evidence, appendices and
index. 23 June 1932. 1931/2 (95) v. House of
Commons.

STEELE, J.
Report on excise restrictions in force in the West
Indies and British Guiana. 1903. 1903 Cd.1681 xliv.
Colonial Office.

STEPHEN, A. C.
Preliminary survey of the Scottish waters of the
North Sea by the Petersen grab. 1922. (Sci.invest.,
1922, no.3) Fishery Board for Scotland.

STEPHEN, Harry Lushington
Departmental committee on the principles for scales
of salary for teachers in elementary schools.
Report. Vol.1. 20 Dec.1917. 1917/8 Cd.8939 xi.
Report. Vol.2. Summaries of evidence and
memoranda. 1918 Cd.8999 ix. Board of
Education.
Departmental committee on the principles to
determine the fixing of salaries for teachers in
secondary and technical schools, schools of art,
training colleges and other institutions for higher
education.
Report. Vol.1: 31 July 1918. 1918 Cd.9140 ix.
Report. Vol.2: Summaries of evidence. 1918
Cd.9168 ix. Board of Education.

STEPHENS, J. V.
Wells and springs of Derbyshire. 12 Feb.1929.
(Mem.Geol.Surv.) Geological Survey.

STEPHENS, T. A.
Report on intermediate education in Ireland. 15
Feb.1905. 1905 Cd.2546 xxviii. Board of Education.

STEVEN, H. M.
Nursery investigations. June 1928. (Bull., no.11)
Forestry Commission.

STEVENS, Patrick William Joseph
Report on the cultivation of tea in the Caucasus,
Russia. 7 Jan.1905. (Dip.cons.reports: misc.ser.,
no.628) 1905 Cd.2237-9 lxxxvi. Foreign Office.
Report on the tea industry of the Caucasus, Russia.
28 May 1903. (Dip.cons.reports: misc.ser., no.593)
1903 Cd.1387-6 lxxvi. Foreign Office.

STEVENS, W. C.
Machinery and equipment used for bending wood.

July 1938. (F.P.R. Records, no.25) Department of
Scientific and Industrial Research.
The practice of wood bending. May 1936. (F.P.R.
Records, no.10) Department of Scientific and
Industrial Research.

STEVENSON, James
Committee on pensions and passage expenses of
colonial officers.
Report on pensions. 7 Jan.1924. (Colonial, no.1)
(no others identified) Colonial Office.
Committee on the rubber situation in British
colonies and protectorates.
Report. 19 May 1922. 1922 Cmd.1678 xvi.
Supplementary report. 2 Oct.1922. 1922 Session
2 Cmd.1756 ii. Colonial Office.

STEVENSON, William David Henderson
Studies on the cultivation of vaccinia on the chorio-
allantoic membranes of chick embryos. Oct.1938.
(Rep.Pub.Health & med.Subj., no.87) Ministry of
Health.

STEVENSON, William Flack
Report on the surgical cases noted in the South
African War, 1899-1902. 16 Feb.1905. War Office.

STEWART, C. D.
The measurement of upper wind velocities by
observations of artificial clouds. Nov.1924.
(Prof.Notes, no.38) Meteorological Office.

Stewart, C. S. H. V-T. SEE: Vane-Tempest-Stewart, C.
S. H., 7th Marquess of Londonderry

STEWART, Charles John
Safeguarding of industries committee.
Report on leather gloves, fabric gloves and glove
fabric. 6 July 1925. 1924/5 Cmd.2531 xv. Board
of Trade.
Report on snap fasteners and hooks and eyes. 22
Aug.1922. Board of Trade.
Report on wire nails. 22 Aug.1922. Board of
Trade.

STEWART, Percy Malcolm
Commissioner of special areas, England and Wales.
Reports. SEE: Gillett, G. M.

STEWART, William
Departmental committee on certain questions
arising under the Workmen's Compensation Acts.
Report. 13 Jan.1938. 1937/8 Cmd.5657 xv.
Home Office.

STEWART-MURRAY, John George, 8th Duke of
Atholl
Committee of the Privy council on the question of
contributions to Imperial funds from the islands of
Jersey, Guernsey and Man.
Report. 29 Jan.1926. 1926 Cmd.2586 viii. Privy
Council.
Committee on the utilisation of Edinburgh Castle for
a Scottish national war memorial.
Report. July 1919. 1919 Cmd.279 xxi. Scottish
Office.

STEWART-MURRAY, Katherine Marjory, Duchess of
Atholl
Consultative council on highlands and islands.
Report on the reform of local health
administration. May 1923. (IN: Consultative
Council on local health administration and
general health questions. Report on reform of
local health administration, 1923) Scottish
Board of Health.

STEWART—MURRAY: Katherine Marjory, *Duchess of Atholl* (continued)

Departmental committee on examinations for part-time students.
> Report. 13 July 1928. Board of Education.

Imperial education conference, 1927.
> Report of proceedings. Dec.1927. Board of Education.

STILES, W. S.
Thermionic emission; a survey of existing knowledge with particular reference to the filaments of radio valves. Jan.1932. (R.R.B. special rep., no.11) Department of Scientific and Industrial Research.

STILES, Walter
The preservation of food by freezing, with special reference to fish and meat: a study in general physiology. Dec.1921. (F.I.B. special rep., no.7) Department of Scientific and Industrial Research.

STILL, George Frederick
London committee on ante-natal and post-natal problems of child life.
> Report on social conditions and acute rheumatism. 15 Jan.1927. (S.R.S., no.114) Medical Research Council.

STILLWELL, S. T. C.
The moisture content of wood with special reference to furniture manufacture. Dec.1929. (F.P.R. Bull., no.5) Department of Scientific and Industrial Research.

STIRLING—MAXWELL, John
Departmental committee on forestry in Scotland.
> Report with appendices and evidence. Dec.1911. 1912/3 Cd.6085 xxix. Scottish Office.

Departmental committee on lands in Scotland used as deer forests.
> Report. 11 Nov.1921. 1922 Cmd.1636 vii. Scottish Office.

Inter-departmental home-grown timber committee.
> Interim report. Sept.1933. (no others identified) Forestry Commission.

National forest park committee.
> Report. Nov.1935. Forestry Commission.

Report on the demand for timber for box and packing-case manufacture in Great Britain. Dec.1934. Forestry Commission.

STOCK, Philip Graham
Preliminary report on the use of hydrogen cyanide for fumigation purposes. Aug.1923. (Rep.Pub.Health & Med.Subj., no.19).

Effect on food of fumigation with hydrogen cyanide. Sept.1930. (Rep.Pub.Health & Med.Subj., no.60) Ministry of Health.

STOCKMAN, Stewart
Departmental committee on foot-and-mouth disease. 1914. 20 Sept.1914. 1914 Cd.7270 xii. Board of Agriculture and Fisheries.

STOCKS, Mary Danvers
Committee on cooperation between the Unemployment Assistance Board, the local authority and voluntary associations in Liverpool.
> Report. Nov.1937. Ministry of Labour.

STOKES, Frederick Wilfred Scott
Standing committee on prices. Sub-committee on motor fuel.
> First report. 12 Feb.1920. 1920 Cmd.597 xxiii.
> Second report. 23 Nov.1920. 1921 Cmd.1119 xvi. Board of Trade.

Stonehaven, *Lord. SEE:* Baird, J. L., *1st Viscount*

STOPES, Marie Carmichael
Monograph on the constitution of coal. April 1918. Department of Scientific and Industrial Research.

STORDY, Robert J.
Report on veterinary work in British East Africa and Uganda protectorates for the years 1898-1900. 23 May 1901. (Diplomatic and consular reports, misc., no.551) 1901 Cd.430-6 lxxx. Foreign Office.

STOREY, Harold
The Paris conference and trade after the war. 1916. Ministry of Information.

STORRS, Ronald
Disturbances in Cyprus in October 1931. 11 Feb.1932. 1931/2 Cmd.4045 vi. Colonial Office.

STRACHEY, Edward
Departmental committee on the British export trade in live-stock with the Colonies and other countries.
> Report. 4 Sept.1911. 1911 Cd.5947 xxii.
> Minutes of evidence with a digest of the evidence, appendices and an index. 1912/3 Cd.6032 xxv. Board of Agriculture and fisheries.

Select committee on butter trade.
> Report, proceedings, evidence, appendix and index. 9 July 1906. 1906 (245) vii. House of commons.

STRADLING, Reginald Edward
Effects of moisture changes on building materials. July 1928. (B.R.B. Bull., no.3) Department of Scientific and Industrial Research.

Fire resistant construction. Jan.1927. (B.R.B. special rep., no.8) Department of Scientific and Industrial Research.

STRAHAN, Aubrey
The coal of south Wales; with special reference to the origin and distribution of anthracite. 17 Feb. 1908. (Mem.Geol.Surv.) Geological Survey.

The geology of the south Wales coalfield.
> Part 1: The country around Newport, Monmouthshire. 25 Nov.1899. (Mem.Geol.Surv.)
> Part 2: The country around Abergavenny. 16 June 1900. (Mem.Geol.Surv.)
> Part 3: The country around Cardiff. 21 April 1902. (Mem.Geol.Surv.)
> Part 4: The country around Pontypridd and Maes-Têg. 28 Feb.1903. (Mem.Geol.Surv.)
> Part 5: The country around Merthyr Tydfil. 20 April 1904. (Mem.Geol.Surv.)
> Part 6: The country around Bridgend. 4 Nov.1904. (Mem.Geol.Surv.)
> Part 7: The country around Ammanford. 8 April 1907. (Mem.Geol.Surv.)
> Part 8: The country around Swansea. 22 March 1907. (Mem.Geol.Surv.)
> Part 9: West Gower and the country around Pembrey. 7 Feb.1907. (Mem.Geol.Surv.)
> Part 10: The country around Carmarthen. 19 Jan.1909. (Mem.Geol.Surv.)
> Part 11: The country around Haverford West. 1 July 1913. (Mem.Geol.Surv.) Geological Survey.

Geology of the Thames Valley near Goring. 18 Jan.1924. (Mem.Geol.Surv.) Geological Survey.

Guide to the geological model of the Isle of Purbeck. 4 Jan.1906. (Mem.Geol.Surv., England & Wales) Geological Survey.

Guide to the model of Ingleborough and district. 5

STRAHAN, Aubrey (continued)
Sept.1910. (Mem.Geol.Surv.) Geological Survey.

Iron ores: pre-carboniferous and carboniferous bedded ores of England and Wales. 18 May 1919. (Special reports on the mineral resources of Great Britain, vol.13) (Mem.Geol.Surv.) Geological Survey.

Lead and zinc ores of Durham, Yorkshire and Derbyshire, with notes on the Isle of Man. 17 May 1922. (Special reports on the mineral resources of Great Britain, vol.26) (Mem.Geol.Surv.) Geological Survey.

Lignites, jets, kimeridge, oil-shale, mineral oil, cannel coals, natural gas. 12 June 1918. (Special reports on the mineral resources of Great Britain, vol.7) (Mem.Geol.Surv.) Geological Survey.

Potash-felspar, phosphate of lime, alum shales, plumbago or graphite, molybenite, chromite, talc and steatite (soapstone, soaprock and potstone) and diatomite. 3 March 1916. (Special reports on the mineral resources of Great Britain, vol.5) (Mem.Geol.Surv.) Geological Survey.

STRANG, Herbert
Great Britain and the war; a book for boys and girls. 1918. Ministry of Information.

STRANGE, Edward Fairbrother
Departmental committee on the wholesale food markets of London.
First report. 23 Feb.1920. 1920 Cmd.634 xvii.
Second report. 10 May 1920. 1920 Cmd.713 xvii.
Third report: Fish supplies and distribution. 11 Oct.1920. 1921 Cmd.1168 xii.
Fourth report: Wholesale fruit and vegetable markets. 14 Feb.1921. 1921 Cmd.1341 xii.
Fifth report: Meat supplies and distribution. 7 March 1921. 1921 Cmd.1341 xii.
Final report: Influence of wholesale market facilities on food prices. 7 March 1921. 1921 Cmd.1341 xii. Ministry of Food.

STRAWN, Silas H.
Commission on extra-territoriality in China.
Report. 16 Sept.1926. (China, no.3, 1926) 1926 Cmd.2774 viii. Foreign Office.

STREATFIELD, Lucy Anne Eavely Deane
Commission of enquiry on women's army auxiliary corps in France.
Report. 20 March 1918. Ministry of Labour.
Women's advisory committee.
Report on women holding temporary appointments in government departments. 3 Jan.1919. 1919 Cmd.199 xxix. Ministry of Reconstruction.

STREET, Philip Whistler
Royal commission on the meat export trade of Australia.
Report with appendices. 14 Nov.1914. 1914/6 Cd.7896 xlvi. Colonial Office.

STRONGE, Francis
Report on the mines and mineral resources of Colombia. June 1909. (Dip.cons. reports: misc.ser., no.667) 1909 Cd.4447-5 xcii. Foreign Office and Board of Trade.

STRUTHERS, J.
Inter-departmental committee on the model course of physical exercises.
Report. 10 March 1904. 1904 Cd.2032 xix. Board of Education and Committee of the Privy Council on Education in Scotland.

STRUTT, Edward Gerald
Committee on the Pembrey farm settlement.
Report. 12 June 1920. 1920 Cmd.851 ix. Ministry of Agriculture and Fisheries.

Departmental committee on duration of buildings for smallholdings.
Report. 25 Nov.1912. 1912/3 Cd.6536 xlvi. Board of Agriculture and Fisheries.

STRUTT, John, 3rd Baron Rayleigh
Committee on vibration produced by the working of the traffic on the Central London Railway.
Report. Jan.1902. 1902 Cd.951 xxiii.
Appendices. 1902 Cd.975 xxiii. Board of Trade.

Departmental committee on gas testing in the metropolis.
Report. 19 May 1904. 1904 Cd.2118 xxiv.
Evidence and appendices. 1904 Cd.2203 xxiv. Board of Trade.

STRUTT, Robert John, 4th Baron Rayleigh
Radium sub-committee of the committee of Civil Research.
Report. 7 March 1929. 1928/9 Cmd.3303 v. Treasury.

STUART-WORTLEY, Charles Beilby, 1st Baron Stuart of Wortley
Advisory committee on military service (civil liabilities) grants.
Interim report: May 1916 to 25 May 1918. 1 Oct.1918. 1919 Cmd.39 x. (no others identified) Local Government Board.

Select committee on Post Office (telephone agreement).
Report, proceedings, evidence, appendix and index. 31 July 1905. 1905 (271) vii. House of Commons.

STURDEE, Edwin Lawrance
A disease of parrots communicable to man (psittacosis). Oct.1930. (Rep.Pub.Health & Med.Subj., no.61) Ministry of Health.

STURDY, R. V.
Report on legislation in regard to gambling in 'options' and 'futures'. 17 Aug.1907. 1908 Cd.3863 cviii. Foreign Office.

SUHRAWARDY, Abdullah Al-M'amun.
Supplementary note to the report of the Indian Constitutional reforms central committee. 18 Feb.1930. 1929/30 Cmd.3525 x. India Office.

Sumner, Lord. SEE: Hamilton, J.A., Baron Sumner.

SUTCLIFFE, R. C.
Barometer fluctuations at Malta. June 1931. (Prof. Notes, no.62) Meteorological Office.

SUTER-LERCH, H. J.
Germany her own judge; reply of a cosmopolitan Swiss to German propaganda. 1918. Ministry of Information.

Sutherland, Lord. SEE: Leveson-Gower, G.G.S., 5th Duke of Sutherland

SUTHERLAND, Angus
Scottish departmental committee on the North Sea fishing industry.
Part 1: Report with appendices. 8 Jan.1914. 1914 Cd.7221 xxxi.
Part 2: Evidence. 1914 Cd.7462 xxxi. Scottish Office.

SUTHERLAND, Charles Lindsay
Report on an inquiry into the occurrence of disease of the lungs from dust inhalation in the slate

SUTHERLAND, Charles Lindsay (continued)
industry in the Gwyrfai District. June 1930. Mines Department.

Report on the incidence of silicosis in the pottery industry. 26 July 1926. Home Office.

Report on the occurrence of silicosis amongst granite workers. 19 May 1930. Home Office.

Report on the occurrence of silicosis among sandstone workers. 7 Nov.1928. Home Office.

SUTHERLAND, John Ebenezer
Scottish sea fisheries committee.
Report. 30 Sept.1917. Scottish Office.

SUTTON, William
Sickness and mortality experience deduced from quinquennial returns made by registered friendly societies 1856-1880. April 1912. Friendly Societies Registrar.

SUWAIDY, Sayyid Taifiq al
Committee on correspondence between Sir Henry McMahon, H.M. High Commissioner in Egypt, and the Sharif of Mecca in 1915 and 1916.
Report. 16 March 1939. 1938/9 Cmd.5974 xiv. Colonial Office.

SWEETING, Richard Deane Roker
Report on a recent epidemic of scarlatina in Burnham-on-Crouch, U.D., Essex. 21 Jan.1908. (Rep.Med. Insp., no.298) Local Government Board.

Report on a re-inspection of Ilkeston Borough, with reference to the use of the hospital for infectious diseases there. 8 Feb.1911. (Rep.Pub.Health & Med.Subj., no.50) Local Government Board.

Report on an outbreak of enteric fever at the villages of Edlesborough and Eaton Bray. 28 Nov.1904. (Rep.Med.Insp., no.203) Local Government Board.

Report on the sanitary conditions of Bedford R.D. 22 Aug.1911. (Rep.Pub.Health & Med.Subj., no.58) Local Government Board.

Report on the sanitary conditions of Crickhowell R.D., with reference to the prevalence of enteric fever in the Parish of Llanelly, Breconshire. 8 Dec.1910. (Rep.Pub.Health & Med.Subj., no.44) Local Government Board.

Report on the sanitary conditions of the Dartford registration district, with reference to the prevalence of fatal diphtheria. 30 July 1900. (Rep.Med.Insp., no.150) Local Government Board.

Report on the sanitary conditions of Huntingdon R.D., with reference to flooding of the district by the River Ouse. 9 Sept.1907. (Rep.Med.Insp., no.278) Local Government Board.

Report on the sanitary conditions of the Leith Borough, Lancashire, with reference to the prevalence of enteric fever. 12 Feb.1908. (Rep.Med.Insp., no.301) Local Government Board.

Report on the sanitary conditions of the Milton registration district, with reference to recent prevalence of diphtheria and enteric fever. 2 Oct.1901. (Rep.Med.Insp., no.167) Local Government Board.

Report on the sanitary conditions of Ramsey U.D., with reference to the prevalence of scarlatina. 8 Nov.1909. (Rep.Pub.Health & Med.Subj., no.19) Local Government Board.

Report on the sanitary conditions of the Rotherham Borough, with reference to continued prevalence of enteric fever. 2 April 1909. (Rep.Pub.Health & Med.Subj., no.3) Local Government Board.

Report on the sanitary conditions of St.Neot's and Eaton Socon R.D.'s. 27 Feb.1907. (Rep.Med.Insp., no.253) Local Government Board.

Report on the sanitary conditions of Tavistock R.D., with special reference to an outbreak of diphtheria at Princetown. 22 Aug.1906. (Rep.Med.Insp., no.240) Local Government Board.

Report on the sanitary conditions of the Weymouth Borough and Melcombe Regis and on recent prevalence there of scarlatina. 30 Aug.1901. (Rep.Med.Insp., no.164) Local Government Board.

SWETTENHAM, Frank Athelstane
Mauritius royal commission.
Part 1: Report and appendix A. 28 April 1910. 1910 Cd.5185 xlii.
Part 2: Appendix B. Minutes of proceedings and evidence. 1910 Cd.5186 xlii.
Part 3: Appendix C. Copies of certain documents received. 1910 Cd.5187 xlii.

SWIFT, Rigby Philip Watson
Committee on re-arrangements of the circuits to promote economy and the greater dispatch of the business of the High Court.
Report. 23 Feb.1923. 1923 Cmd.1831 ix. Lord Chancellor's Office.

County court staff committee.
Report. 28 July 1920. 1920 Cmd.1049 xiii. Lord Chancellor's Office.

SWINBURNE, James
Report on draft regulations for the generation, transformation, distribution, and use of electrical energy (in factories and workshops). 18 Dec.1908. 1909 Cd.4462 xxi. Home Office.

SWINTON, George Sitwell Campbell
Delhi town planning committee on the choice of a site for the new Imperial capital.
First report. 13 June 1912. 1913 Cd.6885 xx.
Second report. 11 March 1913. 1913 Cd.6888 xx.
Final report. 20 March 1913. 1913 Cd.6889 xx. India Office.

Sydenham of Combe. SEE: Clarke, G.S., 1st Baron Sydenham of Combe.

SYKES, Alan John
Commission appointed to review the permits under which alien enemies are allowed to reside in prohibited areas.
Report. 26 Oct.1916. 1916 Cd.8419 iv. Home Office.

SYKES, Frederick
Broadcasting committee
Report. 23 Aug.1923. 1923 Cmd.1951 x. Post Office.

SYLVEN, Nils
The influence of climatic conditions on type composition. June 1937. (Bull., no.21) Imperial Bureau of Plant Genetics. Herbage Plants.

SYNGE, M.B.
Provision made for children under compulsory school age in Belgium, France, Germany and Switzerland. Dec.1908. 1909 Cd.4477 xviii. (Special reports on Educational Subjects, vol.22) Board of Education.

TAIGEL, P. G.
Back-stays for use in mines. Jan.1940. (S.M.R.B.Paper, no.103) Mines Department.

**TAIT, John B.**
Surface water drift in the Northern and middle areas of the North Sea and in the Faroe-Shetland Channel.

> Part 1. (Sci.invest., 1930, no.2) 1930.
> Part 2, sect.1. (Sci.invest,1930, no.4) 1930.
> Part 2, sect.2. (Sci.invest., 1931, no.3) 1931.
> Part 2, sect.3. (Sci.invest., 1937, no.1) 1937.
> Fishery Board for Scotland.

**TAITE, Charles Davis**
Committee on measures to prevent the emission of soot, ash and grit from chimneys of electric power stations. July 1932. Electricity Commission. Ministry of Transport.

**TALBOT, Charles Alexander Price**
Report on the mining industry in the province of Galicia, Spain. 17 Sept.1900. (Dip.cons.reports: misc.ser., no.538) 1900 Cd.353-3 xci. Foreign Office.

**TALBOT, George John**
Commission to inquire into the case of ex-inspector John Syme of the Metropolitan police.

> Report. 8 June 1924. 1924 Cmd.2193 xii. Home Office.

Committee on the Restoration of Order in Ireland Act, 1920.

> Report. 1 Aug.1924. 1924/5 Cmd.2278 xiv. Home Office.

**TALBOT, J. E.**
Report of a public inquiry on provision of a new public elementary school in the parish of Llanasa, county of Flint. 7 Jan.1907. 1907 Cd.3320 lxiv. Board of Education.

**TANSLEY, K.**
Adaptation of the eye: its relation to the critical frequency of flicker. 18 June 1929. (S.R.S., no.134) Medical Research Council.

**TATE, William H.**
Advisory committee on the welfare of the blind.
> Report of the sub-committee on home teaching. 9 Dec.1936. Ministry of Health.

**TAYLOR, A. E.**
Report on the conditions of diet and nutrition in the internment camp at Ruhleben. 3 May 1916. (Misc., no.18, 1916.) 3 May 1916 Cd.8259 xv. Foreign Office.

**TAYLOR, A. K.**
The effect of different systems of lighting on output and accuracy in fine work (typesetting by hand). Nov.1927. Medical Research Committee.

**TAYLOR, G. Stevenson**
Memorandum on chairs and other lifting appliances. Dec.1914. Home Office.

**TAYLOR, J. R.**
Report on Greater London drainage. Dec.1934. Ministry of Health.

**TAYLOR, T. H. C.**
The biological control of an insect in Fiji: an account of the coconut leaf—mining beetle and its parasite complex. 1937. Imperial Institute of Entomology.

**TAYLOR, William**
Inquiry committee on the standardisation of the elements of optical instruments.
> Report. Sept.1920. Department of Scientific and Industrial Research.

**TAYLOR, William Francis Kyffin**
Committee on appeals from division of courts of summary jurisdiction.
> Report. 25 April 1933. 1932/3 Cmd.4296 x. Home Office.

**TCHERNAVIN, V.**
The absorption of bones in the skull of salmon during their migration to river. 1938. (Salmon Fish., 1938, no.6) Fishery Board for Scotland.

**TEBB, A. E.**
An inquiry into the prevalence and aetiology of tuberculosis among industrial workers, with special reference to female munitions workers. 18 Oct.1918. (S.R.S., no.22) Medical Research Committee.

**TEMPANY, Harold Augustin**
Agriculture in the West Indies, compiled from documents supplied to the West India Royal Commission, 1938/9 and other sources. Sept.1940. (Colonial, no.182). Colonial Office.

**TEMPERLEY, Harold William Vazeille**
Report on political conditions in Montenegro. 12 Oct.1920. (Misc., no.1, 1921) 1921 Cmd.1123 xliii. Foreign Office.

Tempest-Stewart, C. S. H. V. *SEE:* Vane-Tempest-Stewart, C.S.H., *7th Marquess of Londonderry*

**TEMPLE, Charles Lindsay**
Report on the State of Amazonas, Brazil. 4 June 1900. (Dip.cons.reports: misc.ser., no.530) 1900 Cd.2-13 xci. Foreign Office.

Report on the State of Maranhao, Brazil. 18 Jan.1901. (Dip.cons.reports: misc.ser., no.547) 1900 Cd.430-2 lxxx. Foreign Office.

**TENNANT, Harold John**
Committee on the scientific and statistical investigations now being carried out in relation to the fishing industry of Great Britain.
> Report. Aug.1908. 1908 Cd.4268 xiii.
> Minutes of evidence, and appendices. 1908 Cd.4304 xiii. Treasury.

Committee on the special reserve.
> Interim report. 22 Oct.1913. 1914 Cd.7250 lii. (no others identified) War Office.

Select committee on registration of nurses.
> Report, proceedings, minutes of evidence and appendix. 26 July 1904. 1904 (281) vi.
> Report, proceedings, evidence, appendix and index. 25 July 1905. 1905 (263) vii. House of Commons.

**TENNANT, May**
Report of an enquiry regarding the conditions of marriage off the strength. 3 Dec.1913. 1914 Cd.7441 li. War Office.

**TENNYSON, Hallam, *2nd Baron Tennyson***
Committee on settling within the Empire ex-servicemen who may desire to emigrate after the war.
> Report. 28 July 1917. 1917/8 Cd.8672 x. Colonial Office.

Departmental committee on agricultural settlements in British Colonies.
> Vol.1: Report. 31 May 1906. 1906 Cd.2978 lxxvi.
> Vol.2: Minutes of evidence, appendices, analysis and index. 1906 Cd.2979 lxxvi. Colonial Office.

THESIGER, Frederick John Napier, *1st Viscount Chelmsford*
Committee on education and supply of biologists.
Report. 20 May 1931. Economic Advisory Council. Treasury.

Committee on the British Industries Fair.
Report. 13 Nov.1930. 1930/1 Cmd.3726 x. Board of Trade.

Departmental committee of inquiry on the Miners' Welfare Fund.
Report. 14 Dec.1932. 1932/3 Cmd.4236 xv. Mines Department.

Departmental committee on regional development.
Interim report. 26 March 1931. 1930/1 Cmd.3915 xvii. (no further reports identified) Ministry of Health.

Juvenile employment inquiry.
Report. 23 July 1921. Ministry of Labour.

Report on Indian constitutional reforms. 22 April 1918. 1918 Cd.9109 viii. India Office.

Select committee on Irish land purchase (pledges by ministers of the Crown).
Report, evidence and appendix. 2 Aug.1926. 1926 (H.L.162) vi. House of Lords.

Select committee on the nationality of married women.
Report, proceedings, evidence and appendices. 24 July 1923. 1923 (115) vii. House of Commons.

THEWLIS, J.
The structure of teeth as shown by X-ray examination. 14 Feb.1940. (S.R.S., no.238) Medical Research Council.

Thomas, Bruce. *SEE:* Thomas, W. B.

THOMAS, D. Lleufer
Commission of enquiry into industrial unrest.
Report of commissioners for Wales. *SEE:* Barnes, G. N.

THOMAS, Gretta Mary
A report on cancer of the skin. May 1933. (Rep.Pub.Health & Med.Subj., no.70) Ministry of Health.

Thomas, H. Preston. *SEE:* Preston-Thomas, H.

THOMAS, Herbert Henry
The geology of Ardnamurchan, north-west Mull and Coll. (Sheet 51 and part of 52) 15 May 1930. (Mem.Geol.Surv., Scotl.) Geological Survey, Scotland.

Refractory materials; petrography and chemistry. 27 Nov.1919. (Special reports on the mineral resources of Great Britain, vol.16) (Mem.Geol.Surv.) Geological Survey.

THOMAS, Ivor
The British carboniferous producti; I: genera *postula* and *overtonia*. 6 June 1914. (Mem.Geol.Surv., Palaeont, vol.1, part 4) Geological Survey.

The British carboniferous orthotetinae. 5 Nov.1910. (Mem.Geol.Surv., Palaeont, vol.1, part 2) Geological Survey.

THOMAS, James Henry
Committee on new industrial development.
Report. 28 June 1932. Economic Advisory Council. Treasury.

THOMAS, R. Arthur
Advisory committee for the metalliferous mining and quarrying industry.

Report on the possibilities of developing or reviving the working of metalliferous and associated deposits in Great Britain. 4 May 1932. Mines Department.

THOMAS, T. S. E.
The ignition of firedamp by the filaments of broken electric lamp bulbs. Nov.1933. (S.M.R.B. Paper, no.80) Mines Department.

The pressures produced by the striking of momentary arcs in closed vessels. Sept.1932. (S.M.R.B. Paper, no.77) Mines Department.

THOMAS, W. N.
Effect of temperature on the setting times of cements, and on the strength of cements, mortars and concretes. Jan.1929. (B.R.B. special rep., no.13) Department of Scientific and Industrial Research.

The use of calcium chloride or sodium chloride as a protection for mortar against frost. Oct.1929. (B.R.B. special rep., no.14) Department of Scientific and Industrial Research.

Thomas, W. R. *SEE:* Rees-Thomas, W.

THOMAS, William Bruce
Charges (railway control) consultative committee.
Report on increase of fares upon the services of the London Passenger Transport Board. 20 May 1940. Ministry of Transport.
Report on increasing charges of the Railway companies and the London Passenger Transport Board. 18 Sept.1940. Ministry of Transport.

THOMPSON, Beeby
The water supply of Bedfordshire and Northamptonshire from underground sources. 21 March 1908. (Mem.Geol.Surv.) Geological Survey.

THOMPSON, D'Arcy Wentworth
North Sea fisheries investigation committee.
*General.* Reports of the British delegates attending the international conferences on fishery and hydrographical investigations in the North Sea and correspondence. 31 Jan.1902. 1902 Cd.1313 xv.
Reports of the British delegates attending the meetings of the International Council for the Exploration in the Sea in 1903, 1904 and 1905.
Vol. 1. May 1906. 1906 Cd.2966 xviii.
Vol.2. General report of the International Council for 1902-4. May 1906. 1906 Cd.3033 xviii.
Report of the British delegates attending the meeting at Amsterdam in 1906 and reports relating thereto. 18 July 1906. 1906 Cd.3165 xviii.
Reports of the British delegates attending the meetings of the International Council for the Exploration of the Sea, in 1907, 1908 and 1909 and reports relating thereto. Dec.1910. 1910 Cd.5032 xxx.

*Northern Area.*
Report on fishery and hydrolographical investigations in the North Sea and adjacent waters, 1902-3. June 1905. 1905 Cd.2612 xiv.
Second report on fishery and hydrographical investigations in the North Sea and adjacent waters, 1904-5. Part I. Hydrography . 11 Jan.1907. 1907 Cd.3358 xii.
Third report, 1904-06. Sept.1908. 1908 Cd.4350 xvi.
Fourth report, 1906-08. Hydrography. Aug.1909. 1909 Cd.4893 xxiv.

THOMPSON, D'Arcy Wentworth (continued)
Fifth report, 1908-11. 16 May 1913. 1913 Cd.6950 xxv.

*Southern Area.*
First report. 2 Aug.1905. 1905 Cd.2670 xiv.
Second report, 1904-05. Part I: 15 Oct.1907. 1908 Cd.3837 xvi.
Part II: 31 March 1909. 1909 Cd.4641 xxiv.
Third report, 1906-08. 15 Feb.1911. 1911 Cd.5546 xxv.
Fourth report on fishery (plaice and trawling) and hydrographical investigations in the North Sea and adjacent waters conducted by the Marine Biological Association of the United Kingdom, 1909. 23 Feb.1912. 1912/3 Cd.6125 xxviii. Prime Minister's Office.

On mean sea level and its fluctuations. 1914. (Sci.invest., 1914, no.4) Fishery Board for Scotland.

On saithe, ling and cod in the statistics of the Aberdeen trawl-fishery, 1901-1929. 1931. (Sci.invest., 1931, no.2) Fishery Board for Scotland.

On the surface temperature of the North Sea and of the north Atlantic. 1916. (Sci.invest., 1916, no.1) Fishery Board for Scotland.

On whales landed at the Scottish whaling stations during the years 1908-1914 and 1920-1927. 1928. (Sci.Invest., 1928, no.3) Fishery Board for Scotland.

Report on herring fishery in the Firth of Clyde. 17 Dec.1902. 1903 Cd.1674 xiv. Fishery Board for Scotland.

THOMPSON, Ernest
British economic mission to the Far East.
Report. 17 March 1931. Department of Overseas Trade.
Cotton Mission.
Report. 17 March 1931. Board of Trade.

THOMPSON, H. N.
Report on the forests of the Gold Coast. Jan.1910. (Colonial reports: misc., no.66) 1910 Cd.4993 lxv. Colonial Office.

THOMPSON, Harold
Problems in haddock biology.
1. Preliminary report. (Sci.invest., 1922, no.5) 1923.
2. Frequency and distribution of the age classes in 1923. (Sci.invest., 1924, no.1) 1924.
3. Metabolism of haddock and other gadoid fish in the aquarium. (Sci.invest., 1926, no.2) 1924.
4. The haddock of the north-western North Sea. (Sci.invest., 1927, no.3) 1928.
5. General features in the biology of the haddock in Icelandic waters, 1903-1926. (Sci.Invest., 1928, no.5) 1929. Fishery Board for Scotland.
The tunicata of the Scottish area.
Part 1. (Sci.invest., 1930, no.3) 1930.
Part 2. (Sci.invest., 1931, no.1) 1931.
Part 3. (Sci.invest., 1932, no.2) 1933.
Part 4. (Sci.invest., 1934, no.1) 1934. Fishery Board for Scotland.

THOMPSON, John H. R.
Pulmonary tuberculosis; mortality after sanitorium treatment. 21 June 1919. (S.R.S., no.33) Medical Research Committee.

THOMPSON, W. R.
The biological control of insect and plant pests. June 1930. (E.M.B. 29) Empire Marketing Board.

THOMSON, Francis Vernon
Administrative committee on tramp shipping.
Interim report. Oct.1935. 1934/5 Cmd.5004 xi.
Second report. Feb.1936. 1935/6 Cmd.5084 xiii.
Third report. Oct.1936. 1935/6 Cmd.5291 xiii.
Fourth report. Jan.1937. 1936/7 Cmd.5363 xiii.
Fifth report. Sept.1937. 1936/7 Cmd.5555 xiii.
Sixth report. May 1938. 1937/8 Cmd.5750 xiii.
Board of Trade.

THOMSON, J. H.
Departmental committee on acetylene generators.
*SEE:* Boys, C. V.

THOMSON, James, *Sir*
Indian excise committee, 1905-06.
Report. 4 July 1906. 1907 Cd.3327 lviii. India office. Treasury.

THOMSON, Joseph John
Committee on the position of natural science in the educational system of Great Britain.
Report. 19 Feb.1918. 1918 Cd.9011 ix. Prime Ministers' Office.

THOMSON, St.Clair
Tuberculosis of the larynx: ten years' experience in a sanatorium. Feb.1924. (S.R.S., no.83) Medical Research Council.

THOMSON, Theodore
Report on an outbreak of enteric fever in the Borough of Mansfield. 4 March 1907. (Rep.Med.Insp., no.254) Local Government Board.

Report on prevention of contamination of the supply of water furnished by the Cambridge University and Town Waterworks Co. 12 Oct.1908. Local Government Board.

Report on recurrent prevalences of enteric fever in Folkstone urban sanitary district. 6 March 1902. (Rep.Med.Insp., no.171) Local Government Board.

Report on the recent prevalence of diphtheria in the Prestwich U.D. 26 Sept.1901. (Rep.Med.Insp., no.165) Local Government Board.

Report on the sanitary conditions of Hambledon R.D. 3 April 1907. (Rep.Med.Insp., no.257) Local Government Board.

Report on the sanitary conditions of Holsworthy U.D. 1901. (Rep.Med.Insp., no.161) Local Government Board.

Report on the sanitary conditions of Yeovil Borough. 26 July 1907. (Rep.Med.Insp., no.274) Local Government Board.

Report on the sanitary conditions of Yeovil R.D. 13 Sept.1907. (Rep.Med.Insp., no.280) Local Government Board.

THOMSON, W. S.
Report on insect infestation of stored cacao. Dec.1929. (E.M.B.24) Empire Marketing Board.

THORMAN, G. L.
The distribution of mean annual maxima and minima of temperature over the globe. Nov.1928. (Geophys.Mem., no.44) Meteorological Office.

THORNTON, J. P.
The use of uniform and instruction in tailoring in reformatory and industrial schools. Nov.1916. Home Office.

THORNTON, J. S.
Schools public and private in the North of Europe.
May 1907. (Special reports on educational subjects,
vol.17) 1907 Cd.3537 xxii. Board of Education.

THORNTON, Lewis Henry Douglas
A report on an outbreak of food poisoning due to
salmonella, type 'Dublin' and conveyed by raw milk.
March 1938. (Rep.Pub.Health & Med.Subj., no.82)
Ministry of Health.

THORNTON, William Mundell
Committee on the amendment of the general
regulations governing the use of electricity in mines
under the Coal Mines Act, 1911.
Report. 13 Sept.1940. Mines Department.

THORNTON, William Mundell
Report on electric signalling with bare wires as
regards the danger of ignition of inflamable gaseous
mixtures by the break-flash at the signal wires. 1
June 1916. Home Office.

THORPE, Jocelyn Field
Oxygen research committee.
Report. Sept.1923. Department of Scientific
and Industrial Research.

THORPE, T. Edward
Departmental committee on electric mains
explosions.
Report. 22 May 1914. 1914 Cd.7481 xxix. Board
of Trade.

Report on the work of the Government Laboratory
on the question of the employment of lead
compounds in pottery. May 1901. 1901 Cd.679 x.
Home Office.

Use of lead in the manufacture of pottery.
Reports. 1901. 1901 Cd.527 x. Home Office.

THRESH, John Clough
The water supply of Essex from underground
sources. 10 Dec.1915. (Mem.Geol.Surv.) Geological
Survey.

THURN, Everard F.
Report on the Fiji hurricane of March, 1910. 16
April 1910. (Colonial reports: misc., no.72) 1910
Cd.5216 lxv. Colonial Office.

TIDDEMAN, R. H.
The water supply of Oxfordshire. 12 April 1910.
(Mem.Geol.Surv.) Geological Survey.

TIDESWELL, F. V.
Gob fires.
Part 1: Explosions in sealed-off areas in non-
gassy seams. Aug.1932. (S.M.R.B. Paper,
no.75)
Part 2: The revival of heatings by inleakage of
air. Aug.1932. (S.M.R.B. Paper, no.76) Mines
Department.

TIDY, Henry Letheby
Report on the investigation of an epidemic caused by
bacillus aertrycke. 14 Nov.1918. (S.R.S., no.24)
Medical Research Council.

TOCHER, J. F.
Variations in the composition of milk. Nov.1925.
Scottish Board of Health.

TOLKOWSKY, S.
The Jewish colonisation in Palestine. 1918. Ministry
of Information.

TOMLIN, Thomas James Cheshire, *Baron Tomlin of
Ash*
Child adoption committee.
First report. 6 April 1925. 1924/5 Cmd.2401 ix.

Second report. 6 July 1925. 1924/5 Cmd.2469
ix.
Third and final report. 19 April 1926. 1926
Cmd.2711 viii. Home Office.
Committee on district probate registries.
Report. 18 July 1923. 1923 Cmd.1968 xii, pt.2.
Lord Chancellor's Office.
Dormant funds committee.
Report. 15 July 1932. 1931/2 Cmd.4152 vii.
Lord Chancellor's Office.
Land registration committee.
Report. 4 April 1930. 1929/30 Cmd.3564 xv.
Lord Chancellor's Office.
Land transfer committee.
Report. Jan.1935. 1934/5 Cmd.4776 x. Lord
Chancellor's Office.
Royal commission on the civil service.
Report. 8 July 1931. 1930/1 Cmd.3909 x.
Minutes of evidence and index. 1929-1932.
Appendix. 16 parts. 1930.
Selections from statements. 2 parts. 1931.
Treasury.

TOMLINSON, George John Frederick
Colonial students committee.
Report. Dec.1938. (Colonial, no.161) 1939.
Colonial Office.

TONGUE, Alfred and Co.
Report on the coal industry. 9 Feb.1920. 1920
Cmd.555 xiii. Prime Minister's Office.

TONKS, L. H.
The geology of Manchester and the south-east
Lancashire coalfield. (Sheet 85) 30 March 1931.
(Mem.Geol.Surv.) Geological Survey.

TOPHAM, H.
Committee on prevention of accidents in paper
mills.
First report: machinery accidents. 5 Aug.1937.
(no others identified) Home Office.

TOULMIN, George
Select committee on motor traffic.
Report and proceedings. 13 Feb.1913. 1912/3
(519) ix.
Report and proceedings. 11 Aug.1913. 1913
(278) viii.
Evidence. Vol.1: 17 December to 3 April 1913.
Vol.2: 8 April to 18 July 1913, with appendices.
1913 (278) viii, ix. House of Commons.

TOWNLEY, Walter Beaupré
Report on the German colonial estimates for 1900.
31 March 1900. (Dip.cons. rep. misc., ser., no.524)
1900 Cd.2-7 xci. Foreign Office.

Report on the German colonies for the year ending
June 30, 1899. 25 May 1900. (Dip.cons.rep:
misc.ser., no.528) 1900 Cd.2-11 xci. Foreign Office.

TOYNBEE, Arnold J.
The Belgian deportations. 1917. Ministry of
Information.

The murderous tyranny of the Turks. 1917. Ministry
of Information.

TRACEY, Richard E.
Committee on the training and examination of
junior naval officers.
Report. 23 May 1898. 1901 Cd.508 xlii.
Admiralty.

TRANASS, V.
Royal (Norwegian) Commission on Norwegian
salmon fisheries, 1896-1898.
Report. 10 June 1898. 1901 Cd.452 xii.

TREFUSIS, Charles John Robert Hepburn-Stuart-Forbes, *21st Baron Clinton*
Departmental committee on the Fertilizers and Feeding Stuffs Act, 1906.
Report. 27 March 1924. 1924 Cmd.2125 ix. Ministry of Agriculture and fisheries.

Fertilisers and feeding stuffs advisory committee.
Report. 3 July 1925. 1924/5 Cmd.2470 xii. Ministry of Agriculture and Fisheries.

Inter-departmental committee on forestry education.
Report. 1 Feb.1921. 1921 Cmd.1166 xii. Colonial Office.

TRENCHARD, Hugh Montague, *1st Viscount*
Advisory committee on the scientific investigation of crime.
Report. 24 June 1936. Home Office.

TREVELYAN, Charles Philips
Departmental committee on educational endowments.
Vol.1: report. 31 March 1911. 1911 Cd.5662 xvii.
Vol.2: minutes of evidence, appendices and index. 1911 Cd.5747 xvii. Board of Education.

Departmental committee on the acceptance, by the Board of Education, of dental certificates from unregistered practitioners. July 1914. 1914 Cd.7538 xxv. Board of Education.

Inter-departmental committee on partial exemption from school attendance.
Vol.1. Report. 23 July 1909. 1909 Cd.4791 xvii.
Vol.2. Minutes of evidence, appendices and index. 1909 Cd.4887 xvii. Board of Education.

Trevethin, *Lord. SEE:* Lawrence, A. T., *1st Baron*

TRIFFITT, M. J.
Helminthology in its application to agriculture and horticulture. 1933. (Notes and Memo., no.8) Imperial Bureau of Agricultural Parasitology.

TROTTER, F. M.
The geology of the Brampton district. (Sheet 18) 1 June 1932. (Mem.Geol.Surv.) Geological Survey.

Gosforth district. (Sheet 37 N.S.) (Mem.Geol.Surv.) Geological Survey.

TROTTER, Henry
Despatch on the operations of the European Commission of the Danube during the years 1894-1906, with a resume of its previous history. 17 July 1907. (Commerical, no.9, 1907.) 1907 Cd3646 lxxxvii. Foreign Office.

TROUP, Charles Edward
Departmental committee on cremation regulations.
Report. 28 Jan.1903. 1903 Cd.1452 xxiii. Home Office.

TRYON, George Clement
Departmental committee of inquiry on the machinery of administration of the Ministry of Pensions..21 June 1921. Ministry of Pensions.

TUDESQ, Andree
Brother Tommy; the British offensives on the western front, January to June, 1917. 1917. Ministry of Information.

TULLOCH, William John
Further investigations on the variola-vaccinia flocculation reaction. 30 April 1931. (S.R.S., no.156) Medical Research Council.

TURNBULL, Hubert Maitland
The accuracy of Wassermann tests applied before and after death, estimated by necropsy. 1: The Wassermann test applied before death. 22 Jan.1920. (S.R.S., no.47) Medical Research Committee.

TURNER, Ben
Standing committee on trusts.
Report of a sub-committee on uniform clothing. 19 April 1921. 1921 Cmd.1339 xvi. Board of Trade.

TURNER, Christopher Hatton
Advisory committee on rural cottages.
Report, appendices and reduced plans. 24 Aug.1914. Board of Agriculture and Fisheries.

Departmental committee on buildings for small holdings in England and Wales.
Report with abstract of the evidence, appendices, index and plans, and specifications. 22 March 1913. 1913 Cd.6708 xv. Board of Agriculture and Fisheries.

TURNER, F. G.
Concrete road construction on the Reichsautobahnen; notes on a visit to Germany. July 1937. Ministry of Transport.

TURNER, John
Standing committee on prices.
Report of a sub-committee on the price of matches. 21 June 1920. 1920 Cmd.924 xxiii. Board of Trade.

TURPIN, William Gibbs
American dollar securities committee.
Report. 4 June 1919. 1919 (212) xiii, pt.1. Treasury.

TYNDALE, W. C.
The latest developments of practical treatment of sewage. June 1903. War Office.

TYRRELL, G. W.
The geology of Arran. (Sheet 21 and 13) 31 Oct.1927. (Mem.Geol.Surv., Scotl.) Geological Survey, Scotland.

Ullswater, *Lord. SEE:* Lowther, James William, *1st Viscount Ullswater*

UNDEN, M.
Report on the question of the Turco-Irak frontier. 16 Dec.1925. (Misc., no.20, 1925) 1924/5 Cmd.2565 xxxii. Foreign Office.

UNWIN, William Cawthorne
Report on the sixth congress of the International Association for Testing Materials at New York, 1912. Nov.1912. 1914 Cd.7185 xlviii. Board of Trade.

UPCOTT, G. C.
Committee on common seniority lists for men and women.
Report. 7 March 1924. Treasury.

USSHER, W. A. E.
The geology of the country around Bodmin and St. Austell. (Sheet 347) 30 Sept.1909. (Mem.Geol.Surv.) Geological Survey.

The geology of the country around Exeter. (Sheet 325) 27 Sept.1901. (Mem.Geol.Surv.) Geological Survey.

The geology of the country around Kingsbridge and Salcombe. (Sheet 355 and 356) 7 April 1904. (Mem.Geol.Surv.) Geological Survey.

The geology of the country around Newton Abbot. (Sheet 339) 11 Dec.1912. (Mem.Geol.Surv.) Geological Survey.

USHER, W. A. E. (continued)

The geology of the country around Plymouth and Liskeard. (Sheet 348) 7 Oct.1907. (Mem.Geol.Surv.) Geological Survey.

The geology of the country around Torquay. (Sheet 350) 9 June 1903. (Mem.Geol.Surv.) Geological Survey.

The geology of the country between Wellington and Chard. (Sheet 311) 28 Nov.1906. (Mem.Geol.Surv.) Geological Survey.

The geology of the country around Wybridge and Modbury. (Sheet 349) 2 July 1912. (Mem.Geol.Surv.) Geological Survey.

The geology of the country near Sidmouth and Lyme Regis. (Sheets 326 and 340) 21 March 1906. (Mem.Geol.Surv.) Geological Survey.

The geology of the Quantock hills and of Taunton and Bridgewater. (Sheet 295) 7 Nov.1907. (Mem.Geol.Surv.) Geological Survey.

UTHWATT, Augustus Andrews

Committee on liability for war damage to the subject-matter of contracts.
Report. 2 Sept.1939. 1938/9 Cmd.6100 xv. Lord Chancellor's Office.

Committee on the principles of assessment of war damage.
First report. 3 Nov.1939. 1939/40 Cmd.6136 v.
Final report. 1 March 1940. 1939/40 Cmd.6197 v. Treasury.

Committee on the responsibility for the repair of premises damaged by hostilities.
Report. 26 Sept.1938. 1938/9 Cmd.5934 xv. Lord Chancellor's Office.

VALLOTTON, Benjamin

In the land of death. 1917. Ministry of Information.

VALLOW, Harold

Tuberculosis in insured persons accepted for treatment by the City of Bradford Health Committee. 24 Feb.1923. (S.R.S., no.76) Medical Research Council.

VAN SOMEREN, Vernon D.

A preliminary investigation into the causes of scale absorption in salmon. 1937. (Salmon Fish., 1937, no.2) (no others identified) Fishery Board for Scotland.

VAN ZEELAND, Paul

Report on the possibility of obtaining a general reduction of the obstacles to international trade. 26 Jan.1938. (Misc., no.1, 1938) 1937/8 Cmd.5648 xv. Foreign Office.

VANE, Christopher William, *10th Baron Barnard*

Agricultural education conference.
Report. Agricultural education for women. 29 July 1915. Board of Agriculture and Fisheries.

VANE-TEMPEST-STEWART, Charles Stewart Henry, *7th Marquess of Londonderry*

Royal commission on London squares.
Report. 11 Sept. 1928. 1928/9 Cmd.3196 viii.
Minutes of evidence. 15 Nov. 1927 to 28 Feb.1928. 1927-8. Ministry of Health.

VASSAR-SMITH, Richard Vassar

Committee on financial facilities.
Report. 21 Nov.1918. 1918 Cd.9227 x. Treasury.

VAUGHAN-WILLIAMS, Richard Lomax.

Royal commission on the church of England and other religious bodies in Wales and Monmouthshire.

Vol.1, part 1: report. 1 Nov.1910. 1910 Cd.5432 xiv.
Vol.1, part 2: appendices. 1910 5432-I xiv.
Vol.2: minutes of evidence (questions 1-17,874) 1910 Cd.5433 xv.
Vol.3: minutes of evidence (questions 17,875-34,376) 1910 Cd.5434 xvi.
Vol.4: minutes of evidence (questions, 34,377-48,615) 1910 Cd.5435 xvii.
Vol.5: appendices to minutes of evidence. 1910 Cd.5436 xviii.
Vol.6: nonconformist county statistics. 1910 Cd.5437 xviii.
Vol.7: appendix to minutes of evidence (nonconformists) 1910 Cd.5438 xix.
Vol.8: indexes. 1910 Cd.5439 xix.

VECCHIO, Giorgio del

The moral basis of Italy's war. 1917. Ministry of Information.

VERDIER, J. W.

Committee on the cost of production, prices, *etc.*, of clogs.
Report. 27 Nov.1919. 1920 Cmd.541 xxiii. Board of Trade.

VERNEY, Harry C. W.

Departmental committee on land settlement for sailors and soldiers. *SEE:* Hobhouse, H.

VERNON, Horace Middleton

Fatigue and efficiency in the iron and steel industry. 20 Jan. 1920. (I.H.R.B. Rep., no.5) Medical Research Council.

The influence of alcohol on manual work and neuro-muscular co-ordination. 30 May 1919. (S.R.S., no.34) Medical Research Committee.

The influence of hours of work and of ventilation on output in tinplate manufacture. July 1919. (I.H.R.B. Rep., No.1) Medical Research Committee.

Investigation into the factors concerned in the causation of industrial accidents. Feb.1918. (Health of munition workers committee. Memo., no.21) 1918 Cd.9046 xv. Ministry of Munitions.

On the extent and effects of variety in repetitive work. Feb.1924. (I.H.R.B. Rep., no.26) Medical Research Council.

The speed of adaptation of output to altered hours of work. April 1920. (I.H.R.B. Rep., no.6) Medical Research Council.

Statistical information concerning output in relation to hours of work. July 1916. (Health of munitions workers committee. Memo., no.12) 1916 Cd.8344 xxiii. Ministry of Munitions.

Further statistical information concerning output in relation to hours of work, with special reference to the influence of Sunday labour. April 1917. (Health of munition workers committee. Memo., no.18) (appendix to Memo., no.5). 1917/8 Cd.8628 xx. Ministry of Munitions.

Two contributions to the study of accident causation. Nov.1922. (I.H.R.B. Rep., no.19) Medical Research Council.

Two investigations in potters' shops. March 1922. (I.H.R.B. Rep., no.18) Medical Research council.

Two studies on rest pauses in industry. Feb.1924. (I.H.R.B.Rep., no.25) Medical Research Council.

VERNON, M. D.

The movements of the eyes in reading. 25 July 1930. (S.R.S., no.148) Medical Research Council.

VERNON, P. E.
The assessment of psychological qualities by verbal methods. May 1938. (I.H.R.B. Rep., no.83) Medical Research Council.

Vernon-Thomson, F. SEE: Thomson, F. V.

VIAUD, Louis Marie Julian
The trail of the barbarians. 1917. Ministry of Information.

VICARS, Edward
Report for the year 1907 on the chemical, metal and mining industries of the consular district of Lyons. Nov.1908. (Dip.cons.reports: misc.ser., no.669) 1908 Cd.3728-5 cviii. Foreign Office and Board of Trade.

VICKERY, J. R.
The yellowing of the abdominal fat of frozen rabbits. May 1932. (F.I.B. special rep., no.42) Department of Scientific and Industrial Research.

VIGOUREUX, P.
Quartz oscillators and their applications. July 1939. Department of Scientific and Industrial Research.

VILLIERS, Albert George Child, 7th Earl of Jersey.
Committee on the Board of Trade and the Local Government Board.
Report. 10 May 1904. 1904 Cd.2121 lxxviii. Treasury.

Departmental committee on railway rates (preferential treatment).
Report. 6 April 1906. 1906 Cd.2959 lv.
Minutes of evidence, appendices and index. 1906 Cd.2960 lv. Board of Agriculture and fisheries.

VILLIERS, George Herbert Hyde, 6th Earl of Clarendon.
Report on visit to Canada in connection with British settlement. Oct.1926. 1926 Cmd.2760 xv. Colonial Office.

VINCENT, Charles Edward Howard
Committee of inquiry into the Dublin Metropolitan Police.
Report. 11 Oct.1901. 1902 Cd.1088 xlii.
Evidence and appendix. 1902 Cd.1095 xlii. Irish Secretary's Office.

Committee of inquiry into the Royal Irish Constabulary.
Report. 10 Oct.1901. 1902 Cd.1087 xlii.
Evidence and appendix. 1902 Cd.1094 xlii. Irish Secretary's Office.

VINCENT, Edgar, 1st Viscount D'Abernon
Advisory committee on the action of alcohol.
Report. Alcohol: its action on the human organism. Dec.1917. Central Control Board (Liquor Traffic).

Royal commission on national museums and galleries.
Interim report. 1 Sept.1928. 1928/9 Cmd.3192 viii.
Final report. Part I: general conclusions and recommendations. 20 Sept. 1929. 1929/30 Cmd.3401 xvi.
Final report. Part 2: conclusions and recommendations relating to individual institutions. 1 Jan.1930. 1929/30 Cmd.3463 xvi.
Evidence, memoranda and appendices. Oct.1929.

Royal commission on the Dominions.
First interim report. 28 Dec.1912. 1912/3 Cd.6515 xvi.
Minutes of evidence, part 1: migration. 1912/3 Cd.6516 xvi.
Minutes of evidence, part 2: natural resources, trade and legislation. 1912/3 Cd.6517 xvi.
Evidence taken in New Zealand in 1913. 1914 Cd.7170 xvii.
Evidence taken in Australia in 1913. Parts 1 and 2. 1914 Cd.7171, Cd.7172 xvii.
Evidence taken in London, November 1913, and papers. 1914 Cd.7173 xviii.
Second interim report. 16 Jan.1914. 1914 Cd.7210 xviii.
Evidence taken in London, January 1914, and papers. 1914 Cd.7351 xviii.
Third interim report. 25 June 1914. 1914 Cd.7505 xviii.
Evidence taken in the Union of South Africa in 1914. 1914/6 Cd.7706, Cd.7708 xiii.
Evidence taken in London in June and July 1914 and papers laid. 1914/6 Cd.7710 xiii.
Fourth interim report. 9 Dec.1914. 1914/6 Cd.7711 xiv.
Evidence taken in Newfoundland in 1914. 1914/6 Cd.7898 xiv.
Evidence taken in the Maritime provinces of Canada in 1914. 1914/6 Cd.7971 xiv.
Memorandum and tables on the food and raw materials requirements of the United Kingdom. 1914/6 Cd.8123 xiv.
Memorandum and tables on the trade statistics and trade of the self-governing Dominions. 1914/6 Cd.8156 xiv.
Fifth interim report. 31 January 1917. 1917/8 Cd.8457 viii.
Evidence taken in the Central and Western provinces of Canada in 1916. 1917/8 Cd.8458, Cd.8459 viii, ix.
Papers laid before the commission, 1914-1917. 1917/8 Cd.8460 ix.
Memoranda and tables on the chief harbours of the British Empire and certain foreign countries and the Suez and Panama canals. 1917/8 Cd.8461 ix.
Final report. 21 Feb.1917. 1917/8 Cd.8462 x.

VISCHER, H.
The system of education in northern Nigeria. Dec.1913. (Imperial education conference papers) Board of Education.

VON DONOP, S. B.
Notes on mechanism as applied to artillery. May 1902. War Office.

VYVYAN, Arthur Vyell
Court of inquiry appointed by the Air Council.
Report and evidence. Aug.1919. 1919 Cmd.347 xxxiii. Air Council.

VYVYAN, George Rawlinson
Trinity House fog-signal committee.
Report on experiments at St. Catherine's point, Isle of Wight. 1901. 1902 Cd.848 xcii. Board of Trade.

WADE, John
Report on the destruction of rats and disinfection on shipboard. 10 Nov.1904. (Rep.Med.Insp., no.201) Local Government Board.

WADE, Thomas Williams
Report on an investigation into the mortality rate from tuberculosis of the respiratory system among quarrymen and state workers in the Gwyrfai rural district. 6 May 1927. (Rep.Pub.Health & Med.Subj., no.38) Ministry of Health.

WADE, Thomas Williams (continued)
Report on the occurrence of bacillary dysentery in the Ogmore and Garw urban districts in the county of Glamorgan. Oct.1922. (Rep.Pub.Health & Med.Subj., no.14) Ministry of Health.

WADSWORTH, J.
The relation between haze and relative humidity of the surface air. Oct.1921. (Prof.Note, no.26) Meteorological Office.

The relation between the height reached by a pilot balloon and its ascending velocity. April 1923. (Prof.Notes, no.31) Meteorological Office.

Studies of wind and cloud at Malta. March 1928. (Geophys.Mem., no.37) Meteorological Office.

A study of visibility and fog at Malta. July 1930. (Geophys.Mem., no.51) Meteorological Office.

WAINWRIGHT, W. H.
A graphical cost analysis of cottage building. April 1922. (B.R.B. Special rep., no.6) Department of Scientific and Industrial Research.

WAKELY, John
Vice-regal committee on the Clerk of the Crown and Peace, county court registrars and local registrars of title in Ireland.
Report. 17 June 1920. 1920 Cmd.805 xiii. Irish Secretary's Office.

WALKER, Alexander
Departmental committee on area gas supply.
Report. 31 March 1930. Board of Trade.

Departmental committee on gas supplies in the West of Scotland.
Report. 2 Nov.1936. Board of Trade.

WALKER, E. Eaton
Reports on the geology of the East Africa Protectorate. Aug.1903. 1904 Cd.1769 lxii. Foreign Office.

WALKER, G. W.
Graphical construction for the epicentre of an earthquake. Dec.1911. (Geophys.Mem., no.3) Meteorological Office.

WALKER, Norman
Consultative council on medical and allied services.
Report on hospital services. 19 Jan.1933. Department of Health for Scotland.

WALKER, Samuel
Irish inland fisheries commission.
Report. 14 Jan.1901. 1901 Cd.448 xii.
Appendix, Part I: Minutes of evidence. 1901 Cd.450 xii.
Appendix, Part II: Documents. 1901 Cd.451 xii.
Appendix, Part III: Translation of the report of the Royal Commission on Norwegian Salmon Fisheries 1896-1898 and of a treatise by Mr. Landmark on hatcheries and the rearing of fry. 1901 Cd.452 xii. Irish Secretary's Office.

WALKER, Thomas Hollis
Report of inquiry on St. Helens County Borough police force held in March and April 1928. 27 April 1928. 1928 Cmd.3103 xii. Home Office.

WALKER, W. F.
The frame working of fruit trees. April 1938. (Occ. paper, no.5) Imperial Bureau of Fruit Production.

WALKER, William
Departmental committee on washing and drying accommodation at mines.
Report. 20 March 1913. 1913 Cd.6724 xxxiv. Home Office.

Mine rescue apparatus research committee.
First report. Aug.1918.
Second report. June 1920.
Third and final report. Jan.1924. Department of Scientific and Industrial Research.

Miners' lamps committee.
Minutes of evidence, index and appendix. 1922.
Memo.no.1: Record of research on the passage of flame of an explosion through wire gauze. May 1920.
Memo.no.2: Report on the use of celluloid in the construction of miners' electric lamps. 24 Dec.1920.
Memo.no.3: Report on the supply of spare parts for the repair and renewal of safety lamps. 9 Feb.1921.
Memo.no.4: Record of research on the passage of flame through perforated tubes and through tubes of small diameter. 25 Nov.1921.
Memo.no.5: Record of research on the passage of flame of an explosion from within miners' lamps fitted with chimneys. 25 Nov.1921.
Memo.no.6: Lamproom organisation and the upkeep of safety lamps. 21 Dec.1921.
Memo.no.7: Report on the general use by workmen of safety lamps which give no indication of inflammable or noxious gasses. 14 Dec.1922.
Memo.no.8: Record of research on the testing of wire gauzes in currents of explosives mixtures. 4 Sept.1923.
Memo.no.9: Report on the relighting of lamps underground. 11 Oct.1923.
Memo.no.10: Report on testing for firedamp. 31 Dec.1923.
Memo.no.11: Final report. June 1924. Mines Department.

Miners' lamps committee.
Report of the sub-committee on the glasses used in flame safety lamps. 2 Oct.1922. Mines Department.

WALLACE, David Euan
Report of investigation into the industrial conditions in certain depressed areas. 2: Durham and Tyneside. 27 July 1934. 1933/4 Cmd.4728 xiii. Ministry of Labour.

WALLACE, T.
Technique in pot culture for fruit plants. 1933. (Occ. paper, no.1) Imperial Bureau of Fruit Production.

WALLACE, W. Reeve
Costs in Privy Council appeals; precedents and notes. July 1911. Privy Council Office.

WALLENSTEIN, Abraham
Jews and Germanism. 1918. Ministry of Information.

WALLER, Augustus Désiré
Report on the food supply of the United Kingdom. 29 July 1916. 1916 Cd.8421 ix. Board of Trade.

WALLER, M. L.
Departmental committee on the supply of books to prisoners.
Report. 27 Oct.1910. 1911 Cd.5589 xxxix. Home Office.

WALROND, William Hood
Committee on the constitution of the consular service.
Report. 2 July 1903. 1903 Cd.1634 lv. Foreign Office.

WALSH, Gerald
Report on dock labour in relation to poor law relief. 1 Sept.1908. 1908 Cd.4391 xcii. Local Government Board.

WALSH, Stephen
Departmental committee on building byelaws.
    Report. 28 Sept.1918. 1918 Cd.9213 vii.
    Evidence and index. 1918 Cd.9214 vii. Local Government Board.

WALTER, A.
Results of observations on the direction and velocity of the upper air current over the south Indian Ocean. Dec.1927. (Geophys.Mem., no.39) Meteorological Office.

WALTERS, John Tudor
Committee on building construction in connection with the provision of dwellings for the working classes.
    Report. 24 Oct.1918. 1918 Cd.9191 vii. Local Government Board *and* Scottish Office.

WARBURG, H. D.
Instructions for reducing and analysing tidal stream observations. June 1929. (Hydrographic publication H.D.290) Admiralty.

WARBURTON, Cecil
Preliminary investigation on flock as a possible distributor of vermin, and on the life history of the body-louse. 9 March 1909. (Rep.Pub.Health & Med.Subj., no.2) Local Government Board.

WARD, Edward Willis Duncan
Committee on civil employment of ex-soldiers and sailors.
    Report with appendix. 2 July 1906. 1906 Cd.2991 xiv.
    Minutes of evidence, digest and index. 1906 Cd.2992 xiv. War Office.

Committee on the provision of officers (a) for service with the regular army in war, and (b) for the auxiliary forces.
    Interim report. 22 Feb.1907. 1907 Cd.3294 xlix.
    Minutes of evidence and appendix. 1907 Cd.3295 xlix. (no others identified) War Office.

Report on the National Scheme of Co-ordination of Voluntary Effort, resulting from the formation of the Department of the Director-General of Voluntary Organisations. 31 May 1919. 1919 Cmd.173 x. War Office.

Report on the service of the Metropolitan Special Constabulary. 1 Aug.1919. 1920 Cmd.536 xxii. Home Office.

Report of the work of the Camps' Library. June 1919. 1919 Cmd.174 x. War Office.

War Office Committee on the treatment of soldiers invalided for tuberculosis.
    Report. 16 Nov.1908. 1908 Cd.3930 xi. War Office.

WARD, William
England and the present war. 1914. Ministry of Information.

Memorandum on German cement. 17 Dec.1904. (Dip.cons.reports: misc.ser., no.624) 1905 Cd.2237-5 lxxxvi. Foreign Office.

Memorandum on German ceramic industries and German trade in ceramic products. 5 July 1906. (Dip.cons.reports: misc.ser., no.653) 1906 Cd.2683-17 cxxii. Foreign Office.

Report on the German machinery import and export trade and industry. 6 Dec.1904. (Dip.cons.reports: misc.ser., no.622) 1905 Cd.2237-3 lxxxvi. Foreign Office.

Report on the German paper industry and export trade. 22 Oct.1905. (Dip.cons.reports: misc.ser., no.642) 1906 Cd.2683-6 cxxii. Foreign Office.

WARD, William Humble, *2nd Earl of Dudley*
Committee on the question of continuous discharge certificates for seamen.
    Vol.1: Report. 7 March 1900. 1900 Cd.133 lxxvii.
    Vol.2: Minutes of evidence, appendix and index. 1900 Cd.136 lxxvii. Board of Trade.

Royal commission on congestion in Ireland.
    First report. 14 Nov.1906. 1906 Cd.3266 xxxii.
    Appendices, minutes of evidence and documents. 1906 Cd.3276 xxxii.
    Second report. 20 Nov.1906. 1907 Cd.3318 xxxv.
    Appendix, minutes of evidence and documents. 1907 Cd.3319 xxxv.
    Third report. 23 Feb.1907. 1907 Cd.3413 xxxv.
    Appendix, minutes of evidence and documents. 1907 Cd.3414 xxxv.
    Fourth report. 22 April 1907. 1907 Cd.3508 xxxvi.
    Appendix, minutes of evidence and documents. 1907 Cd.3509 xxxvi.
    Fifth report. 25 June 1907. 1907 Cd.3629 xxxvi.
    Appendix, minutes of evidence and documents. 1907 Cd.3630 xxxvi.
    Sixth report. 30 Aug.1907. 1908 Cd.3437 xxxix.
    Appendix, minutes of evidence and documents. 1908 Cd.3738 xxxix.
    Seventh report. 30 Sept.1907. 1908 Cd.3784 xl.
    First appendix, minutes of evidence and documents. 1908 Cd.3785 xxxix.
    Second appendix: statistics of the number, valuation, acreage and population of holdings in Ireland. 1908 Cd.3786 xl.
    Eighth report. 30 Oct.1907. 1908 Cd.3838 xli.
    Appendix, minutes of evidence and documents. 1908 Cd.3839 xli.
    Ninth report. 25 Nov.1907. 1908 Cd.3844 xli.
    Appendix, minutes of evidence and documents. 1908 Cd.3845 xli.
    Tenth report. 28 Feb.1908. 1908 Cd.4006 xlii.
    Appendix, minutes of evidence and documents. 1908 Cd.4007 xlii.
    Eleventh report. 14 April 1908. 1908 Cd.4088 xlii.
    Appendix, minutes of evidence and documents. 1908 Cd.4089 xlii.
    Final report. 5 May 1908. 1908 Cd.4097 xlii.
    First appendix: Index to evidence. 1908 Cd.4098 xliii.
    Second appendix: Digest of evidence. 1908 Cd.4099 xliii.

WARDEN, R.
A survey of the air currents in the Bay of Gibraltar, 1929-30. Nov.1933. (Geophys.Mem., no.59) Meteorological Office.

WARDLAW, Claude W.
Banana storage; an account of recent investigations into the storage behaviour of several varieties. Sept.1933. (E.M.B.72) Empire Marketing Board.

The behaviour and diseases of the banana in storage and transport. Jan.1931. (E.M.B.36) Empire Marketing Board.

Control of wastage in bananas; with special

WARDLAW, Claude W. (continued)
reference to time and temperature factors. Sept.1932. (E.M.B.60) Empire Marketing Board.

Panama disease of bananas. July 1929. (E.M.B.20) Empire Marketing Board.

The storage of tropically-grown tomatoes. Sept.1932. (E.M.B.59) Empire Marketing Board.

Transport and storage of bananas with special reference to chilling. Nov.1931. (E.M.B.45) Empire Marketing Board.

WARE, Fabian
The immortal heritage; an account of the work and policy of the Imperial War Graves Commission during the years, 1917-1937. 24 July 1937. Cambridge University Press for Imperial War Graves Commission.

WARMINGTON, Cornelius Marshall
Company law amendment committee.
Report. 18 June 1906. 1906 Cd.3052 xcvii.
Appendix. 1906 Cd.3053 xcvii. Board of Trade.

WARNER, Frank
Committee on British industries fairs.
Report. 9 April 1921. Board of Trade.

Committee on flax seed and flax growing in the United Kingdom.
Interim report: Flax seed. 18 Nov.1924. (no further identified) Board of Trade.

Indian trade enquiry.
Reports on jute and silk. 14 Aug.1918. Imperial Institute.

WATKIN, G.
Report of delegates to enquire as to openings in New Zealand for women from the United Kingdom. Aug.1920. 1920 Cmd.933 xxii. Colonial Office.

WATKINS, C. M.
The durability of slates for roofing. Feb.1932. (B.R.B. Bull., no.12) Department of Scientific and Industrial Research.

The use of asphalt mastic for roofing. Oct.1936. (B.R.B. special rep., no.25) Department of Scientific and Industrial Research.

WATKINS, Frederick Henry
Report on the Caicos Islands sisal industry. 29 June 1907. 1908 Cd.3766 lxx. (Colonial rep.misc.no., 43) Colonial Office.

Report on the salt industry of the Turks and Caicos Islands. 7 July 1908. 1908 Cd.4326 lxx. (Colonial rep.misc.no. 56) Colonial Office.

WATKINS, W. H.
Standing committee on trusts.
Report of a sub-committee on vinegar. 6 May 1920. 1921 Cmd.1355 xvi. Board of Trade.

WATSON, Alfred W.
Actuarial report on the Education (Scotland) (Superannuation) Act, 1925. 12 July 1935. 1934/5 (122) xvii. Treasury.

Actuarial report on the Teachers (Superannuation) Act, 1925. 30 March 1935. 1934/5 (78) xvii. Treasury.

Committee on pensions to widows and orphans of officers in the colonial Service and on colonial provident funds.
Report. 20 April 1936. 1935/6 Cmd.5219 vii. Colonial Office.

Committee on the collection and presentation of official statistics.
Report. 8 Feb.1921. Treasury.

Departmental committee on the application of the Government of Ireland Act to national health insurance.
Report. 7 Dec.1921. 1922 Cmd.1575 ix. National Health Insurance Joint committee.

Inter-departmental committee on health and unemployment insurance.
First and second interim reports. 24 Feb. and 17 March 1922. 1922 Cmd.1644 ix.
Third interim report. 23 Feb.1923. 1923 Cmd.1821 xii pt.2. (last report issued) Ministry of Labour *and* Ministry of Health.

Memorandum on the Washington draft convention concerning the employment of women before and after childbirth. 28 June 1920. 1921 Cmd.1293 xxxi. Ministry of Health.

Mortality experience of government life annuitants, 1900-1920.
Report of the government actuary. 1924. Treasury.

National health insurance (international arrangements) board.
Report. 1 March 1927. 1927 Cmd.2965 xi. Ministry of Health.

Report on an examination of the sickness and disablement experience of a group of approved societies, 1921-27. 31 Jan.1930. 1929/30 Cmd.3548 xxv. Ministry of Health.

Report on police pensions. 31 Dec.1930. Home Office.

Report on teachers in contributory service in schools which are not grant-aided. 31 Oct.1935. 1935/6 (14) ix. Treasury.

Report on the Buntingford Union Association. 12 Dec.1911. 1911 Cd.6001 lxxiii. Treasury.

Report on the clauses of the Economy (Miscellaneous Provisions) Bill relating to national health insurance. 10 March 1926. 1926 Cmd.2603 xxiii. Treasury.

Report on the financial effect of the new provisions (for pensions for soldiers). 18 April 1918. 1918 Cd.9054 xii. Ministry of Pensions.

Report on the financial provisions of the National Health Insurance and Contributory Pensions Bill, 1935. 17 May 1935. 1934/5 Cmd.4906 xiv. Ministry of Health.

Report on the financial provisions of the National Health Insurance Bill, 1920. 1 March 1920. 1920 Cmd.612 xxxvii. Ministry of Health.

Report on the financial provisions of the National Health Insurance Contributory Pensions Bill. 3 May 1932. 1931/2 Cmd.4073 xiv. Ministry of Health.

Report on the financial provisions of the Unemployed Workers' Dependants (Temporary Provision) Bill. 20 Oct.1921. 1921 Cmd.1529 xviii. Ministry of Labour.

Report on the financial provisions of part I of the Unemployment Bill, relating to unemployment insurance. 6 Nov.1933. 1932/3 Cmd.4447 xv. Ministry of Labour.

Report on the financial provisions of the Unemployment Insurance Act, 1920, Amendment Bill. 19 Feb.1921. 1921 Cmd.1164 xviii. Ministry of Labour.

Report on the financial provisions of the Unemployment Insurance (Agriculture) Bill, 1935.

WATSON, Alfred W. (continued)
20 Dec.1935. 1935/6 Cmd.5050 xvii. Ministry of Labour.

Report on the financial provisions of the Unemployment Insurance Bill, 1920, as amended by Standing Committee C. 25 June 1920. 1920 Cmd.796 xxxix. Ministry of Labour.

Report on the financial provisions of the Unemployment Insurance Bill. 25 March 1922. 1922 Cmd.1620 ix. Ministry of Labour.

Report on the financial provisions of the Unemployment Insurance Bill, 1927. 21 Oct.1927. 1927 Cmd.2966 xix. Ministry of Labour.

Report on the financial provisions of the Unemployment Insurance Bill. 14 Nov.1929. 1929/30 Cmd.3437 xxv. Ministry of Labour.

Report on the financial provisions of the Unemployment Insurance (no.2) Bill. 8 June 1921. 1921 Cmd.1336 xviii. Ministry of Labour.

Report on the financial provisions of the Unemployment Insurance (no.2) Bill, 1924.
    Report. 4 April 1924. 1924 Cmd.2109 xix.
    Further report. 24 June 1924. 1924 Cmd.2170 xix. Ministry of Labour.

Report on the financial provisions of the Widows', Orphans and Old Age Contributory Pensions Bill. 1 May 1925. 1924/5 Cmd.2406 xxiii. Ministry of Health.

Report on the Widows' Orphans' and Old Age Contributory Pension Acts, 1925-1932. 15 April 1935. 1934/5 (82) xii. Treasury.

Sub-committee of the permanent consultative committee on official statistics.
    Report: statistics relating to health and mortality in the mercantile marine. 30 June 1926. Board of Trade.

Valuation of the assets and liabilities of approved societies.
    Interim report. 31 Dec.1921. 1921 Cmd.1130 xv.
    Report. 31 March 1922. 1922 Cmd.1662 ix.
    Second valuation. 25 Nov.1926. 1926 Cmd.2785 xiv.
    Third valuation. 10 Nov.1931. 1931/2 Cmd.3978 xiv. Ministry of Health.
    (Fourth valuation SEE: Epps, G. S. W.)

WATSON, Duncan
Poultry technical committee for Great Britain.
    Report. 12 Jan.1938. Ministry of Agriculture and fisheries and Department of Agriculture for Scotland.

WATSON, Eugene
Departmental committee on food production in Scotland.
    Report. Aug.1915.
    Minutes of evidence and index. 1915.
    Second report. 29 Dec.1916.
    Third report. 12 April 1917. (no others identified) Scottish Office.

WATSON, H. H.
Physical methods for the estimation of the dust hazard in industry. 18 Jan.1935. (S.R.S., no.199) Medical Research Council.

WATSON, Hugh Dudley Richards
The navigation of the upper Yangtse.
    Report. 1900. (H.D.176)
    Appendix. 1901. (H.D.180)
    Further report. Jan.1902. (H.D.181) Admiralty.

WATSON, R. A.
Electric potential gradient measurements at Eskdalemuir. March 1928. (Geophys.Mem., no.38) Meteorological Office.

WATSON, R. E.
A comparison of the records from British magnetic stations, underground and surface. May 1927. (Geophys.Mem., no.35) Meteorological Office.

Measurements of the effective electric conductivity of the air and the earth's electric field. March 1929. (Geophys.Mem., no.45) Meteorological Office.

Pyrheliometer comparisons at Kew Observatory, Richmond. Aug.1923. (Geophys.Mem., no.21) Meteorological Office.

WATT, Ernest
Interim report on artificial light and X-ray therapy. Nov.1925. (no further reports identified) Scottish Board of Health.

WATT, R. A. Watson
The use of light filters in the observation of pilot balloons. March 1921. (Prof.Notes, no.16) Meteorological Office.

WATTS, Francis
Report on the agricultural industries of Montserrat. April 1906. (Colonial rep.misc., no.34) 1906 Cd.2877 lxxvi. Colonial Office.

Report on the Mauritius sugar industry. 20 Dec.1929. 1929/30 Cmd.3518 viii. Colonial Office.

Report on the sugar industry in Antigua and St. Kitts-Nevis, 1881-1905. April 1906. (Colonial rep.misc., no.35) 1906 Cd.2878 lxxvi. Colonial Office.

WATTS, Philip
Committee on load lines of merchant ships and the carriage of deck cargoes of wood goods.
    Report. 3 Dec.1915. 1916 Cd.8204 xiii. Board of Trade.

WEAKLEY, Ernest
Report on conditions and prospects of British trade in Syria. June 1911. 1911 Cd.5707 lxxxvii. Board of Trade.

Report on the mining industries and forestry in Turkey. 17 Jan.1903. (Dip.cons.reports: misc.ser., no. 589) 1903 Cd.1387-2 lxxvi. Foreign Office.

WEATHERILL, H.
Report showing results of investigation of the assets and liabilities of the benefit branch of the Royal Irish Constabulary Force Fund. 18 June 1914. 1914 Cd.7549 lxvii. National Debt Office.

WEBB, Aston
Committee on the proposed alteration of the flower beds of Hampton Court Gardens.
    Report. 20 June 1919. 1919 Cmd.326 xxii. Board of Works.

Stone preservation committee.
    Report. Aug.1926. Department of Scientific and Industrial Research.

WEBB, Sidney James, 1st Baron Passfield
Report of the conference on the operation of dominion legislation and merchant shipping legislation. 4 Dec.1929. 1929/30 Cmd.3479 xvi. Colonial Office.

Standing committee on trusts.
    Findings by a committee on road transport rates. 31 Dec.1919. 1920 Cmd.549 xxiii. Board of Trade.

WEBB, Sidney James, *1st Baron Passfield* (continued)
Findings by a committee on a trade combination in the tobacco industry. 13 Dec.1919. 1920 Cmd.558 xxiii. Board of Trade.

WEBSTER, C. K.
The Congress of Vienna, 1814-15. Dec.1918. Foreign Office.

WEBSTER, Richard Everard, *1st Baron Alverstone*
Departmental committee on the County of London quarter sessions.
Vol.1: Report and appendices. 28 July 1909. 1909 Cd.4828 xxxi.
Vol.2: Minutes of evidence. 1909 Cd.4829 xxxi. Home Office.

Royal commission on sentences passed under martial law (South Africa).
Report. Nov.1902. 1902 Cd.1364 lxix.

WEDD, C. B.
The geology of the country around Flint, Hawarden and Caergwrle. (Sheet 108) 1 Dec.1923. (Mem.Geol.Surv.) Geological Survey.

The geology of the country around Oswestry. (Sheet 137) 24 March 1929. (Mem.Geol.Surv.) Geological Survey.

The geology of the country around Stoke-upon-Trent. (Sheet 123) 19 July 1902. (Mem.Geol.Surv.) Geological Survey.

The geology of the country around Wrexham. (Sheet 121) (Mem.Geol.Surv.)
Part 1: Lower palaeozoic and lower carboniferous rocks. 2 Aug.1926.
Part 2: Coal measures and newer formations. 15 March 1927. Geological Survey.

The geology of Liverpool with Wirral and part of the Flintshire coalfield. (Sheet 96) 21 Dec.1922. (Mem.Geol.Surv.) Geological Survey.

The geology of the northern part of the Derbyshire coalfield. (Sheet 112 and the southern part of Sheet 100) 14 June 1913. (Mem.Geol.Surv.) Geological Survey.

WEDGWOOD, Josiah Clement
Committee on House of Commons personnel and politics.
Interim report. 7 Oct.1931. 1931/2 Cmd.4130 x. (no other reports identified) Treasury.

WEIR, William D., *1st Viscount Weir*
Advisory committee on civil aviation.
Report on government assistance for the development of civil aviation. 19 April 1920. 1920 Cmd.770 ix. Air Ministry.

Report on imperial air routes. 30 Oct.1919. 1919 Cmd.449 x. Air Ministry.

Committee on main line railway electrification.
Report. 24 March 1931. Ministry of Transport.

Committee on the amalgamation of services common to the Navy, Army and Air Force.
Report. 2 Jan.1923. 1926 Cmd.2649 viii. Cabinet Office.

Committee on the national problem of the supply of electricity.
Report. 14 May 1925. Ministry of Transport.

Conference on war damage to property.
Report. 3 Oct.1939. 1938/9 Cmd.6116 xv. Treasury.

WEISS, André
The violation by Germany of the neutrality of Belgium and Luxembourg. 1915. Ministry of Information.

WELBY, Charles Glynne Earle
Committee on horse purchase in Austro-Hungary.
Report, minutes of evidence and appendices. Aug.1901. 1902 Cd.882 x. War Office.

WELBY, Reginald Earle, *1st Baron.*
Royal commission on the administration of the expenditure of India.
First report. vol.I. 1896, c.8258, xv.
Minutes of evidence and appendices. vol.II. 1896, c.8259, xvi.
Minutes of evidence. vol.III. 1900 Cd.130 xxix.
Final report. 1900. vol.IV. 1900 Cd.131 xxix.

WELCH, E.
Teaching of drawing in a secondary school. April 1924. (Educational pamphelts, no.45) Board of Education.

WELCH, F. B. A.
British regional geology: Bristol and Gloucester district. 1935. Geological Survey.

WELCH, John Joseph
Text book of naval architecture for use of officers of the Royal Navy, rev. and enlg. ed. (first ed.1889); second rev. and enlg. ed., 1907. Admiralty.

WELLER, H. O.
Sand-lime and other concrete bricks. March 1921. (B.R.B. Special Rep., no.1) Department of Scientific and Industrial Research.

WENHAM, Douglas
Standing committee on trusts. Sub-committee on the principle of fixed retail prices. 30 March 1920. 1920 Cmd.662 xxiii. Board of Trade.

Wenlock, *Lord. SEE:* Lawley, B., *3rd Baron*

WESSELS, Johannes Wilhelmus
Witwatersrand disturbances commission.
Report. Sept.1913. 1914 Cd.7112 xlix. Colonial Office.

WEST, Cyril
Brown heart: a functional disease of apples and pears. 1 July 1923. (F.I.B. special rep., no.12) Department of Scientific and Industrial Research.

Functional diseases of apples in cold storage. Aug.1925. (F.I.B. special rep., no.23) Department of Scientific and Industrial Research.

The problems of apple transport overseas. Nov.1924. (F.I.B. special rep., no.20) Department of Scientific and Industrial Research.

WESTERN, George Trench
Report upon 878 cases of bacillary enteritis received from the eastern Mediterranean. 2 Feb.1917. (S.R.S., no.5) Medical Research Committee.

WESTON, Frank, *Bishop of Zanzibar 1908-1925*
The black slaves of Prussia. An open letter to General Smuts. 7 Nov.1917. Ministry of Information.

WESTON, H.C.
The effect of different systems of lighting on output and accuracy in fine work, (typesetting by hand). Nov.1927. Medical Research Committee.

Effect of eyestrain on the output of linkers in the hosiery industry. Feb.1927. (I.H.R.B. rep., no.40) Medical Research Council.

The effects of conditions of artificial lighting on the performance of worsted weavers. Dec.1937. (I.H.R.B. Rep., no.81) Medical Research Council.

WHITAKER, William (continued)

On the design of machinery in relation to the operator. April 1926. (I.H.R.B. Rep., no.36) Medical Research Council.

On the relief of eyestrain among persons performing very fine work. April 1928. (I.H.R.B. Rep., no.49). Further experiments on the use of special spectacles in very fine processes. Aug.1929. (I.H.R.B. Rep., no.57) Medical Research Council.

The performance of weavers under varying conditions of noise. 11 Jan.1935. (I.H.R.B. Rep., no.70) Medical Research Council.

The relation between illumination and efficiency: the effect of the size of work. June 1935. Medical Research Council.

Some observations on bobbin winding. June 1920. (I.H.R.B. Rep., no.8) Medical Research Council.

A study of the efficiency in fine linen weaving. Dec.1922. (I.H.R.B. Rep., no.20) Medical Research Council.

WHARTON, John Lloyd

Departmental committee on vagrancy.

    Vol.1:   Report. 21 Feb.1906. 1906 Cd.2852 ciii.

    Vol.2:   Minutes of evidence, digest and index. 1906 Cd.2891 ciii.

    Vol.3:   Appendix with charts and maps. 1906 Cd.2892 ciii. Local Government Board.

WHEATON, S. W..

Preliminary report on enteric fever in the County of Durham. 12 May 1910. (Rep.Pub.Health & Med.Subj., no.35) Local Government Board.

Report on a re-inspection of Pewsey R.D. 23 July 1908. (Rep.Med.Isp., no.306) Local Government Board.

Report on diphtheria in Enfield U.D. 14 June 1909. (Rep.Pub.Health & Med.Subj., no.10) Local Government Board.

Report on diphtheria in the Borough of Darwen. 17 March 1902. (Rep.Med.Insp., no.173) Local Government Board.

Report on diphtheria in the Borough of Denbigh. 22 June 1903. (Rep.Med.Insp., no.187) Local Government Board.

Report on enteric fever among hop pickers in Staffordshire and Worcestershire in 1909. 1 May 1910. (Rep.Pub.Health & Med.Subj., no.30) Local Government Board.

Report on enteric fever in Barnstaple Borough. 17 June 1912. (Rep.Pub.Health & Med.Subj., no.69) Local Government Board.

Report on enteric fever at Stroud in Rochester Borough in 1912. 7 March 1913. (Rep.Pub.Health & Med.Subj., no.79) Local Government Board.

Report on enteric fever in the Swanage U.D. in 1910. 11 Jan.1911. (Rep.Pub.Health & Med.Subj., no.47) Local Government Board.

Report on smallpox in the Dewsbury Union. 12 Dec.1904. (Rep.Med.Insp., no.204) Local Government Board.

Report on the sanitary conditions of Abertillery U.D. 20 Feb.1906. (Rep.Med.Insp., no.228) Local Government Board.

Report on the sanitary conditions of Bishop Auckland U.D. 23 April 1901. (Rep.Med.Insp., no.158) Local Government Board.

Report on the sanitary conditions of Fishguard and Goodwick in Haverfordwest R.D., with reference to the recent prevalence of diphtheria. 16 Dec.1901. (Rep.Med.Insp., no.170) Local Government Board.

Report on the sanitary conditions of Helmsley R.D. 29 Aug.1907. (Rep.Med.Insp., no.277 ) Local Government Board.

Report on the sanitary conditions of Llandilofawr R.D., Carmarthenshire. 28 Aug.1901. (Rep.Med.Insp., no.163) Local Government Board.

Report on the sanitary conditions of Maesteg U.D. 13 Aug.1908. (Rep.Med.Insp., no.308) Local Government Board.

Report on the sanitary conditions of Narberth R.D. 5 May 1906. (Rep.Med.Insp., no.233) Local Government Board.

Report on the sanitary conditions of Neath R.D. 30 June 1911. (Rep.Pub.Health & Med.Subj., no.54) Local Government Board.

Report on the sanitary conditions of Strood R.D., Kent. 2 Oct.1901. (Rep.Med.Insp., no.166) Local Government Board.

Report on the sanitary conditions of Winchcomb R.D. and on prevalence of diphtheria. 28 Oct.1907. (Rep.Med.Insp., no.291) Local Government Board.

Report on the water supply of Holderness in the East Riding of Yorkshire. 30 Jan.1905. Local Government Board.

Report on water supplies in the Norton R.D. 14 May 1903. (Rep.Med.Insp., no.184) Local Government Board.

WHEELER, Edward Gidleigh

Tables of chemical and physical constants. July 1918. Ministry of Munitions.

WHEELER, Richard Vernon

Coal dust explosions. The effect of release of pressure on their development. Sept.1925. (S.M.R.B. Paper, no.14) Mines Department.

Coal dust explosions, Eskmeals, 1923; a descriptive account. Jan.1924. (S.M.R.B. Paper, no.3) Mines Department.

The combustion of coal dust. April 1931. (S.M.R.B. Paper, no.73) Mines Department.

The composition of coal; plant cuticles in coal. Oct.1925. (S.M.R.B. Paper, no.17) Mines Department.

The electric ignition of firedamp; alternating and continuous currents Oct.1925. (S.M.R.B. Paper, no.20) Mines Department.

Firedamp explosions within closed vessels; the effects of turbulence. July 1925. (S.M.R.B. Paper, no.10) Mines Department.

Firedamp explosions within closed vessels: "pressure piling". March 1928. (S.M.R.B. Paper, no.49) Mines Department.

Flame-proof electrical apparatus for use in coal mines.

    First report: Flange protection. Sept.1924. (S.M.R.B. Paper, no.5)

    Second report: Perforated plate protection. Feb.1926. (S.M.R.B. Paper, no.21)

    Third report: Ring-relief protection. Feb.1927. (S.M.R.B. Paper, no.35)

    Summarising report. April 1929. (S.M.R.B. Paper, no.60) Mines Department.

WHEELER, Richard Vernon (Continued)

The ignition of firedamp. July 1925. (S.M.R.B. Paper, no.8) Revised May 1929. (S.M.R.B. Paper, no.53) Mines Department.

The ignition of firedamp by broken electric lamp bulbs: the appearance of the filaments. Oct.1934. (S.M.R.B. Paper, no.89) Mines Department.

The ignition of firedamp by the heat of impact of coal cutter picks against rocks. Jan.1931. (S.M.R.B. Paper, no.70) Mines Department.

The ignition of firedamp by the heat impact of metal against rock. April 1929. (S.M.R.B. Paper, no.54) Mines Department.

The ignition of firedamp by the heat impact of rocks. May 1928. (S.M.R.B. Paper, no.46) Mines Department.

The ignition of firedamp by the impact of hand picks against rock. Sept.1930. (S.M.R.B. Paper, no.62) Mines Department.

The ignition of gases by hot wires. June 1927. (S.M.R.B. Paper, no.36) Mines Department.

The inflammation of coal dusts: the effect of the chemical composition of the dust. March 1927. (S.M.R.B. Paper, no.33) Mines Department.

The inflammation of coal dusts: the effect of the fineness of the dust. Jan.1936. (S.M.R.B. Paper, no.95) Mines Department.

The inflammation of coal dusts: the effect of the nature of added incombustible dust. June 1933. (S.M.R.B. Paper, no.79) Mines Department.

The inflammation of coal dusts: the effect of the presence of firedamp. Sept.1930. (S.M.R.B. Paper, no.64) Mines Department.

The inflammation of coal dusts: the value of the presence of carbon dioxide and combined water in the dusts. Jan.1936. (S.M.R.B. Paper, no.96) Mines Department.

The lag on ignition of firedamp. July 1925. (S.M.R.B. Paper, no.9) Mines Department.

The lighting power of flame safety-lamps. Sept.1927. (S.M.R.B. Paper, no.40) Mines Department.

The limits of inflammability of firedamp and air. Sept.1925. (S.M.R.B. Paper, no.15) Mines Department.

Monograph on the constitution of coal. April 1918. Department of Scientific and Industrial Research.

The movement of flame in firedamp explosions. June 1933. (S.M.R.B. Paper, no.82) Mines Department.

The pressures produced by electric arcs in closed vessels. Aug.1927. (S.M.R.B. Paper, no.39) Mines Department.

The prevention of ignition of firedamp by the heat of impact of coal-cutter picks against hand rocks. July 1933. (S.M.R.B. Paper, no.81) Mines Department.

The pressures produced on blowing electric fuse links. July 1927. (S.M.R.B. Paper, no.38) Mines Department.

Report on battery-bell signalling systems as regards the danger of ignition of firedamp-air mixtures by the break-flash at the signal wires. 20 Jan.1915. Home Office.

Report on electric signalling with bare wires as regards the danger of ignition of inflammable gaseous mixtures by the break-flash at the signal-wires. 1 June 1916. Home Office.

Report on experiments into means of preventing the spread of explosions of carbonaceous dust. Nov.1934. Home Office.

Report on the inflammability and capacity for transmitting explosions of carbonaceous dusts liable to be generated on premises under the Factories and Workshop Acts. 12 Dec.1912. 1912/3 Cd.6662 xxvi. Home Office.

The relative inflammability and explosibility of coaldusts. Sept.1928. (S.M.R.B. Paper, no.48) Mines Department.

The relative inflammibility of coal dusts: a laboratory study. May 1929. (S.M.R.B. Paper, no.56) Mines Department.

The spontaneous combustion of coal: the most readily oxidizable constituents of coal. July 1926. (S.M.R.B. Paper, no.28) Mines Department.

Stone dust as a preventative of coal dust explosions: comparative tests. Sept.1925. (S.M.R.B. Paper, no.13) Mines Department.

The treatment of flue gases of Battersea Power Station. *SEE:* Robertson, R.

WHETHAM, William Cecil Dampier
Departmental committee on lighting in factories and workshops. *SEE:* Wilson, D. R.

WHINNEY, Arthur F.
Report on the fares and working expenses of the London General Omnibus Co. Ltd. 13 June 1919. 1919 Cmd.209 xxv. Home Office.

Safeguarding of industries.
Report of the committee on superphosphate. 24 June 1925. 1924/5 Cmd.2475 xv. Board of Trade.

Report of the committee on worsteds. 22 Feb.1926. 1926 Cmd.2635 xv. Board of Trade.

WHIPPLE, Francis John Welsh
Point discharge in the electric field of the earth. May 1936. (Geophys.Mem., no.68) Meteorological Office.

WHITAKER, James Smith
Departmental committee on conditions imposed on the supply of medicines to insured persons.
Report. 9 June 1913. 1913 Cd.6853 xxxvi.
Evidence and appendices. 1913 Cd.6854 xxxvi.
National Health Insurance Joint Committee.

WHITAKER, William
The water supply of Buckinghamshire and Hertfordshire from underground sources. 8 Jan.1921. (Mem.Geol.Surv.) Geological Survey.

The water supply of Cambridgeshire, Huntingdonshire and Rutland from underground sources. 31 March 1921 . (Mem.Geol.Surv.) Geological Survey.

The water supply of Essex from underground sources. 10 Dec.1915. (Mem.Geol.Surv.) Geological Survey.

The water supply of Hampshire (including the Isle of Wight) with records of sinkings and borings. 10 Feb.1910. (Mem.Geol.Surv.) Geological Survey.

The water supply of Kent, with records of sinkings and borings. 29 Sept.1908. (Mem.Geol.Surv.) Geological Survey.

WHITAKER, William (continued)

The water supply of Norfolk from underground sources. 18 Oct.1920. (Mem.Geol.Surv.) Geological Survey.

The water supply of Suffolk from underground sources. 6 Feb.1906. (Mem.Geol.Surv.) Geological Survey.

The water supply of Surrey from underground sources. 1 April 1912. (Mem.Geol.Surv.) Geological Survey.

The water supply of Sussex from underground sources. 31 Oct.1898. Supplement. 2 Oct.1910. (Mem.Geol.Surv.) Geological Survey.

Water supply of Wiltshire from underground sources. 19 Oct.1925. (Mem.Geol.Surv.) Geological Survey.

Wells and springs of Dorset. 8 April 1926. (Mem.Geol.Surv.) Geological Survey.

WHITBREAD, Samuel Howard

Select committee on bastardy orders.
Report, proceedings, evidence and appendix. 27 July 1909. 1909 (236) vi. House of Commons.

WHITE, H. J. Osborne

The geology of the country around Alresford. (Sheet 300) 2 June 1910. (Mem.Geol.Surv.) Geological Survey.

The geology of the country around Basingstoke. (Sheet 284) 22 May 1909. (Mem.Geol.Surv.) Geological Survey.

The geology of the country around Henley-on-Thames and Wallingford. (Sheet 254) 5 Aug.1908. (Mem.Geol.Surv.) Geological Survey.

The geology of the country around Hungerford and Newbury. (Sheet 267) 20 June 1907. (Mem.Geol.Surv.) Geological Survey.

The geology of the country around Marlborough. (Sheet 266) 5 Dec.1924. (Mem.Geol.Surv.) Geological Survey.

The geology of the country around Winchester and Stockbridge. (Sheet 299) 26 June 1912. (Mem.Geol.Surv.) Geological Survey.

The geology of the country near Brighton and Worthing. (Sheets 318 and 333) 7 Jan.1924. (Mem.Geol.Surv.) Geological Survey.

The geology of the country near Fareham and Havant. (Sheet 316) 3 Nov.1913. (Mem.Geol.Surv.) Geological Survey.

The geology of the country near Hastings and Dungeness. (Sheets 320 and 321) 5 Dec.1927. (Mem.Geol.Surv.) Geological Survey.

The geology of the country near Lewes. (Sheet 319) 27 April 1926. (Mem.Geol.Surv.) Geological Survey.

The geology of the country near Lymington and Portsmouth. (Sheets 330 and 331) 26 Feb.1915. (Mem.Geol.Surv.) Geological Survey.

The geology of the country near Ramsgate and Dover. (Sheets 274 and 290) 29 Oct.1928. (Mem.Geol.Surv.) Geological survey.

The geology of the country near Saffron Walden. (Sheet 205) 18 Dec.1931. (Mem.Geol.Surv.) Geological Survey.

The geology of the country south and west of Shaftsbury. (Sheet 313) 20 Jan.1923. (Mem.Geol.Surv.) Geological Survey.

A short account of the geology of the Isle of Wight. 18 Oct.1920. (Mem.Geol.Surv.) Geological Survey.

WHITE, James Dundas

Committee on war organisation in the distributing trades in Scotland.
First report. 1 July 1915. 1914/6 Cd.7987 xxxvii.
Second report. 28 March 1916. 1916 Cd.8220 xv. Scottish Office.

WHITE, Oswald

Report on Japanese labour. March 1919. (Commercial no.1, 1920) 1920 Cmd.511 xxxix. Board of Trade.

Report on Japanese paper-making. 19 May 1905. (Dip.cons.reports: misc.ser., no.635) 1905 Cd.2237-16 lxxxvi. Foreign Office.

Report on Japanese paper mills. May 1907. (Dip.cons.reports: misc.ser., no.660) 1907 Cd.3284-4 lxxxvii. Foreign Office.

WHITE, P. Bruce

Food poisoning; a study of 100 recent outbreaks. 30 Jan.1925. (S.R.S. no.92) Medical Research Council.

An investigation of the salmonella group with special reference to food poisoning. 15 Dec.1924. (S.R.S., no.91) Medical Research Council.

Further studies of the salmonella group. (Supplement to S.R.S., no.91) July 1926. (S.R.S.103) Medical Research Council.

Report on an outbreak of dysentery in the urban district of Lynton, Devon. July 1923. (Rep.Pub.Health & Med.Subj., no.20) Ministry of Health.

WHITEHEAD, James

Committee of investigation for England on complaints as to the operation of the milk marketing scheme, 1933.
Report. 2 April 1936. Ministry of Agriculture and Fisheries.

WHITEHEAD, Talbot H.

British regional geology. The Welsh borderland. 1935. Geological Survey.

The country between Stafford and Market Drayton. (Sheet 139) 8 Jan.1927. (Mem.Geol.Surv.) Geological Survey.

The country between Wolverhampton and Oakengates. (Sheet 153) 4 April 1928. (Mem.Geol.Surv.) Geological Survey.

The geology of the southern part of the south Staffordshire coalfield. 28 Aug.1926. (Mem.Geol.Surv.) Geological Survey.

WHITLEY, Arthur

Russian banks and communist funds.
Report of an inquiry into certain transactions of the Bank for Russian Trade, Ltd. and the Moscow Narodny Bank Ltd. with a memorandum by the Moscow Narodny Bank. 1 June 1928. 1928 Cmd.3125 xii. Home Office.

WHITLEY, John Henry

Committee on relations between employers and employed.
Interim report on joint standing industrial councils. 8 March 1917. 1917/8 Cd.8606 xviii.
Supplementary report: works committees. 18 Oct.1917. 1918 Cd.9001 xiv.
Second report, on joint standing industrial councils. 18 Oct.1917. 1918 Cd.9002 x.
Report on conciliation and arbitration. 31 Jan.1918. 1918 Cd.9081 vii.

WHITLEY, John Henry (continued)
Report on conciliation and arbitration (in substitution of Cd.9081) 31 Jan.1918. 1918 Cd.9099 vii.
Final report. 1 July 1918. 1918 Cd.9153 viii. Ministry of Reconstruction.

Royal commission on labour in India.
Report. 14 March 1931. 1930/1 Cmd.3883 xi.
Vol.1. Evidence Bombay Presidency: written and oral evidence. 2 vols. 1931.
Vol.2: Punjab, Delhi and Ajmer-Merwara: written and oral evidence. 2 vols. 1931.
Vol.3. Central and United Provinces: written and oral evidence. 2 vols. 1931.
Vol.4. Bihar and Orissa with coalfields: written and oral evidence. 2 vols. 1931.
Vol.5. Bengal: written and oral evidence. 2 vols. 1931.
Vol.6. Assam and the Dooars. 1931.
Vol.7. Madras Presidency and Coorg: written and oral evidence. 2 vols. 1931.
Vol.8. Railways: written and oral evidence. 2 vols. 1931.
Vol.9. London. 1931.
Vol.10. Burma. 1931.
Vol.11. Supplementary. 1931. India Office.

WHITSON, Thomas Barnby
Scottish departmental committee on housing.
Report. 8 Dec.1933. 1933/4 Cmd.4469 xii. Department of Health for Scotland.

WHITTAKER, Thomas Palmer
Select committee on home work.
Report, proceedings, evidence, appendix and index. 8 Aug.1907. 1907 (290) vi. House of Commons.

Report, proceedings, evidence, appendix and index. 22 July 1908. 1908 (246) viii. House of Commons.

Select committee on House of Commons (Procedure).
Report, proceedings, evidence and appendices. 22 July 1914. 1914 (378) vii. House of Commons.

Select committee on land values.
Report, and proceedings. 22 Dec.1919. 1919 (243) v. House of Commons.

WHYTE, Alexander
Report on recent travels along the sea-coast belt of the British East Africa protectorate. May 1903. 1903 Cd.1534 xlv. Foreign Office.

WHYTE, Alexander Frederick
Committee on constitutional reforms for Burma.
Report. 14 Dec.1921. India Office.

WHYTE, R. O.
Erosion and soil conservation. March 1938. (Bull., no.25) Imperial Bureau of Plant Genetics: Herbage Plants.

Grassland and forage crops in Thuringia, Czechoslovakia and Hungary. Aug.1934. (Bull., no.15) Imperial Bureau of Plant Genetics: Herbage Plants.

Research on grassland, forage crops and the conservation of vegetation in the United States of America. Sept.1939. (Bull., no.26) Imperial Bureau of Pastures and Forage Crops.

Vernalization, or Lyssenko's method for the pre-treatment of seed. March 1933. (Bull., no.9) Imperial Bureau of Plant Genetics: Herbage Plants.

WHYTE, William Edward
Consultative council on local health administration and general health questions.
Report on the steps necessary to secure that state-aided houses will in future be let only to persons of the working classes. Oct.1932. Department of Health for Scotland.

WIDDOWSON, E. M.
The chemical composition of foods. 8 Nov.1939. (S.R.S., no.235) Medical Research Council.

WILCOCKSON, W. H.
Tungsten ores. Dec.1919. (Mono.Min.resour.) Imperial Institute.

WILEMAN, A. E.
Report for the year 1908 on the sugar industry of South Formosa. Feb.1909. (Dip.cons.reports: misc.ser., no.675) 1909 Cd.4447-3 xcii. Foreign Office and Board of Trade.

WILKIE, David Percival Dalbreck
Report on medical treatment of men burned in colliery explosions. 6 June 1933. Mines Department.

WILKINS, L.
Sub-committee on employment of women in agriculture in England and Wales.
Report. Dec.1919. Board of Agriculture and Fisheries.

WILKINS, V-E.
Agricultural research and the farmer: a record of recent achievement. 27 Feb.1922. Ministry of Agriculture, Fisheries and Food.

Research and the land: an account of recent progress in agricultural and horticultural science in the United Kingdom. 28 July 1926. Ministry of Agriculture and Fisheries.

WILKINSON, S. B.
The geology of Islay, including Oronsay and portions of Colonsay and Jura. (Sheets 19 and 27 and the western part of 20) 3 May 1907. (Mem.Geol.Surv.Scotl.) Geological Survey, Scotland.

WILLIAMS, Ernest T.
Electric lighting committee.
First report: principles adopted for electric lighting in H.M. naval service. 1924. (no other reports identified) Admiralty.

WILLIAMS, John Fischer
Departmental committee on imprisonment by courts of summary jurisdiction in default of payment of fines and other sums of money.
Report. 30 June 1934. 1933/4 Cmd.4649 xi. Home Office.

Royal commission on tithe rent charge.
Report. 26 Nov.1935. 1935/6 Cmd.5095 xiv.
Minutes of evidence, appendices and index. 1934-6. Home Office.

WILLIAMS, R.
Committee on the staffing and methods of work of the National Savings Committee.
Report. 27 Jan.1921. 1921 Cmd.1461 xvii. Cabinet Office.

WILLIAMSON, Archibald
Committee on electric power supply.
Report. 28 April 1918. 1918 Cd.9062 viii. Board of Trade.

Committee of enquiry on artificial limbs.
Report. 28 July 1921. Ministry of Pensions.

Committee on the telegraph service on staff to

WILLIAMSON, Archibald (continued)
operate machine telegraphs.
Report. 6 May 1915. Post Office.

Departmental committee on protection of shipping from the dangers of floating derelicts and sunken obstructions.
Report, evidence and appendices. 21 Jan.1913. 1913 Cd.6699 xix. Board of Trade.

Departmental committee on taxi-cab fares.
Report. 10 June 1911. 1911 Cd.5782 xli.
Minutes of evidence. 1911 Cd.5875 xli. Home Office.

Select committee on short weight.
Report, proceedings, evidence and appendices. 15 July 1914. 1914 (359) x. House of Commons.

WILLIAMSON, H. Charles
On the eggs of certain skates (RAIA). 1912. (Sci.Invest., 1912, no.1) Fishery Board for Scotland.

Report on diseases and abnormalities in fishes. 1911. (Sci.Invest., 1911, no.2) Fishery Board for Scotland.

Report on larvae and later stages of certain decapod crustacea. 1909. (Sci.invest., 1909, no.1) Fishery Board for Scotland.

Report on the reproductive organs of *sparus centrodontus, etc.* 1910. (Sci.invest., 1910, no.1) Fishery Board for Scotland.

Retardation of the development of the ova of the herring. 1910. (Sci.invest., 1910, no.2) Fishery Board for Scotland.

Short resume of the researches into the European races of herrings and the method of investigation. 1914. (Sci.invest., 1914, no.1) Fishery Board for Scotland.

WILLIAMSON, Isobel J. F.
External disinfection of fish ova with reference to the prophylaxis of furunculosis. 1930. (Salmon Fish., 1930, no.2) Fishery Board for Scotland.

Furunculosis of the salmonidae. 1928. (Salmon Fish., 1928, no.5) Fishery Board for Scotland.

Further observations on furunculosis of the salmonidae, 1928. 1929. (Salmon Fish., 1929, no.1) Fishery Board for Scotland.

Identification of *bacillus salmonicida* by the complement-fixation test; a further contribution to the study of furunculosis of the salmondial. 1930. (Salmon Fish., 1930, no.1) Fishery Board for Scotland.

Observations on experimental infection of trout by *bacillus salmonicida.* 1931. (Salmon Fish., 1931, no.7) Fishery Board for Scotland.

A study of bacterial infection in fish and certain other lower vertebrates. 1929. (Salmon Fish., 1929, no.2) Fishery Board for Scotland.

Willingdon, *Lord. SEE:* Freeman-Thomas, F., *1st Viscount Willingdon*

WILLIS, Frederick James
Committee on the administration of Queen Alexandra Hospital, Cosham, Hampshire.
Report. 27 Nov.1929. Ministry of Pensions.

Conference on lunacy reform, 19 and 20 January 1923.
Report. Feb.1922. Home Office.

Departmental committee on ethyl petrol.

Interim report. 16 July 1928. 1928 Cmd.3159 ix.
Minutes of evidence. 1928.
Final report. 10 Feb.1930. Ministry of Health.

Departmental committee on the composition and description of food.
Report. 20 March 1934. 1933/4 Cmd.4564 xii. Ministry of Health.

Report of a public inquiry into the administration of the guardians of the hamlet of Mile End Old Town. 21 Jan.1908. 1908 Cd.4011 xcii. Local Government Board.

Report on the work undertaken by the British government in the reception and care of Belgian refugees. *SEE:* Hatch, E. F. G.

WILLMORE, John Stephen
The welfare of Egypt. 1917. Ministry of Information.

WILLOUGHBY, Digby Wentworth Bayard, *9th Baron Middleton*
Central committee on the scheme for establishing scholarships and maintenance grants for the sons and daughters of agricultural workmen and others. Aug.1926. Ministry of Agriculture and fisheries.
Committee on the adequate supply of horses suitable for military purposes.
Report. 8 Oct.1915. 1914/6 Cd.8134 xxxix. Board of Agriculture and Fisheries.

WILLOUGHBY, Gilbert Heathcote-Drummond, *2nd Earl Ancaster*
Departmental committee on allotments.
Report. Jan.1922. Ministry of Agriculture.

WILLS, L. J.
Records of London wells. 8 Oct.1912. (Mem.Geol.Surv.) Geological Survey.

WILLS, William
Report on draft regulations for casting brass. 21 March 1908. 1908 Cd.4154 xii. Home Department.

WILSON, A. K.
Sheffield industrial mission to South America.
Report. 26 Jan.1931. Department of Overseas Trade.

WILSON, Duncan-Randolph
Departmental committee on lighting in factories and workshops.
First report.
Vol.1. Report and appendices. May 1915. 1914/6 Cd.8000 xxi.
Vol.2. Minutes of evidence, *etc.* 1914/6 Cd.8001 xxi.
Vol.3. Records of observations in factories. Nov.1915.
Second report. June 1921. Cmd.1418 xii.
Third report. March 1922. 1922 Cmd.1686 vii.
Fourth report. 21 Sept.1938. Home Office.
Fifth report. 19 June 1940. Ministry of Labour.

Report on conferences between employers and inspectors concerning methods for suppressing dust in asbestos textile factories. 10 April 1931. Home Office.

WILSON, G. H.
Study of hypoglycaemic shock treatment in schizophrenia. July 1936. Board of Control.

WILSON, G. S.
The bacteriological grading of milk. 30 Oct.1935. (S.R.S., no.206) Medical Research Council.

Tuberculous bacilliaemia. 22 June 1933. (S.R.S., no.182) Medical Research Council.

WILSON, G. V.
The Ayrshire bauxitic clay. 3 April 1922. (Mem.Geol.Surv., Scotl.) Geological Survey, Scotland.

The concealed coalfield of Yorkshire and Nottinghamshire. 25 Feb.1913. (Mem.Geol.Surv.) Geological Survey.

The lead, zinc, copper and nickel ores of Scotland. 8 Sept.1920. (Special reports on the mineral resources of Great Britain, vol.17) (Mem.Geol.Surv., Scotl.) Geological Survey, Scotland.

WILSON, J. S.
A printing method of recording road surface texture. Aug.1939. (Road Res. Bull., no.3) Department of Scientific and Industrial Research.

WILSON, J. S. Grant
The geology of the lower Strathspey. (Sheet 85) 16 Jan.1902. (Mem.Geol.Surv., Scotl.) Geological Survey, Scotland.

WILSON, J. W.
Committee on war charities.
Report. 19 June 1916. 1916 Cd.8287 vi. Home Office.

WILSON, James, *Sir*
Farm workers in Scotland.
Report. Sept.1920. Board of Agriculture for Scotland.

WILSON, John, *Lord Ashmore*
Departmental committee on messengers-at-arms and sheriff officers.
Report. 15 Oct.1923. Scottish Office.

Report on house accommodation available for workers employed at Rosyth and their families; and on the provision for sickness and accident. 11 July 1911. Local Government Board for Scotland.

Special report on the design, construction and materials of various types of dwellinghouses in Scotland. 9 Sept.1915. 1917/8 Cd.8760 xiv. Royal Commission on Housing in Scotland.

WILSON, John Dover
Humanism in the continuation school. 1918. (Educational pamphlets, no.43) Board of Education.

WILSON, John William
Committee on Sir Hugh Lane's pictures.
Report. 28 Jan.1925. 1926 Cmd.2684 xiii. Colonial Office.

Committee on summer time.
Report. 22 Feb.1917. 1917/8 Cd.8487 xviii. Home Office.

Departmental committee on the superannuation of teachers.
Report on the first reference. 3 April 1914. 1914 Cd.7364 xxv.
Report on the second reference. 20 March 1914. 1914 Cd.7365 xxv. Board of Education.

Select committee on remuneration of ministers.
Report, proceedings, evidence and appendices. 15 Dec.1920. 1920 (241) viii. House of Commons.

WILSON, Malcolm
The phomopsis disease of conifers. July 1925. (Bull., no.6) Forestry Commission.

WILSON, Roderick Roy
British Guiana Commission.
Report. 5 April 1927. 1927 Cmd.2841 vii. Colonial Office.

Select committee on the western highlands and islands of Scotland.
Report, proceedings, evidence, appendices and index. 24 July 1928. 1928 (117) vi. House of Commons.

WILSON, Samuel Herbert
Report on visit to East Africa, 1929. 2 July 1929. 1929/30 Cmd.3378 viii. Colonial Office.

Report on visit to Malaya, 1932. 25 Feb.1933. 1932/3 Cmd.4276 x. Colonial Office.

WILSON, William Combe
The tannic acid treatment of burns. 16 Sept.1929. (S.R.S., no.141) Medical Research Council.

WILSON, William Deane
Report on the medical arrangements in the South African war. 18 Dec.1903. War Office.

WILSON, Woodrow
America and freedom; being statements of President Wilson. 1917. Ministry of Information.

The challenge accepted; address to Congress. 2 April 1917. Ministry of Information.

WILSON-FOX, Henry
Select committee on transport.
First report. 6 Nov.1918. 1918 (130) iv.
Second report, proceedings, evidence, appendices and index. 14 Nov.1918. 1918 (136) iv. House of Commons.

WILSON-GOODE, J. L.
Report on the trade in the protectorate of South-West Africa. 23 Dec.1919. 1920 Cmd.842 xxxiii. Department of Overseas Trade.

Wimborne, Viscount. SEE: Guest, Ivor Churchill, *Viscount Wimborne*

Winchester, *Bishop of. SEE:* Garbett, C. F.

WINDHAM, William
British oversea settlement delegation to Australia.
Report. May 1924. 1924 Cmd.2132 xi. Colonial Office.

British oversea settlement delegation to New Zealand, 1923.
Report. June 1924. 1924 Cmd.2167 xi. Colonial Office.

Windsor, *Baron. SEE:* Windsor-Clive, Robert George, *1st Earl of Plymouth*

WINDSOR-CLIVE, Ivor Miles, *2nd Earl of Plymouth*
Committee on broadcasting services in the colonies.
Interim report. July 1936. (Colonial no.139)
First supplement. July 1936. (Colonial no.139) Colonial Office.

Committee on leave and passage conditions for the Colonial service.
Report. 2 Aug.1934. 1933/4 Cmd.4730 ix. Colonial Office.

Tsetse fly committee.
Report. 5 Dec.1932. Economic Advisory Council. Treasury.

WINDSOR-CLIVE, Robert George, *1st Earl of Plymouth*
Committee of inquiry on the Royal Hibernian Academy and the Metropolitan School of Art, Dublin.
Report, evidence, appendices and index. 1 Nov.1906. 1906 Cd.3256 xxxi. Treasury.

Committee on the design for completing the rebuilding of the quadrant, Regent Street.

WINDSOR-CLIVE, Robert George, *1st Earl of Plymouth* (continued)

Report. 6 Feb.1913. 1912/3 Cd.6660 xlvi. Home Office.

Departmental committee on celluloid.

Report. 22 Nov.1913. 1914 Cd.7158 xv. Evidence and appendices. 1914 Cd.7159 xv. Home Office.

Joint select committee on London underground railways.

Report, minutes of evidence, appendix and index. 23 July 1901. 1901 (279) vi. House of Commons *and* House of Lords.

WISE, Bernhard R.

The freedom of the seas. 1915. Ministry of Information.

WISE, K. S.

Report on the Nastin treatment for leprosy at the Mahaica Leper Asylum, British Guiana, 1908-1910. 30 March 1911. 1911 Cd.5583 liii. Colonial Office.

WITHERS, Hartley

The need for saving in peace time. 1919. (National Economy series, no.1) National War Savings Committee.

WITTS, Leslie John

Respirators (poliomyelitis) committee.

Report on "breathing machines" and their use in treatment. 22 Nov.1939. (S.R.S., no.237) Medical Research Council.

WOLFE, Humbert

Report by the delegates on the International Labour Conference, 8th session, Geneva, 26 May to 5 June 1926. Oct.1926. 1926 Cmd.2749 xxx. Ministry of Labour.

Report of the delegates on the International Labour Conference, 9th session, Geneva, 7 to 24 June 1926. Oct.1926. 1926 Cmd.2750 xxx. Ministry of Labour.

Report by the delegates to the International Labour Conference, 10th session, 25 May to 16 June 1927. Nov.1927. 1927 Cmd.2995 xxvi. Ministry of Labour.

Report by the British delegates on the International Labour Conference, 11th session, Geneva, 30 May—16 June 1928. Nov.1928. 1928/9 Cmd.3226 xxiii. Ministry of Labour.

Report of the British delegates on the International Labour Conference, 12th session, Geneva, 30 May to 21 June 1929. April 1930. 1929/30 Cmd.3558 xxxii. Ministry of Labour.

Report of the British delegates on the International Labour Conference, 13th session, geneva, 10 to 26 October 1929. April 1930. 1929/30 Cmd.3559 xxxii. Ministry of Labour.

WOOD, A. H.

Joint committee on mental deficiency.

Report, part 1: General. 1929.
Part 2: The mentally defective child. 19 Jan. 1929.
Part 3: The adult defective. 1929.
Part 4: Investigation into the incidence of mental deficiency in six areas, 1925-1927, by E. O. Lewis. 1929. Board of Education *and* Board of Control.

WOOD, Edward Frederick Lindley, *3rd Viscount Halifax*

Report of the United Kingdom delegates on the League of Nations, 17th Assembly. 31 Dec.1936. (misc., no.2, 1937) 1936/7 Cmd.5365 xxviii. Foreign Office.

Report on visit to the West Indies and British Guiana, December 1921—February 1922. May 1922. 1922 Cmd.1679 xvi. Colonial Office.

WOOD, Ethel Mary

Committee on the supply of female domestic servants.

Report. 19 Oct.1923. Ministry of Labour.

WOOD, Henry

Aircraft experiments for the locating of herring shoals in Scottish waters, 1924. (Sci.Invest., 1925, no.1) Fishery Board for Scotland.

Movements of herring in the northern North Sea. 1937. (Sci.invest., 1937, no.3) Fishery Board for Scotland.

Observations on the Scottish summer herring fishing of 1922 . 1923. (Sci.invest., 1923, no.2) Fishery Board for Scotland.

Race investigation of the herring population of Scottish waters. 1936. (Sci.invest., 1936, no.3) Fishery Board for Scotland.

Scottish herring shoals; pre-spawning and spawning movements. 1930. (Sci.invest., 1930, no.1) Fishery Board for Scotland.

WOOD, Thomas McKinnon

Advisory committee on liquor trade finance, Scotland.

Report on proposals for the state purchase of the licensed liquor trade. April 1916. 1916 Cd.8319 xii. Scottish Office.

Committee of enquiry into the Royal Ordnance Factories, Woolwich.

Reports. 6 Nov.1918, to 13 March 1919. 1919 Cmd.229 xxxi. Ministry of Munitions.

WOOD, Walter

The playground movement in America and its relation to public education. July 1913. (Educational pamphlets, no.27) Board of Education.

WOODGATE, Alfred

Board of guardians of West Ham Union.

Report on their administration 20 July to 30 October 1926. 1926 Cmd.2786 xv.
Second report, 1 November 1926 to 31 May 1927. June 1927. 1927 Cmd.2900 xi.
Third report, 1 June 1927 to 31 May 1928. 8 June 1928. 1928 Cmd.3142 xii. Ministry of Health.

WOODHEAD, D. W.

The estimation of firedamp: flame caps. May 1927. (S.M.R.B. Paper, no.37) Mines Department.

A flame safety-lamp of high candle-power. Sept.1930. (S.M.R.B. Paper, no.65) Mines Department.

The lighting power of flame safety-lamps. Sept.1927. (S.M.R.B. Paper, No.40) Mines Department.

The pressure wave sent out by an explosion: spark photographs with permitted explosives. March 1934. (S.M.R.B. Paper, no.88) Mines Department.

WOODHEAD, John Ackroy

Palestine partition commission.

Report. 19 Oct.1938. 1937/8 Cmd.5854 xiv. Colonial Office.

WOODHOUSE, Arthur

Report on the waterway between the Baltic and Black Sea. 6 June 1900. (Dip.cons.reports: misc.ser., no.529) 1900 Cd.2-12 xci. Foreign Office.

WOODHOUSE, Horace Marton
Standing committee on prices.
Findings by a committee on the cost of production and distribution of wool, tops and yarns and the profits. Jan.1920. 1920 Cmd.535 xxiii.
Second report 1921. 1921 Cmd.1192 xvi. Board of Trade.

WOODHOUSE, Stewart
Typhoid fever in Limerick City and prison. 18 Sept.1902. 1902 Cd.1331 xlvii. Local Government Board for Ireland.

WOODRUFF, Douglas
The story of the British colonial empire. 1939. Colonial Office.

WOODS, A. R. T.
Engineering committee. Sub-committee on refrigerator cars and barges.
Interim report: Railway cars. 15 Jan.1919. (F.I.B. special report no.1)
Report: Insulated and refrigerator barges. April 1923. (F.I.B. special report, no.15) Department of Industrial and Scientific research.

WOODS, H. M.
Alcohol and inheritance: an experimental study. 15 June 1932. (S.R.S., no.168) Medical Research Council.

WOODS, Henry George
Advisory committee on University Colleges (Great Britain) Grant in aid.
Report. 6 June 1907. 1907 (267) lxiv.
Report. 24 July 1908. 1909 (182) lxix. Treasury.

Advisory committee on grants to University Colleges.
Report. 16 March 1910. 1910 (110) lxxii. Treasury.

WOODS, Hilda M.
Epidemiological study of scarlet fever in England and Wales since 1900. 4 May 1933. (S.R.S., no.180) Medical Research Council.

The incidence of industrial accidents upon individuals with special reference to multiple accidents. Aug.1919. (I.H.R.B. Rep., no.4) Medical Research Committee.

WOODS, Wilfred Wentworth
Mui Tsai in Hong Kong and Malaya.
Report of the commission. 23 Jan.1937. (Colonial, no.125) Colonial Office.

WOODWARD, E. M.
Precis of information concerning the Uganda Protectorate. Sept.1902. War Office.

WOODWARD, Horace Bollingbroke
The geology of the country near Sidmouth and Lyme Regis. (Sheets 326 and 340) 29 March 1906. (Mem.Geol.Surv.) Geological Survey.

The geology of the London district. 19 Oct.1909. (Mem.Geol.Surv.) Geological Survey.

The water supply of Bedfordshire and Northamptonshire, from underground sources. 21 March 1908. (Mem.Geol.Surv.) Geological Survey.

Water supply of Lincolnshire from underground sources. 23 Nov.1904. (Mem.Geol.Surv.) Geological Survey.

WOOLCOCK, William James Uglow
Dyestuffs industry development committee.
Report on the present position and development of the dyestuffs manufacturing industry in Great

Britain. 2 July 1930. 1930/1 Cmd.3658 xi.
Third report: Present position of the dyestuffs manufacturing industry in Great Britain, 1932. 25 Oct.1932. 1931/2 Cmd.4191 viii. (first report not published) Board of Trade.

Safeguarding of industries.
Report of the committee on brooms and brushes. 30 Nov.1925. 1924/5 Cmd. 2549 xv. Board of Trade.

Report of the committee on handkerchiefs and household linen goods. 23 April 1928. 1928 Cmd.3096 xii. Board of Trade.

Wortley, Charles Beilby Stuart SEE: Stuart-Wortley, Charles Beilby.

WRAY, D. A.
British regional geology: the Pennines and adjacent areas. Geological Survey.

Geology and mineral resources of the Serb-Croat-Slovene state. Jan.1921. Department of Overseas Trade.

Geology of the country around Wem. (Sheet 138) 7 Aug.1924. (Mem.Geol.Surv.) Geological Survey.

WRENACRE, H.
Report on the coal mining industry in the Hokkaido, Japan. June 1912. (Dip.cons.reports: misc.ser., no.682) 1912/3 Cd.6006-1 xciv. Foreign Office and Board of Trade.

Wrenbury, Lord: SEE: Buckley, Henry Burton, 1st Baron Wrenbury.

WRIGHT, H. L.
Observations of smoke particles and condensation nuclei at Kew Observatory. Dec.1932. (Geophys.Mem., no.57) Meteorological Office.

Some notes on readings at Kew Observatory of the Gorczynski pyrheliometer, the sunshine recorder and the black bulb thermometer. May 1935. (Prof.Notes, no.68) Meteorological Office.

WRIGHT, Robert Alderson, Baron Wright of Durley
Departmental committee on coroners.
Report. 17 Jan.1936. 1935/6 Cmd.5070 viii. Home Office.

Law revision committee.
Fifth interim report: Statutes of limitation. Dec.1936. 1936/7 Cmd.5334 xiii.
Sixth interim report: Statute of frauds and the doctrine of consideration. May 1937. 1936/7 Cmd.5449 xiii.
Seventh report: Rule in Chandler v. Webster. May 1939. 1938/9 Cmd.6009 xii.
Eighth report: Contributory negligence. June 1939. 1938/9 Cmd.6032 xii. Lord chancellors' Office. (for previous reports See: Pollock, E. M.)

WRIGHT, W. B.
The geology of Killarney and Kenmare. 25 July 1916. (Mem.Geol.Surv., Ireland) Department of Agriculture and Technical Instruction.

The geology of the Ballycastle coalfield, County Antrim. Oct.1923. (Mem.Geol.Surv., Ireland) Department of Agriculture and Technical Instruction for Ireland.

The geology of the Rossendale anticline. (Sheet 76) 5 Nov.1926. (Mem.Geol.Surv.) Geological Survey.

WRIGHT, W. D.
A re-determination of the trichromatic mixture data. 18 Oct.1929. (S.R.S., no.139) Medical Research Council.

WROTTESLEY, Frederick John
Gas legislation committee.
Interim report. 22 March 1932. 1931/2 Cmd.4065 ix.
Second interim report. 5 Dec.1932. 1932/3 Cmd.4237 xii.
Final report. 24 March 1933. 1932/3 Cmd.4288 xii. Board of Trade.

WYATT, Frank B.
Actuarial report on the position of persons in the naval and military service of the Crown. (Clause 36 of the National Insurance Bill) 26 July 1911. 1911 Cd.5809 lxxiii. Treasury.

Actuarial report on proposed government amendments to clause 36 of the National Insurance Bill (Special provision with regard to persons in the naval and military service of the Crown) 6 Nov.1911. 1911 Cd.5943 lxxiii. Treasury.

Report of the actuaries in relation to the National Insurance Bill as amended in committee. 28 Nov.1911. 1911 Cd.5983 lxxiii. Treasury.

Report of the actuaries in relation to the scheme of insurance against sickness, disablement, *etc.,* embodied in the National Insurance Bill, 1911. 20 May 1911. 1911 Cd.5681 lxxiii. Treasury.

Report of the actuaries on the rate of sickness prevailing in the agricultural districts of Scotland. 16 Nov.1911. 1911 Cd.5966 lxxiii. Treasury.

WYATT, S.
Atmospheric conditions in cotton weaving. Oct.1923. (I.H.R.B.Rep., no.21) Medical Research Council.

Individual differences in output in the cotton industry. June 1920. (I.H.R.B. rep., no.7) Medical Research Council.

Inspection processes in industry; a preliminary report. May 1932. (I.H.R.B. Rep., no.63) Medical Research Council.

Rest-pauses in industry; a review of the results obtained. March 1927. (I.H.R.B., Rep., no.42) Medical Research Council.

Some observations on bobbin winding. June 1920. (I.H.R.B. Rep., no.8) Medical Research Council.

Studies in repetitive work with special reference to rest-pauses. Nov.1925. (I.H.R.B.Rep., no.32) Medical Research Council.

Variations in efficiency in cotton weaving. March 1923. (I.H.R.B. Rep., no.23) Medical Research Council.

WYLER, Edwin Joseph
A method of increasing the sensitiveness of the Wassermann test. Dec.1931. (Rep.Pub.Health & Med.Subj., no.67) Ministry of Health.

On serological tests for syphilis with very small amounts of patients' serum. Sept.1934. (Rep.Pub.Health & Med.Subj., no.74) Ministry of Health.

The Wassermann test; technical details of no.1 method M.R.C. (modified). 1 March 1929. (S.R.S., no.129) Medical Research Council.

WYNDHAM, Percy
Report on the beet sugar industry in the United States. 1 Feb.1901. (Dip.cons.reports: misc.ser., no.548) 1901 Cd.430-3 lxxx. Foreign Office.

WYNN-CARRINGTON, Charles Robert, *1st Earl Carrington*
Memorandum on agricultural education in England and Wales. 22 Sept.1909. 1909 Cd.4886 lxvii. Board of Agriculture and Fisheries.

WYNNE, Frederick Horton
Overwind prevention committee.
Report. 7 March 1935. Mines Department.

WYNNE, G. C.
History of the Great War. Military operations. France and Belgium, 1915. 2 vols. and 2 vols. maps. 1927-8. War Office.

WYNNE-FINCH, John Charles
National forest park committee.
Report on Snowdonia. Nov.1937. Forestry Commission.

Report on the Forest of Dean. Nov.1938. Forestry Commission.

YATES, L. K.
The woman's part; a record of munitions work. 1918 Ministry of Information.

YORKE, Horatio Arthur
Committee on appliances designed to diminish danger to men employed in railway service (railway employment safety appliances).
Reports and appendices. 28 May 1907. 1907 Cd.3638 lxxiv. Board of Trade.

Report on a visit to America (concerning railways), September 19 to October 31, 1902. 6 Dec.1902. 1903 Cd.1466 lx. Board of Trade.

Report on the *chemin de fer metropolitain de Paris,* with remarks on shallow tunnels. 8 Jan.1902. 1902 Cd.977 xxiii. Board of Trade.

Report on the construction and working of light railways in Belgium. 7 March 1912. 1912/3 Cd.6158 lxxv. Board of Trade.

YOUNG, Alfred H. F.
Committee on the standard uniform for the Mercantile Marine.
Report. 14 Dec.1917. 1918 Cd.9030 xii. Board of Trade.

YOUNG, Edward Hilton, *1st Baron Kennet of the Dene*
Commission on closer union of the dependencies in eastern and central Africa.
Report. 17 Oct.1928. 1928/9 Cmd.3234 v. Colonial Office.

Committee on the restoration of land affected by iron ore working.
Report. 31 March 1939. Ministry of Health.

Committee on the staffing and methods of work of the Board of Trade.
Report. 17 Jan.1921. 1921 Cmd.1461 xvii. Cabinet Office.

Departmental committee on the University of London.
Report. March 1926. 1926 Cmd.2612 x. Board of Education.

Departmental committee on scholarships and free places.
Report. 22 July 1920. 1920 Cmd.968 xv. Board of Education.

Report of the United Kingdom delegates on the League of Nations, 13th Assembly. 1 Nov.1932. (Misc., no.13, 1932) 1932/3 Cmd.4212 xxviii. Foreign Office.

Royal commission on Indian currency and finance.

YOUNG, Edward Hilton, *1st Baron Kennet of the Dene* (continued)

> Report. 1 July 1926. 1926 Cmd.2687 xii.
> Vols. 2 and 3: Appendices to the report. 1926.
> Vols. 4 and 5: Minutes of evidence. 1926.
> Vol. 6: Index to the report. 1926. India Office.

YOUNG, F. S.

Report on the cattle trade in Kansas. 13 Aug.1900. (Dip.cons.reports: misc.ser., no.537) 1900 Cd.353-2 xci. Foreign Office.

YOUNG, J.

A course of practical chemistry: quantative and qualitative. Dec.1913. War Office.

YOUNG, Matthew

Appendicitis; a statistical study. 10 Feb.1939. (S.R.S., no.233) Medical Research Council.

Facial growth in children, with special reference to dentition. 1932. (S.R.S., no.171) Medical Research Council.

YOUNG, May R.

Helminth parasites of New Zealand. 1938. Imperial Bureau of Agricultural Parasitology.

YOUNGER, Robert, *Baron Blanesburgh*

Advisory committee on the welfare of the blind.
> Report on the unemployable blind. 17 July 1929. Ministry of Health.

Aliens repatriation committee.
> Report. 21 Oct.1919. 1919 Cmd.383 x. Home Office.

Committee on applications for release of property of ex-enemy aliens in necessitous circumstances.
> Interim report. 5 May 1922. 1922 Cmd.1687 vii.
> Special report. 24 Dec.1923. 1924 Cmd.2046 vii. Board of Trade.

Committee on parliamentary, *etc.,* candidature of Crown servants.
> Report. 31 March 1925. 1924/5 Cmd.2408 ix. Treasury.

Committee on the treatment by the enemy of British prisoners of war.
> Report on the typhus epidemic at Gardelegen, 1915. 13 Sept.1916. (Misc., no.34, 1916) 1916 Cd.8351 xv. Foreign Office.

> Report on the conditions at Wittenberg camp during the typhus epidemic of 1915. 6 April 1916. (Misc., no.10, 1916) 1916 Cd.8224 xv. Foreign Office.

Departmental committee on unemployment insurance.
> Report. Vol.1. Jan.1927.
> Minutes of evidence. Vol.2. 1927. Ministry of Labour.

Report of a public inquiry held under the Education Acts at Menai Bridge, 31 July 1912. 26 Aug.1912. Board of Education.

Report of a public inquiry held under the Education Acts at Neath, 23 March 1914. 6 June 1914. Board of Education.

Royal commission on mining subsidence.
> First report: Doncaster area. 21 Dec.1925. 1926 Cmd.2570 xiii.
> Second and final report. 23 June 1927. 1927 Cmd.2899 xi.
> Minutes of evidence, 1st to 21st days. 1923-1925. Mines Department.

YULE, George Udny

Function of statistical method in scientific investigation. Oct.1924. (I.H.R.B. Rep., no.28) Medical Research Council.

ZAIMAN, A.

The manufacture of clay roofing tiles in France, Belgium and Holland. April 1928. (B.R.B. Bull., no.4) Department of Scientific and Industrial Research.

Economic and manufacturing aspects of the building brick industries. July 1933. (B.R.B. special rep., no.20) Department of Scientific and Industrial Research.

ZIMMERMAN, A. E.

The economic weapon in the war against Germany. 1918. Ministry of Information.

ZIMMERMAN, Emil

The German Empire of Central Africa. Feb.1918. Ministry of Information.

# APPENDIX

## Alphabetical list of Royal Commissions and Distinctive titles of Committees, 1900-1940

The name of the chairman follows the title of the committee or commission so that reference may be made directly to the main body of the index to determine the full details. The date of report is inserted after the title when required to distinguish committees of the same title, but which were appointed and reported at separate times. The Royal commissions have the designation "R. com." placed at the end of the title, so they are interfiled with the committees.

Accidents to Railway servants R. com.
James, Henry, *1st Bn. James of Hereford.*

Adhesives research committee.
O'Gorman, Mervyn

Administration of the Port of London R. com.
Baring, John, *2nd Bn. Revelstoke.*

Administrative committee on tramp shipping.
Thomson, Francis Vernon.

Admiralty transport arbitration board.
Lawrence, Alfred Tristram, *1st Bn. Trevethin.*

Afforestation in the Lake District; joint informal committee.
Robinson, Roy Lister.

Agricultural costing committee.
Peat, Harry William Henry.

Agricultural economics in the Empire committee.
Elliot, Walter.

Agricultural education conference.
Vare, Christopher William, *10th Bn. Barnard.*

Agricultural industry in G.B., R. com.
Peat, William Barclay.

Agricultural Marketing reorganisation commission for eggs and poultry for Scotland.
Sprot, Mark.

Agricultural tribunal of investigation.
Ashley William James.

Agriculture R. com.
Peat, William Barclay.

Agriculture in India R. com.
Hope, John Victor Alexander, *2nd M. of Linlithgow.*

Air mails committee.
Moore-Brabazon, John Theodore Cuthbert.

Air raid shelter policy.
Anderson, David.

Aircraft insurance committee.
Jackson, Frederick Huth.

Alien immigration R. com.
James, Henry, *1st Bn. James of Hereford.*

Aliens repatriation committee.
Younger, Robert, *Bn. Blanesburgh.*

American aviation mission.
Crowell, Benedict.

American dollar securities committee.
Turpin, William Gibbs.

Anti-typhoid committee.
Martin, Charles James.

Arandora Star inquiry.
Snell, Henry, *1st Bn. Snell.*

Army agricultural committee.
Harcourt, Lewis, *1st Vct. Harcourt.*

Army and airforce courts-martial committee.
Oliver, Roland Gifford.

Army council (Halakite) enquiry.
Shearman, Montagu.

Arrest and subsequent treatment of Mr. Francis Shehy Skeffington, Mr. Patrick Dickson and Mr. Patrick James McIntyre R. com.
Simon, John Allesbrook.

Arterial drainage commission, Ireland.
Binnie, Alexander Richardson.

Automatic train control committee.
Pringle, John Wallace.

Bankruptcy committee.
Hansell, E. W.

Belfast University R. com.
MacAlister, Donald.

Boundary commission for England and Wales; Ireland; Scotland.
Lowther, James William, *1st Vct. Ullswater.*

Bridge stress committee.
Ewing, James Alfred.

British cellulose enquiry committee.
Hamilton, John Andrew, *Bn. Sumner.*

British economic mission to the Far East.
Thompson, Ernest.

British Guiana commission.
Wilson, Roderick Roy.

British Guiana constitutional commission.
Douglas-Jones, Crawford Douglas.

Broadcasting committee 1923.
Sykes, Frederick.

Broadcasting committee 1926.
Lindsay, David Alexander Edward, *27th E. of Crawford.*

Broadcasting committee 1935.
Lowther, James William, *1st Vct. Ullswater.*

Budget disclosure inquiry.
Porter, Samuel Loury, *Bn. Porter.*

Burma round table conference, 1931-32.
Peel, William Robert Wellesley, *1st E. Peel.*

Business of courts committee.
Pollock, Ernest Murray, *1st Bn. Hanworth.*

Business of courts committee.
Pollock, Ernest Murray, *1st Bn. Hanworth.*

Canals and inland navigations of the U.K. R. com.
Kay-Shuttleworth, Ughtred James, *1st Bn. Shuttleworth.*

Care and control of the feeble-minded R. com.
Pleydell-Bouverie, Jacob, *6th E. Radnor.*

Chancel repairs committee.
Inskip, Thomas Walker Hobart.

Channel tunnel committee.
    Peacock, Edward Robert.

Charges (railway control) consultative committee.
    Thomas, William Bruce.

Child adoption committee.
    Tomlin, Thomas James Cheshire, *Bn. Tomlin of Ash.*

Church of England in Wales and Monmouthshire R. com.
    Vaughan-Williams, Richard Lomax.

Churches (Scotland) R. com.
    Bruce, Victor Alexander, *9th E. of Elgin and Kincardine.*

Churches (Scotland) Act, 1905, R.com.
    Bruce, Victor Alexander, *9th E. of Elgin and Kincardine.*

Civil aerial transport committee.
    Baird, John Lawrence, *1st Vct. Stonehaven.*

Civil air transport subsidies committee.
    Hambling, Herbert.

Civil aviation advisory board.
    Leveson-Gower, George Granville Sutherland, *5th D. of Sutherland.*

Civil service reorganisation committee.
    Ramsay, Malcolm Graham.

Civil service R. com. 1915.
    MacDonnell, Anthony Patrick, *1st Bn. MacDonnell.*

Civil service R. com. 1931.
    Tomlin, Thomas James Cheshire, *Bn. Tomlin.*

Civil war workers committee.
    Bellhouse, Gerald.

Coal conservation committee.
    Haldane, Richard Burdon, *1st Vct. Haldane of Cloan.*

Coal industry R. com. 1919.
    Sankey, John, *1st Vct. Sankey.*

Coal industry R. com. 1926.
    Samuel, Herbert Louis.

Coal mines reorganisation commission.
    Gowers, Ernest Arthur.

Coal Suppliers R. com.
    Jackson, William Lawies, *1st Bn. Allerton.*

Coast erosion, reclamation of tidal lands and afforestation in the U.K. R. com.
    Guest, Ivor Churchill, *Vct. Wimbourne.*

Colonial films committee.
    Snell, Henry, *1st Bn. Snell.*

Colonial students committee.
    Tomlinson, George John Frederick.

Colonial survey committee.
    Bottomley, William Cecil.

Company law amendment committee 1906.
    Warmington, Cornelius Marshall.

Company law amendment committee, 1918.
    Buckley, Henry Burton, *1st Bn. Wrenbury.*

Congestion in Ireland R. com.
    Ward, William Humble, *2nd E. of Dudley.*

Cost of living committee.
    Meiklejohn, Roderick Sinclair.

Cotton mission.
    Thompson, Ernest.

Council on art and industry.
    Pick, Frank.

Council for art and industry, Scottish committee.
    Bilsland, Alexander Steven.

County court staff committee.
    Swift, Rigby Philip Watson.

Court of Session and the office of Sheriff Principal (Scotland) R. com.
    Clyde, James Avon, *Lord.*

Credit insurance committee.
    Hills, John Waller.

Crinan canal committee.
    Raeburn, William Norman.

Cross-river traffic in London R. com.
    Lee, Arthur Hamilton, *1st Vct. Lee of Fareham.*

Decimal currency R. com.
    Emmott, Alfred, *1st Bn. Emmott of Oldham.*

Delay in the King's Bench Division R. com.
    Hicks-Beach, Michael Edward, *1st Vct . St. Aldwyn.*

Delhi town planning committee on the choice of a site for the new Imperial capital.
    Swinton, George Sitwell Campbell.

Despatch of business at common law R. com.
    Peel, William Robert Wellesley, *1st E. Peel.*

Distribution of the industrial population R. com.
    Barlow, Montague, *sir.*

Divorce and matrimonial causes. R. com.
    Barnes, Henry Gorell, *2nd Bn. Gorell.*

Dormant funds committee.
    Tomlin, Thomas James Cheshire, *Bn. Tomlin of Ash.*

Dublin disturbances commission.
    Henry, Denis Stanislaus.

Dublin University, R. com.
    Palles, Christopher.

Duties of Metropolitan police R. com.
    Jones, David Brynmor.

Dystuffs industry development committee.
    Woolcock, William James Uglow.

East Africa sub-committee of the tsetse-fly committee.
    Hemming, Francis.

East African commission.
    Ormsby-Gore, William George Arthur.

East African guaranteed loan committee.
    Jackson, Richard Hoyle.

Eastern mail service committee.
    Cecil, Evelyn, *1st Bn. Rockley.*

Ecclesiastical discipline R. com.
    Hicks-Beach, Michael Edward, *1st Vct. St. Aldwyn.*

Economics of small farms and small holdings in Scotland.
    Conacher, H. M. *and* Scott, W. R.

Editorial committee on the international code of signals.
    Smith, Walter R.

Educational policy in British tropical Africa.
    Ormsby-Gore, William George Arthur.

Electoral systems R. com.
    Cavendish, Richard Frederick.

Electric lighting committee.
Williams, Ernest T.

Electrification of railways advisory committee.
Kennedy, Alexander Blackie William.

Empire cotton growing committee.
Birchenough, Henry.

Empire flax growing committee.
Smith, Frederick Henry, *1st Bn. Colwyn.*

Engineering trades (new industries) committee.
McLaren, Henry D.

Existence of corrupt practices at the last election for the city of Worcester R.com.
Atkinson, Edward Tindal.

Explosives in mines research committee.
Nathan, Frederick L.

Fabrics co-ordinating research committee.
Pickard, Robert Howson.

Fabrics research committee.
Pickard, Robert Howson.

Fair wages committee.
Murray, George Herbert.

Farm workers in Scotland.
Wilson, James, *sir.*

Fertilisers and feeding stuffs advisory committee.
Trefusis, Charles John Robert Hepburn-Stuart-Forbes, *21st Bn. Clinton.*

Finance and currency (East Indies) R. com.
Chamberlain, Joseph Austen.

Fire brigades and fire protection R. com.
Laurence, Percival Maitland.

Fish preservation committee.
Maurice, Henry G.

Fishing industry committee.
Scott, W. R.

Food council.
Peto, Geoffrey Kelsall.

Food preservatives committee.
Munro, Horace Cecil.

Food prices R. com.
Geddes, Auckland Campbell.

Foot and mouth disease research committee.
Arkwright, Joseph A.

Freshwater fisheries committee.
Grenfell, William Henry, *1st Bn. Desborough.*

Fuel for motor transport.
Nathan, Frederick L.

Furunculosis committee.
Mackie, Thomas Jones.

Gas cylinders research committee.
Carpenter, H. C. Harold.

Gas legislation committee.
Wrottesley, Frederick John.

Gas traction committee.
Redwood, Boverton, *sir.*

Glasgow tribunal of inquiry, 1933.
Anderson, Andrew McBeth, *Lord.*

Gold production committee.
Mackay, James Lyle, *1st Bn. Inchcape of Strathnaver.*

Government factories and workshops committee.
Murray, George Herbert.

Health and safety of miners R. com.
Monkswell, Robert Collier, *2nd Bn. Monkswell.*

Health of munitions workers committee.
Newman, George.

Highlands and islands medical service committee.
Dewar, John Alexander.

Honours R. com.
Murray, Andrew Graham, *1st Bn. Dunedin.*

Housing financial assistance committee.
Hobhouse, Henry.

Housing of the industrial population of Scotland, rural and urban, R. com.
Ballantyne, Henry.

Humber conservancy commission.
Digby, Kenelm Edward.

Imperial committee on economic consultation and co-operation.
Skelton, Oscar Douglas.

Imperial Institute committee of inquiry.
Ormsby-Gore, William George Arthur.

Imperial shipping committee.
Mackinder, H. J.

Imperial wireless telegraphy committee, 1920.
Norman, Henry.

Imperial wireless telegraphy committee, 1924.
Donald, Robert.

Import duties advisory committee.
May, George Ernest, *1st Bn.*

Income tax codification committee.
MacMillan, Hugh Pattison, *Bn. Macmillan of Aberfeldy.*

Income Tax R. com.
Smith, Frederick Henry, *1st Bn. Colwyn.*

India irrigation commission.
Scott-Moncrieff, Colin Campbell.

India reforms enquiry committee.
Mudiman, Alexander Phillips.

Indian constitutional reforms committee.
Sankaran Nair, Chettur.

Indian currency and finance R. com.
Young, Edward Hilton, *1st Bn. Kennet.*

Indian Decentralisation R. com.
Hobhouse, Charles Edward Henry.

Indian enquiry commission, Union of South Africa.
Solomon, William Henry.

Indian excise committee.
Thomson, James, *sir.*

Indian expenditure R. com.
Welby, Reginald Earle, *1st Bn. Welby.*

Indian factory labour commission.
Morison, William Thomson.

Indian federal finance committee.
Percy, Eustace, *Lord.*

Indian financial enquiry.
Niemeyer, Otto Ernst.

Indian fiscal commission.
Rahimtoola, Ibrahim.

Indian franchise committee.
Kerr, Philip Henry, *11th M. of Lothian.*

Indian industrial commission.
Holland, Thomas Henry.

Indian jails committee.
    Cardew, Alexander Gordon.

Indian Plague Commission.
    Fraser, Thomas R.

Indian police commission.
    Fraser, Andrew Henderson Leith.

Indian retrenchment committee.
    Mackay, James Lyle, *1st Bn. Inchcape of Strathnaver.*

Indian Sandhurst committee.
    Skeen, Andrew.

Indian States committee, 1929.
    Bulter, Spencer Harcourt.

Indian States enquiry committee, 1932.
    Davidson, John Colin Campbell.

Indian statutory R. com.
    Simon, John Allesbrook.

Indian wheat committee.
    Acland, Francis Dyke.

Industrial transference board.
    Fisher, Norman Fenwick Warren.

Intermediate education in Ireland.
    Molony, Thomas Francis.

Investments advisory committee.
    Murray, George Herbert.

Irish boundary commission.
    Feetham, Richard.

Irish coal industry committee.
    O'Connor, James.

Irish distress committee.
    Hoare, Samuel.

Irish Free State compensation committee.
    Murray, Andrew Graham, *1st Bn. Dunedin.*

Irish grants committee.
    Percy, Eustace, *Lord.*

Irish inland fisheries commission.
    Walker, Samuel.

Irish milk commission.
    O'Neill, Patrick J.

Irish peat inquiry committee.
    Griffith, John Purser.

Irish police forces reorganisation and pay com.
    Ross, John.

Irish Public Health Council.
    Bigger, Edward Coey.

Juvenile employment inquiry.
    Thesiger, Frederick John Napier, *1st Vct. Chelmsford.*

Juvenile organisations committee.
    Lewis, John Herbert.

Kenya land commission.
    Carter, William Morris.

Labour conditions in West Africa.
    Orde-Browne, Granville St. John.

Labour conditions in the West Indies.
    Orde-Browne, Granville St. John.

Labour in India R. com.
    Whitley, John Henry.

Land drainage in England and Wales R. com.
    Bathhurst, Charles, *1st Vct. Bledisloe*

Land registration committee.
    Tomlin, Thomas James Cheshire, *Bn. Tomlin of Ash.*

Land Transfer Acts R. com.
    Hicks-Beach, Michael Edward, *1st Vct. St. Aldwyn.*

Land transfer committee.
    Tomlin, Thomas James Cheshire, *Bn. Tomlin of Ash.*

Landing of arms at Howth on July 26th, 1914 R. com.
    Shaw, Thomas, *Bn. Shaw.*

Lands settlement commission, South Africa.
    Arnold-Forster, Hugh Oakley.

Lathe tools research committee.
    Day, Charles.

Law revision committee, 1934.
    Pollock, Ernest Murray, *1st Bn. Hanworth.*

Law revision committee, 1936-1939.
    Wright, Robert Alderson, *Bn. Wright of Durley.*

Legal education committee.
    Atkin, James Richard, *Bn. Atkin.*

Licensing (England and Wales) R. com.
    Mackenzie, William Warrender, *1st Bn. Amulree.*

Licensing (Scotland) R. com.
    Mackay, Alexander Morrice.

Light railways investigation committee.
    Gibb, Alexander.

Lighthouse administration R. com.
    Blafour, Gerald William.

Local government committee.
    MacLean, Donald.

Local government R. com.
    Onslow, Richard William Alan, *5th E. of Onslow.*

Local government in the Tyneside area R. com.
    Scott, Angus Newton.

Local government in great London R. com.
    Lowther, James William *1st Vct. Ullswater.*

Local taxation R. com.
    Bruce, Alexander Hugh, *6th Bn. Balfour of Burleigh.*

London and home counties traffic advisory committee, 1925-29.
    Maybury, Henry percy.

London and home counties traffic advisory committee, 1934.
    Jackson, Henry.

London squares R. com.
    Vane-Tempest-Stewart, Charles Stewart Henry, *7th M. of Londonderry.*

London Traffic R. com.
    Barber, David Miller, *sir.*

Lotteries and betting R. com.
    Rowlatt, Sidney Arthur Taylor, *sir.*

Lubricants and lubrication inquiry committee.
    Donkin, S. B.

Lunacy and mental disorder R. com.
    Macmillan, Hugh Pattison, *Bn. Macmillan.*

Machinery of government committee.
    Haldane, Richard Burdon, *1st Vct. Haldane of Cloan.*

Malta R. com.
    Askwith, George Rankin, *1st Bn. Askwith.*

Malta (finances, economic position, and judicial procedure) R. com.
Mowatt, Francis, *sir.*

Martial law sentences in South Africa R. com.
Webster, Richard Everard, *1st Bn. Alverstone.*

Mauritius R. com.
Swettenham, Frank Athelstane.

Meat export trade of Australia R. com.
Street, Philip Whistler.

Mechanical transport committee (War Office).
Holden, Henry Capel Lofft.

Medical committee on adenoids and enlarged tonsils.
Newman, George.

Mental deficiency committee.
Wood, A. J.

Merchandise marks committee.
Greer, Harry.

Merchant shipping advisory committee, 1908.
Cross, S.

Merchant shipping advisory committee, 1922.
Spencer, Thomas.

Merthyr Tydfil R. com.
Lowry, Arthur Belmore.

Mesopotamia war R. com.
Hamilton, George Francis, *Lord.*

Metalliferous mines and quarries R. com.
Cunnynghame, Henry Hardinge S.

Meteorological grant committee.
Maxwell, Herbert Eustace, *6th Bn Monreith.*

Metropolitan poor law inspectors' advisory committee on the homeless poor.
Oxley, J. S.

Mid-Scotland ship canal committee.
Chapman, Sydney John.

Military hospitals in South Africa R. com.
Romer, Robert, *sir.*

Military service committee.
Carr, R. H.

Militia and volunteers R. com.
Fitzalan-Howard, Henry, *15th D. of Norfolk.*

Mine rescue apparatus research commission.
Walker, William.

Miners' lamps committee.
Walker, William.

Miners' mystagmus committee.
Haldane, John Scott.

Mines R. com.
Monkswell, Robert Colliers, *2nd Bn. Monkswell.*

Mining subsidence R. com.
Younger, Robert, *Bn. Blanesborough.*

Motor cars R. com.
Gully, William Court, *1st Vct. Selby.*

*Mui Tsai* in Hong Kong and Malaysia commission.
Woods, Wilfred Wentworth.

National and imperial defence committee.
Balfour, Arthur James, *1st Bn. Balfour.*

National forest park committee, 1935.
Stirling-Maxwell, John.

National forest park committee, 1937-38.
Wynne-Finch, John Charles.

National fuel and power committee, 1928.
Mond, Alfred Morits, *1st Bn. Melchett and* Hodges, Frank.

National health insurance R. com.
Lawrence, Charles Napier, *1st Bn. Lawrence.*

National museums and art galleries R. com.
Vincent, Edgar, *1st Vct. D'Abernon.*

National Park committee.
Addison, Christopher.

Native affairs commission, Natal.
Campbell, Henry Cooke.

Natural resources, trade and legislation of the dominions R. com.
Vincent, Edgar, *1st Vct. D'Abermon.*

Naval reserves committee.
Grey, Edward, *1st Vct. Grey of Fallodon.*

Newfoundland R. com.
MacKenzie, William Warrender, *1st Bn. Amulree.*

Newport (Mon.) harbour extension committee.
Mason, Robert.

Nitrogen products committee.
Goold-Adams, Henry Edward Fane.

North Charterland concession, Northern Rhodesia, inquiry.
Maughan, Frederick Herbert, *1st Vct. Maughan.*

North Sea fisheries investigation committee.
Thompson, D'Arcy Wentworth.

Northern Ireland special arbitration committee.
Smith, Frederick Henry.

Nursing homes committee.
Ramsay, Malcolm Graham.

Oil fuel committee.
Bell, Thomas.

Overwind prevention committee.
Wynne, Frederick Horton.

Oxford and Cambridge universities R. com.
Asquith, Herbert Henry.

Oxygen research committee.
Thorpe, Jocelyn Field.

Palestine partition commission.
Woodhead, John Ackroy.

Palestine R. com.
Peel, William Robert Wellesley, *1st E. Peel.*

Patents committee.
Jenkins, Walter St. David.

Petroleum filling stations committee.
Earle, Lionel.

Physical training (Scotland) R. com.
Murray, William David, *5th E. of Mansfield.*

Poisoning by arsenic R. com.
Kelvin, William Thomson, *1st Bn. Kelvin.*

Police pay of new entrants committee.
Higgins, George Herbert.

Police powers and procedure R. com.
Lee, Arthur Hamilton, *1st Vct. Lee of Fareham.*

Poor laws and relief of distress R. com.
Hamilton, George Francis, *Lord.*

Poor persons (divorce jurisdiction) committee.
Schuster, Claud.

Poor persons procedure committee.
Merriman, Frank Boyd.

Post-graduate medical committee, 1921.
    Cambridge, Alexander Augustus Frederick William Alfred George, *1st E. Athlone.*

Post graduate medical education committee, 1930.
    Greenwood, A. C.

Poultry technical committee for Great Britain.
    Watson, Duncan.

Primary education in Ireland.
    Morris, M. H. F., *2nd Bn. Killanin.*

Private manufacture of and trading in arms R. com.
    Banks, John Eldon, *sir.*

Proportional representation R. com.
    Lowther, James William, *1st Vct. Ullswater.*

Protection and training; departmental committee on the treatment of young offenders.
    Morton, George.

Protection of the New Forest committee.
    Robinson, Roy Lister.

Public libraries in England and Wales committee.
    Kenyon, Frederick George.

Public records R. com.
    Pollock, Frederick, *sir.*

Public services (East Indies) R. com.
    Dickson-Poynder, John Poynder, *1st Bn. Islington.*

Public trustee (infants damages) committee.
    Branson, George Arthur Harwin.

Quarter sessions committee.
    Bodkin, Archibald Henry.

Railway advisory council.
    Metcalfe, Charles.

Railway conciliation and arbitration scheme of 1907 R. com.
    Harrel, David, *sir.*

Railway electrification committee.
    Pringle, John Wallace.

Railway employmment safety apparatus.
    Yorke, Horatio Arthur.

Railway pool committee.
    Clode, Walter Baker.

Rates advisory committee.
    Gore-Browne, Frank.

Rebellion in Ireland R. com.
    Hardinge, Henry Charles, *3rd Vct. Hardinge.*

Registration of title in Scotland R. com.
    Murray, Andrew Graham, *1st Bn. Dunedin.*

Reinforced concrete structures committee.
    Humphreys, George William.

Respirators (poliomyelitis) committee.
    Witts, Leslie John.

Rhodesia-Nyasaland R. com.
    Bathurst, Charles, *1st Vct. Bledisloe.*

Rural education conference.
    Hobhouse, Henry.

Russian banks and communist funds enquiry.
    Scott, Harold *and* Whitley, Arthur.

Safety in coal mines R. com.
    Cecil, Evelyn, *1st Bn. Rockley.*

St. Louis International Exhibition, 1904, R. com.
    Peel, Arthur Wellesley, *1st Vct. Peel.*

Salmon fisheries R. com.
    Bruce, Victor Alexander, *9th E. of Elgin and Kincardine.*

School epidemics committee.
    Newman, George.

Scottish architectural advisory committee.
    Richmond, John Ritchie.

Scottish fat stock marketing reorganisation commission.
    Sprot, Mark.

Scottish freshwater fisheries committee.
    Campbell, Gavin, *1st M. of Breadalbane*

Scottish housing advisory committee.
    Ross-Taylor, Joshua P.

Scottish sea fisheries committee.
    Sutherland, John Ebenezer.

Sea fish commission.
    Duncan, Andrew Rae.

Secondary school examinations council.
    Norwood, Cyril.

Selection of justices of the peace R. com.
    James, Henry, *1st Bn. James of Hereford.*

Severn barrage committee.
    Moore-Brabazon, John Theodore Cuthbert.

Sheffield industrial mission to South Africa.
    Hodgson, C. R.

Shipping "rings" and deferred rebates R. com.
    Cohen, Benjamin Arthur.

Ships replacement committee.
    Innes, Charles Alexander.

Shops committee
    Harmsworth, Cecil Bisshopp.

Shot-firing committee.
    Ritson, John Anthony Sydney.

Sir John Jackson, Ltd., R. com.
    Channel, Arthur M.

South Wales regional survey committee.
    Seager, William Henry.

Southampton harbour commission.
    Bateman, Alfred Edmund.

Springs research committee.
    Hutchinson, Thomas Massie.

Steel structures research committee.
    Hindley, Clement D. M.

Steering gear committee.
    Gresley, Herbert Nigel.

Stone preservation committee.
    Webb, Aston.

Store cattle R. com.
    Finlay, Robert Bannatyne, *1st Vct. Finlay.*

Straits settlements currency committee.
    Barber, David Miller.

Street offences committee.
    Macmillan, Hugh Pattison, *Bn. Macmillan of Aberfeldy.*

Superannuation in the civil service R. com.
    Courtney, Leonard Henry.

Superior civil services in India R. com.
    Lee, Arthur Hamilton, *1st Vct. Lee of Fareham.*

Superannuation committee.
    Rae, James.

Supply of food and raw material in time of war R. com.
    Bruce, Alexander Hugh. *6th Bn. Balfour of Burleigh.*

Support of workings in mines committee.
    Mottram, Thomas Harry.

Supreme court fee committee.
MacNaughten, Malcolm Martin.

Television committee.
Mitchell-Thomson, William, *1st Bn. Selsdon.*

Temporary staffs committee.
Hodgson, E. H.

Textile factories labour committee on factory labour in India.
Freer-Smith, Hamilton Pym.

Tithe rent charge R. com.
Williams, John Fischer, *sir.*

Town and country planning advisory committee.
Maude, Evelyn John

Trade disputes and trade combinations R. com.
Murray, Andrew Graham, *1st Bn. Dunedin.*

Trade relations between Canada and the West Indies R. com.
Bruce, Alexander Hugh, *6th Bn. Balfour of Burleigh.*

Transport advisory council.
Griffith-Boscawen, Arthur Sackville Trevor.

Transport R. com.
Griffith-Boscawen, Arthur Sackville Trevor.

Transvaal concessions commission.
Lyttleton, Alfred.

Transvaal labour commission.
Niven, A. Mackie.

Trinity College, Dublin R. com.
Geikie, Archibald.

Trinity College, Dublin, and the University of Dublin R. com.
Fry, Edward, *sir.*

Trinity House fog-signal committee.
Vyvyan, George Rawlinson.

Trustee securities committee.
Lawrence, Paul Ogden.

Tsetse fly committee.
Windsor-Clive, Ivor Miles, *2nd E. of Plymouth.*

Tuberculin committee.
Douglas, Stewart Rankin.

Tuberculosis R. com.
Power, William Henry.

Unemployment grants committee.
Philipps, John Wynford, *1st Vct. St. Davids.*

Unemployment insurance R. com.
Gregory, Holman.

Unhealthy areas committee.
Chamberlain, Arthur Neville.

University education in Ireland R. com.
Robertson, James Patrick Bannerman, *Bn. Robertson.*

University education in London R. com.
Haldane, Richard Burdon, *1st Vct. Haldane.*

University education in Wales R. com.
Haldane, Richard Burdon, *1st Vct. Haldane.*

University of Durham R. com.
Guinness, Walter Edward, *1st Bn. Moyne.*

Venereal diseases R. com.
Clarke, George Sydenham, *1st Bn. Sydenham.*

Vivisection R. com.
Gully, William Court, *1st Vct. Selby.*

Voluntary hospitals committee, 1921.
Cave, George, *1st Vct. Cave.*

Voluntary hospitals committee, 1923-28.
Onslow, Richard William Alan, *5th E. Onslow.*

War Office (reconstruction) committee.
Brett, Reginald Baliol, *2nd Vct. Esher.*

War relief funds committee.
Collins, Richard Henn.

War in South Africa R. com.
Bruce, Victor Alexander, *9th E. of Elgin and Kincardine.*

War stores in South Africa, R. com.
Farwell, George.

Water power resources committee.
Snell, John Francis Cleverton.

Water power resources, Ireland sub-committee.
Griffith, John Purser.

Welsh in education and life, departmental committee.
Bruce, William Napier.

West Indian currency committee.
Ormsby-Gore, William George Arthur.

West Indian shipping committee.
Amery, Leopold Charles Maurice Stennet.

West Indian sugar commission.
Olivier, Sydney, *1st Bn. Olivier.*

West Indies closer union commission.
Fergusson, Charles.

West Indies R. com.
Guinness, Walter Edward, *1st Bn. Moyne.*

Whisky and other potable spirits R. com.
James, Henry, *1st Bn. James of Hereford.*

Wireless telegraphy commission.
Mitchell-Thomson, William, *1st Bn. Selsdon.*

Witwatersrand disturbances commission.
Wessels, Johannes Wilhelmus.

Women's advisory committee on the domestic service problem.
Emmott, Gertrude, *Lady Emmott.*

Women's employment committee.
Hills, John Waller.

Women's house-planning committee.
Kerr, Helen L.

Women's housing sub-committee of the housing advisory council.
Emmott, Gertrude, *Lady Emmott.*